SMITHSONIAN INSTITUTION

BUREAU OF AMERICAN ETHNOLOGY: J. W. POWELL, DIRECTOR

BULLETIN 26

KATHLAMET TEXTS

BY

FRANZ BOAS

WASHINGTON
GOVERNMENT PRINTING OFFICE
1901

MRS. WILSON, A

KATHLAMET WOMAN

CONTENTS

ILLUSTRATION

KATHLAMET TEXTS

Told by
CHARLES CULTEE

Recorded and translated by
FRANZ BOAS

INTRODUCTION

The following texts were collected in the summers of 1890 and 1891 and in December, 1894. So far as I have been able to ascertain, the Kathlamet dialect is spoken by three persons only—Charles Cultee and Samson, both living at Bay Center, Washington, and Mrs Wilson, who lives at Nemah, on Shoalwater bay. Unfortunately neither Samson nor Mrs Wilson were able to give me any connected texts, so that Charles Cultee was my only informant. This is unfortunate, as he told me also Chinook texts, and is, therefore, the only source for two dialects of the Chinookan stock. In order to ascertain the accuracy of his mode of telling, I had two stories which he had told in the summer of 1891 repeated three and a half years later, in December, 1894. These stories will be found on page 54 and page 182 of the following texts. They show great similarity and corroborate the opinion which I formed from internal evidence that the language of the texts is fairly good and represents the dialect in a comparatively pure state. Cultee lived for a considerable number of years at Cathlamet, on the south side of Columbia river, a few miles above Astoria, where he acquired this dialect. His mother's mother was a Kathlamet, his mother's father a Xuilā'paX; his father's mother was a Klatsop, and his father's father a TkulXiyogoā'ikc, which is the Chinook name of the Tinneh tribe on upper Willapa river. His wife is a Chehalis, and at present he speaks Chehalis almost exclusively, this being also the language of his children.

Cultee (or more properly Q¦Eltē') has proved a veritable storehouse of information. I obtained from him the texts which were published in an earlier bulletin of the Bureau of American Ethnology,[1] as well

---

[1] Chinook Texts; Washington, 1894.

as the material embodied in the present paper. The work of translating and explaining the texts was greatly facilitated by Cultee's remarkable intelligence. After he had once grasped what was wanted, he explained to me the grammatical structure of sentences by means of examples, and elucidated the sense of difficult periods. This work was the more difficult as we conversed only by means of the Chinook jargon. It will be noticed that the periods of the later dictations are much more complex than those of his earlier dictations.

The following pages contain nothing but the texts and translations. These collections of texts will, it is expected, be followed by a grammar and dictionary of the language, which will contain a comparison of all the known dialects of the Chinookan stock.

The Kathlamet is that dialect of the Upper Chinook which was spoken farthest down the river. Its territory extended from Astoria on the south side and Grey's Harbor on the north side of the river to Rainier. Cultee stated that above Kalama the pronunciation was slightly different. He mentioned the following tribes as speaking the Kathlamet dialect: The Wā'qa-iqam of Grey's Harbor; the ʟā'cgᴇnᴇmaxîx· about opposite Cathlamet (on the north side); the Kʟā'ecaʟxîx·, at the present town of Cathlamet; the ʟā'qaʟala, about three miles above Oak point on the north side of the river; the ʟctā'mēctîx·, half a mile below the mouth of Cowlitz river; the ʟā'k¡alama, at Kalama; the Tē'iaq¡ōtcoē, three miles above Oak point, on the south side of the river; the Kʟā'gulaq, two miles below Rainier; and the Kʟā'mōîx·, at Rainier

Alphabet

a, e, i, o, u	have their continental sounds (short).
ā, ē, ī, ō, ū	long vowels.
ᵃ, ᵉ, ⁱ, ᵒ, ᵘ	vowels not articulated, but indicated by position of the mouth.
ᴀ, ᴇ, ɪ, ᴏ, ᴜ	obscure vowels.
ä	in German Bär.
â	aw in law.
ô	o in German voll.
ê	e in bell.
î	i in hill.
-	separates vowels which do not form diphthongs.
ai	i in island.
au	ow in how.
l	as in English.
ll	very long, slightly palatized by allowing a greater portion of the back of the tongue to touch the palate.
ʟ	posterior palatal l; the tip of the tongue touches the alveoli of the lower jaw, the back of the tongue is pressed against the hard palate; sonant.

L	the same, short and exploded, surd (Lepsius's t̪).
L!	the same with very great stress of explosion.
q	velar k.
k	English k.
k·	palatized k (Lepsius's k'), almost ky.
kX	a posterior palatal k, between k and k·.
x	ch in German Bach.
X	x pronounced at posterior border of hard palate.
x·	palatal x as German ich.
s, c	are evidently the same sound, and might be written s· or c·, both being palatized; c (English sh) is pronounced with open teeth, the tongue almost touching the palate immediately behind the alveoli; s is modified in the same manner.
d, t b, p g, k	as in English, but surd and sonant are difficult to distinguish.
h	as in English.
y	as in year.
w	as in English.
m	is pronounced with semiclosure of the nose and with very slight compression of the lips; it partakes, therefore, of the character of b and w.
n	is pronounced with semiclosure of the nose; it partakes, therefore, of the character of d.
!	designates increased stress of articulation.
2, 4	designate excessive length of vowels, representing approximately the double and fourfold mora.
'	indicates a pause.

Words ending with a short vowel are contracted with the first vowel of the next word. The last consonant of a word is united with the first vowel of the next word to one syllable.

NEW YORK, *November, 1895.*

MYTHS

Myth of Aq¡asXē'nasXēna (told 1890)

There was [a woman and] her husband. She had a small child. Now she was angry and left her husband. She made a small house and there she stayed. After some time he began to sing his shaman's song. After a while the people went to see him. Now the people danced. She went out of her house. She went out in the evening and listened. Now she thought: "I will go. No, I had better not go, else my child might cry." Now it was night again. She washed her child and put it in the cradle. The child fell asleep; then she went to look. She remained standing at the door and tried to look through a hole. But she did not see her husband. She entered the house and danced among [the people]. When it was nearly daylight she remembered her child. "Oh, my child! perhaps it is crying. I

TK¡ANĀ'MÎKC

Aq¡asXē'nasXēna Itcā'k¡anē

Aq¡asXē'nasXēna Her Myth

Cxēlā'itîX itcā'kikala. Aqa Lstā'xan iLō'koantsX. Aqa
There was her husband. Then her child small. Then

kalā'lkuilē igā'xôx. Aqa igigE'ltaqL itcā'kika. Aqa igE'tôx
angry she became. Then she left him her husband. Then she made it

itō'koa-îts tqu'Lē. Aqa kopā igō'La-it. Lă'lê, aqa igē'ktcxam: lā'lê
small house. Then there she stayed. Long, then, he sang shaman's songs; long

aqa igoxōilō'tcxam tê'lXam. Aqa igoXuiwē'yutck tê'lXam. Aqa
then they went to see the people. Then they danced the people. Then

igō'pa. Xā'pîX aqa igō'pa. Aqa igaxamē'laq. Aqa igaXLō'xoa-it:
she went out. In the evening then she went out. Then she listened. Then she thought:

"Qōi nō'ya? Qā'txō nîct anō'ya, yā'okîX qaLktcā'xamx LgE'Xan."
"Must I go? Better not I go, else it will cry my child."

Aqa wit'ax agon ā'pōl. Aqa ikLō'qoat Lgā'Xan. Lă ikLacî'lutk
Then again one night. Then she washed it her child. Long she put it into the cradle

Lgā'xan. Aqa iLoqō'ptit Lgā'xan. Aqa igō'ya. IgaxElō'tcxam. Aqa
her child. Then it slept her child. Then she went. She went to see. Then

igō'La-it icî'qe. Kē'nuwa igagē'qamîtck nLxoā'pîXpa. Năct
she stayed doorway. Try she looked hole at. Not

igē'qalkEl itcā'kika. Aqa igā'ckupq. Aqa gikatē'x· igō'wîtck. Lă2,
she saw him her husband. Then she entered. Then among them she danced. Long,

aqa q¡oa'p alitcū'ktiya. Aqa iLā'lqaL Lgā'xan. "Ō LgE'xan. LXuan
then nearly it was going to become day. Then its remembrance her child. "O my child. Perhaps

will go home." Then she went home. When she approached her house her child was crying. She entered and took it. She took it [in her arms] and, behold, it was a stick! "Oh, my poor child! Perhaps Aq¡asXē'nasXēna carried it away."

Now Aq¡asXē'nasXēna carried that child. She took it home to the house [which she herself] and the Crane [inhabited]. Now they stayed there. The child grew up. Then she always carried the boy on her back. After some time she grew tired and one day she left him at home. Then the Crane said to him: "Come here. I will give you food." He gave him trout to eat. Now he told him and said to him: "Do you think she is your mother? She is another [woman]; she is not at all your mother. She carried you away. Her name is Aq¡asXē'nasXēna." After some time she came home. Now her boy was angry. "What did you say to your nephew, Crane?" "I said to him: 'She is your mother.' You made him sick." "Oh, younger brother, thus shall you speak to your nephew." On the next day she went again and carried him. In the evening she came home. On the

---

ʟō'qulqt ʟgᴇ'xan. Tgt¡ō'kti nXk¡uā'ya." Aqa igō'ya, igā'Xk¡oa.
cries my child. Good I go home." Then she went, she went home.

Q¡oā'p iktō'xam tqu'ʟē, aqa ʟō'qulqt ʟgā'xan. Aqa igō'pqam. Aqa
Near she came house, then cried her child. Then she entered. Then

igᴇ'ʟgᴇlga ʟgā'xan. Aqa ā'wa igᴇ'ʟôx. Aqa ē'mᴇqō: "Ō ʟgᴇ'xan
she took it her child. Then thus she did it. Then a stick: "O my child

ʟgoā'ʟi. ʟXuan Aq¡asXē'nasXēna ikʟōtā'mit." Aqa igᴇ'ʟukʟ
poor. Perhaps Aq¡asXē'nasXēna carried it away." Then she carried it

Aq¡asXē'nasXēna ʟaXi ʟk'ā'skas. Aqa ikʟō'kʟam tᴇ'ctaqʟ k¡a
Aq¡asXē'nasXēna that child. Then she carried it to their house and

iq¡oā'cqoac. Ā'2qa icxē'la-îtX kō'pa. Aqa iʟā'qa-iʟ igîʟxᴇ'lôx
the crane's. Then they two stayed there. Then large became

ʟaXi ʟk'ā'skas. Aqa igᴇ'ʟōkʟ ikʟō'ctxoax. Lē'lē aqa tᴇl igā'xôx.
that child. Then she carried him she carried him on her back. Long then tired she became.

Aqa ēXt wē'koa iqʟqᴇ'loqʟq. Aqa itciō'lXam iq¡oā'qoac: "Mā'tē,
Then one day he was left. Then he said to him the crane: "Come,

mā'tē! iamî'lqoîm." Itcayî'lqoîm ā'q¡ēx·ᴇnē. Aqa igixēlgu'ʟîtck.
come! I will give you food." He gave him food trout. Then he told.

Itciō'lXam: "Mxʟō'Xuana wā'maq ā'Xau? AXᴇlō'ita. Nîcqē'
He said to him: "Do you think your mother that one? She is another one. Not at all

wā'maq. Igᴇmutā'mit. Itcā'XᴇIēu Aq¡asXē'nasXēna." Lā aqa
your mother. She carried you away. Her name is Aq¡asXē'nasXēna." Long then

igaxatgoā'mama. Aqa iXᴇ'ʟXaôkt itcā'Xan. "Qā mioxō'la
she came home. Then he was angry her son. "How did you speak to him

imē'ʟatXᴇn, iq¡oā'cqoac." "Qā2 niuxō'la? Niuxō'la wā'maq ā'xauē.
your nephew, crane!" "How did I speak to him? I spoke to him your mother that.

Itcā'tcqum qamiā'îtx." "Ā4, ā, ā, ā'owē! k¡oaʟqā'4 amioxō'lalᴇma
Sick she always makes you." "Ah, ah, ah, younger brother! thus speak to him to

imē'ʟatXᴇn." Aqa wi igē'tcuktiX. Aqa wi igō'ya. Aqa wi
your nephew." Then again it became day. Then again she went. Then again

igē'yuctx. Tsō'yustîX ickoā'mam. Aqa wi igē'tcuktîX. Aqa
she carried him. In the evening she came home. Then again it got day. Then

following day she left him again. The Crane said again: "Come here." Then he gave him food. Now he gave him a knife, and said: "If you want to kill her, take her inland. When you find white pines, then kill her. If you want to kill her, cut her neck. Then something round will jump out. Catch it. She will say to you: 'Kill *me*.' But you must catch that round thing. She will die when you break it." On the following day she carried him again. He said: "We will go inland." Then they went inland and arrived on a mountain. There were many white pines. Now he took hold of a tree. Then she bent her neck and he cut it. Now a round thing jumped [out and ran about]. She said: "Kill *me*." Then he took it and squeezed it. She was dead. Now spruce trees and hemlock trees fell down. He climbed up that white pine. He ascended it and went up. There he was near the sky. Then he took his arrows and shot at the sky. Now he shot his arrow. He shot more. Now his arrows formed a

---

wi iqiqᴇ'ltaqʟ. Aqa wi itciō'lXam iq¦oā'sqoas: "Mā'tē." Aqa
again he was left. Then again he said to him the crane: "Come." Then

wit'ax itcē'lqoēm. Aqa itcā'ilōta aqewē'qē. "Ma'nîx amuwā'qoa,
again he gave him food. Then he gave it to him a knife. "When you kill her,

aqa ʟxē'leuX amō'kʟa. Ma'nîx amiusgā'ma iqā'mᴇn, aqa kōpā'
then inland carry her. When you find it white pines, then there

amuwā'qoa. Ma'nîx amuwā'qoa, ʟ¦q¦ōp amiō'xoa itcā'tuk. Aqa
kill her. When you kill her, cut do it her neck. Then

atsupnā'ya lō'ᴇlō. Aqa ya'xka amix·ᴇluwā'lalᴇm. Kē'nuwa
it will jump out a round thing. Then it catch it. Try

agᴇmulx·ā'ma: 'Nai'ka ntō'waq.' Amix·ᴇluwā'lalᴇma yaxi lō'ᴇlō.
she will say to you: 'Me kill.' Catch it that round thing.

Ma'nîx ʟk¦ōp amiō'xoa, aqa alō'mᴇqta." Aqa wit'ax igē'tcuktē.
When squeeze you do it, then she will die." Then again it got day.

Aqa wit'ax igē'yuctx. Aqa itcō'lXam: "Atxō'ya ʟxē'2leuX."
Then again she carried him. Then he said to her: "We will go inland."

Aqa îctō'ya ʟxē'2leuX. Aqa îcgiō'skam cā'xalîX ē'lX ipā'kalpa.
Then they went inland. Then they found up country mountain on.

Aqa ē'xowē iqa'mᴇn ixēnXā't. Aqa itcē'kᴇlka ē'mᴇqō. Aqa ē'wa
Then many white pines stood there. Then he took it a stick. Then thus (bent)

igī'yux itcā'tuk. Aqa ʟq¦ōp itcī'axôx itcā'tuk. Aqa itcî'sōpᴇna
she made it her neck. Then cut he did it her neck. Then it jumped

lō'ᴇlō. Aqa itcix·ᴇluwā'lalᴇmtck. Aqa igiō'lXam: "Ō, nai'ka
the round thing. Then he caught it. Then she said to him: "Oh, me

ntō'waq!" Aqa itcē'kᴇlka k¦a ʟk¦ōp itcī'yuX. Aqa igō'maqt. Aqa
kill me!" Then he took it and squeeze he did it. Then she was dead. Then

iō'îtcō ē'maktc. Aqa iō'îtcō iqā'ētᴇma. Aqa iōquē'wulXt iqā'mᴇn-
fell down the spruce trees. Then fell down the hemlock firs. Then he ascended a white pine

oqpā'tîx·. Aqa iō'ya cā'xalîX, ioquē'wulXt. Q¦oā'p igō'cax aqa
there. Then he went up, he ascended. Near the sky then

itcō'kuika tiā'qamatcX. Iā'maq itcē'lax igō'cax. Aqa itcā'maq
he took them his arrows. Shooting it he did it the sky. Then shooting it

itciā'lôx ayā'qamatcX. Wē't'ax itcā'maq atciā'lôx. Āqa ē'2taʟqt
he did it with it his arrow. Again shooting it he did it with it. Then long

long line. He had used all his arrows. Then he tied his bow [onto them] and went up. He arrived in the sky. Now he made a hole in the sky and found another country. Now he went and met an old woman. "What do you carry on your back, old woman? I am hungry; give me to eat." "I am the darkness; I am the darkness." "You must give me to eat." "I am the darkness, O, chief, I am the darkness." Now he jumped [at her] and took away her load. Then he pulled out the stopper. Now it became dark. "Close it! close it, O, chief, close it!" Then he closed her load and it became light again.

He went on and again he met people. They were black. "Where are you going?" "We are going down. We go into the hair of the people." [They were the lice.]

He went on. He met more people. He said to them: "Where are you going?" "We are going down. We are going to live on the bodies of the people." [They were the itch.]

He went on and again he met people. They were pretty people.

---

tiā'qamatcx. Aqa itixā'tqoam tiā'qamatcx. Aqa k¡au itcō'xoa
his arrows. Then he finished them his arrows. Then tie he did it
ayā'pL¡ikē. Aqa iuquē'wulXt.
his bow. Then he ascended.
Aqa iō'yam igō'caxpatîX. Aqa Lxoā'p itcī'yax igō'cax. Aqa
Then he arrived sky at there. Then hole he made it the sky. Then
iō'yam igō'caxpa. Aqa itciū'skam ēlX. Ixalō'ita ēlX. Aqa iō'ya.
he arrived sky in. Then he found it a country. Another country. Then he went.
Aqa itcLō'skam Lq¡eyō'qt Lqagē'lak. "Tān mnē'ctxula, aq¡eyō'qt?
Then he found it an old one a woman. "What your load, old woman?
Wa'lō gE'nuxt; nē'tqoîm." "Anp¡ōnmā'x, anp¡ōnmā'x." "Qā'txō
Hungry I am; give me to eat." "I am the darkness, I am the darkness." "Must
amnElqoē'ma." "Anp¡ōnmā'x, qē'ctāmX, anp¡ōnmā'x." Aqa
you give me to eat." "I am the darkness, O, chief, I am the darkness." Then
itcī'sōpEna; itcē'gElka itcā'ctxula. Aqa Lāq itcā'yôx ayā'k¡ektcōtē.
he jumped; he took it her load. Then out he took it its stopper.
Aqa igō'pōnEm. "Ē'xpō, ē'xpō, ē'xpō, qē'ctamX, ē'xpō." Aqa
Then it got dark. "Close it, close it, close it, O, chief, close it." Then
itcē'xpō itcā'stxula. Aqa tuwā'x igē'xauxîx.
he closed it her load. Then light it got.
Aqa wit'ax iō'ya. Aqa wit'ax L¡ap itcī'tôx tê'lXam; tLlE'XumaX
Then again he went. Then again find he did them people; black
tê'lXam. "Qāmta amcō'ya?" "Ā, antcō'ya gē'gualîX. Antcō'ya
people. "Where are you going?" "Ah, we go down. We go to
tê'lXam LE'gaqcō."
the people their hair."
Aqa wit'ax iō'ya. Aqa wit'ax itctō'skam tê'lXam tgatē't. Aqa
Then again he went. Then again he found them people coming. Then
itctō'lXam: "Qā'mta amcō'ya?" "Ā, antcō'ya gē'gualîX. Antcō'ya
he said to them: "Where are you going?" "Ah, we go down. We go to
tê'lXam ī'taLq."
the people their bodies."
Aqa wi iō'ya. Aqa wit'ax itctō'skam tê'lXam tgatē't;
Then again he went. Then again he found them people coming;
tgt¡ō'ktēmax tê'lXam. "Qā'mta amcō'ya?" "Ā4, gē'gualîX
pretty people. "Where are you going?" "Ah, down
antcō'ya. LE'gaqcō Natē'tanuēpa antcō'ya."
we go. Their hair the Indians to we go."

"Where are you going?" "Oh, we are going down to live in the hair of the people."

Then he went on again. He heard people singing. He came up to them. "Where are you going?" "We are going down. We are going to eat the blood of the people." [They were the fleas.]

Again he went on. He heard people whispering. He met them. "Oh, where are you going?" "We are going down; we shall drink the blood of the people."

Then he went a long way. He met a man. Two arrows were sticking in his body. After a little while he met another man. He said: "O, my son-in-law, did you see my game?" "I did not see anything. I only met a person in whose body two arrows were sticking." "What [kind of animals] do you hunt? [I am hunting men.] When you go on, take our road; do not go the other way." Now he went a short distance. Then he met a mountain goat. Two arrows stuck in it. Then he saw another person. He said to him: "Did you see my game, son-in-law?" "Yes, I saw it." "Take our road there."

Aqa wi iō'ya. Itcauitcî'maq tê'lXam ōkualā'lam: "Ā4!" Aqa
Then again he went. He heard them people singing: "Ah!" Then

ioquā'quam tê'lXam: "Qā'mta amcō'ya?" "Antcō'ya gē'gualîX.
he met them people: "Where are you going?" "We go down.

NtckLXElEmō'xoma tê'lXam Lgā'qawulqt."
We go to eat the people their blood."

Aqa wi iō'ya. Aqa wit'ax itcauitcî'maq tê'lXam:
Then again he went. Then again he heard them people:

"Ā, ā, ā, ā, ā, ā." Lq¡āp itcî'tôx. "Ā, qā'mta amcō'ya?" "Ā,
"Ā, ā, ā, ā, ā, ā!" (whispered.) Meet he did them. "Ah, where are you going?" "Ah,

antcō'ya gē'gualîX. Tê'lXam Lgā'qawulqt antckLōqu'mcta."
we go down. The people their blood we shall drink."

Aqa wi iō'ya kElā'îX. Itcî'LqElkEl LēXā't LgoaLē'lX. Ā, môkct
Then again he went far. He saw him one person. Ah, two

tqā'matcX tElgā't. Koala' aqa wi Lgōn LgoaLē'lX itcî'LqElkEl.
arrows were in him. A little while, then again another person he saw him.

"Ō, ē'qsîX. Imē'qElkEl tci itcî'naqan?" "K'ā'ya nîct inē'qElkEl.
"Oh, son-in-law! You saw [int. part.] my game?" "Nothing not I saw it.

Lā'ema LgoaLē'lX, môkct tqā'matcX tElgā't." "Tāntxō ma'yax
Only a person, two arrows were in him." "What then you

imē'naqan? Ma'nîx amō'ya tayaX intcā'yixatk, a'qa ta'yax ē'Xatk
your game? When you go that our road, then that road

amilō'ya. Nîct amō'ya ē'wata ixalō'ita ē'Xatk." Aqa iō'ya. Mank
go on it. Not go there the other road." Then he went. A little

kElā'îX iō'ya; itciū'skam ē'cîXq. Môkct tqā'matcX tElgā't. Aqa
far he went; he found it a mountain goat. Two arrows were in it. Then

wi Lgōn LgoaLē'lX itcî'LqElkEl. Aqa wit'ax iLgiō'lXam:
again another person he saw him. Then again he said to him:

"Imē'qElkEl itcî'naqan, ē'qcîX?" "Ā, inē'qalkEl." "Ēwatā'x
"Did you see my game, son-in-law?" "Ah, I saw it." "There

antcā'iXatk, ēwatā' amalō'ya."
our road, there go on it."

He went on and came to a parting of the roads. Then he walked the road to the left. He went and went. Then he found human bones. He went a short distance and [the road] was stinking. He walked on and saw a house. He entered and searched for urine. He found it and washed himself. After he had finished washing he searched for a comb, but he could not find one. He saw a large basket, and thought: "Perhaps there is a comb in that basket." He untied the basket and took it down. He took out a mountain-goat blanket. Then he took out another one. He took out five in all. Then he found a woman,—oh, a pretty woman! Bones of children were tied to her hair. She gave him a comb which was made of human bones. Now he combed himself, and he put back the mountain-goat blankets. Then he hung her up there. He stayed there. Soon the noise of falling objects [was heard] five times. A person was thrown into the house. Another one was thrown into the house. Still another one was thrown into the house. Five [dead] people were

---

Aqa iō'ya wē't'ax. Aqa itcō'skam cī'iXatk. Aqa iā'loya ē'wa
Then he went again. Then he found them two roads. Then he went on it there

q¡ēq¡ê'tcktan ē'Xatk. Aqa iō'ya. Iō'ya, aqa itctō'skam tᴇ'gaq¡ōtcō
the left the road. Then he went. He went, then he found them bones

mᴇmalō'ctîkc. Mank kᴇlā'îX iō'ya, aqa ka'nauwē ī'takcti. Lā4 iō'ya.
of dead ones. A little far he went, then all stinking. Long he went.

Aqa itcō'quikᴇl tqu'ʟē. Iō'pqam. Itcʟō'naxʟ ʟō'ᴇnō. Aqa itcʟō'ckam
Then he saw it a house. He entered. He searched for urine. Then he found it

ʟō'ᴇnō. Aqa igᴇxᴇ'qoat. Lā2, iʟᴇ'Xōʟq igᴇxᴇ'qoat. Aqa itcʟō'nᴇxʟ
urine. Then he washed. Long, he finished he washed. Then he searched for

ʟktcā'ma. Näct itcʟō'skam ʟktcā'ma. Aqa itcē'qᴇlkᴇl iqā'giltk. Aqa
a comb. Not he found it a comb. Then he saw it a basket. Then

igîXʟō'xoa-ît: "ʟXuan kōpā' ʟktcā'ma." Aqa stuXᵘ itcī'yuX iqā'giltk.
he thought: "Perhaps there a comb." Then untie he did it the basket.

Aqa itciō'tXᴇm gē'gualîX. ʟāq° itcî'ʟôx ʟēXt ʟqoa'k. Aqa wi
Then he placed it down. Out he did it one mountain-goat blanket. Then again

ʟgōn ʟāq° itcî'ʟôx. Quî'numa ʟāq° itcî'tôx. Aqa itcʟō'skam
one more out he did it. Five out he did them. Then he found her

ʟqagē'lak. Ō, ʟt¡ō'kti ʟqagē'lak. Ō4, k¡au'k¡au tᴇ'ʟguXt tᴇ'q¡ōtcō.
a woman. Oh, pretty a woman. Oh, tied were on her bones.

Pāʟ iʟā'q¡akctaq tᴇ'q¡ōtcō, tqā'tōtēnîkc tᴇ'gaq¡ōtcō. Aqa iʟkʟē'lōt
Full her head bones, children their bones. Then she gave it to him

ʟktcā'ma. ʟmē'mᴇlōs tᴇ'ʟaq¡ōtcō. Aqa iʟēxalgᴇ'tcam. Aqa wi
a comb. Dead people their bones. Then he combed himself. Then again

itcawē'kitk taXi tqoā'kᴇmax. Aqa wi itcup¡ō'nit kōpā'. Aqa
he put back those blankets. Then again he hung her up there. Then

iō'ʟa-ît. Koala aqa qul. Aqa wi qul, aqa wi qul, aqa
he stayed. Soon then noise of falling objects. Then again noise of falling objects, then again noise of falling objects, then

wit'ax qul. Quā'nᴇmîX qul. Iqʟxā'ma ʟgoaʟē'lX tqu'ʟēpa.
again noise of falling objects. Five times noise of falling objects. It was thrown down a person house in.

Aqa wi ʟgōn iqʟxā'ma. Aqa wi ʟgō'nax iqʟxā'ma. Aquî'nᴇmîkc
Then again another was thrown down. Then again another was thrown down. Five

tê'lXam iqoxoā'ima tqu'ʟēpa. Iʟxā'la-it iā'qoq itco'yuct.
persons were thrown down the house in. They stayed his sons the evening star's.

thrown into the house. Then the Evening Star's children stayed there. The basket began to swing. Then the old man said: "Ah!" Again [the basket] began to swing. Then he said again: "Ah! O my children! Quick; take your sister down. Something evil has been done to her." Now they took her down and placed her near [the visitor]. Now they gave him a basket filled with human eyes. He thought: "I will leave them." The next morning all his brothers-in-law went out.

Then he went out. He went back. He found a road and went along. There was a good smell there. He went a long distance. Then he found the bones of mountain goats. He went a little while and found a house. He entered. Now he desired to wash himself. He searched for urine and he found it in a basket. Then he washed himself and entered again. He searched for a comb, but he did not find it. Again he untied a large basket and took out one blanket. He took out another one. He took out five in all. Now he saw a

---

Igēxᴇlā'lalᴇmtck iqā'giltk. Aqa igē'kîm iq¡eyō'qt: "Ā4!" Wī't'ax
It swung the basket. Then he said the old man: "Ah!" Again

igēxᴇlā'lalᴇmtck. Aqa wi igē'kîm: "Ā4, ō ā'qoamax! Ai'aq
it swung. Then again he said: "Āh, o children! Quick

gē'gualîX amcî'kôX amcā'mtXîX. Aqa itcā'mᴇl itciā'lôx." Aqa
down make your sister. Then her badness he made it on her." Then

gē'gualîX iʟᴇ'kôx. Aqa iʟgāigᴇmʟā'ētᴇmit. Aqa iqtē'lᴇqoîm aēXt
down they did her. Then they placed her near him. Then they gave him to eat one

at¡ā'ks tê'lXam sgā'xôst. Ā4qa igîXʟō'xo-ît: "Tgt¡ō'kti
Cowlitz basket people their eyes. Then he thought: "Good

anʟgᴇlō'qʟqa." Aqa igē'tcuktîX. Aqa wi iʟō'ya ʟkanauwē'tîkc
I leave them." Then it got day. Then again they went all

ʟiā'xqēXināna.
his brothers-in-law.

Aqa iō'pa. Aqa iō'ya, igiXᴇ'takoa. Aqa ʟap itcō'xôx ā'eXatk.
Then he went out. Then he went, he turned back. Then find he did it a road.

Aqa iō'ya, iā'loya. Aqa ka'nauwē q¡ᴇs wuX¡ ā'eXatk. Kᴇlā'îX
Then he went, he went on it. Then all good smell that road. Far

iō'ya, aqa ictō'skam tᴇ'q¡ōtcō. Aqa ē'cîXk tē'iaq¡ōtcō. Aqa iō'yam
he went, then he found them bones. Then mountain goats their bones. Then he arrived

mank kᴇlā'îX. Aqa itco'quikᴇl tqu'ʟē. Aqa iō'pqam. Aqa wit'ax
a little far. Then he saw it a house. Then he entered. Then again

tq¡ēx itcî'tôx aliXqoā'tē. Aqa wi itcʟō'naxʟ ʟō'ᴇnō. Aqa wi
wish he did them he would wash. Then again he searched for it urine. Then again

itcʟō'skam at¡ā'kspa ʟā'luXt. Aqa wit'ax igēxō'qoat. Aqa wi
he found it a Cowlitz basket in it was in it. Then again he washed himself. Then again

iō'pqam. Aqa wi itcʟō'naxʟ ʟktcā'ma. Näct itcʟō'skam ʟktcā'ma.
he entered. Then again he searched for it a comb. Not he found it a comb.

Aqa wi stuX^{u} itcī'yuX iqā'giltk. ʟāq° itcî'ʟux ʟēXt ʟqoā'k. Aqa
Then again untie he did it the basket. Out he did it one mountain-goat blanket. Then

wi ʟgō'nax ʟāq° itcî'ʟux. Quā'nᴇma tqoā'k ʟāq° itcî'tux. Aqa
again another out he did it. Five mountain-goat blankets out he did them. Then

woman—a pretty woman. Her hair was full of dentalia. She gave him a comb and he combed himself. When he had finished, he put back all the blankets and hung her up there. Then he remained there. Now the noise of falling objects was heard. It was heard five times. Then five men came in, [the sons of the Morning Star. They had caught mountain goats.] They stayed there a long time. Then the basket began to swing. The old man said: "Ah!" Again it began to swing. Then he said again: "Ah!" He spoke to his children: "Take your sister down. Something bad has been done to her." Then they took out their sister and took her to [the visitor]. Now he took her and they stayed there for a long time. [She was the Sun.]

Now one night the Evening Star's sons made war upon them. They shot arrows. [His daughter,] the Moon, was ashamed. Now they went home. [The Sun] said to her: "When people go to defecate, you shall light them. You are not as good as I am. I shine when chiefs exchange presents." Now the Moon went home.

---

itcLō'skam Lqagē'lak. Ō, Lt¡ō'kti Lqagē'lak. Ō4, La'ktēmax
he found it a woman. Oh, pretty a woman. Oh, dentalia

pāL LE'Laqcōpa. ILkLē'lōt Lktcā'ma. ILēxElga'tcam. ILē'XuLq
full her hair at. She gave it to him a comb. He combed himself. He finished

iLēxalga'tcam. Aqa wi itcauwē'kitk ka'nauwē tqoā'kEmax. Aqa wi
combing himself. Then again he put them back all mountain-goat blankets. Then again

itcup¡ō'nit kōpā' wit'ax. Aqa iō'La-it. Lā'lê; aqa qul igē'xōXîX.
he put her up there again. Then he stayed. Long; then noise of falling objects it became.

Aqa wi qul igē'xōXîX. Qoā'nEmîX qul igēxōXîX.
Then again noise of falling objects it became. Five times noise of falling objects it became.

ILa'skatpq Lkanamquî'numîkc. ILxē'la-ît. Lā'lê iLxē'la-it. Aqa
They entered all five. They stayed. Long they stayed. Then

igēxElā'lalEmtck iqā'giltk. Aqa igē'kîm iq¡eyō'qt: "Ā4." Wē't'ax
it swung the basket. Then he said the old man: "Ah." Again

igēxElā'lalEmtck. Aqa wi igē'kîm: "Ā4." ItcLō'lXam iā'qôq:
it swung. Then again he said: "Ah." He said to them his children:

"Ai'aq Lāq° mcî'kôx amtcā'mEtXîX." Aqa itcā'mEl itciā'lôx. Aqa
"Quick off make her your younger sister." Then her badness he made it on her. Then

Lāq° iLE'kôx aLā'mEtXîX. LgāigEmLā'etamēt. Ā'qa itcō'ckam. Ā'qa
off they did her their younger sister. They put her near him. Then he took her. Then

icxē'la-ît. Lā'lā, lā'lā îcxē'la-ît.
they two stayed. Long, long they two stayed.

Aqa Xā'pîX aqa sāq° iqE'Lôx. Aqa iLxE'maqt. IgaXEmā'sa-ît
Then evening then war was made on them. Then they were shot. She was ashamed

akLE'mēn, aqa iLE'Xk¡oa. Iqō'lXam: "Qiā'x k¡a LkLōtsā'tsamx, tcXua
the moon, then she went home. She was told: "If they defecate, then

waX qamLgElō'xoax. Nîct xE'lgatcX. Nai'ka, qiā'x tkanā'xîmc
shine you do. Not like me. I, if chiefs

tkilē'ma gEnoxoā'xax, tcXua wāX qanLukuē'xa." Aqa iLî'Xk¡oa
exchange they do, then shine I do for them." Then she went home

akLE'mēn. Aqa icxē'la-ît kōpa'.
the moon. Then they two stayed there.

They stayed there a long time. Then she gave birth to two boys who were grown together at their abdomens. Now they began to grow. [One day she said to her husband:] "Come; I will louse you." Now she loused him outside. He sat bending down and dug the ground with his hands. Then he made a hole in the ground and looked down. Now he saw houses, and he thought: "Oh, that is my father's town." He said to his wife: "Let me alone." He entered the house and lay down for a long time. It grew night. [Then the Morning Star said to his daughter:] "Did you scold your husband?" "No, I did not scold him. He is homesick." "Heigh, my son-in-law! Why does he not say so? Quick; take some willow bark to that old woman." Now they brought willow bark and she made a large basket. They brought her more willow bark and she made ropes. After she had finished the ropes they put blankets into the basket and filled it. Then they put them on top of the blankets. Then they let them down and they arrived on the ground.

Now a child was shooting at a target. Then he took his arrow

Lā, aqa igakxE'tōm. Cmōkct ikcoxu'tōm. Gipā' cXq;oā'LqōX
Long, then she gave birth. Two she gave birth to. Here grown together

ictā'wanpa. Aqa mank stā'qa-iL stā'xan igicxE'lôx. "Ai'aq
their belly at. Then a little big the two children became. "Quick

aLamgē'qcta!" Aqa ikLigE'kiqct Lā'XanîX. Aqa LE'kLEk itcī'yuX
I will louse you!" Then she loused him outside. Then dig he did it

ēlX. Aqa Lxoa'p itcī'yuX ēlX. Aqa igē'kîkct ē'wa gē'gualîX.
the ground. Then hole he made it the ground. Then he looked there down.

Aqa itcō'quikEl tqLē'max. Aqa igîXLō'xoa-ît: "Ō, ala'xti itcEmā'm
Then he saw them houses. Then he thought: "Oh, then my father

iā'lXam." Aqa itcō'lXam ayā'kika: "Iāc nE'xa!" Aqa iō'pqam.
his town." Then he said to her his wife: "Let alone do me." Then he entered.

Aqa igexō'kcit. Lā2, igō'pōnEm. "Ēmiō'mElatci imē'kikal?"
Then he lay down. Long. it got dark. "You scold [int. part.] your husband?"

"K;ā'ya nîct iniō'mEl. Ikā'k;ᵘL; tcī'yuxt." "Hē, itcī'qcîX! qātsqē
"No not I scold. Homesickness makes him. "Heigh, my son-in-law! why

nîct igē'kîm? Ai'aq. ā'lukL amō'tan tau aq;cyō'qt." Iqā'lukL
not he speaks? Quick, bring her willow bark that old woman." It was brought to her

aqa amō'tan aq;cyō'qt. Aqa igī'yux iā'qa-iL iqō'mxōm. Aqa wi
then willow bark the old woman. Then she made it a large basket. Then again

iqā'lukL amō'tan. Aqa atā'xtax igE'tôx tE'pa-it. Aqa ka'nauwē
it was brought to her willow bark. Then next she made them ropes. Then all

ikLō'koaLq tE'pa-ît. Aqa iqau'wēkitk tqoā'kEmax. PāL igē'xôx
she finished them ropes. Then they were put into it mountain-goat blankets. Full became

iqō'mxōm. Aqa iqLxēlā'itEmē, caxala' iqLxēlā'itEmē. Aqa
the basket. Then they were put into it, on top they were put into it. Then

iqLō'xo-iktcō. Aqa iLō'yam gē'gualîX ē'lXpadîX.
they were let down. Then they arrived below country on that.

Aqa Lk'ā'skas wā'q;pas Lkēx. Aqa itcā'kîlka aLā'qamatcX. Aqa
Then a boy target he made. Then he took it his arrow. Then

itcaLxa'pcōt. "Ā'nēt agE'qamatcX, iqē'sqēs, tgE'kiūtgoax. Ā'nēt
he hid it from him. "Give me my arrow, blue-jay, I am poor. Give me

and hid it. "Give me my arrow, Blue-jay: I am poor. Give me my arrow, Blue-jay: I am poor." "Come here! Who are you?" "Oh, I was not yet born when Aq;asXē'nasXēna took away my elder brother." "Oh, [I am your elder brother.] It is I." "I think it is you, Blue-jay." Now his sister-in-law took him and blew upon his eyes. Then his eyesight was restored. Now she gave him a small mountain-goat blanket. "Quick; go home and bring your father and your mother." The boy went home. When he arrived at the house he said: "Oh, my elder brother came home." His mother began to cry: "I think Blue-jay is deceiving you." "Well, feel of my blanket." Then she felt of his blanket. It was soft. "Perhaps he came back, indeed." "Indeed, it is true. I came to fetch you. My sister-in-law sent me." Now he took his mother and father to them. She washed their faces and their eyesight was restored. "Quick; go and sweep our house and make a fire." They swept the house. After they had finished they went to fetch those who had just arrived. Now they carried all the property [into the house]. They stayed there. Now Blue-jay opened the door and defecated in the doorway. [He was told:] "Take a

agᴇ'qamatcX iqē'sqēs, tgᴇ'kiutgoax." "Nî'Xua mᴇ'tē! ʟān mā'yax?"
my arrow, blue-jay, I am poor." "Well! come! who you?"

"Ō, nai'ka akoa nîct qā ngoaʟē'lX igiutā'mit Aq;asXē'nasXēna
"Oh, I, thus not when person, she took him away Aq;asXē'nas-Xēna

ī'tcîlX." "Ō4, nai'ka, nai'ka!" "K;ā mai'ka iqē'sqēs." Aqa
my elder brother." "Oh, I, I!" "And you blue-jay." Then

igē'kᴇlka ayā'potexan. Pō'pō igī'yuX siā'xôst. Tuwā'x, igē'kîket.
she took him his sister-in-law. Blow she did him his face. Light, he saw.

Aqa iqʟē'lōt iʟō'koa-îts ʟqoā'k. "Ai'aq, mu'Xkoa, cgā'lᴇmam
Then he was given a small mountain-goat blanket. "Quick! go home! fetch them

amē'qō k;a wē'mam. Aqa igē'Xk;oa ik;ā'skas. Iō'yam tqu'ʟēpa.
your mother and your father. Then he went home the boy. He came home the house to.

"Ō, igitē'mam ē'tcîlX." "Ō2," agᴇ'tcax wā'yaq. "K;ā iqē'sqēs lā'xlax
"Oh, he came my elder brother." "Oh," she cried his mother. "And blue-jay deceive

tcī'mōxt." "Nî'Xua aʟᴇ'gᴇlga ʟgᴇ'pasiskoa." Aqa igᴇ'ʟgᴇlga
he did you." "Well, feel of my blanket." Then she felt of

ʟiā'k;ētē. Aqa ʟmᴇn ʟiā'k;ētē. "Â4, ʟXuan ā'qanuwē igitē'mam."
his blanket Then soft his blanket. "Ah, perhaps indeed he came."

"Ō, ā'qanuwē, ā'qanuwē. Iamtgā'lᴇmam. Igᴇntō'koatck
"Oh, indeed, indeed I came to fetch you. She sent me

agᴇ'pōtexan." Aqa itcī'cukʟ wā'yaq k;a wī'yam. Itcō'kʟam.
my sister-in-law." Then he took them his mother and his father. He brought them.

Aqa ikcōmē'nak;ua, aqa icᴇ'kîket. "Ai'aq amtktōq;oē'la tᴇ'lxaô.qʟ.
Then she washed their faces, then they saw. "Quick sweep it our house

Amtktōq;oē'la, aqa alamtXîlgē'ʟxa." Aqa îcktō'q;oē'la tᴇ'ctaqʟ. Aqa
sweep it, then make fire." Then they swept it their house. Then

iʟkcō'koaʟ tᴇ'ctaqʟ. Aqa iʟkcōguā'lᴇmam ctaXi ctē'mam. Aqa
they finished it their house. Then they went to fetch them those who came. Then

iʟkᴇ'tokwē ka'nauwē taXi ʟā'kʟᴇlā'lᴇmax. Aqa iʟxelā'itX. Aqa
they carried it all that their property. Then they stayed. Then

itca-ixᴇ'lᴇqʟ iqē'sqēs. Aqa itcʟō'tsatsa icī'qēpa. "Ā'kᴇlka wuX
he opened the door blue-jay. Then he defecated on the door "Take it that

firebrand." [He took it and] struck it against his backside. "Ananā! I am burnt. Maybe his elder brother came back, and he burnt me." He looked back and there he saw chiefs sitting there. "Oh, our chief has come back." Now he went to all the houses and told the people.

They stayed there for a long time and the two boys grew up. Now they called the people. They saw the children. They arose together and sat down together. "What do you think, Robin? I will cut them apart. Then we shall have two chiefs." "Ha, do you alone see that? Why don't you be quiet?" Three times Blue-jay said he would cut them, but Robin did not like it. One day Blue-jay cut them. Then one went to one side and one to the other. They fell down and their intestines were pulled out. Then the woman looked at him and Blue-jay caught fire. His hair was all burned. "Eh, Blue-jay, now I must go home upward;" and she said: "Itc¡xiā'nē shall be your name. You shall go into the water. Now I will go up. When a chief is about to die, one of my children shall be seen. When two chiefs are going to die, both will be seen [together]." [The Twins are the Sundogs.]

ā'tōL." Itca-igE'qoaLq iā'pōtcpa. "Anananananā'! inE'xLEl. Aqa LX
fire." He pushed it his anus at. "Anananananā'h! I am burnt. Then maybe

igigā'tkoam ē'yalXt. Aqa itcinXLE'lama." Ē'wa igē'xôx, igiXE'nakoa.
he arrived his elder brother. Then I am burnt." Thus he did, he looked back.

Aqa itcō'quikEl tkanā'xîmet oxoēlā'itX. "Ō, ilxā'xak¡Emana
Then he saw them chiefs were there. "Oh, our chief

igitē'mam." Aqa iō'ya ka'nauwē tqLē'max. Aqa igiXgu'Lîtck
returned." Then he went all houses. Then he told

iqē'sqēs. Lā'2lā aqa iLxē'la-it. Ctā'qa-iL igicxE'lôx. Aqa iqō'xoaktck
blue-jay. Long then they stayed. Large they became. Then they called them

tē'lXam. Ā4qa iqcō'qomitck sk¡ā'skas. Aqa istō'tXuîtx skanasmô'kst,
the people. Then they were seen the two boys. Then they arose two together,

aqa istōLā'itx skanasmô'kst. "Wuska qā'da imēXata'koax skā'sait?
then they sat down two together. "Ha, how your mind, robin?

Lq¡ōp antcō'xoa. ALqi smôkst skak¡Emā'na acxō'xa." "Wā'ska
Cut I will do them. Later on two chiefs they will be." "Ha,

mai'ma na mcō'qomē? Qa'nsîx qān mxōx?" Lō'nîX igē'kîm
you only [int. part.] do you see them? When quiet you are?" Three times he spoke

iqē'sqēs, Lq¡ōp atcō'xoa. Kā'sait nîct tq¡ēx itcî'tôx. Ā'eXt aqaLā'x
blue-jay, cut he will them. Robin not like he did it. One day

aqa Lq¡ōp itcî'cux iqē'sqēs. Iō'ya ē'wata ēXā't, igiXē'maxit.
then cut he did them blue-jay. He went there one, he fell down.

Tiā'q¡ameuke Lāx igō'xôx. Ē'wata eXā't igiXē'maxit. Tiā'q¡ameuke
His intestines out came. Then one fell down. His intestines

Lāx igō'xôx. Egî'uket wuX aqagē'lak. Aqa igē'XumLXa. Liā'qcō
out came. She looked at him that woman. Then he caught fire. His hair

ka'nauwē LE'XumLXa. "Ē, iqē'sqēs, aqa nîXkuā'ya sā'xalîX." Aqa
all burnt. "Eh, blue-jay, then I return upward." Then

igiō'lXam: "Itc¡Xiā'nē imē'xaleu mai'ka. Ltcu'qoapa mō'ya. Aqa
she said to him: "Itc¡Xiā'nē your name you. Water in you go. Then

nai'ka nō'ya sā'xalîX. Manē'x aLō'mEqta Lgak¡amā'na, aqa LēXā't
I I go upward. When he will die a chief, then one

LgE'xan aqLqElkElā'ya. Manē'x amô'ketîke ckanā'xîmet aluxuaLā'ita,
my child will be seen. When two chiefs will die,

aqa skanasmô'kst aqsqElkElā'ya."
then both will be seen."

Myth of Nikciamtcā'c (told 1890)

There was a maiden. The Panther was the chief of one town. Now Blue-jay said to the maiden: "Go and look for the Panther; he is an elk hunter." One day she went. She went a long distance and came to a house. She entered. Now the house was all painted. She stayed at the bed of the Beaver. She stayed there. In the evening the Mink came home and carried trout. Then the Otter came; he carried steel-head salmon. Then the Raccoon came; he carried crawfish. Then the Muskrat came; he carried flags. The Lynx came; he carried ducks. The Mouse came home; she carried camass-roots. All came home. Only their eldest brother was not there. "Maybe our elder brother fell down." The woman thought: "Oh, maybe he is a canoe builder." In the evening a man came groaning. He came home. His belly was that large [indicating]. After some time he went near

---

Nikciamtcā'c Itcā'k¡anē

Nikciamtcā'c Her Myth

Lxelā'etîX aēXā't aLā'hat¡au, awā'wa. Ik¡oa'yawa iLā'Xak¡Emana
There was one maiden, it is said. The panther their chief

La-îtci ēXt giLā'lXam. Aqa itcō'lXam iqē'sqēs aLā'hat¡au, inā'xLam
those one people of a town. Then he said to her blue-jay the maiden: "Search for

ik¡oa'yawa, imō'lEkumax iā'k¡etēnax. Igō'n ē'kua aqa igō'ya.
the panther, elks hunter." One day then she went.

Igō'ya, kElā'îX igō'ya. Igogoā'qoam tqu'Lē. Igā'ekupq. Aqa
She went, far she went. She arrived at a house. She entered. Then

ka'nauwē itā'kēmatck taXi tqu'Lē. Aqa iqā'nuq iā'lXemitk igō'La-it.
all painted that house. Then beaver his bed she stayed.

Igō'La-it. Tsō'yustîX igiXatk¡oā'mam kō'sa-it. Itcā'Lam ā'q¡EXEnē.
She stayed. In the evening he came home the mink. He brought a trout.

Igitē'mam ē'nanaks. Itcî'Lam iq¡oanē'X. IgiXatk¡oā'mam iLatā't.
He came the otter. He brought a steel-head salmon. He came home the raccoon.

ItcLî'tam LqaLxā'la. IgiXatk¡oā'mam its¡Enē'sts¡Enēs. ItctE'Lam
He brought crabs. He came home the muskrat. He brought

tElkoā'tē. IgiXatk¡oā'mam ipu'koa. ItctE'Lam tguēXguē'Xukc.
flags. He came home the lynx. He brought ducks.

IgaXatk¡oā'mam ā'cō. IktE'Lam tE'lalX. Ka'nauwē iguXoatk¡oā'mam.
She came home the mouse. She brought camass. All came home.

Aqa k¡ā'ya ē'LalXt. "LXuan igēXgē'itcomē ē'lxalXt." IgaxLō'Xa-ît
Then none their elder brother. "Perhaps he fell upon his own body, our elder brother." She thought

aqagē'lak: "IkEnī'm Lqa Laxōtck¡ē'na." Xā'pîX aLXilqā'yax LgoaLē'lX
the woman: "Canoe I think a builder." At dark he groaned a person

Ltēt. Aqa iLî'tpqam LgoaLē'lX. Ē'4wa iā'qa-iL iLā'wan. Lä2, aqa
coming. Then he entered the person. Thus large his belly. Long, then

her. "Go and take my trout, woman," he said. Now she went down to the beach. All the canoes were lying there. She searched for trout, but she could not find any. Then she found a bundle of willow branches. She went to the house and entered. "Did you bring trout?" "I did not see any; I found only this bundle of willow branches." "What kind of salmon do you take? [Willows are my salmon.]" After some time night came, and they went to sleep. Now her husband slept. She put her hand on his stomach. Now it was full of sticks. Then he awoke, and his stomach felt sick. He sang: "Trout, trout broke my bones, they broke my ribs!" Then the woman arose. Now she went to the end of the town. There she found a small house. There she lay down. Now it grew day.

The Beaver said to the Mink: "Go and bring your sister-in-law. Say to her: 'Will you keep me, or shall I take you to him?'" Now the Mink went. "I came to fetch you, Nikciamtcā'c! Your husband

---

iLagE'mLa-ît. "Tgā'lEmam tE'q¡ēxEnē, aqagē'lak!" Aqa igō'Lxa
he approached her. Fetch the trouts, woman!" Then she went to the beach

aqagē'lak. Aqa ka'nauwē akE'nim ōlā'kaôX. Aqa iktō'naxL
the woman. Then all canoes were there. Then she searched for them,

tE'q¡ēxEnē. K¡ā'ya, nîct iktō'cgam. Aqa igiō'ckam ēlā'îtk. K¡au
the trouts. Nothing, not she found them. Then she found them willows. Tied

igē'xôx. Aqa igā'xk¡oa tqu'Lēpa. Igō'pqam. "Tsō'Xoa, tE'q¡ēXEnē
they were. Then she went home house to. She came in. "Well, trouts

imtE'Lam tci?" "K¡ā nîct inō'quikEl. Iā'ema elā'itk k¡au ikē'x
you brought them [int. part.]?" "Nothing not I saw them. Only willows tied were

iniū'ckam." "Tāntxō mā'yax tE'mēq¡EXEnē?" Lä2, aqa igō'ponEm.
I found them." "What your trouts?" Long, then it got dark.

ILkLqā'yoXuit aqa ioqō'ptit itcā'kikal. A'qa ē'wa igī'yux iā'wan.
They went to sleep then slept her husband. Then thus she did it his belly.

IkLikxā'ema LE'gakci. Aqa tE'mqō pāL iā'wan. Aqa kōpa'
She put on to it her hand. Then sticks full his belly. Then there

igiXî'qo-îtq. Aqa iā'tcqEm iā'wan. Aqa igē'ktcxEm:
he awoke. Then sick his belly. Then he sang his conjurer's song:

"K¡ēXana, k¡ēXana, k¡ēXana āiqtē'nElXala, taXi tgē'kEmtōmax."

"Trout, trout, trout broke my bones those my ribs."

Aqa igaxa'latck wuX aqagē'lak. Aqa igō'ya yaXi kE'mukitîX.
Then she arose that woman. Then she went that end of town.

Aqa iktō'cgam itō'qoa-îts tqu'Lē. Aqa kōpā' igaxaō'kcit. Aqa
Then she found it a small house. Then there she lay down. Then

igē'tcuktîX: "Anetā'2m amē'pōtcxan, kō'sa-it! AmulXā'mam:
it got day: "Fetch her your sister-in-law, mink! Go and say to her:

'Mai'ka tci namxā'Lx, nai'ka tci qamanā'Lx?'" Aqa iō'ya
'You [int. part.] do you take me for yourself, I [int. part.] do you take me to him?'" Then he went

kō'sa-it. "Ayamtgā'lEmā'm, Nikciamtcā'c! ItcEnōlXā'm ēmē'kikal:
mink. "I came to fetch you, Nikciamtcā'c! He said to me your husband:

'Mai'ka tci namxā'Lx, nai'ka tci qamanā'Lx?'" "Ō, nîct tq¡ēx
'You [int. part.] do you take me for yourself, I [int. part.] do you take me to him?'" "Oh, not like

said to me: 'Will you keep me, or shall I take you to him?'" "Oh, I don't like you. You are stingy." Mink went home. "She is lazy."

"Quick, Otter, fetch her. Say to her: 'Will you keep me, or shall I take you to him?'" Then the Otter went. "Oh, I came to fetch you. Your husband has sent me. He said to me: 'Will you keep me, or shall I take you to him?'" She did not speak. Then he said again: "I came to fetch you; I came to fetch you." "Oh, I don't like you. You are stingy." The Otter went home. "Oh, she is lazy."

Then he said to the Black-bear: "Go and fetch your sister-in-law." The Black-bear went. "Oh, I came to fetch you. Your husband said to me: 'Will you keep me, or shall I take you to him?'" "Oh, I don't like you. You are stingy."

He said to the Raccoon: "Go, Raccoon, and fetch your sister-in-law." Raccoon went. "Oh, I came to fetch you. Your husband said to me: 'Will you keep me, or shall I take you to him?'" "Oh," she said to him, "I don't like you. You are stingy. You do not give me any crawfish."

"Oh, Muskrat, go and fetch your sister-in-law. Go and say to her: 'Will you keep me, or shall I take you to him?'" The Muskrat went. "Oh, I came to fetch you. Your husband said to me: 'Will

---

iā'môxt, tᴇmē'onîm." Igē'xk¡oa kō'sa-it. "Ā, q¡am īgā'xôx."
I do you, you are stingy." He went home mink. "Oh, lazy she is."

"Ai'aq agā'lᴇmam, ē'nanakc! AmulXā'mam: 'Mai'ka tci namxā'ʟx,
"Quick fetch her, otter! Go and say to her: 'You [int. part.] do you take me for yourself,

nai'ka tci qamanā'ʟx?'" Aqa iō'ya ē'nanakc. "Ayamtga'lᴇmā'm,
I [int. part.] do you take me to him?'" Then he went the otter. "I came to fetch you.

Nikciamtcā'c. Itcintō'koatck imē'kikal. Itcᴇnō'lXam: 'Mai'ka tci
Nikciamtcā'c. He has sent me your husband. He said to me: 'You [int. part.]

namxā'ʟx, nai'ka tci qamanā'ʟx?'" Nāctqa igā'kim. Aqa wē't'ax
do you take me for yourself, I [int. part.] do you take me to him?'" Not at all she spoke. Then again

itcō'lXam: "Iamtgā'lᴇmam, iamtgā'lᴇmam." Aqa igiō'lXam: "Ō,
he said to her: "I came to fetch you, I came to fetch you." Then she said to him: "Oh,

nēct tq¡ēx iā'mᴇtxt, tᴇmē'onim." Igē'Xk¡oa ē'nanakc. "Ā, q¡am
not like I do you, you are stingy." He went home the otter. "Ah, lazy

igā'xôx."
she is."

Itciō'lXam iskē'ntXoa: "Agā'lᴇmam amē'pōtcXan, iskē'ntXoa!
He said to him the bear: "Go and fetch her your sister-in-law, bear!

AmulXā'mam: 'Mai'ka tci,'" etc., etc.
Go and say to her: 'You [int. part.],'" etc., etc.

Itciō'lXam iʟatā't: "Agā'lᴇmam amē'pōtcXan, iʟatā't!
He said to him the raccoon: "Go and fetch her your sister-in law, raccoon!

AmulXā'mam: 'Mai'ka tci,'" etc., etc. . . . "Nīct tq¡ēx iā'môxt,
Go and say to her: 'You [int. part.],'" etc., etc. . . . "Not like I do you,

tᴇmē'onim. Nict imᴇnᴇ'lqo-im ʟmē'xaʟxēla."
you are stingy. Not you give me to eat your crabs."

Itciō'lXam its¡ᴇnē'sts¡ᴇnēs: "Agā'lᴇmam amē'pōtcXan,
He said to him the muskrat: "Go and fetch her your sister-in-law,

you keep me, or shall I take you to him?'" "I don't like you. You are too stingy. You don't give me any flags."

He said to the Mouse: "Go and fetch your sister-in-law. Say to her: 'Will you keep me, or shall I take you to him?'" The Mouse went. "Oh, Nikciamtcā'c! I came to fetch you. Your husband said to me: 'Will you keep me, or shall I take you to him?'" "I don't like you. You are stingy. You don't give me any camass."

Then he said to the Panther: "Go and fetch your sister-in-law. Go and say to her: 'Will you keep me, or shall I take you to him?'" Then the Panther went. "Oh, Nikciamtcā'c! I came to fetch you. Your husband said to me: 'Will you keep me, or shall I take you to him?'" She did not speak to him. He said so again. "I came to fetch you." He said so twice. "Oh, be quiet; come in!" The Panther entered. They lay down on the bed.

He remained away a long time. "Quick, go to look after them, Mink!" The Mink went. And there they were lying down. The Mink returned and said: "They are lying down in bed."

Now the Beaver cried and cried for five days. Now all the land

---

its¡Enē'sts¡Enēs! AmulXā'mam: 'Mai'ka tci, etc., etc. . . .
muskrat! Go and say to her: 'You [int. part.],' etc., etc. . . .

"Ō, nîct tq¡ēx iā'môxt. Txāla tEmē'onim. Nîct imEnE'lqo-im
"Oh, not like I do you. Too you are stingy. Not you gave me to eat

tEmē'lkoati."
your flags."

Itcō'lXam ā'cō: "Agā'lEmam amē'tōm, ā'cō! AmulXā'mam:
He said to her the mouse: "Go and fetch her your sister-in-law, mouse! Go and say to her:

'Mai'ka tci,'" etc., etc. . . . "Ō, nîct tq¡ēx iā'môxt. Nîcqē
'You [int. part.].'" etc., etc. . . . "Oh, not like I do you. Not at all

imEnE'lqo-îm tE'lalX."
you gave me to eat camass."

Aqa itciō'lXam ik¡oaya'wa: "Agā'lEmam amē'pōtcxan, ik¡oaya'wa!
Then he said to him the panther: "Go and fetch her your sister-in-law, panther!

AmulXā'mam: 'Mai'ka tci namxā'Lx, nai'ka tci qamanā'Lx?'"
Go and say to her: 'You [int. part.] do you take me for yourself, I [int. part.] do you take me to him?'"

Nāeqa igā'kim. Wē't'ax itcō'lXam: "Ō, iamtgā'lEmam." Mô'kctîX
Not at all she spoke. Again he said to her: "Oh, I came to fetch you." Twice

itcō'lXam. "Ō, qān mE'xôx. Ā'ckatpq!" Iā'ckupq ik¡oaya'wa.
he said to her. "Oh, silent be. Come in!" He entered the panther.

Aqa icxō'keit ilxE'm'ēpa.
Then they two lay down the bed on.

Lē'lē k¡ā'ya igē'xôx. "Ai'aq ci'ketam kō'sa-it!" Iō'ya kō'sa-it,
Long nothing he was. "Quick go and look at them mink!" He went mink,

aqa ickE'Lqayū. IgîXk¡oā'mam kō'sa-it. Igixgu'Litck kō'sa-it:
then they were lying down. He came home mink. He told mink:

"Icgā'Lqayu ilxE'm'ēpa." Aqa igigE'tcax iqā'nuq. IgigE'tcax,
"They are lying down bed on." Then he cried the beaver. He cried,

igigE'tcax qui'num Lkā'etax. Aqa iLē'kta-îX ka'nauwē ēlX. Koala'
he cried five days. Then it was flooded all land. Soon

was flooded. After a little while the houses were covered. Then the Beaver dived. Then they went aboard their canoes, and all the country was covered by water. It reached nearly to the sky. One year the water was high. "Now dive, Blue-jay!" Blue-jay dived, but his tail remained above the water. He floated. Then all the animals tried to dive. "Now, Mink! you dive next." He dived. After a little while he came up again. "Now, Otter! you dive next." The Otter dived. After a long time he came up again. He did not find the ground. "Now you dive, Muskrat!" Then the Muskrat said: "Tie the canoes together!" Now they tied the canoes together. They laid planks across them. Then the Muskrat threw off his blanket. "I shall lift the world. My belly is just like that of Beaver; my belly is just like that of Beaver. My belly is large." Five times he sang his song. Then he dived. He remained under water for a long time. After a little while flags came up. Then it became summer, and the

aqa L¡lāp itgī'ya tqu'Lē. Aqa igiktē'mEnq iqā'nuq. Aqa
then under water went the house. Then he dived the beaver. Then

iLagE'la-it aLā'Xanim. Aqa L¡lāp igē'xôx ē'lX ka'nauwē.
they went aboard their canoes. Then under water became country all.

K¡oā'pa igō'caxpa iLō'yam. ĒXt iqē'tak iLE'xôx cā'xalîX.
Nearly sky to they arrived. One year it was up.

"NîXua amktē'mEnq, iqē'sqēs!" Igiktē'mEnq iqē'sqēs. Lāx
"Well, dive, blue-jay!" He dived blue-jay. Out

iā'pōts aqa wi iuXu'nitek. Aqa iLktē'mEnq; Lkanauwē'tîke
his back-side then again he floated. Then they dived; all

kē'nuwa iLktē'mEnq. "Tca amktē'mEnq kō'sa-it amā'et¡ax."
try they dived. "Now dive mink you next."

Igiktē'mEnq. Lē'lē mank igiktē'mEnq. Lāx igē'xôx. "Amai't¡ax
He dived. Long a little he dived. Out he became. "You next

ē'nanakc amktē'mEnq!" Igiktē'mEnq ē'nanakc. Lē'2lē igiktē'mEnq.
otter dive!" He dived the otter. Long he dived.

Lāx igē'xôx. Nā2ct iō'yam ē'lXpa. Aqa: "Tca! amai't¡ax
Out he became. Not he arrived the ground at. Then: "Now! you next

its¡enē'sts¡enēs amktē'mEnq!" Aqa igē'kim its'enē'sts'enēs: "K¡au
muskrat you dive!" Then he spoke the muskrat: "Tie

mcī'kôx akE'nim." Aqa k¡au iLī'kôx akE'nim. Aqa iLgakxā'ema
do them the canoes." Then tie they did them the canoes. Then they put them across

aqē'nXak. Aqa iLexē'ma Liā'k¡ētē its¡Enē'sts¡Enēs:
planks. Then he took it off his blanket the muskrat:

"Qanutā'mitatskoa walayō', itsu'wan aqa iqā'nuq, itsu'wan aqa iqa'nuq, 
"I begin to lift it the day, my belly like the beaver, my belly like the beaver,

itsu'wan aqa LEngE'sges, itsu'wan aqa LEngE'sges." 
my belly large belly my belly large belly."

Qui'numîX itctō'ckam tiā'qewam. Aqa igiktē'mEnq. Lā4,
Five times he took them his songs. Then he dived. Long,

k¡ā'ya igē'xôx. Koalā'4 itgatXuni'tekoam tElkoā'tē. Ō qōct ā'qa
nothing he was. Soon they came up floating flags. Oh, behold then

canoes went down with the waters. It became dry. The canoes landed on the ground.

Then the Grizzly-bear jumped out of the canoe. "You lost your tail." "I shall buy another one." The Black-bear jumped out. "You lost your tail." "I shall buy another one." The Otter jumped out. "You lost your tail." He returned, took his tail, and put it on. Now the Mink jumped out. "You lost your tail." He returned, took his tail, and put it on. The Muskrat jumped out. "You lost your tail." He returned, took his tail, and put it on. The Panther jumped out. "You lost your tail." He returned, took his tail and put it on. They went ashore.

---

tcā'qoa-îX. Aqa igō'ya gē'gualîX akᴇ'nim. Iʟō'ya gē'gualîX
summer. Then they went downward the canoes. It went down

ʟtcu'qoa. Cpāq igē'xoXîX. Igōlā'kᴇXuit akᴇ'nim.
the water. Dry it became. They grounded the canoes.

Itsî'sōpᴇna icā'yîm. "Ā amē'itc imakᴇ'lōqɪ." "Ā'ʟqa
He jumped the grizzly bear. "Oh, your tail you lost it." "Later on

agō'nax anōmᴇlā'lᴇma." Itcî'sōpᴇna iskē'ntxoa. "Ā amē'itc
another one I shall buy it." He jumped the black bear. "Oh, your tail

imakᴇ'lōqɪ." "Ā'ʟqa agō'nax anōmᴇlā'lᴇma." Itcî'sōpᴇna
you lost it." "Later on another one I shall buy it." He jumped

ē'nanakc. "Ā amē'itc imakᴇ'lōqɪ." IgiXᴇ'takoa, itcā'kᴇlka
the otter. "Oh, your tail you lost it." He returned, he took it

ayā'itc. Iga-ixᴇlgā'mit. Itcî'sōpᴇna kō'sa-it. "Ā amē'itc
his tail. He put it on. He jumped mink. "Oh, your tail

imakᴇ'lōqɪ." IgiXᴇ'takoa, itcā'kᴇlka ayā'itc. Iga-ixᴇlgā'mit.
you lost it." He returned, he took it his tail. He put it on.

Itcî'sōpᴇna its;ᴇnē'sts;enēs. "Ā amē'itc imakᴇ'loqɪ." IgiXᴇ'takoa,
He jumped the muskrat. "Oh, your tail you lost it." He returned,

itcā'kᴇlka ayā'itc. Iga-ixᴇlgā'mit. Itcî'sōpᴇna ikoayawa'. "Ā
he took it his tail. He put it on. He jumped the panther. "Oh,

amē'itc imakᴇ'lōqɪ." IgiXᴇ'takoa, itcā'kᴇlka ayā'itc. Iga-ixᴇlgā'mit.
your tail you lost it." He returned he took it his tail. He put it on.

Ka'nauwē aʟᴇkᴇ'lōʟx.
All they went inland.

Sun Myth (told 1891)

There was a chief of a town. His relatives lived in five towns. In the morning he used to go outside and stay out to look at the Sun. The Sun was about to rise. He said to his wife: "What would you think if I went to see the Sun?" His wife said to him: "Do you think he is near that you want to go there?" On the following day he went out again. Again he saw the Sun. It was nearly sunrise. He said to his wife: "Make me ten pairs of shoes. Make me ten pairs of leggings." The woman made ten pairs of shoes and ten pairs of leggings. The next morning he went. He went far away. He used up his shoes and his leggings. Then he put on another

---

Aqalā'x itcā'k;anē

The Sun His Myth

Oxoēlā'etîX taîtci gitā'lXam. Qoā'nEma tgā'lXamēmax tiā'euXtîkc
There were those people of a town. Five his towns his relatives

yaXi ictā'mEx. Kawē'X aqa iopā'X k;a Lā'xanîX aqa iuLā'îtX
that chief. Early then he used to go out and outside then he stayed

aqa itcō'qumîtx wuXi aqaLā'x. Q;oā'pîX Lāx[a] naxō'xoax wuXi
then he saw him that sun. Nearly visible became that

aqaLā'x. Aqa itcō'lXam ayā'kikal: "Qa'da imē'x·atakoax, pēno
sun. Then he said to her his wife: "How your mind, if

inō'xLam wuXi aqaLā'x." Igiō'lXam ayā'kikala: "MxLō'Xuan tei
I go to seek that sun." She said to him his wife: "Do you think [int. part.]

q;oā'pîX k;a amxtō'kuala amō'ya wuXi aqaLā'xpa?"
near and you wish to go you go that sun to?"

Igō'n ē'ka-it. wit'ax kawē'X iō'pa. Aqa wit'ax itcō'qumitck
Another day, again early he went out. Then again he saw him

wuXi aqaLā'x. Q;oā'pîx· yaXī Lāx igā'xatx wuXi
that sun. Nearly here visible becomes that

aqaLā'x. Itcō'lXam ayā'kikala: "AmtEnlō'xoa tqē'Lpa
sun. He said to her his wife: "Make them for me moccasins

itā'LēlXam. AmtEnlō'xoa tqiLā't;awulXtîX: itā'LēlXam tê'lXam
ten. Make them for me leggings; ten people

tgā'xēLat;awulXtîX." Aqa iktē'lôx ayā'kikala itā'LēlXam
their leggings." Then she made them for him his wife ten

tE'gaqēLpa tê'lXam. kopā'2t tgā'xēLat;awulXtîX. Wē't'ax
their moccasins people, as many their leggings. Again

igē'tcuktîX, aqa iō'ya. KElā'îX iō'ya. Igoxoa'LXōm
it got day, then he went. Far he went. He finished them

tiā'qēLpa. Igoxoa'LXōm tiā'xēLat;awulXtîX. Tgō'nax q;uL
his moccasins. He finished them his leggings. Other ones put on

pair of shoes and leggings. He went for five months. Then he had used five pairs of shoes and five pairs of leggings. He went for ten months. Then he was near the place where the Sun was rising and he had used all his shoes. Then he found a large house. He opened the door. There was a girl. He entered and stayed there. He saw arrows hanging on one side of the house. Quivers full of arrows were hanging there. There were hanging shirts of elk skin, wooden armor, shields, stone axes, bone clubs, and head ornaments. Implements used by men were hanging on the one side of the house. On the other side were mountain-goat blankets, dressed elkskin blankets, buffalo skins, dressed buckskins, long dentalia, shell beads, and short dentalia. Near the doorway some large thing was hanging. He did not know it. He asked the girl: "Whose are these quivers?" [She said:] "They are my father's mother's property. When I am grown

---

itixE'lux tiā'qēLpa ka tiā'xēLat!awulXtîX. Qoā'nEma
he did them his moccasins and his leggings. Five

Lkaemu'kc iō'ya. Qoā'nEma tiā'qēLpa igoxoā'LXōm. Qoā'nEma
months he went. Five his moccasins he finished them. Five

tiā'xēLat!awulXtîX igoxoā'LXōm. ILā'2LēlXam Lkaemu'kc iō'ya.
his leggings he finished them. Ten months he went.

Aqa q!oā'pîX nopā'x wuXi aqaLā'x. Igoxoā'LXōm tiā'qēLpa, aqa
Then near he came out that sun. He finished them his moccasins, then

iogoā'qxoam tqu'Lē; itā'qa-iL tqu'Lē. ItcixE'laqLqîX, aqa Lōxt
he reached it a house; a large house. He opened the door, then there was

LqLā'pLxîX. Iā'ckōpq, iō'La-it. Aqa itctō'qōmitck ē'wa tE'nat
a girl. He entered, he stayed. Then he saw them there one side

taXi tqu'Lē qu'LquL tā'wixt tqā'matcx, qu'LquL Lā'wîxt Lq!ē'tsxō
that house hanging there were arrows, hanging there were quivers

pā'LEmax tqā'matcx. Qu'LquL Lā'wîxt Lgē'luqtē. Qu'LquL tā'wîxt
full of arrows. Hanging there were elkskin armors. Hanging there were

tE'qLkX; qu'LquL tā'wîxt tE'gēla; qu'LquL tā'wîxt txewā'exewaē;
wooden armors; hanging there were shields; hanging there were stone axes;

qu'LquL Lā'wîxt Ltamq!ā'Lkc; qu'LquL tā'wîxt tk!ē'cgEla.
hanging there were bone war clubs; hanging there were head ornaments.

Ka'nauwē tkalā'ktē ē'wa tE'nat taXi tqu'Lē. Ē'wa tE'nat taXi
All man's property thus one side that house. There the other side that

tqu'Lē qu'LquL tā'wîxt tqoā'kEmax; qu'LquL tā'wîxt tpaē'x^ukc;
house hanging there were mountain-goat blankets; hanging there were painted blankets made of two elk skins;

qu'LquL iā'wîxt itō-ihē'max; qu'LquL tā'wîxt tsEqsE'quks; qu'LquL
hanging there were buffalo skins; hanging there were curried buckskins; hanging

iā'wîxt iqauwik!ē'Lē; qu'LquL iā'wîxt ē'q!ōtcō; qu'LquL iā'wîxt
there were long dentalia; hanging there were shell beads; hanging there were

ikupku'p. Aqa icī'qē q!oā'p quL iā'wîxt yaXi ē'wa giā'qa-iL tā'nki.
short dentalia. Then the door near hanging there was that thus large something.

ItcixE'LEluXt. A'qa itcuqu'mtcxogoa wuXi aqLā'pLxîx: "Lān Lā'kti
He did not know it. Then he asked her that girl: "Whose things

LaXi Lq!ē'tsxō?" "AgE'k!ēe tgā'kti. LgE'q!ēlawulXEm kLgE'lōtkt."
those quivers?" "My grandmother's things. When I get mature she will give them away."

up, she will give them away." "Whose are these elkskin armors?" "They belong to my father's mother. When I am grown up, she will give them away." "Whose are these arrows?" "They belong to my father's mother. When I am grown up, she will give them away." "Whose are these wooden armors?" "They belong to my father's mother. When I am grown up, she will give them away?" "Whose are these shields and war clubs?" "They belong to my father's mother. When I am grown up, she will give them away." "Whose are these stone axes?" "They belong to my father's mother." Then also he asked about the things on the other side of the house: "Whose are these buffalo skins?" "They belong to my father's mother and to me. When I am grown up, she will give them away." "Whose are these mountain-goat blankets?" "They belong to my father's mother. When I am grown up, she will give them away." "Whose are these dressed buckskins?" "They belong to my father's mother. When I am grown up, she will give them away." "Whose are these deerskin blankets?" "They belong to my father's mother. When I am grown up, she will give them away." "Whose are these shell beads?"

"Lān Lā'kti taXi tgē'luqtē?" "AgE'k¡ēc tEntā'ktē. LgE'q¡ēlawulXEm
"Whose things those elkskin armors?" "My grandmother's our things. When I get mature

kLgE'lōtkt." "Lān Lā'kti taXi tqā'matcX?" "AgE'k¡ēc tEntā'kti.
she will give them away." "Whose things those arrows?" "My grandmother's our things.

LgE'q¡ēlawulXEm kLgE'lōtkt." "Lān Lā'kti taXi tEqLkX?"
When I get mature she will give them away." "Whose things those wooden armors?"

"AgE'k¡ēc tEntā'kti. LgE'q¡ēlawulXEm kLgE'lōtkt." "Lān Lā'kti
"My grandmother's our things. When I get mature she will give them away." "Whose things

taXi tE'kēla k¡a LaXi Ltameq¡ā'Lkc?" "AgE'k¡ēc tEntā'kti." "Lān
those shields and those war clubs?" "My grandmother's our things." "Whose

Lā'kti taXi tqēwā'ēxēwaē?" "AgE'k¡ēc tEntā'kti." Aqa wi tgōn
things those stone axes?" "My grandmother's our things." Then again the other

tE'nat tqu'Lē: "Lān iLā'kti yaXi ito-ihē'max?" "AgE'k¡ēc
one side that house: "Whose things those buffalo skins?" "My grandmother's

intā'to-ihē'max. LgE'q¡ēlawulXEm giLgE'lōtkt." "Lān Lā'kti
our buffalo skins. When I get mature she will give them away." "Whose things

taXi tqoā'kEmax?" "AgE'k¡ēc tEntā'ktē. LgE'q¡ēlawulXEm
those mountain-goat blankets?" "My grandmother's our things. When I get mature

kLgE'lōtkt." "Lān Lā'kti taXi tsEqsE'qukc?" "AgE'k¡ēc
she will give them away." "Whose things those buckskins?" "My grandmother's

tEntā'ktē. LgE'q¡ēlawulXEm kLgE'lōtkt." "Lān Lā'kti taXi
our things. When I get mature she will give them away." "Whose things those

tpayi'xama?" "AgE'k¡ēc tEntā'ktē. LgE'q¡ēlawulXEm kLgē'lotkt."
deer-skin blankets?" "My grandmother's our things. When I get mature she will give them away."

"Lān iLā'ktē yaXi ē'q¡otcō?" "AgE'k¡ēc intā'ktē.
"Whose things those shell beads?" "My grandmother's our things.

"They belong to my father's mother. When I am grown up, she will give them away." "Whose are these long dentalia?" "They belong to my father's mother. When I am grown up, she will give them away." "Whose are these short dentalia?" "They belong to my father's mother. When I am grown up, she will give them away."

He asked about all those things, and thought: "I will take them." When it was evening, the old woman came home. She hung up something that pleased him. It was shining. He stayed there a long time and took that girl. They remained there. Every morning the old woman disappeared. At night she came back. She brought home all kinds of things. She brought home arrows. Sometimes she brought mountain-goat blankets and elkskin shirts. She did so every day. He stayed there a long time; then he grew homesick. For two days he did not rise. She asked her granddaughter: "Did you scold him and is he angry?" "No, I did not scold him; he is homesick." Then she asked her son-in-law: "What do you wish to have when you go home? Do you want these buffalo skins?" He said: "No." "Do you want these mountain-goat blankets?" He

---

ʟgᴇ′q¡ēlawulXᴇm giʟgᴇ′lōtkt." "ʟā′n iʟā′ktē yaXi ēqauwik¡ē′ʟē?
When I get mature she will give them away." "Whose things those long dentalia?

ʟān iʟā′ktē yaXi ikupku′p?" "Āgᴇ′k¡ēc itcā′ktē.
Whose things those short dentalia?" "My grandmother's her things.

ʟgᴇ′q¡ēlawulXᴇm giʟgᴇ′lōtkt."
When I get mature she will give them away."

Ka′nauwē taXi tā′nᴇmax itctaxqa′mᴇtcxōgoa. Igixʟō′xoa-ît:
All those things he asked about them. He thought:

"Anucgā′ma." Xā′pîX aqa igaxk¡oā′mam wuXi aq¡eyō′qt. Aqa
"I will take it." In the evening then she came home that old woman. Then

wi ēXt quʟ igiā′wîX yaXi q¡āt ktcī′yuxt ʟiā′kᵘtgoamax yaXi
again one hang up she did it that like he did it shining that

tā′nki. Iâ′2ʟa-ît kōpa′. Ē′yaʟqtîX iō′ʟa-it kōpa′. Aqa itcō′ckam
something. He stayed there. Long time he stayed there. Then he took her

wuXi ak¹ā′pʟxîx·. Iʟxē′la-it kōpa′. Kawī′X, ā′nqa k¡ᴇm wuXi
that girl. They stayed there. Early, already nothing that

aq¡eyō′qt. Tsō′yustîX naXk¡oā′mamx. Aktō′kʟamx tktē′max.
old woman. In the evening she came home. She brought them things.

Aktō′kʟamx tqā′matcx; anā′ tqoā′kᴇmax aktō′kʟamx. Anā′
She brought them arrows; sometimes mountain-goat blankets she brought them. Sometimes

igē′luqtē agiō′kʟamx. Ka′nauwē ʟkā′etax ā′kua. Ē′yaʟqtîX
elkskin armors she brought them. All days thus. Long time

iō′ʟa-it, aqa ikā′kᵘʟ itcī′yôx. Mô′kctîX iō′qoya nîct igixᴇ′latck.
he stayed, then homesickness acted on him. Twice his sleeps not he arose.

Igō′lXam wuXi agā′gian wuXi aq¡eyō′qt: "Emiō′mēlatci k¡a
She said to her that her grandchild that old woman: "You scolded him [int. part.] and

ēx·ᴇ′ʟXaqt?" "K¡ā′ya, nîct ēniō′mela; ikā′kᵘʟ tcī′yôxt. Aqa
he is angry?" "No, not I scolded him; homesickness acts on him. Then

igiō′lXam itcā′qcîX: "Tān amiō′k¹a namXk¡oā′ya? YaXi tci
she said to him her son-in-law: "What will you carry when you go home? That [int. part.]

ito-ihē′max amiō′k¹a?" Itcō′lXam k¡ā′ya. "TaXi tci tqoā′kᴇmax
buffalo skins you carry them?" He said to her, "No." "Those [int. part.] mountain-goat blankets

said: "No." "Do you want these elkskin shirts?" He said: "No." She showed him all that was on the one side of the house. Next she showed him the ornaments. She showed him everything. He liked that great thing that was hanging there. When that thing turned around it was shining so that one had to close one's eyes. That he wanted. He said to his wife: "The old woman shall give me only her blanket." His wife said to him: "She will not give it to you. The people tried to buy it, but she will not give it away." Then he became angry. After some days she asked him again: "Will you take this?" She showed him everything. She showed him all the implements used by men. When she came to that thing that was hanging there, she was silent. Then she became tired and said: "Take it, but look out if you carry it. You wanted it. I wished to love you and I do love you." Then she hung it onto him and she

---

amtō'k·ia?" Itcō'lXam **k¡ā'ya.** "**YaXi** tci igē'luqtē ka'nauwē
will you carry them?" He said to her, "No." "Those [int. part.] elkskin armors all

amiō'k·ia?" Itcō'lXam k¡ā'ya. Ka'nauwē taXi tᴇ'nat tqu'ʟē
will you carry them?" He said to her, "No." All those one side the house

kē'nuwa iktᴇxᴇ'nēma. Atā'xt¡ax taXi tktē'max. Ka'nauwē-ł kē'nuwa
try she showed them to him. Next those things. All try

iktēxᴇ'nēma. Yā'Xka q¡āt tcī'yuxt yaXi tā'nki giā'qa-iʟ, yaXi
she showed them to him. That like he did it that something large, that

qiup¡ō'nētîX. Ma'nix lā'xo nixō'xoax yaXi tā'nki qiup¡ō'nētîX
hanging up. When turn it did that something hanging up

niktē'qoXuitqiX, nau'i tsXᴇp qacxō'xoax siā'xôst. ʟiā'kt¡oma yaXi
it turned round, at once closed eyes did his eyes. Shining that

tā'nki. Aqa ya'Xka yaXi q¡āt tcī'yuxt. Itcō'lXam ayā'kikal:
something. Then that that like he did it. He said to her his wife:

"Aginlō'ta ēXt yaXi itcā'k¡etē wuXi aq¡eyō'qt." Igiō'lXam
"She shall give me one that her blanket that old woman." She said to him

ayā'kikala: "Nîct qantsî'x agimᴇlō'ta. Kē'2nuwa qiamᴇlā'lᴇmx,
his wife: "Never she will give it to you. Try it is bought,

nîct qantsî'X agiō'tx." Aqa wit'ax nîx·ʟx·ā'qoax. Tcā'xiX
never she gives it away." Then again he became angry. Several

qayoqoē'XiX, aqa wit'ax agioqu'mtcxōguax: "YaXi' tci
his sleeps, then again she asked him: "That [int. part.]

amiō'k·ia?" agiōlXā'mx. Ka'nauwē kē'nuwa aktixᴇnē'max tax·i
will you carry it?" she said to him. All try she showed them to him those

tgā'ktemax. Aktixᴇnē'max kē'nuwa tax·i tkalā'kte. Ka'nauwē
their things. She showed them try those man's things. All

kē'nuwa aktixᴇnē'max. Naikō'quamx yaXi qiup¡ō'nētix·. Aqa
try she showed them to him. She arrived at that hanging up. Then

qān naxō'xoax, ma'nîx naikō'quamx yaXi qiup¡ō'nētix·. Aqa
silent she became, when she arrived that hanging up. Then

tᴇll igē'xôx ē'tcamxtc. Aqa igiō'lXam: "Qā'txa amiō'k·ia!
tired it became her heart. Then she said to him: "Shall you carry it!

Qā't¡ōcXᴇm! qēn amiō'k·ia. Mai'ka imē'Xaqamit. Kē'nuwa tq¡ēx
Take care! if you carry it. Your your mind. Try like

iā'mōxt, tcqē tq¡ēx iā'mxōxt." Quʟ igē'lôx. Ka'nauwē quʟ
I do you, then like I do you." Hang she did it on him. All hang

gave him a stone ax. She said: "Now go home." Now he went home.

He did not see a town until he came near his uncle's town. Now the thing which he carried in his hands shook, and said: "We shall strike your town." Then he lost his senses, and he broke his uncle's town and killed all the people. Now he recovered. He had broken all the houses. His hands were full of blood. Then he thought: "Oh, what a fool I was! The thing I wanted is bad." He tried to throw it away, but it stuck to his flesh. Then he went. He went a short distance and again he lost his senses. He came to the town of another one of his uncles. Again the thing said: "We shall strike your town." He tried to keep quiet, but he could not do it. He tried to throw it away, but his hands closed. Then he lost his senses, and broke all the houses. He recovered and the town of his uncle was destroyed. The people lay there dead. Then he cried and tried to strip it off in the fork of a tree, but it did not come off at all. It

---

igē'lôx. Aqa igē'lōt iqewā'exēwaē. Igiō'lXam: "Mᴇ'Xk¡oa ā'qa!"
she did it on him. Then she gave him a stone ax. She said to him: "Go home now!"

Iō'pa, aqa iō'ya, igē'Xk¡oa. Nēct itciō'qumitck ēlX. Q¡oā'p itciō'xam
He went out, then he went, he went home. Not he saw it a country. Near he arrived

iā'mōt iā'lXam. Aqa igē'Xᴇlta yaXi qtcigᴇlgā't. Aqa igē'kîm
his uncle his town. Then it shook that what he had on. Then it spoke

yaXi qtcigᴇlgā't: "Atxîlgā'mita imē'lXam, atxîlgā'mita imē'lXam,"
that what he had on: "We shall strike it your town, we shall strike it your town,"

yaXi qtcigᴇlgā't igē'kîm. K¡ᴇm igō'xax tiā'xatakoax. Itcī'yux
that what he had on spoke. Nothing became his reason. He did it

iā'lXam iā'mōt. ʟ¡mān, ʟ¡mān, ʟ¡mān itcī'yux. Ka'nauwē tē'lXam
his town his uncle's. Break, break, break he did it. All people

itctō'tēna. ʟ¡pāq igē'xôx. Ka'nauwē taXi tqʟē'max ʟ¡mᴇ'nʟ¡mᴇn
he killed them. Recover he did. All those houses broken

ōguakē'x. Pāʟ ʟqā'wulqt tē'iakci. Igixʟō'xoa-ît: "Ō, nai'ka nᴇ'ʟ¡ala.
were. Full blood his hands. He thought: "Oh, I fool!

Koaʟqē'ʟ¡ iā'lko-ilē gi tā'nki qa gi tq¡ē'x iqē'nxôx." Kē'nuwa
Thus behold bad that something and that like I did it." Try

ʟāq igēxō'lalᴇmtck ka ē'yaʟq nixk¡ā'Xitx. Aqa wi iō'ya, as
take off he took it off and his flesh it pulled. Then again he went, and

nōʟ¡îX iō'ya, aqa wi k¡ᴇm igō'xoax tiā'xatakoax. Q¡oā'p
a little while he went, then again nothing became his reason. Near

itciō'xam igō'nax iā'mot iā'lXam. Aqa wit'ax igē'kîm: "Atxîlgā'mita
he arrived another his uncle his town. Then again it spoke: "We shall strike it

imē'lXam, atxîlgā'mita imē'lXam." Kē'nuwa pᴇt qatciō'xax.
your town, we shall strike it your town." Try quiet he did it.

Nāct qa'ntcîx pᴇt nixō'xoax. Kē'nuwa qatcixē'max, gwā'nîsum
Never quiet it was. Try he threw it away, always

taXi tē'iakci noxo-iʟxē'yux. Aqa wi k¡ᴇm igō'xax tiā'xatakoax.
those his fingers bent. Then again nothing became his reason.

Aqa wi itcī'yux iā'mōt iā'lXam. Ka'nauwē ʟ¡mᴇ'nʟ¡mᴇn itcī'yux.
Then again he did it his uncle his town. All break he did it.

ʟ¡pāq igē'xôx. K¡ᴇm iā'lXam iā'mot. Ka'nauwē ō'xoaxt ōXoā'ʟa-it
Recover he did. Nothing his town his uncle. All there were they were dead

tē'lXam. Aqa igigᴇ'tcax. Kē'nuwa kcigᴇnʟ¡ē'qīkiXpa ē'mᴇqō,
the people. Then he cried. Try branch in tree,

stuck to his body. He tried to strike what he wore on a stone, but he could not break it. Then he went on. He came near the town of another one of his uncles, and again the thing which he carried shook. "We shall strike your town," it said. Then he lost his senses. He broke the houses of his uncle's town. He destroyed his uncle's town. Then he recovered. He cried, because he made his relatives unhappy. He tried to dive in order to take it off, but it stuck to his body. He rolled himself in a thicket, and he tried to break on a stone what he wore. Then he gave it up. He cried. He went on and came to the town of another uncle. Again the thing which he carried shook: "We shall strike your town." He lost his senses. He broke all the houses and killed all the people. Then he recovered. All the people were killed, and the town was destroyed. His arms and his hands were covered with blood. He cried: "Kā! kā! kā! kā!" and tried to break what he

---

kōpa' kē'nuwa qāyaxauiq!ā'yakoax, kē'nuwa ʟāq nixō'lalᴇmx. Nēctqē
there try he squeezed himself through it, try come off it did. Not at all

ʟāq nixō'xoax, ka ē'yaʟq nîxk!ā'Xîtx. Kē'nuwa qatciuguicē'mᴇX
come off it did, and his flesh it pulled it. Try he struck it

ʟqᴇ'nakcpa yaXi kteigᴇlgā't. Nēct qa'nsîx ʟ!mᴇ'nʟ!mᴇn nîxō'xoax.
a stone on that what he had on. Never break it did.

Wē't'ax qayō'îx. Q!oā'p qatciyō'xoamx igō'nax iā'mōt iā'lXam.
Again he went. Near he arrived another his uncle his town.

Aqa wi nîxᴇlā'lalᴇmx yaXi qtcigᴇlgā't. "Atxîlgā'mita imē'lXam,
Then again it shook that what he had on. "We shall strike it your town,

atxîlgā'mita imē'lXam." K!ᴇm noxoā'xax tiā'Xatakoax. Qatciō'xax
we shall strike it your town." Nothing became his reason. He did it

iā'lXam iā'mōt. ʟ!mān, ʟ!mān, ʟ!mān, ʟ!mān, kanauwē'2 qatciuʟXō'mx
his town his uncle. Break, break, break, break, all he finished it

iā'lXam iā'mōt ka tê'lXam qatctuʟXō'mx. ʟ!pāq nîxō'xoax.
his town his uncle and the people he finished them. Recover he did.

Nikteā'xamx qatcuxāwalōtā'-îtx tiā'cuXtike. Kē'nuwa nîktē'mᴇnqᴇmx
He cried all the time he made them unhappy his relatives. Try he dived always

ʟtcu'qoapa. Kē'nuwa ʟāq nîxō'lalᴇmx ka ē'yaʟq nîxk!ā'Xîtx.
water in. Try come off it did and his flesh it pulled it.

Kē'nuwa niā'mᴇla-îx·pa nîxcgē'lalᴇmx. Kē'nuwa qatciuguicē'mx
Try a thicket in he rolled about. Try he struck it

yaXi kteigᴇlgā't ʟqᴇ'nakcpa. Tā'menua nîxō'xoax. Aqa nîkteā'xamx.
that what he had on a stone on. Give up he did. Then he cried all the time.

Wit'ax qayō'îx. Aqa wi igō'nax qatcigō'qoamx ē'lXam, iā'mōt
Again he went. Then again another he arrived at a town, his uncle

iā'lXam. Aqa wi nixᴇlā'lalᴇmx yaXi qtcigᴇlgā't. "Atxîlgā'mita
his town. Then again it shook that what he had on. "We shall strike it

imē'lXam, atxîlgā'mita imē'lXam." K!ᴇm noxoā'xax tiā'Xatakux.
your town, we shall strike it your town." Nothing became his reason.

Qatciō'xax ē'lXam, ʟ!mān, ʟ!mān, ʟ!mān, ʟ!mān, ka tê'lXam.
He did it the town, break, break, break, break, and the people.

ʟ!pāq nîxō'xoax. Tᴇmᴇ'mm ka'nauwē tê'lXam ka ē'lXam.
Recover he did. None all the people and the town.

Lā'ema ʟqā'wulqt tē'yaqō k!a tē'yakcē. Nîxō'xoax qā! qā! qā! qā!
Only blood his arms and his hands. He did qā! qā! qā! qā!

nîkteā'xomx. Kē'2nuwa qatciuguicē'ʟx tqᴇ'nake. Nēct ʟ!mᴇ'nʟ!mᴇn
he cried. Try he struck them stones. Not break

wore on a stone, but it did not break. He tried to throw it away, but his hands closed. He went on, and he came near his own town. He tried to remain standing, but it was as if his feet were pulled toward it. Then he lost his senses and destroyed the whole town and killed his relatives. Then he recovered. The whole town was destroyed, and the ground was full of bodies. Then he cried again: "Kā! kā! kā! kā!" He bathed and tried to take off what he wore, but it stuck to his body. Sometimes he struck it against stones and thought it might get broken. Then he gave it up. He cried.

Now he looked back, and there the old woman was standing. She said to him: "I tried to love you; I tried to be kind to your people; why do you cry? You wished for it and wanted to wear my blanket." Now she took it off and left him. She went home. He stayed there; he went a short distance and built a small house.

---

nîxō'xoax yaXi qtcigElgā't. Kē'nuwa qatcixē'max yaXi
it did that what he had on. Try he threw it away that

qtcigElgā't. Koā'nesum tikq!oā'Lkux tē'yakci. Wē't'ax qayō'îx.
what he had on. Always became bent his hands. Again he went.

Aqa iā'xt!ax iā'lXam. Q!oā'p qatciyō'xax iā'lXam, kē'nuwa
Then his own next his town. Near he did it his town, try

qayō'tXuîtx ya'Xka L!a aqoxoak!ā'x tiā'qo-it. K!Em noxoā'xax
he stood he behold it pulled them his feet. Nothing became

tiā'xatakoax, qatciō'xax iā'lXam, L!mān, L!mān, L!mān, L!mān.
his reason, he did it his town, break, break, break, break.

Ka'nauwē qatciuLXō'mx iā'lXam ka tiā'cuXtîkc qatctuLXō'mx.
All he finished it his town and his relatives he finished them.

L!pāq nîxō'xoax; k!Em iā'lXam. PāL ēlX ō'xoaxt tmēmElō'ctîkc.
Recover he did; nothing his town. Full the ground were corpses.

Nîxō'xoax qā! qā! qā! qā! nîktcā'xamx. Kē'nuwa nîxqoā'tx. Kē'nuwa
He did qā! qā! qā! qā! he cried. Try he bathed. Try

Lāq° nîxō'lalEmx yaXi iqE'ltit, ka ē'yaLq nîxk!ā'Xîtx. Anā'
come off he did that what he wore, and his flesh it pulled. Sometimes

LqE'nakcpa nîxcgē'lalEmx. NîxLuXoā'îtx, k!ō'ma cā'ca alîxō'xoa.
stone on he struck it. He thought, perhaps break it will.

Tā'menua nîxō'xoax. Aqa wi niktcā'xamx ka iō'qulqt.
Give up he did. Then again he cried and he wept.

Nix·Enā'qoax, aqa-igEmtXuē'la wuXi aq!eyō'qt. "Mai'ka,"
He looked back, then she stood there that old woman. "You,"

agiō'lXam, "mai'ka. Kē'nuwa tq!ēx iā'mxôx, kē'nuwa tq!ēx
she said to him, "you. Try like I did you, try like

ntôx tEmē'cuXtîkc. Qā'tcqē mō'qulqt? Mai'ka imē'Xaqamit, aqa
I did them your relatives. Why you weep? You your mind, then

imē'Luk yaXi itcî'k!etē." Aqa igē'kElka. Lāq° igē'xôx yaXi
you carried it that my blanket." Then she took it. Take off she did it that

qtcigElgā't. Aqa iga-iqE'ltaqT; igā'Xk!oa. Iō'La-it kōpa'. Iō'ya
what he had on. Then she left him; she went home. He stayed there. He went

mank kElā'îX. Kōpa' tqu'Lē itcî'tôx, itō'qoa-îts tqu'Lē.
a little far. There a house he made it, a small house.

MYTH OF THE SWAN (TOLD 1894)

The people tried to buy a maiden, but her father did not give her away. Then the chief of the Swans bought her. They gave her to him. It became winter. Now the people had eaten all their provisions, and they became hungry. The Swan had a double dish. His mother gave him food. Dry broken salmon was in one dish, and pounded salmon bones were in the other. Then the Swan ate the dry salmon, and his wife ate the salmon bones. Every evening they received food in this way. His wife did not know what her husband was eating. She thought all the food might be salmon bones. For a whole year they ate in this manner. When she chewed, there was a noise of breaking bones. When he ate, there was a noise of meat being munched. Then she began to notice it. After some nights she took her husband's

---

IQĒʟŌ'Q IĀ'K;ANĒ

SWAN HIS MYTH

Ē̆wa' kē'nuwa qomᴇlā'lᴇmx wuXi ahā't;au. Nāct qaqō'tx. Ā'qa
Thus intending she was bought that virgin. Not she was given away. Then

ʟqelō'q iʟā'Xak;ᴇmana qatcumᴇlā'lᴇmx. Aqa qa-ilō'tx. Aqa
the swans their chief bought her. Then she was given to him. Then

tcā'xᴇlqʟîX ninō'xoaxîx. Qatktūʟxō'mx tgā'ʟxalᴇmaēmax tē'lXam;
winter it became. They finished their food the people;

aqa walō' aktō'xax. Aqa sx·umt;ē't sq;u'nam, sī'aq;unam iqelō'q.
then hunger acted on them. Then two fastened together wooden dishes, his wooden dishes the swan.

Aqa agē'lqoēmx ayā'qō iqelō'q. Tk;ē'lak aē'Xt aq;u'nam. tk;anā'ʟkʟîX
Then she gave him food his mother the swan. Dried salmon one dish, dried and broken salmon bones

aē'Xt aq;u'nam. QatiXᴇlᴇmō'xumx taXi tk;ē'lak iqelō'q. Wu'Xi
one dish. He ate it that dried salmon the swan. That

ayā'kikala tk;anā'ʟkʟîX qataxalᴇmō'xumx. Ka'nauwē tsō'yustîX
his wife dried and broken salmon bones she ate them. Every evening

k;oaʟqē' aqeîlquē'muX. Nîct alō'XuîX wuXi ayā'kikala. Axʟō'Xuan
thus they two were given food. Not she knew it that his wife. She thought

ka'nauwē tk;anā'ʟkʟîX taXi aqeîlquē'muX. Ē'Xt iqē'taq,
all dried and broken salmon bones that they two were given food. One year,

ataxalᴇmō'xumx, sxōp, sxōp, sxōp, sxōp yaXi itcā'kcXapa. YaXi
they ate it, noise of eating hard food that her mouth in. That

iqelō'q nîxʟxᴇ'lᴇmux, tc;kuā'k, tc;kuā'k iā'kcXa. Aqa xā'xa
swan he ate noise of eating soft food his mouth. Then notice

igiō'xoax yaXi itcā'kikala. Qantcī'xʟx qanā'pōl aqa agigᴇlgā'x
she did him that her husband. Several nights then she took it

dish, and she saw that he was eating dry salmon. "Oh," she thought, "he has treated me ill. He gave me bones to eat, and, behold, my husband is eating dried salmon! I will go home to my people."

Early the next morning she made herself ready and went home. She arrived at her father's and her mother's house. She said: "Oh, they treated me ill. They gave me pounded salmon bones to eat, while my husband was eating dried salmon." Then she lay down; she was ashamed. For five nights she lay on one side. After five nights she turned over and laid her head on the other side. Then she arose. She was quite white, and no hair was on either side of her head. Then she sang her conjurer's song. Now snow began to fall. It fell for five days. Then she said to the young men of the village: "Take that dip-net down to the water and move it five times up and down there at sea." Then she sang a song conjuring the smelt, and the young men went. Five times they went up and down in their canoe; then it was full of smelt. They went ashore, and the people gathered the smelt. Their houses were full. Now the water began to freeze, and the

---

yaXi ā'yaq¡unampa itcā'kikal tān yaXi ixelā'x. Agtuk¡omā'nanEmx,
that his dish in her husband what that he ate. She looked at it,

aqa tk¡ē'lak. "Ō, qEnxguā'mit," naxLuXuā'itx. "TE'q¡ōtcō
then dried salmon. "Oh! I am made unhappy," she thought. "Bones

aqtnElqoē'muX. Qōct, tk¡ē'lak tîxelā'x itcī'kikal. Tgt¡ō'kti
I was given to eat. Behold, dried salmon he ate it my husband. Good

anXk¡oā'ya itcī'lXampa." Wāx igē'tcuktē, igaXa'ltXuîtck,
I go home my town to." Next day it got day, she made herself ready,

aqa igā'Xk¡oa. Igō'yam wī'tcampa k¡a agā'qopa. "Ō,
then she went home. She arrived her father at and her mother at. "Oh,

qanXguā'mit, tk¡anā'LkLîX iqtnElquē'mEnîLtck. Itcī'kikal
I was made unhappy, dried and broken salmon bones I was always given to eat. My husband

aqa tk¡ē'lak aqtîlquē'muX." Aqa igaxō'kcît igaxEmā'sa-it.
then dried salmon he was given to eat." Then she slept she was ashamed.

Quī'nEmîX igō'qoya, aqa igaxā'iktqo-îX, wi quī'nEmîX igō'qoya
Five her sleeps, then she turned over, again five her sleeps

ē'wa ē'natîX Lgā'qakctaq. Aqa igaxE'latck. Nō'ē tk¡ōp, nEct
thus on the other side her head. Then she arose. At once white, not

LE'gaqcō ē'wa ē'nata itcā'q¡aqcta. Kanā'mtEmaX nō'i k¡ā LE'gaqcō.
her hair thus one side her head. Both sides at once no her hair.

Aqa igā'ktcxEm. Aqa Ltga iLE'xôx. ILō'La-it Ltga. Qoā'nEm
Then she sang. Then snow it became. It was snow. Five

Lkā'etax iLō'La-it Ltga. Iktō'lXam tq¡ulîpXunā'yu: "Ai'aq
days was snow. She said to them youths: "Quick

amsgitē'mam mā'LnîX yaXi itcō'itk. Qoā'nEmîX Lāq amcxō'xoa
take to the water that dip net. Five times to and fro do

gipā' mā'LnîX." Aqa igā'ktcxam. Iqamiā'îtx igī'yux. Aqa itgī'ga
there seaward." Then she sang her conjurer's song. Iqamiā'îtx she made. Then they went

ta-îtci tq¡ulîpXunā'yu. Qoā'nEmîX Lāq itgī'yux itā'xEnim. Aqa
those youths. Five times to and fro they did it their canoe. Then

pāL igē'xôx iLXE'na. Itxē'gela-îx. Aqa itgiup¡ē'yaLx iLXE'na
full it became smelts. They landed. Then they gathered smelts

giLā'lXam. Pā'LEmax igō'xoax tgā'qLēmax. Aqa itcē'lpo-îx. Aqa
the people of the town. Full became their houses. Then frozen. Then

canoes could not go out, because the water was all frozen. Then the Swans died of hunger. Now their chief heard: "Oh, your wife conjured the smelts." Thus he was told: "Their houses are full of smelts." Then the Swan said: "We will go and I will take my wife back." Thus he spoke to his relatives.

Early in the morning the Swans made themselves ready. They had two canoes. They went. The people said: "Canoes are coming." Then the Swans landed. The woman was told: "Maybe your husband comes to fetch you." She said: "Lock the house. Do not let them enter." Then indeed they locked it, and the Swans were standing outside. The woman said: "Quick! Roast five smelts; I want to eat them." Five smelts were roasted. Then the woman said: "The heads of my smelts are roasted." The Swan replied: "The heads of our smelts are roasted." "The bellies of my smelts are turned over." The Swan said: "The bellies of our smelts are turned over." "The backs of my smelts are turned over." The Swan said: "The backs of our

---

xā'oqxaʟx ikᴇ'nim qā'xpa qa iō'yîx. Ka'nauwē itcē'lpo-îx. Aqa wa'lō
can not canoe anywhere went. All frozen. Then hunger

iʟxᴇ'la-it ʟqelō'q. Ā4, aqa igēxᴇltcī'maq ʟqelō'q iʟā'Xak!ᴇmana.
they died the swans. Ah, then he heard the swans their chief.

"Ā2, amē'kikal Iqamiā'îtx igī'yux," iqiō'lXam. "Pāʟ ʟā'qʟēmax
"Ah, your wife Iqamiā'itx she made," he was told. "Full their houses

iʟxᴇ'na." Igē'kîm iqēlō'q: "Alxō'ya, anuguā'lᴇmama agᴇ'kikal,"
smelts." He said the swan: "We will go, I will fetch her my wife,"

itctō'lXam tiā'cuXtîke.
he told them his relatives.

Wāx igē'tcuktîX, aqa iʟxᴇ'ltcXuîtck ʟqēlō'q. Môket aʟā'Xanim.
Early it got day, then they made themselves ready the swans. Two their canoes.

Iʟōyā'4. "Ā2, akᴇnī'm atē't," igugoā'kîm tê'lXam. Iʟxē'gila-îX.
They went. "Ah, canoes are coming," they said the people. They landed.

"Ā2, ʟqelō'q iʟxē'gela-îX. Imē'kikal ʟXuan itcîmtgā'lᴇmam,"
"Ah, the swans landed. Your husband perhaps he came to fetch you,"

iqō'lXam. "Amegaʟxpō'ya," igā'kîm. "Nîct aʟacgā'tpqa."
she was told. "Shut the door," she spoke. "Not they will enter."

A'qa ā'qanuwē iqā'ʟxpō. Aqa kopā' ʟā'xanîX iʟxē'la-it. Aqa
Then indeed it was shut. Then there outside they stayed. Then

igā'kîm wuXi aqagē'lak: "Ai'aq aqō'lktca quī'nᴇm aʟxᴇ'na.
she spoke that woman: "Quick roast five smelts.

Anᴇlguā'x." Aqa aqō'lktca qui'nᴇm aʟxᴇ'na. "Ēwā'
I want to eat." Then they were roasted five smelts. "Thus

tgā'q!aqstakuks aqō'lᴇktca wuX agᴇ'ʟxana." Aqa igē'kîm yaXi
their heads are roasted those my smelts." Then he spoke that

iqelō'q: "Ewā' tgā'q!aqstakuks aqō'lᴇktca agᴇ'kikal antā'ʟxana."
swan: "Thus their heads are roasted my wife our smelts."

"Ēwā' tgā'unake aqa-iqtqwā'yayaXtîX agᴇ'ʟxana." "Ēwā'
"Thus their bellies are turned my smelts." "Thus

tgā'unake aqa-iqtqwā'yayaXtîX agᴇ'kikal antā'ʟxana," igē'kîm
their bellies are turned my wife our smelts," said

iqelō'q. "Ēwā tga'gōtcXîke aqa-iqtqwā'yayaXtîX agᴇ'ʟxana."
the swan. "Thus their backs are turned my smelts."

"Ēwā' tgā'gōtcXîke aqa-iqtqwā'yayaXtîX agᴇ'kikal antā'ʟxana."
"Thus their backs are turned my wife our smelts."

smelts are turned over." "The tails of my smelts are turned over." The Swan said: "The tails of our smelts are turned over."

Then the Swans who were staying outside became cold. They were shut out. Now the smelts were done. Then the woman ate. She said: "Now roast a smelt on five single spits." A smelt was roasted on five single spits. She said: "Make fire of pitch wood when you roast the smelt." Now the smelt was roasted on five spits. They burned pitch wood. Then the smelt became black with soot. It was done. Then she said: "Now open the door that they may enter." Then the door was opened for the Swans, and they entered. They entered, and they were given the smelt, but it smelled of pitch. While they were eating, wings began to grow on them. Then they began to fly. The woman said: "Swan shall be your name; you shall not eat dry salmon. When you smell smelts, you shall fly away. You shall eat only roots and rushes; never shall you eat dry salmon;

"Ē̆wā' tgā'lictîkc aqa-iqtqwā'yayaXtîX agᴇ'ʟxana." "Ē̆wā'
"Thus their tails are turned my smelts." "Thus

tgā'lictîkc aqa-iqtqwā'yayaXtîX agᴇ'kikal antā'ʟxana," igē'kîm
their tails are turned my wife our smelts," said

iqelō'q. Aqa tsᴇs ʟgē'xôx ʟqēlō'q. ʟxelā'etîX ʟā'XanîX aʟxpō't.
the swan. Then cold became the swans. They stayed outside they were shut out.

Igō'2kst wuXi aʟxᴇ'na. Aqa igaxᴇ'lᴇmuX wuXi aqagē'lak
They were done those smelts. Then she ate that woman

ayā'kikal iqēlō'q. "Ai'aq aqa amcgē'lᴇktca iʟxᴇ'na, quî'nᴇm
his wife the swan's. "Quick then roast a smelt, five

ʟq!oatsā'ma." Aqa iqē'yōlᴇktc quî'nᴇm ʟq!oatsā'ma. "ʟq!axō'cgan
single spits." Then it was roasted five single spits. "Pitch wood

amckʟigᴇmgē'ʟxa, manîx namcgiō'lᴇktca yaXi iʟxᴇ'na." Aqa
burn, when you roast it that smelt." Then

ā'qanuwē iqē'yolᴇktc, quî'nᴇm ʟiā'q!oatsᴇma yaXi iʟxᴇ'na. Aqa
indeed it was roasted, five its single spits that smelt. Then

iqʟigᴇ'mugiʟx ʟq!axō'cgan. Aqa iga-ik!ᴇmʟlā'mx·ît yaXi iʟxᴇ'na.
it was burnt pitch wood. Then it was blackened that smelt.

Iō'kst yaXi iʟxᴇ'na. Aqa igā'kîm: "A'yaq aqa qaʟxᴇ'laqʟ,
It was done that smelt. Then she said: "Quick then open the door,

aʟacgā'tpqa." Aqa iqaʟxᴇ'laqʟ ʟqēlō'q. Iʟā'ckōpq ʟqēlō'q. Aqa
they may come in." Then it was opened for the swans. They entered the swans. Then

iqiʟᴇ'lqo-îm yaXi iʟxᴇ'na. ʟā'ema ʟq!axō'cgan ē'yaqtckc. Kē'nuwa
they were given food that smelt. Only pitch its smell. Try

igitxᴇ'lᴇmux. Ā4, ʟā'k!ēntq itxaʟᴇ'lux. Aqa iʟō'koa ʟkanawē'tîkc
they ate it. Ah, wings came to be on them. Then they flew all

ʟaXi ʟqēlō'q. Igā'kîm wuXi aqagē'lak: "ʟqēlō'q îmcā'xalēu.
those swans. She said that woman: "Swans your name.

Nîct qa'ntsîX tk!ē'lak atᴇmcxᴇlᴇmō'xum. Manē'x alēmciʟā'ya
Never dry salmon you shall eat. When you will smell

iʟxᴇ'na, kanauwē'4 amcîxuwā'xita. Ā'ema atsqᴇmē'mîX
smelt, all you will fly away. Only Indian potatoes

alamcᴇlᴇmō'Xuma; ā'ema ā'qᴇmxᴇm tgā'kciu atᴇmcxᴇlᴇmō'Xuma.
you will eat; only water plants their roots you will eat them.

Nāct qa'ntsîx tk!ē'lak atᴇmcxᴇlᴇmō'xuma. Nāct qa'ntsîx
Never dry salmon you will eat them. Never

you shall not make people unhappy. When smelts are caught in the evening, you shall fly away on the following morning. You shall go inland."

---

amēguXuakuā'mita	tê'lXam.	Manē'x	Xā'pîX	aqiup;iā'ʟxa	iʟxᴇ'na,
you will make poor	people.	When	in the evening	it is gathered	a smelt,

ka	wuXa'	ka'nauwē	amcîXuwā'Xita.	Amcō'ya	cā'xala	tagı	ēlX."
then	in the morning	all	you shall fly away.	You shall go	up	this	country."

The Copper is Speared (told 1894)

There were many people. Their chief had two children—two girls. All the year round they went hunting a thing that was on the water. That thing was far out at sea. It shone like the sun. The people came together and tried to shoot it, but they could not hit it. They did so all the year round. Their best marksmen tried to hit it, but they could not hit it. Then the people gave it up.

One day these girls said: "Let us take our father's arrows secretly." Thus said the younger one. The elder one did not reply. She spoke to her five times. All day long they were digging potentilla roots. The people came together and always tried to shoot that something. The girls took secretly the bow and arrows and the harpoon shaft. They tied their hair here on the forehead.

ĒwaXō'mit Aqlē'itqcq

Copper is Speared

Oxoelā'etîX ta-îtci tê'lXam. Cmôket ciā'Xan yaXi iLā'Xak!Emana
There were those people. Two his children that their chief

sqagē'lak. Ka'nauwē Lqētā'kEmaX aqiXEluwā'lalEma-îtx yaXi
girls. All years they always went to hunt that

tā'nki Ltcu'qoapa. Mā'LnîX ē'maLpa, Lā'xanîX ō'xoax yaXi tā'nki.
something water on. At sea sea on, outside it was that something.

Liā'k"t!ōmax L'a aqaLā'xti. Kē'nuwa nuXuā'qoaxt tê'lXam, kē'nuwa
Shining like the sun. Try they assembled the people, try

tiā'maq aqtilō'xoax, nîct qantsî'x iā'maq aqelō'xoax. Ka'nauwē
shooting it it was done, never hit it was. All

Lqētā'kEmaX kē'nuwa nuxoā'qoax gā'taxaL!ē, kē'nuwa tiā'maq
years try they assembled the best archers, try hit

aqtelō'xoax. Nē2ct qantsî'x iā'maq aqelō'xoax. Tē'menua nuxoā'xax
they did it. Never hit it was. Give up they did

tê'lXam. QāqLqanē'gua aqa qacgē'mx sta'Xi sqagē'lak staXi
the people. One day then they spoke those women those

shā't!au: "Qoē qatxktutā'mitx tiā'qamatcx ē'txam," nagē'mx wuX
virgins: "Must we take away his arrows our father's," she said that

axgE'sqax. Nā2ct aktaxuwā'tckuax wuX ā'galXt. Qoā'nEmîX
younger one. Not she answered that elder sister. Five times

agōlXā'mx. Ka'nauwē Lkā'etax qaLcolā'lEpLa-îtx ik!Enā'tan. Aqa
she spoke. All days they always gathered potentilla roots. Then

wi nōXuā'qoax tê'lXam. Aqa wi aqiXEluwā'lalEmX yaXi tā'nki.
again assembled the people. Then again they went to hunt that something.

QaLkcōtā'mitx LpL!ikē' k!a tqā'matcx k!a itcō'Lq qacgiutā'mîtx.
They took away the bow and the arrows and the harpoon they took them away from him.

K!au'k!au qaLkcō'xoax Lî'ctaqcō gipā'tîX actā'tcpuXpa.
Tie they did it their hair here their foreheads on.

The people tried to hit that thing, but they missed it by a long way. The two girls were seen. The elder one shot and hit quite near. Next the younger one shot and nearly hit it. Now all the people went home. They arrived at their houses. "Who are these youths who almost hit it?" said the people. "We do not know them. Maybe they have just come." In the evening the girls came home. Then Blue-jay said: "Maybe our girls hit that strange thing. They have been away [all day]." Thus said Blue-jay to the girls.

On the next day they went again to hunt that thing. They tried to hit it. After some time a canoe was seen and those two youths were in it. The people said: "Those are the youths who nearly hit it." The elder one shot first. Ah, he nearly hit it! Next the younger one shot. He nearly hit its back. The people went home. It became evening. The people came home. Then again

---

Kē'nuwa tiā'maq atqtilō'xoax yaXi tā'nki. Kᴇlā'îX aqiyukʟpā'x.
Try hit they did it that something. Far it was missed.

Aqcqᴇlgᴇ'lx. Iā'maq agilō'xoax wuX axgᴇ'kunq. Q¡oā'p iā'maq
They were seen. Shoot she did that elder one. Nearly hit

agēlō'xoax. Alā'xta wuX axgᴇ'sqax iā'maq agelō'xoax. Q¡oā'4p
she did it. Next that younger one shoot she did it. Nearly

iā'maq agelō'xoax. NuXuak¡uā'x ka'nauwē ta-îtci tê'lXam.
hit she did it. They went home all those people.

NuXuitcō'x ta-îtci tê'lXam. "Qa'wa-îtc ta-u tq¡ulipXunā'yu,
They talked together those people. "Who these youths

ta-u ā'koapō iā'maq itgē'lôx?" igugoā'kim ta-îtci tê'lXam.
who nearly hit did it?" said those people.

"NtcgōXuē'ʟᴇluXt, koalē'wi ʟXuan itgatē'mam." Xā'pîX aqa
"We do not know them, just perhaps they arrived." In the evening then

qack¡uā'mamx staXi shā't¡au. Nigē'm iqē'sqēs: "Stā'xka ʟXuan
came home those virgins. He said blue-jay: "They may be

sgi sga'hat¡au iā'maq asgilō'xoa yaxi tā'nki itk¡ēnuwā'i. Koalē'wi
these my virgins hit did it that something strange. Just

k¡ā'ya icgē'xax," itccō'lXam ctaXi chā't¡au iqē'sqēs.
nothing they were," said to them those virgins blue-jay.

Wāx igē'tcuktîX, aqa wi qiXᴇluwā'lalᴇmtck yaXi tā'nki. Kē'nuwa
Next day it got day then again they went to hunt it that something. Try

tiā'maq iqtē'lôx. Lā'2lē, aqa wi iqē'qalkᴇl ikᴇ'nîm. Aqa wi
shoot it it was done. Long, then again it was seen a canoe. Then again

ctā'xka staxi sq¡u'lipX ctēt. Igugoā'kim ta-îtci tê'lXam: "CtaXē'
those two youths came. They said those people: "They

ctaXi cq¡u'lîpX ta-u ā'koapō iā'maq icgē'lôx." Iā'maq igē'lôx
they the youths who nearly hit did it." Shoot she did it

wuX axgᴇ'kunq ā'newa. Ā'2koapō iā'maq igē'lôx. Alā'xt¡ax wuX
that elder one first. Nearly hit she did it. Afterward that

axgᴇ'sqax iā'maq igē'lôx. Q¡oā'4p iā'kalitas iā'maq igē'lôx wuX
younger one shoot she did it. Near its back hit she did it that

axgᴇ'sqax. Igō'Xoak¡oa ta-îtci tê'lXam. Tsō'yustîX igē'xoxoîx;
younger one. They went home those people. Evening it became;

aqa igō'Xoak¡oa ta-îtci tê'lXam. IgōXoak¡oā'mam ka'nauwē. Aqa
then they went home those people. They came home all. Then

wi igō'Xo-îtcō tê'lXam: "Ō ta-u sq¡u'lîpX ctā'xka aʟqē iā'maq
again they spoke together the people: "Oh, these two youths they later on hit

they talked together. "Oh, these youths will hit it in course of time. Whence did they come? These youths are pretty. They have much hair." In the evening the two girls came home. Blue-jay said: "LE! These girls always disappear. I think they will shoot that strange thing."

For four days these young men were seen and they almost hit it. On the fifth day the people talked together again: "Where may these youths come from who always come near hitting it?" In the evening the two girls came home. They carried only few potentilla roots. Then the people said: "To-morrow we will go to hunt. We shall recognize these youths." In the morning the people made themselves ready. They prepared their arrows. Then they went down to the water to hunt that something. They grew tired. All the time they were trying to hit it. Then the two youths were seen. A person said: "The two youths who nearly hit it are coming." It came in sight and

---

acgelō'xoa yaXi tā'nki. Qā'mtēwa qîctē'mam? T!ō'kti tq!ulîpXunā'yu.
will do it that something. Whence they come? Good youths.

Lgā'pEla LE'qaqcō." Xā'pîX aqa wi icgoā'mam ctaXi chā't!au.
Much their hair." In the evening then again came home these virgins.

Igē'kim iqē'sqēs: "LE! Qulî'tc k!ā'ya ckēx cgi cgā'hat!au. Ctā'xka
He said blue-jay: "LE! Always nothing are these my virgins. They

aLqi iā'maq acgElō'xoa yaXi tā'nki itk!ē'nuwa-i."
later on hit they will do it that something strange."

Lakt Lguā'max iqE'cqElkEl ctaXi cq!u'lîpX. Ā'koapō iā'maq
Four days they were seen those youths. Nearly hit

acgilō'xoax ctaXi cq!u'lîpX. Ē'LaquinEmîX iō'qoya aqa wit'ax
they did it those youths. The fifth sleep then again

igō'Xuitcu ta-îtci tê'lXam: "Ō, qā'mtaLq ictē'mam ta-u cq!u'lîpX?
they talked together these people: "Oh, whence come these youths?

Gwā'nEsum ctā'xka ā'koapō iā'maq icgē'lôx." Xā'pîX qack!oā'mamx
Always they nearly hit they do it." In the evening they came home

ctaXi chā't!au. Nō'L!Emax ictā'k!ewula yaXi ik!Enā'tan. Igugoā'kim
these virgins. Little their load those potentilla roots. They said

ta-îtci tê'lXam: "Ō'la aqcxEluwā'lalEm aqcugulā'qLka qā'xLqa qa
those people: "To-morrow they go to hunt they will be recognized whence

tq!ulîpXunā'yu."
the youths."

Kawī'X oguXualā'yutck ta-îtci tê'lXam. T!ayā'ta itgE'tux
Early they made themselves ready those people. Good they made them

tgā'qamatcX. Aqa wi itgE'Lxa ta-îtci tê'lXam. Aqa wi
their arrows. Then again they went down those people. Then again

aqixEluwā'lalEmtck yaXi tā'nki. Tā2l igō'xoax ta-îtci tê'lXam.
they went to hunt that something. Tired became those people.

Kē'nuwa tiā'maq iqtilxō'lalEmtck. Aqa wi iqE'cqElkEl ctaXi
Try hitting it they always did. Then again they were seen those

cq!u'lîpX. Aqa iLE'kîm LgoaLē'lX: "Aqa wi ctēt ctaXi cq!u'lîpX.
youths. Then he said a person: "Then again come those youths.

Ctā'xka ctaXī'yax q!oā'p iā'maq acgilō'xoax ctaXi cq!u'lîpX." Lāx
They these nearly hit they do it those youths." Visible

the elder one shot. She nearly hit it. Then it came in sight again and the younger one shot. TEP! there stood her arrow. She had hit it. She said to her elder sister: "Paddle!" and she paddled. They reached that thing; they speared it and put it into their canoe. The people tried to pursue them, but they left them all behind. They came down the river.

Now all the people were sorry because the two youths got the better of them. Blue-jay said to his chief: "Search for those two youths. Give them your children." He replied to Blue-jay: "Your advice is good." Now all the people came home. They were all sorry because they were conquered. "Where may those youths have come from who hit that strange thing?" When it turned one way, it looked red; then it looked green, then white. The girls had disappeared. In the evening they came home. They went to bed right away. In the morning Blue-jay went in. "LE! These girls," said Blue-jay. "See

---

igē'xôx; iā'maq igē'lôx wuX axgE'qunq. Q¡oā'łp iā'maq igē'lôx.
it became; shoot she did it that elder one. Nearly hit she did it.

Wē't¡ax Lāx igē'xôx; alā'xt¡ax wuX axgE'cqax iā'maq igē'lôx.
Again visible it became; afterward that younger one hit she did it.

TEP iga-igō'tXuit wuX agā'qamatcX wuX axgE'cqax. Igō'lXam
Noise of hitting it stood that her arrow that younger one. She said to

wuX ā'galXt: "MkLē'watck," igō'lXam. Aqa ikLē'watck.
that her elder sister: "Paddle." she said to her. Then she paddled.

Ictigō'qoam; aqa icgē'lkēqcq. Icgiaqxā'ema ictā'xanimpa. Kē'nuwē
They reached it; then they speared it. They put it into the canoe their canoe into. Try

iqE'cuwa; ictō'qo-iqLq ka'nauwē ta-îtci tē'lXam. Ewā qā'eqamîX
they were pursued; they left them behind all those people. Then down the river

ictō'ya.
they went.

Ō ka'nauwē ta-îtci tē'lXam nîct it¡ō'kti igē'xôx ē'tamxtc.
Oh all those people not good was their heart.

IqE'tōLq. Itciō'lXam iqē'sqēs iā'Xak¡Emana: "Ō amcōnā'xLa ctaXi
They were conquered. He said to him blue-jay to his chief: "Oh search for them those

cq¡u'lîpX. Amclō'ta cmē'Xan." Iqiō'lXam iqē'sqēs: "Q¡oā'L yaXi
youths. Give them your daughters." He was told blue-jay: "All right that

imE'kîm." IguXuak¡oā'mam ka'nauwē ta-îtci tē'lXam. LE'gaxax
you say." They came home all those people. Sorry

ka'nauwē. LE'gaxax iqE'tōLq, sxE'lk¡atcX iqE'tōLq. "Qā'mtā2Lqa
all. Sorry they were conquered, just as though they were conquered. "Whence

itgatē'mam ta-u tq¡ulîpXunā'yukc ta-u iā'maq itgē'lôx ta-u tā'nki
came those youths who hit they did it that something

itk¡ēnuwā'-i?" Anā' niktE'qoXwitXix, anā' Lpîl nîxō'xoax, anā' ptcîx
strange?" Sometimes it turned, sometimes red it was, sometimes green

nîxō'xoax, anā' tk¡ōp nîxō'xoax yaXi tā'nki. K¡ayā' ckē'xax ctaXi
it was, sometimes white it was that something. Nothing were those

chā't¡au. Xā'pîX aqa ick¡oā'mam. Nā'wi ickLkā'yuXuit ctaXi
virgins. In the evening then they came home. At once they went to bed those

chā't¡au. Kawī'X iō'pqam iqē'sqēs: "LE, cgi cga'hat¡au," igē'kîm
virgins. Early he entered blue-jay: "LE, these our virgins!" he said

how long they are sleeping. Certainly two men have been with them." Thus he spoke to the chief's daughters. The people talked together. They searched for those youths, but they did not find them. It grew dark. Then the girls brought to the house what they had caught. They placed it under their bed. They arose early. Their father was lying down. He was ashamed. He was wondering who might have hit that thing. His daughters went up to him. They had bathed and warmed themselves. The elder one said to her father: "Arise!" Their father arose. They said to him: "Go and bathe!" Then he went down to the water to bathe. He came back again. They said to their mother: "Give us a large good mat." They put the mat in the middle of the house. Then they took what they had caught and put it down in the middle of the house. There it was just like the sun. Blue-jay came in. He closed his eyes right away. That thing was shining. "I thought so," said Blue-jay; "our chief's daughters hit it." He went out. "Ah, don't you notice, our chief's daughters

---

iqē'sqēs. "Qē qᴇ'cgulqulē tantxo lē'lē icqē'wîtXit," itccō'lXam 1
blue-jay. "If two women to whom two men went secretly therefore long they sleep." he said to them

iʟā'Xak|ᴇmana ciā'xan. Igō'Xuitcu ta-îtci tē'lXam. Qcō'naXʟ 2
their chief his daughters. They talked together those people. They were searched for

ctaXi cq|u'lîpX. Nēst qiqcō'cgam. Igō'ponᴇm. Aqa îcgiukoā'lᴇmam 3
those youths. Not they were found. It got dark. Then they brought to the house

yaXi îctā'k|ētēnax ctaXi chā't|au. Icgī'yutk gē'kuala ēlXᴇ'mē. 4
that what they had shot those virgins. They placed it under the bed.

Kawī'X aqa icxᴇlā'yutck. Yōkᵘtk yaXi wē'ctam; ēxᴇ'm'as. 5
Early then they arose. He was lying down that their father; he was ashamed.

Tkadā'koax itctuxō'la, qa'wa-itc iā'maq itgē'lôx yaXi tā'nki. 6
Thoughts he made, who hit they did it that something.

Icī'tptckam ciā'Xan. Ctoqoā'tîx· icxcqoā'mit. Igiō'lXam yaXi 7
They went inland his daughters. They bathed, they warmed themselves. She said to him that

wē'tcam wux axgᴇ'qunq: "Mxᴇ'latck." Igixᴇ'latck yaXi wē'ctam. 8
her father that elder one: "Arise." He arose that their father.

Icgiō'lXam: "MXk|oā'tam." Aqa iyō'ʟxa, igîxk|oā'tam. 9
They said to him: "Go and bathe." Then he went to the water, he went to bathe.

Igē'tptcgam. Icgō'lXam wā'ctaq: "Ē'ʟuk iq|ā'pᴇnX, iā'qa-îʟ 10
He came up. They said to her their mother: "Give a mat, a large

iq|ā'pᴇnX, qē it|ō'kti iq|ā'pᴇnX." Iqioʟā'maq kā'tcᴇk tqu'ʟē yaXi 11
mat, if good a mat." It was put middle house that

iq|ā'pᴇnX, aqa ʟāqᵒ icgī'yux yaXi ictā'k|ētēnax. Iqexē'ma kā'tcᴇk 12
mat, then out they took that what they had caught. They placed it middle

tqu'ʟē. Iā'ɬxka ʟ'a aqaʟā'x iā'lkuilē yaXi tā'nki. Ia'skupq yaXi 13
house. That as sun like that something. He entered that

iqē'sqēs. Ō, na'wi igîsxpō'Xuît sī'axôst. ʟiā'ktōmaX yaXi tā'nki. 14
blue-jay. Oh, at once he closed his eyes. It was shining that something.

"K|oaʟqē' nxʟō'Xua-ît," igē'kîm iqē'sqēs. "Stā'xka ilxā'Xak|ᴇmana 15
"Thus I thought," said blue-jay. "They our chief

sī'aXan iā'maq icgē'lôx." Iō'pa iqē'sqēs: "Ā nîst tci imsā'xaxomît? 16
his children shoot they did it." He went out blue-jay: "Ah not [int. part.] do you notice?

have hit that strange thing?" Then the people were called together. All of them were called. They cut that thing and distributed it. Its blood was distributed among the birds, and they all received a little red to put on their heads. They all received something. Some were painted green, others white, and others black. Only Blue-jay was given the best. Then he danced. He was glad, and said: "I am better than you; I have received the best." He showed it to the Clam, who took it and jumped out into the water. Blue-jay took a long stick. He struck downward with it and said: "Now that Clam is dead." The Clam made the water boil, and Blue-jay said: "He is dead." But Robin said: "Do you think he is dead? He is laughing at you." Then they took the excrements of that thing out of its belly and put them on Blue-jay. First he had received the best, but the Clam took it away from him.

---

cElxā'Xak¦Emana iā'maq îcgē'lōx gi tā'nki itk¦ē'nuwayu." Aqa
our two chiefs shoot they two did it this something strange." Then

iqō'Xoaqtck tê'lXam. Ka'nauwē4 iqō'Xoaqtck. Aqa iqē'yuxc yaXi
they were called together the people. All were called together. Then it was cut that

tā'nki. Aqa iqiawē'mak ka'nauwē4 gi qtkgā'la; iqiawē'mak LaXi
something. Then it was distributed among all these fliers; it was distributed that

Liā'qawulqt. NōL¦ pEl aqLō'xoax. NōL¦ pEl aqLō'xoax ka'nauwē
its blood. A little red they were made. A little red they were made all

tp¦Esp¦E'suks. IguXoā'LXum ka'nauwē. Anā' ptcîX aqLō'xoax
birds. They finished all. Sometimes green it was made

Lp¦E'sp¦Es, anā' tk¦ōp aqLō'xoax Lp¦E'sp¦Es, anā' LEl aqLō'xoax.
a bird, sometimes white it was made a bird, sometimes black it was made.

Yā'ema iqē'sqēs it¦ō'ktē iqēlEmā'q¦euL. Igē'wîtck iqē'sqēs.
Only blue-jay good it was given to him as a present. He danced blue-jay.

K¦wa'nk¦wan igē'xôx. Igē'kîm: "QāL mE'saika. It¦ō'kti
Glad he was. He said: "How behold you! Good

iqēnElEmā'q¦euL." Itcick¦E'lukti cE'qawawa. IcgixE'cgam.
I am given as a present." He showed it the large round clam. He took it from him.

Isgî'sōpEna cE'qawawa Ltcu'qoapa. Itcē'kElka ē'mEqō iqē'sqēs;
He jumped the clam water into. He took it a stick blue-jay;

ē'yaLqt yaXi ē'mEqō. Itcîlgē'qcqalalEmtck gē'gualîX. Itciō'lXam:
long that stick. He speared it down. He said to him:

"Aqa ictō'maqt ctaXi cE'qawawa." LEp icE'xôx cE'qawawa
"Now is dead that clam." Boil it did the clam

Ltcu'qoapa. Igē'kim iqē'sqēs: "Aqa ictō'maqt." Igē'kim skā'sa-ît:
water in. He said blue-jay: "Now he is dead." He said robin:

"AmxLō'Xuan tci ictō'maqt? CkEmōquā'nēmx yā'Xauē." Ā'qa
"You think [int. part.] he is dead? He is laughing at you he." Then

iqē'kElka iā'wanpa iā'qēxElē yaXi tā'nki. Aqa yāq iqē'lôx iqē'sqēs.
it was taken its belly in its excrements that something. Then put on it was done (on) blue-jay.

Iā'nēwa it¦ō'kti yaXi itk¦ē'nuwai iqē'lōt, k¦a iqēxE'cgam. CE'qawawa
First good that strange thing he was given, and it was taken away from him. The clam

icgixE'cgam.
took it away from him.

Myth of the Coyote (told 1891)[1]

When he had finished on this side of the river, he went up the river. He arrived up there. Then he and his younger brother, the Snake, went fishing salmon with their nets. They fished with their net, but did not catch anything. They went home. Coyote was angry; he defecated. "Why did those salmon disappear?" "Oh, that bandy-legged one. Do you think the custom is the same here? It is another country. These people speak another language. Untie your net, take out two meshes, and turn around the buoys." Coyote said: "You have told me enough." Thus he spoke to his excrements. He said to his brother, the Snake: "Quick! Let us untie it!" They untied the net and took out two meshes. Then they tied it again to the buoys. Then they finished. The following day they went to catch salmon.

It!ā'lapas Iā'k!anē

Coyote His Myth

Iʟā'cXōʟq	kata	ē'nat	ō'maʟ.	Aqa	wi	ictō'suwulX.	Ictō'yam
They two finished it	there	one side	the river.	Then	again	they went up the river.	They arrived

sā'xalîX.	Aqa	wi	icxēnauwā'itgēmam.	Kē'nuwē	icî'xēnauwāîtgē.
up.	Then	again	they went fishing with their net.	Try	they fished with the net.

Nā2ct	tān	îcgē'waq.	Icā'Xk!oa.	IgiXᴇ'ʟXa	it!ā'lapas.	Itcō'ts!ats!a:
Not	anything	they killed.	They went home.	He was angry	coyote.	He defecated:

"Qātcqi	k!ā	gi	tgu'nat?"	"Ā	taya'x	tiā'qo-îtqux	itk!ī'yuktax.
"Why	nothing	these	salmon?"	"Ah	that	his legs	crooked.

Amxʟō'Xuana	k!oaʟqā'	yaXi	qā'eqamîX?	Ixelō'ita	gi	ēlX
Do you think [int. part.]	the same as	that	down the river?	Another	this	country

qē'wa	axᴇlō'ita	atā'wawa	tatā'-îtci	tē'lXam.	Stu'XstuX	tᴇ'xa
therefore	another	their language	those	people.	Untie	do them

tatā'X	tᴇmē'nauwa-îtk.	Môkct	ʟckʟā'kux	ʟāq°	amʟō'xoa.
those	your nets.	Two	meshes	out	take them.

Amʟîktqoā'yayaXtiX	ʟmē'kōlaq."	Igē'kîm	it!ā'lapas:	"Kopᴇ't
Turn them round	your buoys."	He said	coyote:	"Enough

aqa	imxanᴇlgu'ʟîtck,"	itciō'lXam	iā'qexalē.	Itciō'lXam	iā'mXîX,
then	you told me,"	he said to them	his excrements.	He said to him	his younger brother,

aqiō'lXam	itcī'yau:	"Ai'aq	stu'XstuX	atxktō'xoa."	Stu'XstuX
he was told	the snake:	"Quick	untie	we will do it."	Untie

icgᴇ'tôx	ctā'nauwa-îtk;	môkct	ʟkaʟā'qux	ʟāqo	icgî'ʟôx.	Aqa
they did it	their net;	two	meshes	out	they did them.	Then

wi	ickʟawē'xētq	ctā'nauwa-îtk.	Ickʟō'koaʟq	ctā'nauwa-îtk.
again	they tied it to the buoys	their net.	They finished	their net.

Igōnē'gua	îcxēnauwā'itgēmam.	ʟgā'pᴇla	îcktō'tēna.	ÎcXk!oā'mam.
Another day	they went fishing with their net.	Many	they killed them.	They came home.

---

[1] Continuation of the Coyote myth told in "Chinook Texts" (bulletin of the Bureau of Ethnology), Washington, 1894, pp. 92–106.

They killed many. They came home. The Newt carried them up to the house on her back. Then they put them down, and cut them in the afternoon. They were roasted. Then they put the roasted salmon aside. On the following day they went fishing. They tried to fish, but they were unsuccessful. They went home. Coyote was angry. He defecated, and asked his excrements: "Why did those salmon disappear?" "Ah, you lean fellow. Do you think it is the same as down the river? This is a different country; these people speak another language. When you have killed salmon, and you come ashore, you must carry them to your house on your back yourself. Women are not allowed to carry them. You must carry all you have caught. Then you must cut them while you still have your belt on. Do not press the salmon's face. When you put them into the canoe, you must lay them on their backs." Coyote said: "You have told me enough."

On the following day they went to catch salmon and killed many. They went home and Coyote did in this manner: When he had killed a salmon, he put it into the canoe belly upward. They came ashore. As soon as they landed he went to take a large basket and carried the

---

Iktō'etxoniLtek aq;asE'na. Aqa iLgō'xoatk, yaXī'pa aqaLā'x, aqa
She carried them much on her back | the newt. | Then | they put them down on the ground, | there | the sun, | then

iLgE'tòxe. Itgā'kst ka'nauwē. IciLgā'tōtk taXi qtgEkst tgu'nat.
they cut them. | They were done | all. | They put them up | those | done | salmon.

Wāx igē'tcuktē. Lxēnauwā'itgēmam. Kē'nuwa iLi'xēnauwa-itk;
Next day | it got day. | They went fishing with their net. | Try | they fished with the net;

acuwā'tka. ILi'Xk;oa. Kalā'lkuilē igē'xôx it;ā'lapas. Itcō'ts;ats;a.
they were unsuccessful. | They went home. | Angry | he was | coyote. | He defecated.

Itciuqu'mtsxōgoa iā'qēxalē: "Qāteqī k;ā igō'xoax gi tgu'nat?"
He asked them | his excrements | "Why | [illegible] | became | [illegible] | salmon?"

"Yā, tayax qiō'L;lEx. AmxLō'Xuana k;oaLqā' qā'eqamiX? IxElō'ita
[illegible]

tayaX ēlX. axalō'ita atā'wawa tatā'-itci tē'lXam. Manix amtotē'na
[illegible]

tgu'nat. ac amxigē'lā yayaXtiX. aqa amtō'etXuniLa LXE'leuX.
[illegible]

Ka'nauwē amtō'etXua. Nau'i a'yaq amtō'xoa akuamuguā'lEkuX.
[illegible]

Nāet iā'xōt mixatc;ē'naqoax igu'nat. Amiakxaemā'ya, ē'caxala iā'wan."
[illegible]

Igē'kim it;ā'lapas: "KopE't aqa imxanElgu'Litek." Igē'teuktiX.
He said | coyote | [illegible] | It got day

ILxōnauwā itgē'mam. Lgā'pEla iLktō'tēna tgu'nat. ILi'Xk;oa.
[illegible] | Many | they killed them | [illegible] | [illegible]

K;oaLqā' igē'xōx it;ā'lapas qaLgiwā'qoax igu'nat, ēwā' ē'caxala iā'wan
[illegible]

qatcie'kxaē'max. ILXk;oā'mam. as iLxē'gela-iX. Itcugua'lEmam
[illegible] | [illegible] | and | they landed | [illegible]

salmon up. He carried up all he had caught. Then he took his knife and cut them all. They roasted them. Now they were done. Then they finished eating. They invited the people. They came to eat salmon and put aside what they had left over.

On the following day they went again to catch salmon. They tried to fish. The flood tide came and they had been unsuccessful. They went home. Coyote scolded. He defecated. "Why do those salmon disappear?" "I told you, you lean fellow. Do you think it is the same as down the river? These people speak another language. When you have killed salmon, and you come home and you distribute them among the people, you must give each one a stick of roasted salmon. When there are many people in a family, you must give them two sticks. If any are left over, you must dry them right away. Do not dry them at ebb tide, but at low water. Extinguish your fire at once." Coyote said: "You have told me enough."

Early the next morning they went again to catch salmon. They laid their net. There were many in it. They put their whole net

---

etc!ēct. Itctō'ctxunēʟtck taXi tgu'nat. Kanauwā' itcī'tōctx
a large basket. He carried them much on his back those salmon. All he carried them on his back

ʟxᴇ'leuX. Itcā'gᴇlga ayā'qēwiqē, igixᴇ'lk!ēxc. Ka'nauwē
inland. He took it his knife, it was cut. All

itcī'tuxc taXi tgu'nat. Iʟᴇ'xēlᴇktc. Iʟxik!ē'kst. Iʟā'ʟXōʟq
he cut them those salmon. They were roasted. They were done. They were finished

iʟā'ʟxalᴇm. Iʟgoguēxē'mam tê'lXam iguXuētxᴇ'lᴇmtck. Iʟgᴇ'tōtk
they ate. They invited them the people they came to eat. They put them up

taXi ʟxk!ā'ētix·it. Wāx igē'tcuktīX. Iʟxēnauwā'itgemam.
those what was left over. The next day it got day. They went fishing with their net.

Kē'nuwa iʟᴇ'xēnauwāitgē, ac iʟtuwē'tckoam. Acuwā'tka.
Try they fished with the net, and it got flood tide. They were unsuccessful.

Iʟī'Xk!oa. iʟīXk!oā'mam. Kalā'lkuilē igē'x it!ā'lapas.
They went home, they came home. Angry was coyote.

Itcʟō'ts!ats!a: "Qātcqī k!ā igō'xoax gi tgu'nat?" "Iamō'lXam,
He defecated: "Why nothing become those salmon?" "I told you,

gi qiō'ʟ!lᴇxt. Amxʟō'Xuan tci k!oaʟqā' qā'eqamīX? Axᴇlō'ita
this lean one. Do you think [int. part.] the same as down the river? Another

atā'wawa tatā'-itci tê'lXam. Ma'nīx amtōtē'na tgu'nat,
their language those people. When you kill them salmon,

amXatk!oā'mama, ma'nīx amtawēmā'kua tê'lXam, tē'Xtᴇma
you get home, when you distribute them among people, one to each

tgā'xēt!ēlalᴇma; ma'nīx tgā'pᴇlatīkc aē'Xt gatā'xayamē, aqa môkct
their roasting spits; when many one family, then two

tgā'xēt!ēlalᴇma amtawiqoē'ma. Ma'nīx atumxk!ā'etix·ita, nau'i
their roasting spits you give them to eat. When they are left over, at once

a'yaq ak!ē'lak amō'xoa. Nāct aʟxᴇltā'kua, aqa alaxcā'ya ak!ē'lak.
quick dry salmon do them. Not ebb tide, then low water dry salmon.

Nā'wi tcXup amō'xoa amē'tōʟ." Igē'kîm it!ā'lapas: "Kopᴇ't
At once extinguish do it your fire." He said coyote: "Enough

aqa ımxanᴇlgu'ʟītck." Kawu'X iʟxēnauwā'itgēmam. Iʟī'xanx·a.
then you told me." Early they went fishing with their net. They laid their net.

into the canoe. Then they put the salmon into the canoe. They tried to lay the net again, but they did not catch anything. They went home. They came home. They roasted them at once and dried them at once. Then he defecated, and said: "Why did those salmon disappear?" His excrements scolded him. "I told you," they said to Coyote. "When you kill salmon, and you have laid your net for the first time and you put it back into your canoe, you must take it at the part where the two nets are tied together. That part you must put first into the canoe. You must lay all your salmon belly upward. When you lay your net, then you must stay in the canoe for a long time. Then you may lay your net again." Coyote said: "You have told me enough."

On the following morning they went to catch salmon. Their canoe was full of salmon. They went home. Coyote had his belt on. Then they were cut. He roasted all the salmon and gave much to the people up the river. When there were many in a family, he gave them three spits. When there were few, he gave them two spits. He fed

---

LGā'pEla iLĕ'la-it. ILktā'kXatk Lā'nauwa-ītk. Ka'nauwē
Many were in it. They put it into the canoe their net. All

iLktā'kXatk Lā'nauwa-itk. Atā'xt¡ax Lā'gunat iLktā'kXatk.
they put it into their canoe their net. Next them their salmon they put them into their canoe.

Kē'nuwa iLī'xēnauwa-ītgē. K¡ā nīct tān iLgē'waq. ILī'Xk¡oa.
Try they fished with the net. Nothing not anything they killed it. They went home.

ILXk¡oā'mam. Nā'wi a'yaq iLī'xēluktc. Nā'wi ak¡ē'lak iLE'kôx.
They came home. At once quick they roasted it. At once dry salmon they made.

Itcīō'ts¡ats¡a, igē'kîm: "Qātsqī k¡ā igō'xoax taXi tgu'nat?"
He defecated, he said: "Why nothing became those salmon?"

Itciō'melē iā'qexalē. "Iamō'lXam," qiō'lXam it¡ā'lapas: "Ma'nîx
They scolded him his excrements. "I told you," he was told coyote: "When

amtōtē'na tgu'nat, t¡ō'tsnîX amxEnxā'ya, amtakXatqoā'ya
you kill them salmon, for the first time you lay your net you put it into the canoe

tEmē'nauwa-ītk qayawip¡ō'tpa, aqa amtakXatqoā'ya tEmē'gunat,
your net at the place where it is tied, then you put them into the canoe your salmon,

ka'nauwē tga'unakc ti'caxala amtō'xoa. Ma'nîx amxEnxā'ya, aqa
all their bellies upward do them. When you lay your net, then

lē'lē amxgā'mitaqoa, tcXua wi qamxEnxā'x." Igē'kîm it¡ā'lapas:
long you stay in the canoe, then you lay your net." He said coyote:

"KopE't imxanElgu'Lîtck." Igē'tcuktîX. ILxēnauwā'itgEmam.
"Enough you told me." It got day. They went fishing with their net.

Pāl iLā'Xanim tgu'nat. ILī'Xk¡oa. Iuguā'lqux it¡ā'lapas. Aqa
Full their canoe salmon. They went home. His belt was on coyote. Then

igixE'lk¡îxc. ItgE'kst ka'nauwē taXi tgu'nat. Itctō'mak ka'nauwē
they were cut. They were done all those salmon. He gave much all

ē'wa cā'xalîX ē'lXam. Manē'x Lgā'pElatîkc aēXt gatā'xayamē,
there up town. When many one family,

Lōn tgā'xēt¡ēlalEma. Qatctawiqoē'mx. Manēx anō'L¡katîkc, aqa
three their roasting spits. He gave them to eat. When few, then

môkct tgā'xēt¡ēlalEma. Ka'nauwē qatctōmā'kuax ē'wa cā'xala
two their roasting spits. All he distributed them there up

all the people of the upper part of the river. A little was left over and he dried it all. Now he knew all the tabus. Coyote said: "Thus shall be the tabus for all the generations of Indians. Even I got tired. No murderer shall eat salmon, no girl, no menstruating woman, no widower, nobody who prepares corpses for burial, and no woman who has just given birth to a child. It is forbidden. Even I got tired. When men work on their net and make a small mistake, they shall not catch anything. When a louse is on a net, the owner shall not catch anything."

ē'lXam. NōL|ka qatiXk|ā'etix·itx. Ka'nauwē ak|ē'lak qatetō'xoax.
town. A little only they left over. All dry salmon he made them.

Ka'nauwē qatēlō'Xuix·itx tk|ē'Lau. Nigē'mx it|ā'lapas:
All they were known tabus. He said coyote:

"AluXumapā'ya Natē'tanuē k|oaLqē' Lgā'k|ēLau. Ā'la nai'ka,
"Generations Indians thus their tabus. Even I,

ā'la tEll inE'xôx. Năct aliLxElEmō'xoma gaLā'k|auk|au igu'nat.
even tired I became. Not he shall eat it a murderer salmon.

Nă'ct aliLxElEmō'xoma Lq|elā'wulX, năct aliLxElEmō'xoma LqLā'Xit.
Not she shall eat it a girl who is just mature, not she shall eat it a menstruating woman.

Năct aliLxElEmō'xoma LE'pLqau. Năct aliLxElEmō'xoma Lmē'mElōct
Not they shall eat it widowers and widows. Not he shall eat it corpses

Lē'XLēX LgE'Loxt. Năct aliLxElEmō'xoma t|ō'tsnîX qaLqtō'mEx.
prepare who does it. Not she shall eat it just who gave birth to a child.

Tgā'k|ēLau. Ā'la nai'ka, ā'la tEll inE'xôx. Manîx
Their taboo. Even I, even tired I became. When

nauwā'itk aLktuxō'lalEma, nōL| aLgō'k|umamEkua, năct tān
a net they make it, little they make a mistake, not anything

Lgēwā'qoamEniLa-îtx. Ma'nîx ōguaLā'lētEma-îtx āqtē'xa nauwā'itk,
they always catch. When they are on it shirt lice a net,

năct tān Lgēwā'qoamEniLx qLā'nauwa-îtk."
not anything they always catch those having the net."

Myth of the Salmon. I (told 1891)

The people of mythical times were dying of hunger. They had only sagittaria-roots to eat. They had only small sagittaria-roots and skunk-cabbage and —— roots and rush roots to eat. In the spring of the year the Salmon went up the river. They had first arrived with many companions. They went some distance. Then the Skunk-cabbage said: "At last my brother's son has arrived. If it had not been for me, your people would have been dead long ago." Then the Salmon said: "Who is that who is talking there?" "Oh, that is the Skunk-cabbage who is talking." "Let us go ashore." They went ashore and gave him one elkskin armor. They gave him five elk skins and put war clubs under his blanket, one on each side. They put two clubs under the blankets. Then they carried him inland and placed him among willows.

Igu'nat Iā'k¡anē. I

Salmon His Myth

IguXuā'La-it wa'lō ts¡ak¡ā'nEX. Tā'ema tsq¡ēmē'mix·
They died of hunger the people of the myths. Only sagittaria-roots

qatoxoēmō'xEmx k¡a LEmq¡ā'emax k¡a LE'qalpō k¡a tqanā'pcupcū
they ate them and small sagittaria-roots and skunk-cabbage and (a root)

qatoxoēmō'xumx k¡a Lp¡E'nxaLX. Tcā'goa-îX igē'xoxîX, aqa
they ate it and rush-roots. The spring of the year it became, and

iō'suwulX igu'nat. T¡ō'tsnîX qayō'yamx igu'nat Lgā'pElatîkc
he went up the river the salmon. First he arrived the salmon many

iLā'cgēwal. Qā'xpaL qiō'yam, aqa igē'kîm ē'qalpō: "Koala ctcā'qa
his companions. When he arrived, then said the skunk-cabbage: "At last

qayō'yamx itcE'wulX. Qē nîc nai'ka inE'xôx pān qigōXoā'La-it
he arrived my nephew. If not I I had been, (then) had died

tmē'lXam." Igē'kîm igu'nat: "Lān LaXi ā'koa Lxō'la?" "Ā, ē'qalpō
your people." He said the salmon: "Who that thus talking?" "Ah, skunk-cabbage

yaXi ā'kua iXō'la." "Alxē'gela-îX, alxē'gela-îX!" ILxē'gela-îX.
this one thus talking." "Let us go ashore, let us go ashore!" They went ashore.

Iqē'lōt ēXt igē'luqtē. Qoā'nEm tgē'luqtē iqtē'lōt. Iqa-igE'mōlX
He was given one elkskin armor. Five elkskin armors they were given to him. It was put under his blanket

aē'Xt atā'mq¡aL kat aē'Xt iqa-igE'mōlX igōn ē'nat ē'yaLq. Môkct
one club and one was put under his blanket other one side his body. Two

Ltā'mq¡aL iqLigE'mōlX. Iqē'yuk·i LxE'lēuX. Iqēyō'tXamit kā'tcak
clubs were put under his blanket. He was carried inland. He was put middle

ēlā'itkpa.
willows in.

The Salmon and his people went on ascending the river. Then another person said: "At last my brother's son arrived, whose buttocks are full of maggots. If it had not been for me, your people would be dead." "Who is talking there?" said the Salmon. "Oh, your aunt, the Sagittaria-root." He put some small dentalia on her buttocks and gave her three woodchuck blankets. Then they left her. They went some distance.

Then another person said: "Oh, at last my brother's son has arrived, whose buttocks are full of maggots. If it had not been for me, all your people would be dead." The Salmon said: "Who is talking there?" "Oh, your aunt, the large Sagittaria-root." "Let us go ashore." He put large dentalia on her buttocks and gave her five woodchuck blankets. He placed her in the mud.

Then they continued going up the river. They had gone some distance. Another person spoke: "Oh, at last my brother's son has arrived, whose buttocks are full of maggots. If it had not been for me, all your people would be dead." "Who is talking there?" "Oh, your uncle, the Rush-root." "Let us go ashore," said the Salmon. They

---

Aqa wit'ax iʟō'suwulX igu'nat k¡a tiā'xelawēmax. Aqa wi ʟgō'nax
Then again he went up the salmon and his people. Then again another

iʟᴇ'xalᴇtcō ʟgoaʟē'lX: "Koala ctcā'qa qayō'yamx itcī'tkēu iā'pōtc
spoke person: "At last he arrived my nephew his anus

gā'yamoa. Qē nīc nai'ka inᴇ'xôx ngoaʟē'lX pān oguXoā'ʟa-it
having maggots. If not I I had been I person, (then) had died

tmē'lXam." "ʟān ʟaXi ā'kua ʟxō'la?" igē'kîm. "Ā, amē'ʟak
your people." "Who that thus talking?" he said. "Ah, your aunt

aʟᴇmq¡ā'emax." Itcalgā'mit akupku'p itcā'potcpa. Itcī'caltē cq¡u'la.
small sagittaria-root." He put on to her small dentalia at her anus. He put on to her a woodchuck blanket.

ʟōn itcī'caltē ʟq¡ola'. Iʟᴇqa'luqʟq. Kᴇlā'îX mank iʟō'ya.
Three he put on to her woodchuck blankets. They left her. Far a little they went.

Aqa wi ʟgō'nax iʟî'xᴇlatcō ʟgoaʟē'lX: "Koala ctcā'qa qayō'yamx
Then again another spoke person: "At last he arrived

itcī'tkeu, iā'pōtc gā'yamoa. Qē nēkctx nai'ka inᴇ'xôx ngoaʟē'lX,
my nephew, his anus having maggots. If not I I had been I person,

pān qigoXuā'ʟa-it tmē'lXam." Igē'kîm igu'nat: "ʟān ʟaXi ā'kua
(then) had died your people." He said the salmon: "Who that thus

ʟxō'la?" "Ā, amē'ʟak atsq¡emē'mîx· wuXi ā'koa axō'la."
talking?" "Ah, your aunt, sagittaria-root she thus talks."

"Alxē'gela-îX!" Itcîlgā'mit iqawik¡ē'ʟē itcā'pōtcpa. Qoā'nᴇma
"Let us go ashore!" He put on to her long dentalia her anus at. Five

tq¡ulā'max itcī'taᴇltē. Itcō'k'ɪ ē'ʟ¡uwᴇlkʟ¡uwᴇlkpa. ItcuʟA'etamit.
woodchuck blankets he put on to her. He carried her mud to. He put her down.

Aqa wit'ax iʟō'suwulX. Kᴇlā'îX iʟō'yam. Aqa wi iʟᴇ'xᴇltcu
Then again he went up the river. Far he arrived. Then again he spoke

ʟgoaʟē'lX: "Koala ctcāqa qayō'yamx itcō'wulX iā'pōtc gā'yamoa.
a person: "At last he arrived my nephew his anus having maggots.

Qē nēkctx nai'ka inᴇ'xôx ngoaʟē'lX, pān qigoXuā'ʟa-it tmē'lXam."
If not I I had been I person, (then) had died your people."

Igē'kîm: "ʟān ʟaXi ā'kua ʟxō'la?" "Ā, emē'mot ip¡ᴇ'nxaʟX."
He said: "Who that thus talking?" "Ah, your uncle rush-root."

gave him an elkskin shirt and put feather ornaments on his head. He put him into a swamp. Then they continued going up the river.

They went some distance, and another person spoke: "Oh, at last my brother's son arrived, whose buttocks are full of maggots. If it had not been for me, all your people would be dead." "Who is talking there? Let us go ashore." "Oh, your uncle, the ——, is talking." They gave him five raccoon blankets and placed him on the bank of the river.

Then they met a canoe. The Salmon said: "Ask the people in that canoe." There were three people in the canoe. A man was in the stern, a woman in the middle of the canoe. She said: "——." The Salmon replied: "What does that woman say?" And the man in the stern of the canoe answered: "Oh, she said: 'They went up with the flood tide and arrived at the Cascades; they came down again with the ebb tide.'" "Stop the canoe. Why does she lie? How do the people who go up to the rapids come back?" They stopped them. The

---

"Alxē'gela-îX," igē'kîm igu'nat. Iqē'ltē ēXt igē'luqtē. Tiā'k¡ēckEla
"Let us go ashore," said the salmon. It was put on to him one elkskin shirt. A feather head ornament

iqtē'lôx. Iqiū'tXEmitam L¡mE'nL¡mEn ē'lXpa.
was put on to him. He was placed soft ground in.

Aqa wi iLō'suwulX. Qā'xpa iLō'yam aqa wit'ax iLE'xaltcu
Then again they went up the river. When they arrived then again he spoke

Lgoalē'lX: "Koala ctcāqa qayō'yamx itcō'wulX iā'pōtc gā'yamoa.
a person: "At last he arrived my nephew his anus having maggots.

Qa nāketx nai'ka inE'xôx ngoaLē'lX, pān qigoXuā'lа-it tmē'lXam."
If not I I had been I person, (then) had died your people."

"Alxē'gela-îX. Lā'n LaXi ā'kua LXō'la?" "Ā, tqanā'pcupcū imē'mōt
"Let us go ashore. Who that thus talking?" "Ah, (a root) your uncle

yaXi ā'kua ixō'la." Quî'nEm iqE'tēltē tqanō'qoakc. QiuLā'etEmitam
that thus talking." Five were put on to him raccoon blankets. They went to place him

tkmā'epa.
shore line at.

Aqa iLō'suwulX cā'xalîX. Lq¡āp iLgī'yôx ikE'nim. Igē'kîm
Then they went up the river up. Meet they did it a canoe. He said

igu'nat: "AmcgiqE'mtcxōgua yaXi ikE'nim." Tā'k¡aLōnîkc ta-îtci
the salmon: "Ask them that canoe." Three in the canoe those

tê'lXam. LE'kala LE'qēyamit. ILE'xaltcō LaXi kā'tcak q¡Iā'guxt:
people. A man in the stern. He spoke that middle being in the canoe:

"Laq¡ā'lakīawā', Laq¡amō'cq¡amōc, Laq¡apā'wapawa." Igē'kîm
"——." He said

igu'nat: "Qā igElxoxō'la wuXi aqagē'lak?" ILE'kîm LaXi
the salmon: "What does she say that woman?" He said that

LE'qēyamit: "Ā, axō'lal, iLtō'wîtck, aqa iLō'sowulX, iLō'yam
the one in the stern: "Ah, she says, it got flood tide, then they went up, they arrived at

ikē'catck, aqa igiLxē'takua, aqa wi iLE'stsō." "Lq¡up îmcgē'LxoxîX.
Cascades, then the waters returned, then again they went down the river." "Stop do them.

Qā'tcqē iL¡mē'nXut tcōxtx? Qantsī'X pō nuXuatā'kam ta-îtci
Why lies she makes? How many if they return those

Flounder was in the bow of the canoe. They took him by his head and twisted it so that his face was turned around and his mouth stood crosswise. They took hold of the Crow and pulled her head; her face was turned around. They took Blue-jay; they pulled him and twisted his neck; his face was turned around. They said to them: "How do people return who go to the Cascades?"

They left them. "Future generations shall always need five days to get to the Cascades."

---

ikē'catck qtgēX?" ʟq¡up iqē'ʟxoxîX. Iqʟgō'qoam. Ā'k¡amitX
Cascades going?" Stop it was done. They came to them. In the bow of the canoe

apkē'cX. Iqē'gᴇlga itcā'q¡akctak. Iqayî'lōtk. Ē'wa ictiktᴇ'qoXuitîX
the flounder. It was taken her head. She was twisted. Thus they turned it round

sgā'xōst. Ē'wa iutc¡ē'qʟko-ît itcā'kᵘcXat. Iqā'gᴇlga at¡ā'ntsa.
her face. Thus it became crosswise her mouth. She was taken the crow.

Iqʟā'nXuktē, ictiktᴇ'qoxuitîX sgā'xōst. Iqē'gᴇlga iqē'sqēs.
She was pulled at her head, they turned it round her face. He was taken blue-jay.

Iqʟē'nXuktē, iqayî'lōtk iā'tuk. Ictiktᴇ'qoXuitîX sī'axôst.
He was pulled at his head, it was twisted his neck. They turned it round his face.

Iqʟō'lXam: "Qantcā'x pō nuXuatā'koam ikē'catck qtgē'îx."
They were told: "How many if they return Cascades going."

Iqʟgē'lōqʟq. "AluXumapā'ya tē'lXam qoā'nᴇmîX atîlqō'ya yaXtîX,
They were left. "Generations of people five times they shall go there,

tcXua atgē'yama ikē'catck."
then they shall arrive at Cascades."

Myth of the Salmon. II (told 1894)

The Spring Salmon went up the river for the first time. A person was standing there. When he came past, he said: "Oh, at last my nephew has arrived, whose buttocks are full of maggots. If it had not been for me, all your people would be dead." "Who is that who is talking there?" "Your uncle, the Skunk-cabbage, is talking there." "Quick, go ashore!" The Salmon went ashore and put an elkskin armor on him. He put five elkskin armors onto the Skunk-cabbage and one club under each side of the blanket. He carried him up from the water and placed him among willows.

He continued going up the river. A woman was standing there. "Oh, at last my nephew has arrived, whose buttocks are full of maggots. If it had not been for me, all your people would be dead." "Who is

---

Igu'nat Iā'k;anē. II

The Spring Salmon His Myth

Iō'suwulXt igu'nat. T;ō'tsnîX igitē'mam ka iō'suwulXt. Aqa LōtXuē'la LgoaLē'lX. "Koala etca'qa qayō'yamx iteō'wîlX iā'pute goā'yamoa. Qē nēketx nai'ka inE'xôx ngoaLē'lX, pān qigōXuā'La-it tmē'lXam." Igē'kim: "Lān LaXi ā'koa Lxō'la?" "A, imē'mut iā'Xauē ē'qalpō yaXi ixō'la." "A'yaq amexē'gela-iX." IyaqE'lōtx igu'nat. Iqē'ltē igē'luqtē, qoī'nEm igē'luqtē iqē'ltē ē'qalpō. Iqa-igE'mōlX atā'muq;aL, ē'nata ē'yaxō kada ē'nata ē'yaxō agōn ā'ēXt atā'muq;aL. Iqē'yukL LxE'lēuX. Iqeyō'tXamit kā'teak ēlā'-itkpa.

Aqa wi iLō'suwulXt. Aqa wi iqE'LqElkEl Lqagē'lak LōtXuē'la. "Koa'la etcā'qa qayō'yamx itcī'tkEn iā'pōte goā'yamoa. Qē nēketx nai'ka inE'xôx ngoaLē'lX, pān qigōXuā'La-it tmē'lXam." Igē'kim:

it who is talking there?" "Oh, your aunt, the small Sagittaria-root." "Quick, let us go ashore!" They put onto her a deerskin blanket and put small dentalia onto her buttocks. "Later on they will buy you for small dentalia." He carried her inland and put her in the mud.

Then they continued going up the river. Again he saw a person. "Oh, at last my nephew has arrived, whose buttocks are full of maggots. If it had not been for me, all your people would be dead." "Quick, go ashore!" The Salmon continued: "Who is it who is talking there?" "Your uncle the Rush-root is talking." He put buckskins onto him.

They went up again. Then another person was seen. "Oh, at last my nephew has arrived, whose buttocks are full of maggots. If it had not been for me, all your people would be dead." The Salmon said: "Who is talking there?" "Ah, the Indian potato is talking." "Quick, let us go up!" They landed and put a woodchuck blanket onto her. They gave her three woodchuck blankets and put long dentalia onto

---

"LĀn LaXi ā'kōa LXō'la?" "Ā ā'xka amē'Lak aLEmq¦ā'emax."
"Who that thus talking?" "Ah, she your aunt small sagittaria-root."

Aqa: "A'yaq lxē'gela-iX." IqE'cEltī cpā'iX, mâkct iqE'talti
Then: "Quick we will go ashore." It was put onto her a double deer-skin blanket, two were put onto her

tpā'îX. Iqalgā'mita akupku'p itcā'pōtspa. "Ā'Lqi aqEmōmElā'lEma,
deerskin blankets. It was put on her small dentalia her anus at. "Later on you will be bought,

ikupku'p amtXLā'ita aqEmtXumk¦ē'nuapa." Iqō'kLa LXE'lēuX
small dentalia will be put up for you you will be exchanged for them." She was carried inland

ē'L¦uwalkL¦uwalkpa. IqōLā'etamit.
mud to. She was put down.

Aqa wi iLō'suwulXt. Aqa wi iqE'LqElkEl LgoaLē'lX:
Then again he went up. Then again he was seen a person:

"Koala ctcā'qa qayō'yamx itcō'wîlX iā'putc goā'yamoa. Qē nē'ketx
"At last he arrived my nephew his anus having maggots. If not

nai'ka inE'xôx ngoaLē'lX, pān qigoXuā'La-it tmē'lXam." Igē'kîm
I I had been I person, (then) had died your relatives." He said

igu'nat: "LĀn LaXi ā'kua LXō'la?" "Ā yā'xka imē'mut ip¦E'nxaL
the salmon: "Who that thus talking?" "Ah he your uncle rush-root

yaXi ākua ixō'la." Iqē'ltē asE'qsEq. Mākct iqE'tEltē tsEqsE'quks.
that thus talking." It was put onto him a buckskin. Two were put on him buckskins.

Aqa wit'ax iLō'suwulXt. Aqa wi Lgō'nax iqE'LqElkEl LgoaLē'lX:
Then again he went up. Then again one more he was seen a person:

"Koala ctcā'qa qayō'yamx itcî'tkēu, iā'putc goā'yamō. Qē nē'ketx
"At last he came my nephew, his anus having maggots. If not

nai'ka inE'xôx ngoaLē'lX, pān qigōXuā'La-it tmē'lXam." Igē'kîm
I I had been I person, (then) had died your relatives." He said:

igu'nat: "LĀn LaXi ā'kua LXō'la?" "Ā—y—ā'xka amē'Lak
the salmon: "Who that thus talking?" "Ah, she your aunt

atsq¦emē'mîX ā'kua axō'la." "Ai'aq alxgiā'kela." Aqa
Indian potato thus talks." "Quick let us land." Then

iLxē'gela-îX. IqE'cEltē eq¦ula'. Lōn tq¦ulā'max iqE'tEltē.
they landed. It was put onto her woodchuck blanket. Three woodchuck blankets were put onto her.

Iqalgā'mita iqawik¦ē'Lē. Itcā'potcpa iqalgā'mit. "Manē'x
It was put onto her long dentalia. Her anus at they were put. "When

her buttocks. "You will be bought for long dentalia and for woodchuck blankets." Then she was placed in the mud.

They went on again. They went a long distance and found a person. "Oh, at last my nephew has arrived, whose buttocks are full of maggots. If it had not been for me, all your people would be dead." "Who is talking there?" said the Salmon. They gave him five raccoon blankets and placed him near the water.

Then they went up again. They went far up the river. They came to St Helens. There they saw a canoe coming down the river. The canoe came near. Ah, Blue-jay and the Crow were in it, and the Flounder in the bow of the canoe. They were asked: "Where do you come from?" They did not reply. They were asked a second time. Then the Crow answered and said: "———." The Salmon said: "What does she say?" One person said: "She said they went up with the flood tide and they came to Cascades. Then with the ebb tide they went down the river." "Ha! the Crow is lying! No canoe

---

aqᴇmomᴇlā'lᴇma iqawik;ē'ʟē amtXʟā'eta, tq;ulā'max aqamtXᴇmō'ta."
you will be bought / long dentalia / will be put up for you, / woodchuck blankets / will be put up for you."

Iqō'kʟa ē'ʟ;uwᴇlkʟ;uwᴇlkpa. Iqoʟā'etamit.
She was carried / mud to. / She was put down.

Aqa wi iʟō'suwulXt. Kᴇlā'îX iʟō'ya. Aqa wi iʟaʟgō'qoam
Then / again / he went up. / Far / he went. / Then / again / they met him

ʟgoaʟē'lX ʟōXt. "Koala ctcā'qa qayō'yamx itcō'wîlX iā'potc
a person / there was. / "At last / he arrived / my nephew / his anus

goā'yamoa. Qē nēkctx nai'ka inᴇ'xôx nguaʟē'lX, pān
having maggots. / If / not / I / I had been / I person, / (then)

qigoXuā'ʟa-it tmē'lXam." "ʟān ʟāXi ā'koa ʟxō'la?" igē'kîm
had died / your relatives." / "Who / that / thus / talking?" / said

igu'nat. Ā tq;anā'pcupcū yaXi ā'kua ixō'la." "A'yaq alxē'gēla-îx."
the salmon. / Ah / (a root) / that / thus / talking." / "Quick / let us land."

Iqā'teltē quî'nᴇm tqanō'qoakc. Iqēguʟā'etamit q;oā'p ʟtcu'qoapa.
They were put onto her / five / raccoon blankets. / He was put / near / water at.

Iʟō'suwulXt, aqa cā'xalîX iʟō'ya. Iʟō'yam Nā'yagōgo-îXpa.
They went up, / then / up / they went. / They arrived / St Helens at.

Iqiʟgē'qᴇlkᴇl ikᴇ'nīm ēstsX. Q;oā'p igī'yôx yaXi ikᴇ'nim.
It was seen / a canoe / going down the river. / Near / it came / that / canoe.

Ā iqē'sqēs ʟaʟā'itc ʟēstsX k;a at;ā'ntsa, k;a apkē'cX ā'k;amîtX.
Ah, / blue-jay / these / come down the river / and / the crow, / and / the flounder / in the bow of the canoe.

"Ā qā'mtēwa amctē'mam?" iqʟōqu'mtcxōkua. Nāct iʟᴇ'xᴇltcō.
"Ah / whence / you came?" / they were asked. / Not / they told.

Wē't'ax iqʟōqu'mtcxōkua. Mô'ktîX iqʟōqu'mtcxōkua. Aqa
Again / they were asked. / Twice / they were asked. / Then

igā'xaltco at;ā'ntsa. Igā'kîm: "ʟaq;ā'lakiawā', ʟaq;amō'cq;amōc
she told / the crow. / She said: / "——— / ———

ʟaq;apā'wapawa." Igē'kîm igu'nat: "Qa'yax igā'kîm?" Iʟᴇ'kîm
———." / He said / the salmon: / "What / does she say?" / He spoke

ʟeXā't ʟgoaʟē'lX: "Iʟᴇ'witck kawu'X aqa iʟo'suwulXt. Iʟō'yam
one / person: / "At flood tide / early / then / they went up. / They came to

ikē'catck, aqa igiʟxē'takoa aqa wi iʟᴇ'stsō." "Itcā'ʟ;mēnXut
Cascades, / then / they returned (the waters) / then / again / they went down the river." / "She is telling lies

ever came back from Cascades (in one day). It takes five to go and come back from Cascades. Let us put our canoe alongside of theirs." Then they went alongside their canoe. They took Blue-jay, pulled his head, and twisted his face. They took the Crow, pulled her head, and twisted her face backward. They took the Flounder, who was in the bow of the canoe. They put her mouth crosswise. "Later generations shall never come back from Cascades in one day." Blue-jay was thrown inland and the Crow was thrown inland. "Crow shall be your name; you shall not talk the Wasko language." The Flounder was thrown into the water and was told: "Go down the river to the beach, and lie down flat. Your name shall be Flounder."

---

at!ā'ntsa. Nîct qa'ntsîX nîXtā'kuax ikᴇ'nim ikē'catckpa.
the crow. Never returns a canoe Cascades from.

Qui'nᴇmîX qayoqō'ix ikᴇ'nim qayō'suwulXᴇmX, tcXua qiyō'yam
Five sleeps a canoe goes up, then it arrives at

ikē'catck. A'yaq, alxgē'ʟqamᴇla." Aqa iʟgē'ʟqamᴇla iqē'sqēs.
Cascades. Quick let us go alongside their canoe." Then they went alongside the canoe blue-jay.

Iqʟē'nxuktē iqē'sqēs. Ē'wa ictiktᴇ'qoXuitîX sī'axôst. Iqā'gᴇlga
He was taken at his head blue-jay. Thus they twisted his face. She was taken

at!ā'ntsa, iqʟā'nxuktē. Ictiktᴇ'qoXuitiX sgā'xost. Iqʟā'nxuktē
the crow, she was taken at her head. They twisted her face. She was taken at her head

apkē'cX ā'k!amitx. Ēwā' iuk!ulā'tx·it itcā'kᵘcXat. "Alōxoā'xa
the flounder in the bow of the canoe. Thus he put it crossways her mouth. "Generations of

tê'lXam näct qa'ntsîx aluXoatā'koa ēXt wē'koa ikē'catckpa.
people never they shall return one day Cascades from.

Iqēxē'ma iqē'sqēs ʟxᴇ'lēuX. Iō'koa iqaxē'ma at!ā'ntsa ʟxᴇ'lēuX.
He was thrown blue-jay inland. There she was thrown the crow inland.

"At!ā'ntsa imē'xalēu, nēct qa'ntsîX ʟuxolē'mᴇt amxᴇltcuwā'ya."
"Crow your name, never Wasko language you shall speak it."

Iqalē'maʟx apkē'cX. iqō'lXam apkē'cX: "Mē'ya qā'ēqamîX
She was thrown into the water the flounder, she was told the flounder: "Go down the river

ʟkamilā'lᴇqpa. Amsînq!oyā'yayaxtîx·. Apkē'cX imē'xalēu."
beach to. You shall lie down flat. Flounder your name."

Myth of the Elk (told 1894)

There were five brothers. One day the eldest one said: "I shall go out to-morrow and look for people." "Do as you like," said the younger brothers. He arose early, took his arrows and went. He went far. Then he saw a house. He reached it and opened the door. There was an old man on his bed. "O, grandson," he said; "you have come at last. I am starving. There are many elks here; [kill some] and leave me some food [before you go on]." "All right; I shall leave some food for you," said he. Then he went. [The old man] said to him: "Stand here." He stood there. Then a person shouted: "It is coming!" He saw an elk. He shot at it and shot at it again. Then the elk jumped at him and devoured him. The elk took off its skin. It was that old man who had become an elk. It grew dark, and [the eldest brother] did not come home.

Imō'lak Iā'k;anē

The Elk His Myth

Lxelā'itîX Lquî'numîke. Aqa igē'k·îm yaXi ixgE'qunq: "Ō'la
There were five men. Then he said that the eldest one: "To-morrow

aqa nō'ya ewata'. Antō'naxLama tē'lx·am." "Mai'ka ē'mEmxte,"
then I shall go there. I shall go to look for them people." "You your mind,"

itgiō'lXam tiā'muXîkc. Kawī'x· aqa igixE'latck. Itcō'kuiga
they said to him his younger brothers. Early then he arose. He took them

tiā'qamatex. Aqa iō'ya; iō'4ya. KElā'îx· iō'ya. Aqa itcō'quikEl
his arrows. Then he went; he went. Far he went. Then he saw it

tqu'Lē. Itcuguā'qum ta'Xi tqu'Lē. Itca-ixE'laqLqîx·. Aqa Lōxt
a house. He reached it that house. He opened the door. Then there was

Lq;eyō'qt iLā'lXamepa. "Ō, qā'cō, imtē'mamL. Aqa wa'lō
an old man his bed on. "O, grandson, you came indeed. Then hunger

inō'maqt. Liā'pEla imō'lakEmaX gipā'tîx·. AmEnElgē'tatkea."
I die. Many elks here. You shall leave food for me."

"Q;oā'L ayamElgē'tatkea," itcLō'lXam. Aqa iō'ya. ILgiō'lXam:
"All right I shall leave food for you," he said to him. Then he went. He said to him:

"Gipā'tîx· amō'tXuita." Aqa iō'tXuit gōpa'. IgaLxE'lqamX
"Here stand." Then he stood there. He shouted

LguaLē'lîX: "Ā2, yaXi iōittā'2!" Itcē'qalkEl imō'lak itē't.
a person: "Ah, that is coming!" He saw it an elk came.

Iā'maq itcē'lax. Wē't;ax iā'maq itcē'lax. Itcē'kEnpE:a yaXi
Shooting it he did it. Again shooting it he did it. It jumped at him that

imō'lak. Ā4, aqa iqē'wulq yaXi iguaLē'lX. Aqa itcixē'ma
elk. Ah, then he was devoured that person. Then it took it off

iā'k;itē yaXi imō'lak. Qōet iā'Xka yaXi iq;eyō'qt yaXi imō'lak
its clothing that elk. Behold! he that old man that elk

igē'xôx. Igō'ponEm. Nā2et igiXk;uā'mam.
became. It got dark. Not he came home.

Then said the [next] younger brother: "I will go to-morrow and look for our elder brother." It became day. Then he took his arrows and went. He went far. He saw a house and reached it. There was an old man. [He said:] "O, grandson; you have come at last. Your elder brother was here. Look at the elk skin which he left here for me. He slept here. Many women went picking berries, and he went to look for them. I wish you would also leave some food for me before you go away. There are many elks near by here." [The young man] said: "I shall leave some food for you." Then they two went inland. [The old man] said: "Stand here." He stood there. After a little while a person shouted: "Ah, an elk is coming there!" He saw an elk coming. He shot at it and shot at it again. Twice he shot at it. Then the elk jumped at him and devoured him. The old man took off the [elk] skin and went home. He carried his skin on his back.

Now three brothers remained. The next one said: "To-morrow I

Igē'k·îm yaXi igō'n iXā't iā'muXîX: "Ō'la niolā'xʟama
He said that other one his younger brother: "To-morrow I shall go to look for him

ē'lxalXt." Igē'tcuktē; itcō'guiga tiā'qamatcx. Aqa wi iō'ya.
our elder brother." It became day: he took them his arrows. Then again he went.

Iōyā'4; kᴇlā'2îx· iō'ya. Itcō'quikᴇl tqu'ʟē. Iugoā'qoam ta'Xi
He went; far he went. He saw it a house. He reached it that

tqu'ʟē. Aqa ʟōXt ʟa'Xi ʟq¡eyō'qt. "Ō2, qā'cō, imtē'mamʟ.
house. Then there was that old man. "O, grandson, you came indeed!

Igitē'mam ē'mîlXt. Ē'kcta iā'p¡askwal imō'lak, itcinᴇ'ltatkc.
He came your elder brother. Look at it its skin the elk, he left it as food for me.

Tē'ka iō'qoya. ʟgā'pᴇlatîkc tᴇ'nᴇmckc ōxuik¡ē'wula, ē'watka
Here he slept. Many women they always pick berries, there only

wi iō'ya itctōnā'xʟam tᴇ'nᴇmckc, k¡a wi amnᴇlgē'tatkca, tcXua
also he went he went to look for them the women, and also you shall leave food for me, then

qamᴇnqᴇlō'qʟqax. Gipā' q¡oā'pîx· gimō'lᴇkᴇmaX." Itciō'lXam:
you leave me. There near having elks." He said to him:

"Ayamᴇlgē'tatkca," Aqa ictō'ptcka. Itciō'lXam: "Gipā'
"I shall leave food for you." Then they two went inland. He said to him: "Here

mō'tXuita." Ayō'tXuit. Koala' aqa iʟgē'loma ʟgoaʟē'lX: "Ā4,
stand." He stood. A little while then shouted a person: "Ah,

aqa yaXi iō'itt imō'lak." Itcē'qElkᴇl imō'lak itē't. Iā'maq
then that it comes the elk." He saw it an elk came. Shooting it

itcē'lax. Wē't¡ax iā'maq itcē'lax; mô'kctîX iā'maq itcē'lax.
he did it. Again shooting it he did it; twice shooting it he did it.

Itcē'kᴇnpᴇna yaXi imō'lak. Gōpā' aqa iqē'wulq yaXi iguaʟē'lX.
It jumped at him that elk. There then he was devoured that person.

Itcixē'ma iā'p¡askwal yaXi iq¡eyō'qt. Aqa igē'Xk¡oa yaXi
He took it off his skin that old man. Then he went home that

iq¡eyō'qt. Itsī'yustx yaXi iā'p¡askwal.
old man. He carried it on his back that his skin.

Aqa ʟō'nikc iʟuk¡oā'itîXt ʟā'-itci ʟtctā'muXîkc. Igē'kîm
Then three remained those their younger brothers. He said

shall look for our two elder brothers." "Do as you like," said his younger brothers. He arose early and made himself ready. He took his arrows and went far away. He saw a house. He thought: "Oh, my brothers are probably at this house." He went [on] and arrived at that house. He opened the door. There was an old man. He entered. Then the old man said: "O, grandson; you have come at last. [Your brothers] left this elk skin for me. They went to the place where the women are picking berries. You also shall leave food for me. I always try to shoot elks, but I can not kill them." "All right" [said the young man], "I shall leave food for you here." Then they went inland. [The old man] said: "Stand here." He stood there. Then a person shouted: "Ah, an elk is coming!" He looked; an elk was coming. He shot at it; he shot at it again. Then it jumped at him. Then it devoured him right there. [The old man] took off his [elk] skin and carried it back home, where he dried his skin.

---

yaXi igō'n iXā't: "Ō'la aqa antconā'XLa cī'lxalXt."
that other one: "To-morrow then I shall look for our two elder brothers."

"Mai'ka ē'memXte," icgiō'lXam ciā'muXîX. Kawī'X igixE'latck.
"You your mind," they two said to him his two younger brothers. Early he arose.

IgixE'ltXuîtck. Itcō'kuiga tiā'qamatcX. Iō'ya, kElā'2îx· iō'ya.
He made himself ready. He took them his arrows. He went, far he went.

Itcō'quikEl tqu'Lē. IgîxLō'xoa-it: "Ō, gōpa' cī'kElXt ekē'xax ta'Xi
He saw it a house. He thought: "Oh, there my two elder brothers are that

tqu'Lēpa." Iōyā'4; iō'yam ta'Xi tqu'Lēpa. Itca-ixE'laqLqîx·. Aqa
house at." He went; he arrived that house at. He opened the door. Then

LōXt Lq!eyō'qt. Iā'ckupq. "Ō, qā'cō, imtē'mamL," iLgiō'lXam
there was an old man. He entered. "O, grandson, you came indeed," he said to him

LaXi Lq!eyō'qt. "YaXi imō'lak iā'p!askwal icginE'ltatkc.
that old man. "That elk its skin they two left for me.

Lgā'pElatîkc tE'nEmckc oxwik!ē'wula gōpa' ictō'ya; k!a wi
Many women always pick berries there they two went; and also

mai'ka amEnElgē'tatkca. Liā'pEla imō'lEkEmaX kē'nuwe iā'maq
you leave food for me. Many elks try shooting them

qanilō'XoaX, nāct qa iō'mEqtx." Itciō'lXam: "Q!oā'L;
I always do, not anyhow dead." He said to him: "All right;

ayamElgē'tatkca." Aqa ictō'ptcga. Itciō'lXam: "Gipā' mō'tXuita,"
I shall leave food for you." Then they two went inland. He said to him: "Here stand."

Iō'tXuit gōpa'. Aqa iLgē'loma LgoaLē'lX: "Ā, aqa yaXi iō'itt
He stood there. Then shouted a person: "Ah, then that comes

imō'lak." Igē'kîkct. imō'lak itē't. Iā'maq itcē'lax. Wē't!ax
elk." He looked. an elk came. Shooting it he did it. Again

iā'maq itcē'lax. Aqa itcē'kEnpEn. Gopā'2 aqa iqē'wulq yaXi
shooting it he did it. Then it jumped at him. There then he was devoured that

igoaLē'lX. Lāqᵘ itcī'yux yaXi iā'p!ackwal. Itcī'yustx; igē'Xk!ua.
person. Take off he did it that his skin. He carried it on his back; he went home.

Itcîx·cā'mît iā'p!askwal.
He dried it his skin.

Now two [brothers] remained; three were killed. Then one of them said again: "To-morrow I shall go. I shall look for our elder brothers." He arose early. Then he took his arrows and went. He went far and saw a house. He thought: "Oh, here are my elder brothers." He went [on] and arrived at that house. He opened the door. There was an old man. He entered. [The old man] said: "O, grandson; you have come at last. Your elder brothers are near by. They left me this elk skin. You must also leave some food for me." [The young man] said: "All right; I shall leave food for you." Then they went inland. [The old man] said: "Stand here." And after a little while a person shouted: "Ah, an elk is coming!" He looked; an elk was coming. He shot at it; he shot at it again. Then it jumped at him and devoured him right there. Then the old man took off that skin and carried it home.

Now one only remained. Only the youngest brother remained. Then he made arrows and arrowpoints. The boy's grandmother was

---

Aqa smôkst ictuk!oā'ētîx·t; aqa ʟō'nîkc aqʟō'tēna. Aqa wi
Then two remained; then three were killed. Then again

igē'k·îm yaXi iXā't: "Ō'la aqa nai't!ax anō'ya. Anʟōnā'xʟama
he said that one: "To-morrow then I also I shall go. I shall go and look for them

ʟî'txalXtkc." Kawī'x· aqa igixᴇ'latck. Itcō'kuiga tiā'qamatcX.
our two selves' elder brothers." Early then he arose. He took them his arrows.

Aqa iō'ya. Iō'ya; kᴇlā'îx· iō'ya. Itcō'quikᴇl tqu'ʟē. Igîxʟō'Xoa-ît:
Then he went. He went; far he went. He saw it a house. He thought:

Ō, kōpā' ʟkēx ʟᴇ'kᴇlXtkc. Iō'ya. Iō'yam ta'Xi tqu'ʟēpa.
Oh, there are my elder brothers. He went. He arrived that house at.

Itca-ixᴇ'laqʟqîx·. ʟōXt ʟq!eyō'qt. Iā'ckupq. "Ō, imtē'mamʟ,
He opened the door. There was old man. He entered. "Oh, you came indeed,

qā'cō. Gipā' ʟkē'xax q!oā'pîx· ʟᴇ'mēlXtkc. YaXi' iʟginᴇ'ltatkc
grandson. Here are near your elder brothers. This they left for me

imō'lak iā'p!ackwal, k!a wi mai'ka amᴇnᴇlgē'tatkca," itciō'lXam.
elk its skin, and also you you shall leave for me," he said to him.

Itciō'lXam: "Q!oā'ʟ ayamᴇlgē'tatkca." Aqa ictō'ptcga. Itciō'lXam:
He said to him: "All right I shall leave food for you." Then they two went inland. He said to him:

"Gipā' mᴇ'tXuit." As nō'ʟ!îx·, aqa iʟgē'lōma ʟgoaʟē'lX: "Ā4,
"Here stand." And a little while, then shouted a person: "Ah,

yaXi iō'itt imō'lak." Igē'kikct, aqa itē't yaXi imō'lak. Iā'maq
that comes the elk." He looked, then came that elk. Shooting it

itcē'lax, wit!ax iā'maq itcē'lax. Aqa itcē'kᴇnpᴇn. Gōpa' iqē'wulq
he did it, again shooting it he did it. Then it jumped at him. There he was devoured

yaXi igoaʟē'lX. ʟāq° igē'xuX yaXi iā'p!askwal yaXi iq!eyō'qt.
that person. Take off he did it that his skin that old man.

Itcī'yuctx, igē'Xk!ua.
He carried it on his back, he went home.

Aqa iXā'tka iuk!uā'itîXt. Iā'ima iʟā'muXîX iuk!uā'itîXt. Aqa
Then one only remained. He alone their younger brother remained. Then

itcî'tux tqā'matcX. Itcī'yux ik!ē'lXtcu, tqā'matcX itā'k!ēlXtcu.
he made them arrows. He made them arrowpoints, arrows their arrowpoints.

there [also]. Then he broke the arrowpoints to pieces and threw them into the fire. He said to his grandmother: "Stand there." The old woman stood there and shook herself [standing] over the fire. Then the arrowpoints which were thrown into the fire were transformed into a dog. Then the boy said to his grandmother: "Turn into a crow and help me." At night he dreamed that a person spoke to him: "Your brothers were killed by a monster. Do you think it is an elk? It is a monster. When you go there, scratch the fat of the dried elk skin." Early in the morning he made himself ready. He cried. He went with his dog. He saw a house and thought: "That is the monster's house." He went [on] and arrived at that house. He opened the door. There was an old man who said: "O, grandson; you have come at last! My grandson has a dog made of flint." Then [the boy] became afraid. [The old man] said: "Your brothers have gone to where the women are singing. They left me this elk." Then [the boy] scratched the fat

---

Ō̆Xt ayā'k¡îc yaXi ik¡ā'skas. L¡EME'nL¡EmEn itcī'yuX yaXi
There was | his grandmother | that | boy. | Broken | he made them | those

ik¡ē'lXtcu. Aqa itcixE'lgiLx ā'tōLpa. Itcō'lXam ayā'k¡îc:
arrowpoints. | Then | he threw them into the fire | fire in. | He said to her | his grandmother:

"ME'tXuit gipā'." Igō'tXuît; aqa tō'tō igā'xux ā'tōLpa aq¡eyō'qt.
"Stand | there." | She stood; | then | shake | she did (herself) | fire over | the old woman.

Aqa Lk¡ō'tk¡ōt iLE'xôx yaXi igixE'lgiLx igē'lXtcu. Aqa itcō'lXam
Then | a dog | became | that | thrown into fire | arrowpoints. | Then | he said to her

wuX ayā'k¡îc: "Ō, mt¡ā'ntsa amxō'xoa. AmEngElgē'cgam." Aqa
that | his grandmother: | "Oh, | you crow | you will be. | You help me." | Then

igiXgē'qawaqa Xā'pîX. ILgiō'lXam LgoaLē'lX: "IqLō'2tena
he dreamed | at night. | It said to him | a person: | "They were killed

LE'mēlXtkc. Iqcxē'Lau itcLō'tena. AmcxLō'Xuan tci imō'lak?
your elder brothers. | A monster | killed them. | You think | [int. part.] | an elk?

Iqcxē'Lau. Yā'xka iā'p¡askwal yaXi iXcā'mit, ma'nîx amō'ya,
A monster. | That | its skin | that | dried, | when | you go,

aqa tc¡u'X amiō'Xoa yaXi iā'pXaleu." Kawī'X, aqa igixE'ltXuîtck.
then | scratch | do it | that | its fat." | Early, | then | he made himself ready.

Iō'qulqt. Aqa iō'ya. K¡a Liā'k¡utk¡ut ictō'ya. Ictō'ya.
He cried. | Then | he went. | And | his dog | they two went. | They two went.

Itcō'quikEl tqu'Lē. Aqa igiXLō'xoa-ît: TaXī'yaX tē'yaqL yaXi
He saw it | a house. | Then | he thought: | That | his house | that

iqcxē'Lau. Iō'ya; iō'yam ta'Xi tqu'Lē. Itca-ixE'laqLē. LōXt
monster. | He went; | he arrived | that | house. | He opened the door. | There was

Lq¡eyō'qt. "Ō, qā'cō, imtē'mamL," iLgiō'lXam. "Ō, Liā'k¡utk¡ut
an old man. | "O, | grandson, | you came indeed," | he said to him. | "Oh, | he has a dog

ē'tcqcEn. Ik¡ē'lEXtcutk Liā'k¡utk¡ut ē'tcqcEn." Aqa k¡wac igē'xôx
my grandson. | Flint | his dog | my grandson." | Then | afraid | he became

ē'yamxtcpa. "Ō," itciō'lXam, "gipā' ōkualā'lam tE'nEmckc, [ac
his mind in. | "Oh," | he said to him, | "here | sing | the women, | [and

wāx igē'tcuktē], gopā' Lkēx LE'mēlXtkc." Itciō'lXam: "Ō, ya'Xau
early | it gets day], | there | are | your elder brothers." | He said to him: | "Oh, | this

imō'lak iLginE'ltatkc." Ya'Xi iā'pXEle-u yaXi imō'lak iā'p¡askwal
elk | they left for me." | That | its fat | that | elk | its skin

of that elk skin. The old man gave a sudden start [because it pained him]. Once more he scratched the fat. The old man gave again a sudden start. He said: "The elk and myself have one skin in common." He said: "You shall leave me some elk before you leave." [The boy] said: "All right; I shall leave [some food] for you. I will go out first." Then he went out with his dog. Then the youth made five lakes. He said to his dog: "Beware! Keep up your courage! The monster will devour us!" He had five quivers full of arrows. He placed one quiver near each lake. Then he re-entered the house. The old man said: "Come! Let us go inland and hunt elks!" They went inland. [The old man] said: "Stand here." The youth stood there. Then the old man shouted: "Ah, here it is coming!" The youth looked, and, indeed, an elk came. He shot, shot, shot, and shot at it all day long. Then he finished his arrows. He went to one lake and took one of his quivers. Then he shot, shot, shot, and shot at it,

---

tc¡uX itcī'yôx. ʟēk¡^{u} igē'xôx yaXi iq¡eyō'qt. Wī't¡ax tc¡uX
scratch he did it. Start with pain he did that old man. Again scratch

itcī'yôx yaXi iā'pXᴇleu. Wi k¡waʟqē' ʟēk¡^{u} igē'xôx yaXi
he did it that its fat. Again thus start with pain he did that

iq¡eyō'qt. Igē'k·îm yaXi iq¡eyō'qt: "Antxᴇluwā't itcî'p¡askwal
old man. He said that old man: "Our two selves' common property my skin

imō'lak iā'p¡askwal." Itciō'lXam: "Aᴍᴇɴᴇlgā'tatkca imō'lak,
the elk its skin." He said to him: "You shall leave it for me elk,

tcXu qamᴇɴqᴇlō'qʟqax." Itciō'lXam: "Q¡oā'ʟ ayamᴇlgā'tatkca.
then you leave me." He said to him: "All right I shall leave it for you.

Anupā'yatcXua." Aqa ictō'pa k¡a iā'k¡utk¡ut. Aqa itcî'ʟux
I will go out first." Then they two went out and his dog. Then he made them

quî'ɴᴇᴍ ʟkak¡ōʟē'tXᴇmaX yaXi iq¡u'lîpX. Itciō'lXam iā'k¡utk¡ut:
five lakes that youth. He said to him his dog:

"Ō, qā't¡ucXᴇᴍ! ē'mēmxtc q¡ᴇ'lq¡ᴇl ē'xa ē'mēmxtc. Atctxuwᴇ'lqam
"Oh, beware! your heart strong make it your heart. He goes to devour us

iqcxē'ʟau." Quî'ɴᴇᴍ ʟgā'q¡ētsxō tiā'qamatcX. ĒXt ikak¡ō'ʟîtX
the monster." Five their quivers his arrows. One lake

ēXt itā'q¡ētsxō tiā'qamatcX qatctō'tXemîtx. Aqa wi iā'ckupq
one their quiver his arrows he placed near it. Then again he entered

taXi tqu'ʟēpa. Aqa igē'k·îm yaXi iq¡eyō'qt: "Tca! txō'ptcga,
that house in. Then he said that old man: "Come! let us go inland,

atxigᴇlō'ya imō'lak." Aqa ictō'ptcga. Itciō'lXam: "Gipā'
we will go hunting elk." Then they two went inland. He said to him: "Here

mᴇ'tXuit!" Iō'tXuit yaXi iq¡u'lipX. Aqa igigē'loma yaXi
stand!" He stood that youth. Then he shouted that

iq¡eyō'qt: "Ā2, ya'Xauē aqa iō'itt." Igē'kikct yaXi iq¡u'lipX.
old man: "Ah, this then comes." He looked that youth.

Itcē'qalkᴇl ā'qanuwē imō'lak itē't. Tiā'maq itctē'lux, tiā'maq
He saw it indeed an elk came. Shooting it with them he did it with them, shooting it with them

itctē'lux, tiā'maq itctē'lux, tiā'maq itctē'lux, ka'nauwē wē'koa.
he did it with them, shooting it with them he did it with them, shooting it with them he did it with them, all day.

Iguxoā'ʟXum tiā'qamatcX. Iō'ya ikak¡ō'ʟîtXpa. Itcō'kuiga
He finished them his arrows. He went lake into. He took them

until he finished his arrows. He jumped into the lake. Then the monster drank all the water in the lake. [The youth] ran to another lake. He took the next quiverful of arrows. Again he shot, shot, shot, and shot at it, until he finished his arrows. His dog helped him. Then the youth jumped again into a lake. Again the monster drank all the water in that lake. Again the youth ran to another lake. He took the next quiverful of arrows. Then he shot at it again. He finished his arrows, and again he jumped into a lake. Again the monster drank all the water in the lake. The youth ran to the next lake. He took the next quiverful of arrows and shot at it. When he had finished his arrows, he jumped into the lake and dived with his dog. Again the monster drank all the water in the lake. There, in the

---

tiā'qamatcX ēXt itā'q!ētsxō. Aqa wi't!ax tiā'maq itctē'lux.
his arrows one their quiver. Then again shooting it with them he did it with them,

tiā'maq itctē'lux, tiā'maq itctē'lux, tiā'maq itctē'lux. Iguxoā'ʟXum
shooting it with them he did it with them, shooting it with them he did it with them, shooting it with them he did it with them. He finished them

tiā'qamatcX. Itcī'sōpᴇna ikak!ō'ʟītXpa. Itcʟō'qumct yaXi
his arrows. He jumped lake into. It drank it that

iqcxē'ʟau ʟaXi ʟtcu'qoa ikak!ō'ʟītX ʟē'iacq. Itcʟō'ʟXum ka'nauwē.
monster that water lake being in it. He finished it all.

Igē'kta wi't!ax igō'n ikak!ō'ʟītX. Aqa wi itcō'kuiga tiā'qamatcX
He ran again other lake. Then again he took them his arrows

ēXt itā'q!ētsxō. Aqa wi tiā'maq itctē'lux, tiā'maq itctē'lux,
one their quiver. Then again shooting it with them he did it with them, shooting it with them he did it with them,

tiā'maq itctē'lux, tiā'maq itctē'lux. Iguxoā'ʟXum tiā'qamatcX.
shooting it with them he did it with them, shooting it with them he did it with them. He finished them his arrows.

ʟgēkīlkē'cgᴇliʟ ʟiā'k!utk!ut. Aqa wi itcī'sōpᴇna ikak!ō'ʟitXpa
It helped him his dog. Then again he jumped lake into

yaXi iq!u'līpX. Aqa wi itcʟō'qumct yaXi iqcxē'ʟau ikak!ō'ʟītX
that youth. Then again he drank it that monster the lake

ʟē'iacq. Kanauwē itcʟō'ʟXum. Aqa wi igē'kta yaXi iq!u'līpX
(water) being in it. All he finished it. Then again he ran that youth

igō'n ikak!ō'ʟītX. Aqa wi itcō'kuiga ēXt itā'q!ētsxō tiā'qamatcX.
another lake. Then again he took them one their quiver his arrows.

Aqa wi tiā'maq itctē'lux. Kanauwē' iguXoā'ʟXum tiā'qamatcX.
Then again shooting it with them he did it with them. All he finished them his arrows.

Aqa wi itcī'sōpᴇna ikak!ō'ʟītXpa. Aqa wi itcʟō'qumc iqcxē'ʟau
Then again he jumped lake into. Then again it drank the monster

ka'nauwē ʟa'Xi ʟtcu'qoa ikak!ō'ʟītX ʟē'iasq. Aqa wi igē'kta
all that water lake being in it. Then again he ran

yaXi iq!u'līpX, igō'nax ikak!ō'ʟītX. Aqa wi itcō'kuiga ēXt
that youth, one more lake. Then again he took it one

itā'q!ētcXō tiā'qamatcX. Aqa wi tiā'maq itctē'lux. Kanauwē'2
their quiver his arrows. Then again shooting it with them he did it with them. All

iguxoā'ʟXum tiā'qamatcX. Aqa wi itcī'sōpᴇna ikak!ō'ʟītXpa.
he finished his arrows. Then again he jumped lake into.

ʟ!lap iō'ya k!a iā'k!utk!ut. Aqa wi itcʟō'qumc iqcxē'ʟau
Under water he went and his dog. Then again drank it the monster

ikak!ō'ʟītX ʟē'iasq. Gōpa' lā'ktīx· aqa iqē'wulq iā'k!utk!ut. Aqa
the lake (the water) being in it. There the fourth then it was devoured his dog. Then

fourth lake, the monster devoured the dog. Then he ran into another lake. He took his arrows and shot at it. "Ieh!" the monster said; "you can not conquer me. I shall devour both of you." The youth shot all his arrows; then he jumped into the water. He had a small knife. Then the monster devoured him, saying. "I told you that you could not conquer me."

[Meanwhile] the Crow was sitting on top of a spruce tree [and sang]:

"Make light, light, light, light!
Grandchild light, grandchild light!
Grandchild light, grandchild light!"[1]

Then the monster said to the Crow: "I wish you were down here, that I might devour you." Then the youth cut the monster below its heart. Before long it felt sick. The dog helped, and they killed the monster. The Crow helped them. When the monster was dead, the youth and the dog went out. They took off the skin of the monster. They cut it up and threw the pieces of skin away. They

---

igē'kta igō'n ikak!ō'LîtX. Itcō'kuiga tiā'qamatcX. Aqa wi
he ran another lake. He took them his arrows. Then again

tiā'maq itctē'lux. "Iē'4!" Igē'k·îm yaXi iqcxē'Lau: "Ō, xā'oqxaLX
shooting it with them he did it with them. "Iē!" He said that monster: "Oh, can not

amtgEnō'LXoa. Ayamtowu'lq!ama ā'Lqē." Iguxoā'LXum
you two win over me. I shall devour both of you later on." He finished them

tiā'qamatcX, aqa itcî'sōpEna Ltcu'qoapa. Itsō'koa-its ayā'q!ewiqē.
his arrows, then he jumped water into. Small his knife.

Aqa itcē'wulq!. "Ō, ayamtō'lXam xā'oqxaLX amtgEnō'LXoa."
Then he devoured him. "Oh, I told you can not you two win over me."

Aqa igō'La-it at!ā'ntsa ē'maktcpa sā'xalîX iā'qap ē'maktc:
Then it stayed the crow spruce tree on up its top spruce tree:

"Tuwā'X, tuwā'X, tuwā'X, tuwā'X.
"Light, light, light, light.
Kā'yu tuwā'X, kā'yu tuwā'X;
Grandchild light, grandchild light;
Kā'yu tuwā'X, kā'yu tuwā'X."
Grandchild light, grandchild light."

Aqa itcō'lXam iqcxē'Lau: "Ō, qō'i gē'gualîX mkēX! pō
Then said to her the monster: "Oh, I wish (you were) below you were! if

iamō'lEq!." Aqa Lq!ō'pLq!ōp itcī'yux gē'gualîXpa ē'yamxtcpa yaXi
I should swallow you." Then cut he did it below at his heart at that

iq!u'lîpX. Ō2, nēct lē'lē, aqa iā'tcqEm igixE'lôx. ItcigElgē'cgEliL
youth. Oh, not long, then its sickness was on it. It helped him

iā'k!utk!ut. Ā, aqa icgē'waq yaXi iqcxē'Lau. IkcgElgē'cgEliL
his dog. Ah, then they two killed it that monster. She helped them two

at!ā'ntsa. Aqa iō'maqt yaXi iqcxē'Lau. Ictō'pa. Aqa Lāq°
the crow. Then it died that monster. They two went out. Then take off

icgī'yux yaXi iā'p!askwal yaXi iqcxē'Lau. Ō4, aqa Lq!u'pLq!up
they did it that its skin that monster. Oh, then cut

---

[1] This means: "Cut the elk's stomach, so that it will become light inside."

cut it in pieces, some large and some small. The pieces of skin were transformed into prairies; the large pieces became large prairies, the small pieces became small prairies.

---

icgī'yux.	Ka'nauwē	qāx	icgiXu'qo-iq	yaXi	iā'p;askwal	yaXi
they did it.	Every	where	they two threw it away	that	its skin	that

iqexē'ʟau.	ʟq;u'pʟq;up	icgī'yux.	anā'	iā'qa-iʟ,	anā'	iō'k;oa-its.
monster.	Cut	they two did it,	sometimes	large,	sometimes	small.

Ka'nauwē	qāx	gi	ē'lX	qa	tᴇmqā'emaX	ige'xux	yaXi	iā'p;askwal
Every	where	this	country	where	prairies	became	this	its skin

yaXi	iqexē'ʟau.	Manē'x	iā'qa-iʟ	ʟq;ōp	qasgiō'xoax.	aqa	itā'qa-iʟ
that	monster.	When	large	cut	they two did it,	then	large

tᴇmqa'emaX.	Manē'x	iō'k;oa-its	ʟq;ōp	qasgiō'xoax,	aqa	itō'k;oa-its
prairie.	When	small	cut	they two did it,	then	small

tᴇmqā'emaX.
prairie.

Myth of the Southwest Wind (told 1894)

There were five Southwest winds. The people were poor all the year round. Their canoes and their houses were broken. The houses were blown down. Then Blue-jay said: "What do you think? We will sing to bring the sky down." He continued to say so for five years. Then their chief said: "Quick! call the people." All the people were called. Then they sang, sang, and sang, but the sky did not move. They all sang, but the sky did not move. Last of all the Snow-bird(?) sang. Then the sky began to tilt. [Finally] it tilted so [that it touched] the earth. Then it was fastened to the earth and all the people went up. They arrived in the sky. Blue-jay said: "Skate, you had better go home. You are too wide. They will hit you and you will be killed. Quick! go home."

Ikā'qamtk Iā'k¡anē

Southwest Wind Its Myth

Quī'num yaXi ikXā'la ikā'qamtq. Ka'nauwē4 Lqētā'qEmaX
Five those winds southwest winds. All years

tgā'kiutqoax ta-itci tê'lXam. Atā'xanim L¡mE'nL¡mEn naxō'xoax.
poor those people. Their canoes broken got.

Tgā'qLēmax L¡mE'nL¡mEn naxoā'xax, qatctupē'xoaXîX. Ā2qa
Their houses broken got, they were blown down. Then

igē'k·îm yaXi iqē'sqēs: "Wu'ska, qā'Lqa tEmsā'Xadakoax, pō
he said that blue-jay: "Well, how your minds, if

ilxE'ktcxam, aqa pō gē'gualîX igē'tē igō'cax." Quā'nEm
we sing, then if down comes the sky." Five

Lqētā'qEmaX guā'nEsum k¡oaLqē' nigē'mx iq¡ē'sqēs. Aqa igē'k·îm
years always thus said blue-jay. Then said

iLā'Xak¡Emana: "Ō2, a'yaq aqōXuā'qtcga tê'lXam." Aqa
their chief: "Oh, quick call them the people." Then

iqō'Xoaktck tê'lXam. Ka'nauwē2 tê'lXam iqō'Xoaqtck. Aqa
they were called the people. All the people were called. Then

igō'goatcxEm, igō'goatcxEm, igō'goatcxEm. Nē'ct igē'xEla igō'cax.
they sang, they sang, they sang. Not it moved the sky.

Ka'nauwē2 igō'goatcxEm. Nā'ct igē'xEla igō'cax. ALā'xt¡ax
All they sang. Not moved the sky. Last

Lgō'goatsmēnqan iLî'ktcxam. Aqa lāX igē'xax igō'cax. LāX
the snow-bird(?) sang. Then tilt did the sky. Tilt

iLgī'yax Lgō'goatsmēnqan. Ā'qa ēlX pāt lāX igē'xôx igō'cax.
he made it the snow-bird(?). Then ground real(?) tilt did the sky.

Aqa k¡au iqē'yux gē'gualix·. Aqa ituquē'wulXt tê'lXam
Then tied it was below. Then they went up the people

ka'nauwē. Aqa itgī'yam cā'xalîX igō'caxpa. Igē'k·îm iq¡ē'sqēs:
all. Then they arrived up sky in. He said blue-jay:

"Ō, tgt¡ō'kti amxk¡oā'ya ēaiai'yu! txal ē'mēxalxt, a'Lqē kElā'-îx·
"Oh, good go home skate! too you wide, later on far

acxamgēlēmā'ya, ai'aq ēmē'maq aqēmElō'xoa. Ai'aq mu'Xk¡oa!"
they will hit you, quick shooting you you will be. Quick go home!"

The Skate said: "Shoot at me; afterward I will shoot at you." The Skate stood up. Blue-jay took his bow and shot at him. But the Skate turned sideways and Blue-jay missed him. Then he told Blue-jay: "Now I shall shoot at you." Blue-jay stood up. The Skate said: "Raise your foot before your body; if I should hit your body, you would die." Blue-jay held up his foot. Then the Skate shot him right in the middle of his foot. He fell down crying. Now the people had arrived in the sky. It was cold. When it got dark, they said to the Beaver: "Quick! go and fetch the fire." The Beaver went up to the town. Then he swam about in the water. [Soon] he was seen, and one person said: "A Beaver is swimming about." Then a man ran down to the water, struck the Beaver, and killed him at once. He hauled him to the house, and said: "What shall we do with that Beaver?" "We will singe him." They placed him over the fire and the sparks caught in his fur. Then he arose

---

Igē'k·îm ēaiai'yū: "Nî'Xua ētcî'maq ē'nitX, kē'qamt ēmē'maq
He said the skate: "Well shooting me be able to do. afterward shooting you

ayamᴇlō'Xoa." Iō'tXuit ēaiai'yu. Itcā'kᴇlga ayā'pʟ¡ikē iq¡ē'sqēs.
I shall do you." He stood the skate. He took it his bow blue-jay.

Iā'maq itcē'lax; igixk¡ᴇlatā'mit ēaiai'yū. Iqē'yukʟp ēaiai'yū.
Shooting him he did him; he turned round the skate. He was missed the skate.

Iqiō'lXam iq¡ē'sqēs: "Tca mai't¡ax ēmē'maq ayamᴇlō'Xua."
He was told blue-jay: "Well, you also shooting you I shall do you."

Iō'tXuit iqē'sqēs. Igē'k·îm ēaiai'yu: "ʟᴇ'mēpe ē'wi ʟᴇ'xa,
He stood blue-jay. He said the skate: "Your foot thus do it,

cā'xalîX ʟᴇ'xa, yā'wukîX qamō'mqtx, ma'nîx ē'miʟq ēmē'maq
up do it, else you die, when your body shooting you

ayamᴇlō'Xua." Ē'wi cā'xalîX itcî'ʟôx ʟē'yape iqē'sqēs. Iā'maq
I do you." Thus up he did it his foot blue-jay. Shooting him

iqē'lux ʟē'iapepa. Lē katsᴇkpā' iā'maq iqē'lôx. Kōpā' iqē'sqēs
he was done his foot in. Just middle in shooting him he was done. Then blue-jay

ēyuʟuwā'iqoxo-it, igigᴇ'tcax. Ā4, itgī'am cā'xalîX ta-îtci
he slipped down, he cried. Ah, they arrived above those

tê'lXam. Itsō'mit igē'xax. Igō'ponᴇm. Iqiō'lXam iqoa-inē'nē:
people. Cold it was. It became dark. He was told the beaver:

"Ai'aq ā'tōʟ agā'lᴇmam." Iō'ya cā'xalîX iqoa-inē'nē yaXi
"Quick fire go and take." He went up the beaver that

ē'lXampa. Aqa iō'k¡uiXa ʟtcu'qoapa. Iqē'qᴇlkᴇl iqoa-inē'nē.
town to. Then he swam water in. He was seen the beaver.

Iʟᴇ'k·îm ʟgoaʟē'lX: "Iqoa-inē'nē yaXi iuk¡uē'Xala." Iʟᴇ'kXta
He said a person: "A beaver that swims about." He ran

mā'ʟnîX ʟgoaʟē'lX. Iqiō'qwîlX iqoa-inē'nē. Gōpā' iō'maqt,
toward the water a person. He was hit the beaver. There he was dead,

nau'i iō'maqt. Iqiō'ʟata ʟxᴇ'le-u. Iʟᴇ'k·îm ʟa'Xi ʟgoaʟē'lX:
at once he was dead. He was hauled inland. He said that person:

"Qā aqiō'Xoa iqoa-inē'nē?" "Ā, aqiaʟk¡tsx·imā'ya." Iqiaʟqxā'ema
"How shall be done the beaver?" "Ah, he shall be singed." He was put

ā'tōʟpa. Ē'ka ikq¡oā'yuʟqoXuit ā'tōʟ ē'yaqeō. Igixᴇ'latck
fire on. Thus it struck him the fire his hair. He arose

iqoa-inē'nē. Igē'kta ʟā'xanē. Iō'k¡uiXa mā'ʟnîX. Itcō'k^{u}ʟa wuX
the beaver. He ran outside. He swam toward the water. He carried it that

and ran outside. He swam away from the shore, carrying the fire. [Soon] he arrived at [the place where] his relatives [were staying] and brought them the fire. The people made a fire. Then they said to the Skunk: "Go and examine the house, and try to find a hole where we can enter in the night." The Skunk went and laughed, running about under the houses. Then an old man said: "Behold! there is a Skunk. Never before has a Skunk been here, and now we hear it. Search for it. Kill it." They looked for the Skunk. Then it ran home [because] it became afraid. They told Robin: "Quick! go and look at the house. See if there is a hole where we can enter at night." Robin went and entered a small house. There were two old women. He warmed himself and remained there. Then they said to the Mouse and to the Rat: "Quick! go and look for Robin." The Mouse and the Rat went. They entered the last house. Then they cut the bowstrings and the strings of the coats of the women. They did so in all the houses. They cut all the bowstrings. Then they went home.

ā'tōL. Iō'yam tiā'cuXtîkcpa. Itcō'k^{u}Lam wuX ā'tōL. Igōxuē'kiLx
fire. He arrived his relatives at. He brought it that fire. They made a fire

ta-itci tê'lXam. Iqō'lXam ap¡ē'cxac: "Ai'aq amē'ya atE'ktctam
those people. She was told the skunk: "Quick go go and look for

tqu'Lē, manē'x qā'xpa alxacgō'pqa Xā'pîX, ma'nix amtucgā'ma
the house, when where we go in at night, when you find it

qā'xpa Lxoa'p ōguakē'x tqu'Lē." Igō'ya ap¡ē'cxac: "Hā'2, hê, hê, hê."
where hole is the house." She went the skunk: "Ha, he, he, he."

ka'nauwē qāx gē'gualîX tqLē'maX kaxq¡ayā'wulalEmtck. ILE'k·îm
every where below the houses she laughed. He said

Lq¡eyō'qt: "Ō, nîet qa'nsîx ap¡ē'cxac nō'yamx dē'ka. Tatc¡a dē'ka
an old man: "Oh, never a skunk arrived here. Behold! here

iqaltcî'mElē. Mcgā'naxL mcgā'waq!" Iqō'naxL wuX ap¡ē'cxac.
she is heard. Search for her kill her!" She was searched for that skunk.

Aqa igā'Xk¡oa: k¡wac igā'xōx. "Ai'aq," iqiō'lXam skā'sa-it, "ai'aq
Then she went home; afraid she got. "Quick," he was told robin, "quick

mē'ya tE'ktctam tqu'Lē qā'xpa Lxoa'p ōguakē'x, gōpa' Xā'pîX
go go and look at the house where hole is, there at night

alxō'pqa." Iō'ya skā'sa-it. Iō'pqa itō'k¡oa-its tqu'Lē. Gōpa'
we will go in." He went robin. He entered a small house. There

mô'ketîke tq¡eyō'qtîke oxoēlā'etîX. Gōpa' igixckoā'mit skā'sa-it.
two old ones were. Then he warmed himself robin.

Guā'nEsum iō'ya skā'sa-it. "Ai'aq mE'tēya," iqcō'lXam ā'cō k¡a
Always he was gone robin. "Quick you two go," they two were told mouse and

iqā'lEpas. "Amtgenā'xLam skā'sa-it." Ictō'ya ā'cō k¡a iqā'lapas.
rat. "Go and look for robin." They two went mouse and rat.

Ictō'pqa kE'mkitîX tqu'Lē; ictō'pqa. Aqa Lq¡ō'pLq¡ōp icgE'Lux
They two entered the last house; they two entered. Then cut they did them

LpL¡î'kē Lgā'LanEmax. Lq¡ō'pLq¡ōp icgE'tux tE'nEmckc tgā'LanEmax
the bows their strings. Cut they two did them the women their strings

tgā'q¡ēLxap. Ā4, ka'nauwē ta'Xi tqLē'maX ā'kua icgE'tôx.
their coats. Ah, all those houses thus they did them.

Icktō'LXum Lgā'LanEmax LpL¡î'kē. Aqa icE'Xk¡oa. "Ā, aqa
They finished them their strings the bows. Then they two went home. "Ah, then

[They said:] "We cut all their bowstrings." Robin had disappeared, and they said: "Perhaps they have killed him." Then they attacked the town. After a while Robin went home. His belly was burnt red by the fire. Then these people were killed. They tried to span their bows, but they had no strings. The women intended to put on their coats and to run away, but the strings were cut. They stayed there and they were killed. The Eagle took the eldest Southwest wind by its head; the Owl took another one, the Golden Eagle a third one, the Turkey the fourth one, and the Chicken-hawk took the youngest one by its head. After a little while the four [elder ones] were killed. Then the youngest one escaped from the Chicken-hawk. The one which the Turkey [held] would have escaped, if they had not helped him. Only the youngest Southwest wind escaped from them. Then the people went home. Blue-jay went down first. His foot was sore.

---

ka'nauwē Lq¡ō'pLq¡ōp intgE'LLux Lgā'LanEmax LpL¡î'kē." K¡ayā'
all cut we did them their strings the bows." Nothing

ikē'x skā'sa-it. "Ō," igugoā'kim, "LXuan iqē'waq skā'sa-it."
became robin. "Oh," they said, "perhaps he is killed robin."

Aqa sāq¡ itgī'yux yaXi ē'lXam. Koalē' wi skā'sa-it igē'Xk¡oa.
Then war they made on that town. Then after a while again robin went home.

Ka'nauwē iā'wan Lpîl igē'xôx. Ā'tōL Lpîl igī'yux. Aqa iqtōtē'na
All his belly red became. The fire red made it. Then they were killed

ta-itci tê'lXam. Kē'nuwa qaLgāgElgā'x aLā'pL¡ikē, k¡a nîct
those people. Intending they spanned their bow, and not

itcā'Lana. Kē'nuwa Lqagē'l aLuwā'Xita; qaLgagElgā'x aLā'q¡îLxap,
its string. Intending women ran away; they took them their coats,

ka'nauwē k¡u'tk¡ut itcā'Lan. Gōpā' qaLōLā'-itx, gopā' qLuwā'qoax.
all cut their strings. There they stayed, there they died.

ItcLē'nxuktē yaXi ixgE'kXun iqā'qamtk, atc¡îqtc¡ē'q ikLē'nxuktē.
He took him at his head that oldest one southwest wind, the eagle took him at his head.

ItcLē'nxuktē ikā'uXau yaXi igō'n ikā'qamtk. ItcLē'nXuktē itc¡ē'nu
He took him at his head the owl that one southwest wind. He took him at his head the golden eagle

yaXi igō'n iXā't ikā'qamtk. ItcLē'nXuktē iq¡elē'q¡elē yaXi igō'n
that other one southwest wind. He took him at his head the turkey that other

iXā't ikā'qamtk. IkLē'nXuktē apE'ntcaqL yaXi ixgE'sqax. As
one southwest wind. He took him at his head the chicken-hawk that youngest one. And

nō'L¡îX aqa iqtō'tēna ka'nauwē lakt. Āqa apE'ntcaqL igā'xoya
a little while then they were killed all four. Then the chicken-hawk it escaped from her

yaXi ixgE'sqax ikā'qamtk. Iq¡elē'q¡elē ā'kua pō igē'xoya qē nîket
that youngest one southwest wind. The turkey thus if he escaped from him if not

qigElgē'cgam ĒXtka ikā'qamtk igē'LXoya. Yā'ima ixgE'sqax
he was helped. One only southwest wind escaped from them. Only he the youngest one

ikā'qamtk igē'LXoye. Aqa igō'Xoak¡oa ta-îtci tê'lXam. Iā'newa
southwest wind escaped from them. Then they went home those people. He first

iq¡ē'sqēs iō'qo-itco. Lē'iapc iLā'tcqEm iLE'lôx. Aqa itqE'qētcu
blue-jay he went down. His foot its sickness was on it. Then they went down

Then the people descended. The Skate was still above. Then [Bluejay] cut the rope and the sky sprang back. Part of the people were still above. They became stars. [Therefore] all kinds of things are [in the sky]—the Woodpecker, the Fisher, the Skate, the Elk, and the Deer. Many things are there. Only the youngest Southwest wind is alive nowadays.

---

ta-îtci tê'lXam. Gōpā' ikē'x ēaiai'yu cā'xalîX. Aqa Lq¡up
those people. There was the skate above. Then cut

itcī'yuX yaXi iā'Lan igō'cax. Ēyuʟā'taXit sā'xalîX igō'cax.
he did it that its rope the sky. It sprang up the sky.

Gōpā' aqā'watîkc tê'lXam cā'xalîX. Gōpā' tq¡ēXā'nap igō'xoax
There part of them the people above. There stars they became

cā'xalîX. Gōpā' ka'nauwē tā'nki: întiawī'ct cā'xalîX; gōpā'
above. There all things: the woodpecker above; there

ēqatē'tîX cā'xalîX; ēaiai'yū gōpā' cā'xalîX; imō'lak gōpā' cā'xalîX;
the fisher above; the skate there above; the elk there above;

ēmā'cEn gōpā' cā'xalîX. ʟgā'pEla tā'nEmax cā'xalîX. Gōpā' aqa
the deer there above. Many things above. There then

iXā'tka ikā'qamtk tē'kōtcîX; iā'ema ixgE'sqax.
one only southwest wind nowadays; he only the youngest one.

Rabbit and Deer (told 1894)

The mother of the Rabbit was the Deer. They used to gather wood and berries every day. The Rabbit was playing about in the woods. He was eating roots all the time. Then he found short rotten branches. He took those rotten branches and broke off *Polypodium* leaves. The Rabbit thought: "Oh. I wish those branches would be transformed into people." Then he tied the branches and made them look just like men. Then he pulled the branches out and carried them to the water. He hid them near the house. He came home. There was his mother. She said to him: "Where have you been? You have been away a long time." He said: "I have been in the woods. I have been gathering roots." The next morning his mother rose.

IkanaXmE'nē k¡a Imā'cEn Ictā'k¡anē

The Rabbit and the Deer Their Myth

Wā'yaq ikanaXmE'nē k¡a imā'cEn. Ka'nauwē Lkā'ētax
His mother the rabbit and the deer. Every day

nEXElk¡ē'wulalEma-îtx. Aqa ikanaXmE'nē nîxk¡ayā'wulalEma-îtx.
she gathered roots and berries. Then the rabbit always played about.

Yîxē' LXE'lēu qayō'yîx qadîxElEmō'xuma-îtx tkanatskuē'. Ā2qa
There inland he went and always ate roots (sp.?). Then

qateLuegā'mx LE'puke Ltexoā'Lap. LEgEnxā't wuXi ā'lEmlEm
he took them branches rotten sticks. He placed them on that rotten wood

LaXi LE'puke. Aqa LE'xLEx atcō'xoax ā'qElqEl. NîXLoXoā'it
those branches. Then break he did them polypodium leaves. He thought

ikanaXmE'nē: Ō teXua tē'lXam ōguakē'x gi LE'puke. Aqa
the rabbit: O, if people became these branches. Then

k¡au'k¡au qateLō'xoax LaXi LE'puke. L¡a tē'lXam qaLxō'xoax LaXi
tie he did them those branches. Just as people he made them those

LE'puke. Aqa Lu'xLux qateLō'xoax ka'nauwē LaXi LE'puke. Aqa
branches. Then pull out he did them all those branches. Then

qateLō'k^{u}Lx mā'LnîX. Q¡oā'p tE'etaqL. aqa qateLupeū'tx LaXi
he carried them to the water. Near their town. then he hid them those

LE'puke. NîXk¡oā'mamx. Ōxt wā'yaq. Igiō'lXam: "Qā'mta imō'ya?
branches. He came home. There was his mother. She said to him: "Where did you go?

Lē'lē k¡aya imE'xôx." Igē'k·im: "LXē'2leu inō'ya. Tkanatskuē'
Long nothing you were." He spoke: "Inland I went. Roots (sp.?)

intonā'xILam." Wāx igē'tcuktîX. Kawī'X aqa igaxE'latck wā'yaq.
I searched for them." Next morning it became day. Early then arose his mother.

She went to gather roots. They had one large canoe. The Rabbit launched it and went down the river. There was a town down the river. There were many houses, and the people had dried salmon. The people were silent. Now they heard war-cries. They said: "Oh, maybe somebody is making war on us." All the people ran away. The Rabbit landed and went up to the houses. There were no people there; they had all run away. Then he stole. He stole their winter salmon. His canoe was full. He stole their roe; he stole all kinds of things. He went home and came to his house. He carried up the different kinds of food. In the evening his mother came home. "Oh, where did you take that food?" she said to him. "I made war on those people down the river." "Oh, then you will be killed," said his mother. "Oh, I am not going to die. When they strike me, I shall rise again." Then they ate, and they had much food in their house.

They stayed there five days. Then he went down the river again. He put those branches into his canoe. Then he went down to

---

IgaxElk¡ē'wulalEmam. ĒXt ictā'Xanīm, iā'qa-iL ictā'Xanīm. Aqa
She went to gather roots and berries. One their canoe, large their canoe. Then

itciō'cgiLX yaXi ictā'Xanīm. Aqa iō'stsX qā'eqamîX ikanaXmE'nē.
he launched it that their canoe. Then he went down the river down the river the rabbit.

Ē'lXam qā'eqamîX igē'xax, Lgā'pEla tqLē'max. Ōxuēkᵘ'cE'mal
A town down the river was, many houses. They were drying salmon

ta-îtci tê'lXam. Kā4 oxoēlā'itîx· ta-îtci tê'lXam; aqa ē'Lutk igē'xox.
those people. Where were those people; then war-cries became.

Igogoā'kim: "Ō Lqōct sāq° iqE'lxôx." Itgwā'Xit kanauwē' ta-îtci
They said: "Oh behold! war is made on us." They ran away all those

tê'lXam. Igixē'gela-îx· ikanaXmE'nē. Iō'ptcka LXE'leuX taXi
people. He landed the rabbit. He went up inland those

tqLē'mapa. K·¡ôm tê'lXam. Ka'nauwē itgwā'Xit. Aqa
houses to. No noise people. All had run away. Then

igē'kuXtk ikanaXmE'nē. Itcî'tuXtk tE'q¡awan. Pā2L iā'xanim
he stole the rabbit. He stole them winter salmon. Full his canoe

itcî'tux. Akibō't itcō'Xtka. Kā'nauwē tā'nki itcî'yuXtk.
he made them. Salmon roe in skins he stole it. All things he stole them.

Igē'Xk¡oa. Iō'yam · tE'ctaqLpa. Iō'ptcga. Itctō'kuîptck taXi
He went home. He arrived that town at. He went up. He carried them up those

LXElEmā'emax. Tsō'yustîX igaXk¡oā'mam wā'yaq: "Ō, qā'xpa
kinds of food. In the morning she came home his mother: "O, where at

imō'guiga gi LXElEmā'emax?" igiō'lXam. "Ā, sāq° inE'tôx
did you take them these kinds of food?" she said to him. "Ah, war I made on them

ta-îtci qā'eqamîX tê'lXam." "Hē, aqamuwā'qoa," igiō'lXam
those down river people." "Heh, you will be struck," she said to him

wā'yaq. "Ō, nîct qantsî'x anō'mEqta manîx aqEnuwā'qoa." Aqa
his mother. "Oh, never I shall be dead when I am struck." Then

icLXLXE'lEmEtck. Aqa Lgā'pEla tctā'LXElEmaēmax tE'ctaqLpa.
they two ate. Then many their kinds of food their house in.

Qoā'nEmîX iō'qoya-îX aqa wi iō'ya, iō'stsō. Aqa wit
Five times he slept then again he went, he went down the river. Then again

the place where those people were staying. Now they heard war-cries. One person said: "Do you see many people?" A youth looked out, and said: "Oh, there are many people. There is a canoe full of people;" and all those people ran away. The Rabbit landed and went up. There were no people. He stole all kinds of food. His canoe was full. He stole salmon backs; he stole dried salmon; he stole all kinds of things. Then he went home. He came to their house. Then he carried up that food. In the evening his mother came home. She said to him: "Where did you take that food?" "Oh, I made war on those people down the river?" "Oh, they will kill you." "Be quiet; I am not going to die when they strike me."

After five days he went down the river again. Those people said: "When these people come again we will fight them." The people were quiet and war-cries were heard. Then they said: "The people are coming." A person looked out. "Oh, many people are coming;

---

itcLakElā'etamit LaXi LE'pukc. Aqa wi iō'stsō, kā oxoēlā'etîx·
he put them into the canoe | those | branches. | Then | again | he went down the river, | where | were

ta-îtci tê'lXam. Aqa wi ē'Lutk igē'xôx. ILE'k·îm LēXā't LgoaLē'lX:
those | people. | Then | again | war-cry | became. | He said | one | person:

"Amcgē'qamitck Lgā'pElatîkc tci tê'lXam?" ILE'kik·ct LeXā't
"Do you see | many | [int. part.] | people?" | He looked | one

Lq¡u'lîpX Lā'Xanē. ILE'k·îm: "Ō, Lgā'pElatîkc ac pāL yaXi
youth | outside. | He said: | "Oh, | many people | and | full | that

ikE'nim tê'lXam." Itgwā'Xit ta-îtci tê'lXam ka'nauwē. Igixē'gela-i
canoe | people." | They ran away | those | people | all. | He landed

ikanaXmE'nē. Iō'ptcga. K·¡ôm tê'lXam ka'nauwē. Aqa igē'kuXtk.
the rabbit. | He went up. | No noise | people | all. | Then | he stole.

Itcî'tuXtk txElEmā'emax. Pā'L iā'Xanim itcî'tuXt. LXōikō'tcX
He stole them | kinds of food. | Full | his canoe | he stole it. | Salmon backs

itcî'LuXtk. AlXgu'la itcō'Xtga. Ka'nauwē tā'nki itci'yuXtk.
he stole them. | Dried salmon split along back | he stole them. | All | things | he stole them.

Igē'Xk¡oa. IgîXk¡oā'mam tE'ctaqLpa. Itctō'kuîptck taXi
He went home. | He came home | their house to. | He carried them up | those

txalEmā'emax. Tsō'yustîX igaXk¡oā'mam wā'yaq. Igiō'lXam:
kinds of food. | In the evening | she came home | his mother. | She said to him:

"Qā'xpa imō'guiga gi LXElEmā'emax?" "Ā, sāq" inE'tux ta-îtci
"Where at | did you take them | these | kinds of food?" | "Ah, | war | I made on them | those

qā'eqamîX tê'lXam." "Ō, aqamuwā'qoa." "Ac pEt mE'xôx. Ā,
down river | people." | "Oh, | you will be struck." | "And | quiet | be. | Ah,

manîx aqEnuwā'qoa, nict qantsî'x anō'mEqt."
if | I am struck, | never | I die."

Qoā'nEmîX iō'qoya-îX aqa wit'ax iō'stsō. Igōguā'kîm ta-îtci
Five times | he slept | then | again | he went down river. | They said | those

tê'lXam: "Manîx wit'ax atgutē'mam ta-îtci tê'lXam, aqa
people: | "When | again | they arrive | those | people, | then

lXktomā'qta." Kā oxoēlā'etîx· ta-îtci tê'lXam; aqa wi ē'Lutk
we will fight with them." | Where | were | those | people; | then | again | war-cry

igē'xôx. Igōguā'kîm: "Aqa tgatē't tê'lXam." ILE'kikct LeXā't
became. | They said: | "Then | they are coming | the people." | He looked | one

they are paddling. Let us run away." All the people ran away. The Rabbit landed and went up. There were no people. Then he stole much food. He went home; and when he came home he carried up that food. In the evening his mother came home. "Oh, don't fight those people any more; they will kill you." "I am not going to die. When they strike me, I shall recover."

After five days he went down the river again. He twisted spruce limbs and tied those branches. He pulled out many branches, and they were all moving when he was paddling.[1] He came near the town. Then war-cries were heard. Now those people took their arrows and went out. They said: "There are many people coming; let us run away," and all the people ran away. The Rabbit landed and began to steal. He stole all kinds of food. Then his canoe was full. Then he went home. He came home and carried all the food

---

ʟgoaʟē'lX ʟā'xanîX: "Ā, ʟgā'pᴇlatîke tê'lXam tgatē't;

person outside: "Ah, many people are coming;

ōguakʟē'wala. A'yaq lXwā'Xita." Itgwā'Xit ka'nauwē ta-îtci

they are paddling. Quick let us run away." They ran away all those

tê'lXam. Igixē'gela-iX ikanaXmᴇ'nē. Iō'ptcga. K·!ôm ka'nauwē

people. He landed the rabbit. He went up. No noise all

tê'lXam. Aqa wi igē'kuXtk. Itcî'ʟuXtk ʟgā'pᴇla ʟXᴇlᴇmā'emax.

people. Then again he stole. He stole them many kinds of food.

Igē'Xk!oa. IgîXk!oā'mam. Itctō'kuîptck taXi ʟXᴇlᴇmā'emax.

He went home. .. came home. He carried them up those kinds of food.

Tsō'yustîX igaXk!oā'mam wā'yaq. "Ō, kopᴇ't aqa sāq° mtō'xoam

In the evening she came home his mother. "Oh, enough now war make on them

tê'lXam. Aqamuwā'qoa." "Aqanuwā'qoa, ma'nîx anō'mᴇqta aʟqē

the people. You will be struck." "I am struck, when I am dead by and by

atcînalXatā'kua."

I shall recover."

Wi qoā'nᴇmîX iō'qoya-îX aqa wi iō'stsō. Xā'Xa

Again five times he slept then again he went down the river. Twist

itcî'tôx tpē'naʟX, aqa k!au'k!au itcî'ʟôx ʟaXi ʟᴇ'pukc.

he did them spruce limbs, then tie he did them those branches.

Qatcixk!a'goatcko··x aqa qaʟXᴇlā'yuwalalᴇmx ʟaXi ʟᴇ'pukc.

He pulled them out much then they moved much those branches.

Q!oā'p itciō'Xoam yaXi ē'lXam. Aqa wi ē'ʟutk itcī'yux.

Near he came it that town. Then again war-cry he made it.

Itgō'guiga tgā'qamatcX ta-îtci tê'lXam. Itgᴇ'pa. Igōgoā'kîm:

They took them their arrows those people. They went out. They said:

"Ō tgā'pᴇlatîke ta-îtci tê'lXam. Tgt!ō'kti lxwā'Xita!"

"Oh many those people. Good we run away!"

Itguwā'Xit ka'nauwē ta-îtci tê'lXam. Igixē'gela-i ikanaXmᴇ'nē.

They ran away all those people. He landed the rabbit.

Aqa wi igē'kuXtk. Itcî'tuXtk kanauwē' ʟXᴇlᴇmā'emax. Pāʟ

Then again he stole. He stole them all kinds of food. Full

iā'xanim, aqa wi igē'Xk!oa. IgîXk!oā'mam. Itctō'kuîptck taXi

his canoe, then again he went home. He came home. He carried them up those

ʟXᴇlᴇmā'emax. Tso'yustîX igaXk!oā'mam wā'yaq. Igiō'lXam

kinds of food. In the evening she came home his mother. She said to him

---

[1] They were tied to his paddles so that they all moved up and down with his motions, looking like so many people.

up to his house. In the evening his mother came. She said to him: "You went again." He said to her: "Yes, I went. All those people ran away." "Oh, stop going," said his mother.

After five days he went again. The people were quiet and they heard war-cries. They took their arrows and all went out. They saw the canoe. "Oh, many people are coming. They are uttering war-cries." Then the people ran away. But one old man hid under the bed. The Rabbit landed and entered the house. The old man saw him. He looked secretly. Behold, the Rabbit was stealing. He threw down one salmon roe. He ate it. His teeth were full. Then he rolled about and shut his eyes. The old man took a stick. He hit him here in his face, just across his eyes, and there the Rabbit lay dead. The old man hauled him out of the house and shouted. "Come down!" said the old man. "Behold, the Rabbit has been stealing from us." Now the people came down. They said: "Behold the

---

wī't'ax: "ʟ¡a imō'ya." Itcō'lXam: "Ā2, inō'ya. Ka'nauwē ta-îtci
again: "Behold you went." He said to her: "Ah, I went. All those

tê'lXam qatᴇnXuwā'xitx." "Ō aqa kopᴇ't imō'ya," igiō'lXam
people always run away." "Oh now enough you go," she said to him

wā'yaq.
his mother.

Wi qoä'nᴇmîX iō'qoya-îX aqa wi iō'ya. Kā2 oxoēlā'ētîx·
Again five times he slept then again he went. Silent were

ta-îtci tê'lXam. Aqa wi ē'ʟutk igē'xôx. Itgō'guiga tgā'qamatcX
those people. Then again war-cry became. They took them their arrows

ta-îtci tê'lXam. Itgᴇ'pa ka'nauwē. Iqē'qᴇlkᴇl yaXi ikᴇ'nim.
those people. They went out all. It was seen that canoe.

"Ō ʟgā'pᴇlatîkc tê'lXam tgatē't. Ē'ʟutk tgioxō'la." Ā'qa
"Oh many people are coming. War-cry they say much." Then

itguwā'Xit ta-îtci tê'lXam ka'nauwē. ʟeXā't ʟq¡eyō'qt ʟXᴇ'pcut
they ran away those people all. One old man hid

gē'gualîX ilXᴇ'mē. Igixē'gela-îx ikanaXmᴇ'nē. Ia'ckupq taXi
under the bed. He landed the rabbit. He entered that

tqu'ʟēpa. Aʟgiō'qumit ʟaXi ʟq¡eyō'qt, ʟxē'k¡ᴇlpsōt. Ō, ʟqōct
house in. He looked that old man, he looked secretly. Oh, behold!

ikanaXmᴇ'nē igigō'Xtgᴇla. Itcaxē'ma aēXt aᴋ·cbō't gē'gualîX.
the rabbit was stealing much. He threw down one salmon roe put up in a skin down.

Aqa iʟᴇxᴇ'lᴇmuX ʟaXi ʟᴇ'qāpt. Pā'ʟᴇmax iʟᴇ'xôx ʟiā'qatcX.
Then he ate that salmon roe. Full got his teeth.

Aqa igixcgē'lalᴇmtck isînp¡ō'Xuit. Iʟgē'gᴇlga ē'mᴇqō ʟaXi
Then he rolled about he shut his eyes. He took it a stick that

ʟq¡ēyō'qt, iʟgigᴇ'ltcîm gipā'tîx· siā'Xôstpa, siā'xôst qasxᴇnᴇmō't.
old man, he hit him right here his face on, his eyes across.

Kōpā' iō'maqt ikanaXmᴇ'nē. Iʟgiō'ʟata ʟā'xanîX ʟaXi ʟq¡eyō'qt
There he was dead the rabbit. He hauled him outside that old man

ka ʟxᴇ'lqamx. "Amcā'ʟx, amcī'ʟxa!" iʟᴇ'k·îm ʟaxi ʟq¡eyō'qt.
and shouted. "Come down to the water, come down to the water!" said that old man.

"ʟqōct ikanaXmᴇ'nē gitcᴇlxō'Xtgᴇla." Aqa itgᴇ'ʟxa ta-îtci
"Behold the rabbit he stole from us." Then they went toward the water those

tê'lXam. "Ō," igugōā'kim, "ʟqōct ikanaXmᴇ'nē." Iqiō'kctam
people. "Oh," they said, "behold the rabbit." They went to see it

Rabbit!" They went to look at the canoe and saw that it was full of branches. *Polypodium* leaves were tied to them. Then they skinned the Rabbit and took off his hide. In the evening his mother came home. Her son was not there. "Oh, my son is killed," she thought. The Rabbit was thrown into the water near the beach. He had no skin. Early in the morning his mother went down the river to search for him. She cried while she was going. She went down the river and came to the water in front of the town. There she saw something white lying on the ground. She went to look at it. Behold, her child was lying there! She carried him to her canoe and put him into it. Then she went up the river crying. She went a long distance. Then she said to her child: "Rise! Are you dead, indeed? Rise!" She said this often. When she was near her house the Rabbit rose. "Oh," he said, "I slept a long time and I got cold. I have no blanket. His mother said to him: "Did you sleep? You were dead. You were killed. You were skinned, and your skin was taken away from you." "Let us return to get my skin." "Oh, maybe we shall

---

iā'xanim mā'LnîX, aqa LE'puke pāL yaXi ikE'nīm. K¡au'k¡au
his canoe at the water, then branches full that canoe. Tied

ā'qElqEl aLE'lôxt. Aqa sEXᵘ iqī'yux. Lāq iqē'xux iā'p¡askwal.
polypodium leaves were. Then skinned he was. Off was made his skin.

Tsō'yustîX igaXk¡oā'mam wā'yaq. K¡ā itcā'xan. "Ō,
In the evening she came home his mother. None her son. "Oh,

aqa iqē'waq itcî'xan," igaXLō'xoa-ît. Aqa iqēxē'ma Ltcu'qoa
then he is killed my son," she thought. Then he was thrown water

qaLXumwē'la ikanaXmE'nē. Aqa k¡ā iā'p¡askwal. Kawē'x aqa
shore line the rabbit. Then none his skin. Early then

igō'stsō wā'yaq igiunā'xLam. Ō'qulqt igō'ya. Igō'stsō. Igō'yam
she went down the river his mother she searched for him. She wailed she went. She went down the river. She arrived at

yaXi ē'lXam ayā'maLnîX. Igē'qElkEl tā'nki tk¡ōp ixē'mat. Igō'ya,
that town toward the water from it. She saw it something white lay there. She went,

igiō'ktam. Lqōct itcā'xan yaXi ixē'mat. Igē'yukL mā'LnîX
she went to look at it. Behold! her son that lay there. She carried him seaward

igiō'kLa ictā'Xanimpa. Igiakxā'yîm, aqa igō'suwulX. Ō'qulqt.
she hauled him her canoe into. She put him into the canoe, then she went up the river. She cried.

KElā'îX igō'ya. Igiō'lXam itcā'xan: "MxE'latck! Ā'qanuwē tci
Far she went. She said to him her son: "Rise! Indeed [int. part.]

imō'maqt? MxE'latck!" Ē'xawitiX igiō'lXam. Q¡oā'p tE'ctaqLpa
you dead? Rise!" Often she said to him. Near their house at

aqa igixE'latck ikanaXmE'nē. "Ō," igē'kim, "ē'yaLqtîX inoqō'ptē.
then he rose the rabbit. "Oh," he said, "long I slept.

Aqa tsEs inE'xôx. Qāx itcî'k¡ētē?" Igiō'lXam wā'yaq:
Then cold I got. Where my blanket?" She said to him his mother:

"ImEqō'pti tci? Imō'maqt, iqamō'waq. Ts¡Exᵘ iqē'yôx imē'k¡etē,
"You slept [int. part.]? You were dead, you were killed. Skinned was done your blanket,

iqEmxE'cgam." "Tgt¡ō'kti atxtā'koa, aniogoā'lEmam itcî'k¡ētē."
it was taken from you." "Good we return, I will go and take my blanket."

be killed," said his mother. Then they returned. They went down the river. They arrived at the beach in front of that town. Then the Rabbit took his arrows. He spoke: "Give me my skin, or I shall kill you." One person said: "Maybe he will kill us, indeed. Behold, he arose although he has no skin." They tried to give him a raccoon skin, but he said: "It is bad. I do not want it." They tried to give him a beaver skin. He said: "It is bad." They tried to give him a lynx skin. He tried to put it on, but he said: "It is bad; it hurts me." They tried to give him an otter skin. It was bad, he did not want it. They gave him one-half of his skin. Then he pulled it on one side so that it became thin. Then it fitted him. He put it on. Now he and his mother went home. They came to their house. She said to him: "Do not go any more; you will be killed for good." Then he did not go any more, because he had been troubled; he was afraid. That is the story; to-morrow we shall have good weather.

"Ō LXuan aqtxōtē'na," igā'kim wā'yaq. Aqa wi icXE'takua
"Oh, perhaps we shall be killed," she said his mother. Then again they returned

ictō'stsō. Ictō'yam yaXi ē'lXam ayā'maLna. Itcō'guiga
they went down the river. They arrived at that town toward the water He took them from it.

tiā'qamatcX ikanaXmE'nē. "Ō2, mcgē'nōt itcî'k¡etē," igē'kîm.
his arrows the rabbit. "Oh, give me my blanket," he said.

"Ayamcotē'na." "Ō," iLî'kîm LeXā't LgoaLē'lX, "LXuan
"I shall kill you." "Oh," said one person, "Perhaps

ā'qanuwē atcîlxotē'na. Nest iā'p¡askwal, tatc¡a itcîlXā'takua."
indeed he will kill us. Not his skin, behold! he recovered."

Iqē'lot kē'nuwa iLatā't iāp¡askwal. Igē'kîm: "Iā'mEla, nîct tq¡ēx
He was given try raccoon his skin. He said: "It is bad, not like

inī'yôx." Iqē'lot kē'nuwa iqoa-inē'nē iā'p¡askwal. "Iā'mEla,"
I do it." He was given try beaver his skin. "It is bad,"

igē'kîm. Iqē'lōt kē'nuwa ipu'koa iā'p¡askwal. Kē'nuwa igē'xaltē.
he said. He was given try lynx his skin. Try he put it on.

"Iā'mEla," igē'kîm, ā'yatcEqtcEq." Iqē'lōt kē'nuwa ē'nanak^{u}c
"It is bad," he said, "It is prickly." He was given try otter

iā'p¡askwal. Iā'mEla. Ka'nauwē2 itcuq¡oē'yupa. Iqē'lot ē'cit¡îXka,
his skin. It was bad. All he refused them. He was given one-half only,

ē'natka. K¡ā ē'nat. Aqa itcē'xka, itcē'xka, itcē'xka. P¡ē'Xoat
one side only. Nothing the other side. Then he stretched it, he stretched it, he stretched it. Thin

igē'xôx, tcXu igēxE'k¡ak; yaxi igē'xalte. Aqa icE'Xk¡ua
it got, then it fitted; that he put it on. Then they went home

wā'yaq. IcXk¡oā'mam tE'ctaqL. Igiō'lXam: "Kapā't aqa imō'ya
his mother. They came home their house. She said to him: "Enough then you went

qā'cqamîX. Aqamō'LEm ātcuwa." Aqa iLē'XoLq ikanaXmE'nē.
down the river. You will be killed for good." Then he finished the rabbit.

Icē'xangEna. K¡wac igē'xôx. K¡wanē'k¡wanē; ō'la sa-igā'p.
He went no more because he feared trouble. Afraid he was. The story, to-morrow good weather.

Coyote and Badger (told 1891)

There were Badger and Coyote. They were catching birds all the time. Coyote caught two, while Badger always caught many. Now Coyote said: "What do you think, shall we send word to the Sturgeon?" Badger replied: "I think so." Then they tied a rope of cedar bark around Coyote's waist, and he went to the water. A canoe passed. He shouted: "Tell the Sturgeon to come and see our younger brother!" The people said: "We will tell him." They stayed there some time. Then Coyote saw a canoe. He went to tell his younger brother: "A canoe is coming." Now the Sturgeon went ashore. He stayed a little while, and Badger was groaning all the time and said: "I want to go out! I want to go out!" Then Coyote spoke: "He always tells me to haul him and carry him

---

It!ā'ʟapas Ictā'k!anē k!a Ip!ē'cxac

Coyote Their Myth and Badger

Cxēlā'etîX	ip!ē'cxac	k!a	itā'lapas.	Ka'nauwē	ʟkā'etax
There were	badger	and	coyote.	All	days

tp!ᴇcp!ᴇ'cukc	qictōp!iā'ʟxa-îtx.	Môkct	iā'k!ētēnax	it!ā'lapas.
birds	they gathered.	Two	his game	coyote.

Guā'nsum	ʟgā'pᴇla	iā'k!etēnax	ip!ē'cxac.	Aqa	nigē'mx	it!ā'lapas:
Always	many	his game	badger.	Then	he said	coyote:

"Wu'ska	qa	imē'Xaqamit	pō	itxgiō'qōimʟ	inā'qōn?"	Igē'kîm
"Come!	how	your mind	if	we send word to	the sturgeon?"	He said

ip!ē'cxac:	"K!oaʟqā'	nXʟō'Xuan."	K!au	iʟixᴇ'lux	ʟqē'cō
badger:	"Thus	I think."	Tie	he did it	cedar bark

cī'yaqtcqıkpa.	Aqa	iō'ʟa-it	mā'ʟnîX	it!ā'lapas.	Igē'xkoa	ikᴇ'nim.
his waist to.	Then	he stood	at the water	coyote.	It passed him	a canoe.

Itcigē'loma	it!ā'lapas.	Igē'kîm	it!ā'lapas:	"Amsxîlkʟā'2tcgō
He called it	coyote.	He said	coyote:	"Tell him

inā'qōn,	atcī'tketama	întā'mXîX."	Igogoā'kim	ta-îtci	tê'lXam:
the sturgeon,	he shall come and see	our younger brother."	They said	those	people:

"Antcxîlkʟā'tcgoa."	Lā'2lē	iō'ʟa-it	it!ā'lapas;	iā'ʟqtîX	iō'ʟa-it.
"We shall tell him."	Long	stayed	coyote;	long	he stayed.

Atcē'qᴇlkᴇl	ikᴇ'nim.	Igēxîlkʟē'tcgoam	iā'mXîX:	"Ā,	ikᴇ'nim
He saw it	a canoe.	He told him	his younger brother:	"Ah,	a canoe

itē't,"	itciō'lXam	iā'mXîX.	Igixā'gela-îX	inā'qōn.	Iō'ptcgam
is coming,"	he said to him	his younger brother.	He landed	the sturgeon.	He came up

inā'qōn.	Nō'ʟ!îX	iō'ʟa-ît.	Iga-iXilqā'yalalᴇmtck	ip!ē'cxac.	Igē'kîm
the sturgeon.	A little	he stayed.	He groaned	the badger.	He said

ip!ē'cxac:	"P!ayā'	p!ayā'."	Igē'kîm	it!ā'lapas:	"K!oaʟqā'	gi
badger:	"P!ayā'	p!ayā'."	He said	coyote:	"Thus	this

qatsnō'xoayatx	as	qaniuʟā'tax	qaniuktcpā'x.	Tsō'xoa	mangᴇlgē'sgama!
he always does to me	and	I haul him	I carry him out.	Come!	help me!

out. Oh, help me! Let us carry him out. Take hold of his legs." The Sturgeon rose. He took the feet; Coyote took the head. They carried him out. When his legs came out Badger broke wind and the Sturgeon fell down dead. Badger rose. They cut the Sturgeon; his roe was white.

After several days they got hungry again, and Coyote said: "What do you think? We will send word to the Beaver." Then Badger said: "I think so." Then Coyote stood by the water and saw a canoe passing. He shouted: "Tell the Beaver to come and see our younger brother!" The people said: "We will tell him." Coyote stayed there some time, till he saw a canoe with one man in it. Now the Beaver landed. He stayed a little while; then Badger groaned and said: "I want to go out! I want to go out!" Then Coyote spoke: "He always tells me to haul him and carry him out. Oh, help me! Let us carry him out. Take hold of his legs." The Beaver rose. He took hold of the feet; Coyote took the head. They carried him out. When his legs came out Badger broke wind and

---

Atxgiuktcpā'ya. E'wa tiā'qo-ît amigᴇlgā'ya." Iō'tXu-ît inā'qōn.
We will carry him out. Thus his legs you take them." He stood the sturgeon.

Itcē'gᴇlga ē'wa tiā'qo-ît. It¡ā'lapas ē'wa ʟiā'q¡aketaq itcē'gᴇlga.
He took him thus his feet. Coyote thus his head he took it.

Aqa icgī'uktcpa. ʟāx igō'xoax tiā'qo-ît ē'wa ʟā'xanîX;
Then they carried him out. Out became his feet thus outside;

iga-ixᴇ'lqo-îcqo-îc ip¡ē'cxac, ac kōpā' igexē'maxit, iō'maqt
he farted badger, and there he fell down, he was dead

inā'qōn. Igixᴇ'latck ip¡ē'cxac. Icgē'yuxc inā'qōn. Tk¡ᴇp iā'qapt.
the sturgeon. He arose badger. They cut it the sturgeon. White its roe.

Qā'watîX iō'qoya-îX, aqa wi wa'lō igî'cux. "Wu'ska, qada
Several his sleeps, then again hunger acted on them. "Come! how

imē'Xatakoax, ā'oē. Atxgiuqoē'mʟa iqā'nuk." Igē'kim ip¡ē'cxac:
your mind, younger brother. We will send word to the beaver." He said badger:

"K¡oaʟqā' nXʟō'Xuan." Iōʟā'eta mā'ʟnîX it¡ā'lapas. Itcē'qᴇlkᴇl
"Thus I think." He stayed at the water coyote. He saw it

ikᴇ'nim. Igē'cxgoa. Itcigē'loma. "AmegiulXā'm iqā'nuk
a canoe. It passed them. He called it. "Tell him the beaver

atcē'ketama intā'mXîX." Igugoā'kim ta-îtci tê'lXam:
he shall come and see our younger brother." They said those people:

"AntcxilkʟĀ'2tcgoa." Lā'2lē iō'ʟa-it it¡ā'lapas. Itcē'qᴇlkᴇl
"We will tell him." Long he stayed coyote. He saw it

ikᴇ'nim. ʟāk¡ā'ex·at. Igixā'gela-îX aqa iqā'nuk. Nō'ʟ¡îX
a canoe. One person in a canoe. He landed then the beaver. A little

iō'ʟa-ît iqā'nuk. Iga-ix·îlqā'yayalemtck ip¡ē'cxac. "P¡ayā'2 p¡ayā',"
he stayed the beaver. He groaned badger. "P¡ayā', p¡ayā',"

igē'kîm ip¡ē'cxac. Igē'kîm it¡ā'lapas: "K¡oaʟqā' qatsnō'xoayatx,
he said badger. He said coyote: "Thus he always does to me,

as qaniuʟā'tax qaniuktcpā'x. Amᴇngᴇlgē'cgama atxgiuktcpā'ya.
and I haul him I carry him out. Help me we will carry him out.

Ē'wa tiā'qo-it amigᴇlgā'ya!" Iō'tXuit iqā'nuk, aqa icgī'yuktcpa.
Thus his feet take!" He stood up the beaver, then they carried him out.

ʟāx igō'xoax tiā'qo-it yaXi ip¡ē'cxac ē'wa ʟā'xanē.
Out became his feet that badger thus outside.

the Beaver fell down dead. Badger rose and laughed. They skinned the Beaver. After two days they had finished it, and they became hungry again.

Then he said to his younger brother: "What do you think? We will send word to the Seal." Badger said: "I think so." Coyote went to the water. He stayed a little while and saw a canoe. He shouted: "Tell the Seal to come and see our younger brother!" Coyote stayed there some time, when he saw a canoe. He told his younger brother: "A canoe is coming, with one man in it. I think that is the Seal. Look out!" Now the Seal got up to the house. He stayed a little while in Coyote's house. Then Badger groaned: "I want to go out! I want to go out!" "Thus he always tells me, and he makes me tired. He asks me to haul him and carry him out. Help me. Let us carry him out." Then the Seal rose. Coyote told him: "You take his feet." Then they carried him out. When his feet came outside he broke wind and the Seal fell down dead. Badger

---

Iga-ixE'lqo-îcqo-îc. Kopä'4 igixē'maXit iqā'nuk. IgixE'latek
He farted. There he fell down the beaver. He arose

ip¡ē'exac. Igixk¡ayā'wulalEmtek yaXi ip¡ē'exac. IexE'lk¡ēxc,
badger. He laughed much that badger. They cut,

iegī'yuxe yaXi iqā'nuk. Mā'ketîX ictō'qoya, aqa iegiō'LXōm.
they cut him that beaver. Two their sleeps, then they finished it.

Aqa wi wā'lō ieXE'La-it. Aqa wi iteiō'lXam iā'mXîX: "Qa'da
Then again hunger they died. Then again he said to him his younger brother: "How

imē'Xatakoax? Atxgōqoē'mLa aqē'sgoax." Igē'kîm ip¡ē'exac:
your mind? We will send word to the seal." He said badger:

"K¡oaLqā' nXLō'Xuan." Aqa wi iō'La-it mā'LnîX it¡ā'lapas.
"Thus I think." Then again he stayed at the water coyote.

Nâ'L¡îX iō'La-it. Atcē'qElkEl ikE'nim. Iteigē'loma ikE'nim
A little he stayed. He saw it a canoe. He called it the canoe

it¡ā'lapas. "AmegulXā'ma aqē'sgoax agē'tketama intā'mXîX."
coyote. "Tell him the seal she shall come and see our younger brother."

Lā'2lē iō'La-it; ē'aLqtîX iō'La-it. Itcē'qElkEl ikE'nim.
Long he stayed; long he stayed. He saw it a canoe.

QiXilEkLē'tcgam iā'mXîX: "Lāk¡ā'eXat Ltēt. LXuan aqē'sgoax.
He was told his younger brother: "One person in a canoe is coming. Perhaps the seal.

Qā't¡ōcXEm." Igā'tptckam aqē'sgoax. Nâ'L¡îX igō'La-ît tE'etaqLpa
Take care." She came up the seal. A little she stayed their house in

it¡ā'lapas. Iga-iXElqā'yalalEmtek ip¡ē'exac. "P¡ayā', p¡ayā',"
coyote. He groaned the badger. "P¡ayā', p¡ayā',"

igē'kîm. "K¡oaLqā' gi qatsnō'xoa-itx, aqa tEll qatsnō'xoa-itx,
he said. "Thus this he always does to me, then tired he makes me,

qē as qaniuLā'tax qaniuktspā'x. AmEngElgē'sgama.
if and I haul him I carry him out. Help me.

Atxgiuktspā'ya." Igō'tXuit aqē'sgoax. Iteō'lXam it¡ā'lapas:
We will carry him out." He stood up the seal. He said to her coyote:

"Ē'wa tiā'qo-it amigElgā'ya." Aqa iegī'yuktepa. Lāx igō'xoax
"Thus his feet take them!" Then they carried him out. Out became

tiā'qo-ît Lā'xanîX. Iga-ixE'lqo-îcqo-îc, ac kopā'2 igaxē'maXit
his feet outside. He farted, and there she fell down

rose and laughed. Then Coyote spoke: "We will always do so when we get hungry; we shall catch everything." They singed the Seal. After several days they finished it. They got hungry again. "What do you think, younger brother? We will send word to the Porpoise." Badger said: "I think so." Coyote went again to the water. He stayed a little while. A canoe passed. He shouted: "Tell the Porpoise to come and see our younger brother!" The people said: "We will tell him." Coyote stayed a long while, then he saw a canoe. He told his younger brother: "A canoe is coming. I think it is the Porpoise." Now the Porpoise landed and went up. A little while he stayed. Then Badger groaned. He said: "I want to go out! I want to go out!" Then Coyote said: "He always tells me so and makes me tired. He asks me to haul him and carry him out. Help me. Let us carry him out." Then the Porpoise arose. Coyote told him: "You take his feet." Then they carried him out. When his feet came outside he broke wind and the

---

aqē'sgoax. IgixE'latck ip¦ē'cxac. Igixk¦ayā'wulalEmtck. Igē'kîm
the seal. He arose badger. He laughed much. He said

it¦ā'lapas: "Ksta k¦oaLqā' atxō'xoa, manē'x wa'lō aktxō'xoa.
coyote: "Then thus we shall do, when hunger acts on us.

Ka'nauwē tā'nEmax atktōqoē'mLa." IcgaLk¦E'tsXēma wuXi
All things we shall send for." They singed her that

aqē'sgoax. Qā'watîX Lq iō'qoya-îX aqa icgō'LXum.
seal. Several maybe his sleeps, then they finished her.

Aqa wi wā'lō igî'cux. "Wu'ska qa imē'Xaqamit, ā'oē?
Then again hunger acted on them. "Come, how your mind, younger brother?

Atxgoqoē'mLa akō'tckōtc." Igē'kîm ip¦ē'exac: "K¦oaLqā'
We will send word to the porpoise." He said badger: "Thus

nXLō'Xuan." Aqa wi iuLā'eta mā'LnîX it¦ā'lapas. Nâ'L¦îX
I think." Then again he stayed at the water coyote. A little

iō'La-it; igē'xkoa ikE'nim. Itcigē'loma. "AmcgulXā'ma akō'tckōtc.
he stayed; it passed him a canoe. He called it. "Tell her the porpoise.

Agē'tkstama intā'mXîX." Lā'lē iō'La-it. Itcē'qElkEl ikE'nim.
She shall come and see our younger brother." Long he stayed. He saw it a canoe.

IgixElkLē'tckoam iā'mXîX. "IkE'nim itē't," itciō'lXam iā'mXîX.
He told him his younger brother. "A canoe is coming." he said to him his younger brother.

"LXuan akō'tckōtc." Igaxā'igela-îX akō'tckōtc. Igā'tptckam.
"Perhaps the porpoise." She landed the porpoise. She went up.

Nâ'L¦îX igō'La-ît. Iga-iXElqa'yalalEmtck ip¦ē'cxac. "P¦ayā', p¦ayā',"
A little she stayed. He groaned badger. "P¦ayā', p¦ayā',"

igē'kîm ip¦ē'cxac. Igē'kîm it¦ā'lapas: "K¦oaLqā' gi qatsEnō'xoa-îtx.
he said badger. He said coyote: "Thus this he always does to me.

Aqa tEll qatcEnō'xoa-îtx, as qaniuLā'tax qaniuktcpā'x.
Then tired he makes me, and I haul him I carry him out.

AmEngElgē'cgama. Atxgiuktcpā'ya." Igō'tXuit akō'tckōtc. Igē'kîm
Help me. We will carry him out." She stood up the porpoise. He said

it¦ā'lapas: "Ēwa' tciā'qo-itāt amigElgā'ya." Aqa icgī'uktcpa. Lāx
coyote: "Thus his feet take them." Then they carried him out. Out

tgō'xoax tiā'qo-it ē'wa Lā'xanîX. Iga-ixE'lqo-îcqo-îc, ac kopā'
came his feet thus outside. He farted, and there

Porpoise fell down dead. Coyote said: "Thus we will do when we get hungry." They cut up the Porpoise, and after several days they had finished it.

They got hungry again, and Coyote said: "What do you think? We will send word to the Sea-lion." Badger replied: "I think so." Then Badger tied a rope around his waist, and Coyote went seaward, where he stood by the water. He stayed a long time. He saw a canoe passing. He shouted: "Tell the Sea Lion to come and see our younger brother!" They said to Coyote: "We will tell him." Coyote went up to the house and said to his younger brother: "Take care!" He stood there a long time, then he saw a canoe with one man in it. The Sea-lion landed and went up. He tried to enter Coyote's house, but he stuck in the doorway. They took out two vertical planks; then he was able to go in. The Sea-lion stayed a long time. Then Badger began to groan and said: "I want to go out! I want to go out!" Coyote said: "He always tells me so and makes me tired. He asks me to haul him and carry him out. Help

---

igaxē'maXit wuXi akō'tekōtc. Igē'kîm it¡ā'lapas: "K¡oaLqā'
she fell down | that | porpoise. | He said | coyote: | "Thus

atxō'xoa ma'nîx wa'lō aktxō'xa." Icî'kôxe wuXi akō'tekōtc.
we shall do | when | hunger | acts on us." | They cut | that | porpoise.

Qā'watîX Lq ictō'qoya, aqa wi icgō'LXum.
Several | maybe | they slept, | then | again | they finished it.

Aqa wi wā'lō igî'cux.' Igē'kîm it¡ā'lapas: "Qa'da
Then | again | hunger | acted on them. | He said | coyote: | "How

imē'Xatakoax? Atxgioqoē'mLa igē'pîXLX." Igē'kîm ip¡ē'exac:
your mind? | We will send word to | the sea-lion." | He said | badger:

"K¡oaLqā' nxLō'Xuan." IgixE'kilq ip¡ē'exac. Iō'Lxa it¡ā'lapas.
"Thus | I think." | He tied a rope around his waist | badger. | He went down to the water | coyote.

IoLā'ita mā'LnîX. Lē'lē iō'La-it. Itcē'qElkEl ikE'nîm. Igē'Xkoa.
He stood | at the water. | Long | he stayed. | He saw it | a canoe. | It passed him.

Itcigē'loma: "AmcxElkLē'tek igē'pîXLX atcē'tketama intā'mXîX."
He called it: | "Tell him | the sea-lion | he shall come to see | our younger brother."

Iqiō'lXam it¡ā'lapas: "AntcxElukLā'tekoa." Iō'ptcka it¡ā'lapas.
He was told | coyote: | "We shall tell him." | He went up | coyote.

IgiXElkLē'tekoam iā'mXîX. Itciō'lXam iā'mXîX: "Qā't¡ōcXEm."
He went to tell him | his younger brother. | He said to him | his younger brother: | "Take care."

Lā'lē iō'La-ît. Atcē'qElkEl ikE'nîm, Lāk¡ā'ēXat. Igixē'gela-îX
Long | he stayed. | He saw it | a canoe, | one person in a canoe. | He landed

aqa igē'pîXLX. Iō'ptcgam. Kē'nuwa iā'ckupq tE'ctaqL
then | the sea-lion. | He came up to the house. | Try | he entered | their house

it¡ā'lapas. Iginq¡u'stix·itē yaXi î'ctacq. Lāqᵘ icgî'tôX môkct
coyote's. | He stuck in | that | door. | Out | they made them | two

tq¡Ekoacî'max. Aqa kōpa iā'ckupq. Lā'lē iō'La-ît yaXi igē'pîXL.
vertical wall planks. | Then | there | he entered. | Long | he stayed | that | sea-lion.

Iga-iXElqā'yayalEmtck yaXi ip¡ē'exac. Igē'kîm it¡ā'lapas:
He groaned | that | badger. | He said | coyote:

"K¡oaLqā' gi qatsnō'xoa-îtx, aqa tEll qatsEnō'xoa-îtx, as
"Thus | this | he does to me, | then | tired | he makes me, | and

me. Let us carry him out." Then the Sea-lion rose. Coyote told him: "You take his feet." Then they carried him out. When his feet came outside he broke wind and the Sea-lion fell down dead. Then Badger rose. They cut the Sea-lion up. Their house was full of meat and fat. Coyote spoke: "Thus we shall always do when we get hungry." They ate a long time and finished it.

Then they became hungry again. Now the people began to know it: "Behold! Coyote and Badger are killing people." Coyote went to the water. A canoe passed. He tried to send word, but they did not speak to him. Still he stood near the water, but he did not see anyone. Then he gave it up and went up to the house. For two days he tried to send word. Then he gave it up and went up to the house. He did not see anything.

Now they were hungry. Coyote mended his arrows. They went to shoot birds. Early in the morning they went. At night they came home. Badger had killed many, Coyote had killed one duck.

---

qaniuʟā'tax qaniuktepā'x. Amᴇngᴇlgē'egama. Atxgiuktepā'ya."
I haul him I carry him out. Help me. We will carry him out."

Iō'tXuit igē'pîXʟX. Icgē'yuktcpa. ʟāx igō'xoax tiā'qo-ît ē'wa
He stood up the sea-lion. They carried him out. Out came his feet thus

ʟā'xanîX. Iga-ixᴇ'lqo-îcqo-îc ip;ē'exac. Kōpā'4 igixē'maXit yaXi
outside. He farted badger. Then he fell down that

igē'pîXʟX. Igixᴇ'latck ip;ē'exac. Icxᴇ'lk;ēxc. Pāʟ igō'xax
sea-lion. He arose badger. They cut. Full became

tᴇ'ctaqʟ ʟqulē'max. Pāʟ apxᴇ'lēu tᴇ'ctaqʟ. Igē'kîm it;ā'lapas:
their house meat. Full grease their house. He said coyote:

"K;oaʟqā' atxō'xoa ma'nîx walō' aktxō'xoa." Iō'ʟqtîX
"Thus we will do when hunger acts on us." Long

icgixᴇ'lᴇmuX, aqa icgiō'ʟXum.
they ate, then they finished it.

Aqa wi wā'lō igī'eux. Āqa ikcilō'Xuix·ît. "ʟqōct! icktōtē'niʟ
Then again hunger acted on them. Then they knew it. "Behold! they killed them

tē'lXam it;ā'lapas k;a ip;ē'exac." Kē'nuwa iuʟā'itam it;ā'lapas
the people coyote and badger." Try he stayed coyote

mā'ʟnîX. Igē'xkō ikᴇ'nim. Kē'nuwa itcigᴇlgē'kim. Nā2ct wā'wa
at the water. It passed a canoe. Try he spoke to them. Not spoken

iqē'yux it;ā'lapas. Kē'nuwa iō'ʟa-it mā'ʟnîX. Nā2ct tān
he was to coyote. Try he stayed at the water. Not anything

itcē'qᴇlkᴇl. Tā'mēnua igē'xôx, aqa iō'ptcga. Mâkct ʟkā'etax
he saw it. Give up he did, then he went up. Two days

kē'nuwa igiXᴇlgē'kim. Tā'mēnua nixō'xoax, qa-iō'ptckax. K;ā
try he spoke. Give up he did, he went up. Nothing

nîct tā'n qatciqᴇlkᴇ'lx.
not anything he saw it.

Ā'qa wā'lō igᴇ'eux. T;ayā' itcī'tux tiā'qamatcX it;ā'lapas, aqa
Then hunger acted on them. Good he made them his arrows coyote, then

tp;ᴇcp;ᴇ'cukc acktup;iā'ʟxa. Kawī'X qactō'îX. Tsō'yustîX
birds they gathered. Early they went. Evening

qacXk;oā'mamx. ʟgā'pᴇla qatctotē'nax ip;ē'exac, aē'Xt it;ā'lapas
they came home. Many he killed them badger, one coyote

Next morning they went again to shoot birds. At night they came home. Coyote had killed two, Badger had killed many. On the following day they went again and came back at night. Coyote had nothing. Badger had shot many. Thus it was every day. One night Coyote thought: "Let us exchange our buttocks," and he said: "What do you think? Let us exchange our buttocks." Badger replied: "I like my own buttocks. I know them; you do not know them." The next day they went again and came back in the evening. Badger had caught many, and Coyote had two. Badger had no arrows. He just broke wind at those birds. Coyote had arrows, and behold, he got nothing. On the following morning it was just the same. Badger got many. He merely broke wind, and they were dead. Coyote sometimes got one, sometimes none. At night he said again: "Let us exchange our buttocks." Badger said: "No." Every evening Coyote said the same thing and made his brother tired.

---

iā'k¡etēnax aqo-î'xqo-îx. Wāx wit'ax qactō'îx. Qactoguē'x
his game duck. Next day again they went. They went to hunt

tp¡Ecp¡E'cukc. Tsō'yustîX qacXk¡oā'mamx. Mâkct iā'k¡etēnax
birds. Evening they came home. Two his game

it¡ā'lapas. Lgā'pEla iā'k¡etēnax ip¡ē'cxac. Wāx wi qactō'îx.
coyote. Many his game badger. Next day again they went.

Tsō'yustiX qacXk¡oā'mamx. Acuwā'tka it¡ā'lapas nîXk¡uā'mamx.
Evening they came home. Unsuccessful coyote he came home.

Lgā'pela iā'k¡etēnax ip¡ē'cxac. Ka'nauwē Lkā'etax ā'kua.
Many his game badger. All days thus.

Qāxtkanā'pōl igixLō'xa-ît it¡ā'lapas: "Qō intgE'cx·Emk¡ēnuwapa
One night he thought coyote: "Wish we will exchange them

cîntā'pōte." "Qā ē'mēmxte, ā'oē? AtxgE'cXEmk¡ē'nuwapa etxā'pōte."
our buttocks." "How your mind younger brother? We will exchange them our buttocks."

Igē'kîm ip¡ē'cxac: "Tq¡ēx nE'LōXt LgE'pōte." Igē'kîm: "NE'Lōkull
He said badger: "Like I do them my buttocks." He said: "I know them

LgE'pōte, nE'cqē mai'ka mE'Lukull." Wi igē'tcuktîX, wi't'ax ictō'ya.
my buttocks, not at all you you know them." Again it got day, again they went.

Ictō'guiga tp¡Ecp¡E'cukc. Tsō'yustîX icXatk¡oā'mam. Lgā'pEla
They went to catch them birds. Evening they came home. Many

iā'k¡etēnax ip¡ē'cxac, mâkct it¡ā'lapas iā'k¡etēnax. K¡ā nîct ayā'pL¡ikē
his game badger, two coyote his game. Nothing not his bow

ip¡ē'cxac, ac qatcawiqoē'cqo-îcx taXi tp¡Ecp¡E'cuks. Tiā'qamatcX
badger, and he farted at them those birds. His arrows

it¡ā'lapas; yaXi qayō'îx, tatc¡a qacē'x·EmgEnā'x. Wāx qactō'îx,
coyote: that one he went, behold he did not get anything. Next day they went,

wī k¡oaLqā'. Lgā'pEla iā'k¡etēnax ip¡ē'cxac ac qatcawiqoē'cqo-îcX,
again thus. Many his game badger and he farted at them,

aqa nuXuaLā'îtx. Ā'ēXt iā'k¡etēnax it¡ā'lapas, anā' acuwā'tka.
then they died. One his game coyote, sometimes he was unsuccessful.

Nupō'nEmx aqa wi qatciōlXā'mx: "AtxgE'cxEmk¡ēnuwapa
It got dark, then again he said to him: "Let us exchange them

etxa'pōte." Nigē'mx ip¡ē'cxac: "K¡ā'ya." Ka'nauwē Lpōlakē'lEmax tEll
our buttocks." He said badger: "No." All nights tired

qatciō'xoax. YaXi iā'mXîX tEll aqiō'xoax ip¡ē'cxac. Aqa nigē'mx
he made him. That his younger brother tired he was made badger. Then he said

Then Badger said: "You make me tired. Let us exchange them." Then they exchanged their buttocks. Now Coyote was glad. He was awake, and thought: "Now I have fooled you, Badger. Now I shall get many." He rose early and quickly. Then he broke wind. He arose and went out. He went with long strides and broke wind: pō, pō, pō, pō. He made slow steps and broke wind: pu, pu, pu, pu. When he stepped with long strides, he broke wind loudly; when he went slowly, he broke wind slowly. Now they went to hunt birds. They came home in the evening. Coyote had nothing, but Badger had caught many. Coyote tried to go up to the birds with long steps, but every time he stepped he broke wind: pō, pō, pō. On the following day they went again and came back in the evening. Coyote had nothing, and Badger had killed many. Then Coyote thought: "I made a mistake; I will return his buttocks to him." He said: "What do you think? I will return your buttocks to you." Badger did not say anything. Coyote tried to

---

ip;ē'exac: "Aqa tEll ēmE'nôx. Qā'txa txgE'eXEmk;ē'nuwapa."
badger: "Then tired you make me. Let us we will exchange them."

Aqa icgE'eXEmk;ē'nuwapa etā'pōtc. IgixE'gElEmtck it;ā'lapas.
Then they exchanged them their buttocks. He awoke coyote.

K;wa'nk;wan igē'xôx it;ā'lapas. IgîxLō'xoa-ît: "Aqa lā'xlax iā'mux,
Glad became coyote. He thought: "Now deceive I do you,

ip;ē'exac. Aqa nai'ka Lgā'pEla antup;iā'Lxa tp;Ecp;E'cuke."
badger. Then I many I shall gather them birds."

IgixE'latck kawu'X; ai'aq igixE'latck. Pō2, iga-ixE'lqō-îcqō-îc.
He arose early; quick he arose. Blow, he farted.

Iō'tXuît, iō'pa. Tc;pāq itcXō'tkalukLtck: Pō, pō, pō, pō. Lā'wa
He stood up, he went out. Strongly he stepped: Blow, blow, blow, blow. Slowly

itcXō'tkakoax: Pu, pu, pu, pu; Lā'wa itcXō'tkalukLtck. Tc;pāq
he stepped: Blow, blow, blow, blow; slowly he stepped. Strongly

qatcXō'tkakoax, pō, nēxElqoē'cqo-îc. Lawā' qatcXō'tkakoax, pō, pō,
he stepped, blowing. he farted. Slowly he stepped, blowing, blowing,

nēxElqoē'cqo-îc; Lawā' nēxElqoē'cqo-îc. Aqa ictō'guiga tp;Ecp;E'cuke.
he farted: slowly he farted. Then they went to hunt birds.

Igō'pōnEm, isXatk;oā'mam. Acuwā'tka it;ā'lapas. Iā'ēma ip;ē'exac
It got dark, they came home. Unsuccessful coyote. Only badger

iā'k;etēnax, Lgā'pEla iā'k;etēnax. Kē'nuwa nîxk;"Luwā'x it;ā'lapas;
his game, many his game. Try he crept near coyote;

tc;pāq qatcXō'tkalukLx, pō, pō, pō, nēxElqoē'cqo-îc. Kopā'2tîX
strongly he stepped, blow, blow, blow, he farted. As often as

qatcXō'tkakoax, kopā'tîX naēxElqoē'cqo-îcx. Igō'n ē'ka-ît wi
he stepped, as often he farted. Another day again

qactō'îx; tsō'yustîX qacXk;oā'mamx. Acuwā'tka it;ā'lapas
they went; evening they came home. Unsuccessful coyote

qaciXumgEnā'x. lā'ema ip;ē'exac Lgā'pEla iā'k;etēnax. IgixLō'xa-ît
he had not got anything. Only badger many his game. He thought

it;ā'lapas: "Pō'XuēcL;k inE'xôx. AnLēlXaktcguā'ya gi Liā'pōtc."
coyote: "Mistake I made. I will return to him these his buttocks."

"Qā imē'Xaqamit, ā'oē? ALamîlXaktcguā'ya gi LEmē'pōtc."
"How your mind, younger brother? I will return it to you these your buttocks."

keep his buttocks closed, but he could not do it. He almost reached the ducks; then they smelled him and flew away. Again they came home, and he said: “I will return your buttocks to you.” But Badger was angry. “You make me tired,” he said. “I gave them to you. Now you are making me tired again. Take out yours first.” Coyote took out the buttocks of Badger. Then Badger took out those of Coyote and threw them into the water, while he put his own buttocks into himself. Now Coyote's buttocks drifted down the rapid creek. Coyote pursued them. Badger went away.

Coyote pursued his buttocks. He came to one place; there he lay down to sleep. He rose early. He came to a town. He asked: “Did my buttocks pass here?” The people said: “Yesterday there was something which the boys tried to hit with spears.”

Coyote went on. His buttocks called: “Pähêhê, pähêhê, pä!” He went a long way and slept again. He rose early and went on.

Nā2ct aqa igē'kîm ip¡ē'cxac. Kē'nuwa qatcigElgā'x iā'pōte,
Not then he spoke badger. Try he held his buttocks,

nîxk¡ᵘLuwā'x; q¡oā'p qatctō'xamx taXi tqoēqoē'xukc, qatgēiLā'x.
he crept near; near he reached them those ducks, they smelled him.

Ka'nauwē nuxuawā'xitx. Wit'ax îcXk¡oā'mam, wī't'ax itciō'lXam:
All escaped. Again they came home, again he said to him:

“ALamî'lXaktckuā'ya gi LEmē'pōte.” IgiXE'LXaq ip¡ē'cxac.
“I will return to you these your buttocks.” He became angry badger.

“Mai'ka tEll ēmE'nôx,” itciō'lXam. “Aqa iLā'melōt, aqa wi tEll
“You tired you make me,” he said to him. “Then I gave them to you, then again tired

amEnō'xoax.” Iqiō'lXam it¡ā'lapas: “Mā'nēwa Lāq LE'mxôx.”
you make me.” He was told coyote: “You first out make them.”

Lāqᵘ iLē'xôx it¡ā'lapas LaXi ip¡ē'cxac Liā'pōte. Lāqᵘ iLē'xôx
Out he made them coyote that badger his buttocks. Out he made them

kē'qamtq ip¡ē'cxac LaXi it¡ā'lapas Liā'pōte. ItcLalē'maLx.
afterward badger that coyote his buttocks. He threw them into the water.

IqLalē'maLx it¡ā'lapas Liā'pōte. ILix·E'q¡oaLk ip¡ē'cxac Liā'pōte.
They were thrown into the water coyote his buttocks. He put them onto himself badger his buttocks.

ILō'Xunē it¡ā'lapas Liā'pōte. Lēiā'sEla yaXi ē'qaL. Itcî'Luwa
They drifted coyote his buttocks. Rapid that creek. He pursued them

Liā'pōte it¡ā'lapas. Aqa iō'ya kElā'îX ip¡ē'cxac. Aqa itcē'2Luwa
his buttocks coyote. Then he went far badger. Then he pursued them

Liā'pōte it¡ā'lapas. Qā'xpa Lq iō'yam iō'qoya. Kawī'X igixE'latck,
his buttocks coyote. Somewhere he arrived he slept. Early he rose.

igigō'qoam ēXt ē'lXam. “Tcō'Xᵘ iLE'mcxgoa LgE'pōte?”
he reached one town. “Well, did they pass you my buttocks?”

itctuqu'mtcxōkoa ta-îtci tē'lXam. “Ā taqE'L,” aqiō'lXam.
he asked them those people. “Ah, yesterday,” was said to him.

“Tā'nki tkLilâqsqalalEmtck tqā'totinîke.”
“Something they threw it often with spears the boys.”

Iō'ya wit'ax it¡ā'lapas. ItcLgilō'mEniLtck Liā'pōte: “P¡ā'hêhê,
He went again coyote. They spoke his buttocks: “P¡ä'hêhê,

p¡ā'hêhê, p¡ā,” igē'xôx it¡ā'lapas. KElā'iX iō'ya, aqa iō'qoya.
p¡ähêhê, p¡ä,” did coyote. Far he went, then he slept.

Again he came to a town, and asked: "Did my buttocks pass you?" "A short time ago something drifted down, and the boys tried to hit it with spears."

Coyote went on. "Pähêhê, pähêhê, pä," said his buttocks. "Pähêhê, pähêhê, pä," said they slowly. After he had gone some distance, he slept again. Early he rose and went on. He went some distance and reached another town. "Did my buttocks pass here?" "Yes; at noon yesterday something drifted down, and the boys tried to hit it with spears."

Again Coyote went. "Pähêhê, pähêhê, pä," said his buttocks. He went a long distance and slept a fourth time. The next morning he went on. He had not gone far, when he came to a town. He saw the boys throwing spears at something. He came to that town and asked: "Did not my buttocks pass here?" "Something just drifted down."

Again he went. "Pähêhê, pähêhê, pä," said his buttocks. He

Kawī'X igixᴇ'latck. Aqa wi iō'ya. Itcigō'qoam ēXt ē'lXam.
Early he rose. Then again he went. He reached it one town.

"TcōXᵘ ēʟᴇ'mexgoa ʟgᴇ'pōte?" "Ā koalē'wē yaXi tā'nki
"Well, did they pass you my buttocks?" "Ah, just that something

iō'goatcō. Tkʟēlō'qsqalalᴇmtck tqā'totinîke."
went down the river. They threw it often with spears the boys."

Wit'ax iō'ya it¡ā'lapas. "P¡ähêhê, p¡ähêhê, p¡ä," itcʟgilō'mᴇniʟtck
Again he went coyote. "P¡ähêhê, p¡ähêhê, p¡ä," spoke

ʟiā'pōte. P¡ähêhê, p¡ähêhê, ʟawā' itcʟgilō'mᴇniʟtck. Qā'xpa ʟq
his buttocks. P¡ähêhê, p¡ähêhê, slowly they spoke. Somewhere

wit'ax iō'qoyō. Kᴇlā'îX iō'qoyō. Kawī'X igixᴇ'latck. Iō'ya;
again he slept. Far he slept. Early he rose. He went;

kᴇlā'iX mank iō'ya. Itcigō'qoam igō'n ē'lXam: "TcuXᵘ iʟᴇ'mexgoa
Far a little he went. He reached it another town: "Well! did they pass you

ʟgᴇ'pōte?" "Ā, taqᴇ'ʟ pā wē'koa tā'nki tkʟēlō'qeqalalᴇmtck
my buttocks?" "Ah, yesterday noon , something they threw it often with spears

tqā'tōtēnîke gipā' mā'ʟnîX."
the boys there in the water."

Aqa wi iō'ya it¡ā'lapas. "P¡ähêhê, p¡ähêhê, p¡ä," itcʟgilō'mᴇniʟtck
Then again went coyote. "P¡ähêhê, p¡ähêhê, p¡ä," spoke

ʟiā'pōte. Kᴇlā'îX iō'ya, aqa wi iō'qoya ī'ʟalaktîX. Kawī'X iō'ya.
his buttocks. Far he went, then again he slept the fourth time. Early he went.

Mank kᴇlā'îX iō'ya. Q¡oā'p itcī'yux ēXt ē'lXam. Itkʟilō'qeqala
A little far he went. Near he came it one town. They were throwing it with spears

yaXi tā'nki itcō'qo-ikᴇla ta-îtci tqā'tōtēnîke. Igigō'qoam igō'n ēXt
that something he saw them those boys. He reached another one

ē'lXam. "TcuXua ʟgᴇ'pōte iʟᴇ'mexgoa?" "Ā yaXi koalē'wē
town. "Well! my buttocks did they pass you?" "Ah, that just

tā'nki iō'goatcō."
something went down the river."

Wī't'ax iō'ya it¡ā'lapas. "P¡ähêhê, p¡ähêhê, p¡ä," itcʟgilō'mᴇniʟtck
Again he went coyote. "P¡ähêhê, p¡ähêhê, p¡ä," spoke

ʟiā'pōte. Kᴇlā'îX iō'ya; iō'qoya. Kawī'X aqa wi iō'ya, as
his buttocks. Far he went; he slept. Early then again he went, and

went a long way and slept. He went on early. He went a short distance and came to a town. He came near to boys who were throwing spears at something. Now the people saw him, and they all went up. Coyote asked them: "Did not my buttocks pass you?" "Just now something passed down here. The boys threw spears at it."

Coyote went on. "Pähêhê, pähêhê, pä," said his buttocks. He reached them. Now his buttocks were small, and all torn by the thrusts of spears and sticks. He put them on, and at last they fitted. "Badger shall be your name—you who fooled me. Future generations of men shall fear your winds only. You shall not kill birds." Then Coyote went on. He kept on going.

---

nō'ʟ¡îX	iō'ya,	aqa	wi	itciō'cgam	ē'lXam.	Q¡oā'p	itcî'tôx	taXi
a little	he went,	then	again	he found it	a town.	Near	he came them	those

tqā'tōtēnîkc,	aqa	tā'nki	itkʟilō'qcqala.	Q¡oā'p	itctō'xoam.	Aqa
boys,	then	something	they were throwing it with spears.	Near	he reached them.	Then

itgē'qᴇlkᴇl.	Itgᴇ'ptcga	ka'nauwē	ta-îtci	tqā'tōtēnîkc.	Iō'yam
they saw him.	They went up	all	those	boys.	He arrived

it¡ā'lapas,	itctuqu'mtcxōkoa:	"TcuXoa	ʟgᴇ'pōtc	iʟᴇ'mcxgoa?"
coyote,	he asked them:	"Well!	my buttocks	did they pass you?"

"Ā,	yaXi	koalē'wē	tā'nki	iō'koatcō,	tqō'tātēnîkc	ktqʟilō'qcqala."
"Ah,	that	just	something	went down the river,	boys	threw at it with spears."

Iō'ya	it¡ā'lapas:	"P¡ähêhê,	p¡ähêhê,"	itcitᴇlqᴇ'muXʟōtck	ʟiā'pōtc.
He went	coyote:	"P¡ähêhê,	p¡ähêhê,"	spoke	his buttocks.

Itcʟtā'qoam	ʟiā'pōtc.	Aqa	iʟō'k¡oa-îts	ʟaXi	ʟiā'pōtc.	Ka'nauwē
He reached it	his anus.	Then	small	that	his anus.	All

ʟ¡mᴇ'nʟ¡mᴇn	iqᴇ'ʟôx	yaXi	iqʟō'qcqalalᴇmtck.	Iʟîx·i'q¡oaʟk
soft	it was made	that	thrown with spears.	He put it onto himself

ʟiā'pōtc.	Qalā'tcXua	iʟXᴇ'q¡ak.	"Ip¡ā'2cxac	imē'xalēu	tau
his anus.	At last	it fitted him.	"Badger	your name	who

itcinᴇxᴇnᴇmō'tXᴇmtck.	AluXumapā'ya	tê'lXam	ā'cma
fooled me.	Generations	people	only

amē'qo-îcqo-îc	k¡wac	acxaxō'xoa.	Näct	amtp¡iā'ʟxax
your farts	afraid	make them.	Not	you will gather them

tp¡ᴇcp¡ᴇ'cukc."	Aqa	iō'ya	kᴇlā'îX	it¡ā'lapas.	Guā'nᴇsum	iō'ya.
birds."	Then	he went	far	coyote.	Always	he went.

Panther and Lynx (told 1891)

There were the Panther and his younger brother, the Lynx. Every morning the Panther went hunting elk. In the evening he came home. He told his younger brother: "Don't leave our fire." He left him often; then the Lynx went to play, and played a long time. When he came home, the fire had gone out. Then he thought: "I will swim across to get some fire." He swam across and opened the door of the house. There was an old blind woman. She could not see anything. She tended the fire of the Grizzly Bears. Lynx took a firebrand and put it down at some little distance. The old woman looked after the firebrands. Now she had lost one. Then she spread her legs and struck her vulva often, crying: "You, you, you have eaten it, you have eaten it, the fire, the fire, vulva, vulva!" Then Lynx looked at the

---

Ik¡oayawa' Ictā'k¡anē k¡a Ipu'koa

The Panther Their Myth and the Lynx

Icxelā'-itîX	ik¡oayā'wa	k¡a	ipu'koa,	iā'mXîX	ik¡oayā'wa.	Wāx
There were	the panther	and	the lynx,	his younger brother	the panther's.	The next morning

qayō'îx:	imō'lEkEmax	nigElō'îx.	Tsō'yustîX	niXk¡oā'mamx.
he went:	elks	he went to hunt.	In the evening	he came home.

Itciō'lXam	iā'mXîX:	"Näct	amaqElō'qLqa	atxā'tōL."	Qā'watîX
He said to him	his younger brother:	"Not	leave it	our fire."	Several times

Lx	igiqE'lōqLq.	Aqa	iō'ya	igixk¡ayā'wōlalEmam.	Ē'yaLqtîX
maybe	he left him.	Then	he went	he went to play.	Long time

igixk¡ayā'wōlalEmtck.	Igē'Xk¡oa.	IgîXk¡oā'mam.	Ā'nqa
he played.	He went home.	He came home.	Already

tcXup	igā'xôx	actā'tōL.	IgîxLō'xoa-ît	ipu'koa:	"Anuk¡oē'x·ia
extinguished	was	their fire.	He thought	the lynx:	"I will swim

ē'wa	k¡anatē'tōL.	AnugoāʼlEmam	ā'tōL."	Iō'k¡uiXa	ipu'koa.
thus	across.	I will fetch it	fire."	He swam	the lynx.

Igigâ'ptckamîX.	IteixE'laqLkîX.	Ā.	Lōxt	Lq¡ēyō'qt
He came up to the house.	He opened the door.	Ah.	there was	an old woman

aLā'p¡onE'nkau.	Nî'cqē	iLā'gēqamē.	Ā.	cEk¡Enx'ā't	wuXi	aLā'tōL
a blind one.	Not at all	she saw.	Ah.	tied together lengthwise	that	their fire

Lcayî'muke.	Itcā'gElga	ā'ēXt	wuXi	aqā'lEptckîX.	Itcaxē'ma	mank
the grizzly bears.	He took it	one	that	firebrand.	He placed it	a little

kElā'îX.	Iktuk¡umā'nanEmtck	wuXi	aq¡eyō'qt	taXi	tqā'lEptckîX.
far.	She looked at them	that	old woman	those	firebrands.

Igonā'xLatck	ā'ēXt.	L¡āk	igE'tôx	tgā'qo-ît.	ILaxElqē'lîXLtck
She had lost	one.	Spread	she did them	her legs.	She slapped herself

LE'gakci:	"Mai'ka	maikā'	mō'wElq;	mōwā'lq;.	wa'tuL	watū'L,
her hands:	"You	you	you ate it	you ate it.	the fire	the fire,

old woman. He took that firebrand and put it back. Now the old woman looked after the fire, and the firebrands were all there. Then the Lynx took again one firebrand. Then the old woman looked again after the firebrands and found that she had lost one. She spread her legs and struck her vulva, crying: "You, you, you have eaten it, you have eaten it, the fire, the fire, vulva, vulva!" Now Lynx went out and took away that firebrand. He swam across. He came home to the house of his elder brother and made a fire. In the evening his elder brother came home. When he came near the house, he smelled the smoke. It smelled different, and the Panther thought: "Maybe our fire went out; maybe he stole fire." Then he came home. There was his younger brother. He spoke to him: "Why does our smoke smell different?" Lynx replied: "You are a liar, it is the same fire!" They slept. Early in the morning the Panther arose and went to wash himself. He put grease on his hair and stayed a little while.

---

wi'qēctq, wiqā'ctq." Itk¡ē'nuwa itcō'xoa yaXi ipu'koa wuXi
vulva, vulva." Sitting and looking he did at her that the lynx that

aq¡eyō'qt. Aqa wit'ax itcaxē'ma wuXi aqā'lEptckîX kōpā' yaXi
old woman. Then again he put it down that firebrand there that

ā'nqa naxē'mat. Aqa wit'ax iktuk¡umā'nanEmtck wuXi aq¡eyō'qt.
before it lay. Then again she looked at them that old woman.

Ka'nauwē taXi tgā'qalEptckîX. Aqa wit'ax itcā'gElga wuXi ā'ēXt
All those firebrands. Then again he took it that one

aqā'lEptckîX ipu'koa. Aqa wi iktuk¡umā'nanEmtck wuXi aq¡eyō'qt.
firebrand the lynx. Then again she looked at it that old woman.

Igonā'xLtck ā'ēXt. L¡āk igE'tôx tgā'qo-ît. ILExE'lqilX LE'gakci:
She had lost it one. Spread she did them her legs. She slapped herself her hands:

"Mai'ka maikā' mō'wElq¡ mōwā'lq¡ wa'tuL watū'L, wi'qēctq,
"You you you ate it, you ate it the fire the fire, vulva,

wiqā'ctq." Iō'pa ipu'koa, itcutā'mit wuXi ā'ēXt aqā'lEptckîX.
vulva." He went out the lynx, he took away that one firebrand.

Iō'k¡oîX iō'ya. Iō'yam tE'ctaqLpa ē'yalXt. Iga-iXE'lgiLx.
He swam he went. He arrived their house at his elder brother's. He made a fire.

Tsō'yustîX igē'Xk¡oa ē'yalXt. Q¡oā'p itctō'xoam tE'ctaqL, aqa
In the evening he went home his elder brother. Near he reached it their house, then

itē'iLa taXi tXtE'lē, ctā'XtElē. Aqa ixalā'ita ē'taqtckc.
he smelled it that smoke, their smoke. Then different its smell.

IgixLō'xoa-ît ik¡oayā'wa: "LXuan tcXup igā'x antā'tōL. LXuan
He thought the panther: "Perhaps extinguished was our fire. Perhaps

itcō'Xtkam ā'tōL. IgîXk¡oā'mam tE'ctaqLpa. Iō'xt iā'mXîX.
he stole it fire." He came home their house to. There was his younger brother.

Itciō'lXam: "Qā'tsqē ōxoalō'ita ē'taqtckc gi txa'XtElē?" Igē'kîm
He said to him: "Why different its smell this our smoke?" He said

ipu'koa: "Qanā'qa imē'L¡mēnXut, ā'2xka atxā'tōL." Ictō'qo-ē.
the lynx: "To no purpose you lie, that our fire." They slept.

Kawī'X igixE'latck ik¡oayā'wa. Igîxq¡oā'tam. ILixE'lôx Lqā'tcao
Early he arose the panther. He went to bathe. He put onto it grease

Swans were flying there. Then he spoke to the Lynx: "Go and see why these swans are flying away." Lynx went to see and entered again. His elder brother asked him: "What did you see?" "I did not see anything but swans flying away because a snag drifted down the river." Then the elder brother looked. He saw that the Grizzly Bear had come nearly up to the house. The Panther came in and said: "Put that kettle over yourself, the monster is almost here." Then the Lynx covered himself with a kettle. The Grizzly Bear opened the door and stood in the doorway. "Who took our grandmother's fire? I will eat him." The Lynx became afraid and trembled. The Grizzly Bear said: "Give me your little brother; I will eat him." The Panther replied: "You are talking all the time. Come in." They began to fight. Then the Panther said: "Where are you? The monster will kill me." Then the Lynx threw off the kettle. He took an adz and danced around. "Elder brother, the

---

LĒ'yaqcōpa as nō'L;îX icxē'la-it. Iguxoawā'Xit tqelō'q. Iqiō'lXam
his hair on and a little they stayed. They flew away swans. He was told

ipu'koa: "Amgē'ketam tā'nki tcuXoā'wula tqelō'q." Igigē'ketam
the lynx: "Go and look something make fly away swans." He went to look

ipu'koa. Igē'tpqam ipu'koa. "Tcu'Xoa ṭān imē'qElkEl?"
the lynx. He came in the lynx. "Well what did you see?"

itciōqu'mtcxōkoa ē'yalXt. "K;ā'ya nîct tān inē'qElkEl. Tā'ema
he asked him his elder brother. "Nothing not anything I saw it. Only

tqēlō'q ī'taxul. Lā'ema gi LE'tcin Lā'tgatcX." Igē'kîket ē'yalXt.
swans their cries, only that snag drifts down." He looked his elder brother.

Q;oā'p aligō'ptegama ya'XtîX icā'yim. Iō'pqa ik;oayā'wa.
Near he came up there the grizzly bear. He entered the panther.

"Ā'mXoalak;oa wuXi aq;u'tan. Q;oā'p iLgE'txôx Lqexē'Lau."
"Cover yourself with that kettle. Near comes the monster."

Igā'iXoalak;oa wuXi aq;u'tān yaXi ipu'koa. ItcixE'laqLq yaXi
He covered himself with that kettle that lynx. He opened the door that

icā'yim. Iō'La-it icî'qēpa. "Lān iLgā'xaL wuntcā'k;ēc wōgā'tōL?
grizzly bear. He stayed door in. "Who took from her our grandmother her fire?

ALEnxElgā'ewapqoē'cx." Aqa k;wāc igē'xôx ipu'koa. Igē'xallta.
(?) " Then afraid became the lynx. He trembled.

"LEnē't, LEnē't," igē'kîm icā'yîm, "wēLEmēmXē'X
"Give him to me, give him to me," said the grizzly bear, "your younger brother

aLEnxēlā'ewapqoē'cx." "Wā'koa amxEltcuwā'ya," igē'kîm
(?) " "All day you will talk," said

ik;oayā'wa. "Ā'ckatpq." Iā'ckupq icā'yim. Aqa icxE'lgayu.
the panther. "Come in." He entered the grizzly bear. Then they fought.

Itciō'lXam iā'mXîX: "Ā, qā'xpa mkē'xax? ALgEnuwā'qoa
He said to him his younger brother: "Ah, where are you? He will kill me

Lqexē'Lau." Itcaxē'ma ā'yaq;tan ipu'koa. Itcē'gElga ē'qa-îtk.
the monster." He threw off his kettle the lynx. He took it an adz.

IgicqLā'nukLtck:
He danced about much:

"Ē'k;ilxoā'q wuiLā'qo-it wuLqexē'Lau ā'pxō, ēk;îlxoā'q!"
"Water lilies his legs the monster, elder brother, water lilies!"

monster's legs are like water lilies," he sang. He struck the Bear's legs with the adz and then they threw him down. Then they cut his neck and hauled him out of the house.

The next morning the Panther went hunting again. He went to hunt elks, and told his brother: "Do not go away, else our fire will go out." He went out and the Lynx went to play. Then he thought of the fire. He went home and the fire was low. He tended it and went out again to play. Then he forgot his fire. A long time he played, then he remembered it. He went into the house, but the fire was already out. Again he swam across. He went ashore and opened the door of the house of the Grizzly Bears. He entered. Now the old woman had four fires. He took one firebrand and put it aside. Then she looked after the fires. She spread her legs, struck her vulva, and said: "You, you, you have eaten it, you have eaten it, the fire, the fire, vulva, vulva!" Then he put that firebrand back again. The old

---

Itcîlgā'mit yaXi ē'qa-îtk iā'qo-îtpa. Kopā' icgigE'LA-ît. Iā'tuk
He struck it that adz his legs at. Then they threw him down. His neck

Lq¡up îcgē'xôx. Icgiō'Lata Lā'xanîX.
cut they did it. They hauled him outside.

Wāx igē'tcuktîX. Aqa wit'ax iō'ya ik¡oayā'wa. Imō'lak
The next morning day came. Then again he went the panther. Elk

igigE'loē. Itciō'lXam iā'mXîX: "Nāct qā'mta mō'ya, iā'okîX
he went to hunt. He said to him his younger brother: "No where go, else

tcXup naxō'xoax atxā'tōL." Iō'pa ipu'koa igîxk¡ayā'wōlalEmtck.
extinguished will be our fire." He went out the lynx he always went to play.

Igayî'lkaLx ayā'tōL. Igē'Xk¡oa, aqa itsō'koa-îts ayā'tōL akē'x.
He thought of his fire. He went home, then small his fire was.

Iga-iXE'lgîLx. Aqa wi iō'ya igixk¡ayā'wōlalEmam. Igā'-ilalakuit
He made a fire. Then again he went he went to play. He forgot it

ayā'tōL. Lē'2lē igîxk¡ayā'wōlalEmtck. Igayî'lkaLx ayā'tōL.
his fire. Long he played. He thought of his fire.

Iō'pqam tE'ctaqL. Ā'nqa tcXup wuXi actā'tōL igā'xôx. Aqa wit'ax
He came in their house. Already extinguished that their fire was. Then again

iō'k¡uix'a ē'wa k¡anatē'tōL. Igigō'ptckamîX itcixE'lakLqîX
he swam thus across. He came up to the house he opened the door

Lcayî'muke tE'LaqL. Iā'ckupq. Aqa la'ktka tgā'qalEptckîX wuXi
the grizzly bears their house. He entered. Then four only her firebrands that

aq¡eyō'qt. Itcā'gElga ā'ēXt wuXi aqā'lEptckîX. KElā'îX
old woman. He took it one that firebrand. Far

itcaxē'ma. Iktuk¡umā'nanEmtck taXi tgā'qalEptckîX. L¡āk igE'tôx
he put it down. She looked at them those her firebrands. Spread she did them

tgā'qo-ît. ILaxE'lqilX LE'gakei: "Mai'ka maikā', mō'wElq¡
her legs. She slapped herself her hands: "You you, you ate it

mōwā'lq¡ wa'tuL watū'L, wi'qēctq wiqā'ctq." Aqa wit'ax itcaxē'ma
you ate it the fire the fire, vulva vulva." Then again he put it down

woman looked at the firebrands and there were as many as before. Thus the Lynx fooled the old woman. He looked often when she struck her vulva. Then he took that firebrand. He went home and swam across. He came into the house and made a fire. In the evening his elder brother came home. There was the Lynx. They slept, and the elder brother rose early. He went to wash himself. After a little while he came in. Swans were flying away. He said to the Lynx: "Go and look." The Lynx went. He came in. He was asked: "What did you see?" "I did not see anything but swans flying away because a snag is drifting down." "Do you think that is a snag? That is the Grizzly Bear. Quick, hide yourself under that kettle!" Lynx hid and put the kettle over himself. Then the Grizzly Bear opened the door. "Who took our grandmother's fire? I will eat him. Give me, give me your younger brother; I will eat him." The Lynx became afraid. He trembled under his kettle.

---

wuXi ā'tōL. Aqa wit'ax iktuk;umā'nanEmtek wuXi aq;eyō'qt.
that fire. Then again she looked at them often that old woman.

Kapā't taXi tgā'qalEptckîX. Aqa ala-ix·ēnēmō'tXEma wuXi
As many those her firebrands. Then he made fun of her that

aq;eyō'qt yaXi ipu'koa. Ä'2qoētîx· itcaxē'lōtex, iLaxElqē'lEXLtek
old woman that lynx. Often he looked at her, she slapped herself

LE'gakci. Itcā'gElga wuXi ā'ēXt aqā'lEptckîX. lō'ya, igē'Xk;oa,
her hands. He took it that one firebrand. He went, he went home,

igikE'k;ēx·a-îX. Iō'yam tE'ctaqLpa. iga-ix·E'lgiLX. Tsō'yustē
he swam across. He arrived their house at. he made a fire. In the evening

igē'Xk;oa ēyalXt. IgîXk;oā'mam ik;oayā'wa. Iōxt ipu'koa.
he went home his elder brother. He came home the panther. There was the lynx.

TcXāp ictō'qoya, kawī'X igixE'latck ē'yalXt. Igixqoā'tam.
One night they slept, early he arose his elder brother. He went to bathe.

Igē'tpqam. Nō'L;îX igē'tpqam. IguXoawā'Xit tqēlō'q.
He came in. A little while he came in. They flew away swans.

"ME'k·îket." iqiō'lXam ipu'koa. Igē'k·îket ipu'koa. Igē'tpqam.
"Look." he was told the lynx. He looked the lynx. He came in.

Iqiōqu'mtcxōgoa: "TcuXoa tān imē'qElkEl?" "K;ā'ya nîct tān
He was asked: "Well! what did you see?" "Nothing not anything

inē'qElkEl. Tā'ema tqēlō'q ī'taxul ō'xuîtcX. Lā'ema LE'tcin
I saw it. Only swans their cries come down. Only a snag

Lā2'tgatcX." "LE'tcin amXLō'Xuan? yā'Xka icā'yim yaXi itē't.
is drifting down." "A snag do you think? He the grizzly bear that comes.

Ai'aq amxE'pcut! Ā'mXoalak;oa wu'Xi aq;u'tan." IgixE'pcut
Quick hide yourself! Cover yourself with that kettle." He hid himself

ipu'koa. Igā'iXoalak;oa wuXi aq;u'tan. Itca-ixE'laqLqîX icā'yim.
the lynx. He covered himself with that kettle. He opened the door the grizzly bear.

"Lān iLgā'xaL wuntcā'k;ēc wogatō'L? ALEnxElaēwapqoē'cx."
"Who took from her our grandmother her fire? (?) "

K;wac igē'xôx ipu'koa. Igē'xallta kā ā'yaq;tan. Lā'2lē iō'La-it
Afraid became the lynx. He trembled where his kettle. Long he stayed

icī'qē. "LEnē't, LEnē't wuLmēmXē'X. ALEnxElaēwapqoē'cx."
door. "Give him to me, give him to me your younger brother. (?) "

He stayed in the door for a long time. Then the Panther said: "You are talking all day. Come in; we will fight." The Grizzly Bear entered, and they fought. They fought a long time. Then the Panther said to the Lynx: "Oh, where are you? The monster is making me tired." The Lynx threw off his kettle and danced about. "Elder brother, the monster's legs are like water lilies," he sang. He hit the Bear's leg with the adz. Then they threw him down. They cut his neck and hauled him out of the house. The Lynx was told: "Stop leaving our fire. The monsters will kill us." For two days the Panther did not leave him. Then he went again.

[The same a third and a fourth time.]

Now only the strongest Bear was left. They stayed there five nights. Then the Panther left and said: "Don't forget our fire. He will kill us. The one who is left is really strong." The Lynx said: "I shall not go away." After a little while the Lynx went out, but right away he looked again after the fire. He went out often, then he forgot it. He played about a long time, then he remembered his fire. He went

---

Igē'kîm ik¡oayā'wa: "Wā'2goa amᴇ'xaltcō. Ā'ckatpq, txᴇlgā'yux."
He said the panther: "All day you will talk. Come in, we will fight."

lā'ckupq icā'yîm. Icxᴇ'lgayū. Iō'ʟqtîX icXᴇ'lgayū. Iqiō'lXam
He entered the grizzly bear. They fought. Long they fought. He was told

ipu'koa: "Ā qā'xpa mkē'xax?" Aqa tᴇll iʟgᴇ'nux ʟqcxē'ʟau.
the lynx: "Ah where are you?" Now tired makes me the monster.

Itcaxē'ma ā'yaq¡tan. Itcē'gᴇlga ē'qa-itk:
He threw off his kettle. He took it an adz:

"Ē'k¡ilxoā'q wuiʟā'qo-it wuʟqcxē'ʟau, ā'pxō, ēk¡ilxoā'q!"
"Water lilies his legs the monster, elder brother, water lilies!"

Igîcxʟā'nukʟtck. Itcilgā'mit iā'qo-itpa yaXi ē'qa-îtk. Kopā'
He danced about much. He struck it his leg at that adz. There

icgigᴇ'ʟa-it, iā'tuk ʟq¡up icgē'xox. Icgiō'ʟata ʟā'XanîX. Iqiō'lXam
they threw him down, his neck cut they did it. They hauled him outside. He was told

ipu'koa: "Kapᴇ't amqᴇlō'qʟqa atxā'tōʟ. Atktxotē'na tqcxcʟā'ukc."
the lynx: "Enough leave our fire. They will kill us the monsters."

Mô'kctîX iō'qoya nîcqē igiqᴇ'loqʟq, aqa wi iō'ya ik¡oayā'wa.
Twice he slept not at all! he left him, then again he went the panther.

[The same a third and a fourth time.]

ĒXā'tka igicxk¡ā'ctix·it yaXi ktiā'ʟxēwulX. Aqa îcxē'la-it
One only was left by them two that the strongest one. Then they stayed

quî'nᴇmîX ictō'qoya. Aqa wi igiqᴇ'luqʟq. Itciō'lXam: "Nēct
five they slept. Then again he left him. He said to him: "Not

amaqō'qʟqa atxā'tōʟ. Atctxōtē'na. Yā'Xka wuk¡ ktiā'ʟxēwulX
leave it our fire. He will kill us. He really the strongest one

yaXi iuk¡uā'ctix·it." Igē'kîm ipu'koa: "Nāct qā'mta nō'ya."
that he is left." He said the lynx: "Not anywhere I shall go."

Nō'ʟ¡îX qayupā'x ipu'koa. Ā'nqa wi qatcō'kctamx ayā'tōʟ.
A little he went out the lynx. Already again he looked at it his fire.

Qā'watîX ʟXuan iō'pa. Aqa igā'yelalakuit ayā'tōʟ.
Several times perhaps he went out. Then he forgot it his fire.

IgîXk¡ayā'wōlalᴇmtck: lē'lē igîXk¡ayā'wōlalᴇmtck. Igayî'lkaʟx
He played; long he played. He thought of

home, but it was out. Then he swam across to the house of the Grizzly Bear. The old woman held the fire. For a short time she threw it down and took it up again right away. He did not dare to take it. The old woman threw it down again. Then he jumped at it and took it. He ran out and swam across. He went ashore and came to their house. He had just made a fire when his elder brother came home. "Where did you go? Just now you are making a fire? When the Grizzly Bear comes I shall throw you before him and he will eat you." Lynx did not say anything. "Take care," said the Panther, "he will kill us." Early the Panther arose. He washed himself and tied his hair. Then swans were flying away. He told the Lynx: "See if the monster is coming." The Lynx went and said: "I do not see anything; only a snag is drifting down." "Do you think that is a snag? That is the Grizzly Bear who is coming. Hide yourself, put the kettle over you." Then the Lynx put the kettle over himself. The Grizzly Bear opened the door and said: "Who took my grandmother's fire?

---

1 ayā'tōʟ. Igē'Xk¡oa. Ā'nqa tcXup igā'xôx ayā'tōʟ. Iō'k¡uiXa
his fire. He went home. Already extinguished was his fire. He swam

2 ē'wa k¡anatē'tōʟ. Iō'yam icā'yim tē'iaqʟpa. IgagᴇIgā't wuXi
thus across. He arrived the grizzly bear his house at. She held it that

3 aq¡eyō'qt wuXi ā'tōʟ. Nō'ʟ¡îX agaxē'max, ā'nqa wi agagᴇlgā'x.
old woman that fire. A little she layed it down, already again she took it.

4 Tcxᴇp igē'xôx ipu'koa. Igaxē'ma wit'ax wuXi aq¡eyō'qt wuXi
Not daring became the lynx. She laid it down again that old woman that

5 aqā'lᴇptckîX. Itcî'sōpᴇna ipu'koa. Itcā'gᴇlga wuXi aqā'lᴇptckîX.
firebrand. He jumped at it the lynx. He took it that firebrand.

6 Igē'kta ʟā'xanîX. Igē'Xk¡oa. Iō'k¡uix·a. Igigō'ptckamîX.
He ran outside. He went home. He swam. He came up to the house.

7 IgîXk¡oā'mam tᴇ'ctaqʟpa. Koalē'wa iXᴇlgē'ʟxal aqa igîXk¡oā'mam
He came home their house to. Just he made a fire then he came home

8 ē'yalXt. "Qā'mta imō'ya? Tcqī koalē'wa amxᴇlgē'ʟxal. Ma'nîx
his elder brother. "Where did you go? Then just you made a fire. When

9 alētē'mama icā'yîm ayamxemā'ya. Atcîmxalᴇmō'xuma." Näct qa
he will come the grizzly bear I shall throw you to him. He will eat you." Nothing

10 igē'kîm ipu'koa. "Qā't¡ōcXᴇm!" aqiō'lXam ipu'koa, "atctxōtē'na."
said the lynx. "Look out!" he was told the lynx, "he will kill us."

11 Kawī'X igixᴇ'latck ik¡oayā'wa. Igixᴇ'qoat, iʟix·ᴇ'mᴇlaptck.
Early he arose the panther. He bathed, he tied his hair in a knot over his forehead.

12 IgoXuawā'Xit tqēlō'q. Iqiō'lXam ipu'koa: "Amᴇ'kēkct aqa
They flew away swans. He was told the lynx: "Look there

13 itē't iqcxē'ʟau." Igē'kîkct ipu'koa. "K¡ā nîct tān inē'qᴇlkᴇl.
he is coming the monster." He looked the lynx. "Nothing not anything I see it.

14 ʟā'ema ʟᴇ'tcin ʟā'2tgatcX." "ʟᴇ'tcinna," atciō'lXam, "yā'Xkā
Only a snag is drifting down." "A snag [int. part.]," he said to him, "he

15 icā'yim yaXi itē't. Amxᴇ'pcōt!" Igā'-iXoalak¡oa aq¡u'tan ipu'koa.
the grizzly bear that is coming. Hide yourself!" He covered himself with the kettle the lynx.

16 Itcixᴇ'laqʟq yaXi icā'yim. "ʟān iʟgā'xaʟ wuntcā'k¡ēc wagatō'ʟ?
He opened the door that grizzly bear. "Who took it from her our grandmother her fire?

Give me your little brother; I will eat him." The Panther was silent for a little while. He was afraid. The Grizzly spoke often and asked for the younger brother. Then the Panther spoke: "Do you think a person will give up his own younger brother? Come in; we will fight." Then the Grizzly Bear went in. They fought, and he almost threw the Panther, who got tired. Then he spoke to the Lynx: "Where are you? The monster makes me tired." Then the Lynx threw off the kettle, took an adz, and danced about. "Elder brother, his legs are like water lilies," he sang. "You are dancing when I am tired," said the Panther. Then the Lynx hit his leg. They killed the last one. Then the Lynx swam across and burned the old woman's house. On the following morning the Panther said: "I shall leave you. You shall live on these creeks. You shall catch silver-side salmon. You are bad; therefore I shall leave you. When I kill an elk, then you will eat it." Then the Panther went away and left the Lynx.

LEnē't LEnē't wuLEmē'mXîX. ALEnxelā'ewapqoē'eX." Iō'LqtîX
Give him to me, give him to me your younger brother. (?) " Long

qan igē'xôx ik¡oayā'wa. K¡wac igē'xôx. Ä'4xuētîX igē'kîm
silent he was the panther. Afraid he was. Often he spoke

icā'yim. Iqēxuwā'koatck iā'mXîX ik¡oayā'wa. Lē'lē aqa
the grizzly bear. He was asked for his younger brother the panther. Long then

itciō'lXam: "Qantcē'x Lqa LgoaLē'lX k¡a igaLgE'Lt Lā'mXîX?
he said to him: "How often maybe a person and he gave him up his younger brother?

Ā'ckatpq, atxElgā'yux!" Iā'ckupq icā'yîm. Aqa icxE'lgayū.
Come in, we will fight!" He entered the grizzly bear. Then they fought.

Guē'tax iqē'yux ik¡oayā'wa. Ā'koapō aqikLā'ētx ik¡oayā'wa. TEll
Almost dead he was made the panther. Almost he was thrown the panther. Tired

igē'xôx ik¡oayā'wa. Iqiō'lXam ipu'koa: "Ā qā'xpa mkēx? aqa tEll
became the panther. He was told the lynx: "Ah where are you? then tired

iLgE'nux Lqcxē'Lau." Itcaxē'ma ā'yaq¡tan ipu'koa. Itcē'gElga
he makes me the monster." He threw it off his kettle the lynx. He took it

ē'qa-îtk. Ayuwē'lalalEmtck:
an adz. He danced about much:

"Ē'k¡ilxoā'q wuiLā'qo-it wuLqcxē'Lau, ā'pxō, ē'k¡ilxoā'q!"
"Water lilies his legs the monster, elder brother, water lilies!"

"Wā'2ka-it mō'-îtck aqa tEll ēnE'xôx." Itcîlgā'mit iā'qo-itpa.
"All day you dance then tired I am." He struck it his leg at.

IcgigE'La-ît, icgē'waq; icgiā'k¡LEmatsk. Iō'k¡uiXē ipu'koa.
They threw him down, they killed him: they killed the last one. He swam across the lynx.

ItcuXuē'giLx tE'gaqL wuXi aq¡eyō'qt. Igē'tcuktîX. Igē'kîm
He burnt her house that old woman's. It got day. He said

ik¡oayā'wa: "Aqa ayamqElō'qLqa. Tē'2ka mai'ka amxōxoa gi
the panther: "Then I shall leave you. Here you be these

tqū'Lmaxpa. Amtup¡iā'Lxa tE'q¡awan. Mai'ka imē'mala, tā'ntxo
creeks at. You shall catch silver-side salmon. You you are bad, therefore

ayamqElō'qLqa. Ma'nîx aminegā'ma anēwā'qoa imō'lak, koā'lewa
I shall leave you. When you find it I have killed it an elk, just then

alEmxElEmō'xuma." Iō'ya aqa ik¡oayā'wa. AqiqE'luqLq ipu'koa.
you shall eat it." He went then the panther. He was left the lynx.

Seal and Crab (told 1891)

One day the Crab and her elder sister, the Seal, were hungry. The Crab cried, and her elder sister said: "Sister, let us go and wash ourselves." They went down to the water and bathed. The Crab felt cold and went up again to the house. The Seal dived several times and killed two salmon—large salmon. Then she went up. The Crab was sitting there. The Seal said: "Go and bring that small salmon." The Crab went down and found those salmon. She took them and hung them onto the point of her finger. "How small are these salmon," said she, but they broke her finger. She hung them onto the next finger. It broke also. She broke all her fingers. Then she went up to the house and cried. She opened the door and spoke to her elder sister: "What are you doing? I broke all my fingers."

Aqē'cgoax Ictā'k¡anē k¡a Aqalxē'la

The Seal Her Myth and the Crab

Qā'xʟkanē'ka-it	aqa	walō'	igō'xoa	aqaʟxē'la	ā'galXt	aqē'sgoax.
One day	then	hunger	acted on her	the crab	her elder sister	the seal.

Axgᴇ'qunk	aqē'sgoax	ʟxgᴇ'cqax	ʟqaʟxē'la.	Igagᴇ'tcax,	walō'	igō'xoa
The elder one	the seal	the younger one	the crab.	She cried,	hunger	acted on her

ʟqaʟxē'la.	Igō'lXam	ā'galXt:	"Tᴇ'xōya	atxqoā'ta."	Ictō'ʟxa
the crab.	She said to her	to her elder sister:	"Let us go	let us bathe."	They went to the water

mā'ʟnîX.	Icgᴇ'kXoat.	Ts¡ᴇs	iʟᴇ'xôx	ʟqaʟxē'la.	Iʟō'ptcga.
to the water.	They bathed.	Cold	became	the crab.	She went up.

Qā'watîX	igaktē'mᴇnq	aqē'sgoax.	Iktō'tena	môket	tgu'nat,
Several times	she dived	the seal.	She killed them	two	salmon,

itā'qa-iʟax	tgu'nat.	Igō'ptcga	aqē'sgoax.	Â	ʟâxt	ʟqaʟxē'la.	"A'yaq
large ones	salmon.	She went up	the seal.	Oh,	there was	the crab.	"Quick!

tgā'lᴇmam	taXi	tk¡unā'tᴇmax."	Iʟō'ʟxa	ʟqaʟxē'la.	Iʟuguā'qoam
go and fetch	those	small fish."	She went to the beach	the crab.	She reached them

taXi	tgunā'tᴇmax.	Quʟ	iktā'wîx	tᴇ'gaksi.	"Ksᴇmm	taXi	tk¡unā'tᴇmax
those	salmon.	Hang	she did them on	her fingers.	"Small	those	small fish

ō'xoaxt."	IguXoalā'Xît	tᴇ'gakci.	Tgō'nuē	quʟ	iktā'wax	taXi
are."	They broke	her fingers.	Other ones	hang	she did them	those

tk¡unā'tᴇmax.	IguXoalā'Xit	tᴇ'gakci.	Ka'nauwā2	iguXoalā'Xit
small fish.	They broke	her fingers.	All	broke

tᴇ'gakci.	Igō'ptcga	igagᴇ'tcax.	Â'qulqt	igixᴇ'laqʟqîX.	Igō'lXam
her fingers.	She went up	she cried.	She wept	she opened the door.	She said to

ā'galXt:	"Qā	ēmᴇ'xôx?	Â	igugoalā'Xit	tᴇ'gakci."	Ictō'ʟxa
her elder sister	"How	are you?	Ah,	they broke	my fingers."	They went to the beach

Then the Seal and her younger sister went down to the water. The Crab's fingers were lying there. The Seal took them up and put them on again. Then the Seal carried the salmon up. They cut them up and roasted them. The Crab said: "I will eat their heads. I will eat their tails. I will eat their roe. I will eat their stomachs. I will eat their hearts. I will eat their livers." Now the salmon were done. The Crab ate two hearts and one liver, then she had enough. Her elder sister, the Seal, said to her: "Eat, eat, else you will be hungry." The Seal ate all the salmon. Now the sister closed her house. She closed even the smallest holes. The Seal spoke to her younger sister: "Do not go outside for two days." Now the Seal forgot to look after her sister. She heard her shouting and looked for her. She had disappeared. She had gone out. Then the Seal went out and listened. She heard her sister shouting somewhere down the river, where

---

aqē'sgoax k!a agā'mtX. Ictō'Lxam; ō'xoaxt tE'Lakci LqaLxē'la.
the seal and her younger sister. They came down; there were her fingers the crab.

Igō'guiga aqē'sgoax. Iktā'lox tE'gakci. IqLE'lôx LaXi LqaLxē'la.
She took them the seal. She put them on her her fingers. They were put on her that crab.

IktōLā'taptck aqē'sgoax taXi tgu'nat. IcgE'tôxc taXi tgu'nat.
She carried them up the seal those salmon. They cut them those salmon.

Icî'xēluktc. ILE'kîm LqaLxē'la: "Nai'ka ak!Elā'tcēn
They roasted them. She said the crab: "I the heads

ananxElEmō'xuma. Nai'ka tElē'ct atEnEnxElEmō'xuma. Nai'ka
I will eat them. I the tails I will eat them. I

Lgā'qapt aLnEnxElEmō'xuma. Nai'ka ā'nux ananxElEmō'xuma.
their roe I will eat it. I the stomach I will eat it.

Nai'ka tgā'Xenuwakcke atEnxElEmō'xuma. Nai'ka tgā'p!anaqcke
I their hearts I will eat them. I their livers

atEnxElEmō'xuma." Isxk!ē'kst ka'nauwē. Môkct tkEnuwā'kcke
I will eat them." They were done all. Two hearts

iLxE'lEmux LaXi LqaLxē'la, k!a ēXt ip!ā'naqc, aqa iLō'qctē.
she ate them that crab, and one liver, then she was satiated.

Kē'nuwa igō'lXam agā'mtXîX aqē'sgoax: "AmxLxE'lEmEtck, ā'ōLEL
Try she said to her her younger sister the seal: "Eat much, else

walō'." IgaxLxE'lEmîtck wuXi aqē'sgoax. Ka'nauwē iktō'LXum
hunger." She ate that seal. All she finished them

taXi tgu'nat wuXi aqē'sgoax. Igiō'xoapō tE'ctaqL. Ka'nauwē
those salmon that seal. She closed it their house. All

igiō'xoapō tE'ctaqL. Kōpā' nōL! Lxoā'pîX, kopā' igîxpō'xoîX.
she closed it their house. There a little hole, there she closed it.

Igō'lXam agā'mtXîX aqē'sgoax: "Nēct amōpā'ya. Mô'kctîX
She said to her her younger sister the seal: "Not go out. Twice

ayoqō'ya yaxtîX niet amōpā'ya." Igā'ilalakuit agā'mtXîX aqē'sgoax.
her sleeps then not go out." She forgot her her younger sister the seal.

Igîltcē'maq ilō'mEniL aqē'sgoax. Igō'kcta agā'mtXîX. Ā'nqa
She heard her shouting the seal. She looked for her her younger sister. Already

k!Em, igō'pa. Igō'pa aqē'sgoax igaxamē'laq. Qā'eqamîX
nothing, she had gone out. She went out the seal she listened. Down the river

Blue-jay defecated, at the place where his town was situated. Now the Crab sang: "My sister and I eat what is swimming in the sea."

The people were hungry. It was winter. They made themselves ready and went aboard one canoe. The Seal went and met her younger sister. She was on top of a tree. "Come down," she said. Then the Crab came down. The Seal struck her and they went home. When they came home the Seal said to her younger sister: "Hide yourself." The Seal hid in a cache. The Crab hid, but her face was visible behind the plank which stood near the fire. Now the people landed and went up to the house. They looked for the Seal, but they found only the Crab. They struck her in the nape. Then a salmon heart fell out of her mouth. They struck her again; then another salmon heart fell out of her mouth. They struck her again and a salmon liver fell out of her mouth. They struck her again and again, but she vomited only two hearts and one liver. They tried to

---

agelō'mᴇniʟ agā'mtXîX. Kā itcʟō'ts¡ats¡a iqē'sqēs yaXi qā'eqamîX
she shouted her younger sister. Where he defecated blue-jay that down river

nē'lXam, iʟā'lXam iqē'sqēs. Aqa ʟxō'la ʟqaʟxē'la. ʟxō'la:
where the town his town blue-jay. Then she spoke much the crab. She said much:

"Ä'maʟ ia'xtk¡ēlaXtk¡ēla intgē'wulq¡ wā'gᴇlXt."
"Bay swimming we eat it my elder sister."

Wā'lō igᴇ'tôx ta-îtci tê'lXam. Tcā'xᴇlqʟîX. Igoxoē'tXuîtck
Hunger acted on them those people. It was winter. They made themselves ready

ta-îtci tê'lXam. Itigᴇ'la-ît ēXt ikᴇ'nim. Igō'ya aqē'sgoax.
those people. They were in one canoe. She went the seal.

Igō'cgam agā'mtXîX. YaXī' cā'xalîX ō'guaxt. "Ō'qoētcō!"
She found her her younger sister. That up she was. "Come down!"

igō'lXam. Iʟō'qo-ētcō ʟqaʟxē'la. Igō'waq agā'mtXîX aqē'sgoax.
she said to her. She came down the crab. She struck her her younger sister the seal.

Icî'Xk¡oa. Ictō'pqam tᴇ'ctaqʟpa. "Amxᴇ'pcut," igō'lXam
They went home. They came in their house in. "Hide yourself," she said to her

agā'mtXîX. "Amxᴇ'pcut." Igaxᴇ'pcut aqē'sgoax ik¡oā'yapa.
her younger sister. "Hide yourself." She hid herself the seal the cache in.

Iʟxᴇ'pcut ʟqaʟxē'la. Lāx stā'xōst gēguala' ʟt¡ō'tᴇlatckan.
She hid herself the crab. Out her eyes below the plank at the side of the fire.

Itxē'gela-îX tê'lXam. Itgᴇ'ptcga. Iqcō'naxʟ aqē'sgoax.
They landed the people. They went up to the house. She was searched for the seal.

Iqʟō'cgam ʟqaʟxē'la. P¡āq iqᴇ'ʟôx ʟā'p¡aqa. ʟ¡uX iguʟā'taXit
She was found the crab. Slapped she was her nape in. Falling out fell out

akᴇ'nuwaks. Wit'ax p¡āq iqᴇ'ʟôx. Agō'n ā'ēXt akᴇ'nuwaks
a heart. Again slapped she was. Another one heart

iguʟā'taXit. ʟō'nîX p¡āq iqᴇ'ʟôx. Kē'qamtqîX ip¡ā'naqs
fell out. Three times slapped she was. Afterward a liver

iuʟā'taXit. Kē'nuwa p¡ā'qp¡āq iqᴇ'ʟôx ʟqaʟxē'la. P¡āq p¡āq p¡āq
fell out. Try slapped she was the crab. Slapped and slapped

p¡āq iqᴇ'ʟôx. Môketka tkᴇ'nuwaks k¡a ēXt ip¡ā'naqs iʟktō'mᴇqōk.
she was. Two only hearts and one liver she vomited them.

find the Seal. Then Blue-jay became tired, and went to defecate. Then they dug up the cache. They found the Seal, took her at her head and bent it down. Then she vomited the salmon. The people took them and tied them into bundles. They left only that which was too soft. Blue-jay came home. He became angry and said: "I heard the Crab and you left me only refuse." He tied up the soft parts which they had left. Then the people went home. They approached their town and slept. They made a fire some distance from the water. They said to Blue-jay: "Come and warm yourself." But he replied: "No; I want to stay here in the canoe. I am warm enough here." Then he ate all the meat. Blue-jay finished all the meat that he had taken and tied up rotten wood [in its place]. Early the next morning they went homeward. After some time they reached their home. Then the boys came down to the beach. These people's children and Blue-jay's children came down together. They gave them all those bundles, and Blue-jay gave his children his bundle. The boys went

---

Kē'nuwa iqō'naxL aqē'sgoax. Tā'menua igē'x iqē'sqēs.
Try she was searched for the seal. Give up he did blue-jay.

ItcLōts!ā'ts!am. LE'kLEk iqē'yôx ik!oā'yat. Iqō'cgam aqē'sgoax.
He went to defecate. Dug it was the cache. She was found the seal.

IqLā'nExoktē, ac ē'wa iqē'yôx itcā'q!aqctak. IgagE'mqôq.
She was taken at her head, and thus was done her head. She vomited.

Iktō'mqôq taXi tgu'nat. Itgō'xoaqtck ta-îtci tê'lXam.
She vomited them those salmon. They gathered them those people.

Itguxoak!ē'nianukLtck. Aqa tā'ema taXi manaq!ē' L!mE'nL!mEn.
They tied them in bundles. Then only that too soft.

Aqa iō'pqam iqē'sqēs. Kalā'lkuilē igē'x iqē'sqēs. "Ē'wa nai'ka
Then he came in blue-jay. Angry became blue-jay. "Thus I

inxEtcE'maq; tatc!a tq!ē'ipX iqtEnE'lōt." Itsōxoak!ē'niakoa taXi
I heard; behold! refuse is given to me." He tied it in a bundle that

manaq!ē' L!mE'nL!mEn iqē'sqēs. Aqa igō'Xoak!oa ta-îtci tê'lXam.
too soft blue-jay. Then they went home those people.

Q!oā'p itgiō'xoam ē'lXam, aqa itgî'qoya. IgoXuē'giLx LXE'lēu
Near they reached it town, then they slept. They made a fire inland

ta-îtci tê'lXam. Kē'nuwa iqiō'lXam iqē'sqēs: "ME'tptcga iqē'sqēs.
those people. Try he was told blue-jay: "Come up! blue-jay.

Mxatck!oā'mitam." Igē'kîm iqē'sqēs: "K!ā'ya qatxō tā'ka
Warm yourself." He said blue-jay: "No, must here

gEnā'kuXt. Nusk!oā'it, nō'sk!oa-it gi ikE'nimpa qa nā'kuXt."
I stay in the canoe. I am warm, I am warm this canoe in where I am in the canoe."

ItixE'lEmux ka'nauwē taXi tqLē'lXam. TaXi itctō'mitck!ē
He ate all that meat. That he took it up

tqLē'lXam, itctâ'LXōm, itcaxk!ē'niakoa ā'lEmlEm. Kawī'X aqa
meat, he finished it, he made a bundle rotten wood. Early then

wi itgī'ya igō'Xoak!oa. Nō'L!îX itgī'ya, aqa iguXoak!oā'mam.
again they went they went home. A little they went, then they came home.

Itgā'Lxa tqā'tōtēnîkc itā'qôq ta-îtci tê'lXam, iā'qôq iqē'sqēs.
They went to the beach the boys their children those people, his children blue-jay.

Kātē'x· itgā'Lxa. Itktā'owit ka'nauwē taXi ōxoak!ē'niayuktax
Together they went to the beach. They gave them all those bundles

up. Then the women and the children ate the meat. Blue-jay's children untied their bundle. Then they saw that it was rotten wood. Blue-jay became angry: "They ate all the food and tied up rotten wood. They fooled me." That is the story; to-morrow we shall have good weather.

---

ta-îtci tā'qôq. Itciā'owit iā'qôq iqē'sqēs yaXi qîXk!ē'niak.
these children. He gave it to his children blue-jay that bundle.

Itgᴇ'ptcgam ta-îtci tqā'tōtēnîkc. Itoxoē'mux aqa taXi tqʟē'lXam
They came up those boys. They ate now that meat

ka tᴇ'nᴇmckc ka tqā'tōtēnîkc. StuX^{u} itgī'yux iqē'sqēs iā'qôq
and women and boys. Untie they did it blue-jay his children

yaXi qixk!ē'niak^{u}t. Aqa ā'lᴇmlᴇm. Kalā'lkuilē igē'xôx iqē'sqēs:
that bundle. Then rotten wood. Angry became blue-jay:

"Iqtᴇnxā'owîlq! gi tqʟē'lXam aqa ʟq iqak!ē'niakoa ā'lᴇmlᴇm.
"It was eaten from me this meat then maybe it was tied up rotten wood.

IqînXᴇnᴇmō'tXᴇmtck." K!anē'k!anē'; ō'la asa-igā'p.
I have been fooled." The story; to-morrow good weather.

MYTH OF THE MINK (TOLD 1891)

There was Mink and his elder brother. Every day Mink played itlukum. He lost, but did not want to give up his stakes, and then the children struck him and almost killed him. He went home crying. His elder brother said to him: "Why do you cry?" "Oh, they struck me." Now Mink was hungry. He said to his elder brother: "Brother, I am hungry." His brother replied: "Go to that lake, stretch out your arms, and sit down." Mink went. He sat down and stretched out his arms. Then an arm became visible. Suddenly a horn dish stood on the ground near him. There was one blackberry and one huckleberry, one salmon-berry and one nut in it, one of all kinds of fruits. It was just one handful. Mink went home;

IKŌ'SA-ÎT ITCA'k¡ANĒ

MINKHIS MYTH

Cxēlā'itîX ikō'sa-ît k¡a ē'yalXt. Qāā'xLkanē'gua aqa ē'Lukuma
There were mink and his elder brother. One day then itlukum

qixE'cgam ikō'sa-ît. Iqē'yuLq; itctō'xoaxāmēlakoa. Iqē'waq,
he played mink. They won over him; he refused to give up his stakes. He was struck,

ā'koapō itgiō'mEqtamit ta-îtci tqā'tōtēnîkc. Igē'Xk¡oa. Iâ'qulqt,
nearly they killed him those boys. He went home. He wept,

igîXk¡oā'mam. Itciō'lXam ē'yalXt: "Qā'tcqē mō'qulqt?" "Ā,
he came home. He said to him his elder brother: "Why do you cry?" "Oh,

qE'nuwaq." Aqa walō' igī'yux ikō'sa-ît. Itciō'lXam ē'yalXt:
I was struck." Then hunger acted on him mink. He said to him his elder brother:

"Walō' gE'nuxt, ā'pXō!" Igē'kîm ē'yalXt: "Mē'ya yaXi iLā'lapa.
"Hunger acts on me, elder brother!' He said his elder brother: "Go that lake to.

Ē'wa mtō'xa tE'm'ēxō. AmōLā'ita." Iō'ya ikō'sa-ît. Iō'La-ît; ē'wa
Thus do your arms. Stay there." He went mink. He stayed; thus

itcî'tôx tī'axō, qā'xpa Lq Lāx aLXō'xoa LgoaLē'lx LE'Lakci. Ē'wa
he did them his arms, somewhere visible became a person his hands. Thus

igē'xux, ā'nqa LXE'leuX iuk¡ō'LîtX îcq¡ō'. Ā'ēXt agō'ē aXî'caqt;
he did, already ashore stood a dish. One black-berry was in it;

ā'ēXt ā'qEmukc aXî'caqt; ā'ēXt anuwā'yax aXî'caqt; ā'ēXt
one blackberry was in it; one huckleberry was in it; one

ā'lalX aXî'caqt; ā'ēXt ā'qula agā'mala. Ka'nauwē tqoxoē'max
gamass root was in it; one nut its kernel. All fruits

tē'XtEmax. Aqa pāL ē'yakci. Igē'Xk¡oa ikō'sa-ît. IgiXE'LXaq.
one of each. Then full his hand. He went home mink. He was angry.

he was angry. He came to his brother's house and said: "I wanted to get food. It is not enough for me, what they gave me." His elder brother replied: "Quick, eat it. When you have enough, take the dish to your sisters-in-law. Anyone who eats that will have enough." Mink took it and poured the berries into his hands. He ate them and threw the dish away. He looked at the dish. The berries were still in it. He took it again and again ate all. He threw the dish away. He looked at it. Again the berries were in it. Now his elder brother observed him. Now he put the dish down carefully and he ate all those berries. He became satiated. He had enough. He did not finish all. "Quick! Take that dish and put it on the water for your sisters-in-law. Then come home." Mink went and came to that lake. He took that dish and said: "If a woman should come to take that dish, I will haul her ashore; I will lie down with her all day." Now that lake began to boil. He held the dish, but it disappeared and he

---

Iō'yam tᴇ'ctaqʟ ē'yalXt. Igē'kîm ikō'sa-ît: "Ā'ᴏʟᴇl inuwā'ʟqam,
He came home | their house | his elder brother. | He said | mink: | "Else | I go to get food,

anuqctē'iaʟqa gēqᴇnᴇ'lqo-îm." Igē'kîm ē'yalXt. Iqiō'lXam ikō'sa-ît:
it is not enough for me | what she gave me to eat." | He said | his elder brother. | He was told | mink:

"A'yaq tᴇmxᴇ'lᴇmuX, ma'nîx amuqctē'ya aqa amtᴇlō'kʟa
"Quick | eat it, | when | you have enough | then | bring it to them

ʟmē'potcxᴇnāna. Yā'Xka k!oaʟqē' ʟgā'pᴇla qatēxᴇlᴇmō'Xumx,
your sisters-in-law. | That | just as | much | they eat,

aqa qā'yukctē'x." Itcō'guiga ikō'sa-ît, wax itcʟᴇ'lôx ʟē'iakci.
then | he is satiated." | He took them | mink, | pour out | he did it | his handful.

Itixᴇ'lᴇmux. Itcixē'ma ya'Xi icq!ō'. Itcī'yukct yaXi
He ate it. | He threw it down | that | dish. | He looked at it | that

icq!ō'. Tē'luxt taXi tqoxoē'max. Wit'ax itcē'gᴇlga. Wit'ax
dish. | There were in it | those | fruits. | Again | he took it. | Again

itcuXuē'muX ka'nauwē. Itcixē'ma yaXi icq!ō'; itcī'yukct yaXi
he ate | all. | He threw it down | that | dish; | he looked at it | that

icq!ō'. wi tē'luxt taXi tqoxoē'max. Itciō'qumit yaXi ē'yalXt.
dish, | again | they were in it | those | fruits. | He saw him | that | his elder brother.

Iqiō'qumit ikō'sa-ît. Aqa t!ayā' itciōk!ō'ʟit yaXi icq!ō'.
He saw him | mink. | Then | well | he put it down | that | dish.

Itixᴇ'lᴇmux, itixᴇ'lᴇmux taXi tqoxoē'max. Pā2ʟ igē'x iā'wan.
He ate, | he ate | those | fruits. | Full | became | his belly.

Iō'qctē. Näct itctō'ʟXōm. "Ai'aq iʟᴇ'luk·i yaXi ē'ʟacq!ō,
He was satiated. | Not | he finished them. | "Quick | carry it | that | her dish,

amiaʟk!ō'ʟēta ʟtcu'qoapa ē'ʟacq!ō ʟᴇmē'pōtcxnāna. Aqa
put it down | water in | her dish | your sisters-in-law. | Then

mXatk!oā'ya." Iō'ya ikō'sa-ît. Iō'yam yaXi ikak!ō'ʟitîXpa.
come home." | He went | mink. | He arrived | that | lake at.

Itcē'gᴇlga yaXi icq!ō'. Igē'kîm ikō'sa-ît: "Ma'nîx ʟān aʟgigᴇlgā'ya
He took it | that | dish. | He said | mink: | "When | somebody | takes

gi icq!ō', anʟxk!ā'ya ʟxᴇ'leu. Wā'2gua anʟō'ctga," igē'kîm
this | dish, | I shall haul her | ashore. | All day | I lie down with her," | said

ikō'sa-ît. Lᴇp, lᴇp, lᴇp, lᴇp igē'x yaXi iʟā'la. Kā itcigᴇlgā't
mink. | Boil, | boil! | did | that | lake. | Where | he held

lost it. He did not see anyone. He went home. His elder brother spoke to him: "Why did you insult your sister-in-law?" And Mink thought: "He knows already what I said."

After a few days, Mink's elder brother spoke: "Let us go and see your sister-in-law. We are hungry." On the following morning they went. After they had gone some time they met a person. He bathed to secure good luck in gambling. A tree lay over the water and he was sitting on its end. Mink said to his brother, the Panther: "What do you think? I will push him and see if he will drown." "Oh, let him alone, he will kill us." His elder brother looked and Mink was already swimming toward that man. He carried his quiver under his arm. Now he reached him and pushed him three times. Then the man took him and threw him away. He fell down far away from that place. His elder brother searched for him and found him. He was dead. Then he took some water and blew on him. Mink

---

yaXi icq!ō', k!Em itcionā'xLatck. Nāct itcî'LqElkEl LgoaLē'lX.
that dish, nothing he lost it. Not he saw a person.

Igē'Xk!oa. Itciō'lXam ē'yalXt: "Qā'tsqē aqa mLElgē'xkLalEtcL
He went home. He said to him his elder brother: "Why then you insulted them

LEmē'pōtcxEnāna?" IgixLō'xoa-it ikō'sa-ît: "Ā'nqa L! itēlō'xo-ix·it
your sisters-in-law?" He thought mink: "Already, behold he knows it

tauqā'tk inE'kîm."
what I said."

Aqā'watîX ictō'qoya, igē'kîm ē'yalXt ikō'sa-ît: "Atxō'ya.
Several times they slept, he said his elder brother mink: "Let us go.

Atxgō'kctam amē'pōtcxan. Ō'la atxō'ya." Wāx igē'tcuktîX,
We will go and see your sister-in-law. To-morrow we will go." Next day it became day.

kawī'X aqa ictō'ya. Qā'xpa Lq îctō'yam, iLkcō'ckam LgoaLē'lX,
early then they went. Somewhere they arrived, they met him a person,

iLxqoā'tōL. Ē'Lukuma iLxEgElqoā'tōL. Iā'gîlx·ELqîX yaXi ē'mqō;
he washed himself to obtain a supernatural helper. Itlukum he washed to obtain a supernatural helper for it. It lay with one end over the water that tree;

kē'mkitîX Lē'guxt. ILqLxLā'tak^{u}t: "Qā imē'Xaqamit ā'pXō,
at the end he was sitting. He moved his arms playing itlukum. "How your mind elder brother,

pō inLō'sEmit pō L!lap iLō'ya?" "Ō, iā'c LE'xa, LgoaLē'lX
if I push him if under water he goes?" "Oh, let alone do him, the person

aLktxōtē'na." Igē'kikct ē'yalXt; ā'nqa yuk!uē'Xat ikō'sa-ît.
he will kill us." He looked his elder brother; already swam mink.

IgimElā't iā'q!ētsxō. ItcLgō'qoam LaXi LgoaLē'lX. ItcLō'sEmit.
He carried under his arm his quiver. He reached that person. He pushed him.

Lō'nîX itcLō'sEmit. ILgē'gElga, iLgēxē'ma. L!uX ēyuLā'taXit.
Three times he pushed him. He took him, he threw him away. Falling down he fell down.

KElā'îX igixē'maXitam. Itcionā'xLam ē'yalXt. Iqionā'xLam
Far he came falling down. He searched for him his elder brother. He was searched for

ikō'sa-ît. Iqiō'cgam ikō'sa-ît. Iō'mEqt. Itci'LgElga Ltcu'qoa
mink. He was found mink. He was dead. He took it water

recovered and said: "I have slept; behold, that fellow waked me. Take care; I will shoot him." "Did you sleep? You were dead. That person killed you and threw you away."

They went a long distance. Now the elder brother heard a person. He did not tell his younger brother. Now Mink also heard that person. He was singing: "I sharpen my nails for Mink and his elder brother." Mink said: "What does that person sing about us?" His elder brother replied: "That person is singing: 'I sharpen my nails for Mink and his elder brother.' Be quiet; he will kill us." Now they saw that person sitting on a bluff. He was sharpening his nails. "What do you think?" said Mink, "I will push him. He will be drowned." "Let him alone; he will kill us." Now his elder brother looked back and there was Mink swimming. He pushed that person twice. The person took hold of him right here and threw him away. His arm broke off. His arm fell down at one place, and his body at

---

ē'yalXt ikō'sa-ît. Pō, pō, pō, pō aqē'yux ikō'sa-ît. ʟ!pāq
his elder brother | mink's. | Blow, blow, blow, blow | he was done | mink. | Recover

igē'xôx ikō'sa-ît: "Nō'qxoyō; tatc!a itcinō'qxotcq taya'x. Iā'maq
he did | mink: | "I slept; | behold | he waked me | that one. | Shoot

atc! anilō'xoa." "Mō'qxoyo na?" Iqiō'lXam ikō'sa-ît:
surely | I shall do him." | "You slept | [int. part.]?" | He was told | mink:

"Imō'maqt. Iʟgᴇ'muwaq ʟgoaʟē'lX, iʟgᴇmxē'ma."
"You were dead. | He killed you | the person, | he threw you away."

Aqa wi ictō'ya. Kᴇlā'iX ictō'yam. Igixᴇltcᴇ'maq yaXi
Then | again | they went. | Far | they arrived. | He heard something | that

ē'yalXt. Itcʟtcᴇ'maq ʟgoaʟē'lX. Nā2ct igixᴇlgu'ʟîtck iā'mXîX.
his elder brother. | He heard him | a person. | Not | he told | his younger brother.

Igixᴇltcᴇ'maq ikō'sa-ît. Itcʟtcᴇ'maq ʟaXi ʟgoaʟē'lX. ʟxō'la ʟaXi
He heard something | mink. | He heard him | that | person. | He said much | that

ʟgoaʟē'lX: "Ikō'sa-îta wē'yalXt qa năck!itᴇla wagᴇ'ʟxoatē."
person: | "Mink | and his elder brother | where | I sharpen for them | my nails."

Igē'kîm ikō'sa-ît: "Qā ʟktxoxō'la ʟgoaʟē'lX?" Itciō'lXam ē'yalXt:
He said | mink: | "How | does he talk | the person?" | He said to him | his elder brother:

"ʟxō'la ʟgoaʟē'lX: 'Ikō'sa-îta wē'yalXt năck!itᴇla wagᴇ'ʟxoatē.'
"He says much | the person: | 'Mink | and his elder brother | I sharpen for them | my nails.'

Qā'txōa ac qān mxā'ʟxôx; aʟktxotē'na." Icgᴇ'ʟqᴇlkᴇl ʟaXi
Must | and | quiet | be; | he will kill us." | They saw him | that

ʟgoaʟē'lX itcā'lampa ʟōxt. Iʟgō'k!oala aʟā'ʟxoatē. "Qā
person | bluff on | he was. | He sharpened them | his nails. | "How

imē'Xaqamē?" igē'kîm ikō'sa-ît. "Anʟō'sᴇmita. ʟ!lap aʟō'ya."
your mind?" | said | mink. | "I will push him. | Under water | he will go."

"Iā'c ʟᴇ'xa; aʟktxōtē'na." Ē'wa igē'xôx ē'yalXt, ka yaXī'
"Let alone | do him; | he will kill us." | Thus | did | his elder brother, | and | there

iuk!uē'Xat ikō'sa-ît. Itcʟō'sᴇmit ʟaXi ʟgoaʟē'lX. Mô'kctîX
swam | mink. | He pushed him | that | person. | Twice

itcʟō'sᴇmit. Iʟgē'gᴇlga gipā'tîX, iʟgexē'ma. Nau'i k!ut igē'xox
he pushed him. | He took him | here, | he threw him away. | At once | break | did

another place. His elder brother searched for him and found him. He had only one arm. Then he shot a squirrel and put its arm onto Mink. He blew water on him and he recovered. "I have slept," said Mink, "Behold, you waked me!" "Did you sleep? You were dead." "I will shoot him who waked me."

Now they went again and came to a lake. A swan was swimming there. It had two heads. Mink said to his elder brother: "Shoot that swan." "No, that swan is a monster; you see it has two heads." "Oh, shoot it!" He made his brother tired, and he shot the swan; then it turned over. Mink said: "I will swim and get it." But his elder brother said: "No, they will drown you; you will be drowned in that lake." He looked away and already Mink was swimming in the lake. He reached the swan and took it. Then both of them went down. His elder brother cried: "Oh, poor brother! Now they have

---

ē'yaxō. Kᴇlā'iX iyoʟā'taXit ē'yaxō, kᴇlā'iX yā'xka iqexē'ma.
his arm. Far it fell down his arm, far he fell down.

Itciō'naxʟ ē'yalXt. Iqiō'naxʟ ikō'sa-ît. Iqiō'ckam ikō'sa-ît; aqa
He searched for him his elder brother. He was searched for mink. He was found mink; then

ē'nat k¡ā ē'yaxō. Iā'maq itcē'lôx ik¡ā'ōtᴇn ē'yalXt ikō'sa-ît.
one side none his arm. Shoot he did it a squirrel his elder brother mink.

IqigE'q¡oaʟk ik¡ā'otᴇn ē'yaxō. Iqē'yôx pō, pō, pō, pō, ʟtcu'qoa
It was put on him the squirrel its arm. It was done blow, blow, blow, blow, water

pō'po iqʟē'lôx. ʟ¡pāq igē'xôx: "Nā'qxoyō," igē'kîm ikō'sa-ît.
blown was on him. Recover he did: "I slept," he said mink.

"Tatc¡a iqenō'qōtcq." "Mō'qoyō na? Imō'maqt." "Ē, iā'maq
"Behold I was waked." "You slept [int. part.]? You were dead." "Eh, shoot

atc¡ anēlō'xoa," itciō'lXam ē'yalXt.
surely I shall do him," he said to him his elder brother.

Aqa wi ictō'ya. Qā'xpa qicgiū'ckam iʟā'la. Iuk¡uē'x·ala
Then again they went. Somewhere they found it a lake. It swam

iqelō'q. Cmôkct ciā'q¡aqctaq yaXi iqelō'q. Itciō'lXam ikō'sa-ît
a swan. Two its heads that swan. He said to him mink

ē'yalXt: "Iā'maq ē'lôx yaXi iqelō'q!" "K¡ā'ya, iqcxē'ʟau yaXi
his elder brother: "Shoot do it that swan!" "No, a monster that

iqelō'q. Amiō'qumē môkct ciā'q¡aqctaq." "Qā'txoa iā'maq ē'lôx!"
swan. You see it two its heads." "Must shoot do it!"

Tā‡ll itcī'yux ē'yalXt, aqa iā'maq itcē'lôx. Kopā' igicᴇltcgē'x·it
Tired he made him his elder brother, then shoot he did him. Then it turned over

yaXi iqelō'q. Igē'kîm ikō'sa-ît: "Anuk¡uē'x·iya; aniuguā'lᴇmam."
that swan. He said mink: "I will swim; I will go and take it."

Igē'kîm yaXi ē'yalXt: "K¡ā'ya, aqimō'ʟat¡amᴇnqᴇma
He said that his elder brother: "No, you will be drowned

ē'yagi'ʟat¡ā'mᴇnqîX." Igē'kikct ē'yalXt, ā'nqa yaXi iuk¡uē'Xat
his means of drowning." He looked his elder brother, already that swam

ikō'sa-ît. Itcigō'qoam yaXi iqelō'q. Itcē'gᴇlga. ʟ¡lap ictō'ya
mink. He reached it that swan. He took it. Under water they went

ckanacmô'kct. IgigE'tcax ē'yalXt: "Ō, igoā'ʟᴇlX itcā'mXîX.
both. He cried his elder brother: "Oh, poor my younger brother.

eaten him." He made five fires and heated stones in all of them. When the stones were hot, he threw them into the lake and made the water boil. Now the lake was boiling. He had used all his stones. The lake became dry and all the monsters were lying on the dry bottom. Their mouths were about a fathom long. He cut the bellies of the large monsters. He finished them all, but he did not find his brother. Then he cut the bellies of the smaller monsters. He cut them all, but he did not find his brother. Then the Panther cried again. Finally he cut the bellies of the small monsters. He cut them all. Now there was only one large newt left. He had skipped it. He cried again. He gave up the hope of finding his brother. Now only that newt was left. He stopped crying. Now he cut its belly. There was Mink holding the swan. He carried him to the water; he blew on him and he recovered. He said: "I have slept; behold, he waked me.

Aqa iqē'wulq¡." IgaēXᴇ'lgiʟx; qui'nᴇm tqā'lᴇptckîX itcî'tôx.
Then he is eaten." He made a fire; five fires he made them.

Iʟē'xᴇltq; kanamtqoā'nᴇm taXi tᴇ'tōʟ iʟē'Xᴇltᴇq. Iʟō'tcqa-it
He heated stones; all five those fires he heated stones. They were hot

ʟaXi ʟqᴇ'nakc. Aqa itcī'yutcXᴇm yaXi ikak¡ō'ʟîtX. Aqa lᴇp
those stones. Then he made boil that lake. Then boil

igē'x ya'Xi ikak¡ō'ʟitX. Ka'nauwē ʟaXi ʟqᴇ'nakc iʟXᴇ'ʟXōm.
did that lake. All those stones he used them all.

Aqa q¡ᴇ'cq¡ᴇc igē'x yaXi iʟā'la. Aqa itcō'k¡umaxXacā'îX
Then dry became that lake. Then he hauled on dry land

tqcxēʟā'wukc. ʟXuan itā'nXamax tgā'kᵘcXatkc. ʟ¡ᴇ'xʟ¡ᴇx
the monsters. Perhaps each one fathom their mouths. Cut

itcî'tôx tgā'unakc, ka'nauwē taXi gitā'qa-iʟax tqcxēʟā'wukc.
he did them their bellies, all those large monsters.

Itctō'ʟXum. Nāct itciō'cgam iā'mXiX. Aqa taXi mank ksᴇ'max
He finished them. Not he found him his younger brother. Then those a little small

tqcxēʟā'wukc ka'nauwē ʟ¡ᴇ'xʟ¡ᴇx itcî'tôx tgā'unakc. Itctâ'ʟXum
monsters all cut he did them their bellies. He finished them

ka'nauwē. Nāct itciō'cgam iā'mXîX. Aqa wi igigᴇ'tcax yaXi
all. Not he found him his younger brother. Then again he cried that

ik¡oayawa'. Aqa atā'xt¡ax taXi ksᴇ'max ʟ¡ᴇ'xʟ¡ᴇx itcî'tôx
panther. Then next again those small ones cut he did them

tgā'unakc. Ka'nauwē ʟ¡ᴇ'xʟ¡ᴇx itcî'tôx. AēXt wuXi aq¡asᴇ'na;
their bellies. All cut he did them. One that newt:

itcā'qa-iʟ wuXi aq¡asᴇ'na. Tcaq¡ᴇ'l'ēyîpX ac qayaxkuā'x. Aqa
large that newt. Refuse (left over) and it was skipped. Then

wi igigᴇ'tcax, igigᴇ'tcax. Tᴇ'mēnua igē'xôx atciucgā'm iā'mXîX.
again he cried, he cried. Give up he did he finds him his younger brother.

Aqa ā'ema iguk¡oā'etiXît wuXi aq¡asᴇ'na. Qān igē'xôx; igigᴇ'tcax,
Then only is lying there that newt. Silent he became; he cried,

tcXua ʟ¡ᴇx itcī'yôx itcā'wan. Kōpā' igē'xôx ikō'sa-ît. Itcigᴇlgā't
then cut he did it its belly. There he was mink. He held it

yaXi iqēlō'q. Itcī'yukᴛ ʟtcu'qoapa. Itcī'yux pō, pō, pō, pō,
that swan. He carried him water to. He did him blow, blow, blow, blow,

āc tXu itcilXā'takua. ItcîlXā'takua ikō'sa-ît: "Nō'qxoyō, tatc¡a
and he recovered. He recovered mink: "I slept, behold!

I will shoot him." But his elder brother said: "Did you sleep? You were dead."

Now they went again. They went a long distance. In the afternoon they landed. The Panther said: "We will sleep here," and made a fire. Mink was hungry. He said to his elder brother: "I am hungry." The Panther said: "Strike those spruce trees. A deer will come out. It has long ears." Mink went and struck the spruce trees. Then a mouse ran out of the woods. "Oh, elder brother," he said, "there it runs!" His elder brother arose and looked. Only a mouse passed by. "Did you see it?" said Mink. "Only your grandmother, the mouse, passed me." "They are his grandmothers when I am not hungry."

"Quick, go and strike the spruce trees, a deer will come. If it is a buck it has antlers." Mink went and struck the spruce trees. He shouted to his elder brother: "Oh, elder brother! It is just what you told me, it has antlers." The Panther looked. A snail was crawling

---

itcinō'qotcq. Iā'maq atc; anilō'xoa." Igē'kîm ē'yalXt ikō'sa-ît:
he waked me. Shoot surely I shall do him." He said his elder brother mink:

"Mō'qxoyō na? Imō'maqt."
"You slept [int. part.]? You were dead."

Aqa wi ictō'ya. Kᴇlā'iX ictō'ya. YaXī' aqaʟā'x aqa icxē'gela-îX.
Then again they went. Far they went. There the sun then they landed.

Igē'kîm ik!oayawa': "Tē'ka gi atxōqō'ya." Iga-ixā'lgiʟx. Walō'
He said the panther: "Here this we will sleep." He made a fire. Hunger

igī'yux ikō'sa-ît. "Walō' gᴇ'nuxt," itciō'lXam ē'yalXt. "Ai'aq
acted on him. mink. "Hunger acts on me," he said to him his elder brother. "Quick

amī'ya!" iqiō'lXam ikō'sa-ît. "ʟ!ā'qʟ!āq amtō'xoa taXi
go!" he was told mink. "Strike do them those

tᴇmā'ktcXᴇmax. Ma'nîx ēmā'cᴇn alētī'ya itā'ʟqtax tiā'utcakc."
spruce trees. When a deer will come long its ears."

Iō'ya ikō'sa-ît. ʟ!ā'qʟ!āq itcī'tôx taXi tᴇmā'ktcXᴇmax. Iguā'Xit
He went mink. Strike he did them those spruce trees. It ran out

ā'cō. "Ā, āpXoyā'!" itciō'lXam ē'yalXt, "yaXi aqa iōittā'."
a mouse. "Ah, elder brother!" he said to him his elder brother, "that then coming."

Iō'tXuit ē'yalXt; igē'kikct. Ā'ema ā'cō igā'eXkoa. "Tcō'Xua,"
He stood there his elder brother; he looked. Only a mouse passed him. "Well,"

igē'kîm ikō'sa-ît, "a'ēma wuXi amē'ckîX ā'cō igā'nᴇXkoa."
he said mink, "only that your grandmother the mouse passed me."

"Tiā'ckēXᴇnana taya'x kā nîct walō' gᴇ'nutx."
"His grandmothers those when not hunger acts on me."

"Ai'aq amī'ya, ai'aq amī'ya. ʟ!ā'qʟ!aq amtō'xoa tᴇmā'ktcXᴇmax.
"Quick go, quick go. Strike do them the spruce trees.

Ma'nîx emā'cᴇn, aqa ʟiā'qtcam ma'nîx ē'kala." Iō'ya ikō'sa-ît.
When a deer, then its antlers when a male." He went mink.

ʟ!ā'qʟ!aq itcī'tôx taXi tᴇmā'ktcXᴇmax. Itcigē'lōma ē'yalXt: "Ā,
Strike he did them those spruce trees. He shouted to him his elder brother: "Ah,

āpXoyā'! ʟ!a tau imᴇnō'lXamtē ʟiā'qtcam yaXi iō'itᴇt."
elder brother! Look what you said to me, his antlers that is coming."

there. Mink came and said: "Did you see it?" The Panther replied: "I did not see anything. Only your grandmother, the snail, came there." "Those are his grandmothers," replied Mink. His elder brother said: "The deer jumps in long leaps." Mink went and struck the spruce trees. Then the bullfrog came out of the woods. "Oh, elder brother," said Mink, "there it jumps, just as you told me." The Panther took his bow and arrows, but he saw only a bullfrog. Mink came to his elder brother. "Did it pass you?" "Ah, only your great-grandfather, the bullfrog, passed me jumping." "Those are my great-grandfathers when I am not hungry."

"Quick, quick! Go and strike the spruce trees!" Mink went and struck the spruce trees. Now the rabbit ran out. He shouted to his elder brother: "There he is running!" The Panther arose and looked. Only a rabbit jumped past. Mink said: "Did you see it?" "I did

---

Igē'kiket ik¡oayawa'; ā'ema ats¡Emē'nqan ak¡Lxē't. Igitē'mam
He looked the panther; only a snail came crawling. He arrived coming

ikō'sa-ît. "Tcu'xoa imē'qElkEl?" itciō'lXam ē'yalXt. "K¡ā'ya
mink. "Well did you see it?" he said to him his elder brother. "Nothing

nîct tān inē'qElkEl. Ā'ema ats¡mō'ēqan amē'ckiX wuXi ak¡Lxē't."
not anything I saw it. Only the snail your grandmother that came crawling."

"Tiā'ckiXEnana taya'x," itciō'lXam ē'yalXt. "Ma'nîx ya'Xka
"His grandmothers those," he said to him his elder brother. "When he

emā'cEn aqa Lā'uLāu atsōpEnā'nanEma." Iō'ya ikō'sa-ît.
the deer then in leaps he will jump." He went mink.

L¡ā'qL¡aq itcî'tôx taXi tEmā'ktcXEmax. Iō'ya iq¡oatE'nxēxē,
Strike he did them those spruce trees. It went the bullfrog,

itsōpEnā'nanEmtck. "Ā, āpXoyā'!" igē'kîm ikō'sa-ît. "L¡a tau
it jumped much. "Ah, elder brother!" he said mink. "Look what

imEnō'lXam atsōpEnā'na yaXi iō'itEt." Itcā'gElga ayā'pL¡ikē
you said to me it jumps that is coming." He took it his bow

yaXi ē'yalXt. Iō'tXuit. Iā'ema iq¡oatE'nxēxē itcē'qElkEl.
that his elder brother. He stood there. Only the bullfrog he saw it.

Igitē'mam ikō'sa-ît ē'yalXtpa. "Tcu'xoa igē'mExkoa?" "Iā'ema
He arrived coming mink his elder brother at. "Well did it pass you?" "Only

emē'tc¡Emax iq¡oatE'nxēxē yaXi igē'nExkoa sōpEnā'na."
your great-grandfather the bullfrog that passed me jumping."

"Tiā'tc¡Emaxnāna taya'x kā nîct walō' gE'nuxt."
"His great-grandfathers those when not hunger acts on me."

"Ai'aq, ai'aq amī'ya! L¡ā'qL¡āq amtō'xoa taXi tEmā'ktcXEmax."
Quick, quick go! Strike do them those spruce trees."

Iō'ya ikō'sa-ît. L¡ā'qL¡āq itcî'tôx taXi tEmā'ktcXEmax. Igēwā'Xit
He went mink. Strike he did them those spruce trees. It ran away

ikanaXmE'nē. Itcigē'loma ē'yalXt: "Ā, yaXawē aqa iō'itta."
the rabbit. He shouted at him his elder brother: "Ah, here now it is coming."

Iō'tXuit ē'yalXt. Igē'kiket. Iā'ema ikanaxmE'nē tsōpEnā'na,
He stood there his elder brother. He looked. Only the rabbit it jumped,

igē'xkoa. Igē'kîm ikō'sa-ît: "Tcu'xoa imē'qElkEl?" "K¡ā'ya
it passed. He said mink: "Well did you see it?" "No

not see anything, only your great-grandfather, the rabbit." "Those are my great-grandfathers," said Mink to his elder brother.

"Quick, quick, go!" said the Panther. Mink was angry. He was lazy, and he was told several times to go. Then he went. He struck the spruce trees. Now a buck came out. Then Mink shouted: "There it goes! it has antlers, it jumps." His elder brother looked, and, indeed, a male deer was coming. He shot it and it fell down. They cut it and its stomach was very fat. They cut it and Mink received some fat. Now he ate much. They roasted the deer antlers over the fire and the Panther ate them. Mink looked at his elder brother. His hands were full of grease. He thought: "He is eating all the grease." He said: "He gave me all the dry parts to eat." Then the Panther gave him the antlers. He tried to eat them, but he could not do it, and threw them away. He said: "He gave me something very tough to eat."

It got night, and it was very clear weather. Mink had eaten enough.

---

nîct tān inē'qᴇlkᴇl. Iā'ema imē'tc!ᴇmax ikanaXmᴇ'nē."
not anything I saw it. Only your great-grandfather the rabbit."

"Tiā'tc!ᴇmaxnāna taya'x," itciō'lXam ē'yalXt ikō'sa-ît.
"His great-grandfathers those," he said to him his elder brother mink.

"Ai'aq, ai'aq amī'ya!" iqiō'lXam ikō'sa-ît. IgiXᴇ'ʟXaq ikō'sa-ît.
"Quick, quick go!" he was told mink. He became angry mink.

Iʟēx q!am. Qā'watîX iqiō'lXam, koalē'we iō'ya. ʟ!ā'qʟ!āq itcî'tôx
He was lazy. Several times he was told, only then he went. Strike he did them

taXi tᴇmā'ktcXᴇmax. Aqa iō'ya ē'kala emā'cᴇn. Aqa ixᴇ'lqamx
those spruce trees. Then he went the male deer. Then he shouted

ikō'sa-ît: "Āqa yaXi iōittā'! ʟiā'qtcam; itsōpᴇnā'na." Igē'kîkct
mink: "Now that one is coming! It has antlers; it jumps." He looked

ē'yalXt. Ā'qanuwē ē'kala emā'cᴇn itē't. Iā'maq itcē'lôx ac kopā'
his elder brother. Indeed a male deer came. Shoot he did it and there

igixē'maXit. Icgē'yuxc, ac q!ᴇ'cq!ᴇc ayā'pXᴇleu ē'yamxtcpa.
it lay. They cut it and dry its fat its stomach at.

Aqa icgī'yuxc; iqa-ilqoē'mniʟtck apXᴇ'leu ikō'sa-ît. Aqa
Then they cut it; he was given food grease mink. Then

igixʟxᴇ'lᴇmitck ikō'sa-ît. ʟ!ā'ʟ!a itcî'ʟôx ʟaXi ʟiā'qtcam emā'cᴇn.
he ate mink. Roasted over the fire he made them those its antlers the deer.

Iʟixᴇ'lᴇmux yaXi ik!oayawa'. Itcî'yukct yaXi ē'yalXt ikō'sa-ît.
He ate it that panther. He saw it that his elder brother mink.

Pāʟ ʟqā'tcau taXi tē'yakci. Iā'ema ʟgā'qatcau tixelā'x. Igē'kîm
Full fat that his hands. Only its fat he ate it. He said

ikō'sa-ît: "Nai'ka itcinᴇ'lqoēm acaēq!ᴇ'cq!ᴇc." Iqʟē'lōt ikō'sa-ît
mink: "Me he gave me to eat too dry." He was given mink

ʟaXi ʟqᴇ'tcam. Kē'nuwa iʟxᴇ'lᴇmux. Lāx îtckʟā'koa-it.
those antlers. Try he ate it. He could not do it.

Itcʟxē'ma. "Tā'nki itcinᴇ'lqoîm aca-iq!ᴇ'lq!ᴇl."
He threw it away. "Something he gave me to eat too hard."

Igō'ponᴇm. Iuq!oā'lak; tᴇmᴇ'm iuq!oā'lak. Iō'qcti aqa ikō'sa-ît.
It got dark. It was clear weather; clean it was clear weather. He was satiated then mink.

He asked his elder brother: "What is the name of the place where we sleep?" "It is forbidden to mention the name; it begins to rain when the name is uttered." "Oh, tell me!" "No, the name must not be mentioned in winter. It is forbidden to mention the name, else a long spell of rainy weather will come on." Mink said: "Oh, whisper the name into my ear." "I will tell you the name when we arrive at our next camp." Mink said again: "Oh, whisper that name into my ear." Then his elder brother told him in a low voice: "The name of this lake is Tā'îx,"[1] and Mink said: "That is good; now I know the name of this lake." Now the Panther did not know where Mink had gone. Mink shouted: "Tā'îx is the name of the lake, on the shores of which I and my brother are going to sleep; Tā'îx is its name." He shouted as loud as he could. Then Mink's brother was angry. "Oh, that bad fellow! Quick, gather sticks, that we may sit on top of them!" He gathered sticks. He gathered many. He sat down on top of

---

Itciuqu'mtcxōgoa ē'yalXt: "Qā iā'xElēwîx· qā atxoqō'ya?"
He asked him his elder brother: "How its name where we sleep?"

"Năct aqiupqEnā'xîX. Tgā'k¡ēLau. ImElā'lkuilē alixō'xoa."
"Not it is named. It is forbidden. A rainy spell it will be."

"Qā'txōa amxanElkᴛē'tcgoa." "K¡ā'ya nîct aqiupqEnā'xiX ma'nîx
"Must you tell me." "No not it is named when

tcā'xElqlîX k¡a qa iā'xEleu tayax ikak¡ō'LitîX. Tgā'k¡ēLau
winter what its name that lake. It is forbidden

aqiupqEnā'x. ImElā'lkuilē nîxō'xoax," iqiō'lXam ikō'sa-ît.
it is named. A rainy spell it gets." he was told mink.

"Qā'txoa Lawā' amiupqEnā'ya." "Ā'Lqi anxkᴛē'tcgoa; angē'ma
"Must low voice you call it." "Later on I shall tell you; I shall say

yiXă'pa intō'qoya, k¡oaLqă' iā'xElēwiX." "Ā sā'osao
there we sleep, thus its name." "Ah low voice

amiupqEnā'ya." Aqa itciō'lXam ē'yalXt: "K¡a nîct tc¡pāq
name it." Then he said to him his elder brother: "And not loud

amiupqEnā'ya. Tā'îx iā'xEleu tayax ikak¡ō'LitîX." Igē'kîm
you name it. Tā'îx its name that lake." He said

ikō'sa-ît: "Qoă'L¡ iginlō'Xuix·it iā'xEleu tayax ikak¡ō'LitîX." Aqa
mink: "All right I know it its name that lake." Then

igiunā'xLatck ikō'sa-ît. Itciunā'xLatck ē'yalXt. Iga-ixE'lqEmx
he was lost mink. He lost him his elder brother. He shouted

ikō'sa-ît: "Tā'2îx iā'xEleu ikak¡ō'LitîX antîxqō'ya wē'tcîlXt. Tā'îx
mink: "Tā'îx its name the lake we sleep my elder brother. Tā'îx

iā'xEleu, Tā'îx iā'xEleu." Tc¡pāk iga-ixE'lqamx. IgiXE'LXaq
its name, Tā'îx its name." Loud he shouted. He grew angry

ē'yalXt ikō'sa-ît: "Nā yaXī'yaX tā'nki giā'mEla! Ai'aq tgē'lkuîq
his elder brother mink's: "Oh, this thing bad! Quick those to sit on

tp¡ē'yaLX, Lgā'pEla tE'mqō tp¡ē'yāLX." Itctōp¡ē'yaLX yaXi ē'yalXt
gather them, many sticks gather them." He gathered them that his elder brother

ikō'sa-ît; Lgā'pEla itctōp¡ē'yaLX. Cā'xalîX tgē'lkuîq itixE'lux.
mink; many he gathered them. High that to sit on became.

---

[1] A lake in the mountains near the head of Cowlitz river.

them. Mink gathered only a few and lay down. Now the noise of rain was heard and a freshet came. In the morning Mink had disappeared. He drifted away with the water. Now Mink's elder brother went down the river and cried. He went a long distance and came to a jam. He searched for his younger brother at that jam. There he saw him between the logs. His stomach was full of water. He blew on him and he recovered. "I slept and that fellow waked me. I will shoot him." "Did you sleep? You were dead. You drifted down the river."

Then they came to the Panther's wife and there they stayed. There was an old man, one of the woman's relatives. Mink was teasing him all the time. Now the Panther's wife gave birth to a child. The woman's relative said to Mink: "Let us go to get wood." Mink said: "All right, we will go." Early the following morning they went across the water. There they made a fire at the foot of a fir tree.

NōL ˋka îtctōp!ē'yaLx ikō'sa-ît, aqa kōpa' igixō'kcit. Ictō'ko-iLtē,
A little only he gathered it mink, then there he lay down. It rained,

tc!āc, tc!āc, tc!āc, Luwā' iLE'xôx. Igē'tcuktîX aqa k!ā'ya ikō'sa-ît.
noise of rain, a freshet it became. Day came then nothing mink.

Iō'Xunē. IyagE'La-it ē'yalXt, aqa iō'stsō ē'yalXt ikō'sa-ît.
He drifted. He was there his elder brother, then he went down the river his elder brother mink.

Iō'qulqt, iō'stsō ik!oayawa'. KElā'îX iō'ya. ItcLō'cgam Ltcā'unē.
He cried, he went down the river the panther. Far he went. He found it a jam.

Itciō'naxL iā'mXîX kōpa', LaXi Ltcā'unēpa. Kōpā' itciō'cgam
He searched for him his younger brother there, that jam at. There he found him

iauiq!ā'yaqt LaXi Ltcā'unēpa. PāL iā'wan Ltcu'qoa. Pō, pō, pō,
he was between them that jam at. Full his belly water. Blow, blow, blow,

pō itcī'yux. ItcîlXā'takoa ikō'sa-ît. "Nâ'qxoyō, itcinō'qxotcq
blow he did him. He recovered mink. "I slept, he waked me

taya'x, iā'maq anēlō'xoa." "Mō'qxoyō na? Imō'maqt; imō'Xunē."
that one, shoot I shall do him." "You slept [int. part.]? You were dead; you drifted."

Aqa wi ictō'ya qā'eqamîX.
Then again they went down the river.

Ictō'yam wuXi ayā'kikalpa ik!oayawa'. Aqa kōpa' icxē'la-it.
They arrived that his wife at the panther. Then there they stayed.

Iq!eyō'qt yaXi iā'qôqcîn ikō'sa-ît. Ka'nauwē qā'tgemax qatcē'xax
An old man that his sister-in-law's relative mink. All kinds of ways he did to him

yaXi iā'qôqcîn. Qa-itcix·inEmō'tx·Ema-îtx. Lā4, aqa igakXE'tōm
that his sister-in-law's relative. He always made fun of him. Some time, then she gave birth

ayā'kikal ik!oayawa'. Itciō'lXam iā'qôqcîn: "Ō'la aqa tE'mEqō
his wife the panther. He said to him his relative's brother-in-law: "To-morrow then wood

atxō'ya." Igē'kîm ikō'sa-ît: "Qoā'L! atxō'ya." Kawî'X aqa
we will go for." He said mink: "All right! we will go." Early then

ictē'gōsîx·. Ictigō'samîx·. Aqa icgiā'lEgiLx amqcî'ckan. LXuan
they went across. They came across. Then they burnt it a fir. Perhaps

The tree was *that* thick. After a little while it fell. It fell toward the water. The old man said to Mink: "Run toward the water." Mink ran and the dry fir fell just in that line. It broke to pieces and all the bark came off. The old man thought: "Thus I killed him." Thus he said to Mink. The old man put the dry wood in piles and took off all the bark. Then he went down and came to his canoe. It was almost filled with dry wood. Mink had piled the wood up in the canoe. Then the old man said to him: "Little rascal!" But Mink said: "You are an old man and you are strong, not I." They put the dry wood into the canoe. It was full. Mink thought: "Where shall I stay? The canoe is full." The old man said: "I will put you into the basket with our wedges." He put stones into the bottom of the basket and placed him on top. He put the wedge [basket] on top of the wood. Now they went across. When they came to the middle of the

---

ă'wa itcā'pᴇlatax agā'qalᴇmq, as nō'ʟ!îX aqa igō'itcō. Igō'-itcō
thus thick its bark, and a little while then it fell. It fell

ē'wa maʟnata'. Aqa iqiō'lXam ikō'sa-ît: "Mᴇ'kta ē'wa maʟnata'."
thus toward the water. Then he was told mink: "Run thus toward the water."

Igē'kta ikō'sa-ît. Pā iga-ēlō'yumXit wuXi aqᴇ'lᴇmq igō'itcō.
He ran mink. There just in that line that its bark fell.

ʟ!mā'nʟ!mān igā'x wuXi amqcî'ckan. Ka'nauwē ʟāq igaxā'x
Broken to pieces was that fir. All come off did

agā'qalᴇmq. Igixʟō'Xoa-it yaXi iq!eyō'qt: "Qoā'ʟ! aqa
its bark. He thought that old man: "All right, now

iyamō'waq." Iqiō'lXam ikō'sa-ît. Itcaxtqoā'lalᴇmtck wuXi
I killed him." He was told mink. He piled it up that

aqᴇ'lᴇmq yaXi iq!eyō'qt. Sāq! tc!u'xtc!ux itcō'xoa wuXi
bark that old man. All strip off he did it that

aqᴇ'lᴇmq. Aqa iō'ʟxa. Iō'yam ictā'Xanim. Q!oā'p pāʟ alixō'xa
bark. Then he went down to the water. He arrived at their canoe. Nearly full it was going to be

aqā'lᴇmq. ItcakXatqoā'la ikō'sa-ît. Itciō'lXam iā'qôqcîn: "ʟqa
bark. He had piled it up mink. He said to him his sister-in-law's relative: "Maybe

tānki mxēlâ'l ʟaXi ʟqoē'tgaitgai." Ige'kîm ikō'sa-ît: "Mq!eyō'qt
something you do that little rascal." He said mink: "You are an old man

mā'yax alamxelō'l." Icgā'kXatk wuXi aqᴇ'lᴇmq. Pāʟ ictā'xanim.
you you do it." They put into the canoe that bark. Full their canoe.

IgixʟōʼXoa-it ikō'sa-ît: "Qā'xpa ʟq anakʟā'eta?" Pāʟ igē'xôx
He thought mink: "Where maybe I shall stay?" Full was

ictā'xanim. Itciō'lXam iā'qôqcîn: "Gipā' gi txā'qcqᴇmapa
their canoe. He said to him his relative's brother-in-law: "Here these our wedges to

ayamᴇlgē'tga." Iqō'mxōm tē'loxt taXi tctā'qcqᴇma. Itcʟᴇ'lgitk
I shall put you." A basket they were in those their wedges. He put them into it

ʟqᴇ'nakc. ʟᴇ'gigoala itcʟᴇ'lgītk. Aqa itcē'lgītk iā'qôqcîn.
stones. Below them he put them into it. Then he put him into it his relative' brother-in-law

Iqē'lgītk ikō'sa-ît. Caxala' tᴇ'ctamqōpa itciakxa'ema. Aqa
He was put into it mink. On top their wood he put him into the canoe. Then

bay, the old man made the canoe shake. Mink fell into the water and went down. Then the old man thought: "Now I have killed him." The old man came home. A person was walking up and down. He looked just like Mink. The old man landed. Then Mink came down and said: "You stayed a long time and I brought our wedges and hammers home already." "Ha, this little rascal," said the old man. Mink replied: "You are an old man and you are strong. I am only a boy. I can not do as much as you." Now they carried up all the wood. Then they stayed.

Then again he teased the old man. Sometimes he threw water on him when he was asleep; sometimes he burned him. One night the old man said: "Let us try who will stay awake longest." Mink said: "All right." He went and searched for some rotten wood. When it got dark, he put the rotten wood over his eyes. The old man

---

ictē'gosîx·. Kā'tcEkpa ē'maL ictō'yam. Lāx° itcī'yux ictā'Xanim.
they went across. Middle in the bay they arrived. Rock he did it their canoe.

L!ōX ioLā'tax·it ikō'sa-ît Ltcu'qoapa. L!lap iō'ya ikō'sa-ît.
Fall down he fell down mink the water into. Under water he went mink.

IgixLō'Xoa-it yaXi iq!eyō'qt: "Q!oā'L!, aqa inī'waq." Q!oā'p
He thought that old man: "All right, now I killed him." Nearly

iō'yam yaXi iq!eyō'qt. Aqa Lktā'la LgoaLē'lX. Ya'Xka L!a
he arrived that old man. Then he walked about a person. He behold!

ikō'sa-ît iLā'lkuilē. Igixē'gela-îX yaXi iq!eyō'qt. Igē'Lxam
mink he resembles him. He landed that old man. He came down to the beach

ikō'sa-ît: "Lē'lē k!ā'ya imE'xôx, ā'nqa întE'Lam txā'qeqama k!a
mink: "Long nothing you were, long ago I brought them our wedges and

txā'LxalōLa." "Lqa tā'nki mxelâ'l LaXi Lqoē'tgaitgai."
our hammers." "Maybe something you do that little rascal."

"Mq!eyō'qt mā'yax alamxelō'l. Nai'ka nk!ā'skas Lqa pō nîct
"You are an old man you you do it. I I a boy maybe if not

nxelō'l." Icktō'kuiptck ka'nauwē ta'Xi tE'ctamqō. Aqa wi
I do it." They carried it up all that their wood. Then again

Lxē'la-it.
they stayed.

Ka'nauwē qā'tgemax qatciō'xoa-itx yaXi iā'qôqcîn. Anā'
All kinds of ways he did to him that his sister-in-law's relative. Sometimes

Ltcu'qoa wax qatcLigō'xoax. Kā iō'qxoyō yaXi iq!eyō'qt, aqa
water pour out he did on him. When he slept that old man, then

Ltcu'qoa wāx aqLigō'xoax. Anā' qatcixtElā'max iā'qôqcîn ikō'sa-ît.
water pour out it was done on him. Sometimes he burned him his sister-in-law's relative mink.

Agōnā'pōl itciō'lXam iā'qôqcîn: "AtXumgē'tga, atxE'gElEma."
One night he said to him his relative's brother-in-law: "Let us go, we will be awake."

Igē'kîm ikō'sa-ît: "Qoā'L!." Itconā'xLam ikō'sa-ît apLx·ā'înq.
He said mink: "All right." He went to search for it mink rotten wood.

Igō'ponEm, iga-ixE'lôx siā'xostpa wuXi apLx·ā'înq. Nigē'kctx
It got dark, he put it on his eyes on that rotten wood. He looked

looked and he saw Mink's eyes open all the time. Then it got daylight. "Ha, you little rascal," said the old man. [Mink replied:] "You are an old man and you are strong. I am only a boy. I can not do as much as you." Then the old man gave it up.

He thought: "I will tell him to bring me a wolf; he shall devour him." On the following morning the old man told him: "Quick, go and bring me two wolves. They were my playmates when I was a boy." Mink went and came to the wolf's house. He said: "I come to fetch you. My sister-in-law's relative told me to bring you." They said: "Well." He brought them and threw them down before the old man. They bit him. "Quick, take them away; they do not like me." Mink took them away and carried them back.

Another day, the old man said: "Quick, bring me two bears." Mink went and arrived at the house of the bears. "I came to fetch you." He carried them home and threw them down before the old man. They slapped him with their paws. "Ah, what is he doing, that little rascal?" "You are an old man and you are strong. I am

---

yaXi iq¡eyō'qt. Igē'qamit ikō'sa-ît qatciō'kctx. Igē'qamit ikō'sa-ît.
that old man. He saw (had his eyes open) mink he saw him. He saw (had his eyes open) mink.

Wāx nitcō'ktxîX: "ʟqa tā'nki mxelâ'l ʟaXi ʟqoē'tgaitgai."
Next morning it got day: "Maybe something you do that little rascal."

"Mq¡eyō'qt mai'ka tatc¡a mxelō'l; ʟqa pō nai'ka nk¡ā'skas nîct
"You are an old man you behold! you do; maybe if I I am a boy not

nxēlō'l." Aqa tä'menua igē'x yaXi iq¡eyō'qt.
I do." Then give up he did that old man.

Igîxʟō'Xoa-it yaXi iq¡eyō'qt: "ʟlē'q¡amō aniʟgElō'goatcgoa.
He thought that old man: "Wolves I shall send for them.

K¡ō'ma aqēwu'lq¡ama." Qāxʟkanē'goa itciō'lXam iā'qôqcîn: "Ai'aq
Perhaps he will be killed." One day he said to him his relative's brother-in-law: "Quick

ʟgā'lEmam ʟlē'q¡amō kaqa nk¡ā'skas igE'xēmōtxEmX." Iō'ya
fetch the wolves, when I was a boy I played with them." He went

ikō'sa-ît. Iō'yam ʟlē'q¡amō tE'ʟaqʟ. Itccō'lXam: "Iamtgā'lEmam.
mink. He arrived the wolves their house. He said to two of them: "I came to fetch you two.

Itcî'qôqcîn itcîntō'koatck." Acgiō'lXam: "Tgt¡ō'kti." Itccō'k·ɪam.
My sister-in-law's relative sent me." They two said to him: "Well." He brought them.

ItccilXā'kuēq iā'qôqcîn. Icgē'x·tca yaXi iq¡eyō'qt. "Ai'aq cE'k·ɪa;
He threw them down to his sister-in-law's relative. They two bit him that old man. "Quick carry them;

cgEnEXE'ʟEluxt." Itcî'cukɪ ikō'sa-ît. Itccō'k·ɪam tE'ctaqʟpa.
they do not like me." He carried them mink. He brought them two their house to.

Igonē'gua: "Ai'aq sgā'lEmam skē'ntXoa." Iō'ya ikō'sa-ît.
Another day: "Quick fetch them two two black bears." He went mink.

Itcgō'qoam skē'ntXoa tE'ctaqʟpa. "Iamtgā'lEmam." Itcî'cukɪ,
He arrived at the two bears their home at. "I came to fetch you two." He carried them two,

igē'Xk¡oa. Itccō'k·ɪam. ItccîlXā'kuēq iā'qôqcîn. P¡a'qp¡aq
he went home. He brought them two. He threw them down to his sister-in-law's relative. Slap

icgī'yux. "ʟqa tā'nki mxēlâ'l ʟaXi ʟqoē'tgaitgai!" "Mq¡eyō'qt,
they two did him. "Maybe something you do that little rascal!" "You are an old man,

only a boy. I can not do as much as you." "Quick, take them away." Mink took them away and carried them home to their house.

After a few days he told him to bring two raccoons. Mink went and brought the raccoons. He brought them to the house and threw them down before the old man. They scratched him all over. "Take them away. They do not know me. When I was young they used to know me." He took them away and carried them home. On the following day the woman's relative told him: "Bring me two grizzly bears from that mountain. Long ago I used to play with them." Mink went and came to the mountain. He told the grizzly bears: "I came to fetch you. My sister-in-law's relative wants you." They said: "All right, take us." He carried them home and threw them down before the old man. They scratched and tore his whole body. Then the old man cried much. Mink's elder brother told him to take them away. He took them away and carried them back.

That is the story; to-morrow it will be good weather.

---

ma'yax ālamxēlō'l; ʟqa pō nai'ka nk¡ā'skas pō nîct nxēlō'l."
you you do it; maybe if I I am a boy if not I do it."

"Ai'aq cî'kʟa!" Itccî'cukʟ ikō'sa-ît. Itccō'kʟam tᴇ'ctaqʟpa.
"Quick carry them!" He carried them mink. He brought them their house to.

Qā'watîX ʟq iō'qoya-îX ac tā'xt cʟatā't itccigᴇlō'koatck. Iō'ya
Several times perhaps they slept and next two raccoons he sent him for them. He went

ikō'sa-ît. Itcî'cukʟ cʟatā't. Itccō'kʟam tᴇ'ʟaqʟpa. ItccîlXā'kuēq
mink. He carried them two raccoons. He brought them their house to. He threw them down to

iā'qôqcîn. Icgiō'pēqʟa ka'nauwē. "Cᴇ'kʟa! aqa cgēnxᴇ'ʟᴇluX.
his sister-in-law's relative. They scratched him all. "Carry them two! now they do not like me.

Akoanitsik¡aē'ts aqa cgᴇ'nokul." Itcî'cukʟ cʟatā't. Itccō'kʟam
When I was young then they knew me." He carried them two the two raccoons. He brought them

tᴇ'ctaqʟpa.
their house to.

WāX igē'tcuktîX, itcō'lXam iā'qôqcîn: "Cgā'lᴇmam cā'yim yaXi
Early it got day, he said to him his sister-in-law's relative: "Fetch them two two grizzly bears that

ipā'kalpa. Cgᴇ'xēmōtXᴇmX ā'nqa." Iō'ya ikō'sa-ît. Iō'yam yaXi
mountain on. I played with them long ago." He went mink. He arrived that

ipā'kalpa. Itccō'lXam cā'yim: "Iamtgā'lᴇmam. Itcî'qôqcîn
mountain on. He said to the two two grizzly bears: "I came to fetch you. My sister-in-law's relative

itcîntō'koatck." Icgiō'lXam: "Qoā'ʟ¡ imᴇntgā'lᴇmam." Itcî'cukʟ.
he sent me." They two said to him: "All right, fetch us." He carried them two.

IgiXk¡oā'mam. ItccîlXā'kuēq iā'qôqcîn. Icgiō'pēqʟa; ka'nauwē
He came home. He threw them down to his sister-in-law's relative. They two scratched him; all

ē'yaʟq ʟ¡mᴇ'nʟ¡mᴇn icgî'yux. Icixᴇlqē'ʟxalᴇmtck yaXi iq¡eyō'qt.
his body torn they made it. He cried with pain that old man.

Itciō'lXam ē'yalXt ikō'sa-ît: "Cᴇ'kʟa." Itcî'cukʟ ikō'sa-ît.
He said to him his elder brother mink: "Carry them two." He carried them mink.

Itccaqᴇlō'kctxam. K¡anē'k¡anē, ō'la asa-igā'p.
He carried them back on his back. The story, to-morrow it will be good weather.

Robin and Salmon-berry (told 1891)

Robin and Salmon-berry were sisters. They lived on opposite sides of one house. Every day they went picking berries. In the evening they came home. Robin's berries were all unripe, Salmon-berry's were all ripe. Robin used to eat right away all the ripe ones that she found. They went out often. One day Robin said: "Louse me." Then Salmon-berry loused her. When she had finished, Salmon-berry said: "Now you louse me." Robin loused her and said: "Oh, your louse is sweet." In the evening they went home. On the next day they did the same thing again. First Robin was loused, and afterward she loused Salmon-berry. They went out often and Robin said: "Oh, younger sister, your louse is sweet.

Amē'sgaga ictā'k!anē k!a Ā'lele

Robin Their Myth and Salmon-berry

Agā'mtXiX tēXt tE'ctaqL cī'xak!anatētōL. Ka'nauwē Lkā'etax
Her younger sister one their house they two on opposite sides. All days

qacxElō'kca-îtx. QacXk!oā'mamx. Tsō'yustîX qacXk!oā'mamx.
they picked berries. They came home. In the evening they came home.

Lā'ema kLuwā'qē itcā'k!ēwula amē'sgaga. Ka'nauwē Lōkst
Only unripe what she gathered robin. All ripe

itcā'k!ēwula ā'lele. Manē'x agucgā'mx ōkst amē'sgaga, ā'nqa
what she gathered salmon berry. When she found it a ripe one robin, already

aguwu'lq!amx. Ē'2LaqawatîX ictō'ya. Igā'kîm amē'sgaga:
she ate it. Several times they two went. She said robin:

"Qâi imLEngE'qikct!" Aqa LagE'qikct amē'sgaga. IkLā'qōLq
"Must you louse me!" Then she loused her robin. She finished

LagE'qikct. Iqō'lXam ā'lele: "Amai't!ax aLamgē'qcta!"
she loused her. She was told salmon berry: "You next I louse you."

IqLagiqē'kct ā'lele. Igā'kîm amē'sgaga: "Ā its!ā'ts!emôm
She was loused salmon berry. She said robin: "Ah, sweet

gi ā'mēqct." Tsō'yustîX icī'Xk!oa. Igonē'gua k!oaLqā' wi
this your louse." In the evening they two went home. One day thus again

icī'xôx. Ā'newa amē'sgaga iqLagE'qēkct, kē'qamtqîX ā'lele
they did. First robin was loused, afterward salmon berry

iqLagE'qēkct. Tcā'xēXL qictō'ya. Aqa igō'lXam: "Ō, ā'tcē!
was loused. Several times they went. Then she said to her: "Oh, younger sister!

Its!ā'ts!emôm gi ā'mēqct. Qa imē'Xaqamē pō iamō'wulq!.
Sweet this your louse. How you mind if I eat you.

What do you think, I will eat you. Then I shall wail for you all the time." Salmon-berry replied: "No; your nephews would be poor." They came home and Salmon-berry told her children: "That monster said she would eat me. If she really should eat me, don't stay here any longer. Go away at once, else she will eat you also. If she tries to deceive you, do not believe her." Robin's children were all girls. Salmon-berry's children were all boys.

Robin and her younger sister went out often. One night Robin came home alone. Behold, she had cut the neck of her younger sister. Then Salmon-berry's sons thought: "She has killed her." The name of Salmon-berry's eldest son was Wā'ckōk!umai'hē. Robin said: "Your mother lost her way." One of Salmon-berry's sons was small. He was still an infant. It was night, but Salmon-berry's eldest son remained awake. He thought that Robin might try to eat them when they were asleep. While he was awake, she arose and went out slowly. She threw Salmon-berry's breasts into the fire. Then

---

Ka'nauwē ʟqetā'kemax iamgᴇ'mtcax." Igō'lXam: "K!ā'ya
All years I cry for you." She said to her: "No,

ʟā'gēyutkoax ʟmē'wulXnāna." IcXk!oā'mam. Igaxa-îlgu'ʟîtck
poor your nephews." They came home. She told him

itcā'xan ā'lele: "Igᴇnuxō'la wuXi aqcxē'ʟau aganuwu'lq!ama.
her son salmon berry: "She said to me much that monster she will eat me.

Ma'nîx qēnagᴇnwu'lq!ama, nau'i kᴇlā'îX amcō'ya. Nāct
When she eats me, at once far go. Not

tē'ka amcxelā'-ita, yā'okîX agamcᴇwu'lq!amx. Ma'nîx lā'xlax
here stay, else she will eat you. When deceive

agᴇmcō'xoa, nēct ā'qanuē amxʟuXuā'ita." Ka'nauwe tᴇ'nᴇmckc
she does you, not indeed you think." All females

itcā'qôq amē'sgaga. Ā'lele ka'nauwē tkā'lukc itcā'qôq.
her children robin. Salmon berry all males her children.

Qā'watîX ictō'ya amē'sgaga k!a agā'mtX. Xā'pîX aqa
Several times they went robin and his sister. At dark then

igaXatk!oā'mam amē'sgaga ā'ema. Qōct, ʟq!up igiā'xôx itcā'tuk
she came home robin alone. Behold, cut she did it her neck

wuXi agā'mtXîX. Igixʟō'xoa-it yaXi itcā'xan ā'lele: "Ā'qa
that her younger sister. He thought that her son salmon berry: "Now

igō'waq." Wā'ckōk!umai'hē iā'xaleu yaXi itcā'xan ā'lele yaXi
she killed her." Wā'ckōk!umai'hē his name that her son salmon berry that

ixgᴇ'qunq. Ikʟō'lXam: "Igomā'tako-it wā'mcaq." Iū'k!oa-îts yaXi
the eldest one. She said to him: "She lost her way your mother." Small that

ēXā't itcā'xan ā'lele ixgē'sqax ka igᴇ'tukc. Igō'ponᴇm;
one her son salmon berry the youngest one and he sucked. It got dark;

igixᴇ'gᴇlᴇmtck yaXi ixgᴇ'qunq itcā'xan ā'lele. Igixʟō'Xoa-it
he was awake that eldest one her son salmon berry. He thought

akʟuwᴇ'lq!ama ma'nîx aʟqē'witx·ita. Qā ē'xkᴇl aqa igaxᴇ'latck;
she would eat them when they would sleep. Where he awake then she arose;

ʟāwā' igō'pa. Iktā'ʟkXatq taXi t!ō'max. Igē'kîm yaXi
slowly she went out. She threw them into the fire those breasts. He said that

Salmon-berry's son said: "Oh, my breasts, my breasts!" Robin took the breasts out of the fire and said: "He dreams of his mother's breast. To-morrow I will search for your mother." Five times she tried to throw the breasts into the fire, but that boy saw it every time. He recognized his mother's breasts.

On the following morning she made herself ready and went. Then Salmon-berry's [eldest] son made a fire. He told Robin's children: "Let us play. We will steam each other. You steam us first, then we will steam you. When we say, 'Now we are done,' you must take us out of the hole." Robin's children said: "Well, all right." Salmon-berry's children were put into the hole first. After a little they were hot, and then the eldest brother said: "Now we are done." They were taken out of the hole. They were dug out of the hole. Then they made a fire. When the stones were hot, Robin's children were put into the hole. Then they put dirt on top of them, and put large sticks over them. They said: "We are done," but Salmon-berry's son did not take them out. For a little while they cried. Then they

---

itcā'xan ā'lele: "SE'gEt¡ō, sEgEt¡ō'." Igō'guiga taXi t¡ō'max
her son salmon berry: "My breasts, my breasts." She took them those breasts

iguXuā'kuiq LXE'leuX. Igā'kîm amē'sgaga: "Ā cē'yat¡ō
she threw them away from the fire. She said robin: "Ah, his breasts,

icîXquwā'luqL. Ō'la anōnā'xLama wā'mcaq." Qoā'nEmîX kē'nuwa
he is dreaming of them. To-morrow I will go and search for her your mother." Five times try

itaxE'lgīLx taXi t¡ō'max. Ā'nqa qatcuquigE'lX yaXi ik¡ā'skas.
she threw them into the fire those breasts. Already he saw it that boy.

Qatctukulā'xqLkax wā'yaq tgā't¡ōmax.
He recognized them his mother her breasts.

Igē'tcuktîX. Aqa wi igaxE'ltXuîtck. Aqa wi igō'ya.
It became day. Then again she made herself ready. Then again she went.

Iga-ixE'lgīLx yaXi itcā'xan ā'lele. ItcLō'lXam itcā'qôq amē'sgaga:
He made a fire that her son salmon-berry. He said to them her children robin:

"Tca! alxk¡ayā'wulalEma. Alxelō'tElgEmāyaXtîX; ntcanē'watîkc
"Come! we will play. We will steam each other; us first

amEntcēlō'tgayaXtîX. Kē'qamtqîX mE'caika. Ma'nîx antcgē'ma,
you steam us. Afterward you. When we say,

'Aqa întsō'kst,' aqa Lāq° amEntcō'xoa." ILE'kîm itsā'qôq
'Now we are done,' then take out you do us." They said her children

amē'cgaga: "Qoā'L¡." IqLē'lōtgîX Lā'newatîkc ā'lele itcā'qôq, as
robin: "All right." They were put into the hole first salmon berry her children, and

nō'L¡îX iLō'skoa-ît. "Ā'qa întsō'kst," igē'kîm ya'Xi ē'LalXt. Lāq°
a little while they became hot. "Now we are done," he said that their elder brother. Take out

iqE'Lôx. Aqa wi LE'kLEk itcī'yoxo-îX. Wē't'ax iga-ixE'lgiLx.
they were done. Then again dig he did it. Again he made a fire.

ILō'tcqa-it LaXi LqE'nakc. Aqa aLā'et¡ikc amē'sgaga itcā'qôq
They were hot those stones. Then next robin her children

iqLē'lōtgîX. IqLgE'tkîq ya'Xi ēlX. ItctE'LkXatq taXi tE'mqō
were put into the hole. It was put on top that dirt. They were put on those sticks

gitā'qaēLax. Kē'nuwa iLE'kîm: "A'qa întsō'kst." Näct Lāq°
large ones. Try they said: "Now we are done." Not take out

became silent. They were dead. All of Robin's five children were dead.

Wā'ckōk¡umai'he left them in there until they were all done. Then he took them out. He put the one near the water. He twisted its mouth. The youngest one was put into the water; one he put on top of the house, another one he placed upright near the door. He put one on the ground and placed it as if it were playing with shells. Then he dug a hole and they escaped through the hole and came out again. They left their bitch at the entrance of the hole. Now they ran away. At noon Robin came home. She thought: "I will eat him when I come home." When she approached her house she saw something floating on the water. She went to her house. There she saw her daughter. She pushed her. "Where is your sister?" she said. Her finger went right into her child's flesh. She looked up. Ther was one of her daughters on the roof. "Where is your sister?" She took her arm and pulled it; it came out at once. She looked to the beach where one of her daughters was playing with shells. She

---

itcî'ʟôx; nâ'ʟ¡îX iʟxē'nimtck, aqa qān iʟᴇ'xôx. Iʟxᴇ'ʟa-it
he did them; a little while they cried, then silent they were. They were dead

ʟkanamqoā'nᴇmîkc itcā'qôq amē'sgaga.
all five her children robin.

Lē'lē ʟᴇ'xôx, ka'nauwē iʟō'kst. A'qa ʟāq° itcî'ʟôx.
Long they were, all they were done. Then take out he did them.

Itcʟōʟā'etamit ʟaXi ʟēXā't ʟtcu'qoapa q¡oā'p. Ē'wa itcī'yôx
He placed it that one water at near. Thus he made it

iʟā'kcXat. ʟa'Xi ʟēXā't itcʟalē'maʟx ʟa'Xi giʟō'k¡oa-îts.
its mouth. That one he put it into the water that small one.

Itcʟuʟā'etamit ʟēXā't sā'xalîX tqu'ʟēpa. Itcʟᴇlk¡ē'ktuwulX ʟēXā't
He placed it one up house on. He placed upright one

q¡oā'p icî'qē. Itcō'kʟa aēXā't ʟā'Xamᴇlk¡oēla itcuʟā'etamit.
near the door. He carried her one she played with shells he placed her.

ʟxoa'p itcī'yux ēlX. YaXī'pa tcXoa ʟāx iʟxō'xoam.
Hole he made the ground. There then come out they arrived.

Iʟgaqᴇ'luqʟk aʟā'k¡ōtk¡ot ya'Xi naʟxoā'pîXpa. Iʟî'xawa ā'qa.
They left her their bitch that hole at. They ran away then.

Pawē'goa igā'xk¡oa amē'sgaga. Igaxʟō'Xoa-it: "Anʟuwu'lq¡ama
Noon she home came robin. She thought: "I will eat them

ma'nîx nanXk¡oā'mam." Q¡oā'p igaXk¡oā'mam igā'kikct mā'ʟnîX,
when I come home." Near she came home she looked at the water,

a'qa tā'nki yuXunē'na. Igō'ya ēwā'tkēwa tᴇ'ʟaqʟpa. ŌtXuā'la
then something drifted. She went there their house to. There was

agā'xan icî'qēpa. Igō'sᴇmit. "Qāx amē'mtX?" igō'lXam agā'xan.
her daughter door at. She pushed her. "Where your younger sister?" she said to her her daughter.

Nau'i ʟ¡mā'n ʟᴇ'gakci yaXi ē'tcaʟqpa agā'xan. Igā'kikct cā'xalîX.
At once soft her fingers that her body in her daughter. She looked up.

Ō'guaxt tqu'ʟē agā'xan: "Qāx amē'mtX?" Igē'gᴇlga ē'tcaxō,
There was on the house her daughter: "Where your younger sister?" She took it her arm,

igā'Xatk¡a. Nau'i k¡ut igē'x ē'tcaxō. Igō'ʟxa qā
she pulled it. At once torn out was her arm. She went down where

ʟā'Xamîlk¡uēla agā'xan. Igiō'sᴇmit itcā'q¡aqctaq. "Qāx
played with shells her daughter. She pushed it her head. "Where

pushed her head. "Where is your sister?" she said. Her head broke off at once. She was dead. Then she ran to the water. She saw her daughter. She was drowned. Then she saw the one girl, whose mouth was pulled to both sides, and thought she was laughing. She said: "You are laughing and your sister is drowned." She pulled her hair. It came out at once. She pulled her youngest daughter. Her legs came out at once. Then she tried to pull her ashore. "Oh, Wā'ckōkǀumai'he has killed my children."

She went up to the house and searched for them. "Where did they go?" She did not find their tracks. After some time she found that bitch. "Where did your masters go?" "Wu!" said the bitch, pointing with her mouth in one direction. She ran that way. She tried to smell them, but she did not smell anything. Again she asked the bitch: "Where did your masters go?" "Wu!" said the bitch, pointing another way. Robin ran that way and tried the same thing. Five times the bitch deceived her. Then Robin threw her away and found that hole in the ground. She went into it and found the tracks

---

amē'mtX?" igō'lXam. Nau'i igiXELā'kuit itcā'tuk. Qōct ō'mEqt.
your younger sister?" she said to her. At once broke her neck. Behold she was dead.

Igā'kta mā'LnîX. Igā'qElkEl wuXi agā'xan, axaLnEmō'qǀoyaqt.
She ran seaward. She saw her that her daughter, she was drowned.

Igō'kcta wuXi aēXā't agā'xan axkǀayā'wula. Igō'lXam:
She saw that one her daughter laughing. She said to her:

"Axkǀayā'wula tawā'x. Amē'mtX wuXi qaxatElEmō'qǀoyakwa."
"Laughing that one. Your younger sister that is drowned."

IkLā'nxoktē. Nau'i kǀut igiā'x itcā'qǀaqctaq. Igā'xkǀa wu'Xi
She pulled her hair. At once pull out she did her hair. She pulled her that

axgē'sqax agā'xan; nau'i kǀut igē'x itcā'qo-it. Kē'nuwa
youngest one her daughter; at once torn out was her leg. Try

igā'xkǀa LXE'leuX. "Ō, ya'Xka Lǀ Wa'ckōkǀumai'hē itcLō'tēna
she pulled her ashore. "Oh, he behold Wa'ckōkǀumai'hē he killed them

itcE'qôq."
my children."

Igō'ptcga. Kē'nuwa ikLō'naxL qāmta iLō'ya. Năct igō'cgam
She went up. Try she searched for them where they went. Not she found it

aLā'eXatk. Lā'lē, aqa igō'cgam wuXi aLā'kǀōtkǀōt. "Qā'mta
their trail. Long, then she found it that their bitch. "Where

iLō'ya Lmē'Xanax·îmct?" "Wu," igā'x wuXi akǀō'tkǀōt. Kē'nuwa
went your masters?" "Wu," did that bitch. Try

igā'kta ēwā'tgēwa. ʇ4 igā'xôx. Năct igE'LēLa. Wī't'ax
she ran there. Scent she did. Not she smelled them. Again

igoqu'mtcxogoa wu'Xi akǀō'tkǀōt: "Qā'mta iLō'ya Lmē'Xanax·îmct?"
she asked her that bitch: "Where went your masters?"

"Wu," igā'xôx ē'wa ā'nakᵘcîX. Igā'kta wuXi amē'sgaga.
"Wu," she did thus to the other side. She ran that robin.

Kē'nuwa igā'xôx ʇ4. Qoā'nEmîX lā'xlax igō'xoa wuXi
Try she did scent. Five times deceive she did her that

akǀō'tkǀōt. Igaxē'ma. Aqa igiō'cgam yaXi LXoa'p igē'xôx yaXi
bitch. She threw her away. Then she found it that hole was that

of the boys and pursued them. She shouted much while she was going: "Wā'ckōk|umai'hē! I brought your mother," but they ran on ahead of her.

They ran a long distance, then they all defecated on a log. When one was tired, another one carried their youngest brother. Then they found the skins of two elk bucks. The eldest son of Salmon-berry cut them both and broke the antlers. He boiled the skins in one kettle, the antlers in another one. Then he said to the boiling kettles: "When she reaches you, you must boil violently. Don't cool off too quickly." Then they left the boiling kettles. Robin went and went and went, and pursued them. She came to those excrements. She was hungry and ate them all. Then she went on pursuing them. She came to the kettles. Both of them were boiling. First she scolded the kettles containing the skins: "I will take revenge on your grandmother, wu'lElElElElE, your mother, wu'lElElElElE, and all your

---

ēlX. Iga-i'LXēpq|ēX. Aqa iktō'cgam tLā'Xatk, aqa igE'LUwa.
ground. She went into it. Then she found them their tracks, then she pursued them.

AXElqā'mXLōL igō'ya: "Wā'ckōk|umai'hē, wā'mcaq iamcē'Lam."
She shouted she went: "Wā'ckōk|umai'hē, your mother I bring her to you."

ILE'xaua Lā'newatîkc; iLō'ya.
They ran first; they went.

KElā'îX iLō'ya. ILkLō'ts|ats|a ē'mqōpa Lkanauwē'tîkc. LeXā't
Far they went. They defecated a tree on all. One

tEll qaLXō'xoax aqa wi Lgō'nax qaLgiō'ctxoax yaXi iLā'mXîX.
tired he became then again another carried him on his back that their younger brother.

Qā'xpa LX iLō'yam, iLgiō'cgam imō'lEkEmax ē'yaqcō mâkct;
Where maybe they arrived, they found it elks their skins two;

ikā'lukc imō'lEkEmax. Tc|E'xtc|EX itcī'yux yaXi iqcō'max yaXi
male elks. Cut he did them those elk skins that

ē'LalXt ā'lele itca'qôq. Kanamô'kct tc|E'xtc|EX itcī'yôx.
their elder brother salmon berry her children. Both cut he did them.

L|mE'nL|mEn itcî'Lôx LaXi LqE'tcam. Ā'eXt aq|u'tan itcî'LōtcXEm,
Soft he made them those antlers. One kettle he boiled them,

ā'ēXt aq|u'tan itcī'yōtcXEm yaXi iqcō'max. Itciō'lXam ya'Xi
one kettle he boiled them those skins. He said to it that

iā'tcXEmal: "Ma'nēx alamgā'tqoama, aqa tc|pāk lEp amxō'xoa.
boiling (kettle): "When she reaches you, then strongly boil do.

Nāct a'yaq tsEs amxō'xoa." Aqa wi iLiqE'lōqLk yaXi
Not quick cold become." Then again they left it that

iLā'tcXEmal. Igō'ya, igō'ya, igō'ya, igE'LUwa wu'Xi amē'sgaga.
their boiling (kettles). She went, she went, she went, she pursued them that robin.

Igiō'cgam ya'Xi iLā'qēxElē. Walō' gōxt. IaxE'lEmuX ka'nauwē
She found them those their excrements. Hunger acted on her. She ate them all

ya'Xi iLā'qēxElē. Igō'ya igE'LUwa. Igiō'cgam ya'Xi iLā'tcXEmal
those their excrements. She went she pursued them. She found it that their boiling (kettle)

aqa cigE'pElEpt. Igiō'mēla iā'newîX iqcō'max: "Amē'k|ēc
and it boiled. She scolded them first the skins: "Your grand-mother

wu'lElElElElE, wā'maq wu'lElElElElE, ka'nauwē tiā'cuXtîkc
wu'lElElElElE, your mother wu'lElElElElE, all his relatives

relatives." Then it cooled off, and she ate and ate and ate. She ate it all. Then she scolded the kettle containing the antlers. She said the same again: "I will take revenge on your father, wu'lElElElElE, your uncle, your mother, and all your relatives." Then it cooled off, and she ate the antlers. The food was soft. She finished it all and continued to pursue them.

Now Salmon-berry's children came to a creek. The Crane stood near the water. He carried them across. He told them: "Don't be afraid, grandchildren, go to my house and eat there. Fish have been boiled for you." And they went to the Crane's house. Robin went on for a long time. Then her stomach ached; she was constrained to defecate. Then she defecated and the skin rope came out of her anus. She tried to pull it. There she saw a rope and she tied it to a tree and went around it often. Then she always said: "Wā'LōtEp hē'latEp, wā'LōtEp hē'latEp." Now she had pulled out the one skin and she

---

iktē'kEmoa." Tsās ige'yux. IaxE'lEmux, iaxE'lEmux, iaxE'lEmux.
she takes revenge on them." Cold she made it. She ate it, she ate it, she ate it.

Igiō'LXum. Aqa wi igō'n igiō'mela. ALā'xt!ax LaXi LqE'tcam.
She finished it. Then again another one she scolded it. Next those antlers.

K!oaLqā' wīt'ax igioxō'lalEmtck: "Wē'mam wu'lElElElElE, wēmē'mōt
Just so again she said much: "Your father wu'lElElElElE, your uncle

wu'lElElElElE, wā'maq wu'lElElElElE ka'nauwē tiā'cuXtîkc
wu'lElElElElE, your mother wu'lElElElElE all his relatives

iktē'kEmoa." Tsās igī'yux. ILaXE'lEmuX LaXi LqE'tcam, asa
she takes revenge on them." Cold she made it. She ate them those antlers, and

iL!mE'nL!mEn yaXi iLaXE'lEmuX. IkLō'LXum, aqa wi
soft that what she ate. She finished them, then again

igE'Luwa.
she pursued them.

ILō'yam ē'qaLpa ā'lele itcā'qoq. IaxtXuē'la iqoā'cqoac.
They arrived a creek at salmon berry her children. He was standing near the water the crane.

Itcā'LukT ē'wa k!anatē'tōL. ItcLō'lXam: "Nāct k!wac
He carried them thus to the other side. He said to them: "Not afraid

ogoatkē'xax, qā'comax. AmcxLXE'lEma ma'nîx namcō'pqama.
be, grandsons. You will eat when you enter my house.

Lgā'pEla tgEkst tk!ataqē'." ILō'ya ē'wa tē'yaqLpa iqoā'cqoac.
Many are done fish." They went thus his house to the crane.

Lē'lē igō'ya, igō'ya. Itcā'wan iā'tcqEm igixE'lôx. LE'ts!ats!a
Long she went, she went. Her belly sickness came to be on it. Desire to defecate

iLE'kux. Aqa ikLō'ts!ats!a wu'Xi amē'sgaga. A'qa Lāx igē'x
was on her. Then she defecated that robin. Then come out did

it!ā'lEqama itcā'pōtcpa. Kē'nuwa igē'xk!a. IyukLē'x·it. K!au
a thong her anus at. Try she pulled it. (A rope) lay there. Tie

igiō'koax tE'mqōpa. Aqa iguXuaLā'nukLtc tEXi tE'mqō. Aqa
she did it a tree to. Then she went around it often that tree. Then

igaxō'lalEmtck: "Wā'LōtEp, hē'latEp; wā'LōtEp, hē'latEp."
she always said: "Wā'LōtEp, hē'latEp; wā'LōtEp, hē'latEp."

Igixā'LXōm ya'Xi ēXt iqE'cō nEtc!E'xtc!Ex. Aqa wi igō'ya.
She finished it that one skin the cut one. Then again she went.

went on. After she had gone some distance, her stomach ached again and she was compelled to defecate. She defecated and there lay another skin rope. Again she tied it to a tree and went around it. She said again: "Wā'LŌtEp hē'latEp, wā'LŌtEp hē'latEp." She was tired. Behold, she had pulled out the whole rope. Then she went on pursuing them. She went a long distance, and her stomach ached again. Something very hard came out and pierced her body. She defecated and out came the antlers. They came out with great difficulty. She went some distance, and her stomach ached again. She was compelled to defecate and the other antlers came out. She was almost dead before the second pair of antlers came out. Then she pursued the children and came to a creek. There the crane was standing near the water. "Younger brother, take me across," she said to the crane. She said thus often. Then the crane stretched his legs across the water. At one point his leg was narrow. He said to her: "Don't be afraid, else you might fall into the water." Now she came across

---

KEla'îX igō'yam. Aqa wit'ax itcā'tcqEm iyaxE'lux. LEts¡ā'ts¡a
Far she arrived. Then again her sickness came to be on her. Desiring to defecate

iLE'kuX. Wit'ax ikLŌ'ts¡ats¡a. Aqa wi iyukLē'x·it yaXi
was on her. Again she defecated. Then again (a rope) lay there that

it¡ā'laqEma. Wi k¡au igiō'koax tE'mqōpa. Aqa wit'ax
thong. Again tie she did it a tree to. Then again

igoxoaLā'nukLtck taXi tE'mqō. Wī't'ax igā'xôx: "Wā'LŌtEp,
she went around it often that tree. Again she made: "Wā'LŌtEp,

hē'latEp; wā'LŌtEp, hē'latEp." Tā2ll igā'xôx aqa wi igixE'LXōm.
hē'latEp; wā'LŌtEp, hē'latEp." Tired she became and again she finished it.

Aqa wi igō'ya, igE'Luwa. KEla'îX igō'ya. Aqa iā'tcqEm
Then again she went, she pursued them. Far she went. Then its sickness

igixE'lôx itcā'wan. Ā'koapō Lā'xLāx nîxō'xoax ya'Xi tā'nki
came to be on it her belly. Nearly come out did that something

qca-ēq¡E'lq¡El. IkLŌ'ts¡ats¡a; Lāx iLî'xôx aqa LqE'tcam. Qalā'
very hard. She defecated; come out did then antlers. Hardly

tcXua Lāq° iLā'xôx. Nō'L¡îX nō'îx, aqa wi iā'tcqEm
then come out they did. A little she went, then again its sickness

nîxElō'xoax itcā'wan. Aqa wi ikLŌ'ts¡ats¡ax, aqa wi Lgōn
came to be on it her belly. Then again she defecated, then again other

LqE'tcam Lāx qaLXō'xoax. Ā'koapō igō'maqt, tcXua iLxE'LXōm
antlers come out they did. Nearly she died, then they were finished

LaXi LqE'tcam. Aqa wi igE'Luwa. Igō'yam ya'Xi ē'qaL.
those antlers. Then again she pursued them. She arrived at that creek.

IaXtXuā'la iqoā'cqoac: "Ā'owē, wāx amEnō'xua ē'wa
He was standing near the water the crane: "Younger brother, take across do me thus

k¡anatē'tōL," igiō'lXam iqoā'cqoac. Ä'XuēîX igiō'lXam.
other side," she said to him the crane. Often she said to him.

Aqa itsE'suktē ē'nat iā'qo-it. YaXā'pa qasixts¡ē'Lxakuîtx.
Then he stretched out this side his leg. Here it grew narrow.

Itcō'lXam: "Nîct Lî'cxaLqt amxalē'maLxa." Igā'ekatē yaXi
He said to her: "Not afraid to fall you fall into the water." She crossed on that

walking on the leg. When she came walking to the middle of the creek, she became afraid and he began to shake his leg. He turned his leg and she fell into the water. She drifted down the river. "Robin shall be your name; you shall not eat people." She drifted down. The crane said to her: "Robin shall be your name."

Far away she drifted ashore. A crow found her and began to eat her private parts. Then she recovered. She arose and painted her belly with her blood. It became all red. Then she went inland and came to a willow. She asked the willow: "Is my painting becoming?" "Oh, how bad looks the blood of her private parts," cried the willow. "Oh, you bad thing!" she said, "when your wood is burned it shall crackle." She came to the alder. "Is my painting becoming?" The alder said: "It is becoming." "Ah, sister," she said, "when people make anything they shall dye it red in your bark. When you are dry, you will burn well." She went on and came to the cottonwood. She asked it: "Is my painting becoming?" The

---

iā'qo-it. Qēq!āyakpā' yaXi ē'qaL icā'xōLq. A'qa itcixEltā'mit
leg. Middle on that creek she was afraid to fall. Then he shook it

yaXi iā'qo-it. Aqa icā'xōLq. Lāx° itci'yôx yaXi iā'qo-it.
that his leg. Then she was afraid to fall. Roll he did it that his leg.

Igalē'maLxēx·it. Igō'Xunē aqa qā'eqamîX. "Amā'sgaga imē'xaleu.
She fell into the water. She drifted then down the river. "Robin your name.

Näct tê'lXam amtuwu'lq!Lx." Igō'Xunē ā'qa. Itcō'lXam
Not people you shall eat them." She drifted now. He said to her

iqoā'cqoac: "Amā'sgaga imē'xaleu."
the crane: "Robin your name."

KElā'îX igō'Xunē. IgōXu'nîptck. Igō'cgam at!ā'ntsa. IcgixE'lEmux
Far she drifted. She drifted ashore. She found her the crow. She ate it

yaXi (naqagē'lak) itcā'qo-itXa. Kāqa ixelā'x aqa itcilXā'takōa.
that (vulva) her vulva. When she ate then she recovered.

IgaXE'latck. ILaxElgē'matck LaXi Lgā'qawulqt ka'nauwē
She arose. She painted herself that her blood all

itcā'wanpa, ac Lpāl igē'x itcā'wan. Igō'ya, igō'ptcga. Iga-igō'qoam
her belly at, and red became her belly. She went, she went inland. She reached it

ēlā'itk. "Lā'nkucq tci LgE'qawulqt?" igiō'lXam elā'itk. "Qantcî'x
the willow. "Becoming to me [int. part.] my blood?" she said to it the willow. "When

iqoē'tXa Liā'qawulqt pō qaLcgā'tcqoa-it." "Nā yaXī'yax," igiō'lXam.
a vulva its blood if ugly on a person." "Oh, that one," she said to it.

"Ma'nîx aqamxElgē'Lxa· aqa L!ā'qL!āq amxō'xoa." Igagō'qoam
"When you will be burnt then crackle you do." She reached

aqaxE'miuLx. "Tcu'xoa Lā'nkucq tci LgE'qawulqt?" Igā'kîm
the alder. "Well becoming to me [int. part.] my blood?" It said

aqaxE'miuLx: "LE'mkucq Lmē'qawulqt." "Ā a a ā'tcē," igō'lXam,
the alder: "Becoming to you you blood." "Ah, younger sister," she said to it,

"ma'nîx tā'nki aqiō'xoax aqa Lpāl qioxō'lalEmx amē'qalEmx. Ma'nîx
"when something is made then red it is made (with) your bark. When

amXcā'qoa aqa imē'x·EmaLXat." Igō'ya wī't'ax. Igaēgō'qoam
you are dry then you will burn." She went again. She reached it

cottonwood said: "Oh, how bad looks the blood of her private parts." "Oh, you bad thing! When you are put into the fire, you shall not burn." She came to the spruce tree: "Is my painting becoming?" "Oh, how bad looks the blood of her private parts." "Oh, you bad thing! When you are put into the fire, you shall not burn well, you shall crackle." She left it and came to the cedar. She asked it: "Is my painting becoming?" "It is becoming." "Oh, you speak well to me, younger brother. When people make canoes, they shall exchange them for slaves. They shall use you for making houses, and exchange them for dentalia. They shall use your bark for making coats for women." She left it and came to the fir. She asked it: "Is my painting becoming?" "Ah, it is becoming." "Oh, younger sister," she said, "when a person sings his conjurer's song, you shall be burned. You shall burn well." She came to the maple. "Is my painting becoming?" "It is becoming." "Ah, younger brother, they shall use your bark for making baskets." She left it and came

---

ē'koma. Igiōqu'mtcxōkoa: "ʟä'nkucq tci ʟgᴇ'qawulqt?" Itcō'lXam:
the cottonwood. She asked it: "Becoming to me [int. part.] my blood?" It said to her:

"Qantcē'X ʟqa ēqoē'tXat pō qaʟcgā'tcqoa-it ʟiā'qawulqt."
"When maybe a vulva if it is ugly on a person its blood."

"Nā gi tā'nki giā'mᴇla! Ma'nîx qamxᴇlgē'ʟxalᴇmx näct
"Oh, this something bad! When you are burnt not

amXᴇmʟXā'ya." Igigō'qoam ē'maktc: "ʟänkucq tci ʟgᴇ'qawulqt?"
you shall burn." She reached it the spruce tree: "Becoming to me [int. part.] my blood?"

"Qantcī'X ʟqa ēqoē'tXat ʟiā'qawulqt qaʟcgā'tcqoa-it." "Nā
"When maybe a vulva its blood is ugly on a person." "Oh,

gi tā'nki giā'mᴇla! Ma'nîx aqamxᴇlgē'ʟxa, ā'mēʟaqʟaq.
this something bad! When you are burnt, you crackle.

Näct t¡ā'ya amXᴇmʟXā'ya." Iga-iqᴇ'luqʟ. Igiū'cgam ē'ckan.
Not good you shall burn." She left it. She found it the cedar.

Igiuqu'mtcxōgua: "ʟä'nkucq tci ʟgᴇ'qawulqt?" "Ō, ʟᴇ'mkucq,"
She asked it: "Becoming to me [int. part.] my blood?" "Oh, becoming to you,"

itcō'lXam. "Qoä'2ʟ¡ immō'lXam ā'oē! Ma'nîx ikᴇ'nim aqamō'xoa
it said to her. "Right you speak to me younger brother! When a canoe you are made

aqa tᴇlā'etîX aqamtXᴇmō'ta. Tqoē'ʟē aqamuxō'lalᴇma, iq¡atō'k
then slaves are exchanged for you. House you are made, longest dentalia

aqamtXᴇmō'ta. Aq¡oē'lōʟx aqō'xoa amē'qēco." Ia-iqᴇ'luqʟk.
are exchanged for you. Coat for women is made your bark." She left it.

Igō'cgam amqcî'ckan. Igoqu'mtcxōkua: "ʟä'nkucq tci ʟgᴇ'qawulqt?"
She found it the fir. She asked it: "Becoming to me [int. part.] my blood?"

"Ā ʟᴇ'mkucq ʟmē'qawulqt." "Ā, a a ā'tcē," igō'lXam "ma'nîx
"Ah becoming to you your blood." "Ah, younger sister," she said to it, "when

aʟktcxᴇmā'ya ʟgoaʟē'lX koalē'wa aʟgumXulgē'ʟxa. Imē'XᴇmaʟXat."
he sings his conjurer's song a person then they will burn you. You will burn well."

Igiū'cgam itcunā'q. "TcuXoa ʟä'nkucq tci ʟgᴇ'qawulqt?" "Ā,
She found it the maple. "Well becoming to me [int. part.] my blood?" "Ah,

ʟä'mkucq ʟmē'qawulqt." "Ā, a a ā'owē, iqō'mxōm aqiuxō'lalᴇma
becoming to you your blood." "Ah, younger brother, basket will be made

to the vine maple. "Is my painting becoming?" "Ah, it is becoming." "Oh, younger brother, they shall use you for making small dishes and spoons." Then she came to the hemlock tree. "Is my painting becoming?" The hemlock replied: "How bad looks the blood of her private parts." Thus she asked all the trees. That is the story. To-morrow we shall have fine weather.

---

amē'q!Elō." Iga-iqE'luqLk. Igiū'cgam iq!ē'ntcik. "Tcu'Xoa Lă'nkucq
your bark." She left it. She found it the vine maple. "Well becoming to me

LgE'qawulqt?" "Ā, Lă'mkucq Lmē'qawulqt." "Ā, a a ā'oē, ma'nîx
my blood?" "Ah, becoming to you your blood." "Ah, younger brother, when

Lq!tă'nEmax aqamuxō'lalEma, Lq!a'mctEmax aqamuxō'lalEma."
small dishes you will be made, spoons you will be made."

Igō'cgam aqalō'lEmtk. "Tcu'Xoa Lă'nkucq LgE'qawulqt?" "Qantcē'X
She found it the hemlock tree. "Well becoming to me my blood?" When

Lqa iqoē'tXat Liă'qawulqt pō qaLcgă'tcqoa-ît." Ka'nauwē gi
maybe a vulva its blood if ugly on a person." All these

tE'mqō aktōqu'mtcxōguax. K!anēk!anē'; ō'la asa-igă'p.
trees she asked them. The story; to-morrow fine weather.

Panther and Owl (told 1891)

There was the Owl and his chief. The Owl's chief was hunting elks every day. The people heard that he was always killing elks. Then Blue-jay told his chief's daughter: "Go to see the Owl's chief." In the morning she made herself ready and went. She went a long distance. She crossed five prairies. Then she saw a person. She approached him secretly. Now she reached him. He was dancing, and she hid herself. She looked at the person and thought: "Maybe that is the Owl's chief." The dancer had a flat head. She looked secretly. Now that person jumped, and she saw that he had caught a mouse. He had a mat on his back and put the mice into it. When he saw a tideland mouse he killed it and put it into his mat. That person was dancing all the time. Then a stick hit his nose, and blood

---

Ik¡oayawa' Ictā'k¡anē k¡a Ikā'oXaō

Panther their Myth and Owl

Cxēlā'etiX ikā'oXaō giā'Xak¡Emana. Ka'nauwē Lkā'etax
There were the owl having a chief. All days

imō'lEkEmax qatciup¡iā'Lxa-îtX iā'Xak¡Emana ikā'oXaō. Guā'nEsum
elks always he went to get his chief the owl's. Always

icxEltcî'mElit iā'k¡ētēnax imō'lEkEmax. Aqa igē'kîm iqē'sqēs,
they heard about him hunter elks. Then he said blue-jay,

itcō'lXam iLā'Xak¡Emana ayā'Xan: "Ō, amionā'xLama ikā'oXaō
he said to her their chief his daughter: "Oh, you go and search for him the owl

iā'Xak¡Emana." Igē'tcuktîX igaXE'ltXuîtck. Aqa igō'ya. Igō'ya,
his chief." It became day she made herself ready. Then she went. She went,

kElā'îX igō'ya. Qoā'nEm igō'qoēpa tEmqā'emax. Aqa
far she went. Five she crossed them prairies. Then

igE'LqElkEl LgoaLē'lX. Q¡oā'p igE'Lôx igaxā'Lk¡EnukLuwa.
she saw him a person. Near she came she approached secretly.

Q¡oā'p ikLō'xoam. ILwē'la, igaxaLxE'pcut. IkLō'qumîtck LaXi
Near she arrived. He danced, she hid herself. She looked at that

LgoaLē'lX. IgaXLō'xoa-ît: "LXuan iā'Xka ikā'oXaō iā'Xak¡Emana
person. She thought: "Perhaps he the owl his chief

tayax iuwē'la." ILā'p¡aqa LaXi LgoaLē'lX. Igaxa'Lk¡alEpsut.
that danced." Flathead that person. She looked secretly.

Aqa iLksupEnā'x LaXi LgoaLē'lX. Ā'nqa qaLgagElgā'x wuXi
Then it jumped that person. Already he had taken that

ā'cō. Lq¡ā'pEnX LE'ltē. Kō'pa qaLgawigē'tElgEmx taXi tcō'yîkc.
mouse. A mat he had it on. There he put them into it those mice.

Manîx gitcā'k¡ēwulal qaLguwā'qaôx, qaLgalgē'tgax Lq¡ā'pEnXpa.
When a tideland mouse he killed it, he put it into it the mat in.

QaLuwē'la LaXi LgoaLē'lX. Ē'mqō nitELgā'xitx cî'LaLpXpa.
He danced much that person. A stick hit it his nose at.

came out of it. The person searched and found the woman. He said: "Oh, my wife. Let us go home." So the Owl found her first. She did not know him. Then he brought her to the house. The house was full of meat and grease. The grease on the one side of the house was all white. There at the end of the house the Owl was staying. The grease there was all green. It was the grease taken from the intestines. The Owl went to the end of the house and said: "I will take the grease of the man who is working for me," and gave it to the woman. She ate it, and after she had finished he hid her. In the evening his chief came. The Owl had been there for a long time. The Panther carried one elk and said to the Owl: "Carry our elk into the house." The Owl brought it, and then they cut it. The Panther was going to give him grease, but he did not take it all. He only took some dung and a little fat. It became night. In the morning the Owl's chief made himself ready and went to hunt elks.

Naui wax ʟā'qauwîlqt; qaʟk¡ē'naxʟx ʟaXi ʟgoaʟē'lX. Aqa
At once flowed out blood; he searched that person. Then

qaʟgucgā'mx: "Ō, agᴇ'kikal ʟ¡ tawā'x. A'yaq atXk¡oā'ya."
he found her: "Oh, my wife behold that. Quick let us go home."

ʟqōst, ikā'oXaō yaXi igiucgā'mX iā'nēwa. IgixE'tEluxt, nîcqē
Behold, the owl that she found him first. She did not know him, not at all

ē'iukul. Aqa itcō'kʟa tᴇ'ctaqʟpa. Pā2ʟ ʟqolē'max taXi tᴇ'ctaqʟ,
he was known to her. Then he took her their house to. Full meat that their house,

pāʟ apXᴇ'lēu. Ē'wa taXi tᴇ'nat tqu'ʟē tk¡ōp wuXi apXᴇ'lēu,
full grease. Thus that one side the house white that grease,

ēwa guguā'olîx·, ē'wa yaXi ikā'oXaō qa iō'Xt, qa ptcāX
thus at the end of the house, thus that owl where he was, there green

ka'nauwē wuXi apXᴇ'lēu. Ka'nauwē tq¡ᴇ'mcukc atā'pXᴇlēu.
all that grease. All intestines their grease.

Iō'ya ē'wa guguā'olîX yaXi ikā'oXaō. Igē'kîm: "Anaēxgā'lᴇmama
He went there end of the house that owl. He said: "I will go to take it

itcī'xeyal ayā'pxᴇlēu. Itcangē'waʟqamit wuXi aqagē'lak. Iʟā'Xoʟq
my working-man grease. He fed her that woman. She finished

igaxʟxᴇ'lᴇmîtck aqa itcō'pcut. Tsō'yustîX igiXk¡oā'mam
eating then he hid her. In the evening he came home

iā'Xak¡ᴇmana. Ā'nqa iō'Xt ikā'oXaō. ĒXt imō'lak itciō'kʟam
his chief. Already he was there the owl. One elk he brought it

ik¡oayawa'. Iqiō'lXam ikā'oXaō: "Ē'ckatqᵘtck itxā'mōlak."
the panther. He was told the owl: "Carry into the house our elk."

Itciā'ckoqᵘtck ikā'oXaō. Lā2, icgī'yuxc. Kē'nuwa iqā'elōt wuXi
He carried it into the house the owl. Some time, they cut it. Try he was given that

apXᴇ'lēu. Nā2ct ka'nauwē itcā'xoqtck. Ā'ema wuXi nōʟ¡ gi
grease. Not all he took it. Only that little this

itcā'qexᴇlē, ā'ema itcā'xoqtck wuXi apxᴇ'lēu. Igō'ponᴇm.
its excrements, only he took that grease. It got dark.

Kawī'X igixᴇ'ltXuîtck iā'xak¡ᴇmana ikā'oXaō. Iō'ya, imō'lak
Early he made himself ready his chief the owl. He went, elk

Then the Owl went to steal at the end of the house from his chief. He stole the good grease and gave it to his wife. Then he went out and caught mice. He danced and sang all the time. He sang: "——" At noon the Owl went home and stole some of his chief's grease and meat, and gave it to his wife. In the evening the Panther came home.

The woman made a hole in her mat and saw him. Oh, he was a pretty person. His hair was braided and reached below his buttocks. His face was painted with red stripes. Then the woman thought: "Oh, I made a mistake; I think he is the Owl's chief." Then the Panther said to the Owl: "Bring our elk and lick off its dung." Then the Owl scolded. "Q¡p, q¡p, q¡p," went his lips. The Panther spoke to him twice. Then the Owl rose and brought the elk into the house. They cut it, but the Owl was angry all the time. He received only

---

igigE'loya. Igigō'xtkam ikā'oXaō ē'wa guguā'olîX. Itcixō'xtkam
he went to hunt. He went to steal the owl thus at the end of the house. He went to steal from him

iā'Xak¡Emana. Itca-ixō'xtkam aqa at¡ō'kti apXE'lēu. Itcā'lEqo-îm
his chief. He went to steal it then good grease. He gave it to her to eat

ayā'kikal ikā'oXaō. Aqa iō'ya. Itcō'kuya tcō'yîkc. Aqa wi
his wife the owl. Then he went. He went to catch mice. Then again

igiwē'lalEmtck. Tiā'qēwam yaXi qayuwē'lalEmX. "Hā'yō,
he danced much. His songs that he always danced. "Hā'yō,

hayō' Lawa ctEtcxEntcxē'n, Lawa ctEtcxEntcxē'n." Aqa cā'xalîX
hayō' Lawa ctEtcxEntcxē'n, Lawa ctEtcxEntcxē'n." Then high

aqaLā'x nîXk¡oā'x ikā'oXaō. NîXk¡oā'mam ikā'oXaō.
the sun he went home the owl. He came home the owl.

Atcixō'xtkax iā'xak¡Emana apXE'lēu k¡a Lqolē'max. QatcElqoē'mx
He stole it from him his chief grease and meat. He gave her to eat

ayā'kikal. Tsō'yustîX nîXk¡oā'mamx ik¡oayawa'.
his wife. In the evening he came home the panther.

LXoa'p igiō'xax yaXi icō'lEtc. Agiō'kctx wuXi aqagē'lak. Ō,
Hole she made it that mat. She saw him that woman. Oh,

Lt¡ō'kti Lgoalē'lX Lōxt. LXp¡ō'ctEmtîX LE'Laqcō gipE'tEmaX
pretty person was there. Braided his hair to here

gēguala' iLā'pōtc LE'Laqcō; Luguē'matckuîX anuā'LEma LaXi
below his buttocks his hair; painted red paint that

Lgoalē'lX. Ts¡E'xts¡Ex tE'Lguxt stā'xōstpa. IgaxLō'Xoa-it wu'Xi
person. Stripes were on it his face on. She thought that

aqagē'lak: "Ō, pō'xo-îc gēnE'xôx; iā'Xka Lō'Xoan iā'Xak¡Emana
woman: "Oh, a mistake I made; he perhaps his chief

ikā'oXaō." Iqiō'lXam ikā'oXaō: "Ē'ctatq^{u}tck itxā'molak.
the owl's." He was told the owl: "Carry it into the house our elk.

Iā'qēxElē qamēnEmē'qLx." Kalā'lkuilē igē'x ikā'oXaō. Q¡p, q¡p,
Its dung lick it off." Scold he did the owl: Q¡p, q¡p,

q¡p, ciā'mîct. Mô'ktcîX itciō'lXam. Koalē'wa iō'tXuit ikā'oXaō.
q¡p, his mouth. Twice he said to him. Just then he stood there the owl.

Itciā'cqoq^{u}tck ictā'mōlak. Icgī'yuxc ictā'mōlak. Guā'nEsum
He carried it into the house their elk. They cut it their elk. Always

iXE'LXaqt ikā'oXaō. Ā'ema wuXi mank qat¡ō'kti apXE'leu
he was angry the owl. Only that a little good fat

the poor kind of grease. Then the chief said: "What do you think? Why are you angry all the time, you old Owl?" The Owl did not reply.

The next morning the Panther made himself ready again. Then the woman made a hole in her mat, and she saw him again. Then she was very much pleased with him. He always ate before he went hunting. Something was left over which he put up on the loft, and the woman saw it. In the morning the Owl arose and stole fat at the end of the house. He gave it to his wife. Then he hid her again. He went out. The Panther thought: "What is the matter with the Owl? He is always angry. He was not that way formerly." Thus thought the Panther. "I think I will go home when the sun is still up in the sky." He went home at that time and noticed that the Owl was there already. He said to the Owl: "Behold, you are here already!" "Yes; I am here already. Yes; I gave up hunting because I did not catch anything. Therefore I came home quickly." Then the Panther spoke to the Owl: "Oh, you old Owl; bring our

---

itcā'xoqtck. Itciō'lXam iā'Xak¡Emana: "Qā gi mgēx,
he took it. He said to him his chief: "How this you are,

cā'naXauXau, guā'nEsum amXE'LXaqt?" Nē'ct qa igē'kîm
old owl, always you are angry?" Not anyhow spoke

ikā'oXau.
the owl.

Kawī'X igixE'ltXuîtck ik¡oa'yawa. Aqa wi Lxoa'p igī'yux yaXi
Early he made himself ready the panther. Then again hole she made that

icō'lEtc. Aqa wi igiō'qomîtck. Q¡at igī'yuxt ē'tcamxtcpa.
mat. Then again she saw him. Like she did him her heart in.

IgixLxā'lEmitck, igixk¡ē'tcinktamē. Igîxk¡ā'etîX ya'Xi tā'nki.
He ate, he ate before going out. He left it over that something.

Aqa yaXī'pa itciugak¡ō'Lit cā'xalîXpa. Igiō'qumē wuXi aqagē'lak.
Then there he put it up up at. She saw it that woman.

Igē'tcuktē. IgixE'latck ikā'oXaō. Igigō'xtkam ē'wa guguā'ōlîX.
It got day. He arose the owl. He stole there at the end of the house.

Itcā'lqo-îm wuXi ayā'kikal. Aqa wi itcō'pcōt. Iō'ya.
He gave to her to eat that woman. Then again he hid her. He went.

IgîXLō'xoa-it ik¡oayawa': "Qā ā'Lqi igē'xax ikā'oXaō, tcqi
He thought the panther: "How later on will be the owl, then

guā'nsum iXE'LXaqt. Nī'ct k¡oaLqā' ā'nqa." IgixLō'xoa-ît
always he is angry. Not thus before." He thought

ik¡oayawa': "Nī'Xua ka cā'xalîX aqaLā'x, aqa anXk¡uā'ya."
the panther: "Well when up the sun, then I will go home."

Ka cā'xalîX aqaLā'X aqa igē'Xk¡oa. Xāx itcī'yuxt ē'yamxtcpa.
When up the sun then he went home. Notice he did him his heart in.

IgîXk¡oā'mam; ā'nqa iō'Xt ikā'oXaō. Iqiō'lXam ikā'oXaō: "Ā'nqa
He came home; already there was the owl. He was told the owl: "Already

L¡ imXatk¡oā'mam." "Ā'nqa inXatk¡oā'mam, ka tE'menua inE'xôx,
behold! you came home." "Already I came home, when give up I did,

aqa k¡ā taXi qEntōp¡iā'Lxa-ītx, tāntxo ayā'q inî'Xatk¡oa."
then nothing those I caught them, therefore quick I went home."

Iqiō'lXam ikā'oXaō: "Cā'naXauXau, iā'ckatq^{u}tck itxā'molak."
He was told the owl: "Old owl, bring into the house our elk."

elk into the house." "His ancestors called me that way." Then his lips went: "Q¡p, q¡p, q¡p." "Don't scold, old Owl." A long time he was angry; then he arose and brought in the elk. They cut it. The Panther gave him only the poor kind of fat, and the Owl took it.

Now the Panther really took notice. The two went to bed, but the Panther remained awake. He listened, and he heard the Owl talking in a low voice. All the time he was laughing in a low voice. Now he really took notice.

Early the Panther arose. He ate before he left. Now the woman again made a hole in her mat, and she looked at him when he had finished eating. He put on the loft what he had left. Then the Panther went, and the Owl arose. He said: "I am going to steal from my workman." He stole fat and meat, and gave it to his wife. Then he went. A little while he danced, and he came home again. He had caught only a little. About noon the Panther came back. The

---

"Tiā'yaq¡eyōqtîkc ctē'yinkxal gō'yogōl." Aqa wi igē'xôx q¡p, q¡p,
"His ancestors named me at end of house." Then again it did q¡p, q¡p,

q¡p, iā'mîct. "Hō'ntcîn! nîct kalā'lkuilē ixā'tx, cā'naXauXau,
q¡p, his mouth. "Don't! not scold do, old owl,

cā'naqo îpqo îp." "Tiā'yaq¡eyōqtîkc ctē'yînkxal gō'yōgōl."
old owl." "His ancestors named me at end of house."

Lē'lē kalā'lkuilē igē'x; koalē'wa iō'tXuît. Itcē'ckatq^utck ictā'mōlak,
Long scold he did; just then he stood up. He carried it into the house their elk,

icge'yuxc. Ā'ema wu'Xi mank qat¡ō'ktēmax apXᴇ'leu itcā'xoqtck
they cut it. Only that little good fat he took it

ikā'oXaō.
the owl.

Ā'qa pāt xāx igē'xôx ik¡oa'yawa. Ickʟqā'yoXuit. Igixᴇ'gᴇlᴇmtck
Then really notice he did the panther. They went to bed. He was awake

ik¡oa'yawa. A'qa itciltcî'mᴇlētᴇmtck. Cāu, cāu, cāu, cāu
the panther. Then he listened to them. Speaking in a low voice

igē'xôx ikā'oXaō. Cāu, cāu, cāu, cāu nîxō'xoax. Aqa wi
he did the owl. Speaking in a low voice there was. Then again

nîxk¡ayā'wulalᴇmx. Ā'qa wuk¡ xāx itcī'yôx.
there was (sound of) laughing. Then really notice he did it.

Kawī'X igixᴇ'latck ik¡oayawa'. Igîxk¡ē'tcᴇnktamit. Aqa wi
Early he arose the panther. He ate before going out. Then again

ʟxoā'p igī'yôx wuXi aqagē'l yaXi icō'lᴇtc. Igiō'qumîtck.
hole she made it that woman that mat. He saw him.

Iʟā'2Xōʟq igîxʟxᴇ'lᴇmîtck. Kōpā' itciūgoak¡ō'ʟit ya'Xi
He finished he ate. There he put it up that

igîxk¡ā'etix·it tā'nki. Iō'ya ik¡oayawa'. Igixᴇ'latck ikā'oXaō.
he left it over something. He went the panther. He arose the owl.

Igē'kîm: "Anixō'xtkama itcî'xēyal." Igigō'xtkam apXᴇ'leu k¡a
He said: "I am going to steal from my workman." He went to steal grease and

ʟqolē'max. Itcā'lqo-îm ayā'kikal. Aqa wi iō'ya ikā'oXaō. Nō'ʟ¡îX
meat. He gave her to eat his wife. Then again he went the owl. A little

igē'wîtck, igē'Xk¡oa. Nōʟ¡ giā'k¡ēwula tcō'yîkc. Ka cā'xalîX
he danced, he went home. A little what he had caught mice. When up

Owl was there already. He said: "Why do you always come home first?" Thus spoke the Panther. The Owl replied: "I caught all the mice; therefore I came back." "What do you always whisper in the evening? You keep me awake." The Owl replied: "I was dreaming that mice climb over me. I was dreaming." The Panther said: "Bring our elk, old Owl." The Owl got angry and said: "His ancestors called me by that name." "Quick, old Owl; bring our elk and eat its dung." The Owl scolded for a long time. He did not want to go. Then he went out and carried the elk into the house. The Owl took only the poor kind of grease. "Why do you always scold?" said the Panther to the Owl. The Owl replied: "You always give me all kinds of names." The Panther replied: "For a long time we two have been living all alone; don't scold. You have changed altogether; you are scolding all the time."

---

aqaLā'x, aqa igē'Xk¡oa ik¡oayawa'. Ā'nqa iō'Xt ikā'oXaō.
the sun, then he went home the panther. Already there was the owl.

IgiXk¡oā'mam. Itciō'lXam: "Qā gîmgakē'xax? Mā'newa
He came home. He said to him: "How are you? You first

qamXk¡oā'mamx," iqiō'lXam ikā'oXaō. Itciō'lXam ik¡oayawa'.
you come home," he was told the owl. He said to him the panther.

Igē'kîm ikā'oXaō: "A'qa intō'LXōm ta'Xi tcō'yîkc, tāntxo ayā'q
He spoke the owl: "Then I finished them those mice, therefore quick

qanXk¡oā'x." "Tān, tān, tānki cā'ucāu qatcEmō'xoax Xā'pîX;
I come home." "What, what, something low voice he makes in the evening;

qamEnuqō'tcqEmx." Igē'kîm ikā'oXaō: "Qanîx·gē'quwalukLx
you keep me awake." He spoke the owl: "I dream

tcō'yîkc qatxEnguwā'wulElXLEmx; qatEnx·quwā'lEqLx." Itciō'lXam:
mice are crawling up my body; I dream about them." He said to him:

"Iā'ckatqᵘtck itxā'mōlak, cā'naXauXau." IgiXE'LXaq ikā'oXaō:
"Bring into the house our elk, old owl." He was angry the owl:

"Tiā'q¡eyōqtîkc ctē'yinkxal goyogō'l." "Ayā'q cā'naqo îpqo îp,
"His ancestors named me at end of house." "Quick old owl,

ē'ckatqᵘtck itxā'molak; iā'qexElē qamiomē'qLx." Ikalā'lkuilē
bring into the house our elk; its dung lick it off." Scold

nixō'xoax ikā'oXaō. Lä'2lē q¡ām nixō'xoax ikā'oXaō, koalē'wa wi
he did the owl. Long lazy he was the owl, just then again

qayupā'x. Qatciacgō'qᵘtckax ictā'molak. Qacgiō'xcx. Ā'ema mank
he went out. He carried it into the house their elk. They cut it. Only a little

qat¡ō'kti apXE'leu qatcaxō'qtckax ikā'oXaō. "Qā'2qa gi guā'nsum
good fat he kept it the owl. "Why this always

kalā'lkuilē îmkē'x?" aqiō'lXam ikā'oXaō. Igē'kîm ikā'oXaō:
scold you do?" he was told the owl. He said the owl:

"Mai'ka ka'nauwē qa'dEmax qamEnupqEnā'nanEmx." Iō'LqtîX
"You all ways you name me." Long

igē'kîm ik¡oayawa': "Txē'la-it txā'ema. Näct kalā'lkuilē imE'xôx,
he spoke the panther: "We are we alone. Not scold do,

k¡a iamxE'tEluXt guā'nsum kalā'lkuilē îmkē'xax," iqiō'lXam
and you change toward me, always scold you do," he was told

ikā'oXaō.
the owl.

It grew dark. Then the Panther lay down at the end of the house and the Owl at the other end. The Panther was awake. The Owl asked that woman: "What is that?" "My hair." "Oh, our hair, my wife." "What is that?" he said to her. "My ears." "Oh, our ears, my wife." "What is that?" he said. "My face." "Oh, our face, my wife." "What is that?" "Oh, my eyebrows." "Oh, our eyebrows, my wife." "What is that?" "My forehead." "Oh, our forehead, my wife." "What is that?" "My mouth." "Oh, our mouth, my wife." "What is that?" he said to her. "My nose." "Oh, our nose, my wife." "What is that?" "My throat." "Oh, our throat, my wife." "What is that?" "My arm." "Oh, our arm, my wife." "What is that?" "My hand." "Oh, our hand, my wife." "What is that?" "My belly." "Oh, our belly, my wife." "What is that?" She was silent. Twice he said: "What is that?" He became angry. "What is that, woman?" She said: "My navel." "Oh, our navel, my wife." "What is that?" She did not speak to him. He said to her: "What is that? I shall scratch you." She was

---

Igō'pōnEm. Aqa wi îckLkā'yoXuit ē'wa gōguā'olîX ik¡oa'yawa,
It grew dark. Then again they went to bed thus at end of house the panther,

ē'wa goguā'olîX ikā'oXaō. IgixE'gElîmtck ik¡oa'yawa.
thus at end of house the owl. He was awake the panther.

Itcuqu'mtcxōgoa wuXi aq¡āgē'lak ikā'oXaō: "Tān taya'x?"
He asked her that woman the owl: "What this?"

qatculXā'mx. "LgE'qcō." "Ohō', LE'ntaqcō, agā'yakikal. "Tān
he said to her. "My hair." "Ohō', our hair, my wife. "What

taya'x?" AgiulXā'mx: "Tgē'ucakc." "Ohō', tEntā'ucakc, agā'yakikal.
this?" She said to him: "My ears." "Ohō', our ears, my wife.

Tān taya'x?" qatculXā'mx. "Sgē'xôst," agiulXā'mx. "Ohō',
What this?" he said to her. "My eyes," she said to him. "Ohō',

sEntā'yaxôst, agā'yakikal. Tān tayā'x?" "Tgē'lktsalEmax." "Ohō',
our eyes, my wife. What this?" "My eyebrows." "Ohō',

tEntā'yalktsalEmax, agā'yakikal. Tān taya'x?" "Agē'tcpuX."
our eyebrows, my wife. What this?" "My forehead."

"Ohō', antā'yatcpuX, agā'yakikal. Tā'n taya'x?" "Itcā'kcXat."
"Ohō', our forehead, my wife. What this?" "My mouth."

"Ohō', intā'kcXat, agā'yakikal. Tā'n taya'x?" qatcōlXā'mx.
"Ohō', our mouth, my wife. What this?" he said to her.

"Ētcktc." "Ohō', yī'ntaktc, agā'yakikal. Tān taya'x?"
"My nose." "Ohō', our nose, my wife. What this?"

"Ā'gEmōkuē." "Ohō', ā'ntamokuē, agā'yakikal. Tān taya'x?"
"My throat." "Ohō', our throat, my wife. What this?"

"Ē'tcxō," "Ohō', ē'ntaxō, agā'yakikal. Tān taya'x?" "LE'gakci."
"My arm," "Ohō', our arm, my wife. What this?" "My hand."

"Ohō', LE'ntakci, agā'yakikal. Tān taya'x?" "Itcē'wan." "Ohō',
"Ohō', our hand, my wife. What this?" "My belly." "Ohō',

intā'wan, agā'yakikal. Tān taya'x?" Qān igā'xôx. Mô'kctîX
our belly, my wife. What this?" Silent she was. Twice

igē'kîm. Itcō'lXam: "Tān taya'x?" Kalā'lkuilē igē'xôx. "Tān
he spoke. He said to her: "What this?" Scold he did. "What

taya'x, aqagē'lak?" "Agā'q¡amcō," igiō'lXam. "Ohō', antā'q¡amcō,
this, woman?" "My navel," she said to him. "Ohō', our navel,

agā'yakikal. Tān taya'x?" K¡ā nîctqa igiō'lXam. "Tān taya'x?"
my wife. What this?" Silent, not at all she said to him. "What this?"

silent for a long time. Then she said to him: "My private parts." "Oh, our private parts, my wife." The Panther heard it.

Early he arose, and ate before going. He went. Then the Owl arose. He stole some grease and gave it to his wife. Then he went out for the fifth time. He danced a short time and came home. They left the woman alone. Then she arose and went to the end of the house. She looked at the food which the Panther had put aside. It was elk-marrow. Now she pulled out two of her hairs and tied one around one piece of marrow. She took the other hair and tied it around another piece of marrow. Then she put the food back there and hid in the Owl's bed. The Owl danced for a short while and came home. He stole some grease at the end of the house. At noon the Panther came back, but the Owl was there already. He did not say anything. Now he really took notice. The Panther stayed there some time. Then he took that marrow. He wanted to eat it. He broke it and the hair became loose. He stretched it out. He saw it was one

---

itcō'lXam. "TamEnpē'yaqLawuna." Lē'lē qān igā'xôx. Aqa
he said to her. "I shall scratch you." Long silent she was. Then

igiō'lXam: "Itcā'eqo-itxa." "Hohohoho" igē'xôx, "intā'yaqo-itxa
she said to him: "My vulva." "Hohohoho" he did, "our vulva

agā'yakikal." Itcîxtce'mElē ik¡oayawa'.
my wife." He heard it the panther.

Kawī'X igixE'latck ik¡oayawa'. Igîxk¡ē'tcinktamit. Iō'ya.
Early he arose the panther. He ate before going out. He went.

IgixE'latck ikā'oXaō. Igē'kuXtk, itcā'lqoîm ayā'kikal. Aqa wi
He arose the owl. He stole, he gave to her to eat his wife. Then again

iō'ya ikā'oXaō ē'LaquinEmîX. Nō'L¡îX igē'wîtck. Igē'Xk¡oa.
he went the owl the fifth time. A little he danced. He went home.

IctaqE'loqLk wuXi aqagē'lak. Aqa igaxE'latck. Igō'ya ē'wa
They had left her that woman. Then she arose. She went there

goguā'olîX. Igiuk¡umā'nanEmtck ya'Xi tā'nki qiuk¡ō'LētîX. A'qa
end of house. She looked at it that something that he had put up. Then

imō'lak ayā'mala. K¡ut igE'Lôx môkct LE'gaqcō. IkLā'k¡EnEXta
elk its marrow. Tear out she did them two her hair. She rolled it around

aē'Xt wuXi ā'mala LēXt LqE'cō. Agō'n igā'gElga ikLā'k¡EnEXta
one that marrow one hair. The other one she took it she rolled it around it

LaXi LqE'cō. Aqa wi iguk¡ō'Lit kōpā'. Aqa wi igaxE'pcut
that hair. Then again she put it up there. Then again she hid

iā'lXEmepa ikā'oXaō. Nō'L¡îX igē'wîtck ikā'oXaō. Igē'Xk¡oa.
his bed at the owl. A little while he danced the owl. He went home.

IgîXk¡oā'mam. Igigō'xtkam ē'wa goguā'olîX apXE'leu. Pā wē'gua
He came home. He went to steal there at the end of the house fat. At noon

igē'Xk¡oā ik¡oayawa'. IgîXk¡oā'mam. Ä'nqa iō'Xt ikā'oXaō.
he went home the panther. He came home. Long ago he was there the owl.

Nāctqa itciō'lXam, qē'wa qa pāt xāx itcī'yuxt. Iō'LqtîX iō'La-ît
Not at all he spoke to him, because really notice he did him. Long he stayed

ik¡oayawa'. A'qa itcā'gElga wuXi ā'mala. Ala-ixElEmō'xoma.
the panther. Then he took it that marrow. He was going to eat it.

ItcaxE'lakuc. StuXᵘ iLE'x LaXi LqE'cō. ItcLgē'nXam, ē'LanXa
He broke it. Untied became that hair. He stretched it, one fathom long

fathom long. Then the Panther thought: "Oh, the Owl is hiding a woman." He broke another piece of marrow, and found another hair. After he had eaten, they cut the elk. He did not say anything. The night came on and they lay down. Then he heard the Owl laughing.

The Panther arose early and said: "Why did you laugh, Owl?" The Owl replied: "I dreamt the mice were climbing over me." The Panther went out. He stayed in the woods a little inland from the house. Then the Owl looked secretly and rose. He went out and went around. The Panther saw him. Then the Owl entered again. He spoke much in the house. The Panther heard the two speaking together. After some time the Owl went out again and went to catch mice. The Panther saw the Owl going. When he had gone a little while the Panther entered and searched in the Owl's bed. There he found a woman. He said to her: "Rise!" She rose, and he carried her to his bed. He said to her: "Did you hear about the famous

---

LaXi LqE'cō. IgîxLō'xoa-ît ik!oayawa': "Ō, itcLō'pcu⁺ L! Lqagē'lak
that hair. He thought the panther: "Oh, he hid her behold a woman

ikā'oXaō. Agō'n wit'ax itcaxE'lakua wuXi ā'mala. Wi LēXt LqE'cō
the owl. The other again he took it that marrow. Again one hair

itcLō'cgam. ILā'2XōLq iā'LxalEm ik!oayawa'. Aqa icxE'L!ifxc.
he took it. He finished it he ate the panther. Then they cut (the elk).

Nā2ct qa itciō'lXam. Igō'pōnEm. A'qa îckLqā'yōXuit. Aqa wit'ax
Not at all he spoke to him. It grew dark. Then they went to bed. Then again

igixigElEmē'laq; igîxk!ayā'wulalEmtck ikā'oXaō.
he listened; he laughed much the owl.

Kawī'X igixE'latck ik!oayawa'. Igē'kîm ik!oayawa': "Qanā'x
Early he arose the panther. He said the panther: "How much

igîxk!ayā'wulalEmtck ikā'oXaō?" Igē'kîm ikā'oXaō: "Tā'xka
did he laugh the owl?" He said the owl: "Those

tcō'yîkc qatxEnguwā'wulExLEmx qatnîXquwā'lukᵘLX." Ayō'pa
mice crawled up my body I dreamt about them." He went out

ik!oayawa'. Iō'La-it LxE'leuX tqu'Lepa, atā'mLxEleu tqu'Lē.
the panther. He stayed inland house at, inland from it the house.

Igixē'k!Elopsōt ikā'oXaō. Igā'2tcuktîX. Iō'pa ikā'oXaō.
He looked secretly the owl. Day came. He went out the owl.

Ioxoā'Lakoa tE'ctaqL. Itciō'qumit ik!oayawa'. Iā'ckupq ikā'oXaō.
He went around it their house. He saw him the panther. He entered the owl.

IgēxE'ltcō tqu'Lēpa. IcixE'ltcō aqa cmōkct ixEmē'laqt ik!oayawa'.
He spoke much the house in. They spoke much then two he heard it the panther.

Lē'lē aqa wi iō'pa ikā'oXaō. Iō'ya aqa ikā'oXaō, tcō'yîkc
Long then again he went out the owl. He went then the owl, mice

iō'kuya. Igē'qamit ik!oayawa', itciō'qumit ikā'oXaō. Nō'L!îX
he went to catch them. He looked the panther, he saw him the owl. A little while

iō'ya ikā'oXaō. Iā'ckōpq ik!oayawa'. Igik!ē'naxL ikā'oXaō
he went the owl. He entered the panther. He searched the owl

iā'lXEmitkpa. Itcō'cgam wuXi aqagē'lak. Itcō'lXam:
his bed at. He found her that woman. He said to her:

"AxE'latck!" IgaxE'latck. Itcō'kLa ē'wa iā'lXEmitk. Itcō'lXam:
"Rise!" She rose. He carried her thus his bed. He said to her:

Owl? You went to him." Now the Owl was dancing. A stick struck his nose and it began to bleed. Then he went home. The woman was already at the end of the house. She was lying down with the Panther. Then the Owl was angry. "I bought that woman for him and I went out in the canoe singing to buy the woman for him there at the end of the house." The Owl scolded for a long time.

Then the Panther said to that woman: "Look out! We shall fight. When we fly up higher and higher fighting, we shall kill each other. When green flesh falls down, you must burn it; when red flesh falls down, keep it, and do the same with the bones. When green bones fall down, burn them; when white bones fall down, keep them." The Owl scolded for a long time. Then the Panther said: "You are talking all the time. Come! we will rise to the sky and fight." The Owl made himself ready. He put on five raccoon blankets. The Panther made himself ready. He put on five elkskin blankets. Now

---

"Imxaltcā'mEliLqa tiā'xagElaxElē ikā'oXaō; aqa imigā'tqoam."
"You heard about him his fame the owl; then you came to him."

Ka iwē'la ikā'oXaō, igilgā'Xit ē'mqō cī'aLpXpa. Nau'i Lqā'wulqt
Where he danced the owl, it hit him a stick his nose at. At once blood

wāx cī'aLpX. Igē'Xk|oa ikā'oXaō. Igîxk|oā'mam ikā'oXaō.
pour out his nose. He went home the owl. He came home the owl.

Ā'nqa ayā'kikal qoaqē' akē'x. IcgE'Lqayū gi ik|oayawa'.
Already his wife at the end of the house was. They lay on bed this panther.

Kalā'lkuilē igē'xôx ikā'oXaō: "Ya'Xka inā'yilxewakoa wuXi
Scold he did the owl: "He I bought her for him that

aqagē'lak. AnLā'gitgulamalit yaXi goguā'olîX." Lā'2lē kalā'lkuilē
woman. I went out in a canoe singing to buy her for him that one at the end of the house." Long scold

igē'x ikā'oXaō.
he did the owl.

Itcō'lXam wu'Xi actā'kikal ik|oayawa': "Qā't|ōcXEm! Ma'nîx
He said to her that their wife the panther: "Look out! When

nantxuwā'qoa, ma'nîx antxēlukcqoā'wulXEma igō'cax, ma'nîx
we shall kill one another, when we fly up fighting the sky, when

ptcîx iLqu'l, ayulkᵘtcuwā'ya iLqu'l, aqa alîmxElgā'LXa. Ma'nîx
green flesh, it falls down flesh, then burn it. When

Lpāl iLqu'l ayulkᵘtcuwā'ya, aqa amiō'tga. K|oaLqā' ē'q|ōtcō.
red flesh falls down, then keep it. Thus bones.

Ma'nîx ptcāx ē'q|ōtcō ayulkᵘtcuwā'ya, aqa alîmxElgā'LXa.
When green bones fall down, then burn them.

Ma'nîx tk|ōp ē'q|ōtcō aqa amiō'tka." Lē'lē kalā'lkuilē
When white bones then keep them." Long scold

igē'x ikā'oXaō. A'qa igē'kîm ik|oayawa': "Wā'koa amxEltcuwā'ya.
he did the owl. Then he said the panther: "All day you talk.

ME'tē! atxEluqcqoā'wulXEma igō'cax." IgixE'ltXuîtck ikā'oXaō.
Come! we will fly up fighting the sky." He made himself ready the owl.

Igā'exaltē ayā'qanuq. Qoā'nEmi tē'xaltē tiā'qanoqoakc ikā'oXaō.
He put it on his raccoon blanket. Five were on him his raccoon blankets the owl.

IgixE'ltXuitck ik|oayawa'. Qoā'nEma tgē'luqtē itē'xaltē. KopE't
He made himself ready the panther. Five elkskin blankets were on him. Enough

they began to fight. First they tore their blankets. When they had torn the blankets, they tore their bodies, and they began to rise upward. They flew up to the sky, and the flesh began to fall down. Sometimes green flesh fell down. This the woman burned. When red flesh fell down, she kept it. Now they had torn all the flesh. Finally they tore their bones. When green bones fell down, the woman burned them. When white bones fell down, she kept them and put them into the basket. Then the intestines fell down. They looked just alike; some she burned, some she kept. Now she heard a noise of something falling down. The heads came down biting each other. Then she put a stick between them and tore them apart. She burned the Owl's head. Now she went down to the water and threw the flesh and that head into the water. She went up again. She waited a little while, then she saw her husband, the Panther. He came up to her and said: "Behold, you burned my intestines! These are the Owl's intestines. Go to your brother-in-law, the Bear, and tell him to give you one-half of his intestines." He gave them to her

---

aqa icxE'lkaiū. Tā'newa tctā'k¡etē LE'XLEX icgī'tôx. Icktō'LXum
then they fought. First their blankets tear they did them. They finished them

ctā'k¡etē. A'qa ya'Xi ē'ctaLq. A'qa ictolā'tckuiXit cā'xalîX.
their blankets. Then those their bodies. Then they flew up high.

Icxē'lukcqoā'wulX igō'cax. A'qa itktXuī'yutcō tE'ctaLqul. Anā'
They flew up fighting the sky. Then fell down their flesh. Sometimes

ptcîX iLqu'l qayuluktcō'x, agixElgā'Lxax wu'Xi actā'kikal. Ma'nix
green flesh fell down, she burned it that their wife. When

LpEl iLqu'l, agiō'tgax. IguXuā'LXum tE'ctaLqul. Aqa tāxt¡ax
red flesh, she kept it. It was finished their flesh. Then next

tE'ctaq¡ōtcō qayaluktcō'x. PtcîX ē'q¡otcō qayaxElgē'Lxax; ma'nîx
their bones fell down. Green bone she burned it; when

tk¡ōp ē'q¡otcō, agiō'tkax wu'Xi agā't¡akᵘspa. ItgE'luktcu
white bone, she kept it that her basket in. They fell down

ctā'q¡amcukc. Acuxuē'k¡atcX ctāq¡amcukc. TēXt itaxE'lgiLx,
their intestines. Looking alike their intestines. One she burnt it,

tēXt igE'tōtk. Kā ōXt gEm itgā'Lkᵘtcuwā'mam ctā'q¡aqctaqukc.
one she kept it. When was noise they come falling down their heads.

Ō'xoaqct ta'Xi tq¡ā'qctaqukc. Ē'mqō igîcxE't¡ēqLkua, aqa tc¡uXᵘ
They bit each other those their heads. A stick she stemmed between them, then broken apart

igō'xoax ta'Xi tq¡ā'qctaqukc. IaXE'lgiLx ikā'oXaō iā'q¡aqctaq.
they were those heads. She burned it the owl his head.

Igō'Lxa mā'LnîX. Wāx igE'tôx Ltcu'qoapa ta'Xi tLqul ka ya'Xi
She went down to the water. Pour out she did them water in that flesh and that

iq¡ā'qctaq. Igō'ptcga. Nō'L¡îX igō'La-it, igē'qElkEl itcā'kikal
head. She went up. A little while she stayed, she saw him her husband

ik¡oayawa' ētptckt. Iagā'tqoam. Itcō'lXam: "ItEmxE'lgiLx
the panther he came up. He reached her. He said to her: "You burnt them

LgE'q¡amcukc, Lqōct! Ikā'oXaō tatā'X tiā'q¡amcukc. Ni'Xua
my intestines, behold! The owl those his intestines. Well

amē'ya iskē'ntXoapa ēmē'potcxan. AmiulXā'ma atctEnlō'ta
go the bear to your brother-in-law. Tell him he shall give them to me

and she carried them home. He tried them, but they were not good. They made him feel sick. She carried them back and returned them to the Bear. She said to the Raccoon: "Oh, your elder brother sends word to you to give him your intestines." He gave her one-half. She took them and he tried them, but they were not good. They made him feel sick. He told her: "Carry them back. Tell the Wolf to give you one-half of his intestines." The Wolf gave them to her. She took them home and he tried them, but they were not good. They made him feel sick. He told her: "Go to the Beaver; he shall give me one-half of his intestines. He gave them to her, and the Panther tried the Beaver's intestines, but they were not good. They made him feel sick. He said to her: "Go to the Otter, your brother-in-law. He shall give you his intestines." She told him: "Your elder brother tells you to give him your intestines." He gave her one-half, and she took them home. He tried them, but they were not good. They made him feel sick. He tried all the quadru-

---

tᴇ'cit¡îX tiā'q¡amcukc." Igō'ya ayā'kikal. Igiō'lXam iskē'ntXoa:
one-half his intestines." She went his wife. She said to him the bear:

"Amtilō'ta tᴇ'cit¡îX tᴇmē'q¡amcukc." Itctā'lōt, igᴇ'tukᴛ. Kē'nuwa
"Give them to him one-half your intestines." He gave them to her, she took them. Try

itixᴇ'lôx; năct t¡aya'; iā'tcqᴇm itgē'lôx. Igᴇ'tōkᴛ wī't'ax.
they were on him; not good; his sickness they made on him. She carried them again.

Iktē'lᴇXaktcgua iskē'ntXoa. Igiō'lXam iʟatā't: "Ā, ē'mᴇlXt
She returned them to him the bear. She said to him the raccoon: "Oh, your elder brother

tcumXō'la amtelō'ta timē'q¡amcukc." Itctā'lōt tᴇ'cit¡îX. Igᴇ'tukᴛ.
he tells you you shall give them to him your intestines." He gave them to her one-half. She carried them.

Kē'nuwa itixᴇ'lôx. Năct t¡ā'ya; iā'tcqᴇm itgē'lôx. Itcō'lXam:
Try they were on him. Not good; his sickness they made on him. He said to her:

"Tē'lōkᴛ. AmiulXā'ma ilē'q¡amō, atctᴇnlō'ta tᴇ'cit¡îX
"Carry them. Tell him the wolf, he shall give them to you one-half

tiā'q¡amcukc." Itctā'lōt ilē'q¡amō tiā'q¡amcukc. Igᴇ'tōkᴛ.
his intestines." He gave them to her the wolf his intestines. She carried them.

Kē'nuwa itixᴇ'lôx. Năct t¡ā'ya; iā'tcqᴇm itgē'lôx. Itcō'lXam:
Try they were on him. Not good; his sickness they made on him. He said to her:

"Nî'Xua ik¡oa-inē'nēpa amē'ya. Atctᴇnlō'ta tiā'q¡amcukc
"Well the beaver to go. He shall give them to me his intestines

tᴇ'cit¡îX." Itctā'lōt kē'nuwa ik¡oa-inē'ne tiā'q¡amcukc. Kē'nuwa
one-half." He gave them to her try the beaver his intestines. Try

itixᴇ'lox. Năct t¡ā'ya. Iā'tcqᴇm itgē'lôx. Itcō'lXam: "Amē'ya
they were on him. Not good. His sickness they made on him. He said to her: "Go

ē'nanakcpa imē'pōtcxan. Atctᴇnlō'ta tiā'q¡amcukc." Igō'ya.
otter to your brother-in-law. He shall give them to you his intestines." She went.

Igiō'lXam: "Ā, ē'mᴇlXt tcmōxō'lam amtēlō'ta tᴇmē'q¡amcukc."
She said to him: "Ah, your elder brother he tells you you shall give them to him your intestines."

Itctā'lōt tᴇ'cit¡îX. Iktō'kᴛam. Kē'nuwa itixᴇ'lôx. Năct t¡ā'ya;
He gave them to her one-half. She brought them. Try they were on him. Not good;

peds and asked for their intestines. Last of all he asked the Lynx. She went to take his intestines. She got them and took them home. They were right. They did not make him feel sick.

They stayed there a long time. Then the woman was about to give birth to a child. She became sick, and she gave birth to two children. First she gave birth to an Owl, then to a Panther. The Panther said: "I will kill your owl-child." But the woman said: "No; the poor one. Let them grow up together!" They played together, and the Panther washed his son. The woman washed her son, the Owl. They grew up. The Owl's child killed shrews; the Panther's son killed chipmunks. Now they were really grown up. The Owl's son killed young mice and the Panther's son killed fawns. They did what their fathers had done. That is the story. To-morrow we shall have fine weather.

---

iā'tcqEm itgē'lôx. Ka'nauwē quxauwā'yuwala kē'nuwa
his sickness | they made on him. | All | quadrupeds | try

itctō'xauwā'koatck tgā'q¡amcuke. Kē'qamtq¡îX aqa ipu'koa
he asked them | their intestines. | Afterward | then | the lynx

ayā'xt¡ax. Iktēxgā'lEmam tiā'q¡amcuke. Iktō'kLam, itixE'lox.
last. | She went to take them | his intestines. | She brought them, | they were on him.

Q¡oā'L¡ aqa ya'Xkapa. Nî'cqē iā'tcqEm itgē'lôx.
All right, | then | him on. | Not at all | his sickness | they made on him.

Lā'lē icxē'la-it. Aqa iLagEmLî'lkoatck. Itcā'tcqEm iaxE'lôx
Long | they stayed. | Then | she was about to give birth. | Her sickness | was on her

wuXi aqagē'lak. Igaxā'2tōm. Iā'newa ikā'oXaō ia'Xan
that | woman. | She gave birth. | First | the owl | his son

igioXu'tōm, kē'qamtq¡îX ik¡oayawa' iā'Xan igioXu'tōm. Igē'kîm
she gave birth to him, | afterward | the panther | his son | she gave birth to him. | He said

ik¡oayawa': "Anewā'qoa ya'Xi ikā'oXaō iā'Xan." Igā'kîm wu'Xi
the panther: | "I will kill him | that | the owl | his son." | She said | that

aqagē'lak· "K¡ā'ya, tiā'kiutkoax. A'Lqē ē'XtkatîX actō'mta,
woman: | "No, | the poor one. | Later on | together | they will grow up,

acxk¡ayā'wulalEma." A'qa itciuqoā'tuLtck iā'Xan ik¡oayawa'.
they will play together." | Then | he washed him | his son | the panther.

A'qa igiuqoā'tuLtck wuXi aqagē'lak iā'Xan ikā'oXaō. Ā'qa
Then | she washed him | that | the woman | his son | the owl. | Then

ictā'qa-iLax igixacE'lux. Iq¡anō'mēqL qatciwā'qoax ya'Xi ikā'oXaō
large | they became. | Shrews | he killed them | that | owl

iā'Xan. Aguskuā's qatcuwā'qoax ya'Xi ik¡oa'yawa iā'Xan. Āqa
his son. | Chipmunks | he killed them | that | panther | his son. | Then

pāt ictā'qa-iLax. Ā'cō agā'xan qatcuwā'qoax ya'Xi ikā'oXaō
really | large. | Mouse | its young | he killed them | that | owl

iā'Xan. Aq¡ā'xcap qatcuwā'qoax ya'Xi ik¡oa'yawa iā'Xan.
his son. | Fawns | he killed them | that | panther | his son.

K¡oaLqā' cta'xi cî'ctam, k¡oaLqā' wi ctā'xka icî'xôx. K¡anēk¡anē';
Thus as | those | fathers, | thus | also | they | did. | The story;

ō'la aca-igā'p.
to-morrow | good weather.

The Raccoon (told 1891)

There was the Raccoon and his grandmother. Once upon a time they were hungry. The Crow lived in their house. He said to his grandmother: "Grandmother, I am hungry." She said: "What do you want? Do you want dried salmon?" "It is bad," said the Raccoon. Again he said to his grandmother: "Grandmother, I am hungry." "Do you want paper salmon?"[1] He said to his grandmother: "It is bad." Again he said to her: "Grandmother, I am hungry." "Do you want pounded salmon?" "It is bad." He said again: "Grandmother, I am hungry." "Do you want dried roasted salmon?" She offered him all kinds of food. Afterward she offered him fruits. He said again: "Grandmother, I am hungry." "Do you want gamass?" "It is bad. Grandmother, I am hungry." "Do you want dried blackberries?" "They are bad. Grandmother, I

Ilatā't Iā'k¡anē

The Raccoon His Myth

Cxelā'etîX	ayā'k¡Ec	ictakui'n.	Qā'xLqanē'kua	aqa	walō'	igī'yux.
There were	his grandmother	raccoon.	One day	then	hunger	acted on him.

TēXt	tE'gaqL	at¡ā'ntsa.	Itcō'lXam	ayā'k¡Ec:	"Ā'k¡ec	walō'."
One	her house	the crow.	He said to her	his grandmother:	"Grandmother	hunger."

Igiō'lXam:	"Tān	imElgoā'x?	Tcu'xoa	ēq¡eLē'Lx?"	"Tēia'ck¡ᵘL,"
She said to him:	"What	do you want?	Well	dried summer salmon?"	"It is bad,"

igē'kîm	iLatā't.	Wī't'ax	itcō'lXam	ayā'k¡ec:	"Ā'k¡ec	walō'."
he said	raccoon.	Again	he said to her	his grandmother:	"Grandmother	hunger."

"Tān	imElgoā'x?	Tcu'xoa	emē'nEqan?"	Itcō'lXam	ayā'k¡ec:
"What	do you want?	Well	paper salmon?"	He said to her	his grandmother:

"Tē'iack¡ᵘL."	Wī't'ax	itcō'lXam:	"Ā'k¡ec	walō'."	"Tcu'xoa
"It is bad."	Again	he said to her:	"Grandmother	hunger."	"Well

Lkē'LōL?"	"TE'Lack¡ᵘL."	Wī't'ax	igē'kîm:	"Ā'k¡ec	walō'."
pounded dry salmon?"	"It is bad."	Again	he said:	"Grandmother	hunger."

"Tcu'xoa	ak¡ē'lak?"	"TE'gack¡ᵘL."	Ka'nauwē	ta'Xi
"Well	dried salmon?"	"It is bad."	All	those

tctā'LxalEmā'emax.	Aqa	tā'xt¡ax	tqoxoē'max.	"Ā'k¡ec	walō',"
their kinds of food.	Then	finally	fruits.	"Grandmother	hunger,"

itcō'lXam	ayā'k¡ec.	"Tcu'xoa	tE'lalX?"	"TE'gack¡ᵘL.	Ā'k¡ec
he said to her	his grandmother.	"Well	gamass?"	"It is bad.	Grandmother

walō'."	Igiō'lXam	ayā'k¡ec:	"Tcu'xoa	ā'kEmukc,	aXī'caqt
hunger."	She said to him	his grandmother:	"Well	blackberries.	dry

---

[1] Paper salmon is salmon cut in very thin slices and dried.

am hungry." "Do you want dewberries?" "They are bad." She offered him all kinds of berries. Then his grandmother said: "What do you want? Do you want nuts?" "They are bad." Now she had offered him all the food they had in their house. "Do you want acorns?" she said. Then the Raccoon said: "All right." She gave him his small canoe: "Quick, go down, fill your small canoe and then come up, but close the cache well." She had five caches of acorns. The Raccoon went down and opened one of the caches. Then he ate all the contents of the cache. He opened another one and ate its contents. He emptied two caches. He opened one more and emptied it. He ate all that was in it. He opened the fourth one. He had emptied half of it when the Crow came down to the water. She saw him. "Raccoon is stealing!" Then Raccoon said: "Come, come, I will give you some of it." Thus he spoke to the Crow. She went and he gave her food,

---

ā'kᴇmukc." "Tᴇ'gack!^{u}ʟ. Ā'k!ec walō'." "Tcu'xoa agō'wē,
blackberries." "They are bad. Grandmother hunger." "Well dewberries(?),

aXî'caqt agō'wē?" "Tᴇ'gack!^{u}ʟ." Ka'nauwē ta'Xi tctā'qoxoēmax.
dry dewberries?" "They are bad." All those their fruits.

Agiō'lXam ayā'k!ec: "Tā'ntx imᴇlgoā'x? Tcu'xoa tᴇ'qxola?"
She said to him his grandmother: "What maybe do you want? Well nuts?"

"Tᴇ'gack!ʟ." Iguxoā'ʟXum tctā'ʟXᴇlᴇmā'emax tcēqu'ʟiX.
"They are bad." She finished it their food in the house.

"Tcō'xoa ak!a'nauwē imelgoā'x?" Igē'kîm iʟatā't: "Ā, ya'Xka,
"Well acorns do you want?" He said raccoon: "Ah, that,

ya'Xka." Iksē'lōt ayā'k!ec siā'xanīm: "Ai'aq amᴇ'ʟXa.
that." She gave it to him his grandmother his toy canoe: "Quick go down to the water.

Amasᴇlō'tga pāʟ sta'Xi smē'Xanīm. A'qa amᴇ'tptcga. T!ayā'
Put them into it full that your toy canoe. Then come up. Good

amxpuā'ya ya'Xi ik!uā'yatk." Qui'nᴇma tgā'k!uayatgᴇmax
close it that cache." Five her caches

tk!a'nauwē. Iō'ʟxa iʟatā't. Itcixᴇ'laqʟq ēXt ictā'k!uayatk.
acorns. He went down raccoon. He opened it one their cache.

Itcî'tôx ʟkoā'p, ʟkoā'p, ʟkoā'p, ʟkoā'p. Itixᴇ'lᴇmuX. Itciō'ʟXōm
He did (noise of chewing acorns). He ate them. He finished it

ēXt ik!oā'yatk. Igō'n ēXt itcixᴇ'laqʟq. Itcî'tôx
one cache. Another one he opened it. He did

ʟkoā'p, ʟkoā'p, ʟkoā'p, ʟkoā'p. Môkct tk!uayā'tgᴇmax
(noise of chewing acorns). Two caches

itctō'ʟXom. Igō'n ēXt itcixᴇ'laqʟq ik!uā'yātk iʟā'ʟōn. Itcî'tôx
he finished them. Another one he opened it a cache the third one. He did

ʟkoā'p, ʟkoā'p, ʟkoā'p, ʟkoā'p. Itciō'ʟXōm iʟā'ʟōn. Iʟā'lakt
(noise of chewing acorns). He finished it the third one. The fourth one

itcixᴇ'laqʟq. Kᴇ'tcak igē'xôx ya'Xi ik!uā'yatk. A'qa igō'ya
he opened it. Half became that cache. Then she went

ʟtcu'qoa at!ā'ntsa. Igē'qᴇlkᴇl: "Aligō'Xtga wiʟatā't," igiō'lXam.
the water the crow. She saw him: "He is stealing raccoon," she said to him.

Igē'kîm iʟatā't: "Mᴇ'tē, mᴇ'tē, ayamᴇlqoē'ma, ayamᴇlqoē'ma."
He said raccoon: "Come, come, I will give you to eat, I will give you to eat."

Itcō'lXam wu'Xi at!ā'ntsa. Igō'ya at!ā'ntsa. Itcā'lqo-îm; tā'ema
He said to her that crow. She went the crow. He gave her to eat; only

but he gave her only worms. She left him and stayed at some distance. Again she said: "Raccoon is stealing!" He said to her: "Come, come, I will give you some food." The Crow went. He gave her some food, partly good food and partly worms. Five times the Crow came back. Then she went up and said: "Your grandson is eating all your acorns." "The rascal," said his grandmother, "I forgot him." She went down and took a stick. He saw her coming down. Then he crawled up and hid in one end of their firewood. His grandmother searched for him near the water, then she gave it up. She went up and searched outside around the house. She did not find him. She entered and searched under the beds, but she did not find him. Then she gave it up. Then she thought she would make a great fire. She blew up the fire, and then she saw the Raccoon right there. He squatted on his knees and elbows. Then she took a firebrand, and struck his face and his nose and his neck. Then he ran out and she

---

tgā'qexeLawuke itetā'lqo-îm. Iga-iqE'luqL, kELā'îX igō'tXuit.
her worms he gave them to her to eat. She left him, far she stood.

A'qa wit'ax igā'kîm atj;a'ntsa: "Aligō'Xtka wiLatā't." Itcō'lXam:
Then again she said the crow "He is stealing raccoon." He said to her:

"ME'tē, mE'tē, ayamElqoē'ma, ayamElqoē'ma." Igō'ya atj;ā'ntsa.
"Come, come, I will give you to eat, I will give you to eat." She went the crow.

Itea'lqo-îm. Qa'wat tgtj;ō'kti itetā'lEqo-îm qā'wat tgā'qexēLawuke.
He gave her to eat Part good he gave it to her to eat part her worms.

Qoā'nEmîX igaXE'takua atj;ā'ntsa. Aqa igō'ptega. Igaxgu'Lîtck
Five times she returned the crow. Then she went up. She told

atj;a'ntsa: "Aqa itetō'LXōm tEmtā'kj;anauwē imē'kian." "Nā,
the crow "Then he finished it your acorns your grandson." "Ah,

guiā'xatck! igē'nilalakuit." Igō'Lx ayā'kj;ee, igē'gElga ē'mqō.
rascal! I forgot him." She went down his grandmother she took it a stick.

Itca'qelkel ayā'kj;ee āLxt. Iō'ptck igē'kj;Lxē. Iō'ptegam
He saw her his grandmother she went down to the water He went up he crawled. He came up

iLatā't. igēxE'pcut tetā XalEpteqîX nEXumā'kit. Kē'nuwa
raccoon he hid their firebrands at the end. Try

igakj;e'naxt ayā'kj;ee maLnîX. Tā'2mēnua igā'xôx aqa igō'ptega.
she watched for him his grandmother near the water Give up she did then she went up.

Igakj;e'naxt tāxanîX tE'ctaqL igā'kaLaxana. Nā2ct igiō'cgam.
She watched [illegible] [illegible] [illegible] Not she found him.

Igā'ckupq. Igiō'naxt gē'gualîX LXE'mitk. Kj;ā niet igiō'cgam.
She entered she watched for him below bed Nothing not she found him.

Tā'2mēnua igā'xôx. Aqa igō'La-it. Tj;ā'ya igō'xca agā'tōL:
Give up she did Then she stayed Good she made it her fire:

[illegible] igō'xca. Igē'gElkel iLatā't [illegible] kōpā'2. Itsimqj;ōyā'tiX [illegible]
[illegible] She [illegible] She saw him raccoon there He squatted on knees and elbows near

[illegible] Igā'gElga [illegible] [illegible] [illegible]. Igiō'quîlX
[illegible] She took it [illegible] [illegible] firebrand. She struck him

[illegible] [illegible] [illegible] [illegible] [illegible]. Igiō'quîlX
[illegible] [illegible] she struck him [illegible] [illegible] She struck it

[illegible] [illegible] Aqa [illegible] [illegible]. Aqa [illegible]
[illegible] [illegible] [illegible] [illegible] she struck him. Then he went

struck his backside. He went and cried: "Oh, my grandmother struck me and broke my backbone."

He went a long way and met some boys. The Raccoon was crying. "Oh, Raccoon, come! We are playing ball." Those boys were playing at ball. Raccoon said: "Logs, logs, logs, strike you ——" "Qō'q, Raccoon. You thief. Why do you cry?" Raccoon went on. Again he came to some boys. He cried. Again they shouted: "Oh, Raccoon, come, come! We are playing ball. He replied the same: "Logs, logs, logs, strike you ——"

Then Raccoon went on. He went some distance and looked up. There he saw a hawthorn. He climbed it. Then his grandmother followed him. She said: "Grandchild, my grandchild is going to take a young deer for me." Then a stick broke: "Is that you, grandchild?" she said. Raccoon was climbing about in the tree. Then he saw his grandmother. Then she came to him and looked up. There

---

iLatā't. Iō'qulqt iō'ya: "Agak¡ā'2c ignē'2wax Lē'2kLEk
raccoon. He cried he went: "My grandmother she struck me broken

itcē'2gal itā'2c."
my back-bone is."

KElā'îX iō'ya. Aqa iogoā'qoam tqā'totenîke. Iō'qulqt iLatā't.
Far he went. Then he reached them boys. He cried raccoon.

"Ā wiLatā't! ME'tē. Wā'layō alxcgā'ma." Wā'k¡alkal oxoacgE'liL
"Ah, raccoon! Come. Ball we play." Ball they were playing

ta-îtci tqā'totenîke. Igē'kîm iLatā't: "TEnux tc¡a mē'cam
those boys. He said raccoon: "These then you

LEmuqcEmā'emax LEmcXā'ltcîL tc¡E nā'mcxēlayu'tc¡koax." "Qō2q
logs you often strike yourselves (?) " "Qōq

wiLatā't! Mai'ka imē'qalpas, k¡a mixE'qalqt." Aqa wi iō'ya
raccoon! You you thief and you cry." Then again he went

iLatā't. Wī't'ax iugoā'qoam tqā'tōtēnîke. Iō'qulqt iLatā't. Wī't'ax
raccoon. Again he reached them boys. He cried raccoon. Again

iqigē'loma: "Ā wiLatā't wā'layō alxcgā'ma." K¡oaLqā' wī't'ax
he was called: "Ah, raccoon ball we play." Just so again

igē'kîm. "TEnux tc¡a mē'cam LEmuqcEmā'emax LEmcXā'ltcîL
he said. "These then you logs you often strike yourselves

tc¡E nā'mcxēlayu'tc¡koax."
(?) "

Aqa wi iō'ya iLatā't. Qā'xpaLq iō'yam, igē'kikct cā'xalîX. a'qa
Then again he went raccoon. Somewhere he arrived, he looked up, then

pāL wu'Xi asElā'wa cā'xalîX. Ioqoē'wulXt iLatā't. A'qa igē'wa
full those haws above. He climbed up raccoon. Then she pursued him

ayā'k¡ec. Igō'ya ayā'k¡ec, igē'wa. "Gā'yō witcE'kian, aq¡ē'xcap
his grandmother. She went his grandmother, she pursued him. "Grandson, my grandson, fawn

itcanē'tan witcE'kian." Lāq nîxō'xoax ē'mqō. "Mai'ka tci
he catches it for me my grandson." Break did a stick. "You [int. part.]

gā'yo?" nagē'mx. Igayuk¡oaLxē'goax iLatā't. Aqa itcā'qElkEl
grandson?" she said. He climbed about raccoon. Then he saw her

ayā'k¡ec. Aqa igō'qoam ayā'k¡ec. Igā'kikct ē'wa cā'xalîX,
his grandmother. Then she reached him his grandmother. She looked there up,

he was high up on the tree. His grandmother said: "Throw something down into my mouth, grandchild." He did not look. She spoke five times. Then he looked. He said: "Lie down on your back; close your eyes; open your mouth." Then he made a ball of haws and put thorns into them, and threw the ball down into her mouth. It stuck in her throat. Then she cried: "Water, grandchild; water, grandchild!" Often she said so. Then wings began to grow on her. Now he climbed down and searched for water. He did not find it. Then she began to fly, and he said to her: "Partridge(?) shall be your name. You shall not eat acorns."

Then Raccoon went on. He went a long distance. He came to a house and entered. Then he saw the Grizzly Bear in there. Then he thought: "He will eat me. Behold! I came into the house of a monster." The Grizzly Bear said: "Where do you come from, brother? Your face is painted prettily." The Raccoon said: "I was painted a little while before I came." "Oh, paint me also, brother."

---

aqa yaxī' cā'xalîX iō'goaxt iʟatā't. Igiō'lXam ayā'k¡ec:
then there up he was on it raccoon. She said to him his grandmother:

"Nē2tk¡îxā'ematsō gā'yo!" Nēct itcō'kcta. Qoā'nᴇmîX igiō'lXam,
"Throw down into my mouth grandson!" Not he looked. Five times she said to him,

koalē'wa itcō'kcta. "Mxā'ciltckē," itcō'lXam, "as amᴇnp¡ō'Xuita.
just then he looked. "Lie down on your back," he said to her, "and close your eyes.

ʟ¡āq amiō'X imē'kcXat." A'qa lō'ᴇlō itcō'xoa wu'Xi asᴇlā'wa.
Spread do your mouth." Then round he made them those haws.

Aqa itca-ilā'mit wu'Xi agā'qatc. Itcᴇlxā'ema itcā'kcXapa. Qu'ʟquʟ
Then he put into them those its thorns. He threw it down her mouth into. Stick

nau'i a'gamiguēpa. Igiō'lXam: "ʟtcu'qoa, gā'yō; ʟtcu'qoa, gā'yo!"
at once her throat in. She said to him: "Water, grandson; water, grandson!"

Ē'xauitîX igiō'lXam. Ā'qa tᴇ'gak¡ēntq itaxᴇ'lux. Aqa iō'qo-îtcō.
Often she said to him. Then her wings were on her. Then he went down.

Kē'nuwa itcʟō'naxʟ ʟtcu'qoa. Nā2ct itcʟō'cgam. Ā'2qa igō'koa
Try he searched for it water. Not he found it. Then she flew

ayā'k¡ec. Itcō'lXam: "AXutXuē't imē'xaleu. Nā2ct ā'ʟqē
his grandmother. He said to her: "Partridge (?) your name. Not later on

tᴇmē'k¡anauwē."
your acorns."

A'qa wi iō'ya iʟatā't. Kᴇlā'îX iō'ya. Itcuguā'qoam tqu'ʟē.
Then again he went raccoon. Far he went. He reached it a house.

Iā'ckupq. Itcē'qᴇlkᴇl aqa icā'yîm iō'Xt. Igîxʟō'xa-ît iʟatā't:
He entered. He saw him then the grizzly bear he was there. He thought raccoon:

"Ā'qa aqanuwᴇ'lq¡ama, iqcxē'ʟau ʟqōct gi inigᴇ'lōpq." Igē'kîm
"Then I shall be eaten, a monster behold that I entered." He said

icā'yîm: "Qā'mta ē'wa imtē'mam, ā'oē? Masā'tciʟ ʟqa
the grizzly bear: "Whence then you came, younger brother? Pretty maybe

ēmē'gēmatck." Igē'kîm iʟatā't: "Koalā'2wa iqanoguē'matck. Aqa
the painting on your face." He said raccoon: "Just I was painted. Then

"Yes, as you like," said the Raccoon. "Have you any pitch? They hit me here with a chisel, and then they poured pitch over me." Now he boiled some pitch. He asked the Bear: "Have you a chisel?" The Bear replied: "I have one." Now the pitch was boiling. Then the Bear was told: "Lie down on your back." He lay down. He said: "Oh brother, you will kill me!" The Raccoon replied: "As you like; if you don't wish it, I shall not paint you. You do not need to be painted." But the Bear said: "You must paint me, younger brother." Then he struck him with the chisel here at the forehead. He poured the pitch down over his face. He told him: "Jump into the water." The Bear jumped into the water. There he rolled about.

Then the Raccoon ran away. He went a long distance and met a person. He was dancing. He sang "——"

---

gi inᴇ'tē." "Â tgt!ō'kti amnoguē'matcgoa, ā'oē." "Mai'ka
here I came." "Ah, good you paint me, younger brother." "Your

imē'Xakamit," iqiō'lXam icā'yîm. "K!ā ʟᴇmā'q!axōcgan tcī?"
your mind," he was told the grizzly bear. "Nothing your pitch [int. part.]?"

igē'kîm iʟatā't. "Ē'qa-îtk gipā'tîX iqēnᴇlgā'mit, aqa wāx
he said raccoon. "A chisel here I was struck, then poured

ēqʟᴇ'nkux ʟq!axō'cgan; lᴇp ʟq!axō'cgan. iʟūtcXᴇ'm'ᴇt.
was on me pitch; boiling pitch. They boiled it.

ʟqā'ʟXatcX cxē'lak ʟaXi ʟq!axō'cgan." Aqa lᴇp iqᴇ'ʟôx ʟaXi
Coal mixed that pitch." Then boiled it was that

ʟq!axō'cgan. Lᴇp itcî'ʟôx iʟatā't. Iqiō'lXam icā'yîm: "Ē'mᴇqa-itk
pitch. Boil he did it raccoon. He was told the grizzly bear: "Your chisel

tcī?" Igē'kîm icā'yim: "Ē'tcqa-itk." Lᴇp iʟᴇ'x ʟaXi ʟq!axō'cgan.
[int. part.]?" He said the grizzly bear: "My chisel." Boil it did that pitch.

Iqiō'lXam icā'yim: "Amxā'ciltckī." Yixā'ciltcki icā'yim:
He was told the grizzly bear: "Lie down on your back." He lay down on his back the grizzly bear:

"Ō, ā'oē! amᴇnuwā'qoa." Igē'kim iʟatā't: "Mai'ka imē'Xaqamē.
"Oh, younger brother! you will kill me." He said raccoon: "You your mind.

Ma'nîx nîct tq!ēx mᴇ'tox ayamoguē'matckua, qā'txō nēct
If not like you do it I paint you, must not

ayamoguē'matckoa," igē'kim iʟatā't. Igē'kim icā'yim: "Qā'txō
I paint you," he said raccoon. He said the grizzly bear: "Must

amᴇnoguē'matckua, ā'oē!" Itcilgā'mit ya'Xi ē'qa-itk, gipapā'
you paint me, younger brother!" He hit him that chisel, here

itcilgā'mit. Wāx itcʟᴇ'kuX ʟaXi ʟq!axō'cgan siā'xôstpa.
he hit him. Pour out he did it on him that pitch his face on.

Itciō'lXam: "Sᴇ'pᴇna ʟtcu'qoapa." Itsî'sōpᴇna icā'yîm ʟtcu'qoapa.
He said to him: "Jump water into." He jumped the grizzly bear the water into.

Kōpā' igixcgē'lalᴇmtck icā'yîm.
There he rolled about the grizzly bear.

Igē'kta iʟatā't. Kᴇlā'îX iō'ya; aqa itcʟgō'qoam ʟgoaʟē'lX
He ran raccoon. Far he went; then he reached it a person

ʟuwē'la: "Ā'na tsak!oā'ix·ᴇn, tsak!oā'ix·ᴇn, ā'na tsamō'iXun
he danced: "Sometimes (?) (?) sometimes (?)

Then he recognized the Coyote. The Raccoon said: "Step aside, brother, a monster pursues me." The Coyote replied: "I shall eat you, I shall swallow you." "Oh, elder brother, step aside, a monster pursues me. I shall gather crab apples for you; I shall gather crawfish for you; I shall gather fresh-water clams for you; I shall gather haws for you; I shall gather all kinds of berries for you." Thus he spoke to Coyote. When a Grasshopper jumped up, Coyote snapped at it at once. He said: "Go to my house, put ten stones into the fire—five stones on the one side, and five stones on the other side—and heat them. Then cover yourself with a kettle." Raccoon went and came to Coyote's house. Then he heated the stones, all ten, just as Coyote had told him. Then Coyote danced. Now the Grizzly Bear saw him. "Did that little rascal pass you? He hit me." Then Coyote answered as before: "I shall eat you, I shall swallow you." Coyote sang: "——".

---

tsamō'iXun." Itciugu'laqʟq aqa it¡ā'lapas. Igē'kîm iʟatā't: "A,
(?) ." He recognized him then coyote. He said raccoon: "Ah,

ʟāq mxā'naxôx, ā'pxō. Iqcxē'ʟau itcîntuwā't." Igē'kîm it¡ā'lapas:
step aside do for me elder brother. A monster he pursues me." He said coyote:

"Kᴇlā'îX ʟᴇ'kala k¡oā'ix·ᴇn ayamō'xoa. Lᴇq¡° ayamō'xoa."
"Far man (?) I do you. Swallow I do you."

"Ā, ā'pxō! ʟāq mxā'nᴇxala. Iqcxē'ʟau itcîntuwā't. Nai'ka
"Ah, elder brother! step aside do for me. A monster he pursues me. I

amō'înx ayamᴇlp¡iā'ʟxa. Nai'ka aqaʟxē'la ayamᴇlp¡iā'ʟxa. Nai'ka
crab apples I will gather them for you. I crabs I will gather them for you. I

ʟtᴇ'kē aʟamᴇlp¡iā'ʟxa. Nai'ka asᴇlā'wa ayamᴇlp¡iā'ʟxa.
fresh-water clams I will gather them for you. I haws I will gather them for you.

Ka'nauwē tqoxoē'ma atamᴇlp¡iā'ʟxa," iqiō'lXam it¡ā'lapas,
All fruits I will gather them for you," he was told coyote,

itciō'lXam iʟatā't. Qatssopᴇnā'x ē'ts¡ēlaq, ā'nqa qatciō'qcx ya'Xi
he said to him the raccoon. When jumped a grasshopper already he bit it that

it¡ā'lapas. Aqa igē'kîm it¡ā'lapas: "Amē'ya tᴇ'kqʟpa. Iʟā'ʟēlXam
coyote. Then he said coyote: "Go my house to. Ten

ʟqᴇ'nakc aʟᴇmxᴇlgē'ʟxa, ē'natîX ā'tōʟ qoā'nᴇma aʟᴇmxᴇlgē'ʟxa,
stones heat them, on one side the fire five heat them,

ē'wa ē'natîX ā'tōʟ qoā'nᴇma aʟᴇmxᴇlgē'ʟxa. Ala'mxoalak¡oa
then on the other side the fire five heat them. Cover yourself with

aq¡u'tan." A'qa iō'ya iʟatā't. Iō'yam it¡ā'lapas tē'yaqʟ iʟatā't.
a kettle." Then he went raccoon. He reached coyote his house raccoon.

Itcʟxᴇ'lgiʟx ʟa'Xi ʟqᴇ'nakc. Ka'nauwē iʟā'ʟēlXam k¡oaʟqā ya'Xi
He heated them those stones. All ten just as that

itciō'lXam it¡ā'lapas. Kā ēwē'la it¡ā'lapas a'qa itcē'qᴇlkᴇl icā'yim.
he told him coyote. Where he danced coyote then he saw him the grizzly bear.

"Qā'mta iʟᴇ'mXkoa, ā'oē, ʟqoē'tgaētgaē? Iʟgᴇnū'waq."
"Where did he pass, younger brother, the little rascal? He killed me."

Igē'kîm it¡ā'lapas: "Kᴇlā'îX ʟᴇ'kala. K¡oā'iXᴇn ayamō'xoa.
He said coyote: "Far man. ? I do you.

Lᴇq¡° ayamō'xoa," igā'xax it¡ā'lapas: "Ā'na tsak¡oā'iXᴇn,
Swallow I do you," he did coyote: "Sometimes (?)

Coyote said: "I ate him, I devoured him." Now the Bear spoke: "Well, show him to me." Then Coyote spit and the saliva on his hand looked just like Raccoon. The Grizzly Bear spoke: "It is good that you have eaten that little rascal." Then Coyote said: "Let us go into my house." They entered and came in. Then Coyote said: "Now let us bet. You shall swallow these five stones. I shall swallow the other five." Coyote went out and put a reed into his mouth. It came out again at his buttocks. Then he entered again. He swallowed one stone and the Grizzly Bear swallowed one stone. Grizzly Bear's face became red. Coyote swallowed another stone and the Grizzly Bear swallowed another one. Then Grizzly Bear's face became contorted. Coyote swallowed the third stone and the Grizzly Bear swallowed the third one. Then tears ran down Grizzly Bear's cheeks. Coyote swallowed another stone and the Grizzly Bear swallowed the fourth one. Then Coyote swallowed the fifth one. He blew, and steam came out

---

tsak¡oā'iXEn, ā'na tsamō'iXun tsamō'iXun." Igē'kîm it¡ā'lapas:
(?) , sometimes (?) (?) ." He said coyote:

"K¡oā'iXEn inE'Lôx, lEq¡° inE'Lôx." Igē'kîm icā'yim: "Nî'Xua
" (?) I did it, swallow I did it." He said the grizzly bear: "Well

LEnxatE'n'ema." "X" igē'xôx it¡ā'lapas, tō igē'xôx,
show it to me." "X" he did coyote, spit he did,

itcLō'meqo-ît. Yā'Xka iLatā't igixē'maXit Lē'yakcipa. Igē'kîm
he spat it. That raccoon lay his hand on. He said

icā'yîm: "Q¡oā'L mLō'wîlq¡ Lqoē'tgaētgaē." "Tca! txō'ya
the grizzly bear: "All right you ate him the little rascal." "Come! let us go

tE'kqLpa," igē'kîm it¡ā'lapas. Ictō'ya tē'iaqLpa, tē'iaqL it¡ā'lapas.
my house to," he said coyote. They two went his house to, his house coyote.

Ictō'pqam. "AtxEmgē'tga!" igē'kîm it¡ā'lapas. "Qoā'nEma
They two came in. "Let us bet!" he said coyote. "Five

amLuwu'lq¡ama La'Xi LqE'nakc, qoā'nEma nai'ka nLuwu'lq¡ama."
you will swallow them those stones, five I I will swallow them."

Iō'pa it¡ā'lapas, iga-ixE'luktcō ā'pak. Ē'wa iā'potcpa Lāx igā'xôx
He went out coyote, he put it into (his mouth) a reed. There his anus at come out it did

wu'Xi ā'pak. Wī't'ax iā'ckupq. Itcē'wulq¡ ēXt ya'Xi iqE'nakc
that reed. Again he entered. He swallowed it one that stone

it¡ā'lapas. Itcē'wulq¡ icā'yîm ēXt ya'Xi iqE'nakc. Nauē' LpEll
coyote. He swallowed it the grizzly bear one that stone. At once red

icî'xôx cī'axôst. Igō'n itcē'wulq¡ it¡ā'lapas, iLā'môkst. Igō'nax
became his face. Another one he swallowed it coyote, the second one. Another one

itcē'wulq¡ icā'yim iLā'môkst. Naui' iciktc¡ē'wunX ya'Xi icā'yim.
he swallowed it the grizzly bear the second one. At once his face became contorted that grizzly bear.

ILā'Lōn itcē'wulq¡ it¡ā'lapas. iLā'Lōn itcē'wulq¡ icā'yim. Nau'i
The third one he swallowed it coyote, the third one. he swallowed it the grizzly bear. At once

tiā'laqctk itktXuī'yotco. Igō'n itcē'wulq¡ it¡ā'lapas iLā'lakt.
his tears they ran down. Another one he swallowed it coyote the fourth one.

ILā'lakt itcē'wulq¡ icā'yim ya'Xi iqE'nakc. Ē'LaquinEm itcē'wulq¡
The fourth one he swallowed it the grizzly bear that stone. The fifth one he swallowed it

of his mouth. Now the Grizzly Bear swallowed the fifth stone. Coyote told him: "Now drink water." He drank water. It began to boil and he fell down dead. Then Raccoon threw off the kettle. They cut him and ate him.

Now they were hungry again. Every day Raccoon brought crab apples. Every day he brought fresh-water clams. Every day he brought haws. He brought crawfish and potentilla roots. He brought all kinds of berries. Then the two, Coyote and Raccoon, ate all the time. Now it came to be winter and Raccoon was very fat.

Then the two became hungry, and several times Raccoon went out. He found a cache in which provisions were hidden—paper salmon, dried summer salmon, pounded salmon, dried salmon, salmon backs and dried gamass, dried blackberries, and dried dewberries, and all kinds of fruit. All kinds of fruit were hidden. Now he carried home five salmon backs. He went home. He hid them near the house and

---

itꞁā'lapas. "X" igē'xôx itꞁā'lapas; Xōp iā'kᵘcXat. Iqō'xoan
coyote. "X" he did coyote; it steamed his mouth. Steam

igē'qᴇlpa. Ē'ʟaquinᴇm itcē'wulqꞁ icā'yim ya'Xi iqᴇ'nakc. Igē'kîm
went out of his mouth. The fifth one he swallowed it the grizzly bear that stone. He said

itꞁā'lapas: "ʟtcu'qoa ʟᴇ'qamct!" Itcʟō'qumct ʟtcu'qoa ya'Xi
coyote: "Water drink!" He drank it water that

icā'yîm. ʟᴇp igē'xôx ē'yamxtc. Kopā' igē'kꞁelapx·itîX. Iō'maqt.
grizzly bear. Boil it did his stomach. There he fell over. He was dead.

Itcaxē'ma ā'yaqꞁtan iʟatā't. A'qa icgī'yuxc. Icgiō'ʟXum
He threw it off his kettle raccoon. Then they cut him. They finished him

igîcxᴇ'lᴇmux.
they ate him.

A'qa wā'lō icXᴇ'ʟa-it. Ka'nauwē ʟkā'etax qatcugū'ya-îtx
Then hunger they died. All days he gathered them

amō'înx, qatcʟugū'ya-îtx ʟtᴇ'kē ya'Xi iʟatā't. Qatcugū'ya-îtx
crab apples, he gathered them fresh-water clams that raccoon. He gathered them

asᴇlā'wa, qatcūgū'ya-îtx aqaʟxē'la, qatciugū'ya-îtx ikꞁenā'tan,
haws, he gathered them crabs, he gathered them potentilla roots,

qatctugū'ya-îtx ka'nauwē tqoxoē'max. Qatsxᴇlᴇmō'xuma-îtx
he gathered them all fruits. They ate all the time

itꞁā'lapas kꞁa iʟatā't. A'qa tcā'xᴇlklîX igē'xoxo-îX. A'qa
coyote and raccoon. Then winter it got. Then

ayā'pXᴇleu iga-ixᴇ'lôx iʟatā't.
his fat was on him raccoon.

Ā'2qa walō' icXᴇ'ʟa-it. Ā'2ʟatcixēX ʟqa iō'ya iʟatā't. Aqa
Then hunger they died. Several times maybe he went raccoon. Then

itctō'cgam tkꞁē'pcolē, ʟxᴇlᴇmā'emax tkpcō'tîX, ʟmē'nqan ʟupcō'tîX,
he found it a cache, food was hidden, paper salmon was hidden,

ʟqꞁēʟē'ʟx ʟupcō'tîX, aqē'ʟō upcō'tîX, akꞁē'lak upcō'tîX, tgu'nat
dried summer salmon was hidden, pounded Cascade salmon was hidden, dried salmon was hidden, salmon

ʟgā'kōtcX ʟupcō'tîX, tᴇ'lalX uXoā'caqt tgapcō'tîX, ʟᴇ'kᴇmukc
their backs were hidden, gamass dry was hidden, blackberries

ʟᴇkcᴇ'mᴇt, ʟgō'uē ʟᴇkcᴇ'mᴇt ʟupcō'tîX, ka'nauwē tqoxoē'max
dry; dewberries dry were hidden, all fruits

tgapcō'tîX. Itcî'ʟukʟ qui'nᴇma ʟᴇ'kōtcX. Igē'Xkꞁoa. Qꞁoā'p
were hidden. He carried them five backs. He went home. Near

then he came home. They had only potentilla roots to eat. It grew dark, and they lay down. Coyote had his bed on one side of the house, Raccoon on the other side. Raccoon said: "Oh, if my pillow would be full of five salmon backs to-morrow morning!" Coyote replied: "Yes, if that were so, younger brother! If my pillow would be full of ten salmon backs!" Day came, and then Raccoon searched under his pillow. There were five salmon backs under his pillow. Coyote looked under his pillow, but there was nothing. Now they two ate. Raccoon went again to the cache and ate there all day. Then he went home. He carried five dried summer salmon. Near the house he hid them, and his elder brother had only potentilla roots to eat. Again it grew dark, and Raccoon said: "Oh, if I could find five dried summer salmon under my pillow!" Coyote said: "Indeed, my brother, if that were true! If I could find ten summer salmon under my pillow!" Now Raccoon was awake and Coyote slept.

---

tE'ctaqL, a'qa itcLō'pcut. IgiXk¡oā'mam. Iā'ema ik¡enā'tan
their house, then he hid them. He came home. Only potentilla roots

iā'k¡ewula. Igō'ponEm. IckLqā'yuXuit, ē'wa k¡anatē'tuL
what he had gathered. It grew dark. They lay down, there on one side

tqu'Lē iā'lXEmitk it¡ā'lapas, gata tE'nat tqu'Lē iā'lXEmitk iLatā't.
the house his bed coyote, and on the other side the house his bed raccoon.

Igē'kîm iLatā't: "Ēgatcō'ktîX taya'x aqa qui'nEma LE'kōtcX
He said raccoon: "Early to-morrow oh if then five backs

tgE'XEmaxatcX pāL Lkēx." "Ō, ā'qanuē, tayā'x itsō'XuîX,
my pillow full were." "Oh, indeed, if my younger brother,

nai'ka taya'x iLā'LēlXam," igē'kîm it¡ā'lapas. Wāx igē'tcuktē.
I oh if ten," said coyote. Early day came.

ItcukjEmā'nanEmtck tiā'XEmaxatcX iLatā't. Qui'nEm LE'kōtcX
He looked at it his pillow raccoon. Five backs

gē'guala tiā'XEmaxatcX iLatā't. Kē'nuwa itctuk¡umē'nanEmtck
under his pillow raccoon. Try he looked at it

tiā'XEmaxatcX it¡ā'lapas. K¡ā nEct tān itciō'cgam. A'qa
his pillow coyote. Nothing not anything he found it. Then

icxLXE'lEmîtck. A'qa wit'ax iō'ya iLatā't pā taXi tk¡ē'pcolē.
they two ate. Then again he went raccoon there that cache.

Wē'2goa nixLXE'lEmux kōpa' taXi tk¡ē'pcolēpa. NîXk¡oā'x.
All day he ate then that cache at. He went home.

Qoā'nEma Lq¡eLē'LX qatcLō'k·ix. Q¡oā'p tqu'Lēpa qatcLōpcō'tx.
Five dried summer salmon he carried them. Near the house at he hid them.

Iā'ema ik¡enā'tan qatcilō'k·ix ya'Xi ē'yalXt. Nō'pōnEm wit'ax.
Only potentilla roots he carried them to him that his elder brother. It grew dark again.

A'qa wī't'ax nigē'mx iLatā't: "TcXua tk¡umā'nanEmx
Then again he said raccoon: "Well looking at it

tgE'XEmaxatcX, a'qa qui'nEma Lq¡eLē'LX gē'guala' tgE'XEmaxatcX
my pillow, then five dried summer salmon under my pillow

Lkē'xax." "Ā'qanuē, tā'yax itsō'XuîX, tcXua nai'ka iLā'LēlXam
were." "Indeed, if my younger brother, well I ten

Lq¡ēLē'LX gē'guala tgE'XEmaxatcX." IgixE'gElEmtck iLatā't,
dried summer salmon under my pillow." He was awake raccoon,

He went out slowly and brought those salmon. He lifted his pillow and put them under it. In the morning, when day came, he looked under his pillow and there were five dried summer salmon under it. Coyote looked too, but he did not find anything. Sometimes they wished for gamass, and only Raccoon found it under his pillow. When Coyote looked for it, he did not find anything. Every day he went to the cache and ate. When he went home, he carried their food: sometimes paper salmon, which he hid near the house. In two months they finished all the food. Now Raccoon was fat. Coyote thought: "I will kill him and eat him."

On the next evening Coyote said: "Do not go there, else you will meet warriors. Their name is Wā'LaXLaX. They look just as I do, and they will kill you." After several nights, Raccoon went again

---

iuqō'pti it¡ā'lapas. Lawā' iō'pa iLatā't. ItcLguā'lEmam LaXi
he slept coyote. Slowly he went out raccoon. He fetched them those

Lq¡ēLē'Lx. Itctō¡latck tiā'XEmaxatcX, itcE'LXtk gē'guala.
dried summer salmon. He lifted it his pillow, he put it on the ground underneath.

Wāx igē'tcuktē. Itctuk¡Emā'nanEmtck tiā'XEmaxatcX iLatā't.
Next morning it grew day. He looked at it his pillow raccoon.

Quî'nEma Lq¡eLē'Lx itcLō'cgam, tiā'XEmaxatcX pāL Lkēx.
Five dried summer salmon he found them, his pillow full was.

Kē'nuwa itctuk¡Emā'nanEmtck tiā'XEmaxatcX it¡ā'lapas; k¡ā'ya
Try he looked at it his pillow coyote; nothing

nîct tānki itciō'cgam. Anā' tE'lalX qackcūkEmaLEmā'x, iā'ema
not anything he found it. Sometimes gamass they wished for it, only

iLatā't qatctucgā'mx tiā'XEmaxatcXpa. Kē'nuwa it¡ā'lapas
raccoon he found it his pillow at. Try coyote

qatctuk¡Emā'nanEmx tiā'XEmaxatcX, k¡ā nîct tān qatciucgā'mx.
he looked at it his pillow, nothing not anything he found it.

Ka'nauwē Lkā'etax qayō'îx ta'Xi tk¡ē'pcōlēpa. NîxLxE'lEmamx.
All days he went that cache to. He went to eat.

Qiā'x nîXk¡oā'x tcXua qatctō'kIx ta'Xi txElEmā'emax. Anā'
If he returned then he brought it that food. Sometimes

Lmē'nqan qatcLō'kIx; q¡oā'p tE'ctaqLpa qatcLupcō'tx. Mâkct
paper salmon he brought it; near their house at he hid it. Two

LkLEmEna'kc qacktuLXō'mx ta'Xi txElEmā'emax, aqa
months they finished it that food, then

ayā'pXElēu ya'Xi iLatā't. NîxLoXuā'itx it¡ā'lapas: "Anēwā'qoa;
his fat that raccoon. He thought coyote: "I will kill him;

anînxElEmō'xuma."
I will eat him."

Agōnā'pōl aqa qatciolXā'mx: "Näct ēwata' Ltē'yîm.
One night then he said to him: "Not there go.

Amōgoā'qoama t¡uxulā'yowimax, Wā'LaXLaX itā'xaleu. K¡oaLqē'
You will meet them warriors, Wā'LaXLaX their name. Just as

L¡a nai'ka itā'lkuilē. AtgEmuā'qoa." Tcā'xēX Lqa iō'qoya-îX,
behold I they are similar. They will kill you." Several times maybe he slept,

a'qa iō'ya iLatā't ēwā'tkēwa ya'Xi iqēkE'lxēwa-îX. Aqa
then he went raccoon there that it was forbidden. Then

to the place which had been forbidden to him. He climbed about in the trees and gathered fruits. Now he heard the war-cries of many people, and a person appeared holding a lance. His face was painted red and black. His legs were also painted. When that person came nearer, he recognized Coyote, and Raccoon said: "You want to fool me, Coyote. These are your legs; that is your nose." But Coyote said: "We are Wā'LaXLaX; we look like Coyote." He went around him often. Then he struck Raccoon's belly with his lance and ran home. Now Coyote came home. He washed his face and his legs and lay down near the fire. He blew into the fire and was covered with ashes. In the evening he heard his younger brother groaning. Raccoon entered. Then Coyote arose and said: "My younger brother, I told you not to go there; the Wā'LaXLaX would meet you. They look just like me." Now it got dark and Coyote tried to cure him. The peritoneum protruded from his skin. Then he sucked at it and pulled

---

iuk!oaLxē'koax iLatā't. Itctō'la tptsE'nō. Aqa itcī'ltcī'maq
he climbed about in trees raccoon. He gathered them (a fruit). Then he heard it

ē'nxiaXul ikē'x. Ya'xka L!aq Lgā'pElatikc tē'lXam ē'nxiaXul
war-cries were. That just as many people war-cries

tgiuxō'la. Lāx iLE'xôx LgoaLē'lX. Icqoē'L!Em Lgī'gElgā't.
they made. Visible became a person. A lance he held it.

Lqā'LXatcx LE'lux Lstā'xôst, Lgē'matckuēX qā'wa anuā'LEma, qā'wa
Coal was on it his face, painted partly red paint, partly

Lqā'LXatcx ka Lā'qo-ît Lgē'matckuēX. Q!oā'p iLigā'tqoam LaXi
coal and his legs were painted. Nearly he reached him that

LgoaLē'lX, itciugu'laqLI it!ā'lapas. Igē'kîm iLatā't: "Mai'ka
person, he recognized him coyote. He said raccoon: "You

it!ā'lapas, lā'xlax mE'nôxt. Mai'ka tEmē'qo-it, mai'ka ē'miktc."
coyote, deceive you do me. You your legs, you your nose."

Igē'kîm it!ā'lapas: "NE'saika Wā'LaxLax ntsxElk!ā'yutsxax
He said coyote: "We Wā'LaxLax we resemble each other

it!ā'lapas." Qā'watîX igiXE'Lakoa. Itcilgā'mit ya'Xi icqoē'L!Em
coyote." Several times he went around him. He struck it that lance

iā'wanpa. Igē'kta. Igē'Xk!oa it!ā'lapas. IgēXk!oā'mam it!ā'lapas.
his belly in. He ran. He went home coyote. He came home coyote.

IgixEmē'nak!oa. Itcī'tutcktc tiā'qo-it. Igēxō'kcc q!oā'p ā'tōL. Pō
He washed his face. He washed them his legs. He lay down near the fire. Blow

itcō'xoa wu'Xi actā'tōL. Pā2L tE'kEmxEm igē'xôx. Tsō'yustîX
he did it that their fire. Full ashes he became. In the evening

aqa itcī'ltcī'maq iā'mXîX. Aēx·Elqā'yax. Igē'tpqam iLatā't.
then he heard him his younger brother. He was groaning. He came in raccoon.

IgixE'latck it!ā'lapas: "Ā'oē, itsō'XuîX iamō'lXam, nā'sqē ē'wata
He arose coyote: "Younger brother, my younger brother I told you, never there

amō'yîma. Lq!āp amLō'xoa Wā'LaxLax. Ntsxelk!ā'yutsXax."
go. Meet you would do them Wā'LaxLax; We resemble each other."

Igō'pōnEm. Ayukuilā'eta it!ā'lapas. Iqigelā'ita iLatā't. Lāx
It got dark. He tried to cure him coyote. They tried to cure him raccoon. Visible

ōguakē'x tiā'nawa-îtk ya'Xi iLatā't. ItcikXā'naq. IqikXā'naq
was his peritoneum that raccoon. He sucked at it. It was sucked

it out. Then Raccoon was really dead. Coyote had killed his brother. Coyote said: "Do I know my brother? I am almost starved to death." Now he cut his brother, and after two days he had finished eating him. Then he became hungry again. For five days he was hungry, then he cried: "Oh, what a fool I was to kill him! He used to bring me all kinds of food and I had much to eat." He cried: "Oh, my younger brother ——" He cried. A deer and its young passed him and said: "Coyote, you killed him and now you cry." "The fawn shall be pursued." They had named his dead brother's name.

That is the story. To-morrow we shall have good weather.

---

iLatā't. Iqō'xoak¡a tiā'nawa-îtk iLatā't. PāX iō'maqt iLatā't. Ā'qa
raccoon. It was pulled out his peritoneum raccoon's. Really he was dead raccoon. Then

itcē'waq iā'mXîX it¡ā'lapas. Igē'kîm it¡ā'lapas: "TEnlō'xo-iXEna
he killed him his younger brother coyote. He said coyote: "I know them [int. part.]

tgE'mXîkc, aqa walō' inō'maqt." Itcī'yuxc aqa iā'mXîX. Mākct
my younger brothers, then hunger I die." He cut him then his younger brother. Two

Lkā'etax igixE'lEmux. A'qa itciō'LXōm. Aqa wi walō' igī'yux.
days he ate. Then he finished him. Then again hunger acted on him.

Qoā'nEma Lkā'etax walō' igī'yux. A'qa igigE'tcax: "Ā'qanuē qa
Five days hunger acted on him. Then he cried: "Indeed now

nE'L¡ala, qā'ts¡kē inē'waq, pō k¡a tā'nEmax itcnitkuē't.
I fool, why I killed him, if and things he brought me.

TEnxElā'x." Aqa igigE'tcax:
I ate much." Then he cried:

Awi yaui-tsō'-Xu-iX, awi yaui-tsō-XuiX, ā-LE qalu-wa-ya ā-Le-qa k¡ō yū k¡o yū.
My younger brother, my younger brother, (?) (?) k¡o-yū k¡oyū.

Kā iō'qulqt iLē'xkoa ilā'lax k¡a iā'qxôq. "Kō'k¡u, it¡ā'lapas.
When he cried it went past the deer and its young. "Kō'k¡u, coyote.

Mai'ka imē'waq, k¡a imigE'mEqElqt." "Ān iqE'Luwaya wut¡ē'lqan
You you killed him, and you cry." "Ah he will be pursued the fawn

wutsā'qôq." Lāxi igik¡ē'mxanuL. K¡anē'k¡anē; ō'la asa-igā'p.
his young one." Those he named his dead relatives. The story; to-morrow good weather.

TALES

Tiā'pexoacxoac (told 1890)

There was a maiden. Now a chief bought a wife and he took her. She did not like him. She had a bitch which always slept with her. Wherever she went she carried that dog. She always gave her good food. Her dog was fat. One day she forgot her. Then her husband said: "Quick, kill that bitch." Now her husband's brothers killed the bitch. They singed her and boiled her. Her fat was two fingers thick. Now the dog was put aside. Now she came home. In the evening when she came home her sister-in-law said: "Your brother-in-law killed that seal. They saved this for you." Then she cut the fat and ate it. She ate another piece. She ate five pieces. Now she became qualmish. She threw it aside. "Oh, maybe they gave me my dog to eat."

A'qa ēXā't añā't!au. A'qa itcō'mᴇla ictā'muX; a'qa itcō'cgam.
Then one maiden. Then he bought her a chief; then he took her.

Nîct tq!āx igī'yux. A'qa guā'nᴇsum agā'k!ōtkōt qacqʟqō'yōXuîtx.
Not like she did him. Then always her bitch they two slept together.

Qā'mta nō'îx guā'nᴇsum agō'kᴛx agā'k!ōtkōt. Guā'nᴇsum it!ō'kti
Where she went always she carried her her bitch. Always good

iʟxᴇ'lᴇm agialqō'emuX agā'k!ōtkōt. A'qa agā'pXᴇleu agā'k!ōtkōt.
food she gave it to eat to her her bitch. Then her fat her bitch.

Ā'qa igā'elalakuit. A'qa igē'kîm itcā'kikal: "Ai'aq amcgō'waq
Then she forgot her. Then he said her husband: "Quick kill her

agā'k!ōtkōt." A'qa iʟgō'waq ʟiā'wuXikc itcā'kikal. A'qa
her bitch." Then they killed her his brothers her husband. Then

iʟgaxʟᴇ'lam. ʟä4 aqa iʟᴇ'kōtcXᴇm. Môkct tkci agā'pXᴇleu.
they singed her. Long then they boiled her. Two fingers her fat.

A'qa iqagᴇ'lōtk agā'k!ōtkōt. A'qa igaXatk!oā'mam. Tsō'yustîX
Then it was put aside her bitch. Then she came home. In the evening

igaXatk!oā'mam. A'qa igō'lXam agā'tōm: "Aqē'sgoax itcō'waq;
she came home. Then she said to her her sister-in-law: "A seal he killed it;

imē'pōtcxan itcō'waq. Tau'wax iqamgᴇ'lōtk." ʟq!ōp igī'yuX
your brother-in-law he killed it. This was put aside for you." Cut she did it

itcā'pXᴇleu. Igē'wîlq!. Igō'n wi ēXt igē'wîlq!. Qoā'nᴇma ʟq!ōp
its fat. She ate it. Another also one she ate it. Five cuts

igē'wîlq!. A'qa ē'mqōlkᴛ itcō'xoa. A'qa iā'c igī'yux. "Ō,
she ate them. Then qualmishness did her. Then let alone she did it. "Oh,

ʟXuan ta'u agᴇ'k!ōtkōt iqanᴇ'lqoēm."
maybe this my bitch was given to me to eat."

After some time she was with child. Then her husband was ashamed. "Maybe somebody else made her pregnant. I will leave her." Now she went to pick berries. Then they left her. They took their houses away. They smashed and broke their old canoes. In the evening she came home. There were no people. "Oh, they left me." Now she made a small house, and there she stayed. After some time she gave birth. She brought forth a dog. She kicked it. She brought forth another dog. She brought forth five male dogs and one female. Now she suckled them. They grew up. She always left them at the house.

One day she found the tracks of children at the beach in front of her house. "Where may these children have come from?" She entered, and there were her children. She went again. In the evening she came home. Now there were many tracks of children. Now an arrow was there. She found it and she found a shell lying there. She thought: "There must be one girl among them. Maybe they will kill

---

Lä4, aqa agā'wan igaxᴇ'lôx. A'qa igiXᴇmā'sa-it itcā'kikal.
Long, then her pregnancy was on her. Then he was ashamed her husband.

"ʟXuan ʟxalō'ita agā'wan iʟgā'lôx. Nîcqē nai'ka. Tgt¡ō'kti
"Perhaps another one her pregnancy he made it on her. Not at all I. Good

alxagᴇlō'qʟqa." A'qa wi igō'ya igaxalō'kcam. A'qa
we leave her." Then again she went she picked berries. Then

iʟagᴇ'lōqʟq. Ka'nauwē iʟgᴇ'tukᴛ ʟā'qʟēmax. Ka'nauwē cā'ca
they left her. All they carried them houses. All break

iʟᴇ'kôx gitcā'mᴇlamaX akᴇ'nim. Tsō'yustîX igaxk¡oā'mam. A'qa
they did bad canoes. In the evening she came home. Then

k¡Emm tê'lXam. "Ō, ā'qa ʟqōct iqangᴇ'lōqʟq." A'qa igᴇ'tôx
no people. "Oh, now behold I am deserted." Then she made it

itō'koa-îts tqu'ʟē. A'qa kōpa' igō'ʟa-it. Lä'2lē, aqa igakXa'tōm.
its smallness house. Then there she stayed. Long, then she gave birth.

Igioxô'tōm ik¡ō'tkōt. A'qa igigᴇ'ʟtᴇq. A'qa igō'n igioXô'tōm
She gave birth to it a dog. Then she kicked it. Then another one she gave birth to it

wī ik¡ō'tk¡ōt. Quā'nᴇmîkc tkā'lukc tk¡ōtk¡ō'tkc, aēXā't
again a dog. Five male dogs, one

aqagē'lak iktoxô'tōm. Aqa itaxᴇlt¡ō'kcamit. Ā'2qa itā'qa-iʟax
female she gave birth to them. Then she suckled them. Then large

iō'xo-îx. A'qa guā'nᴇsum nuguē'qʟqax tqu'ʟēpa.
they became. Then always she left them the house in.

A'qa ēXt ē'kua aqa iktō'ckam tqā'tōtenîkc tgā'Xatk agā'maʟna-
Now one day then she found them boys their tracks toward the water from her

pa. "Qā'mta ʟqa itgatē'mam tkci tqā'tōtenîkc?" Igō'pqam;
at. "Where maybe they came these boys?" She came in;

ō'2xoaxt itcā'qōq. Igō'n ē'kua igō'ya. Tsō'yustîX
there were her children. Another day she went. In the evening

igaXatk¡oā'mam. A'qa ʟgā'pᴇlatîkc tqā'totenîkc tgā'Xatk. A'qa
she came home. Then many boys their tracks. Then

axē'mat aqā'matcX. Igō'cgam. A'qa axē'mat ā'mᴇlk¡ē, igō'cgam.
there lay an arrow. She took it. Then there lay a shell, she took it.

IgaxʟŌ'Xa-it: "ʟqagē'lak ʟ¡gi ʟk¡ā'sk¡as ʟēXā't." IgaxʟŌ'Xoa-it:
She thought: "A girl behold this child one." She thought:

my dogs." She entered, but there her dogs were lying. On the following day she went again to pick berries. In the evening she came home. There were many tracks of children. There were many arrows and shells. "Where did these children come from?" She entered and her dogs were there. The following morning she went again to pick berries. She did not go far, and there she picked berries. Now she heard children. When the sun was still high up in the sky she returned. She thought: "I will go home. They might kill my dogs." Then she returned. Then she arrived at home. There were no children, but the beach was all covered with tracks of children. She entered, and there her dogs were lying. She thought: "I will hide to-morrow." In the morning she made herself ready. She went out and remained in the grass. After a little while she heard children in the house. Soon a girl came out, went around the house, and entered again. "Did you see our mother?" "Oh, she went a long time ago. There is nobody outside." Soon a child came out;

"LXuan aqtōtē'na tgE'k¡ōtk¡ōtke." Igō'pqam; ō'xoaxt
"Maybe they will be killed my dogs." She came in; there were

tgā'k¡ōtk¡ōtke. Ā'qa igē'tcuktîX wī't'ax. A'qa wi igō'ya
her dogs. Then day came again. Then again she went

igaxalō'kca. Tsō'yustîX a'qa wi igaXatk¡oā'mam. Ō2, a'qa
she picked berries. In the evening then again she came home. Oh, then

Lgā'pElatîkc tgā'Xatk tqā'tōtēnîkc. Oxoā'xtax tqā'matcx
many their tracks boys. There were arrows

Lgā'pEla. A'qa Lî'XuXt LE'mElk¡ē. Lgā'pEla Lî'XuXt. "Qāmta
many. Then there lay shells. Many lay there. "Where

Lqa itgatē'mam tkei tqā'tōtenîkc?" Igō'pqam; ō'2xoaxt
maybe came these boys?" She came in; there were

tgā'k¡ōtk¡ōtkc. Wāx igō'ya wī't'ax igaxalō'kcam. Q¡oā'pîX
her dogs. Next day she went again she went picking berries. Near

igō'ya. A'qa kōpā' igaxE'lukc. A'qa igauitcE'mlētEmtck
she went. Then there she picked berries. Then she heard them

tqā'tōtenîkc. Kā cā'xalîX aqaLā'x, a'qa igā'Xk¡oa. "Ō, ai'aq
boys. When up the sun, then she went home. "Oh, quick

anXk¡oā'ya. LXuan aqtōtē'na tgE'k¡ōtk¡ōtkc." A'qa igā'Xk¡oa.
I will go home. Perhaps they will be killed my dogs." Then she went home.

A'qa igaXk¡oā'mam. K¡Emm tqā'tōtenîkc. Aqa L¡mēn mā'LnîX
Then she came home. No boys. Then soft at sea

tgā'Xatk tqā'tōtenîkc. Igō'pqam; ō'2xoaxt tgā'k¡ōtk¡ōtkc.
their tracks boys. She came in; there were her dogs.

IgaxLō'Xoa-ît: "Ō'la aqa anxpcō'ta." Igē'tcuktîX,
She thought: "To-morrow then I will hide." Day came,

igaXE'ltXuîtck. Igō'pa. Igō'La-it tE'pcōpa. Koala' aqa
she made herself ready. She went out. She stayed the grass in. Soon then

igauitcE'maq tqā'tōtenîkc tqu'Lipa. Koala' a'qa iLpā'mam
she heard them boys the house in. Soon then she came out

Lqagē'l Lk¡ā'sk¡as. ILuXoā'Lakoa tqu'Lē. A'qa wi iLō'pqa.
a female child. She went around it the house. Then again she entered.

"Tcu'Xoa imā'qElkEl wā'lxaq?" "Ā'nqa igō'ya, k¡ā Lā'xanîX."
"Well you saw her our mother?" "Long ago she went, nobody outside."

Koala' a'qa iLō'pa Lk¡ā'skas. Lgōn iLō'pa. Lgō'nax iLō'pa.
Soon then he went out a boy. Another one went out. Another again went out.

another one came out; still another one came out; five boys and one girl came out. They went straight down to the beach. Then the woman entered. Now she saw the dog blankets. She took them and burnt them. Then she went down to the beach. "Oh, my children. Why did you disguise yourselves before me? Let us go up to the house." Now they all hid their faces. She spoke to them twice. Then five of the children went up. One had a sick leg. He did not go up for a long time, but in the evening he also came. Now her children stayed there; they grew up. Then she and her daughter always went picking berries, and the boys all became hunters. One was a deer hunter, one an elk hunter, one a seal hunter, one a sturgeon hunter, and one a sea lion hunter.

After some time, Tiā'pexoacxoac heard that there was a girl at QaLa'la. He went to buy her, and they gave him that girl. Tiā'pexoacxoac was a bad man. He used to eat blood. If he had not enough, then he ate his wives. When his wife had a male child, he

---

Quā'nEmîkc	tkā'lukc	itgE'pa,	LēXā't	Lqagē'lak.	Nā'2wi
Five	boys	went out,	one	girl.	At once

itgE'Lxa	mā'LnîX.	Igō'pqa	wu'Xi	aqagē'lak.	A'qa	igō'quikEl
they went down	seaward.	She entered	that	woman.	Then	she saw them

tgā'k¡etē.	Tk¡ō'tk¡ōtkc	tgā'k¡etē.	Igō'guiga	itaxE'lgiLx.	A'qa
their blankets.	Dogs	their blankets.	She took them	she burnt them.	Then

igō'Lxa	mā'LnîX.	"Ō2,	itcî'qôq,	qātsqē	mcxanxq¡ā'la?	Ai'aq
she went down	seaward.	"Oh,	my children,	why	you disguised yourselves before me?	Quick

alxō'ptcga."	A'qa	itksē'nq¡oya-îX	ka'nauwē.	Mô'kctîX	iktō'lXam
let us go up."	Then	they hid their faces	all.	Twice	she spoke to them

itcā'qôq.	A'qa	iLō'ptcga	Lqui'nEmîkc.	YaXī'	ēXā't	iā'tcqEm
her children.	Then	they went up	five.	That	one	sick

iā'qo-it,	lē'lē	nEct	iō'ptcga.	Tsō'yustîX	tcXua	wī	iō'ptcga.	A'qa
his leg,	long	not	he went up.	In the evening	then	also	he went up.	Then

iLxē'2la-it	itcā'qôq.	A'qa	iLā'qa-iLax	igiLxE'lôx	itcā'qôq.	A'qa
they stayed	her children.	Then	large	they became	her children.	Then

guā'nEsum	qasxalō'kcaîtx	agā'xan.	Lā4	a'qa	Lka'nauwētîkc
always	they two picked berries	her daughter.	Long	then	all

Lā'xiqLax,	ēXā't	imacE'nukc	iā'k¡ēwula,	ēXā't	imō'lEkEmaX
hunters,	one	deer	his game,	one	elks

iā'k¡ēwula,	ēXā't	aqēsgoā'max	iā'k¡ēwula,	ēXā't	Lnā'qōn	iā'k¡ēwula,
his game,	one	seals	his game,	one	sturgeon	his game,

ēXā't	Lgipē'XLukc	iā'k¡ēwula.
one	sea-lions	his game.

Lā4,	igixaltcî'mаq	Tiā'pexoacxoac	aLā'hat¡au	Lā'qaLala.	Ō2,
Long,	he heard about her	Tiā'pexoacxoac	their maiden	the QaLa'la.	Oh,

a'qa	iō'ya	itcumElā'lEmam.	A'qa	iLgā'elōt	aLā'hat¡au.	Iā'mEla
then	he went	he went to buy her.	Then	they gave her to him	their maiden.	He was bad

Tiā'pexoacxoac.	Lqā'owulqt	iā'LxalEm.	Ma'nîx	nEct	qayu'qctēx,
Tiā'pexoacxoac.	Blood	his food.	When	not	he was satiated,

a'qa	Liā'kikal	qaLiXalEmō'XumX.	Ma'nîx	LE'kala	Liā'xan
then	his wife	he ate her.	When	a male	his child

threw it into the water. When she had a girl, he allowed it to live. His house was full of women.

After some time his wife's brothers brought him five sea lions. He drank their blood, but he had not enough. They gave him five seals. He drank their blood, but he had not enough. They gave him five sturgeons. He drank their blood, but he had not enough They gave him five elks. He drank their blood, but he had not enough. Then the middle one of the brothers said: "Oh, I will kill Ē'nōʟ.[1] My supernatural helper tells me so. To-morrow I will kill Ē'nōʟ." The following morning he saw Ē'nōʟ [on a snag]. He took his harpoon and went down to the water. Then he speared Ē'nōʟ and killed him. Now they pounded his body so that it was full of blood. They made five holes in the skin and closed them with plugs. Then the one who had killed Ē'nōʟ said to his brothers: "Now we shall conquer Tiā'pexoacxoac." They tied five canoes together and put planks across. They put the

---

qatcʟalē'maʟxax; ma'nîx ʟqagē'lak, aqa t!ō'nᴇkᵘ qatcʟō'xoax.
he threw it into the water; when a woman, then good save he did her.

Pāʟ tē'iaqʟ tiā'nᴇmckc.
Full his house his women.

Lāɬ, aqa iʟkʟi'kapōna qui'nᴇm ʟgipē'Xʟukc. Itcʟō'qumst
Long time, then they carried food to him five sea lions. He drank it

ʟā'qauwulqt. Nā2ct iō'qctē. Iʟga'ekapōna qui'nᴇm aqēsgoā'max.
their blood. Not he was satiated. They carried food to him five seals.

Itcʟō'qumst aqēsgoā'max ʟā'qauwulqt. Nā2ct iō'qctē. Iʟkʟi'kapōna
He drank it the seals their blood. Not he was satiated. They carried food to him

qui'nᴇm ʟnā'qōn. Iʟō'qumst ʟā'qauwulqt, nā2ct iō'qctē.
five sturgeons. He drank it their blood, not he was satiated.

Iʟgi'kapōna qui'nᴇm imō'lᴇkᴇmax. Nāct iō'qctē. Itcʟō'qumct
They carried food to him five elks. Not he was satiated. He drank it

ʟiā'qauwulqt imō'lᴇkᴇmax. A'qa igē'kîm ēXā't ē'ʟaXatcak:
their blood the elks. Then he said one their middle one:

"Âɬ, anᴇwā'qoa ē'nōʟ. Itcī'uʟᴇmax itcinō'lXam. Ō'la anewā'qa
"Ah, I shall kill it ē'nōʟ. My supernatural helper told me. To-morrow I shall kill it

ē'nōʟ." Igē'tcuktîX. A'qa igē'qᴇlkᴇl ē'nōʟ. A'qa itcē'gᴇlga
ē'nōʟ." Day came. Then he saw it ē'nōʟ. Then he took it

iā'tcuʟq. A'qa iō'yam mā'ʟnîX. A'qa itcʟē'loqcx ē'nōʟ. A'qa
his harpoon. Then he arrived near the water. Then he harpooned it ē'nōʟ. Then

itcē'waq ē'nōʟ. A'qa iʟgī'yôx ʟāq, ʟāq, ʟāq, ʟāq. Pāʟ iʟgē'xôx
he killed it ē'nōʟ. Then they made it strike, strike, strike, strike. Full it became

ʟqau'wulqt ka'nauwē. Qui'numîX ʟxoā'p itcī'yôx, qui'nᴇm
blood all. Five holes he made them, five

itctîlgā'mit tᴇ'mqō. A'qa itcʟō'lXam ʟī'alXtkc: "A'qa ilxgī'yuʟq
he put into it sticks. Then he told them his brothers: "Now we shall conquer him

Tiā'pexoacxoac." K!au iʟī'kôx qui'nᴇm akᴇ'nim. Aqē'nXa
Tiā'pexoacxoac." Tie they did five canoes. Boards

---

[1] A sea monster.

carcass on top of them. Then they carried it to Tiā'pexoacxoac. Now they were seen. "Ah, Tiā'pexoacxoac, your brothers-in-law are coming." Tiā'pexoacxoac went out. He remained standing in the doorway. His brothers-in-law landed. He said to his people: "Quick, haul up [what they bring]." They hauled it up and placed it before Tiā'pexoacxoac. He pulled out one plug and drank the blood. He drank it all. He pulled out the next one and he drank again. He pulled the third one and drank. After a while he got tired. Then he rested a little while. Then he drank again. He rested twice. Then he drank it all. He pulled out the fourth plug and drank. Now his stomach became full. He said: "Only the people of Qaʟa'la give me enough." Then it thundered. "What did you say? Do not come any more! I have had enough."

Now Tiā'pexoacxoac remained there, and his wife was with child. Soon she became sick and gave birth to a child. "Go and see what she

---

iʟgakxā'ema. A'qa iʟgiakxā'ema caxala'. A'qa iʟgī'yukᴛ. Ā'2qa
they laid over them. Then they laid it on it on top. Then they carried it. Then

iqᴇ'ʟqᴇlkᴇl. "Ā4, Tiā'pexoacxoac. ʟmē'qēXᴇnāna ʟtē'it." A'qa iō'pa
they were seen. "Ah, Tiā'pexoacxoac. Your brothers-in-law are coming." Then he went out

Tiā'pexoacxoac. Iō'ʟa-it icī'qepa. A'qa iʟxē'gela-îX ʟiā'qeXenana.
Tiā'pexoacxoac. He stayed the doorway in. Then they landed his brothers-in-law.

A'qa itctō'lXam tiā'lXam: "Ai'aq amcgiʟā'taptck." A'qa
Then he told them his people: "Quick haul it up." Then

iʟgiuʟā'taptck. A'qa igilxā'ema Tiā'pexoacxoac. ʟuX itcī'xôx
they hauled it up. Then it lay before Tiā'pexoacxoac. Pull out he did it

ēXt ē'mqō. Itcʟō'qumct ʟiā'qauwulqt. Itcʟō'ʟXōm ʟiā'qauwulqt.
one stick. He drank it its blood. He finished it its blood.

Aqa wi igō'n ʟuX itcī'xôx. Aqa wi itcʟō'qumct. lʟā'ʟōn
Then again another one pull out he did it. Then again he drank it. The third one

ʟuX itcī'yux. Itcʟō'qumct. Lā2, a'qa tᴇll igē'xôx.
pull out he did it. He drank it. Long, then tired he became.

Igixʟā'ematck, tcXoa aqa wi't'ax itcʟō'qumct. Mô'ketîX
He rested, then now again he drank. Twice

igixʟā'ematck. Aqa itcʟō'ʟXōm. Igō'nax ʟuX itcī'xôx iʟā'lakt.
he rested. Then he finished it. Another pull out he did it the fourth one.

Aqa wi itcʟō'qumct. A'qa iā'wan iutā'wulX. "Qā'2naqē
Then again he drank it. Then his belly thick. "Only

ʟā'qaʟalē' tcXua iʟgᴇnuqctᴇmē'2." Ai'aq tū4, tumm cxelā'koatck
the Qaʟa'la then they gave me enough to eat." Quick tū, tumm it thundered

igō'cax. "Qā qamxatxōlā'4? Aqa kopā'4t amctī'ya. A'qa
the sky. "How you say? Now enough you came. Now

inō'qetē."
I am satiated."

A'qa iō'ʟa-it Tiā'pexoacxoac. A'qa agā'wan igaxā'lôx ayā'kikala.
Then he stayed Tiā'pexoacxoac. Then her pregnancy came to be on her his wife.

Ai'aq a'qa itcā'tcqᴇm iaxᴇ'lôx. A'qa igakXᴇ'tōm. "Amcgā'ketam
Quick then her sickness was on her. Then she gave birth. "Go and see

tān igioxô'tōm, ʟqagē'lak ʟXuan, ʟᴇ'kala ʟXuan." A'qa
what she gave birth to it, a female perhaps, a male perhaps." Then

brought forth; see if it is a boy or a girl." They went to see. They said: "She brought forth a girl." She had put an apron onto her child. When it had grown a little she carried it away. She ran away right down the river. They searched for her up the river. They did not find her. They searched for her two months, but they did not find her. Then she turned back, and went up the river. Now they searched for her downward. For two months they searched for her everywhere down the river. They did not find her. Then Tiā'pexoacxoac gave it up and remained where he was.

Now the woman washed her son. He became a warrior. He was stronger than his father. One day he said to his mother: "Which of his wives does he like best?" His mother replied: "Two of them he likes best." "Where are their beds?" "Their beds are in the middle of the house. When you go there you must lie down thus [the heel of one foot resting on the toes of the other]." Now he went. He arrived and opened the house. He went and lay down at one side of the house. The woman accepted him. She thought her husband had returned. She believed that he was her husband. Now she lay down

---

iqō'kctam. "Ā, Lqagē'lak ikLoxô'tōm." Lä4, a'qa aLā'q¡iLxap
she was looked at. "Ah, a girl she gave birth to it." Long then a coat

igaLE'lox. A'qa ma'nki iLā'xa-iL iLE'x. A'qa ikLōtā'mit Lgā'xan.
she made it for it. Then a little large it became. Then she carried it away her child.

IkLōtā'mit nau'i qā'eqamîX. Kē'nuwa iqō'naxL cā'xalîX. K¡ā'ya
She carried it away at once down the river. Try she was searched for above. Nothing

nîct iqō'cgam. Môket LkLEmena'ke iqō'naxL, näcqē iqō'cgam.
not she was found. Two months she was searched for, not at all she was found.

A'qa wi igā'xkoa cā'xalîX. A'qa qā'eqamîX iqō'naxL. Môket
Then again she turned back above. Then down the river she was searched for. Two

LkLEmē'nake iqō'naxL qā'eqamîX ka'nauwē qā'xpa. Näct iqō'cgam.
months she was searched for down the river every where. Not she was found.

A'qa tä'menua igē'x Tiā'pexoacxoac. A'qa iō'La-it Tiā'pexoacxoac.
Then give up he did Tiā'pexoacxoac. Then he stayed Tiā'pexoacxoac.

A'qa igigE'qoat itcā'xan aqagē'lak. Aqa it¡ō'xoyal igē'xôx.
Then she washed him her son the woman. Then a warrior he became.

Itcē'yuLq wī'yam. ĒXt wē'kua aqa itcō'lXam wā'yaq: "Lān
He was superior to his father. One day then he said to her his mother: "Whom

tq¡ēx itcî'Lôx Liā'kēkal?" A'qa igiō'lXam wa'yaq: "Cmôket tq¡ēx
like he does her his wife?" Then she said to him his mother: "Two like

itcî'côx ciā'kekal." "Qā'xpa ictā'lXEmē?" "Ā, ē'wa k¡awicE'qē
he does them his wives." "Where their beds?" "Ah, there in the middle of the house

ictā'lXEmē. Ma'nîx amō'ya amxō'kcita, aqa ē'wa mtō'xa tE'mipe."
their beds. When you go you lie down, then thus do your feet."

A'qa iō'ya. Iō'yam. Itcioxoā'laqL tqu'Lē. A'qa igēxō'kcit tE'nat
Then he went. He arrived. He opened it the house. Then he lay down on one side

tqu'Lē. Igē'gElga aqagē'lak. IgaxLō'xoa-it: "IgiXatk¡oā'mam
the house. She took him the woman. She thought: "He came home

with him. Then he arose and went to the other side of the house. Again he lay down with the other woman. He stopped some time. Then he arose and went out. He went right home. In the morning the woman, his father's wife, arose. She looked across the house. Her husband was not there. The other one awoke also. She looked. Her husband was not there. She said to her: "Where did he go? He came home. I thought he was lying down with you. He rose." Now a person went out. He watched the house. He saw footprints. He took a stick and broke it the length of the footprints.

After three days Tiā'pexoacxoac returned. "Oh, we found the footprints of a person. They were *that* long and *that* broad." Then he took the stick and compared it with his foot. It was just as long as his foot. He compared the width, and it was a little wider than his foot. Then Tiā'pexoacxoac lay down. He lay down for two days. Then he

---

itcî'kikal." Igīuku'laqL ya'Xka itcā'kikala. A'qa îcxō'kcit
my husband." She recognized him her husband. Then they lay down

itcā'kikal. A'qa igixE'latck. Iō'ya tE'nat tqu'Lē. A'qa wī't'ax
her husband. Then he arose. He went to the other side the house. Then again

igixō'kcit. Agō'n aēXā't aqagē'lak. Aqa wi icxō'kcit.
he lay down. Another one woman. Then again they lay down.

ItcLā'kōLX. IgixE'latck, iō'pa. Nā'wi igē'Xk¡oa. Igē'tcuktîX.
He left her. He arose, he went out. At once he went home. It grew day.

IgaxE'latck aqagē'lak wī'yam ayā'kikal. Igā'kîkct k¡anatē'tōL.
She arose the woman his father his wife. She looked to the other side.

K¡ā itcā'kikala. IgaxE'latck agō'n aēXā't. Igā'kikct: K¡ā'ya
Nothing her husband. She arose the other one. She looked: Nothing

itcā'kikala. Igō'lXam: "Qā'mta iō'ya tau igîXatk¡oā'mam?
her husband. She said to her: "Where he went who came home?

NxLō'xuan mai'kapa iō'ktikt. IgixE'latck." A'qa iLō'pa LeXā't
I thought you at he slept. He rose." Then he went out one

LgoaLē'lX iLgiugoā'nXôqtîX tqu'Lē. Aqa iLgō'quikEl tiā'Xatk.
person he watched the house. Then he saw them his tracks.

A'qa iLgē'gElga ē'mqō. A'qa iLgiXE'lakoa qansî'X ē'taLqt
Then he took it a stick. Then he broke it how long

tiā'Xatk.
his tracks.

A'qa Lōn Lkā'ētax, a'qa igiXatk¡oā'mam Tiā'pexoacxoac. "Ō2,
Then three days, then he came home Tiā'pexoacxoac. "Oh,

LgoaLē'lX întcktō'cgam tLā'Xatk. Ē'wa ē'taLqt, ē'wa ē'taxalXt."
a person we found them his tracks. Thus long, thus wide."

A'qa itcē'gElga ē'mqō, a'qa itciū'kumak¡ā'metaq tē'iapc. Kopē'2t
Then he took it a stick, then he compared them his feet. Enough

ī'taLqt tē'iapc. Itciukumak¡ā'mētaq ē'taXalXt. Nō'L¡ itā'qa-iLax.
their length his feet. He compared them their widths. A little large.

Itgē'iōLq. Lā2, aqa igixō'kcit Tiā'pexoacxoac. Igixō'kcit môkct
He was superior to him. Long, then he lay down Tiā'pexoacxoac. He lay down two

Lkā'etax. A'qa igixE'latck. "Ō2, LXuan LE'kala ikLotā'mit
days. Then he rose. "Oh, perhaps a male she carried him away

rose. "Oh, I think that woman carried away a male child. Go and search for her." He sent five men down the river. Five he sent up the river. He sent four to go and look near by. Now these four men went up to Qawî'ltk. They saw smoke. When they came there they discovered a house. They went up to it and entered. There was Tiā'pexoacxoac's son. He looked just like Tiā'pexoacxoac. Now they returned. They came home. "Oh, Tiā'pexoacxoac, we found your son. He looks just like you." "That is just what I thought. Go and fetch him." Thus he spoke to his slaves. Five of them went. His son kept four of them, and one only returned. "What did he say to you?" "Oh, he took four men away from you." "Go to-morrow and fetch him." On the following day six men went. He kept five and one returned. "What did he say to you?" "He kept five." Four times they tried to take him; and then he had kept twenty of his slaves. Tiā'pexoacxoac became angry. He called his people: "Let us make war upon your nephew." Now they went in two

---

tau aqagē'lak. Ō2, tgt!ō'kti amckunā'xLama." Itctōtō'koatck
this woman. Oh, good you search for her." He sent them

aqui'nEmîkc qā'eqamîX. Itctōtō'koatck aqui'nEmîkc ē'wa cā'xalîX.
five men down the river. He sent them five men then upward.

Itctotō'koatck alā'ktîkc q!oā'pîX alukuak!ē'naxLa. A'qa itgī'ya
He sent them four men near they shall search. Then they went

ala'ktîkc. Itgī'ya cā'xalîX Qawî'ltkpa. Itgō'quikEl tXtE'llē.
the four men. They went upward Qawî'ltk to. They saw it smoke.

ILō'yam, aqa tqu'Lē itktXuē'la. A'qa iLō'ptcka. ILā'ckōpq.
They arrived, then a house they discovered it. Then they went up. They entered.

A'qa iō'Xt Tiā'pexoacxoac iā'Xan. Ya'Xka Tiā'pexoacxoac,
Then he was there Tiā'pexoacxoac his son. He Tiā'pexoacxoac,

cxE'lk!atcX. A'qa iLE'Xk!oa. ILXk!oā'mam tE'LaqLpa. "Ō4,
they resembled one another. Then they went home. They came home their house to. "Oh,

Tiā'pexoacxoac, imē'Xan întcgiō'cgam. Maniq!ē' imtxE'lk!atcX."
Tiā'pexoacxoac, your son we found him. Exactly you resemble one another."

"Ō, k!oaLqē' nXLō'Xuan. Ō, ai'aq amcgigā'lEmam," itcLō'lXam
"Oh, just so I thought. Oh, quick go and fetch him," he said to them

Liā'qiXEltgeukc. ILō'ya Lqui'nEmîkc. Ā, itci'LgElga Lla'ktîkc.
his slaves. They went five men. Ah, he kept them four.

ĒXā'tka igē'Xk!oa. "Ō, qā itcîmcō'lXam?" "Ā4, itcLumxE'cgam
One only went home. "Oh, how did he say to you?" "Ah, he took from you

Lla'ktîkc." "Ō, tgt!ō'kti ō'la mcō'ya. Amcgiukoā'lEmam."
four men." "Oh, good to-morrow you go. You go and fetch him."

A'qa wi igē'tcuktîX; a'qa wi iLō'ya LtxE'mîkc. A'qa wi
Then again day came; then again they went six men. Then again

itcLEXE'cgam Lqui'nEmîkc. ĒXā'tka igē'Xk!oa. "Ā, qā
he took from them five men. One only he went home. "Ah, how

itcîmcō'lXam?" "Ā, itcLumxE'cgam Lqui'nEmîkc." Lā'ktîX
he said to you?" "Ah, he took them from you five men." Four times

kē'nuwa iqiukoā'lEmam. A'qa itctixE'cgam tiā'qiXEltgeukc
try he is fetched. Then he took them from him his slaves

môkctLā'Lîkc. Ā'2qa kalā'lkuilē igē'X Tiā'pexoacxoac. A'qa
twenty. Then scold he did Tiā'pexoacxoac. Then

hundred canoes. His son was eating. Then one of his slaves went out. "Oh, we are going to be attacked." But he continued to eat quietly. Then he said to his mother: "Quick! go inland." And he said to his slaves: "Quick! go inland." Then his slaves and his mother went inland. He went down, took his arrows, and shot the people. He hit a canoe and it burst. He hit another one. It burst. All the people were drowned. He killed Tiā'pexoacxoac's people. Now there were only a few of his people left. Tiā'pexoacxoac said: "Let us go home; your nephew has conquered me." Then he went home. He said: "Bring your nephew. I will give him some of my wives." Now three men went and said to Tiā'pexoacxoac's son: "Your father sent us. We come to fetch you. He will give you some of his wives." "Oh, I like those two of his wives." Then the three

---

itcō'xoaktck tê'lXam. "Ai'aq, aqa sāq¡ alxgiō'xa imcā'LatXEn."
he sent for them the people. "Quick, then war we will make on him your nephew."

Aqa igō'ya môkct itcā¡k¡amunaq akE'nim. IxLxE'lEmux iā'xan.
Then they went two hundred canoes. He ate his son.

ILō'pa Liā'la-etîX LeXā't. "Ā4, sāq¡ ilxE'xôx." P!ā'la ixLxE'lEmux.
He went out his slave one. "Ah, war is made on us." Quietly he ate.

A'qa itcō'lXam wā'yaq: "Ai'aq, mē'ya LxE'leuX." ItcLō'lXam
Then he said to her his mother: "Quick, go inland." He said to them

Liā'qēXEltgeukc: "Ai'aq, mcī'ya LxE'leuX." A'qa iLō'ptcka
his slaves: "Quick, go inland." Then they went inland

Liā'qēXEltgeukc k¡a wā'yaq. A'qa iō'Lxa. Itcō'guiga tiā'qamatcX.
his slaves and his mother. Then he went down. He took them his arrows.

A'qa itctō'maqt tê'lXam. Iā'maq itcē'lôx ikE'nim, ts¡E'xts¡Ex
Then he shot them the people. Shoot he did it with them a canoe, break

igē'xôx. Igō'n iā'maq itcē'lôx ikE'nim, ts¡E'xts¡Ex igē'xôx. L¡lap
it did. Another shoot he did it a canoe, break it did. Under water

itgī'ya ka'nauwē tê'lXam. Iqtō'tena tiā'lXam Tiā'pexoacxoac. Aqa
went all people. They were killed his people Tiā'pexoacxoac. Then

nō'Lka tiā'lXam Tiā'pexoacxoac. A'qa igē'kîm: "Ō, alxk¡uā'ya.
few only his people Tiā'pexoacxoac. Then he said: "Oh, we will go home.

A'qa itcî'nōLq imcā'LatXEn." A'qa igō'Xuak¡ua. A'qa igîXk¡oā'mam
Then he vanquished me your nephew." Then they went home. Then he came home

Tiā'pexoacxoac. A'qa igē'kîm Tiā'pexoacxoac: "Ō2, imcgigā'lEmam
Tiā'pexoacxoac. Then he said Tiā'pexoacxoac: "Oh, go and fetch him

imcā'LatXEn. Antelō'ta tgE'nEmckc aqā'watîkc." A'qa itgī'ya
your nephew. I will give them to him my women several." Then they went

aLō'nîkc tê'lXam. Iqiō'lXam iā'Xan Tiā'pexoacxoac: "Wē'mam
three people. He was told his son Tiā'pexoacxoac: "Your father

itcinctō'koatck. Iqamtgā'lEmam. ItctEmî'lōt tiā'nEmckc aqā'watîkc."
he sent us. You are fetched. He gives them to you his women several."

"Ō4, ctā'xka cmôkct ciā'kikala tq¡ēx inE'côxt." Ō, iLî'Xk¡oa
"Oh, these two his wives like I do them." Oh, they went home

La-itci Lō'nîkc. "Qā itcimcō'lXam imcā'LatXEn?" "Ō,
those three. "How he said to you your nephew?" "Oh,

men went home. "What does your nephew say to you?" "He said to us that he likes those two of your wives." "Go to-morrow. When the day breaks, go and tell him that I will give them to him, if he will come." Now they went again. They arrived there and entered. "Oh, your father will give you his two wives." "Ah, well then I will go home," said he. "Tell him, he shall leave his house." They went home. When they came home, they said: "Your son will arrive to-morrow. He tells you to go outside and take those two old women, your wives." On the next morning, Tiā'pexoacxoac went out. He took those two old women, his wives. After some time, his son arrived and entered his father's house. Then his wife gave birth to two sons. Now Tiā'pexoacxoac fell sick. He made arrows for his grandsons. They shot their grandfather, and after some time he was dead. Now Tiā'pexoacxoac son had many sons.

---

itcintcō'lXam ctā'xka ctā'Xi cmôkct cmē'kikala tq¡ēx itcî'côx."
he said to us them those two your wives like he does them."

"Ō, tgt¡ō'kti ō'la mcō'ya. Igē'tcuktîX amcgiolXā'mam ā'Lqi
"Oh, good to-morrow you go. Day comes you go and tell him; later on

ancilō'ta ma'nîx alitē'ya." A'qa wi iLō'ya wi't'ax. A'qa wi
I will give them two to him when he will come." Then again they went again. Then again

iLō'yam. ILā'ckupq. "Ā4, itccî'mElōt ciā'kikal wē'mam." "Ā,
they arrived. They entered. "Ah, he gives them to you his two wives your father." "Ah,

tgt¡ō'kti aqa anXk¡oā'ya," igē'kîm. "A'qa ayuXoapā'ya tē'iaqL
good then I go home," he said. "Then he shall go out his house

amcgiolXā'ma." A'qa iLî'Xk¡oa. ILîXk¡oā'mam. "Ā, ō'la alitē'ya
you tell him." Then they went home. They came home. "Ah, to-morrow he will come

imē'xan. Itcmō'lXam amupā'ya Lā'xanîX k¡a ctā'Xi cq¡eyō'qt
your son. He told you you shall go out outside and those two two old women

amcō'kTa cmē'kikala." A'qa igē'tcuktîX, a'qa iō'pa Tiā'pexoacxoac.
you take them your two wives." Then day came, then he went out Tiā'pexoacxoac.

Itcî'cukT ciā'kikala cta'Xi cq¡eyō'qt. Lā4 aqa iō'yam iā'xan. A'qa
He took them his two wives those two two old women. Long then he arrived his son. Then

iō'pqam wî'am tē'iaqL. A'qa icoXô'tōm ayā'kikala cmôkct cE'kala
he came in his father his house. Then she gave birth to two his wife two male

sk¡ā'skas. Ā2qa iā'tsqEm igixE'lôx Tiā'pexoacxoac. A'qa
children. Then his sickness came onto him Tiā'pexoacxoac. Then

tqā'matcX itctcî'lôx. A'qa iā'maq îcgē'lôx ictā'q¡acuc. Lā2, aqa
arrows he made them for them. Then shoot they did him their grandfather. Long, then

iō'maqt iq¡eyō'qt. A'qa iō'maqt. A'qa Lgā'pElatîkc iā'qôq tkā'lukc
dead the old man. Then he was dead. Then many his children males

itixE'lôx.
they were on him.

Ēmōgoā'lekc (told 1891)

There were the people of a town. There were two friends among them, one the son of a chief, the other a common man. There was a girl, the daughter of a chief of another town. She had a girl slave. Then one of the young men said to his friend: "Come! let us go to that town to look for girls." In the morning they went. That slave girl was pretty. The young men came to that town. The slave girl pleased the chief's son. The common man was also pretty and that girl liked him, while the slave girl liked the chief's son. The two went often to see them. Now the youth's father heard about it. The chief heard that his son went after a slave girl. He was ashamed. Every morning he scolded his son. Both he and the young man's mother

---

Oxoēlā'etîX ta-îtci ēXt gitā'lXam. EXā't iʟā'Xak!ᴇmana
There were those one people of a town. One their chief

iā'Xan. Cxā'cîkc k!a eXā't iq!u'lîpX. Ixē'yal ya'Xi ēXā't
his son. Two friends and one youth. A common man that one

iq!u'lîpX. Kanasmô'kst cq!u'lîpX. A'qa ēXt gitā'lXam
youth. Both youths. Then one people of a town

aqagē'lak ayā'Xan ya'Xi iʟā'Xak!ᴇmana ahā't!au k!a agā'laitîX
woman his daughter that their chief a maiden and her slave girl

wī't'ax ahā't!au. A'qa itciō'lXam iā'cîkc: "Qōi qatxō'eX ya'Xi
also a maiden. Then he said to him his friend: "Must we go that

ēXt ē'lXampa. Atxktonā'xʟama tᴇ'nᴇmckc." Igē'tcuktîX, a'qa
one town to. We search for them women." Day came, then

ictō'ya. At!ō'kti wu'Xi agā'laitîX wu'Xi ahā't!au. Ictō'yam
they two went. Good that her slave girl that maiden. They arrived

kō'pa ya'Xi ēXt ē'lXam cta'Xi cq!u'lîpX. Q!āt itcō'xoa wu'Xi
there that one town those youths. Love he did her that

alā'etîX ya'Xi iʟā'Xak!ᴇmana iā'Xan. It!ō'kti ya'Xi iq!u'lîpX
slave girl that their chief his son. Good that youth

ya'Xi ixē'yal. Tq!ēx igī'yôx wu'Xi ahā't!au ya'Xi ixē'yal.
that common man. Like she did him that maiden that common man.

Tq!ēx itcō'xoa wu'Xi alā'etîX ya'Xi iʟā'xak!ᴇmana iā'Xan.
Like he did her that slave girl that their chief his son.

Iō'ʟqtîX ickcXᴇluwā'lalᴇmtck. A'qa itilō'Xuix·it ya'Xi wī'yam
Long they two went often to see them. Then he heard about them that his father

ya'Xi iq!u'lîpX. Itilō'Xuix·it ya'Xi iʟā'Xak!ᴇmana, alā'etîX
that youth. He heard about them that their chief, a slave girl

itcaXᴇluwā'la ya'Xi iā'Xan. Igixᴇmā'sa-it ya'Xi ikak!ᴇmā'na.
he went to see her that his son. He was ashamed that chief.

Wāx itciō'mᴇla ya'Xi iā'Xan. Ka'nauwē ʟkā'etax icgiō'mela
Next day he scolded him that his son. All days they two scolded him

scolded him. Then he and his friend went out. He said: "My heart is tired, friend. I am scolded every day; I shall go away." "Oh," said his friend, "I love you and I shall be unhappy if you go." In the evening they came home. He lay down and did not eat. He rose early and the two went into the woods. They shot at targets. He said again: "Oh, my heart is tired; if you like me you may see me always"; thus he said to his friend. "No, friend, don't leave me; I shall be unhappy." For five days they played shooting at targets. Then they bathed. The young man dived five times. Then he came up far away from the shore. His ears had become very long. He was lying on a snag. Then his friend went ashore and cried and cried a long time. He looked, and his friend was standing there. He smiled at him. "Why do you cry so much, friend? We shall do this way. If you like me, you shall see me. Come to this place and we shall play here; but do not tell them. If you do not like me, then you

---

ckanasmô'kct k!a wā'yaq ya'Xi iq!u'lîpX. Qactō'îX qā'mta ya'Xi
both and his mother that youth. They two went somewhere that

iā'cîkc. "Ā'qa tᴇll igē'x ē'tcamxtc, cîkc. Ka'nauwē ʟkā'etax
his friend. "Now tired gets my heart, friend. All days

qanō'mela. Q!oā'p a'qa qā'mta nō'ya." "Ō," itciō'lXam iā'cîkc,
I am scolded. Nearly then somewhere I go." "Oh," he said to him his friend,

"Ō, tq!ēx iā'môx, cîkc, iā'okîX tgᴇ'giōtkoaX qatxanlō'xoax."
"Oh, like I do you, friend, else my unhappiness will be on me."

Xā'pîX qacXk!oā'mamx. Nā'2wē nîxō'kcitx. Näct nixʟxᴇ'lᴇmuX.
In the evening they two came home. At once he lay down. Not he ate.

Kawī'X nîxᴇlā'tcgoax, qactō'îx golx·ē'yōkuîX. Wā'q!pac
Early he arose, they went into the woods. Target

qacxcgā'mx. Wī't'ax qatciolXā'mx: "Ō, a'qa tᴇll igē'xôx
they played. Again he said to him: "Oh, now tired gets

ē'tcamxtc. Ma'nîx tq!ēx mnxō'lalᴇmx, aqa wi amᴇnqᴇlkᴇlā'ya,"
my heart. When like you do me, then again you will see me,"

qatciolXā'mx ya'Xi iā'cîkc. "K!ā'ya, cîkc, nîcqē amᴇnkᴇlō'qʟqa,
he said to him that his friend. "No, friend, not at all leave me,

tgᴇ'giōtkoax." Qoā'nᴇma ʟkā'etax wā'q!pac icᴇ'xôx. A'qa
my unhappiness." Five days target they did. Then

icxgoā'yōt. Igiktē'mᴇnq ya'Xi iq!u'lîpX. Qoā'nᴇmîX
they bathed. He dived that youth. Five times

igiktē'mᴇnq. ʟāx igē'x yaXī' mā'ʟnîX. Gipā'tᴇma itā'ʟqtax
he dived. Visible he became there seaward. Thus long

tiā'utcakc. Iaxakxā'ema wu'Xi akū'yax. Iō'ptck iā'cîkc.
his ears. He lay on that snag. He went up his friend.

Igigᴇ'tcax, igigᴇ'tcax, igigᴇ'tcax. Ka iō'qulqt igē'kikct
He cried, he cried, he cried. Where he cried he saw

iutXuē'la iā'cîkc. Ixk!ayā'wula. "Tān migᴇ'mqᴇlqt, cîkc?
he stood his friend. He smiled at him. "What you cry, friend?

K!oaʟqā' atxō'xoa. Manîx tq!ēx amtō'xoa amᴇnqᴇlkᴇlā'ya.
Thus we will do. When like you do them you will see me.

A'qa amtā'ya tē'ka. A'qa tē'ka atxk!ayā'wulalᴇma. Nēct
Then come here. Then here we will play. Not

amxkʟē'tcgoa. Ma'nîx nîct tq!ēx mᴇ'nôx tcXua qamxkʟē'tcgoax.
tell. When not like you do me then tell.

may tell them. Come here to-morrow." In the evening the youth went home. The chief's son went into the water and dived.

Then that youth cried and went home. He came home and lay down at once. He rose early and took his arrows. He went to the place where they had shot at targets. He cried. He looked, and there his friend was standing. He said: "Why are you crying all the time? If you like me, come here and we shall play." In the evening he went home again. The chief's son went into the water and dived.

After two days they searched for him. On the third day, when the youth came home, they asked him: "Where is your friend?" He said: "I have not seen him for two days." They searched for him and said: "Somebody must have killed him." They went into the neighboring towns and searched for him, but they did not find him. Early the youth went out again. He stayed on the shore for some time; then he saw his friend standing there. His friend said to him: "Do not tell them; if you do you will see me no more." In the

---

Ō'la mtē'ya tē'kaki." Xā'pîX a'qa igē'Xk¡oa ya'Xi iq¡u'lîpX.
To-morrow come here." In the evening then he went home that youth.

Iō'ʟxa ya'Xi iʟā'Xak¡ᴇmana iā'Xan. Igiktē'mᴇnq.
He went to the water that their chief his son. He dived.

Igigā'tcax ya'Xi iq¡u'lîpX. A'qa igē'Xk¡oa. IgiXk¡oā'mam.
He cried that youth. Then he went home. He came home.

Nā'2wi igixō'kcit. Kawī'X igixᴇ'latck. Itcō'guiga tiā'qamatcX.
At once he lay down. Early he arose. He took them his arrows.

Iō'ya kopā' ya'Xi wā'q¡pas icxᴇ'cgam. Iō'qulqt. Igē'kikct,
He went there that target they played. He cried. He looked,

iutXuē'la iā'cîkc. A'qa itciō'lXam: "Qā'tcxē guā'nsum
there stood his friend. Then he said to him: "Why always

mō'qulqt? Ma'nîx tq¡ēx amᴇnō'xoa a'qa mtā'ya, aqa
you cry? When like you do me then come, then

atxk¡ayā'wulalᴇma." Xā'pîX, aqa wī't'ax igē'Xk¡oa. Iō'ʟxa
we will play." In the evening, then again he went home. He went down to the water

yā'Xka, igiktē'mᴇnq ya'Xi iʟā'Xak¡ᴇmana iā'Xan.
he, he dived that their chief his son.

Mâ'ketîX ictō'qxoya, a'qa iqiunā'xʟatck. IgiXatk¡oā'mam
Twice their sleeps, then he was searched for. He came home

iʟā'ʟōnîX ya'Xi iq¡u'lîpX, a'qa iōqu'mtcxōgoa: "Qā'xpa imē'cîkc?"
the third time that youth, then he was asked: "Where your friend?"

Igē'kîm: "A'qa mô'ketîX iō'qxoya nîct tᴇnlō'xoîX." Iqiō'naxʟ
He said: "Now twice his sleeps not I know." He was searched for

ya'Xi iq¡u'lipX. Iqiō'lXam: "Iqē'waq." Ewā' ēXt ē'lXam
that youth. He was told: "He is killed." Thus one town

aqiōnā'Xʟam. Nā'2cqē iqiō'cgam. Kawī'X iō'ya ya'Xi iq¡u'lîpX.
he was searched for. Not at all he was found. Early he went that youth.

Lē'lē ʟxᴇ'leu igē'xôx. Ē'wa igē'xôx, igē'kîkct, aqa iutXuē'la
Long inland he was. Thus he did, he looked, then he stood

ya'Xi iā'cîkc. Itciō'lXam iā'cîkc: "Nᴇct amxkʟē'tcgoa. Ma'nîx
that his friend. He said to him his friend: "Not tell. If

amxkʟē'tcgoa kopā'2t amᴇnqᴇlkᴇlā'ya." Xā'pîX igē'Xk¡oa ya'Xi
you tell, enough you will see me." In the evening he went home that

evening the youth went home. Then they said: "Perhaps he has killed him and has kept it secret." Five times the youth went; then they followed his tracks. They came there and saw them shooting at a target. His father's slaves came home and said: "He is well. We found them shooting at targets." In the evening, when it grew dark, the young man came home. The other one went into the water. Then they asked the youth: "Why do you keep it a secret where he is?" He did not tell them. The young man went every day. They went after him again. When they came there, the youth said: "People are looking at us secretly. I think you told them." The other one replied: "I did not tell them. They made me tired and asked me much." The youth said: "Tell them that while I stayed my father and my mother were ashamed of me. What do they talk? They always said that they were ashamed of me." In the evening the one went home, the other went into the water. Then they asked him

---

iq!u'lîpX. A'qa iqiō'lXam ya'Xi iq!u'lîpX: "ʟXuan itcē'waq,
youth. Then he was told that youth: "Perhaps he killed him,

tcqē itcioqoā'la." Qoā'nᴇmîX iō'ya ya'Xi iq!u'lîpX.
then he keeps it a secret." Five times he went that youth.

AqixE'luwakoa. Iqcgō'qoam, iqᴇ'cqꜰlkᴇl. Wā'q!pas icxcgᴇ'lēʟ.
He was followed. They were reached, they were seen. Target they played.

IguXoak!oā'mam tiā'qēxᴇltgeukc wī'yam. Iguxoagu'ʟîtck ta-îtci
They came home his slaves his father. They told those

tqēxᴇ'ltgeukc: "P!ā'la îgē'xôx, wāq!pas icxcgᴇ'liʟ.
slaves: "Well he is, target they two play.

Intckcgō'qoam." Xā'pîX igō'ponᴇm. Igē'Xk!oa ya'Xi iq!u'lîpX.
We reached them." In the evening it grew dark. He went home that youth.

Iō'ʟxa ya'Xi ēXā't igiktē'mᴇnq. Iqiō'lXam ya'Xi iq!u'lîpX:
He went to the water that one he dived. He was told that youth:

"Qā'tcqē imiōq!oā'la qā'xpa pā iō'Xt?" Nēct igîxgu'ʟîtck.
"Why did you keep it secret where there he is?" Not he told.

Ka'nauwē ʟkā'etax qayō'yēma-îtx ya'Xi iq!u'lîpX. A'qa wi
All days he went always that youth. Then again

isxā'sk!ᴇnukʟuwa. Itxā'sk!ᴇnukʟuwa tq!ulîpXᴇnā'yu. Iqcgō'qoam.
they followed them two secretly. They followed them secretly the youths. They were reached.

Igē'kîm ya'Xi iq!u'lîpX: "Tē'lXam itktxō'qumē. Itxā'txk!ᴇlpsot.
He said that youth: "People are looking at us. They look at us secretly.

ʟXuan îmxgu'ʟîtck." Igē'kîm: "K!ā'ya, nîcqē' înxgu'ʟîtck. Aqa
Perhaps you told." He said: "No, not at all I told. Then

tᴇll iqᴇ'nux: qanugu'mtcxogoa'la." Igē'kîm iq!u'lîpX: "Ā'oʟᴇʟ
tired I am made: I am asked much." He said the youth: "Nevertheless

itsᴇ'k!emasamit. Itcī'mama amiulXā'ma, k!a agᴇ'kXō amulXā'ma:
I made them ashamed. My father tell him and my mother tell her

tān wit'ax ʟē'qxitcX, ā'oʟᴇʟ k!ā inᴇ'xôx ʟā'itckapa. Iʟgᴇnō'lXam
what more they talk, nevertheless nothing I am them from. They said to me

itsᴇ'k!emasamit." Xapī'X igē'Xk!oa, iō'ʟxa igiktē'mᴇnq. A'qa
I made them ashamed." In the evening he went home, he went down to the water he dived. Then

again: "Why do you keep his whereabouts a secret from us?" The youth spoke: "You make my heart tired. He became a monster. You will not see him again. He is ashamed because you scolded him every day." Then some of his relatives cried. They said: "Oh, tell him that we will buy a chief's daughter for him." The next morning he went. "They say that they will buy a chief's daughter for you," said he to his friend. He replied: "Tell them to be quiet; they were ashamed of me." In the evening his friend went home, and they asked him: "What did he say to you?" "Oh, he asked you to be quiet." On the following morning his friend went again and those people made themselves ready. All the young men went. He said to his friend: "They are surrounding us." The people surrounded them. They tried to approach them secretly, but he went right through them. They saw him dive. There in the water he emerged again and lay on a snag. His ears were *that* long. They

---

wi't'ax aqioqu'mtcxōgoa: "Qāgi imiō'q¡oala qā'xpa igē'x?" A'qa
again he was asked: "Why do you keep it secret where he is?" Then

igē'kîm ya'Xi iq¡u'lîpX: "A'qa tᴇll îmcgī'yux ē'tcamxtc. Iqcxē'ʟau
he said that youth: "Now tired you made it his heart. A monster

igē'xôx. Nîct qa'ntsîx wi't'ax amcqîxqᴇlkᴇlā'ya. Igixᴇmā'sa-it.
he became. Never again you will see him. He is ashamed.

Ka'nauwē ʟkā'etax îmcgiō'mela." Igoxoē'nîmtck tiā'cuxtîkc
All days you scolded him." They cried his relatives

aqā'watîkc. "Ā tgt¡ō'kti amiulXā'ma, antcgōmᴇlā'lᴇma ēXt
part of them. "Ah, good you tell him, we will buy her one

giʟā'lXam iʟā'Xak¡ᴇmana ayā'Xan: antcga-ilXē'wakua." Wāx
people of a town their chief his daughter: we will buy a wife for him." Next day

igē'tcuktîX. lō'ya. "Ā, aqᴇmuxō'la aqumᴇlā'lᴇma wu'Xi
day came. He went. "Ah, you are told she will be bought that

iʟā'Xak¡ᴇmana ayā'Xan." Itciō'lXam iā'cîkc: "AmʟōlXā'ma, ac
their chief his daughter." He said to him his friend: "Tell them, and

qān aʟxanxō'xoa. Ā'oʟᴇʟ itsᴇ'k¡emasamit." Xā'pîX igē'Xk¡oa
silent they shall be. Nevertheless I made them ashamed." In the evening he went home

iā'cîkc. Iqioqu'mtcxōgoa: "Qā itcimō'lXam?" "Ō itcimcō'lXam
his friend. He was asked: "How did he say to you?" "Oh, he said to you

ac qān amcxixō'xoa." Kawī'X iō'ya ya'Xi iā'cîkc. A'qa
and silent you shall be." Early he went that his friend. Then

igoXuē'tXuîtck ta-îtci tê'lXam. A'qa itgī'ya ta-îtci tê'lXam,
they made themselves ready those people. Then they went those people,

ka'nauwē itgī'ya tq¡ulîpXᴇnā'yu. Itciō'lXam iā'cîkc:
all they went the youths. He said to him his friend:

"A'qaktxᴇ'ʟakᵘt." Iqcxᴇ'ʟakoa iguXuā'qoam ta-îtci tê'lXam.
"We are surrounded." They were surrounded they met those people.

Kē'nuwa isxā'sk¡ᴇnukʟuwa. Igē'kta kā'tcᴇkpā'tîx· ta-îtci tê'lXam.
Try they approached secretly. He ran middle there those people.

Iqiō'qumit igiktē'mᴇnq. YaXī' mā'ʟnîX ʟāx igē'xôx wu'Xi
He was seen he dived. Here seaward visible he became that

akū'yaxpa. Ē'wemax etā'ʟqtax tiā'utcakc. Iaxak¡ᴇ'niakoa wu'Xi
snag on. Thus long his ears. He leaned on it that

akū'yax. A'qa igō'xoak¡pa. Igoxoē'nîmtck tê'lXam ā'qa. Igē'kîm
snag. Then they went home. They cried the people then. He said

went home and cried. Then the youth said: "Behold! you said I lied; he became a monster." Then they gathered many people. His friend went; he cried and cried and cried. He cried a long time. He looked and there his friend was standing: "Oh, friend," he said to him, "I am unhappy. I thought you had left me for good." "I shall tell you when they make me tired. Then you may cry. If they will let me alone, we shall do the same all the time; we shall play when you come here." Then he said again to his friend: "They are coming secretly to surround us." The people surrounded them in a double row, trying to catch him, but he ran into the water, dived, and emerged far out at sea. He lay on a snag. Then the people cried. "Go," they said to the youth, "tell him we will buy for him that slave girl whom he liked so much." The following morning his friend went. He cried a long time and saw his friend. He told him what the people had said: "Your father will buy that slave girl for you."

---

ya'Xi iq!u'lîpX: "Tä'tc!a amcgᴇnuxō'la itcî'ʟ!mēnXut ya'Xi
that youth: "Behold you told me I spoke a lie that

iqcxē'ʟau igē'xôx." A'qa wi iqō'xoaqtck tê'lXam. ʟgā'pᴇlatîkc
a monster he became." Then again they were sent for the people. Many

iqō'xoaqtck, a'qa wi iō'ya iā'cîkc. Igigᴇ'tcax, igigᴇ'tcax, igigᴇ'tcax
they were sent for, then again he went his friend. He cried, he cried, he cried

iā'cîkc. Lē'lē igigᴇ'tcax. Igē'kîkct, a'qa iutXuē'la iā'cîkc. "Ō
his friend. Long he cried. He looked, then there stood his friend. "Oh

cîkc," itciō'lXam, "tgᴇ'giōtkoax. Nxʟō'Xuan aqa guā'nᴇsum
friend," he said to him, "my unhappiness. I thought then always

imᴇnqᴇ'lōqʟq." "Manē'x tᴇll aqiō'x ē'tcᴇmxtc, aqa ayamōlXā'ma,
you left me." "When tired is made my heart, then I shall tell you,

tcXua qamktcā'xamx. Ma'nîx ac iā'c aqᴇnō'xoa, a'qa k!oaʟqē'
then you may cry. When and let alone I am done, then just as

atxō'xoa. Ma'nîx tq!ēx amtō'xoa atxk!ayā'wulalᴇma, a'qa mtä'ya
we do. When like you do it we play, then come

tē'ka." A'qa wī't'ax itciō'lXam iā'cîkc: "A'qa wi tgatē't tê'lXam.
here." Then again he said to him his friend: "Now again they are coming the people.

Itxatxk!ētkʟuwā't." A'qa wi iqcxᴇ'ʟakoa. Mâ'kctîX iguXoā'qoam
They approach us secretly." Then again they were surrounded. Twice they met

tê'lXam. A'qa wi kē'nuwa atgigᴇlgā'ya. Kē'nuwa itgē'gᴇlga
the people. Then again try they took him. Try they took him

ta-îtci tê'lXam. Ā'nqa yaXī' mā'ʟnîX igē'kta, igiktē'mᴇnq.
those people. Already there seaward he ran, he dived.

YaXī'2 mā'ʟnîX ʟāx igē'x iaXak!ᴇ'niakoa wu'Xi akū'yax. A'qa
There seaward visible he became he leaned on it that snag. Then

wi igoxoē'nîmtck ta-îtci tê'lXam. A'qa wi iqiō'lXam ya'Xi
again they cried those people. Then again he was told that

iq!u'lîpX: "Ō, tgt!ō'kti amiulXā'ma, antcgōmᴇlā'lᴇma wu'Xi
youth: "Oh, good you tell him, we will buy her that

alā'etîX wu'Xi tq!ēx qtcōxt." Igē'tcuktîX, a'qa wi iō'ya iā'cîkc.
slave girl that like he did her." Day came, then again he went his friend.

Lē'2lē iō'ʟa-ît. A'qa wi itcē'qᴇlkᴇl iā'cîkc. Igixᴇlgu'ʟîtck iā'cîkc:
Long he stayed. Then again he saw him his friend. He told his friend:

He told his friend: "Tell them to be quiet; they were ashamed of me." Then his father said: "Let us put a net into the water. He will dive and the net will catch him." Day came. His friend went out first. Then the people went. Then they put a net into the water near the land. They tied large stones to it so that the net hung down. They surrounded him. They surrounded him in three rows and drew nearer and nearer. The two youths were playing shooting at targets. Then the quickest jumpers tried to jump at him and the people tried to take him, but he had gone into the water. He dived between the net and the land. The net did not shake, and he came up in the water beyond it. His ears were *that* long. Then the people went home. They cried. His father said: "Let us kill him. Perhaps he will be put on the land." They mended their arrows. Early his friend went. He stood a long time and said to his friend: "They will shoot me." Now the people came. They put two nets into the water and tied

---

"Ā, qamuxō'la, atcumᴇlā'lᴇma wē'mam wu'Xi alā'etîX." Itciō'lXam
"Ah, you are told he will buy her your father that slave girl." He said to him

iā'cîkc: "Ō, amʟōlXā'ma ac qān aʟxᴇnxō'xoa. Ā'oʟᴇʟ
his friend: "Oh, tell them and quiet they shall be. Nevertheless

itcᴇ'k!emasamit." Igē'kîm ya'Xi wī'yam: "Nauā'itk aqtō'kʟa.
I made them ashamed." He said that his father: "A net will be carried.

Wuk! aqtō'xoa ʟtcu'qoapa. K!ō'ma aliktē'mᴇnqama, a'qa quʟ
Straight it will be made water in. Perhaps he will dive, then hang

atxelō'xoa." Igē'tcuktîX. Iā'newa iō'ya iā'cîkc. A'qa wī't'ax
they will do him." Day came. First he went his friend. Then again

itgī'ya ta-îtci tê'lXam. A'qa wuk! iqᴇ'tôx taXi nauā'itk
they went those people. Then straight it was made that net

ʟtcu'qoapa q!oā'p ē'lîX. K!au'k!au iqʟō'qoax iʟā'qa-iʟax ʟqᴇ'nakc
water in near the land. Tied were done large stones

ē'wa gē'gualîX taXi nauā'itk. A'qa wi iqcᴇ'ʟakoa. ʟō'nîX
there below that net. Then again they two were surrounded. Three times

iguXoā'qoam ta-îtci tê'lXam. Q!oā'p itgî'côx. Wā'q!pas icxcgē'liʟ.
they met those people. Near they came. Target they two were playing.

Kē'nuwa iqcē'kᴇnpᴇna, cgā'xēlalagᴇmax itkcē'kᴇnpᴇn. Igē'kta.
Try they were jumped at, the quickest ones they jumped. He ran.

Kē'nuwa itgē'gᴇlga ta-îtci tê'lXam, ā'nqa ya'Xi mā'ʟnîX igē'kta.
Try they took him those people, already there seaward he ran.

Igiktē'mᴇnq atā'mʟxᴇleu ta'Xi nauā'itk. Nā2st igō'xoala ta'Xi
He dived landward from it that net. Not it shook that

nauā'itk. YaXī'2 mā'ʟnîX ʟāx igē'xôx. Ē'wemax itā'ʟktax
net. There seaward visible he became. Thus long

tiā'utcakc. Igō'Xoak!oa ta-îtci tê'lXam. Igoxoē'nîmtck. Igē'kîm
his ears. They went home those people. They cried. He said

ya'Xi wī'yam: "Tgt!ō'kti a'qa aqewā'qoa. K!ō'ma ʟxᴇ'leuX
that his father: "Good then he is killed. Perhaps landward

aqiō'tga." Itgᴇ'tôx tgā'qamatcX t!ayā'. Kawī'X iō'ya iā'cîkc.
he will be put." They made them his arrows good. Early he went his friend.

Lē'lē iō'ʟa-it iā'cîkc. A'qa igē'kîm ya'Xi iā'cîkc: "A'qa tgᴇ'maq
Long he stayed his friend. Then he said that his friend: "Now shoot

aqtᴇnlō'xoa." A'qa tgatē't tê'lXam. A'qa môkct nauā'itgᴇmax
I shall be done by them." Then they came the people. Then two nets

many stones to them. Then they went up to them secretly and shot him. His body was full of arrows. In four rows the people surrounded him. They tried to take him, but he ran into the water and dived. The nets did not shake. The arrows drifted on the water where he had dived. All the arrows came out and drifted on the water. The people went home. The youth said: "If you do not let him alone, you will never see him again. If you wish, you may always see him. You may go and see us play." Next day his friend went again. He cried and cried and cried a long time and he saw his friend standing there. "Oh, my poor friend, you will not see me again; my heart is tired." Then they shot at targets again. The people came again; part of them came in canoes. They took arrows. Again they surrounded them. He said to his friend: "They are surrounding us." Again they shot him. Five rows of people surrounded

---

wuk! iqE'tôx Ltcu'qoapa. K!au'k!au iqLō'koax Lgā'pEla LqE'nakc
straight they were made water in. Tied they were done many stones

ta'Xi nauā'itk. A'qa isxā'sk!EnukLuwa. Tiā'maq iqtē'lôx;
that net. Then they approached them secretly. Shoot he was done with them;

ka'nauwē pāL tqā'matcX ē'iaLq. La'ktîX igō'Xomaya tê'lXam.
all full arrows his body. Four times they met the people.

Kōpā' iō'ya, igē'kta. Kē'nuwa itgē'gElga. Ā'nqa ē'wa mā'LnîX
There he went, he ran. Try they took him. Already there seaward

igē'kta. Igiktē'mEnq. Nē2ct igō'xoala ta'Xi nauā'itk. Kōpā'
he ran. He dived. Not they shook those nets. There

yaXī' igiktē'mEnq kōpā' itkXE'nitck ta'Xi tqā'matcX. Ka'nauwē
then he dived there they drifted those arrows. All

Lāq itxē'xôx ta'Xi tqā'matcX. YaXī' mā'LnîX Lāx igē'xôx.
come out they did those arrows. Here seaward visible he became.

Igō'Xok!oa ta-îtci tê'lXam. Igē'kîm ya'Xi iq!u'lîpX: "Manē'x
They went home those people. He said that youth: "When

nEct iā'c amcgiō'xa, a'qa nîct qantsī'X amcgiqElkElā'ya. Manē'x
not let alone you do him, then never you will see him. When

tq!ēx amckto'xoa amcgiō'qumita guā'nEsum, amcō'yima, ac
like you do it you see him always, you go, and

aqEntâ'qumita yaXī' wā'q!pas qantxcgE'līL." Igē'tcuktîX, kawī'X
you look at us there target we play." Day came, early

iō'ya iā'cîkc. IgigE'tcax, igigE'tcax, igigE'tcax. Lē'lē igigE'tcax.
he went his friend. He cried, he cried, he cried. Long he cried.

Igē'kîkct. IutXuē'la iā'cîkc. "Ō, tEmē'giutkoax, cîkc. Ā'2qa
He looked. There stood his friend. "Oh, your unhappiness, friend. Then

kapE't imE'nqElkEl. A'qa tEll igē'xôx ē'tcamxtc." Kōpā' wā'q!pas
enough you saw me. Then tired it became my heart." There target

icxE'cgam. A'qa wi itgī'ya tê'lXam. Aqā'watîkc tcakEnīma'
they two played. Then again they went the people. Several in a canoe

itgī'ya. Ka'nauwē tqā'matcX itgūguigā't ta-îtci tê'lXam. A'qa
they went. All arrows they held them those people. Then

wī't'ax iqcXE'Lakoa. Itciō'lXam iā'cîkc: "A'qa wi iqtxE'Lak^{u}t."
again they were surrounded. He said to him his friend: "Now again we are surrounded."

A'qa wi tiā'maq iqtē'lôx; qui'nEmîX igō'Xomaya tê'lXam
Then again shot he was with them; five times coiled around people

them. He was full of arrows; then he ran to the water. The people tried to take hold of him, but he ran into the water. The people tried to harpoon him. All the arrows came out and he emerged far from the shore. Then his friend said: "Now you may cry; you will never see him again. He will always remain a monster." Then the people cried. They cut their hair, and his friend cried all the time. Five days his friend cried. He looked up and there his friend was standing. "Oh, my poor friend. I am not dead. You are always crying for me. I am in a house like yours. My name is Ēmōgoā'lEkc. A person who sees me will become a chief. Now stop crying." Thus he spoke to his friend.

---

nuXoā'goamx. Pā2L igē'xôx tqā'matcX, a'qa wi igē'kta mā'LnîX.
they met. Full he became arrows, then again he ran seaward.

Kē'nuwa itgē'gElga ta-îtci tê'lXam. YaXī'2 mā'LnîX igē'kta.
Try they took him those people. Here seaward he ran.

Kē'nuwa itkLē'loqck ta-îtci ikE'nimpā qōgoakē'x tê'lXam.
Try they harpooned him those canoe in being in people.

Ka'nauwē Lāq itxē'x tqā'matcX. YaXī'2 mā'LnîX Lāx igē'xôx.
All come out they did the arrows. Here seaward visible he became.

Igē'kîm ya'Xi iā'cîkc: "K¦ō'ma tc¦a amcxē'nîmtck. Nîct qantsî'X
He said that his friend: "Perhaps behold you cry. Never

amcgiqElkElā'ya. A'qa guā'nEsum iqcxē'Lau igē'x." Igoxoē'nîmtck
you will see him. Then always a monster he is." They cried

ta-îtci tê'lXam. Ka'nauwē LE'gaqcō Lq¦ōp itgî'Lôx. Ka'nauwē
those people. All their hair cut they did it. All

Lkā'etax iā'cîkc niktcā'xEma-itx. Qoā'nEmîX iō'qxoya igigE'tcax
days his friend he cried. Five times his sleeps he cried

iā'cîkc. Ē'wa igē'xôx, iutXuē'la iā'cîkc. "Ō, tEmē'giutkoax, cîkc.
his friend. Thus he did, he stood his friend. "Oh, your poverty, friend.

NEcqē nō'maqt, tatc¦a guā'nEsum mEngE'mqElqt. K¦oaLqā' L¦a
Not at all I die, behold always you cry for me. Just so behold

mai'ka tqu'Lipa nōxt. Ēmōgoā'lEkc itcî'xaleu. Qiā'x Lkak¦Emā'na
your house in I am. Ēmōgoā'lEkc my name. If a chief

Lxō'lalEmx tcXua LkEnqElkElē'ma-îtx. Kōpē't aqa imgE'tcax,"
he gets then they will always see me. Enough now you cry,"

itciō'lXam iā'cîkc.
he said to him his friend.

The Brothers (told 1894)

The name of a country is Nagiō'na. Five men and one woman lived in a town there. Every year, in October, they went to Nē'tEl to dry salmon. They never gave their youngest brother any food. They gave him only tail pieces of salmon. They did so every year. They gave him only tail pieces of salmon. For five years they moved from Nagiō'na to Nē'tEl and back again. Then the youngest brother had become a youth. When they were moving to Nē'tEl, he said to his elder brothers: "Leave me here at our house." They had a large house fourteen fathoms long. Then they moved to Nē'tEl and left their youngest brother behind.

They stayed a long time at Nē'tEl; then the eldest one said: "Go and take food to our youngest brother. Take him tail pieces of salmon." One of them went and took his youngest brother tail

---

Nagiō'na iā'xaleu ya'Xi ēlX. Kōpā' iLā'lXam Lquî'nEmîkc 1
Nagiō'na its name that country. There their town five

Lkā'lukc k¡a aēXā't aqagē'lak. NixEltā'qoamxîX tcā'maLîx 2
men and one woman. Every year October

nixō'xoaxîX qaLō'îx Nē'tElpa qaLxElukcEmā'mamx. Nēst qantsî'x 3
it got they went Nē'tEl to they went to dry salmon. Not ever

qaLgilqoē'mX ya'Xi iLā'mXîX. Ma'nîx qaLgilqoē'mX, aqa ctā'ema 4
they gave him to eat that their younger brother. When they gave him to eat, then only

sp¡iā'sX aqcîlqoē'mX. Ka'nauwē Lqetā'qEmax k¡oaLqē'. Ctā'ema 5
salmon tails he was given to eat. All years thus. Only

sp¡iā'sX aqcilqoē'mEniLx. Â, qoā'nEmîX Lqetā'qEmax iLgE'Layu. 6
salmon tails he was given to eat. Ah, five times years they moved.

A'qa iq¡u'lîpX igē'xôx ya'Xi iLā'mXîX. A'qa wi iLgE'Layu ē'wa 7
Then a youth he became that their younger brother. Then again they moved there

Nē'tEl. ItcLō'lXam Lē'yalXtîkc: "Tā'ka amcînqElō'qLqa gi 8
Nē'tEl. He said to them his elder brothers: "Here leave me this

tE'lxaqLpa." Itā'2qa-îL ta'Xi tE'LaqL. Itā'LElXam LE'ganXa igō'n 9
our house at." Large that house. Ten fathoms more

lakt ta'Xi tqu'Lē. A'qa iLaqE'lōqLq iLā'mXîX; iLgE'Layu ē'wa 10
four that house. Then they left him their younger brother; they moved there

Nē'tElpa. 11
Nē'tEl to.

Lē'lē Lxē'la-it Nē'tElpa. Igē'k·îm ya'Xi ixgE'qunq: 12
Long they stayed Nē'tEl at. He said that the eldest one:

"Mcgîlqoē'mam ilxā'mXîX. Amcktîlqoē'mamx tp¡iā'sXîkc." 13
"Go and give him to eat our younger brother. Bring him to eat salmon tails."

Iō'ya ēXā't. Itcîlqoē'mam iā'mXîX tp¡iā'sXîkc. Iō'yam ta'Xi 14
He went one. He brought him to eat his younger brother salmon tails. He arrived that

pieces of salmon. He came to the house, but his youngest brother was not there. Bird skins were hanging in the house. He waited some time, but his youngest brother did not come home. Then that person went home again. He hung up the tail pieces of salmon and left them. In the evening the youngest brother came home. He entered and the tail pieces were hanging there. He thought: "Oh, they came to see me. What shall I do with those tail pieces? They just give me tail pieces of salmon to eat." He hung them up near the door, and skinned the birds which he had found on the beach. All the year round he searched for birds on the beach; he always caught birds on the beach.

His brothers stayed for a long time at Nē'tᴇl. Then the eldest one said again: "Take food to our youngest brother." Tail pieces of salmon were cut again, and another of the brothers went. He arrived at the house and entered. There was nobody there, but one side of the house was full of bird skins. His youngest brother was not there.

---

tᴇ'ʟaqʟpa. K¡ā ya'Xi iā'mXîX. Iā'ema tp¡ᴇsp¡ᴇ'suks cu'XcuX
their house at. Nothing that his younger brother. Only birds skinned

ōguakē'x. Qu'ʟquʟ tā'wîxt tᴇ'ʟaqʟpa. Kē'nuwa itcigî'mʟa-it.
they were. Hang they did their house in. Try he waited for him.

Nāct igiXatk¡oā'mam. Aqa wi igē'Xk¡oa yā'Xi igoaʟē'lX.
Not he came home. Then again he went home that person.

Quʟ itctā'wîX ta'Xi tp¡iā'sXîks. Itcō'qo-iqʟq. Tsō'yustîX,
Hang he did them those salmon tails. He left them. In the evening,

a'qa igîXk¡oā'mam ya'Xi iq¡u'lîpX. Iō'pqa. A'qa quʟ tā'wîXt
then he came home that youth. He entered. Then hang they did

tp¡iā'sXîks. IgîxʟŌ'Xoa-it: "Ō, iqᴇnᴇ'tkctam ʟ¡. Tān
salmon tails. He thought: "Oh, they came to see me, behold! What

ʟqa aniuguē'xa gi tp¡iā'sXîks? Koalē'wa ʟqa tp¡iā'sXîks
maybe shall I do with them these salmon tails? Just maybe salmon tails

iqtnᴇ'lqoîm." Quʟ itctā'wîX k¡awusî'qēpa. A'qa wi cu'XcuX
I am given to eat." Hang he did them near the door. Then again skin

itcî'tux tp¡ᴇsp¡ᴇ'suks. Itctō'mitckē mā'ʟnîX tkamilā'lqpa.
he did them birds. He found them on the beach seaward beach on.

Ka'nauwē ʟqā'etaq qayacktā'goatcgoa-itx. Qatctomē'tck¡ēnanᴇma-îtx
All year he went to search on the beach. He always found them on the beach

tp¡ᴇsp¡ᴇ'suks.
birds.

Lē'lc ʟxē'la-it ʟē'ialXtîkc ya'Xi Nē'tᴇlpa. A'qa wi itcʟō'lXam
Long they stayed his elder brothers that Nē'tᴇl at. Then again he told them

ē'ʟalXt: "Ō, mcgilqoē'mam ilxā'mXîX." A'qa wi ʟq¡u'pʟq¡up
their elder brother: "Oh, bring him food our younger brother." Then again cut

iqᴇ'tux tp¡iā'sXîks. A'qa wi iō'ya igō'n ē'Xat ē'yalXt. Iō'yam
they were salmon tails. Then again he went another one his elder brother. He arrived

tᴇ'ʟaqʟpa. Iā'ckōpq. K¡ᴀmm tê'lXam, tā'ema tp¡ᴇsp¡ᴇ'suks
their house at. He entered. No people, only birds

itā'p¡ackoal pāʟ tᴇ'nat tqu'ʟē. K¡ā ya'Xi iā'mXîX. Nō'ʟ¡îX
their skins full one side the house. Nothing that his younger brother. A little

He stayed a short while and then he hung up the tail pieces. He went home. In the evening the youth came home. He saw the tail pieces and thought: "They always give me tail pieces to eat," and hung them up near the door. Now two strings of tail pieces were there. He did not eat them. All the year round he went to search for birds on the beach. He always caught birds there.

The brothers stayed for a long time. Then the eldest brother said again: "Go and take food to our youngest brother." Then another one went and brought him tail pieces of salmon to eat. He arrived, but his youngest brother was not there. The house was full of bird skins. The birds were skinned, and the tail pieces were hanging there. He thought: "What may our youngest brother eat?" Two strings of tail pieces were hanging there. Their youngest brother had not eaten them. Then that person went home again. In the evening the youth came home. "Oh, behold, they brought me that food!" He took the tail pieces and hung them up. Now three strings of tail pieces were

---

iō'ʟa-it.	Quʟ	itctā'wîX	ta'Xi	tp¡iā'sXîks.	Igē'Xk¡oa.
he stayed.	Hang	he did them	those	salmon tails.	He went home.

Tsō'yustîX	igîXk¡oā'mam	ya'Xi	iq¡u'lîpX.	Itcō'quikᴇl	tp¡iā'sXîks.
In the evening	he came home	that	youth.	He saw them	the salmon tails.

IgîxLō'Xoa-it:	"QulE'tc	sp¡iā'sX	iqᴇnᴇ'lqo-îm."	Quʟ	itctā'wîX
He thought:	"Always	salmon tails	I am given to eat."	Hang	he did them

k¡awusî'qē.	A'qa	mô'ketîX	k¡au	nōguakē'x	ta'Xi	tp¡iā'sXîks.
near the door.	Then	twice	tied	they were	those	tail pieces.

Nāct	itixᴇ'lᴇmuX.	Ka'nauwē	ʟqā'etaq	qayacktā'goatcgoa-itx.
Not	he ate them.	All	year	he went to search on the beach.

Qatctōmē'tck¡ēnanᴇma-itx	tp¡ᴇsp¡ᴇ'suks.
He always found them on the beach	birds.

A'qa	wi	lē'lē	iʟxē'la-it.	A'qa	wi	igē'k·îm	ē'ʟalXt:
Then	again	long	they stayed.	Then	again	he said	their elder brother:

"Amcgîlqoē'mam	îlXā'mXîX."	A'qa	wi	iō'ya	ēXā't	itcîlqoē'mam
"Bring him food	our younger brother."	Then	again	he went	one	he brought him food

tp¡iā'sXîks.	Iō'yam	tᴇ'ʟaqʟpa.	K¡ā	nîct	iōXt	iʟā'mXîX.	Pāʟ
salmon tails.	He arrived	their house at.	Nothing	not	he was there	their younger brother.	Full

ta'Xi	tqu'ʟē	tp¡ᴇsp¡ᴇ'suks	itā'p¡ackoal.	Tc¡u'Xtc¡uX	ōguakē'x.
that	house	birds	their skins.	Skinned	they were.

Quʟ	itctā'wîX	ta'Xi	tp¡iā'sXîks.	IgîxLō'Xoa-it:	"Tān	ʟqa
Hang	he did them	those	salmon tails.	He thought:	"What	maybe

ixelā'x	intcā'mXîX?"	Quʟ	tā'2wîXt	môket	tgā'ʟana.	Nāct
he does	our younger brother?"	Hung	were	two	their ropes.	Not

itixᴇ'lᴇmux	iʟā'mXîX.	A'qa	wi	igē'Xk¡oa	ya'Xi	igoaʟē'lX.
he ate them	their younger brother.	Then	again	he went home	that	person.

Tsō'yustîX	igîXk¡oā'mam	ya'Xi	iq¡u'lîpX.	"Ō,	iqᴇnētqoē'mam
In the evening	he came home	that	youth.	"Oh,	they brought me food

ʟ¡gi!"	Itcō'guiga	ta'Xi	tp¡iā'sXîks.	Quʟ	itctā'wîX.	A'qa	ʟōn
behold this!"	He took them	those	salmon tails.	Hang	he did them.	Then	three

tgā'ʟana	igō'xoax	ta'Xi	tp¡iā'sXîks.	A'qa	ts¡u'Xts¡uX	itcî'tox
their ropes	were	those	salmon tails.	Then	skin	he did them

hanging there. Then he skinned his birds. His house was full of bird skins.

The brothers stayed on. Then the eldest brother said: "Take tail pieces of salmon to our youngest brother." Another one of the brothers went and arrived at their house. His youngest brother was not there. He hung up the tail pieces and went home. In the evening the youth came home. He made a fire and saw the tail pieces. "Oh," he thought, "they brought me food. They give me tail pieces to eat. Such refuse is given to dogs only." He took them and hung them up near the door. Then he skinned the birds which he had found on the beach. There were all kinds of sea birds. He stayed for a long time. All the year round he was searching on the beach, where he caught birds. His house was full of bird skins.

His elder brothers stayed there for a long time and the eldest one said again: "Quick! take food to our youngest brother." Again they

---

tp¡ESp¡E'suks. Lā'xLax itciō'xoax itā'p¡ackoal. A'qa pāL ta'Xi
the birds. Take off he did them their skins. Then full that

tē'yaqL tp¡ESp¡E'suks itā'p¡ackoal.
his house birds their skins.

A'qa wi iLxē'2la-it La-îtci Lē'yalXtîkc. Aqa wi iLE'k·îm:
Then again they stayed those his elder brothers. Then again he said:

"Amcgîlqoē'mam îlxā'mXîX tp¡iā'cXîks." A'qa wi iō'ya ē'Xat
"Bring him food our younger brother salmon tails." Then again he went one

ē'yalXt. Iō'yam tE'LaqLpa. K¡ayā' igē'xôx iLā'mXîX. QuL
his elder brother. He arrived their house at. Nothing became his younger brother. Hang up

itctā'wîX ta'Xi tp¡iā'sXîks. A'qa wi igē'Xk¡oa. Tsō'yustîX
he did them those salmon tails. Then again he went home. In the evening

igîXk¡oā'mam ya'Xi iq¡u'lîpX, iga-ixE'lgiLx. A'qa itcō'kuikEl
he came home that youth. he made a fire. Then he saw them

tp¡iā'cXîks. "Ō, iqenētqoē'mam," igîxLō'Xoa-it. "Koale'wa Lqa
the salmon tails. "Oh, they brought me food," he thought. "Just so maybe

tp¡iā'cXîks iqanE'lqo-îm. Lā'ema Lk¡ō'tk¡ōt tcXua iq¡ē'yip
salmon tails I am given to eat. Only a dog then refuse

aqēLElqoē'muX." Itcō'guiga ta'Xi tp¡iā'sXîks. QuL itctā'wîX
he is given to eat." He took them those salmon tails. Hang he did them

k¡awusî'qē. A'qa wi cu'XcuX itcî'tôx ta'Xi tp¡ESp¡E'suks ta'Xi
near the door. Then again skin he did them those birds those

itctō'mitckē mā'LnîX qa tp¡ESp¡E'suks, ka'nauwē qā'dEmax
he found them on the beach seaward where birds, all kinds

itā'lkuilē tp¡ESp¡E'suks. Lē'lē iō'La-it. Ka'nauwē Lqā'etaq
similar to birds. Long he stayed. All year

nîcktā'guatcgoa-itx. Qatctōmē'tck¡ēnanEma-itx tp¡ESp¡E'suks. A'qa
he searched on the beach. He always found them on the beach birds. Then

pā2L ta'Xi tē'yaqL ya'Xi itā'p¡ackoal tp¡ESp¡E'suks.
full that his house that their skins birds.

Lē'lē iLxē'la-it Lē'yalXtkc. A'qa wi igē'kîm ē'LalXt:
Long they stayed his elder brothers. Then again he said their elder brother:

"Ayā'q îmcgîlqoē'mam îlxā'mXîX." A'qa wi Lq¡u'pLq¡up
"Quick bring him food our younger brother" Then again cut

iqE'tôx ta'Xi tp¡iā'sXîks. A'qa wi iō'ya ya'Xi ēXā't.
they were done those salmon tails. Then again he went that one.

cut tail pieces of salmon and one of them went. He said: "I am going in vain; he will not eat these tail pieces. Those which we gave him before are still there. His house is full of bird skins. Perhaps he will do something with these bird skins." Then the eldest brother said their youngest brother might be feeling lonesome and that for this reason he might play with the bird skins. Now that person went to see their youngest brother. He brought him food. When he reached their house his youngest brother was singing shaman's songs. He thought: "Behold! he is singing." He looked into the house. There he was lying on the bed on his back singing. He sang: "They gave me tail pieces, but I am not discontented." Thus he sang. His face had changed. [The visitor] said to his youngest brother: "Are you singing?" but he did not reply. He spoke to him five times, but he did not reply. Then his brother gave it up and went home. He came home. He felt sorry. His heart was sad. He stayed a long time and did not speak. Then his wife said to him: "What is

---

Igē'k·îm: "Qanā'qa nō'ya. Nā2cqē(t) ixEtElā'x gi tp¡iā'cXîks.
He said: "In vain I go. Not at all he eats them these salmon tails.

Ōguakē'xax tau ā'nqa iqtîlqoē'mam, a'qa pāL tau tE'lxaqL
They are there what before he was given to eat, then full that our house

itā'p¡ackoal tp¡Esp¡E'suks. Tā'nki LXuan atciuguē'xa ya'Xi
their skins birds. Something perhaps he will do with them those

itā'p¡ackoal tp¡Esp¡E'suks." Igē'kîm ya'Xi ē'LalXt: "LXuan
their skins birds." He said that their elder brother: "Perhaps

ē'yamXtc lāx igē'xôx, tāntxo tîxEnEmō'tXumx ta'Xi
his heart lonesome became, therefore he plays with them those

tp¡Esp¡E'suks." Iō'ya ya'Xi ēXā't igoaLē'lX. Itciō'ktcam ya'Xi
birds." He went that one person. He went to see him that

iLā'mXîX; itcîlqoē'mam. Q¡oā'p itctō'xoam tE'LaqL, aqa
their younger brother; he brought him food. Near he reached it their house, then

LēxEnLā'mit iā'mXîX. IgîxLō'xoa-it: "Ō, Lqōst, ē'ktcxam
he sang much his younger brother. He thought: "Oh, behold, singing shaman's songs

intcā'mXîX." ItcickXā'napq tE'LaqLpa. Icîlgā'qōX iā'lXamēpa
our younger brother." He looked into their house in. He lay on his back his bed on

LēxEnLā'mit. Ixō'la: "Spîā'sXîks qnE'lEqoē'2m, tatc¡a, nîctā'2
he was singing much. He said: "Salmon tails I was given to eat, behold, not

agExE'sga." K¡oaLqē' igē'xôx ē'ktcxam. IxElō'ita a'qa
I am discontented." Thus he did he sang. Different then

siā'xôstpa. Kē'nuwa itciō'lXam iā'mXîX. "ME'ktcxam tci?"
his face in. Try he spoke to him his younger brother. "Do you sing [int. part.]?"

Nē4ctqē itciō'lXam. Quā'nEmîX kē'nuwa itciō'lXam. Nā'ct
Not at all he spoke to him. Five times try he spoke to him. Not

itcteqa'watck. Tā'menua igē'xôx ya'Xi ē'yalXt. A'qa igē'Xk¡oa.
he answered. Give up he did that his elder brother. Then he went home.

IgîXk¡oā'mam. Lē'yaxax. Nîct it¡ō'kti igē'xôx ē'yamXtc.
He came home. He was sad. Not good became his heart.

Lē'2lē iō'La-it, nîct igē'xalEtcō. Igiō'lXam ayā'kikala: "Qa
Long he stayed, not he spoke. She said to him his wife: "How

the matter? Why are you sad?" He replied: "It does not stand well with your brother-in-law. I do not know what he is doing; he is singing shaman's songs, or it is something else. Our house there is full of bird skins. I spoke to him, but he did not reply at all. Five times I spoke to him, but he did not answer." Then his wife said: "The one who came home is sad. Maybe the one who is left behind is singing shaman's songs. He spoke to him, but he did not reply. His face has changed." Then the eldest brother said: "Make yourselves ready; to-morrow we will go home. We will go to our youngest brother."

On the next morning they made themselves ready. They went home. They put away their dried salmon and carried a few along. They approached their house. They heard the noise of birds eating in the house. They arrived at the house. Then birds flew around it. They flew down to the beach and out to sea. Part were outside the

---

emE'xôx?	teqī	LE'mexax."	Itcō'lXam:	"Näct	t¡ayā'	ya'Xi
are you?	just	you are sad."	He said to her:	"Not	good	that

imē'pōtexan.	LXuan	ē'ktcxam	tci	qā'tgi	tci?	Pā2L	a'qa
your brother-in-law.	Perhaps	singing shaman's songs	[int. part.]	how	[int. part.]?	Full	then

tau	tE'lxaqL	tp¡Esp¡E'suks	itā'p¡ackoal.	Kē'nuwa	wā'wa	inī'yux,
that	our house	birds	their skins.	Try	talk	I did to him,

nā'2cqē	wā'wa	itcī'nux.	Qoā'nEmîX	kē'nuwa	wā'wa	inī'yux,
not at all	talk	he did to me.	Five times	try	talk	I did to him,

nā'cqē	itctînxa'watck."	Igaxgu'Lîtck	wu'Xi	ayā'kikala.	Igā'k·îm:
not at all	he answered me."	She told	that	his wife.	She said:

"Näct	it¡ō'kti	ē'yamxtc	gigēXatk¡oā'mam.	LXuan	ē'ktcxam
"Not	good	his heart	the one who came home.	Perhaps	singing shaman's songs

tau	ē'lXaq¡awîlXam.	Kē'nuwa	wā'wa	itcī'yux,	nā'ctqē
that	the one whom we deserted.	Try	talk	he did to him,	not at all

itctexa'watck.	Cxelō'ita	siā'xôst	sgē'xôx."	Igē'k·îm	ē'LalXt:
he answered.	Different	his face	became."	He said	their elder brother:

"Ō'la	aqa	amcxEltXuī'tcga.	AlXk¡oā'ya.	Alxigō'qoama
"To-morrow	then	make yourselves ready.	We will go home.	We will go to meet him

îlXā'mXîX."
our younger brother."

Wāx	igē'tcuktîX.	A'qa	iLxE'ltXuîtck.	A'qa	iLE'Xk¡oa.	Kōpā'
Next day	it grew day.	Then	they made themselves ready.	Then	they went home.	There

iLgE'tutk	Lā'txalEma-cmax,	ōXuā'caqt	tE'q¡awan.	Nō'L¡EmaX
they put away	their food,	dry	salmon.	A little

iLgE'tuk'i.	Q¡oā'p	iLō'yam	tE'LaqLpa.	A'qa	tc¡ē4k	tp¡Esp¡E'suks
they carried it.	Near	they arrived	their house at.	Then	(noise of birds eating)	birds

ō'xo-itcX	ta'Xi	tE'LaqLpa.	ILugoā'qoam	ta'Xi	tE'LaqLpa.
they talked much	that	their house in.	They reached	that	their house at

Qoxuā'Lak^{u}t	ta'Xi	tE'LaqL,	toxuā'Lak^{u}t	ta'Xi	tp¡Esp¡E'suks.
They flew around it	that	their house,	they flew around it	those	birds.

A'qa	itgE'Lx	itk^{u}kLā'xitt	mā'LnîX	ē'maLpa.	ItgE'px,	itgE'px,
Then	they went down to the water	they all went together	seaward	the sea to.	They came out,	they came out,

house; part were coming out. Then one of the elder brothers of the youth said: "Did not I tell you that tail pieces were given to slaves only? Our youngest brother became ashamed. He has turned into a supernatural being. You see these birds? They have become his people." The birds all went out to sea. Then they entered the house. It was full of feathers. Their youngest brother had disappeared. He had gone out to sea, and had become a supernatural being. Then one of the elder brothers said: "Oh, our youngest brother! When an Indian finds him, he will give him whale meat." Then they burned their house. When the house was burned, one of them said: "When later generations wish to see supernatural beings, they shall sweep our house and they will find our coals." Then they cried and went far away. They left him.[1]

---

itgᴇ'px, aqā'wa a'qa ʟā'xanîX ōguakē'x. A'qa igē'kîm ya'Xi 1
they came out, part then outside were. Then he said that

ēXā't ē'yalXt ya'Xi iq¡u'lîpX: "Ē'XtîX ʟq inᴇ'k·'îm, ʟā'ema 2
one his elder brother that youth: "Once maybe I told you, only

ʟlā'etîX tcXua tp¡iā'sXîks aqʟᴇlqoē'mᴇniʟ. A'qa igēxᴇmā'sa-it 3
a slave then salmon tails they are given to eat. Then he is ashamed

ilxā'mXîX. A'qa iō'ʟᴇmax igē'xôx. Amcktō'qumit ta'Xi 4
our younger brother. Then a supernatural being he became. You see them those

tp¡ᴇsp¡ᴇ'suks, tiā'lXam itixᴇ'lôx." Ka'nauwē itgᴇ'ʟxa ta'Xi 5
birds, his people they are." All they went down those

tp¡ᴇsp¡ᴇ'suks, ē'maʟpa itgī'ya. Iʟā'ckupq tᴇ'ʟaqʟ. Pā2ʟ wu'Xi 6
birds, the sea to they went. They entered their house at. Full that

ā'kᴇmcō ta'Xi tᴇ'ʟaqʟpa. K¡ā iʟā'mXîX. Iō'ʟxa mā'ʟnîXpa, 7
feathers that their house at. Nothing their younger brother. He went down to the water to the water to,

ē'maʟpa. Ewā' maʟnā' niō'ʟᴇmax· igē'xôx. Igēkîm ya'Xi 8
the sea to. There seaward place of supernatural being he became. He said that

ēXā't ē'yalXt: "Ō, intcā'mXîX. Qiā'x ma'nîx aʟxigᴇlkᴇlā'ya 9
one his elder brother: "Oh, our younger brother. If when he sees him

ʟgoaʟē'lX, a'qa ē'koalē atciʟᴇlqoē'mᴇniʟa ʟiā'tetanuē." A'qa 10
a person, then whale he will give them to eat his Indians." Then

iʟguXuē'giʟx tᴇ'ʟaqʟ. Ka'nauwē igō'XumaʟXa tᴇ'ʟaqʟ. 11
they burnt it their house. All it was burnt their house.

Iʟᴇ'kîm: "Manē'x naloxoā'xa tô'lXam aʟktoqoē'la gi tᴇ'ntcaqʟ, 12
They said: "When generations of people will sweep this our house,

manē'x iō'ʟᴇmax alēxaʟgᴇlō'xoa, aqa aʟgucgā'ma antcā'xaʟxatcX." 13
when supernatural beings they want to see supernatural beings, then they shall find them our coals."

Ā'qa iʟxē'nîmtck; iʟō'ya; kᴇlā'îX iʟgᴇ'ʟayu. 14
Then they cried; they went; far they moved.

---

[1] It is said that when a person who desires to find a supernatural helper weeds the place at Nagio'na called "The House of the Brothers," and then sweeps it, he may find coals. This is a sign that the lost brother will become a helper. If he does not find coals, his endeavor to obtain the supernatural helper will be fruitless.

The War of the Ghosts (told 1891)

There were people at Lgu'laq. One night two young men went to hunt seals. They came down the river. It became foggy and calm. While they were paddling they heard war-cries. They thought: "Maybe there is a war party." They escaped toward the shore and hid behind a log. Now canoes came up and they heard the noise of paddles. When the canoes came opposite them they saw one canoe coming up to them. There were five men in the canoe. They spoke to them: "What do you think? We wish to take you along. We are going up the river to make war on the people." One of the young men said: "I have no arrows." "Arrows are in the canoe." One of them said: "I will not go along, I might be killed. My relatives do not know where I have gone. You may go with them." Thus he spoke to his fellow. The one accompanied them.

Kōpā'	oxoclā'etîX	ta-îtci	tê'lXam	Lgu'laqpa.	QāxLkanā'pōl
There	they were	those	people	Lgu'laq at.	One night

aqesgoā'max	ictagE'loya	cta'Xi	emôket	eq¡u'lîpX.	Qā'eqamîX
seals	they went to hunt	those	two	youths.	Down the river

icî'tē.	A'qa	iga-ikxā'LakoîX.	˥ō	igē'xoXîX.	Aqa	icqLē'wala.
they came.	Then	it became foggy.	Calm	it became.	Then	they paddled.

A'qa	ickauitcE'maq	tê'lXam.	Ē'Lutq	tgioxō'la.	IcxLō'xoa-it:	"Ō,
Then	they heard them	people.	War-cries	they made them.	They thought:	"Oh,

itā'k¡ēsaq	Lqōst!"	Icxē'gela-îX	LXE'leuX.	Icxā'kamEla	wu'Xi
they go to war	behold!"	They landed	inland.	They hid behind	that

ā'mqō	agū'mLXEleu.	A'qa	igā'suwulX	wu'Xi	akE'nim
log	landward from it.	Then	they went up the river	those	canoes

icgaltcE'mElētEmtck.	Xup xup xup	ōgoaqLē'wala.	IgacElō'yîmXit
they heard them.	(Noise of paddling)	they paddled.	They came opposite them

wu'Xi	akE'nim.	Icgē'qElkEl	ēXt	ikE'nim	itē't	ctā'xkapa.
those	canoes.	They saw it	one	canoe	came	them to.

Igicgā'tqoam	aqa	ā'k¡aquinEmîkc.	Iqcō'lXam:	"Qā	imtā'Xaqamit?
It reached them,	then	five men in the canoe.	They were told:	"How	your mind?

Icxamtxā'txam.	Alxk¡ē'saqoama	ē'wa	cā'xalîX."	Igē'kîm	ya'Xi
We will take you along.	We are going to war	there	upward."	He said	that

eXā't:	"NE'cqē	tgE'qamatcX.	K¡ā'ya	tgE'qamatcX."	"Ta'Xi
one:	"Not at all	my arrows.	None	my arrows."	"Those

tqā'matcX	tā'kXaxt."	Igē'kîm	ya'Xi	ēXā't:	"Nai'ka	nākct
arrows	are in the canoe."	He said	that	one:	"I	not

anxEltō'ma,	iā'okîX	aqEnuwā'qoax.	NEcqē'	tgEnlō'xo-îx
I shall go in company,	else	I shall be killed.	Not at all	they know about me

tgE'cēuXtîkc."	"Qā'txō,"	itciō'lXam,	"mā'ema	amxEltō'ma";
my relatives."	"Must,"	he said to him,	"you alone	go in company";

itciō'lXam	gictā'cgewal.	IgixE'ltōm	ya'Xi	ēXā't;	iagE'La-it
he said to him	his companion.	He went in company	that	one;	he went into the canoe

He went into their canoe and the other went home. At midnight he returned and said: "My relative left me. He went to accompany the warriors who went up the river to make war."

Then the warriors went. The people in the canoe talked together. They came to a place on the other side of Kalama. The people went down to the water and they began to fight. He thought they were really people. When one of his fellows was shot, they carried him into the canoe and put him in there. Then the people continued to fight. Now one of them said: "Quick let us go home; that Indian has been shot." Now he thought: "Oh, they are ghosts." He did not feel sick, and they said he had been hit. Then the people went home. They arrived at Lgu'laq. One canoe landed, and that person went ashore. The people went down the river. He went up to the house and made a fire. He said: "Behold I accompanied the ghosts," and he told everything. "We did such and such a thing; we fought.

---

itā'XEnīmpa ta-îtci tê'lXam. Iō'ya, igē'Xk¡oa ya'Xi ēXā't.
their canoe in those people. He went, he went home that one.

Kā'tcEk wā'pōl igîXk¡oā'mam. "Ā, igînqE'loqL itcî'cuX.
Middle night he came home. "Ah, he left me my relative.

IgixE'ltōm; iugumā'tōm gitā'k¡ēsaq."
He went in company; he accompanied them warriors."

Ē'wa cā'xalîX itgī'ya gitā'k¡ēsaq, a'qa itgī'ya ta-îtci gitā'k¡ēsaq.
There upward they went the warriors, then they went those warriors.

Tā'2lXam ō'XuîtcX, ka'nauwē wu'Xi akE'nim. Itgī'yam ē'wa
People were talking, all those canoes. They arrived there

k¡anatē'tōL Tk¡alā'ma. Itgā'Lxa ta-îtci tê'lXam, a'qa igoxoā'maqt.
on the other side of Kalama. They went toward the water those people, then they fought.

IgîxLō'xoa-ît ā'qanuwē tê'lXam. ILā'maq aqitElō'xoax ta-îtci
He thought really people. Shoot they were done those

giLā'cgewal, nä'wi iqLō'k'l̈X ikE'nimpa. IqLEqXaemā'mamx ka
his companions, at once they were carried canoe to. They were put into the canoe and

oxoā'maqt ta-îtci tê'lXam. A'qa iLE'kîm LēXā't: "Ai'aq, a'qa
they fought those people. Then he said one: "Quick, then

alXk¡uā'ya, a'qa iā'maq iqē'lôx ya'Xi itē'tanuē." IgîxLō'Xoa-ît:
we will go home, then shot he is that Indian." He thought:

"Ō, tmēmElō'ctîke L¡!" Näct qā'xpa iā'teqam. Tatc¡a iqiō'lXam
"Oh, ghosts behold!" Not anywhere his sickness. Behold he was told

iā'maq iqē'lôx. A'qa igō'Xoak¡oa ta-îtci tê'lXam. Itgā'2yam
shot he was. Then they went home those people. They arrived at

Lgu'laq. Txē'gela-îX ēXt itā'Xanīm. A'qa iaqE'lōLX ya'Xi
Lgu'laq. They landed one their canoe. Then he went ashore that

igoaLē'lX, ac iaqE'lōLX; a'qa itgE'stsō ta-îtci tê'lXam. Iâ'ptcgam,
person, and he went ashore; then they went down the river those people. He came up,

iga-iXE'lgīLX. Igē'kîm: "TmēmElō'ctîke L¡ gi inugomā'tōm."
he made a fire. He said: "Ghosts behold these I accompanied them."

IgixkᵘLē'lalEmtck: "Ä'wa întcî'xôx. YaXī' întcxE'maqt.
He told much: "Thus we did. There we fought.

went into the canoe and the people went up the river. The other one went home. The people went a long way. On the other side of Kalama they made war upon the people. When one of them was shot, they carried him into the canoe and laid him down there. Just so did those of the other side. The people fought a long time. Then one person said: "Quick! let us go home. That Indian has been hit." The man thought: "Oh, those people I came with are ghosts." They went home. They went to the beach of his town and carried him ashore. He went up. It was nearly daylight when he came to his house. He said: "I went with the ghosts. I was told that I was shot, but I did not feel sick." Then he told them about it. Daylight came in the house. Then he fell down dead. Blood came out of his mouth, and something black came out of his anus. It looked like salal berries. His friend was well. He did not die, because he did not accompany the ghosts.

---

iā'k;aeXat ya'Xi eXā't. A'qa itgī'ya ta-îtci tê'lXam, kELā'-îX
one in canoe that one. Then they went those people, far

itgī'ya. Itgī'ya, itgī'ya, itgī'ya. K;anatē'tuL K;alā'mapa kōpā'
they went. They went, they went, they went. On the other side of Kalama there

xigō igoxoā'maqt ta-îtci tê'lXam. LAXī' iLā'maq aqiLElō'xoax,
when they fought those people. Those shot they were,

nā'wi aqLōk^1 ikE'nimpa. AqLEqxaimā'mamx. K;oaLqē' ta-îtci
at once they were carried the canoe to. They were placed into the canoe. Thus those

ē wa ē'natîX qa'tōXt. Lē'lē iguXoā'maqt ta-îtci tê'lXam. A'qa
there on the other side they did. Long they fought those people. Then

ikE'k·îm La'Xi LeXā't LgoaLē'lX: "A'yaq alxE'xatk;oa, a'qa iā'maq
he said that one person: "Quick let us go home, then shot

iqē'luX ya'Xi Itē'tanuē." A'qa igixLō'Xoa-ît ya'Xi igoaLē'lX:
he is that Indian." Then he thought that person:

"O, tmēmELō'etîke iLgenukomā'tōm." A'qa igō'k;oaxoa ta-îtci
"Oh, ghosts I accompanied them." Then they returned those

tê'lXam. Itgā'2ya aLā'maLnapa, ayā'maLna ya'Xi iLā'lXam. A'qa
people. They went toward the water from it, toward the water from it that his town. Then

iqiaqa'luketx. Iō'ptcga. A'qa q;oā'p ē'k^utElīL, iō'ptcgam tE'LaqLpa.
he was carried ashore. He went up. Then near morning star, he came up the town to.

IgE'k·îm: "Lmē'mElō'etîke iLginukomā'tōm. IqEnō'lXam itcī'maq
He said: "Ghosts I accompanied them. I was told I shot

iqE'nElux k;a nāct qā'xpa itcī'tcqam." A'qa igîxk^uLē'lalEmtck
I was and not anywhere my sickness." Then he told

ya'Xi igoaLē'lX. Tuwā'X igō'xax ta'Xi tqu'Lē; igē'tcuktîX.
that person. Light became that house; day came.

A'qa igixē'maxit iō'maqt. Iā'kcXapa Lqā'wulqt LĀx iLE'xôx.
Then he fell down he was dead. His mouth at blood come out did.

Iā'psteqpa LĀx igē'xôx tā'nki LEllx L;a Lgungu'ntē. P;ā'la iā'cîkc,
His anus at come out did something black just like salal berries. Well his friend,

nāct iō'maqt qē'wa nîct igixE'ltōm. Nîct iugomā'tōm ta-îtci
not he died because not he went in their company. Not he accompanied them those

tmēmElō'etîke.
ghosts.

THE TKULXIYOGOĀ'IKC (TOLD 1894).

There was a chief at Nq¡ulā'was. His name was Pō'XpuX. When a woman had a male child, he threw it into the water. When she had a female child, he allowed it to grow. The chief of the people of Nq¡ulā'was was bad. When one of his wives made a slight mistake, he hit her and killed her. Now a woman gave birth to a boy. Then the chief said: "What is it that my wife gave birth to?" He was told that it was a girl. "Well, let her grow up!" When the child became large, his mother was killed. He used to wear a coat, but behold! he was a male. Now his mother's mother took care of him. Then the two moved a long distance away. Now the boy whose mother had been killed grew up. He bathed in all the lakes. His grandmother sent him to bathe. One night she sent him again to bathe. A lake was

---

TKULXIYOGOĀ'ÎKC LTĀ'XĒXIK¡ALX

THE TKULXIYOGOĀ'IKC THEIR TALE

ĒXā't iLā'Xak¡Emana giLā'q¡ulawas. Pō'XpuX iā'xaleu.
One their chief the people of Nq¡ulā'was. Pō'XpuX his name.

Manē'x LE'kala Liā'xan qatcLalē'maLxax, manē'x Lqagē'lak a'qa
When a male his child he threw it into the water, when a female then

qatcLō'mtamitx. Iā'mEla ya'Xi ikak¡Emā'na, iLā'Xak¡Emana
he raised her. Bad that chief, their chief

giLā'q¡ulawas. Manē'x Liā'kikal, ā'nqa qatcLuwā'qoax; nōL¡
the people of Nq¡ulā'was. When his wife, already he killed her; a little

pō'Xuic niLgElō'xoax, ā'nqa qatcLuwā'qoax. Ā'2qa igakXô'tōm
mistake she made, already he killed her. Then she gave birth

wu'Xi aeXā't aqagē'lak, LE'kala ikLōxô'tōm. A'qa igē'k·îm
that one woman, a male she gave birth to it. Then he said

ya'Xi ikak¡Emā'na: "Tā'nki igioxô'tōm agE'kikal?" Aqiō'lXam:
that chief: "What she gave birth to it my wife?" He was told

"Aqagē'lak." Q¡oā'L aqLō'mtamita. A'qa iLā'qa-iL La'Xi
"A female." All right they raised her. Then large that

Lk¡ā'skas. A'qa iqō'waq wu'Xi wā'yaq ya'Xi ik¡ā'skas.
child. Then she was killed that his mother that boy.

Goā'nEsum ayā'q¡ēLxap, tatc¡a ē'kala. Ā'qa igiō'mtamit. ayā'ckîX.
Always his coat, behold! a male. Then she raised him his grandmother.

A'qa îcgE'Layu, kElā'îX îctō'ya. A'qa wi iqō'waq wā'yaq ya'Xi
Then they two moved, far they two went. Then also she was killed his mother that

ik¡ā'skas. Ā2qa iā'qa-iL igixE'lôx ya'Xi ik¡ā'skas. A'qa
boy. Then large became that boy. Then

igîXqoā'tōLtck, ka'nauwē Lkak¡uLē'tXEmax igîxqoā'tōLtck.
he bathed, all lakes he bathed.

Igiotō'koalalEmtck ayā'ckîX. Agōn ā'pōl igiotō'koatck igîxqoā'tam.
She sent him his grandmother. One night she sent him he went to bathe.

near their house. There the boy used to swim. Now he felt something slippery like a young fish. He felt for it again and tried to catch it. He put his arms together, but it was slippery, and escaped. That thing was very slippery. He often tried to catch it, but it slipped away. Then he went ashore. He pulled out some grass and put it on his chest. Then he caught it again in the water and held it tight. He carried it ashore. He thought it was a young fish. He carried it and went home. He intended to show it to his grandmother. Near the house it fell down. He searched for it, but he could not find it. Then he thought: "I will fetch some pitch wood." Then he entered his grandmother's house and said to her: "Grandmother, have you any pitch wood?" She replied: "There is pitch wood near the door." "I caught a young fish in the lake, and it fell down." She said to him: "Oh, maybe you don't speak the truth. That lake is dry in summer. Where should that fish go? There is no creek into which

---

Q¦oā'pîX ikak¦ō'LitX ta'Xi tE'ctaqL. Kopā' iuk¦uē'XalalEmtck
Near a lake that their house. There he swam

ya'Xi ik¦ā'skas. A'qa tā'nki igē'XgEla luXlu'X, L¦a
that boy. Then something he felt slippery, behold

Lk¦uyā'sXtē. A'qa itciō'naxL kōpā'. Wī't'ax igē'XgEla.
a young fish. Then he searched for it there. Again he felt.

Kē'nuwa itcē'gEIga. Igēxeltā'mit. LuXlu'X igē'xoya. Asa-i
Try he took it. He closed his arms to take it. Slippery it went out of his hands. Very

luXlu'X ya'Xi tā'nki. Ē'xauwitîX itcē'gEIga kē'nuwa.
slippery that something. Often he took it try.

Nîxō'îx. A'qa iō'ptcga LXE'leu. LE'XLEX itcī'tux tE'pcō. A'qa
It went always. Then he went inland inland. Pull out he did it grass. Then

itiXE'qoaLk ta'Xi tE'pcō ayā'qatcpa. A'qa itcē'gElga wī't'ax
he put it on himself that grass his chest at. Then he took it again

Ltcu'qoapa. Ā'qa q¦uL itcē'gElga. Itcī'yukᴵ LXE'leu.
the water to. Then fast he held it. He carried it inland.

IgixLō'Xoa-it Lk¦uyā'sX. Itcī'Lukᴵ. igē'Xk¦oa atcLaxEnēmā'ya
He thought a young fish. He carried it, he went home he was going to show it

ayā'ckîX. Q¦oā'p tE'ctaqLpa a'qa igē'xEluktcō. Kē'nuwa
his grandmother Near their house at then it fell down. Try

itciō'naxL. Nācqē itciō'cgam. IgixLō'Xoa-ît: "AnLEguā'lEmama
he searched for it. Not at all he found it. He thought: "I shall go and fetch

Lq¦axō'ckan." Iōpqam tE'ctaqLpa ayā'ckîX. Itcō'lXam: "Ā'ckîX
pitch wood." He came in their house in his grandmother. He said to her: "Grandmother,

tcu'Xoa Lq¦axō'ckan." Igiō'lXam: "Kōpā' Lxē'mat Lq¦axō'ckan
well pitch wood." She said to him: "There lies pitch wood

k¦awucī'qē." "Lk¦uyā'sX inE'LgElga gi ikak¦ō'LîtXpa k¦a
near the door." "A young fish I took it this lake in and

iLE'nxaluktcō." Igiō'lXam: "LXuan imē'L¦mēnXut. Tcā'koa-îX
it fell down from me." She said to him: "Perhaps you lie. Summer

cpāq nixō'xoax ya'Xi ikak¦ō'LîtX k¦a qā'mta aLtē'mama
dry becomes that lake and where goes

LaXi Lk¦uyā'sX. K¦ā'ya nEct ē'qxaL qā'mta Ltē'mama La'Xi
that young fish. Nothing not creek where goes that

that young fish might go." He said to her: "Well, come help me; we will look for it." Then he lighted the pitch wood. They arrived at the place where the fish had fallen down. Oh, there were long dentalia lying there. Two of them were *that* long. They lay there about *that* high. Then they went down to the lake and all the way the boy had come there were long dentalia on the ground. Then they took a rush basket and a spruce-root basket, and carried all the long dentalia home. Then they made holes below the bed and put the dentalia into them, the long ones and the short ones. In the evening they were all stored away. After two nights the old woman, the boy's grandmother, thought: "I will go and ask for sinew from those people. We will string up the long dentalia." She arose in the morning and went. She entered a house and said: "I come to ask for a present. Please give me some sinew. My grandson's woodchuck blanket is torn." They gave her some sinew, and the old

---

Lk¡uyā'sX." Itcō'lXam: "Nĭ'Xua, amE'tē, amEngElgē'cgam,
young fish." He said to her: "Well, come, help me,

atxLōnā'xLa." A'qa wāx iLgĭ'cōx La'Xi Lq¡axō'ckan. Ictō'yam
we search for it." Then light they did it that pitch wood. They arrived

ya'Xi iLē'xaluktcōpa. Ō, aqa wāx igē'xax iqawik¡ē'Lē, a'qa
that where it fell down at. Oh, then poured out were long dentalia, then

mâkct ā'wimax itcā'Lqtax wu'Xi aqawik¡ē'Lē. A'qa wāx igē'xôx
two thus long those long dentalia. Then poured out they were

LXuan gipE't ā'yaLqt ya'Xi iqawik¡ē'Lē. A'qa ictō'Lxa ē'wa
perhaps thus their thickness those long dentalia. Then they went down there

ikak¡ō'LĭtX. KopE't ya'Xi igē'tē ya'Xi ik¡ā'skas, kopE't wā'xwax
the lake. Thus that he came that boy, thus poured out

igē'x ya'Xi iqawik¡ē'Lē. A'qa icgē'gElga iqā'gēltk k¡a îcwāpcîq.
were those long dentalia. Then they took it a basket made of rushes and grass and a basket made of spruce roots and grass.

A'qa icgī'yukT tqu'Lepa; tE'ctaqLpa ka'nauwē iqawik¡ē'Lē. A'qa
Then they carried them the house to; their house to all the long dentalia. Then

Lk¡oayā'tgEmax icgE'Lux gē'gualîX ilXE'mē. A'qa kōpā'
caches they made them below the bed. Then there

wā'xwax icgī'yux iqawik¡ē'Lē k¡maya ikupku'p. Xā'pîX a'qa
pour out they did them the long dentalia and also the short dentalia. In the evening then

ka'nauwē icgī'yutk. Môket îctō'qoya, a'qa igaxLō'Xoa-ît wu'Xi
all they had put them by. Two their sleeps, then she thought that

aq¡eyō'qt ayā'ckîX ya'Xi ik¡ā'skas: "Qō'i nō'ya aqē'Lata
old woman his grandmother that boy: "Must I go sinew

igEnxElEmā'q¡ēmLam ta-îtci tê'lXampa. Antgixk¡ē'Lia iqawik¡ē'Lē."
I ask for a present those people at. I will string them up the long dentalia."

Kawī'X a'qa igaxE'latck. Igō'ya. Igō'pqam tqu'Lepa: "Aqē'Lata
Early then she arose. She went. She came in the house in: "Sinew

ganxētEmā'q¡ēmLam. Sī'aq¡ula a'qa LE'xLEx sxē'guXt ē'tctgEn."
I come to ask for a present. His woodchuck blanket then torn it is my grandson."

Iqalamā'q¡ēmL wu'Xi aqē'Lata. Igā'Xk¡oa wu'Xi aq¡eyō'qt.
She was given a present that sinew. She went home that old woman.

woman went home. Then she spun the sinew and strung up the long dentalia. Now she had used up all the sinew. The next day she went again, and said to her grandson: "I will go to another house and ask for sinew." The old woman went to another house and said again: "I come to ask for a present. Please give me some sinew. My grandson's woodchuck blanket is torn." Then they gave her much sinew. The old woman went home. When she came home, she spun all day and all night. After she had finished all that sinew, she said again to her grandson: "To-morrow I will go again; I will ask for some sinew at another house." Early in the morning she went again and came to another house. She said: "I come to ask for a present. Please give me some sinew." She received much sinew. Then she went home again. Then one woman said: "How quickly she used all the sinew which she received at that one house. I saw she received much at one house." Thus spoke one woman. The old woman arrived

---

A'qa igājktkEm, igājktkEm, igājktkEm wu'Xi aqē'Lata. A'qa
Then she spun, she spun, she spun that sinew. Then

igexE'k;eLē ya'Xi iqawik;ē'Lē; kanauwē'2 igaxE'LXōm wu'Xi
she strung them up those long dentalia; all it was finished that

aqē'Lata. A'qa wi igō'n ē'goa, aqa wi igō'ya. Igiō'lXam
sinew. Then again one more day, then again she went. She said to him

ē'tcatgEn: "Tgō'nax tqu'Lepa anō'ya, anxElgē'maq;EmLama."
her grandson: "Another house at I go, I shall ask for a present."

Igō'ya wu'Xi aq;eyō'qt tgō'nax tēXt tqu'Lepa. Wī't;ax igā'k·îm:
She went that old woman another one house to. Again she said:

"Aqē'Lata ganxētEmā'q;EmLam. Ē'tcîtgEn sī'aq;ula a'qa LE'XLEX
"Sinew I come to ask for a present. My grandson his woodchuck blanket then torn

exē'guXt." A'qa wi Lgā'pEla iqalEmā'q;emL wu'Xi aq;eyō'qt
it is." Then again much she was given as a present that old woman

wu'Xi aqē'Lata. A'qa wi igā'Xk;oa wu'Xi aq;eyō'qt.
that sinew. Then again she went home that old woman.

IgaXk;oā'mam tE'ctaqLpa. A'qa wi igā'ktkEm, igā'ktkEm,
She came home their house to. Then again she spun, she spun,

igā'ktkEm ka'nauwē Lkā'etax, ka'nauwē Lpō'lEmax. Kanauwā'2
she spun all days, all nights. All

igaxE'LXōm wu'Xi aqē'Lata. A'qa wi igiō'lXam ē'tcatgEn:
it was finished that sinew. Then again she said to him her grandson:

"Ō'la, a'qa wī't'ax anō'ya. AnxElgēmaq;EmLā'ma aqē'Lata
"To-morrow, then again I will go. I will ask for a present sinew

tgō'nax tqu'Lepa." Kawī'X aqa wi igō'ya. Igō'pqam tgō'nax
another house at." Early then again she went. She came in another

tqu'Lē. Igā'k·ēm: "Aqē'Lata Inxētgē'maq;EmLam." IqalEmā'q;ēmL
house. She said: "Sinew, I come to ask for a present." She was given a present

ā'xauwē wu'Xi aqē'Lata. Aqa wi Igā'Xk;oa. ILE'k·îm
much that sinew Then again she went home. She said

LēXā't Lqagē'lak: "A'yaq Lqa Igō'LXum, tēXt tqu'Le
one woman: "Quick maybe she finished it, one house

iqalEmā'q;ēmL aqē'Lata. Ā'xoē iqalEmā'q;ēmL tēXt tqu'Lepa
she was given a present sinew. Much she was given as a present one house in

nō'qumē," iLE'k·îm LēXā't Lqagē'lak. IgaXk;oā'mam wu'Xi
I saw her," she said one woman She came home that

at home and spun again. She spun all day and all night. She had strung up only part of their long dentalia, and the sinew was at an end. Then she said to her grandson: "To-morrow I will go to another house." She arose early and went to another house. She said: "I come to ask for a present. Please give me some sinew. My grandson's woodchuck blanket is torn." Then she received much sinew as a present and went home again. When she came home, she spun all day and all night and strung up the long dentalia. After a little while she had used all the sinew. Then again she said to her grandson: "To-morrow I will go to another house." Early in the morning the old woman arose and went to one house. She entered, and one woman said: "Ha! that old woman is going to ask again for a present of sinew. What is she doing with it? Every day she carries sinew home." Again they gave her sinew, but she was pre-

---

aq¦eyō'qt tᴇ'ctaqʟpa. A'qa wi igā'ktkᴇm: igā'ktkᴇm ka'nauwē
old woman their house to. Then again she spun: she spun all

ʟkā'etax, ka'nauwē ʟpō'lᴇmax. Iā'ema qā'wa a'qa wi
days, all nights. Only part then again

igaxᴇ'ʟXōm wu'Xi aqē'ʟata ya'Xi ictā'qawik¦ēʟē. Igiō'lXam
she finished that sinew that their dentalia. She said to him

ē'tcatgᴇn: "Ō'la wī't'ax anō'ya tgō'nax tqu'ʟepa." Kawī'X
her grandson: "To-morrow again I shall go another house to." Early

igaxᴇ'latck, a'qa wī't'ax igō'ya tgō'nax tqu'ʟepa. Igā'k·îm:
she arose, then again she went another house to. She said:

"Aqē'ʟata înxitgē'maq¦ᴇmʟam. Sī'aq¦ula a'qa ʟᴇ'XʟEX cxē'guxt
"Sinew I come to ask for a present. His wood-chuck blanket then torn it is

ē'tctgᴇn." Iqalᴇmā'q¦ēmʟ ʟgā'pᴇla wu'Xi aqē'ʟata wu'Xi aq¦eyō'qt.
my grandson." She was given as a present much that sinew that old woman.

A'qa wī't'ax igā'Xk¦oa. IgaXk¦oā'mam tᴇ'ctaqʟpa. A'qa wī't'ax
Then again she went home. She came home their house to. Then again

igā'ktkᴇm. Ka'nauwē ʟkā'etax igā'ktkᴇm, ka'nauwē ʟpō'lᴇmax
she spun. All day she spun, all nights

igā'ktkᴇm. A'qa wi igixᴇ'k¦ēʟē ictā'Xawik¦ēʟē. Nō'ʟ¦îX a'qa
she spun. Then again she strung them up their dentalia. A little then

wi igaXᴇ'ʟXōm wu'Xi aqē'ʟata. A'qa wi igiō'lXam ē'tcatgᴇn:
again it was finished that sinew. Then again she said to him her grandson:

"Ō'la a'qa wi tgō'nax tqu'ʟepa anō'ya." Kawī'X igaxᴇ'latck
"To-morrow then again another house to I shall go." Early she arose

wu'Xi aq¦eyō'qt. A'qa wi igō'ya tēXt tqu'ʟepa. Igō'pqam
that old woman. Then again she went one house to. She came in

kōpa' tēXt tqu'ʟepa. Iʟᴇ'k·îm ʟēXā't ʟqagē'lak: "Q¦a,
there one house to. She said one woman: "Ha,

aqē'ʟata igaxitᴇmā'q¦ēmʟam wu'Xi aq¦eyō'qt. Tā'nki
sinew she asks for a present that old woman. What

igiagē'lXalᴇm wu'Xi aqē'ʟata? Ka'nauwē ʟkā'etax igoguē't
does she do with it that sinew? All days she always carried it

tᴇ'ctaqʟpa." Wi iqalᴇmā'q¦ēmʟ aqē'ʟata. A'qa nîct ʟgā'pᴇla
their house to." Again she was given as a present sinew. Then not much

sented with a little only. The old woman went home and spun. Again she used all the sinew. There was one hole for the short dentalia and one for the long dentalia. She said to her grandson: "To-morrow I shall go to another house and ask for some sinew." She arose early in the morning and went again to one house. The people saw her coming. "There that old woman is coming again! Indeed, she comes to ask for a present of sinew. What is she doing with them? Maybe she is stringing up long dentalia." The old woman came to the house and entered. She said: "I come to ask for a present. Please give me some sinew." Now they were tired of that old woman, but finally one woman arose and gave her some sinew as a present. She said: "I have no more; if I had much I should give you more." She arose to go out. When she was near the door one woman said: "She has just asked for a present of sinew. What may she be doing with them? Maybe she is stringing up long den-

---

iqalEmā'q¡ēmL nō'L¡ka. A'qa wi igā'Xk¡oa wu'Xi aq¡eyō'qt.
she was given as a present | a little only. | Then | again | she went home | that | old woman.

A'qa wi igā'ktkEm, igā'ktkEm, igā'ktkEm. Igō'LXum wu'Xi
Then | again | she spun, | she spun, | she spun. | She finished it | that

aqē'Lata. Ka'nauwē wī't'ax igaxE'LXōm. KElā'îX iā'k¡oaya
sinew. | All | again | she finished it. | Far | their hole

ya'Xi giā'sk¡Etxax ikupku'p, kElā'îX iā'k¡oaya iqawik¡ē'Lē
that | short ones | short dentalia, | far | their hole | long dentalia

iā'Lqtax. Igiō'lXam ē'tcatgEn: "Ō'la a'qa wi anō'ya ta'Xi
their length. | She said to him | her grandson: | "To-morrow | then | again | I shall go | that

tēXt tqu'Lepa. Aqē'Lata anxElgē'maq¡EmLam." Kawī'X
one | house to. | Sinew | I go to ask for a present." | Early

igaxE'latck. Igō'ya wī't'ax ta'Xi tēXt tqu'Lepa. Iqā'qElkEl
she arose. | She went | again | that | one | house to. | She was seen

wī't'ax atē't. "Aqā' wi atē't wu'Xi aq¡eyō'qt," iqō'lXam.
again | she came. | "Now | again | she comes | that | old woman," | she was told.

"Q¡a, aqā'Lata axitEmā'q¡ēmLamt. Tān Lqa igiagē'lXalEm gi
"Ha! | sinew | she comes to ask for a present. | What | maybe | she does with it | this

aqē'Lata? LXuan iqawik¡ē'Lē igîxk¡ē'Lēna." Igatā'mam wu'Xi
sinew? | Perhaps | long dentalia | she strings them." | She arrived | that

aq¡eyō'qt ta'Xi tqu'Lepa. Igā'ckupq. Igā'k·îm wu'Xi aq¡eyō'qt:
old woman | that | house to. | She entered. | She said | that | old woman:

"Aqā'Lata nExEtgē'maq¡ēmLam." Nā2ct, iqiagE'nXakuîX wu'Xi
"Sinew | I come to ask for a present." | Not, | the people were tired of her | that

aq¡eyō'qt. A'qa iLō'tXuit LeXā't Lqagē'lak. ILgalEmā'q¡ēmL
old woman. | Then | she stood up | one | woman. | She gave her a present

nō'L¡ka wu'Xi aqē'Lata. ILgō'lXam: "A'qa naqā'yimax
a little only | that | sinew. | She said to her: | "Then | this only

agE'xēLata. Qēc Lgā'pEla pō Lgā'pEla iamElEmā'q¡ēmL."
my sinew. | If | much | then | much | I should give you a present."

Igō'tXuît, igō'pa. Q¡oā'p icî'qē igō'yam. A'qa iLE'k·îm LēXā't
She stood up, | she went out. | Near | the door | she arrived. | Then | she said | one

Lqagē'lak: "Koalē'wi Lqa aqē'Lata axElEmā'q¡ēmEniL. Tān
woman: | "Just | maybe | sinew | she received as a present. | What

Lqa igiagē'lXalEm gi aqē'Lata? LXuan igiank¡ē'Lena
maybe | she does with it | this | sinew? | Perhaps | she strings them

talia which belong to her and to her grandson. She will come again to-morrow and ask for more sinew. Maybe she has not yet strung up all her long dentalia." The old woman went out. She felt offended. She turned back, opened the door, and said: "Do you scoff me? I do string up my grandson's long dentalia, and still you scoff me? We are stringing them up every day." She went home and arrived at their house. She said to her grandson: "Quick, invite the people of our town." Her grandson went and said to the people: "I come to invite you. My grandmother sent me to call you." Then all the people went. Now they took out of one hole the short dentalia and distributed them among the people. They gave them to part of the people, and then the one hole was empty. Then they took them out of another hole and distributed them. Then they had given to all the people.

Now the boy was grown up. Indeed, he had seen spirits. By

---

iqawik!ē'ʟē, ictā'Xawik!ēʟē ʟXuan ē'tcatgᴇn. Â'2la wī't'ax
long dentalia, their long dentalia perhaps her grandson. To-morrow again

alatē'mama. Alaxᴇlgē'maq!ēmʟa aqē'ʟata. ʟXuan nîct
she will come. She will ask for a present sinew. Perhaps not

nixʟXō'mx gi ictā'Xawik!ēʟē icgianʟᴇ'nēʟ aqē'ʟata." Igō'pa
she finished them these their long dentalia they string them sinew." She went out

wu'Xi aq!eyō'qt, icî'qēpa ʟā'xanîX a'qa ē'tcamxtc mᴇlā'
that old woman, the door at outside then her heart annoyed

igē'xôx. IgaXᴇ'takoa wu'Xi aq!eyō'qt. Igixᴇ'laqʟgîX ya'Xi
became. She returned that old woman. She opened the door that

iqabō'tē. "K!a ā'qtcēXul tci?" igā'k·îm. "Ntgîxk!ā'ʟēna
door flap. "And I am ridiculed [int. part.]?" she said. "We string them

ē'tcᴇtgᴇn iqawik!ē'ʟē ka ē'qtcēXul tci? Ka'nauwē ʟkā'etax
my grandson long dentalia and I am ridiculed [int. part.]? All day

ntgîxk!ē'ʟena iqawik!ē'ʟē." A'qa igā'Xk!oa wu'Xi aq!eyō'qt.
we string them long dentalia." Then she went home that old woman.

Igō'yam tᴇ'ctaqʟpa. Igiō'lXam ē'tcatgᴇn: "Ai'aq tgā'lᴇmam
She arrived their house at. She said to him her grandson: "Quick fetch them

ta-îtci tê'lXam gilxā'lXam." Iō'ya ya'Xi ē'tcatgᴇn. Itctō'lXam:
those people the people of our town." He went that her grandson. He said to them:

"Â, iamctgā'lᴇmam. Agᴇ'cgîX igᴇntō'koatck." Itgī'ya ta-îtci
"Ah, I came to fetch you. My grandmother she sent me." They went those

tê'lXam ka'nauwē. ʟāq° icgī'yux ēXt iā'k!oaya ikupku'p.
people all. Take out they did them one their hole short dentalia.

Icgiawē'mak tê'lXam ya'Xi ikupku'p. Aqa'watîkc ta-îtci
They distributed them people those short dentalia. Part of those

tê'lXam a'qa igixᴇ'ʟXōm ya'Xi ēXt ik!oā'ya. A'qa wi·
people then it was at an end that one hole. Then again

igō'n ēXt ik!oā'ya. Icgiawē'mak. Kanauwā'4 ioxoā'k!aq
another one hole. They distributed them. All she gave to all of them

tê'lXam.
the people.

A'qa iā'qa-îʟ igixᴇ'lôx ya'Xi ik!ā'skas. A'qa ā'qanuwē
Then large became that boy. Then indeed

inheritance he became a warrior. He saw the Thunderbird, who became his supernatural helper. The Thunderbird gave him one whale for food. It was given to that Indian. At night the Thunderbird thundered. Then that person was startled. His name was Waq¡awiyā's, the son of Pō'XpuX. That person said: "The Thunderbird has thundered, and he has greatly frightened me. Maybe my supernatural helper will send me something. He told me long ago that he was going to give me a whale when I wanted to eat one." Early the next morning it was calm. When the sun arose, a person looked out on the prairie. There was something lying right in the middle of the prairie. It was shining. The person entered the house and said: "Something is lying on the prairie." The people went out to see it, and said: "Behold! it is a monster." They looked at it for a long time. It was just as large as a house. There was a man from the coast among them, who was living in his wife's village for a time.

---

tiō'ʟᴇma itcō'quikᴇl. It¡ō'xoyal igē'xôx ayā'xt¡ax. Itcā'qᴇlkᴇl
supernatural helpers | he had seen them. | A warrior | became | his inheritance. | He saw him

ikᴇnuwakcō'max iā'iuʟᴇmax. ĒXt ē'koalē itcē'lqo-îm ya'Xi
the thunderbird | his supernatural helper. | One | whale | he gave him to eat | that

ikᴇnuwakcō'max. Iqē'lqo-îm ya'Xi itē'tanue. Igē'xᴇltcu Xā'pîX
thunderbird. | He was given to eat | that | Indian. | He talked | in the evening

ya'Xi ikᴇnuwakcō'ma. A'qa iō'k¡oatck ya'Xi igoaʟē'lX.
that | thunderbird. | Then | he was surprised | that | person.

Waq¡awiyā's iā'xaleu ya'Xi igoaʟē'lX, Pō'XpuX iā'Xan. Igē'k·îm
Waq¡awiyā's | his name | that | person, | Pō'XpuX | his son. | He said

ya'Xi igoaʟē'lX: "Ya'Xi igē'Xaltcu ikᴇnuwakcō'max ʟawā'ʟqa
that | person: | "That one | he talked | the thunderbird | greatly

aqa iqᴇnugoā'mitatck. ʟXuan atcnîlgē'tatkca gi itcī'yuʟmax tau
then | I was frightened. | Perhaps | he will send it to me | this | my supernatural helper | what

ā'nqa k¡oaʟqē' itcinō'lXam. Manî'x anēnᴇlgwā'tckoa ē'koalē a'qa
long ago | thus | he said to me. | When | I wish to eat it | a whale | then

atcînᴇltā'tkca." Kawī'X igē'tcuktîX, a'qa 'lō igē'xaxîX. Lāx igā'xax
he will send it to me." | Early | day came, | then calm | it was. | Come out | did

wu'Xi aqaʟā'x. Iʟᴇ'kîket ʟēXā't ʟgoaʟē'lX ēwā' ta'Xi tᴇmqā'emax.
that | sun. | He looked | one | person | there | that | prairie.

A'qa tā'nki ixē'mat qēq¡aya'q tᴇmqā'emaxpa, ā'yawaxwax. Iʟō'pqa
Then | something | lay there | middle | prairie on, | its glare. | He entered

ʟa'Xi ʟgoaʟē'lX tᴇ'ʟaqʟpa. Iʟᴇ'k·îm: "Tān ya'Xi ixē'mat
that | person | their house in. | He said: | "What | that | is lying there

qēq¡aya'q tᴇmqā'emaxpa?" A'qa itgᴇ'pa ta-îtci tê'lXam,
middle | prairie on?" | Then | they went out | those | people,

itgiō'ketam. Igugoā'kîm: "Ō, ʟqōct iqcxē'ʟau." A'qa
they went to see. | They said: | "Oh, | behold | a monster." | Then

itgiukumā'nanᴇmtck ta-îtci tê'lXam. ʟa tqu'ʟē iā'qa-iʟ ya'Xi tā'nki.
they went to see | those | people. | Like | a house | large | that | something.

Tēka a'qa ʟgoaʟē'lX ʟXᴇldā't kuapa'; iʟᴇ'k·îm: "Ek¡oalē' taya'X".
Here | then | a person | a visitor to his wife's village | there; | he said: | "A whale | that."

He knew it and said: "It is a whale." Then the people cut it, but part of them were afraid. Then that chief made a potlatch. He made a long ditch. He put planks on top of the ditch and covered them with dirt. He made a door at the entrance of the ditch. It was a long hole. There the people went in to dance. They disappeared in the hole underground. They came out again at the door of the ditch. The people from all around went there. Then he became a chief, and Pō'XpuX became an insignificant man. His town was far away. He was the ancestor of the people of Nq!olā'was.[1] His name was Waq!awiyā's.

ILgiugu'laqL. A'qa itgī'uxc ta-îtci tê'lXam, aqā'watîkc a'qa k!wac
He knew it. Then they cut it those people, part of them then afraid

itxē'xôx. A'qa ik!uanō'm itcī'yux ya'Xi ikak!Emā'na. LEX iqī'yux
they were. Then a potlatch he made it that chief. Dig it was done

ya'Xi ēlX. KElā'îX ya'Xi LEX iqī'yux. A'qa aqē'nXak iqā'ikXatk
that ground. Far that dig it was done. Then planks they were put over it

ya'Xi naL!E'xpa ya'Xi ēlX. A'qa wi iqLagE'tkîq wuXi aqē'nxak.
that hole at that ground. Then again they were covered with dirt those planks.

Icî'qēpa Lxoā'p ya'Xi ē'lXpa igē'xôx, k!a yaXi' kElā'îX Lxoa'p
The door at a hole that ground at was, and there far hole

igē'xôx. Ma'nîx a'qa atgiuXtā'mx ta-îtci tê'lXam, kōpā' ya'Xi
was. When then they went to dance those people, there that

naLxoa'p ēlX a'qa k!Em nōxoā'xax. Gipā' icî'qē, q!oā'p icî'qē a'qa
hole ground then nothing they became. Here the door, near the door then

Lāx noxoā'xax ta-îtci tê'lXam. Ka'nauwē qā'xpa tê'lXam igō'xoax
come out they did those people. Every where people came to be

kōpā'. A'qa yā'xka igē'xôx ikak!Emā'na. A'qa Pō'XpuX a'qa
there. Then he became a chief. Then Pō'XpuX then

tE'ltEl igē'xôx. KElā'îX iā'lXam yā'Xka itā'q!eōqt itā'q!ulawas
insignificant he became. Far his town he their ancestor the people of Nq!ulā'was

iā'xEleu Waq!awiyā's.
his name Waq!awiyā's.

---

[1] This is a branch of the Athapascan tribe which formerly inhabited the headwaters of Willapah river.

Pē'lpel (told 1894).

There was a strong man at North river. His name was Pē'LpeL. He made the Willapah poor. When they went to catch sturgeon in their gill nets, and it was near flood tide, then he told his people to go to those people who were catching sturgeon. He took what they had caught. He took also the gill nets of part of them. He did this all the time, and they did not take revenge upon the strong man. When he caught a sturgeon, he just squeezed it and it broke to pieces. When he was seen coming, all the people ran away and went home. When one of them was slow, he overtook him and took away what he had caught. Now a boy was growing up on the South fork of the Willapah among the Lā'qxaLEma. They sent him up the mountains to bathe in ponds. He twisted young hemlock trees and vine maples and young spruce trees. Then he became a youth. Now the old

---

1	Ē̦Xā't	tiā'LXēwulX	ayā'qctxōkL.	Pē'LpeL	iā'xaleu.
	One	strong man	he was a Naqctxō'kL. (of North river)	Pē'LpeL	his name.

2	ItcuXoagoā'mit	Gitā'Xuilapax.	Manē'x	noXuik!anXā'tEmamx
	He made them poor	the Willapah.	When	they went to catch sturgeon in gill nets

3	q!oā'p	qaLuwē'tckoax,	a'qa	qatctutō'goatckoax	giLā'lXam
	nearly	it was flood tide,	then	he sent them	his people

4	qayugoā'qoamx	ta-îtci	gō'Xuik!anXate.	Qatctoxoasgā'mx
	he reached them	those	who fished sturgeon in gill nets.	He took from them

5	itā'k!etēnax.	Aqā'watîkc	aqa	tgā'k!anXatē	qatctōxoacgā'mx.
	what they had caught.	Part of them	then	their gill nets	he took them from them.

6	Ka'nauwē	Lqētā'kemax	k!oaLqē'.	Nā2ct	aqē'nk!ēmEnakoax
	All	years	thus.	Not	it was taken revenge on him

7	tiā'LXēwulX.	Manē'x	qatcigElgā'x	enā'qōn,	kopā'	Lk!up
	he was a strong man.	When	he took it	a sturgeon,	there	squeezed

8	nixō'xoax,	Lq!up	qacxElō'xoax.	Manē'x	aqiqElgE lx	itē't,
	it was,	cut	it was.	When	he was seen	he came,

9	ka'nauwē	qatguwā'xitx,	nuxoak!oā'x.	Manē'x	Lawā'	qaLō'îx
	all	they ran away,	they went home.	When	slowly	he went

10	LēXā't,	qatcLktā'qoamx	qatciLxsgā'mx	iLā'k!ētenax.	Ā'2qa
	one,	he reached him	he took it from him	what he had caught.	Then

11	iLō'mit	LēXā't	Lk!ā'skas	Lā'qxaLEma.	A'qa	iqLōtō'koalalEmtck
	he grew up	one	boy	a Lā'qxaLEma (of South fork of Willapah).	Then	he was always sent

12	iqoā'tōL	Lpakā'lEmaxpa.	XāX	iLgE'tuX	tqā'-etEma,	XāX
	to wash	mountains on.	Twist	he did them	hemlock trees,	twist

13	iLgī'yuX	iq!ē'ncîq,	XāX	iLgE'tux	tEmā'ktXEmax.	Ā'2qa
	he did them	vine maples,	twist	he did them	young spruce trees.	Then

14	Lq!u'lîpX	iLE'xôx	La'Xi	qLā'qxaLEmax.	Aq!eyō'qt	wu'Xi
	a youth	he became	that	Lā'qxaLEma.	An old woman	that

woman, the mother of Pē'LpeL, said to her son: "You must go to the Lā'qxaLEma and take their gill nets. I want to make a coat." He went right away and took their nets. He took them away from the Lā'qxaLEma and from the Willapah. His mother made coats. As soon as her coat began to get a little bad, she threw it away and her son went to take away more nets. Then Pē'LpeL heard that one youth of the Lā'qxaLEma was bathing in order to make himself strong. He said: "Oh, the poor Lā'qxaLEma. I must let them alone. They all run away when they see me." The next summer the old woman said again to her son: "Go and take the nets of the Lā'qxaLEma for me." He went, and when the people saw him, they all ran away. Now the youth said: "I will go to-morrow. Pē'LpeL is getting to be too hopeful because you are afraid of him." Then that day the people went down the river to catch sturgeon. At low water a canoe was seen. That youth had caught a large sturgeon. They had just

---

wā'yaq ya'Xi Pē'LpeL. AgiolXā'mx ya'Xi itcā'xan: "Qō'i
his mother that Pē'LpeL. She said to him that her son: "Must

qamō'ix Lā'qxaLEmapa qamtugoā'lEmamx tk¡anXa'tē. Aq¡ē'Lxap
you go Lā'qxaLEma to fetch them gill nets. A coat

anō'Xua." Ā'nqa qayō'îX qatctugoā'lEmamx tk¡anXā'tē.
I will make it." Already he went he fetched them gill nets.

QatctōXoacgā'mx Lā'qxaLEma k¡a GiLā'XuilapaX. Aq¡ē'Lxap
He took them from them the Lā'qxaLEma and Willapah. A coat

agō'xoax wā'yaq. NōL¡ itcā'mEla qayaxElō'xax agā'q¡ēLxap,
she made it his mother. A little its badness was on it her coat,

ā'nqa agaxē'max. A'qa wi agō'nax qatcugoā'lEmamx ya'Xi
already she threw it away. Then again another one he fetched it that

itcā'xan ak¡anXā'tē. Ā'qa igixEltcE'maq LēXā't Lqoā'tōL
her son a net. Then he heard one he had bathed

Lā'qxaLEmax Lq¡u'lîpX. LxamgElxō'la. "Qō'i iā'c iqE'tôx
a Lā'qxaLEma youth. He had made himself strong against him. "Must let alone they are

qLā'qxaLEma, tgā'giutgoax, aqa ac itgEnqElkElā'ya tguwā'Xita
the Lā'qxaLEma, the poor ones, when they see me they run away

ka'nauwē." Ā'2qa wi itcākoa-îX igē'xoxîx. A'qa wi igiō'lXam
all." Then again summer it became. Then again she said to him

itcā'xan wu'Xi aq¡eyō'qt: "Qō'i qamō'îx qamanē'tam ak¡anXā'tē,
her son that old woman: "Must you go bring me a gill net,

Lā'qxaLEma aLā k¡anXatē." Kē'nuwa qayō'îX ac aqiqElkē'lX.
the Lā'qxaLEma their gill net." Try he went and he was seen.

Aqa tguwā'Xit kanauwē'. A'qa igē'kîm ya'Xi iq¡u'lîpX: "Ō'la
Then they ran away all. Then he said that youth: "To-morrow

a'qa nai'ka anō'ya. K¡wan qē'yuxt Pē'LpeL. K¡wac mcxē'xoxt."
then I I shall go. Hopeful he is made Pē'LpeL. Afraid you are."

Igē'tcuktîX, a'qa wi itgī'ya ta-îtci tē'lXam qā'eqamîX
Day came, then again they went those people down the river

ōXuik¡anXā'tēmam. Q¡ōl, a'qa iqē'qElkEl ikE'nim. ĒXt
they went to fish sturgeon in gill nets. Low water, then it was seen a canoe. One

iā'k¡ētēnax ya'Xi tiā'qxaLEmax ya'Xi iq¡u'lîpX; iā'qa-iL ya'Xi
what he had caught that Lā'qxaLEma that youth; large that

inā'qōn acō'max wu'Xi actā'k¡anXatē. Iqē'qElkEl ya'Xi ikE'nim
sturgeon just that their two selves' net. It was seen that canoe

caught it in their net. Now Pē'ʟpeʟ was seen coming in his canoe. "Oh, he comes to take our nets." And all the people ran away and went home. The companion of the youth said to him: "Quick, haul in your net. That monster is coming." "Be quiet," said he to his companion. The latter was afraid. He spoke to him twice: "Let us take up our nets and go home." But he said: "Be quiet." Now that canoe arrived. The youth was told: "Put your game into my canoe." He did not move. He was told so twice. Then Pē'ʟpeʟ got angry. "Indeed, I heard that he always bathed, preparing to fight me." Now the youth said to his companion: "Haul in our net." They hauled it in and put it into the canoe. The youth was told again: "Quick, put your game into my canoe." But he replied: "Do you think I will give you my fish?" Pē'ʟpeʟ took that sturgeon and put it into his canoe. Then the youth took it at its mouth. He took the sturgeon and the whole mouth was torn. The

---

itē't, Pē'ʟpeʟ ya'Xi itē't: "Ō, tk!anXā'tē qatctgā'lᴇmamt."
came, Pē'ʟpeʟ that he came. "Oh, nets he comes to fetch them."

Igō'Xoak!oa ta-îtci tê'lXam. Ka'nauwē iqîXuwā'Xit. Iʟgiō'lXam
They went home those people. All he was run away from. He said to him

ya'Xi iq!u'lîpX gictā'cgewal: "Ai'aq ʟā'q° axa amē'k!anXatē.
that youth being two companions. "Quick take out do your gill net.

Itē't ya'Xi iqcxē'ʟau." "Qān mxē'xôx," itcʟō'lXam gictā'cgēwal.
He is coming that monster." "Silent be," he said to him being two companions.

K!wac iʟᴇ'xôx gictā'cgewal. Mâ'kctîX kē'nuwa iʟgiō'lXam:
Afraid he was being two companions. Twice try, he said to him:

"ʟāq atxō'Xoa atxā'k!anXatē. AtXk!oā'ya." "Â2, qān mᴇ'xôx,"
"Take out we two will do it our gill net. We two will go home." "Ah, silent be,"

atcʟō'lXam. Igîcgā'tqoam ya'Xi ikᴇ'nim. Iqiō'lXam ya'Xi
he said to him. It reached them that canoe. He was told that

iq!u'lîpX: "Iakatxā'emax yaXi imē'k!ētenax." Nēct igē'xᴇla
youth: "Put it into the canoe that what you caught." Not he moved

ya'Xi iq!u'lîpX. Mâ'kctîX iqiō'lXam. Kalā'lkuilē igē'xôx
that youth. Twice he was told. Scold he did

Pē'ʟpeʟ: "Ō, ā'qanuwē ʟ! gi inxᴇltcî'mᴇlē ixᴇngᴇlqoā'tōʟ."
Pē'ʟpeʟ: "Oh, indeed behold! this one I heard he bathed against me."

Itciō'lXam ya'Xi gictā'cgewal ya'Xi iq!u'lîpX: "Ā'xk!a wu'Xi
He said to him that being two companions that youth: "Haul in that

atxā'k!anxatē." Icgā'xk!a wu'Xi actā'k!anXatē. Icgakxā'ema.
our two selves' net." They two hauled in that their two selves' net. They two put it into the canoe.

A'qa wi iqiō'lXam ya'Xi iq!u'lîpX: "Ai'aq îkxā'ema ya'Xi
Then again he was told that youth: "Quick put it into the canoe that

imē'k!etēnax." Itciō'lXam: "MXʟō'Xuan tci ayamᴇlō'ta ya'Xi
what you caught." He said to him: "Do you think [int. part.] I shall give you that

itcî'k!ētēnax?" Itcē'gᴇlga Pē'ʟpeʟ ya'Xi inā'qōn. Itciakxā'ema
what I caught?" He took it Pē'ʟpeʟ that sturgeon. He put it into his canoe

iʟā'xanimpa. Itcē'gᴇlga ya'Xi iq!u'lîpX, ia'k^{u}cXapa itcē'gᴇlga
his canoe in. He took it that youth, its mouth at he took it

youth said: "Let us go ashore." That youth went ashore. There were six people in Pē'LpeL's canoe. He took hold of the thwarts and right away the canoe broke. "Behold, indeed, you bathed, preparing against me." "Indeed, I bathed, preparing against you," said that youth. He took Pē'LpeL at his clavicles. He moved his hands and tore a hole in his chest. He pushed Pē'LpeL and he fell on his back into the water. "Treat me softly, younger brother," said Pē'LpeL. But the youth said to him: "Rise! Why do you talk that way?" He took hold of him just a little and broke his bones. Pē'LpeL said: "Oh, let me alone, I am poor." The two youths put the sturgeon into their canoe and went home. Pē'LpeL was put into his canoe. He was dead. They went home and carried him to his house. They landed at his town. Pē'LpeL was lost. His companions went up. They told Pē'LpeL's mother: "Go down to the beach. Your son brings your gill net. Make a coat." The old woman went

---

inā'qōn. Nau'i ka'nauwē LEX igē'xôx iā'kᵘcXa ya'Xi inā'qōn.
the sturgeon. At once all broken it became its mouth that sturgeon.

Igē'k·îm ya'Xi iq¦u'lîpX: "LXE'leuX txē'gela-îX." Icxē'gela-îX
He said that youth: "Ashore we will land." They two landed

LXE'leu. IaqE'luLX ya'Xi iq¦u'lîpX. Lā'k¦atxamîkc La-îtci Pē'LpeL.
ashore. He went ashore that youth. Six men in his canoe those Pē'LpeL.

Itcē'gElga ya'Xi its¦iqLqoā'ma ya'Xi iLā'Xanim. Nau'i ts¦EX
He took them those thwarts that his canoe. At once split

igē'xôx ya'Xi ikE'nim. "Ō, ā'qanuwē, L¦ gi! imxangE'lqoat."
it was that canoe. "Oh, indeed, behold this one! you bathed against me."

"IaxamgE'lqoat, ā'qanwē, iaxamgE'lqoat," igē'k·îm ya'Xi
"I bathed against you, indeed, I bathed against you," he said that

iq¦u'lîpX. Iqē'gElga Pē'LpeL gipā'tîx·. Ē'wa itcî'tux ta'Xi
youth. He was taken Pē'LpeL here. Thus he made them those

tē'yakci; nau'i LXoa'pLXoap igē'xôx gipā'tîx· tcî'yatck¦unpa.
his hands; at once holes were here his clavicles at.

Iqiō'samit Pē'LpeL, nau'i iuL¦uwā'ekoXuît Ltcu'qoapa. "Lawā'
He was pushed Pē'LpeL, at once he fell back so that he sat the water in. "Easy

ā'koa mEnō'xoa, ā'wē!" Iqiō'lXam Pē'LpeL: "ME'tXuît. Qā'tsqē
thus do me, younger brother!" He was told Pē'LpeL: "Stand up. Why

ā'koa mxō'la?" Nō'L¦îX iqē'gElga, iguXoalā'Xit tē'yaq¦ōtcō
thus you talk?" A little he was taken, they broke on both sides his bones

Pē'LpeL. Igē'k·îm: "Iā'c nE'xa, tgE'giutgoax." Icgiakxā'ema
Pē'LpeL. He said: "Let alone do me, I am poor." They two put it into the canoe

ictā'naqōn. Icî'Xk¦oa cta'Xi cq¦u'lîpX. A'qa iqiaqxā'ema Pē'LpeL,
their two selves' sturgeon. They two went home those two two youths. Then he was put into the canoe Pē'LpeL,

iō'mEqt. A'qa iLE'Xk¦oa. Iqē'yukT tē'yaqLpa. ILxē'gela-îX
he was dead. Then they went home. He was carried his house to. They landed

gi iLā'lXampa. Iqionā'xLatck Pē'LpeL. ILō'ptcka giLā'cgēwal.
this their town at. He was lost Pē'LpeL. They went up being companions.

Iqō'lXam wā'yaq Pē'LpeL: "A'yaq mE'Lxa," iqō'lXam.
She was told his mother Pē'LpeL: "Quick go down to the water," she was told.

"Ak¦E'nXatē itcamē'Lam imē'xan; aq¦ē'Lxap amō'Xoa." Igō'Lxa
"A gill net he brings you your son; a coat you will make it." She went down to the water

down and saw her son. The canoe was full of blood. Pē'ʟpeʟ was lying dead in his canoe. His mother began to cry, but she died right there.

---

wu'Xi	aq!eyō'qt,	igē'qelkᴇl	itcā'xan.	Pāʟ	ʟqa'wulqt	ya'Xi
that	old woman,	she saw him	her son.	Full	blood	that

ikᴇ'nim.	Iō'mᴇqt	Pē'ʟpeʟ	ikᴇ'nimpa.	Kē'nuwa	igagᴇ'tcax	wā'yaq.
canoe.	He was dead	Pē'ʟpeʟ	the canoe in.	Try	she cried	his mother

Kōpā'	igō'maqt	wā'yaq	Pē'ʟpeʟ.
There	she was dead	his mother	Pē'ʟpeʟ.

The Nisal (told 1894)

The people had a town on each side of the creek. Nisal was the name of the town on the one side, Sunnyside the name of the town on the other side. The people of Sunnyside were all shamans. Now one man at Nisal sang his conjurer's song. A small figure of a supernatural being was made of cedar wood. When this man, who had a supernatural helper, sang, then the cedar figure moved and danced. A woodchuck blanket was put onto it. It was laid double and fitted it. Then the people of Sunnyside became envious because the others could do more than they.

That man who had a supernatural helper continued to sing for two years. Now there were two mean youths at Sunnyside. They did

---

Gilā'lelam Lā'xēxik¦alx

The Nisal Their Tale

Lxēlā'etîX ta-îtci tê'lXam Gilā'lelam Le'xak¦anatētōL; Acuwî'ct
There were those people Nisal on both sides of it; Acuwî'ct (Nisal)

iā'xaleuX ya'Xi ēwa' k¦anatē'tōL; Awā'xamīn iā'xaleuX ya'Xi ēwa'
its name that there on one side; Awā'xamīn (Sunnyside) its name that there

k¦anatē'tōL. Kanauwē' La'qēwamax La-itci Awā'xamīn giLā'lXam.
on the other side. All conjurers there Awā'xamīn their town.

Ā'qa igē'ktcxam ēXā't ksî'aacuwî'ct. A'qa iqē'lox iō'LEmax.
Then he sang a conjurer's song one man of Acuwî'ct. Then it was made a figure of a supernatural being.

Ē'ckan qikē'x. Ma'nîx nîktcxE'mx ya'Xi giā'yuLEmax, a'qa
Cedar it was. When he sang that the one having the figure of the supernatural being, then

nîxElā'lalEmx ya'Xi ē'ckan. Qayuwē'tckoax. Aqcîldē'x cq¦ula'.
it moved that cedar. It danced. It was put on to it a woodchuck blanket.

Q¦up aqcō'xoax cq¦ula'. A'qa q¦oā'L qasîxk¦ā'qoax. Āqa iā'tcqEm
Doubled it was the woodchuck blanket. Then well it fitted. Then its sickness

igixE'lôx ē'Lamxtc gaLā'awaxEmīn. IqE'LōLq. Itcî'LōLq ya'Xi
it was on it their heart the people of Awā'xamīn. They were vanquished. It vanquished them that

ō'LEmax.
upernatural being.

Mâkct tqetā'qEmax igē'ktcxam ya'Xi giā'yuLEmax. A'qa cmôkct
Two years he sang his conjurer's song that the one having a supernatural helper. Then two

ctā'tsxatEmax cq¦u'lîpX Awā'xamīn ictā'lXam, ka'nauwē tā'nki
mean ones youths Awā'xamīn their town, all things

everything that was bad. They were friends. When it became winter again, the men of Nisal let the figure of the supernatural being dance. It danced whenever that man who had a supernatural helper wanted. When he sang, the cedar figure danced. All the people went to see it. They were surprised. Then those two bad youths, those mean men, spoke together. The one said to his friend: "What do you think? We will strike the figure of the supernatural being." The other one replied: "Let us strike it."

On the following day they went inland and searched for a branch. They took it and made a club. When they had finished the club, they went toward the sea and hid near the house. It grew dark. One night the Nisal cried "Eh—" during the dance. They were glad when the figure of their supernatural being danced. The next night, the two youths went across, and when they got across, they crept up secretly to that house. When they came near the door they stopped, and one of them said to his friend: "You lift the door flap; I will strike that supernatural thing."

---

nîcxElō'xoax iā'mEla LXā'cîkc. Wī't'ax tcā'xElkLîx· igē'xôx. Wi
they did bad the friends. Again winter it became. Again

k¡oaLqē' ya'Xi iō'LEmax aqiō'xoax, iLā'yuLEmax Lctā'acuwîct.
thus that figure of a supernatural being it was made, their figure of a supernatural being the Acuwî'ct.

Yā'xka iā'Xaqamit, a'qa iuwē'lalEmx. QatcigEltcxE'mx ya'Xi
He his mind, then it danced. He sang much that

giā'yuLEmax, qayuwē'tckuax ya'Xi ē'ckan. Ka'nauwē tê'lXam
the one having the figure of the supernatural being, it danced much that cedar. All people

qatgixēlō'tcxa-itx. Ac q¡āc nExoā'xax tê'lXam. A'qa icî'k·îm
they went to see it. And surprised they were the people. Then the two said

cta'Xi cq¡u'lîpX cta'Xi gictā'mEla cq¡u'lipX ctā'tcxatEmax.
those two youths those two bad ones two youths the two mean ones.

Itciō'lXam iā'cîkc: "Qa ē'mēmxtc? Atxgiuqoē'lXEma tau
He said to him his friend: "How your mind? We two will strike it that

iō'LEmax." Itciō'lXam iā'cîkc, igē'k·îm ya'Xi ē'Xat: "Tgt¡ō'kti
figure of the supernatural being." He said to him his friend, he said that one: "Good

atxgiuqoē'lXEma."
we two strike it."

Wāx igē'tcuktē. A'qa ictō'ptck LXE'lcuX. Icgō'naxL ā'Lap.
Early day came. Then they two went up landward. They searched for it a branch.

Icgō'cgam ā'Lap. A'qa icî'kux atā'mq¡aL. ILkcā'kōLq atā'mq¡aL.
They two found it a branch. Then they two made it a club. They finished it the club.

A'qa îctō'Lxa. Q¡oā'p tqu'Lepa a'qa icgō'pcut. Igō'ponEm.
Then they went down toward the water. Near the house at then they two hid. It grew dark.

Agōn ā'pōl ē'Lutk qatgiō'xoax kLctā'acuwîct. Ma'nîx
One night crying "Eh" they did the Acuwî'ct. When

qayuwē'tcgoax ya'Xi iLā'yuLEmax, k¡wa'nk¡wan qaLxigElō'xoax.
it danced that their figure of a supernatural being, glad they were.

When the figure of the supernatural being danced, it went to and fro five times in the house. A little while they stayed outside. Then the man who had a supernatural helper began to sing. Then the one said to his friend: "Now they let the figure of the supernatural being dance." After a little while the people in the house began to cry "Eh." The figure of the supernatural being was moving, and then the two youths went to the door. They stayed there. Then they opened the door a little and one of them said to his friend: "There, that supernatural being moves dancing in the house. Look!" Then his friend saw the figure of the supernatural being. Indeed, it was moving. Three times it went to and fro. Then one of them said to his friend: "When it comes again we will strike it. You lift the door

---

A'qa wi igō'ponEm. Aqa îctē'gōsîX cta'Xi cq¡u'lîpX.
Then again it grew dark. Then they two landed those two two youths.

Ictigō'samîx. A'qa icxō'kuikLuwa ta'Xi tqu'Lē. Q¡oā'p icî'qēpa
They arrived on the other side. Then they crept secretly to that house. Near the door at

ictō'yam, aqa icxē'la-it. Itciō'lXam iā'cîke: "Mai'ka amiolā'tcgoa
they arrived, then they two stayed. He said to him his friend: "You you lift it

ya'Xi iqabō'tē. Nai'ka aniuqoē'lXEma ya'Xi iō'LEmax." Manî'x
that door flap. I I will strike it that figure of the supernatural being." When

ayuwē'tcka ya'Xi iō'LEmax, qoā'2nEmîX Lāq¡ nîxō'xoax ya'Xi
it danced that figure of a supernatural being, five times turn round it did that

iō'LEmax ta'Xi tqu'Lēpa manî'x qayuwē'tckoax. Nō'L¡îx· îcxē'la-ît
figure of the supernatural being that house in when it danced. A little while they two stayed

Lā'xanîx· a'qa igē'ktcxam ya'Xi giā'yuLEmax." Itciō'lXam iā'cîke:
outside then he sang his conjurer's song that the one having the figure of the supernatural being." He said to him his friend:

"A'qa aqiwē'mitatcgoa ya'Xi iō'LEmax. Nō'L¡îX a'qa ā'qanuwē
"Now it is caused to dance that figure of the supernatural being. A little while then indeed

ē'Lutk iqioxō'lalEmtck, ē'Lutk tqu'Lepa. A'qa igē'xEla ya'Xi
"Eh" cries were made always, "Eh" cries the house in. Then it moved that

iō'LEmax. A'qa ictō'ya cta'Xi cq¡u'lîpX icî'qēpa. Icxē'la-it
figure of the supernatural being. Then they two went those two youths the door to. They two stayed

icî'qēpa. NōL¡ icgixE'laqLqîX. Atciō'lXam iā'cîke: "A'qa
the door at. A little they two opened it. He said to him his friend: "Now

ayaLituwī'ya ya'Xi iō'LEmax. Nî'Xua, ē'qamîtek!" A'qa itcî'yuket
it comes dancing that figure of the supernatural being. Well, look!" Then he saw it

iā'cîke ya'Xi iō'LEmax. Aqa ā'qanuwē ixElā't ya'Xi iō'LEmax.
his friend that figure of the supernatural being. Then indeed it moved that figure of the supernatural being.

Lō'nîX Lāq¡ igē'xôx iō'LEmax. A'qa itciō'lXam iā'cike: "Wī't'ax
Three times turn it did the figure of the supernatural being. Then he said to him his friend: "Again

aletī'ya a'qa atxiuqoē'lXEma. Cā'xalîX amiulā'tcgoa ya'Xi
it will come then we will strike it. Up you lift that

flap. I will strike it." The other one said: "Yes." Then the figure came dancing. It came to the door. It had two heads. Then it turned back. Now the one lifted the door flap and the other one struck it. The figure of the supernatural being was split. They ran down to the water to their canoe and went across. They said "Heh, we got the better of that Nisal man who had a supernatural helper."

Those people became silent. The two youths came home and they went to bed at once. On the following day the people of Sunnyside heard that the figure of the supernatural being had been struck and killed. "Two men split it. Where may those people have come from?" It got dark and the people of Nisal remained silent. After four days the batons were heard again. Then the people of Nisal said: "Eh." They were told: "Oh, that figure of the supernatural being has been sewed together." One night that shaman who had the

---

iqabō'tē. Nai'ka aniuqoē'lXEma." Igē'k·îm ya'Xi ēXā't:
door flap. I I shall strike it." He said that one:

"A'qanuwē." A'qa igē'tē ya'Xi iō'LEma iaLētō'wîtck. Igîcgā'tqoam
"Indeed." Then it came that figure of the supernatural being it danced. It reached

icî'qēpa. Cmâket ciā'q¡aqctaq ya'Xi iō'LEmax. IgixE'LXēgoa ya'Xi
the door at. Two its heads that figure of the supernatural being. It returned that

iō'LEmax. A'qa itciō'latck ya'Xi iqabō'tē ya'Xi eXā't. Itciō'quîlX
figure of the supernatural being. Then he lifted it that door flap that one. He struck it

ya'Xi ēXā't iq¡u'lîpX. Ts¡Exts¡E'x icxē'lôx ya'Xi iō'LEmax.
that one youth. Split it was in two that figure of the supernatural being.

Icî'xawa mā'LnîX ictā'Xanīmpa. Ictē'gōsîX. Icî'k·îm: "Ku'ca! tau
They two ran toward the sea their canoe to. They two went across. They two said: "Shame! those

giLā'yuLEmax Lctā'acuwîct."
having the figure of a supernatural being the Acuwî'ct."

TcE k¡ā igō'xoax ta-îtci tê'lXam. IcXk¡oā'mam. Nā'wi
And silent were those people. They two came home. At once

ickLqā'yuXuit cta'Xi cq¡u'lîpX. Wāx igē'tcuktē. Ā, iLxEltcî'maq
they two lay down those two two youths. Next day day came. Ah, they heard

gaLā'awaxEmîn: "Ā, iqē'waq ya'Xi iō'LEmax. Iqiō'quîlX. Ts¡Ex
the people of Awā'xamîn: "Ah, it has been killed that figure of a supernatural being. It has been struck. Split

isxē'lôx. Qāmta LXuan qa tê'lXam itgiō'quîlX?" Igō'ponEm tcE
it is in two. Whence maybe where people they struck it?" It grew dark and

k¡ā qLctā'acuwîct. Lā'ktîX iō'qoya-îX, a'qa wī't'ax iqaltcE'maq
silent the Acuwî'ct. Four times their sleeps, then again they were heard

aqcqu'tē. A'qa wi ēLu'tk iLgioxō'lalEmtck Lctā'acuwîct.
the batons. Then again "Eh" cries they always made the Acuwî'ct.

IqLō'lXam Lctā'asuwîct: "Ā, a'qa iLgī'yuptcx iLā'yuLEmax."
They were told the Acuwî'ct: "Ah, then they sewed together their figure of the supernatural being."

Igō'n igō'pōnEm, a'qa igē'k·îm ya'Xi igē'ktcxEm, ya'Xi
Another it grew dark, then he said that he sang conjurer's songs, that

supernatural helper which was killed said: "What shall we do to these Indians? They will be deceived. We will make a bird to attack them." They made a bird which was to attack those two Indians. Now the people thought: "Oh, two persons killed the figure of that supernatural being."

Now indeed snow began to fall. It fell for three days, then it became cold. It was cold for two nights. Then one man of Sunnyside said: "Keep quiet; do not go about much. It is going to be cold." One of the youths who had killed the figure of the supernatural being went toward the water. He looked up the river. Then ice came drifting down the river and two eagles were sitting on it. He went up to the house and said to his friend: "Quick, friend, let us go down to the water. There are eagles drifting down on the ice. They are eating something." His friend said: "Let us go; maybe they are eating a sturgeon." The two went down to the water and launched their canoe. They went to look at the ice on which the eagles were

---

giā'yuLEmax iqē'waq: "Qā aqtE'xa Natē'tanuē? Ā, lā'xlax aqtō'xoa
the one having the figure of the supernatural being / it was struck: / "How / will be done / the Indians? / Ah, / deceive / they will be done

Natē'tanuē. LpǀE'spǀEs aqLuguē'xa." LpǀE'spǀEs aqLcgElō'xoa
the Indians. / A bird / it will be made." / A bird / was made against them two

cta'Xi ctē'tanuē. IguXuiLō'Xoa-ît tê'lXam: "Ō, amâ'kctîkc Lgi
those two / two Indians. / They thought / the people: / "Oh, / two men / these

itgē'waq iō'LEmax."
they killed it / the figure of the supernatural being."

Ā'qanuwē Ltga iLō'La-it. Lō'nîX iō'qoya-îX Ltga iLō'La-it.
Indeed / snow / lay. / Three times / he slept / snow / lay.

A'qa itcē'lpo-îx. Mâ'kctîX iō'qoya-îX itcē'lpo-îX. Igē'k·îm
Then / it was cold. / Twice / he slept / it was cold. / They said

gaLā'awaxEmîn: "Ac pEt amcxō'xoa. Nîct qā'mta
the Awā'xamin: / "And / quiet / be. / Not / anywhere

amcgō'cgēwalEma. Itsō'mit igē'xax." Iō'Lxa ya'Xi ēXā't
go much. / Cold / it gets." / He went down to the water / that / one

iqǀu'lîpX ctā'Xka cta'Xi icgē'waq iō'LEmax. Igē'kîkct ē'wa
youth / they two / those two / they two killed it / the figure of the supernatural being. / He looked / there

cā'xalîX. A'qa ikaba' ē'tgatcX. Mâkct ctcǀîqtcǀî'qukc tigElā'itîX.
up. / Then / ice / drifted down the river. / Two / eagles / were on it.

Iō'ptcga tqu'Lepa. Itciō'lXam iā'cîkc: "A'yaq, cîkc, atxō'Lxa.
He went up / the house to. / He said to him / his friend: / "Quick, / friend, / let us go down to the water.

Tcǀîqtcǀî'qukc tā'nki LXuan ioxoelā'x ē'tgatcX ikabā'pa." Igē'k·îm
Eagles / something / perhaps / they eat / it drifts down the river / the ice on." / He said

iā'cîkc: "A'yaq tE'xoya; LXuan inā'qōn ya'Xi iqixElā'x." Ictō'Lxa
his friend: / "Quick / let us go; / perhaps / a sturgeon / that / it is eaten." / They two went down to the water

mā'LnîX. Icgiō'cgiLx ictā'XEnīm. Icgiō'kctam ya'Xi ikaba' ya'Xi
seaward. / They two launched it / their two selves' canoe. / They two arrived / that / ice / that

sitting. They left the shore and came near the ice. Then the two eagles flew away, and they did not see anything on the ice. They turned their canoe. As they had just turned, the ice began to close, and crushed the canoe. The two youths were drowned together. Those two persons who had killed the figure of the supernatural being were dead. It took revenge upon them. Then the people of Nisal said: "Behold! they killed the figure of our supernatural being. Behold! and we thought men from a far away country did it." It is forbidden to make fun of the figures of supernatural beings. When a person makes fun of one, he will die after a short time.

---

tc¡îqtc¡î'quke tigᴇlā'itîX. Ictō'yam mā'ʟnîX. q¡oā'p îcgī'yux ya'Xi
eagles | they were on it. | They two arrived | on the water. | near | they two came it | that

ikaba'. A'qa ictō'koa cta'Xi ctc¡îqtc¡î'q. K¡ā nîct tān icgē'qᴇlkᴇl
ice. | Then | they two flew | those two | two eagles. | Nothing | not | anything | they two saw it

ya'Xi ikabā'pa. Icgîxē'lakoa ictā'Xanim, as nōʟ¡ îcgixē'lakua
that | ice on. | They two returned | their two selves' canoe, | and | a little | they two had returned

ictā'Xᴇnim. A'qa igîxᴇltcē'mXit ya'Xi ikaba'. IgiXᴇ'mq¡oaʟk
their two selves' canoe. | Then | it closed around the canoe | that | ice. | It crushed it

ya'Xi ictā'Xanim. Kopā' ʟ¡lap ictō'ya cta'Xi cq¡u'lîpX
that | their two selves' canoe. | There | under water | they two went | those two | two youths

ckanacmô'kct. IcXᴇ'ʟa-it cta'Xi icgē'waq iō'ʟᴇmax.
both. | They two were dead | those two | they two killed it | the figure of the supernatural being.

Itcî'nk¡ēmᴇnakoa. Igugoā'k·îm tê'lXam ʟctā'acuwîct: "Ō, ctā'Xka
It took revenge. | They said | the people | the Acuwi'ct: | "Oh, | they two

ʟqōct icgē'waq iō'ʟᴇmax. Tātc¡a ntcʟō'Xua-it kᴇlā'iX qa
behold! | they two killed it | the figure of the supernatural being. | Behold! | we thought | far | where

tê'lXam." Tān txo tgā'k¡ēʟau iō'ʟᴇmax qiXᴇnᴇmō'tXᴇmx. Manē'x
people." | What maybe | it is forbidden | the figure of a supernatural being | it is made fun of it. | When

qaʟgiXᴇnᴇmō'tXᴇmx ʟgoaʟē'lX, nāct iō'ʟqtîX a'qa qaʟō'mᴇqtx.
he makes fun of it | a person, | not | long | then | he dies.

The Spirit of Hunger (told 1894)

There were those people. All the time they were dying of hunger. Many old people were dying. They tried to gather cockles, but there was only water in the shells. They tried to gather mussels, but they were empty. There was no meat in them. Thus it was with everything. They were starving. When a hunter went to kill elks, he did not kill anything. When a hunter went to hunt seals, he did not kill anything. All the hunters were unsuccessful. Behold! The Hunger kept all kinds of bones; those of the beaver, raccoon, sturgeon, and bear. She kept the bones of all kinds of animals, and the shells of sea food.

Now, there were two young friends. In winter the people were hungry again, and after a short while an old man died of hunger, and poor children died of hunger. Then one of these youths said to his

---

Oxoēlā'etîX ta-îtci tê'lXam. Ka'nauwē ʟqētā'kᴇmax wā'lō
There were those people. All days hunger

aktō'xoa-îtx. ʟgā'pᴇlatîkc tq¡eyō'qtîkc nuXoaʟā'îtx. Kē'nuwa
they died. Many old people died. Try

aqʟgᴇlō'-îX ʟpē'xʟᴇnaʟ, ʟā'ema ʟtcā'2qoa qaʟiʟā'eta-îtx
they were taken cockles, only water was on them

āʟaʟt¡āqu'lpa. Kā'nuwa aqigᴇlō'-îX itguē'matk, a'ēma ā'2xᴇmax,
their shells. Try they were taken mussels, only empty,

nîct ē'yatqul. Ka'nauwē tā'nki k¡oaʟqē' nixō'xoax, tcalō'îX.
not their flesh. All things thus were, they were starving.

Kā'nuwa qaʟō'îX ʟā'xēkʟaq imō'lᴇkᴇmax giʟā'k¡ewula, k¡ā nîct
Try they went the hunters elks having for their game, and not

tān qaʟgewā'qoax. Kē'nuwa qaʟō'îX alXayō'maX giʟā'k¡ēwula,
anything they killed it. Try they went seals having for their game,

k¡ā nîct tān qaʟgewā'qoax. A'qa cu'Xumax gᴇnā'x ka'nauwē
and not anything they killed it. Then unsuccessful they were all

tgā'xēqʟax. Qōct Wā'lō, agawigē'tgax ka'nauwē tᴇ'gaq¡ōtcō.
hunters. Behold the Hunger, she kept them all their bones.

K¡oaʟqē' iqoa-inē'nē, k¡oaʟqē' iʟatā't, k¡oaʟqē' inā'qōn. Ka'nauwē
Thus the beaver, thus the raccoon, thus the sturgeon. All

tān tē'yaq¡ōtcō agawigē'tkax Walō'. K¡oaʟqē' iskē'ntXoa.
things their bones she kept them the Hunger. Thus the bear.

Ka'nauwē tmaʟnē'qoxoē'max agawigē'tgax ā'taʟt¡aqul.
All sea food she kept them their shells.

Ā'2qa emôket exā'cikc cq¡u'lîpX. A'qa wi walō' igᴇ'tux
Then two two mutual friends two youths. Then again hunger acted on them

tcā'xᴇlqʟîX. Nō'ʟ¡îX qaʟō'mᴇqtx ʟq¡eyō'qt, walō' akʟuwā'qoax.
in winter. A little while he died an old man, hunger killed him.

ʟk¡ā'skas walō' akʟuwā'qoax, ma'nîx qʟā'giutgoax ʟk¡ā'skas.
A child hunger killed it, when poor a child.

friend: "The Hunger is my supernatural helper. I see her coming. She is carrying a mat on her back. She came round that point of land. She is coming. Don't you see her?" Thus he spoke to his friend. His friend said: "I do not see her. You alone have her for your supernatural helper, and therefore you see her." In the afternoon the children began to cry. They were hungry. On the following day the friends were in bed. They slept long. Then the one said again to his friend: "There, the Hunger is coming again. Do you see her?" The other one said to his friend: "I do not see anything. You alone have her for your supernatural helper; therefore you can see her." But this one of the friends did see her, because she was really his supernatural helper. She was not a very strong supernatural helper of the other one. He was less powerful. He said to his friend: "To-morrow I will take away her mat." "Oh, indeed," said the other one, "our relatives are poor. The old people and the children are poor." On the following day they had only fern

---

A'qa itciō'lXam iā'cîkc ya'Xi iq¡u'lîpX: "Nai'ka gī'yuʟᴇmax
Then he said to him his friend that youth: "I having a supernatural helper

Walō'. Nō'qumit ya'Xi nō'yîX natē'x. Ikʟō'ctxula ʟgā'q¡apᴇnX;
the Hunger. I see her that she goes she comes. She carries it on her back her mat;

ya'Xi iqayō'kt¡itîX stāX naxō'xoax natē'x. TcūX mō'qumit?"
that point of land around she gets she comes. Do you see her?"

itciō'lXam iā'cîkc. Igē'k·îm iā'cîkc: "K¡ā'ya, nîct nō'qumit, tᴇnōX
he said to him his friend. He said his friend: "No, not I see her, only

mai'ka amī'yōʟᴇmaX, tā'ntxo mō'qumit." Lāx naxō'xoax aqaʟā'x,
you your supernatural helper, therefore you see her." Afternoon became the sun,

a'qa noxo-inē'mx tqā'totenîkc. Walō' aktō'xoax. Wāx wi
then they cried the children. Hunger acted on them. Next day again

niktcō'ktxîX, a'qa wi qackʟqā'yuXuîtx iā'cîkc îlXᴇ'mēpa. Lā'lē
day came, then again they two lay down his friend the bed on. Long

qackʟqā'yuXuîtx, a'qa wi itciō'lXam iā'cîkc: "A'qa wi alatē'ya
they two lay down, then again he said to him his friend: "Now again she will come

wu'Xi Walō'. Mō'qumit tci?" Itciō'lXam iā'cîkc: "K¡ā nîct
that Hunger. You see her [int. part.]?" He said to him his friend: "No, not

nō'qumit. TᴇnōX mai'ka amī'yōʟᴇmaX, tā'ntXo mō'qumit."
I see her. Only you your supernatural helper, therefore you see her."

Tatc¡a tcō'qumit ya'Xi iā'cîkc. Ya'Xka wuk¡ ayā'yōʟᴇmaX, ya'Xi
But he saw her that his friend. He really his supernatural helper, that

ēXā't nîct pāt ayā'yōʟᴇmax ac nōʟ¡îX ayā'yōʟᴇmaX. Itciō'lXam
one not strong his supernatural helper and little his supernatural helper, He said to him

iā'cîkc: "Ō'la a'qa anʟaxcgā'ma ʟgā'q¡apᴇnx." Itciō'lXam iā'cîkc:
his friend: "To-morrow then I shall take from her her mat." He said to him his friend:

"Ō, ā'qanuwē, tgā'giutgoax txā'cuXtîkc, tgā'giutgoax tq¡eyō'qtîkc,
"Oh, indeed, poor our relatives, poor the old people,

tgā'giutgoax tqā'totenîkc." Wāx igē'tcuktîX, iā'ema ik¡ē'cana
poor the children." Next day day came, only pteris roots

roots and potentilla roots to eat. Then the friends slept again. In the afternoon the one said again: "There, the Hunger is coming." The other friend had seen her already. The first one said: "I will take her mat away." The other one replied: "Oh, indeed, our poor relatives." This one of the friends had seen her. First she looked into the last house. She looked into all the houses. Now she came to them. He thought: "When will he jump at her? She is looking in now." When she looked into a house the children began to cry of hunger. Then she turned back again and went home. When she had gone some distance, the other friend said: "There, she is going back again; she did not come to us." But the other friend had seen her looking into the house. He thought that she was not a very strong supernatural helper of his friend.

His friend said again: "To-morrow I will take her mat from her," and the other one replied: "Indeed, our poor children and our poor

---

qayuXuimō'Xumx ta-îtci tê'lXam k¡a iā'ema ik¡enā'tan. A'qa wi
they ate those people and only potentilla roots. Then again

ickʟqā'yuXuît iā'cîkc. Lāx aqaʟā'x a'qa wi igē'k·îm: "A'qa wi
they two lay down his friend. Afternoon sun then again he said: "Now again

alatē'ya wu'Xi Walō'." Ā'nqa tcō'qumit ya'Xi iā'cîkc. Igē'k·îm
she will come that Hunger." Already he had seen her that his friend. He said

ya'Xi iā'cîkc: "A'qa anʟaxcgā'ma ʟgā'q¡apᴇnX." "Ō, ā'qanuwē,"
that his friend: "Then I shall take it from her her mat." "Oh, indeed,"

itciō'lXam, "a'qa tgā'giutgoax txā'cuXtîkc." Tcō'qumit ya'Xi
he said to him, "now poor our relatives." He saw her that

iā'cîkc. Tā'newa taXi kᴇ'mkitîX tqu'ʟē igîckXā'napq. A'qa wi
his friend. First that at the end house she looked into it. Then again

tgōn tēXt tqu'ʟē. Ka'nauwē ta'Xi tqʟē'maX igîckXā'napq.
another one house. All those houses she looked into them.

Igaʟgā'tqoam ʟā'îtcgapa. Igîxʟō'xoa-ît ya'Xi iā'cîkc: "Qantsî'x ʟqa
She reached those at. He thought that his friend: "When maybe

gi atsagᴇnpᴇnā'ya igîckXā'napq tᴇ'ʟaqʟpa." IgîckXā'napq, a'qa
this he will jump at her she looks into their house at." She looked into the house, then

iguxoē'nîmtck ta-îtci tqā'tōtenîkc. Walō' igᴇ'tux. Wī igaxᴇ'takoa;
they cried those children. Hunger acted on them. Again she returned;

igā'Xk¡oa. YaXī' kᴇlā'îX igō'yam, a'qa igē'k·îm iā'cîkc: "A'qa
she went home. There far she arrived, then he said his friend: "Then

wi aXaXᴇ'tak^{u}t. Nāct igalxgā'tqoam." Tatc¡a ya'Xi iā'cîkc
again she returns. Not she reached us." But that his friend

tcō'qumit igaʟgō'qoam. IgîckXā'napq tᴇ'ʟaqʟpa. Igîxʟō'Xoa-it
he saw her she reached them. She looked into their house in. He thought

ya'Xi iā'cîkc: "Nîct ʟqōct! pāt ayā'yōʟᴇmaX."
that his friend: "Not behold! strong his supernatural helper."

A'qa wī't'ax igē'k·îm ya'Xi iā'cîkc: "Â'la a'qa anʟaxcgā'ma
Then again he said that his friend: "To-morrow then I shall take it from her

ʟgā'q¡apᴇnX." Itciō'lXam: "Â' kat ā'qanuwē. Tgā'giutgoax
her mat." She said to him: "Ah, indeed. Poor

old people." Day came. In the afternoon they lay in their bed sleeping. The second one of the friends saw the Hunger coming. Then the first one said: "There, the Hunger is coming!" But lo! the other one had seen her already. "Now, I will jump at her when she comes," said the one; "I will take her mat away." Her legs were long and her hair was *thus*. She had only a little hair, but it was long. Then the Hunger came again. She came to the last house and looked into it. The children began to cry, and an old man died of hunger. She looked into all the houses, and came also to the house of the friends. She looked into it. Then the one of the friends thought: "When will he jump at her?" She stood in the door for a long time and turned back again. When she had gone a long distance, the other one of the friends said: "There, she is turning back again. She did not come to us. Maybe she knows that I am going to take her mat away." Then the other friend thought: "Behold! he did not see her. She stood in the door for a long time, but he says she did not come."

---

tqā'totenîkc, tgā'giutgoax tq!eyō'qtîkc." Wāx igē'tcuktîX wī't'ax.
the children, poor the old people." Next day day came again.

Lāx aqaLā'x, a'qa wī't'ax îckLqā'yōXuît ictā'lXamēpa. Ā'nqa
After-noon the sun, then again they two lay down their two selves' bed on. Already

tcō'qumit iā'cîkc atē't wu'Xi Walō'. A'qa wi itciō'lXam ya'Xi
he saw her his friend she came that Hunger. Then again he said to him that

iā'cîkc: "A'qa wi alatē'ya wu'Xi Walō'." Tā'tc!a ya'Xi ēXā't
his friend: "Now again she will come that Hunger." But that one

ā'nqa tcō'qumit wu'Xi Walō'. "A'qa antcakEnpEnā'ya ma'nîx
already he had seen her that Hunger. "Then I will jump at her when

alatē'mam," igē'k·îm ya'Xi ēXā't. "AnLaxcgā'ma Lgā'q!apEnX."
she will arrive," he said that one. "I will take it from her her mat."

Itā'łLqtax ta'Xi tgā'qo-it. K!oaLqē' La'Xi LE'gaqsō, k!a nōL!
Long those her legs. Thus that her hair, and little

La'Xi LE'gaqsō k!a iLā'Lqtax. A'qa wi igā'tē wu'Xi Walō'.
that her hair and long. Then again she came that Hunger.

Igatē'mam ta'Xi kE'mkXitē tqu'Lē. IgîckXā'napqîX. Igoxoē'nîmtck
She arrived at that last house. She looked into it. They cried

tqā'totenîkc. Lō'maqt LēXā't Lq!eyō'qt walō'. Kanauwē' ta'Xi
the children. He died one old man hunger. All those

tqLē'max igîckXā'napq. Igatē'mam tE'LaqLpa, igîckXā'napq
houses she looked into. She arrived their house at, she looked into it

tE'LaqLpa. IgîxLō'Xoa-ît ya'Xi iā'cîkc: "Qantsî'x atsEgEnpenā'ya?"
their house in. He thought that his friend: "When will he jump at her?"

Lē'lē igō'tXuit icî'qēpa. Aqa wi iaXE'takoa. Igō'ya, kElā'îX
Long she stood the door in. Then again she returned. She went, far

igō'yam. A'qa igē'k·îm ya'Xi iā'cîkc: "A'qa wi aXE'taqt. Nāct
she arrived. Then he said that his friend: "Now again she returns. Not

igalxgā'tqoam. LXuan talō'XuîX anLaxcgā'ma Lgā'q!apEnX."
she came to us. Perhaps she knows it I shall take it from her her mat."

IgîxLō'xoa-ît ya'Xi iā'cîkc: "Lqōct nîct tcō'qumit. Ē'yaLqtîX
He thought that his friend: "Behold! not he saw her. Long

igō'tXuit icî'qēpa, tatc!a ixō'la nîct igatē'mam."
she stayed the door in, but he says not she arrived."

For five days she came to their house and the one only saw her. The mat which she carried on her back was small. They were sleeping, and when it was dark the one said to his friend: "Behold! you do not see the Hunger. She stood in the door for a long time, then she turned back." The other one did not reply. Then the first one continued: "To-morrow I will take her mat away. I will help you." The other one replied: "He will take the Hunger's mat, and even I was unable to take it from her." The other one said: "You will see, I shall take her mat away."

On the following day the mother of the one youth said: "What are you whispering all the time?" "We are afraid that the Hunger may kill us." The sun went along and it came to be afternoon. Then that youth tied his hair up on the back of his head. Again they lay down in bed. The one of the friends said: "Now, when she comes again, I shall take her mat." His friend replied: "Well, maybe you

---

Qoā'nEma Lkā'etax igatē'mam tE'LaqLpa. Tcō'qumit ya'Xi eXā't.
Five days she arrived their house at. He saw her that one.

ILō'k;ua-its La'XI Lq;ā'pEnX kLō'stXula. IckLqā'yuXuit Xā'pîX
Small that mat that she carried. They two lay down in the evening

ya'Xi iā'cîkc, a'qa itciō'lXam: "Lqōct nîctqē mō'qumit gi Walō'.
that his friend, then he said to him: "Behold, not at all you saw her this Hunger.

Lā'lē nō'tXuit ē'lxacîqpa, tcXua naXtā'kuax." Näct qa igē'k·îm
Long she stood our door in, then she returned." Not anyhow he spoke

ya'Xi iā'cîkc. Itciō'lXam: "Ō'la a'qa nai'ka anLaxcgā'ma
that his friend. He said to him: "To-morrow now I I shall take it from her

Lgā'q;apEnX." Itciō'lXam iā'cîkc: "AyamgElgē'cgama." "Lê,
her mat." He said to him his friend: "I will help you." "Lê,

îqLaxE'cgam ā'qa Lgā'q;apEnX Walō'. Ā'la nai'ka ta'tc;a nîct
it will be taken from her now her mat the Hunger. Even I, however, not

nLaxE'cgam Lgā'q;apEnX." Itciō'lXam iā'cîkc: "Ā'Lqi
I took it from her her mat." He said to him his friend: "Later on

amaqElkElā'ya, anLExcgā'ma Lgā'q;apEnX."
you will see, I shall take it from her her mat."

Wāx igē'tcuktîX. Igiō'lXam wā'yaq ya'Xi ēXā't iq;u'lîpX:
Next day day came. She said to him his mother that one youth:

"Tān Lqa gi cā'ucau qatcîmtō'xoa-îtx?" "Qōi acXEingEnā'tîX
"What maybe this low voice he always said to you?" "Must they are afraid

walō' alxLā'-ita." Igō'ya aqaLā'x. Lāx igaxō'qoam aqaLā'x.
hunger we shall die." He went the sun. Afternoon he arrived the sun.

A'qa iLîXE'mElaptck ya'Xi iq;u'lîpX. A'qa wi îckLqā'yuXuit
Then he tied his hair on the back of his head that youth. Then again they two lay down

ictā'lXamēpa. Itciō'lXam iā'cîkc: "A'qa nLaxcgā'ma Lgā'q;apEnX
their two selves' bed on. He said to him his friend: "Now I shall take it from her her mat

manî'x alatē'mama wī't'ax." "NîXua'," itciō'lXam iā'cîkc, "ō'la Lqa
when she will arrive again." "Well," he said to him his friend, "to-morrow then

will take her mat away to-morrow." After some time the other one spoke again: "Now the Hunger is coming." Thus spoke the one. But the other one had seen her already. She came and arrived at the last house. There she looked in first, and she looked into all the houses. Now she looked into the house near their own. The children were crying. Then she looked into their own house. Now he jumped outside. It was evening. Then the other one went out also and saw her. His friend almost fell down, but he jumped up again. He fought with the Hunger. Now she threw him, and now he threw her. For a long time he did so, and then he finished. He took her mat away. Then she cried. She liked her mat. She was very lean; she was only bones, but she was strong. She had only a little hair, but it was braided. He hid the mat outside. Nobody saw him fighting the Hunger. It got dark and the friends were in bed again. Then he told his friend about it and they laughed at her. He said: "Thus I did to her, and she almost threw me down.

---

mLExegā'ma Lgā'q;apEnX." Lā, a'qa wi igē'k'îm iā'newa ya'Xi
you will take it from her | her mat." | Long. | then | again | he said | first | that

ēXā't: "A'qa wi atē't wu'Xi Walō'." igē'k'îm ya'Xi ēXā't.
one: | "Then | again | she comes | that | Hunger." | he said | that | one.

Tate;a ā'nqa teō'qumit ya'Xi iā'cîke. Igatē', igatē'mam ta'Xi
But | already | he had seen her | that | his friend. | She came, | she arrived at | that

kE'mkXitē tqu'Lē. Iā'newatîX kōpā' igîckā'napq. A'qa ka'nauwē
last | house. | First | there | she looked into. | Then | all

ta'Xi tqLē'max igîckXā'napq. Ā'qa igîckXā'napq q;oā'p tE'LaqLpa
those | houses | she looked into them. | Then | she looked into it | near | their house at

tēXt tqu'Lē. Igoxoē'nîmtek ta-ftei tqā'totenîke. Ā'qa igîckXā'napq
one | house. | They cried | those | children. | Then | she looked into

tE'LaqLpa. ItcE'sōpEna Lā'xanîX. Tsō'yustîX, ā'qa iō'pa ya'Xi
their house at. | He jumped | outside. | Evening. | then | he went out | that

iā'cîke, a'qa itcō'qumitek, ā'koapō nixē'max·itx, a'qa wi qayō'tXuitx.
his friend, | then | he saw her, | almost | he fell down, | then again | he stood.

IcXE'lgayū k;a wu'Xi Walō'. Ā, kopā' igikLā'itx, ā'qa itcagE'La-it.
They two fought | and | that | Hunger. | Ah, | there | she threw him, | then | he threw her.

Lē'lē ā'koa igē'xōx, a'qa iLE'XōLq. ItcLaxE'egam Lgā'q;apEnX.
Long | thus | he did, | then | they finished. | He took it from her | her mat.

A'qa igagE'tcax. Tq;ē'x igE'Lōx Lgā'q;apEnX. Ō'L;ElXt, ō'L;ElXt,
Then | she cried. | Like | she did it | her mat. | She was lean, | she was lean,

ō'L;ElXt, tā'ema tE'q;ōtcō, ta'te;a tgā'LXēwulX. Nō'L; La'Xi
she was lean | only | bones, | but | she was strong | Little | that

LE'gaqsō, tate;a Lakp;ō'stEmtîX. Kōpā' Lā'xanîX a'qa itcLō'peut
her hair | but | braided | There | outside | then | he hid it

La'Xi Lq;ā'pEnX. Nāct Lan Igiō'qumit ya'Xi icXE'lgayu wu'Xi
that | mat. | Not | any[illegible] | saw him | that | he fought her | that

Walō'. Igā'pōnEm, a'qā wi ickLqā'yuXuit iā'cike. A'qa
Hunger. | It grew dark | then | again | they two lay down | his friend | Then

igixFiklē laiFmtek iā'eîke. A'qa hā'hē icq;ayā'wulalEmtek.
[illegible] | [illegible] | Then | laughing | they two laughed

Itciō'lXam: "Ā wi nō'xos, ā'koapō igingE'La-it, tate;a tā'ema
He said to him | "Thus | I did to her | almost | she threw me, | although | only

Although she is only bones, still she is very strong. I took her mat away. You will see it to-morrow."

The following morning the friends went to bathe in the creek. When they came home they made a fire and opened the roof of the house to admit the light. The mother of that youth said: "Why did you laugh last night?" "Oh, I was just laughing with my friend. Now call the old people." Then she went to call the old people. The old women and the old men were called. All those people were called, and the house of the youth came to be full of people. Then he said to his mother: "Bring me a large mat." His mother brought a good mat. Then he said to his father: "Now look and see what is in this small mat." The youth's father took off his blanket and stood up in the middle of the house. The youth said: "Maybe I deceive you, but maybe it is true. I took the Hunger's mat." Then bones were poured out of the mat upon the large mat in the middle of the

---

tE'q!otsō, tatc!a tgā'LxēwulX. InLaxE'cgam Lgā'q!apEnX. Ā'Lqi
bones, but she is strong. I took it from her her mat. Later on

ō'la amLqElkElā'ya."
to-morrow you will see it."

Wāx igē'tcuktîX. Kawī'X a'qa icXqoā'tam k!a iā'cîkc
Next day day came. Early then they two went to bathe and his friend

ē'qaLpa. Icā'tpqam igacXE'lgīLx, a'qa tuwā'x icktō'xam tqu'Lē.
the creek in. They came into the house they made a fire, then light they made it the house.

Igiō'lXam wā'yaq ya'Xi iq!u'lîpX: "Tān Lqa qamtgitqā'nîmX
She said to him his mother that youth: "What maybe you laughed

Xā'pîX?" "Qanā'qa itcî'cîkc qaniuqoā'nîmX. Nî'Xua,
in the evening?" "To no purpose my friend I laughed at him. Well,

tgā'lEmam tq!eyō'qtîkc." A'qa iqtugoā'lEmam tq!eyō'qtîkc;
fetch them the old people." Then they were fetched the old people;

tā'nEmckc tq!eyō'qtîkc iqtugoā'lEmam, tkā'lukc tq!eyō'qtîkc
the women old ones they were fetched, men the old ones

iqtugoā'lEmam. Kanauwē' ta-îtci tê'lXam iqtugoā'lEmam. PāL
they were fetched. All those people they were fetched. Full

igō'xoax ta'Xi tE'LaqL ya'Xi iq!u'lîpX ta-îtci tê'lXam.
became that their house that youth those people.

Itcō'lXam wā'yaq: "LE'LukT Lq!ā'pEnX, giLā'qa-îL Lq!ā'pEnX."
He said to her his mother: "Bring a mat, a large mat."

Lāq igE'Lūx wā'yaq Lt!ō'kti Lq!ā'pEnX. Itciō'lXam wī'yam:
Take out she did it his mother a good mat. He said to him his father:

"Nî'Xua, Lk!Emā'nanEmtck giLō'k!oa-its Lq!ā'pEnX tā'nki
"Well, look at the small mat what

iLE'lôxt." Itcixē'miak!ētē wī'yam ya'Xi iq!u'lîpX. Iō'La-it
is in it." He took off his blanket his father that youth. He stayed

kā'tcEk tqu'Lē. Igē'k·îm ya'Xi iq!u'lîpX: "Lā'xlax ayamcō'xoa,
middle house. He said that youth: "Deceive I shall do you,

LXuan ā'qanuwē," igē'k·îm. "Walō' Lgā'q!apEnX înLaxE'cgam."
perhaps it is true," he said. "The Hunger her mat I took it from her."

A'qa wāx iqE'tôx ta'Xi tE'q!ōtcō iā'qa-îL iq!ā'pEnXpa qē'q!ayaq
Then pour out they were done those bones a large mat on middle

house. They saw these bones. They were those of the sea-lion, seal, porpoise, sturgeon, beaver, raccoon, otter, elk, bear, and deer—bones of all kinds of animals. And there were shells of clams, cockles, large clams, racer clams, oysters, crabs, mussels, mud clams—shells of all kinds of sea food. Then an old man said: "O grandson! now we shall have food again. Just so it happened long ago, when we also suffered starvation. The Hunger's mat was taken away, and the people were able to procure food again. Everything was attained, when in olden times the people took the Hunger's mat from her." The bones were put into the mat and were poured into the water.

On the following day an elk hunter went inland. After a little while he came down to the water and said: "I have killed three elks." On the following morning a seal hunter went out. After a little while the flood tide came and he landed on the beach of the village. His

---

tqu'LĒ. A'qa iqtuk!umā'nanEmtck ta'Xi tE'q!ōtcō. Igē'pîx·L
house. Then they were looked at those bones. Sea-lion

iā'q!ōtcō, ā'lxayu ī'tcaq!ōtcō, akō'tckōtc ī'tcaq!ōtcō, inā'qōn
its bones, seal its bones, porpoise its bones, sturgeon

iā'q!ōtcō, iqoa-inē'nē iā'q!ōtcō, istak!uē'n iā'q!ōtcō, ē'nanaks
its bones, beaver its bones, raccoon its bones, otter

iā'q!ōtcō, imō'lak iā'q!ōtcō, iskē'ntXoa iā'q!ōtcō, emā'cEn
its bones, elk its bones, bear its bones, deer

iā'q!ōtcō. Ka'nauwē tā'nEmax tE'gaq!ōtcō. Ā'qamuwa
its bones. All things their bones. Large clams

ā'gaLt!aqul, apē'XLnaL ā'gaLt!aqul, iqoā'qunē ā'yaLt!aqul, iqona'
their shells, cockles their shells, cohoes (?) clams their shells, racer clams

ā'yaLt!aqul, iLō'XLōX ā'yaLt!aqul, LkaLXē'la ā'LaLt!aqul, itguē'matk
their shells, oysters their shells, crabs their shells, mussels

ā'yaLt!aqul. Ka'nauwē tmaLnē'qoxoēmax; ai'ē ā'gaLt!aqul. A'qa
their shells. All sea food; mud clams their shells. Then

iLE'k·ī'm LēXā't Lq!eyō'qt: "Ē4, ī'tcîqcîn, a'qa îlxLXE'lEmîtck.
he said one old man: "Eh, my grandson, then we shall eat.

K!oaLqē' ā'nqa wī't'ax aqā'txa Walō'. AqLaxā'tckam Lgā'q!apEnX
Just so long ago also she was done the Hunger. It was taken from her her mat

Walō'. A'qa nEXuitXE'lEmîtck tê'lXam. Ka'nauwē tān
the Hunger. Then they obtained food the people. All things

qaqitp!ē'yaLX. Tā'anēwatîkc qatkLExā'tcgam Lgā'q!apEnX Walō'."
were gathered. The people of olden times (the first ones) they took away from her her mat the Hunger."

Iqawē'kitkL ta'Xi tE'q!ōtcō. Wāx iqtō'xoam mā'LnîX Ltcu'qoapa.
They were put into the mat those bones. Poured they were seaward the water into.

Wāx igē'tcuktîX. Iō'ya LXE'leu ya'Xi iqtiā'XekLax,
Next day day came. He went inland that their hunter,

imō'lEkEmax giā'k!ēwula; as nō'L!îX iō'ya, igē'LXam. Igē'k·îm:
elks having for his game; and a little he had gone, he came to the water. He said:

"Lōn inio'tēna imō'lEkEmax." Wāx igē'tcuktîX. Iō'ya
"Three I killed them elks." Next day day came. He went

alxayō'max giā'k!ēwula. Nō'L!îX iLtuwē'tck!oam, igixē'gela-îX
seals having for his game, A little while it came the flood tide, he landed

canoe was full of seals. The gill nets were made ready. The people went to fish for sturgeon. After a little while the flood tide came and they went home. Their canoes were full of sturgeons. It got dark. Dogs were taken along and they caught raccoons. Two young men became tired out, so heavy was the load of raccoons. The women gathered cockles, large clams, and mussels. Then the people ate much. They had an abundance of everything they had gathered. They searched for bear dens, and two or three were killed in one day. The name of that town is Iqē'lgap!ē, where the mat of the Hunger was taken.

---

aʟā'maʟnapa. (seaward from them at.) Pāʟ (Full) iā'Xanim (his canoe) alxayō'max. (seals.) T!ayā't!a (Good) iqᴇ'tôx (they were made)
tk!anXa'tē. (the gill nets.) IguXuik!anXā'temam (They went to catch sturgeon in gill nets) tê'lXam. (the people.) Nō'ʟ!îX (A little)
iʟtuwē'tsk!oam, (it came the flood tide,) igoXoatk!oā'mam. (they came home.) Pā'ʟᴇma (Full) atā'xᴇnim (their canoes) ʟnā'qōn. (sturgeon.)
Igō'pōnᴇm. (It grew dark.) Iqᴇ'tukᴛ (They were carried) tk!ō'tk!ōtkc, (the dogs,) iqō'koya (they were taken) tʟatā'tukc. (raccoons.) Tā2ll (Tired)
igō'xoax (they became) amô'kctîkc (two) tq!ulîpXunā'yu (youths) itgᴇ'tuctx (they carried them) ta'Xi (those) tʟatā'tukc. (raccoons.)
Tᴇ'nᴇmckc (The women) tkʟup!ē'yaʟx (they gathered them) ʟpē'xtᴇnaʟx (cockles) k!a (and) ʟᴇ'qamuwa (large clams) k!a (and)
itguē'matk. (mussels.) A'qa (Then) igōXuiXᴇ'lᴇmtck (they ate) ta-îtci (those) tê'lXam. (people.) Ē'pʟ!i (Abundance)
iaxā'o-îx (became) ka'nauwē (all) tānki (things) qiqiup!ē'yaʟx. (what was gathered.) Iqtō'naxʟ (They were searched) tiā'qʟema (their dens)
iskîntXuā'max. (bears.) Mâkct (Two) aqiutē'nax (they were killed,) anā' (sometimes) ʟân (three) aqiutē'nax (they were killed) ēXt (one)
wē'koa. (day.) Kōpā' (There) Iqē'lgalp!ē (Iqē'lgalp!ē) iʟā'lXam (their town) iā'XaleuX (its name) qatcʟaxā'tcgam (he took it away from her)
ʟgā'q!apᴇnX (her mat) Walō'. (the Hunger.)

Winter All the Year Round (told 1894)

There were the people of a town. They were forbidden to make fun of certain things. When boys grew up, they were always taught: "Don't strike birds with sticks. It is forbidden." When they stepped on excrements, they said: "I stepped on feathers." It was forbidden to say: "I stepped on excrements."

Now, there was a bad boy. His mother tried to teach him all the time what to do and what not to do. One day he went inland and defecated. He did so with difficulty, and blood was on his excrements. Then he rolled them down the hill and said to them: "There goes the redhead." Then he took them up the hill and rolled them down again. Again he said: "There goes the redhead." He played with

---

Itsōmîqatc ʟgaxē'takuîX

Winter All the Year Round

ʟxēlā'etîX ʟa-îtci giʟā'lXam. Tgā'k;ēʟau qioqoā'nēmx tā'nki
There were those of one town. It was forbidden to them they laugh at anything

ya'Xi iʟā'lXampa. Manē'x qaʟō'mîtx ʟk;ā'skas, aqa ʟxacîlqʟē'lalᴇmx,
that their town in. When he was growing up a boy, then he was always taught,

nē2ct aqîʟkîlcē'mᴇx ē'mᴇqō ʟp;ᴇ'sp;ᴇs, iā'mkîX qaʟxkᵘʟē'tckwax.
not it is struck with it a stick a bird, else it would tell.

Manē'x aqigō'txuit iqē'xalē, aqaʟgē'mx: "Ipqu'lxē inigō'tXuit."
When a person stepped on excrements, he said: "Feathers I stepped on."

Tgā'k;ēʟau manîx qatgē'mx: "Iqē'xalē inigō'tXuit."
It was forbidden to them when they said: "Excrements I stepped on."

Aqa eXā't ik;ā'skas, tiā'tcxatᴇma yaXi ik;ā'skas. Kē'nuwa
Then one boy, his badness that boy. Try

qingē'kiq;ᴇnanᴇma-îtx ka'nauwē ʟkā'etax. Wā'yaq
he is taught always all days. His mother

qakingē'kiq;ᴇnanᴇma-îtx. Igō'n ē'ka-it. qayō'îx sā'xalîX yaXi
taught him always. One day, he went up that

ē'lXpa. Kō'pa qatslōtsā'tsax; qana-inq;ē'kᵘsa-itx. Aqa ʟqā'wulqt
land on. There he defecated; it came with difficulty. Then blood

aʟxᴇlō'xoax. Nau'i ʟqā'wulqt qaʟxᴇlō'xoax. Qatsiō'quîXtā'matsōX
was on it. At once blood was on it. He rolled them down

yaXi iā'qēxalē. Aqa itciō'lXam yaXi iā'qēxalē: "Ayuyayuyā'4
those his excrements. Then he said to them those his excrements: "There goes, goes

kuʟiā'p;atsēu." Aqa wi qatsiugoā'lᴇmamx. Aqa wi qatsiū'kᵘʟ
redhead." Then again he went to take them. Then again he carried them

sā'xalîX. Aqa wi qatsiō'quiXtā'matsōX. Wī qatciō'lXamx:
up. Then again he rolled them down. Again he said to them:

"Ayuyayuyā'4 kuʟiā'p;atsēu." Nîx·ᴇnᴇmō'tXᴇmx yaXi iā'qēxalē.
"There goes, goes redhead." He played with them those his excrements.

his excrements. Then one boy came to him and said: "What are you doing?" He replied: "I am playing with my excrements." "Oh, that is forbidden." "Don't tell, else I shall be scolded." Then the other boy said to him: "Oh, snow will fall and we shall die of hunger." "If you tell the people I shall kill you."

The next night snow began to fall. It fell for two days, and the houses were covered. Then it began to freeze. Now the boy told the people. He said: "I found that boy playing with his excrements; maybe he caused the cold." "Behold!" said an old man, "it is forbidden. All this is forbidden in this country." Then his father and mother were told: "Your child caused the cold. Behold! he played with his excrements, although it is forbidden. That boy found him rolling his excrements down the hill." Then the people became hungry. Then they said: "What do you think? Let us buy that boy from his parents. We will place him on the ice." Thus spoke the

---

Aqa qaLigō'qoamx LeXā't Lk!ā'skas. QaLgiolXā'mx: "Tā'nki
Then he met him one boy. He said to him: "What

mxē'lxalEm?" QatcLōlxā'mx: "Itcī'qēxalē nxēnEmō'tXEmx."
are you doing?" He said to him: "My excrements I am playing with."

QaLgiolXā'mx LaXi Lk!ā'skas: "Hē, tgā'k!ēLau." "Nîct
He said to him that boy: "Heh, it is forbidden." "Not

amxkLē'tcgoa. Aqanomē'la." QaLgiolXā'mx LaXi Lk!ā'skas: "Ā'Lqi
tell. I shall be scolded." He said to him that boy: "Later on

Ltga aLOLā'ita. AlxLā'ita walō'." "Manē'x amxkLē'tcgoa
snow will fall. We shall die of hunger." "If you tell them

ayamowā'qoa."
I shall kill you."

Agōn ā'pōl aqa Ltga qaLŌLā'itx. Mâkct Lkā'etax qaLOLā'itx
One night then snow fell. Two days fell

Ltga. Aqa Llap qatgē'x tqLē'max; qaLugoatgē'koxo-îtx. Aqa
snow. Then covered went the houses; they were covered up. Then

qatcîlbō'xo-îx ayā'xtaxîx. Ō, aqa qaLxkLē'tcgoax LaXi Lk!ā'skas.
cold came. Oh, then he told that boy.

QaLgē'mx kcī'ana: "Inigō'qoam iā'qēxalē ix·EnEmō'tXEmx.
He said the one referred to: "I found him his excrements he played with.

LXuan ia'Xka igitsō'mit itcī'yux." "Ō, Lqōct, ā'qanauwē,"
Perhaps he the cold he made it." "Oh, behold, indeed,"

iLE'kîm LE'Xat Lq!eyō'qt. "Tgā'k!ēLau. Ka'nauwē tgā'k!ēLau
said one old man. "It is forbidden. All is forbidden

ta'yax ēlX." Aqa iqcō'lXam yaXi wī'yam k!a wā'yaq:
this country." Then they two were told that his father and his mother:

"Imtā'xan igitsō'mit itcī'yux. Tgā'k!ēLau. Tā'tc!a tgā'k!ēLau;
"Your son the cold he made it. It is forbidden. But it is forbidden;

ta'tc!a inEmō'tXEmx iā'qēxalē. ILgiō'cgam LaXi LeXā't Lk!ā'skas.
but he played with his excrements. He found him that one boy.

ItsioquiXtā'matsL iā'qēxalē." Aqa wa'lō igE'tux ta-îtci tê'lXam.
He was rolling down his excrements." Then hunger acted on them those people.

Aqa igugoā'kîm: "Wu'ska, alxgiumElā'lEma yaXi ik!ā'skas.
Then they said: "Well, let us buy him that boy.

Qa'da mcā'XadakoaX? AlxgicxamElā'lEma yaXi ictā'xan.
How your mind? We will buy him from them that their son.

people: "Indeed we shall die of hunger if that snow does not disappear." Then they gathered their property and tried to buy the boy, but his parents did not give him away. It was October when the cold began. It got summer again and they began to die of hunger. Many old people died. Hunger killed them. The snow became as hard as stone. The sun tried to come out, but it did not melt the snow. One day the chief opened the door. The door opened high up near the beam of the house. He saw a bird carrying something red in his beak. He struck it with a stick and it let fall what it carried. Then he said to his wife: "Go and fetch what that bird let drop." His wife arose and went to take it. She looked at it. It was a strawberry. Then she said to her husband: "That is a strawberry. The strawberries must be ripe while it is freezing here." She gave her husband the strawberry. Then her husband felt badly about that boy. He said to his wife: "To-morrow I shall leave you. Perhaps

---

AqikLā'itEmita ikapa'." Igugoā'kîm ta-îtci tê'lXam: "Ō,
He shall be placed on ice." They said those people: "Oh,

ā'qanauwē. Walō' alXLā'ita, manîx nîct k¦ā aLxō'xoa gi
indeed. Hunger we die, if not nothing becomes that

Ltga." Aqa itgō'xoaqtck tgā'ktēmax. Kē'nuwa iqiō'mELa yaXi
snow." Then they gathered their property. Try he was bought that

ik¦ā'skas. Nîct iqē'yot. Tcā'maLîx· pEt aqa yaXi itcE'LElbō.
boy. Not he was given away. October really then that cold was on them.

Tatc¦a, wi tcā'koa-îX igē'xoxoē, aqa walō iLXE'La-it.
Behold, again summer it became, then hunger they died.

Lgā'pElatîke tq¦eyō'qtîke qaLō'mEqtx. Walō akLuwā'qoax. Ā'ka
Many old people died. Hunger killed them. Thus

LaXi Ltga Lqā'nake q¦E'lq¦El iLE'xôx. Kē'nuwa aqaLā'x
that snow stones hard it became. Try sun

naxō'xoax, nēct qaLuwī'ntsxax. Qā2xiLqanē'gua, aqa yaXi
it got, not it melted it. One day, then that

ē'tacq taXi tqu'Lē cā'xalîX yixē'pa, q¦oā'p iqē'paqL aqa
its door that house up here, near the beam then

a-ixElā'qLq¦iXix; aqa itcî'Lq¦ElkEl yaXi iLā'Xak¦Emana Lp¦E'sp¦Es,
it opened; then he saw it that their chief a bird,

tā'nki Lgī'yuqst Lpāl. ItcîLgE'ltcēm ē'mEqō. Igē'LxEluktcō
something it carried in its beak red. He hit it with a stick. It fell

yaXi iLgī'yuqct. Itcō'lXam ayā'kikala: "Igā'lEmam tā'nki
that what it carried in its beak. He said to her his wife: "Fetch it something

yaXi igē'Lxaluktcō LaXi Lp¦E'sp¦Es." Igō'tXuît ayā'kikala.
that it let fall that bird." She arose his wife.

Igiugoā'lEmam. Igiuk¦omā'nanEmtck, aqa amō'tē. Igiō'lXam
She went to fetch it. She looked at it, then a strawberry. She said to him

itcā'kikal: "Ā, amō'tē tawā'X. LXuan aqa Lōkst giL'amō'tē
her husband: "Ah, a strawberry this. Perhaps then ripe they having strawberries

gitcî'lxalbōt." Igā'ilōt itcā'kikal wuXi amō'tē. Ō, aqa nîct
we having cold." She gave it to him her husband that strawberry. Oh, then not

it¦ō'kti igē'x ē'yamXtc itcā'kikal yaXi ik¦ā'sk¦aspa. Itcō'lXam
good became his heart her husband that boy to. He said to her

ayā'kikal: "Ō'la aqa ayamteqElō'qLka. Lu'Xuan lE'xaimatîke
his wife: "To-morrow then I shall leave you. Perhaps we alone

it is freezing only here with us." Then in the morning he made himself ready. He put on his leggings. They were *that* long. Then he went there up [the mountains]. He went a long distance and came to a country. That country became visible and there was only a little snow. He went a little farther and came to another country. It was warm there. Then he thought: "Oh, it is freezing weather only with us." He came down to the river on the other side of Wā'k¡anasîsi. There the people were fishing with nets. They hauled the nets ashore and they were full of spring salmon. A person said: "Oh, our net is full of spring salmon." Then they gave a name to that person. "Oh, that Frost," they said to him. Then he was ashamed and went inland. He came to the river at SqE'pōs. There he found ripe strawberries. He took off his leggings and put the strawberries which he picked into them. Then he went home. In the evening he came home and said to his wife: "Oh, it is frost with us only. The Wā'k¡anasîsi are catching salmon." He said to his wife: "Thus they spoke to me.

---

gîtcElxElbō't." Aqa igē'tcuktē. Aqa igiXE'ltXuîtck. ItixE'lox
we having cold." Then it got day. Then he made himself ready. He put them on

tiā'sak¡aluks gipE'tEmax itā'Lqtax. Aqa iō'ya ē'wata, ē'wa
his leggings that long. Then he went there, there

ca'xalata. KElā'îX iō'ya. KElā'îX iō'ya, aqa ēlX itciō'cgam.
upward. Far he went. Far he went, then a country he found it.

Lā'xLax igē'xôx yaXi ēlX. Nō'L¡Emax LaXi Ltga. Iō'ya,
Visible it became that country. Little that snow. He went,

mank kElā'îX iō'ya. Aqa itciō'cgam ē'lX, L¡ō igē'xaxîx.
a little far he went. Then he found it a country, warm it was.

Itcqā'lit igē'xax. Ō, igiXLō'Xoa-it, nE'caimatîkc L¡
A warm day it was. Oh, he thought, only we behold!

gitcintcîlbō't. Iō'Lxam k¡anatē'tōL Wā'k¡anasîsi. Aqa
we are freezing. He came down at the other side of Wā'k¡anasîsi. Then

ōXuinauā'îtgē tê'lXam. Iqō'xoak¡a taXi tnauā'îtk, ac pāL
they fished with nets people. They hauled ashore that net, and full

taXi tgu'nat. ILE'kîm LēXā't LgoaLē'lX: "Ō, pāL igō'xoax
that salmon. He said one person: "Oh, full is

tElxa'naua-îtk." Iqē'yupqEna yaXi igoaLē'lX: "Q¡a, kcē'yana
our net." He was named that person: "Ah, the one referred to

tcLîlbō't," iqiō'lXam. Ō, aqa igixEmā'sa-it. Ayō'ptcga. Iō'ya
freezing," was said to him. Oh, then he was ashamed. He went up. He went

LxE'lēu ē'wa SqE'pōs. Kō'pa aqa itcLō'cgam LaXi L'amō'tē
down the river there SqE'pōs (below St Helens). There then he found them those strawberries

Lōkst. Lāqº itē'x Liā'sak¡aluks. Aqa itcauwē'kitk tcLup¡ē'yaLx
ripe. Off he did them his leggings. Then he put into them what he picked

LaXi L'amō'tē. Aqa igē'Xk¡oa. Xā'piX igîXk¡oā'mam.
those strawberries. Then he went home. In the evening he came home.

"Ō," itcō'lXam ayā'kikal. "Ō, lE'xaimatîkc tcîlxElbō't.
"Oh," he said to her his wife. "Oh, only we we are freezing.

Tgu'nat qtō'wula Wā'k¡anasîsi." Itcō'lXam ayā'kikal: "Ē'wa
Salmon they catch much the Wā'k¡anasîsi." He said to her his wife: "Thus

iqEnō'lXam. IqE'nōpqEna. IqEnō'lXam: 'Q¡a, tcElbō't kcē'yana.'
I was spoken to. I was named. I was spoken to: 'Ah, freezing the one referred to.'

They gave me a name. They called me Frost. Their nets were full. I brought those strawberries." Early the next morning he said to his wife: "Call all the people." Then that woman called all the people. She took a mat and poured out the strawberries. Her husband said: "It is frost with us only. It is summer. You see those strawberries. The Wā'k¡anasîsi are catching salmon and are laughing at us. It is frost with us only. Let us buy that boy." Then they tried again to buy that boy. They gave many dentalia to his father and to his mother. "If you don't sell your boy, you will be killed." Then they gave up that boy. He was carried out to the sea and placed on the ice. Then they heard him cry. At midnight he was dead. Rain began to fall and it rained for a long time. The ice and the snow began to melt. It was good weather. It was midsummer right away. Then the people moved. They went to the bay and caught spring salmon. They caught sturgeon and they ate. Then they dried the salmon and the sturgeon.

Pāʟ igō'xoax taXi tnauā'itk. ʟaXi ʟ'amō'tē înʟî'ʟam." Kawī'X
Full got that net. Those strawberries I brought them." Early

igē'tcuktîX. Aqa itcō'lXam ayā'kikal: "A'yaq tgā'lᴇmam
day came. Then he said to her his wife: "Quick! fetch them

ka'nauwē tê'lXam." Aqa iktugā'lᴇmam ka'nauwē tê'lXam wuXi
all people." Then she fetched them all people that

ayā'kikal. Aqa igᴇ'ʟgᴇlga ʟq¡ā'pᴇnX. Wax igᴇ'ʟôx ʟaXi
woman. Then she took it a mat. Pour out she did them those

ʟ'amō'tē. Aqa igē'kîm yaXi itcā'kikal: "Ō, lᴇ'xaimatîkc
strawberries. Then he said that her husband: "Oh, only we

tcîlxᴇlbō't. Aqa tcā'koa-îX igē'xaxîX. Amcgᴇ'ʟᴇkct gi
are freezing. Then summer it is. You see these

ʟ'amō'tē. Tgu'nat qtō'wula Wā'k¡anasîsi. Qᴇlxoguā'nîmx
strawberries. Salmon they catch much the Wā'k¡anasîsi. We are laughed at

lᴇ'xaimatîkc tcîlxᴇlbō't. Tcā'qa wī't'ax alxgiumᴇlā'lᴇma yaXi
we only are freezing. Come! again we will buy that

ik¡ā'skas." Aqa wit'ax iqiō'mᴇla yaXi ik¡ā'skas. ʟgā'2pᴇla
boy." Then again he was bought that boy. Many

tktē'max îqtcī'lōt wā'yaq k¡a wī'yam. "Ma'nîx nîct amtgiō'ta
dentalia were given to them his mother and his father. "If not you give him away

imtā'xan, aqa qamtōtē'na." Ā'qa îcgī'yōt ictā'xan. Aqa iqē'yukʟ
your son, then you will be killed." Then they gave him away their son. Then he was carried

mā'ʟnîX. Iqikʟā'ētamit ikapa'. Aqa iqᴇltcᴇ'mᴇlit igigᴇ'tcax.
seaward. He was placed on ice. Then he was heard he cried.

Qē'q'ayak wā'pōl aqa iō'maqt. Ā2qa îctō'qoîʟtē, îctō'qoîʟtē4;
Middle night then he died. Then it rained, it rained;

ē'yaʟqtîX ictō'qoîʟtē. Ā'qa iō'sa yaXi ikapa'. Aqa iʟō'sa
long it rained. Then it melted that ice. Then it melted

ʟaXi ʟtga. Ē't¡ōlX igī'xox; ʟqōct, nō'e qē'q¡ayak itcaguā'yam.
that snow. Fair weather it became; behold, at once middle it became summer.

Ā4qa igugwā'ʟayu ta-îtci tê'lXam. Itgī'ya ē'maʟîXpa tgu'nat
Then they moved those people. They went to the bay, salmon

itktōp¡ē'yaʟx; ʟnā'qōn iqʟōp¡ē'yaʟx. Aqa igoʟxuiʟxᴇ'lᴇmtck
they caught; sturgeon they caught. Then they ate

tê'lXam. Ā, aqa igō'Xuikᵘcᴇm; iqa'tōkcᴇm tgu'nat; iqa'ʟōkcᴇm
the people. Ah, then they dried fish; they dried them the salmon; they dried them

ʟnā'qōn.
the sturgeon.

The GiLā'unaLX Maiden who was Carried Away by the Thunderbird (told 1894)

The GiLā'unaLX used to go inland to hunt elks. In the fall of the year they used to go to Saddle mountain. When elks were seen on the prairie of Saddle mountain, they were all killed. There is a narrow trail leading upward. A man who had a strong supernatural helper was placed near the trail. No menstruating woman was allowed to go on that trail. It was forbidden. There on that prairie they gathered onion roots and rush roots. When elks were driven along that small trail, then that person took only a stick. He moved it as though he were going to hit the elk, and it jumped down the precipice at once. Sometimes sixty were killed in this way. When there were few people, then thirty were killed when they were driven down. They were thrown down upon those rocks and their bones were broken. There

---

QatgE'ptckax GiLā'unaLX imō'lEkumax qaLikElō'îX. Kōpā' a'qa
They went inland the GiLā'unaLX, elks they hunted. There then

Lî'taLxîX nixō'xoaxîx Suwalalā'xôstpa. Ma'nîx aqiusgā'mx
August it became Saddle mountain on. When they are found

imō'lEkumax ya'Xi tEmqā'emaXpa Suwalalā'xôst kopā't Liā'pEla
elks that prairie on Saddle mountain just as many

kopā't aqiotē'nax. Iō'k!ua-îts ya'Xi ē'Xatk ya'Xi
as they are killed. Small that road that

iqayoqowî'lXtxpa. Qiā'x wuk; iLā'yuLEmax, tcXua kōpā'
where they go up on. If real his supernatural helper, then there

qayō'tXuîtx ya'Xi ē'Xatkpa. Nē2ct qaLō'îx LqLā'xît ya'Xi
he stands that road on. Not she goes a menstruating woman that

ē'Xatkpa. Tgā'k!iLau. Kōpā' ta'Xi tEmqā'ema cā'xalîX, kōpā'
road on. It is forbidden. Then that prairie on top, there

aqtup!iā'Lxa tkē'qcElEma k!a tqE'pqEp. Manē'x aqiXuwā'x
they are gathered roots (sp.?) and rush roots (?). When they are driven

imō'lEkumax ya'Xi iō'k!ua-îts ē'Xatkpa, a'qa iā'ema ē'mqō
elks that small road on, then only a stick

qaLgigElgā'x La'Xi LgoaLē'lX. QaLgigEntck!oā'mitx ya'Xi ē'mqō
he holds it that person. He stretches it out that stick

ya'Xi imō'lak. Nau'i qatsupEnā'x ē'wa gē'gualîX. Ē'XtEmaxîX
that elk. At once it jumps thus down. Sometimes

tEXEmLāt aqiutē'nax; ma'nîx anō'L!katîkc tê'lXam, a'qa LōnLāL
sixty they are killed; when few only people, then thirty

aqiutē'nax. AqiXuwā'x gē'gualîXpa. AqiukuitXuimē'tatcōX
they are killed. They are driven down to. They are thrown down

ta'Xi tqE'nakcpa. Ac qanā'qa iqēXuwā'x, aqa nuXualā'x·itx
those stones on. And only they are driven, then they are broken

is a trail which the people went down. Then these elks were dried down below.

Now there was a girl who was just mature. That year the GiLā'unaLX went inland to hunt elks. The elks were driven down and forty were killed. Then that person turned aside, and the elks passed going up. The people went down to where the elks were and dried them. That girl was told not to go along to the prairie, where the roots were being gathered. It was forbidden. No girl who had just reached maturity went there. There are two caves in the rock, which are the town of the Thunderbird. There are bones of all kinds of animals. There are bones of whales, of sea-lions, and of all kinds of sea animals. Indeed, the women came to gather roots. That girl did not accompany them. The GiLā'unaLX stayed there a long time. One day a woman said to the girl: "We are going to dig roots. I went

---

tē'yaqǀōtcō. Akā'x itā'eXatk ta-îtci tê'lXam ya'Xi qatukuitcō'Xpa,
their bones. There is their road those people there where they go down on,
kōpa' qatgix·cā'mitx gē'gualîx·pa ya'Xi imō'lEkumax.
there they dry them below at those elks.
Ā'qa nakǀelā'wulXEmx wu'Xi aēXā't ahā'tǀau. Igō'n ēXt iqē'taq
Then she became mature that one maiden. Another one year
wī't'ax qatgE'ptcgax GiLā'unaLX. Imō'lak qaLigElō'îx. A'qa
again they went inland the GiLā'unaLX. Elk they hunted. Then
wī't'ax aqiXuwā'x ya'Xi imō'lEkumax. AqiukuitXuimē'tatcōX.
again they were driven those elks. They were thrown down.
LakLā'L aqiutē'nax, a'qa Lāq aLxō'xoax La'Xi LgoaLē'lX, a'qa
Forty were killed, then turn he did that person, then
qayō'ptckax ya'Xi imō'lEkumax. Qatqqctcō'x gē'gualîX ta-îtci
they went up those elks. They went down below those
tê'lXam ya'Xi nîXLā'etamX ya'Xi imō'lEkumax. Kōpā'
people there they lay those elks. There
qaqiukcE'mx ya'Xi imō'lEkumax. A'qa aqolXā'mx wu'Xi ahā'tǀau:
they dried them those elks. Then she was told that virgin:
"Nēct amxEltō'ma ya'Xi tEmqā'emaXpa ya'Xi tkē'qcElEma
"Not go in company that prairie to that roots (sp.?)
aqtupǀiā'LxaētxPa. Tgā'kǀiLau. Nîct qantsî'x Lqǀēlā'wulX aLō'îx
where they are gathered on. It is forbidden. Not even a girl who menstruates for the first time she goes
kōpa'. Ikēnuwakcō'ma iā'lXam." Lxoa'p ōguakē'x ta'Xi tqE'nakc.
there. The Thunderbird his town." Holes there are those rocks.
Ka'nauwē tā'nki tē'yaqǀōtcō kōpā'. Ē'kǀoalē tē'yaqǀōtcō kōpa'
All things their bones there. Whale its bones there
ō'xoaxt. Mâ'kctîX Lxoā'p ta'Xi tqE'nakc. Igē'pîXL tē'yaqǀōtcō
are. Twice holes those rocks. Sea-lion its bones
kōpa' ō'xoaxt. Kā'nauwē tā'nki mā'LnîX tgatE'qǀōtcō. Ā'qanuwē
there are. All things seaward their bones. Indeed
qatgē'x ta-îtci tE'nEmckc. Qatktupǀiā'Lqamx tkē'qcîlEma. Nāct
they went those women. They went to gather them roots (sp.?). Not
naxEltō'mx wu'Xi aqǀelā'wulX. Lē'lē kōpa' noxoēlā'îtx
she went in company that girl menstruating for the first time. Long there they were
GiLā'unaLX. QāxLkanē'gua qaLgulxā'mx LēXā't Lhā'tǀau: "Ō,
the GiLā'unaLX. One day they said to her that maiden: "Oh,
alxō'ya tkē'qcîlEma. AnqLā'x·it nai'ka, goā'nEsum qanō'îX.
we will go roots (sp.?). I menstruated I, always I went.

up there, although I was menstruating, and nothing happened to me. Perhaps they deceive you only." Then the girl said: "Next time I will go along when you go."

Then they went again and the girl went along. They gathered roots. The women went and gathered roots. When the women went digging roots, the girl had her head covered with long dentalia. Dentalia were tied to her body. Now they lost her. One woman said: "Where is that girl who accompanied us?" They searched for the girl. "Maybe she went to the town of the Thunderbird." A mist covered the prairie. They went to search for the girl near the rocks. They found her near the rocks. All kinds of sea birds were flying around the rocks. At a little distance the noise of the flying birds was heard. They saw that girl and told her: "Come! we will go home." But she did not look. They tried to take her hands and

---

Năct qā qanxō'xoax. ʟXuan qanā'qa lā'xlax qᴇ'muxt." Igā'k·îm
Not anyhow I was. Perhaps to no purpose deceived you are done." She said

wu'Xi aq!elā'wulX: "Wī't'ax amcō'ya, a'qa anxᴇltō'ma."
that girl menstruating for the first time: "Again you will go, then I shall go in company."

A'qa wī't'ax itgī'ya. A'qa igaxᴇ'ltōm wu'Xi ahā't!au.
Then again they went. Then she went in company that maiden.

Tkē'qcîlᴇma itō'guiga. A'qa itgī'ya ta-îtci tᴇ'nᴇmckc, a'qa
Roots (sp.?) they took them. Then they went those women, then

itktup!ē'yaʟx tkē'qcîlᴇma. Kā ōxuik!ē'wula ta-îtci tᴇ'nᴇmckc,
they gathered them roots (sp.?). When they gathered roots those women,

ka'nauwē tgā'ktēma wu'Xi ahā't!au ʟgā'q!aqctaq, ka'nauwē iʟînʟē't
all her ornaments that maiden her head, all they put on her hair

iqawik!ē'ʟē. Ē'tcaʟq ka'nauwē k!au'k!au tā'lôXt ktē'max. A'qa
long dentalia. Her body all tied were to it ornaments. Then

iʟgonā'xʟatck wu'Xi ahā't!au. Iʟᴇ'k·îm ʟēXā't ʟqagē'lak:
they lost her that maiden. She said one woman:

"Qā'xpa gilxā'ctewal tau ahā't!au?" A'qa iʟgō'naxʟ wu'Xi
"Where our companion that maiden?" Then they searched for her that

ahā't!au. "ʟXuan igō'ya ya'Xi ikᴇnuwakcō'ma iā'lXampa."
maiden. "Perhaps she went that Thunderbird his town to."

A'qa iga-ikxā'ʟaqo-îx ta'Xi tᴇmqā'emaXpa. A'qa iʟgonā'xʟam
Then it became foggy that prairie on. Then they went to search for her

wu'Xi ahā't!au ta'Xi tqᴇ'nakcpa. Q!oā'pîX ta'Xi tqᴇ'nakc, a'qa
that maiden those rocks at. Near those rocks, then

iqō'cgam ō'Xtgoapa. Tixᴇ'lak^{u}t ya'Xi iqᴇ'nakc kanauwē'
she was found where she was at. They flew around them those rocks all

mā'ʟnîX qa tp!ᴇcp!ᴇ'cukc. ʟXuan qā'xpa kᴇlā'îX, iqawitcᴇ'mᴇlit
seaward where birds. Perhaps where far, it was heard

ā'taXulam: tᴇmm wu'Xi ā'taXulam. A'qa iktō'qumit wu'Xi
their noise: tᴇmm that their noise. Then they saw her that

aq!elā'wulX. Iqō'lXam: "Mᴇ'tē alXk!oā'ya." Nēct igā'kikct.
girl menstruating for the first time. She was told: "Come, we will go home." Not she looked.

Kē'nuwa iqō'guiga tᴇ'gaxō. Kē'nuwa iqa'xk!a, nēct
Try they were taken her arms. Try she was pulled, not

to pull her, but she did not move. Her face was changed. Then her companions gave it up and left her. They told their companions: "Oh, that girl became crazy. She became a monster. We are all weak of fright." Then one old woman said: "Why did you take that girl along? It is forbidden. No girl who is just mature goes there." Then the people cried. The next morning they went to look for her, but they did not find her. Feathers of sea birds were lying there, *that* high. When it becomes foggy, she is heard singing shaman's songs in the rocks. Thus she did: When they came to the place where she was, she sang shaman's songs. Then the people gave up the search and went home. The chief of the GiLā'unaLX said: "Let us go home," and the GiLā'unaLX went home. Therefore it is forbidden to take girls who are just mature up Saddle mountain, because that girl was taken away. The Thunderbird took her.

---

igaxElā'lalEmtck, aqa sxElō'-ita sgā'xôst sgē'xa. Tē'menua
she moved, then different her face became. Give up

igō'xoax giLā'cgewal, a'qa iqagE'ltaqL. Igōxoagu'Lītck giLā'ckēwal:
they did her companions, then she was left. They told her companions:

"Ā, k!oalalā'k igā'xôx tau aq!elā'wulX. Iqcxē'Lau ā'koa itcō'xoa.
"Ah, crazy she became that girl menstruating for the first time. A monster thus he made her.

Ka'nauwē nE'saika tE'ltEl intcî'xôx." ILE'k·îm LēXā't Lq!eyō'qt:
All we weak (of fear) we became." He said one old person:

"Qā'tcqī mcî'kukt wu'Xi aq!elā'wulX? Tgā'k!iLau. Nîct qantsî'x
"Why you carried her that girl menstruating for the first time? It is forbidden. Never

Lq!elā'wulX qaLō'yîX kōpa'." Ā, aqa oxoē'nîmtck ta-îtci
a girl menstruating for the first time goes there." Ah, then they cried those

tê'lXam. Igē'tcuktîX, kē'nuwa iqō'kctam. K!Em nîcqē' iqō'cgam.
people. Day came, try they went to see her. Nothing not at all she was found.

Gipē't ā'kaLqt wu'Xi ā'kEmc tp!Ecp!E'cukc ā'taXEmc gi mā'LnîX
That high those feathers birds their feathers these seaward

qa tp!Ecp!E'cukc. Aqa manē'x na-ikxaLā'koaxîX aqaltcî'mElitEmx
where birds. Then when it grows foggy she is heard

ta'Xi tqE'nakcpa. qaLaxEnLā'mita-îtx. K!oaLqē' igā'xôx ya'Xi
that rock in. she begins to sing a conjurer's song. Thus she did that

iqō'cgam ōXtpa LaxEnLā'mit. Tē'menua igō'xox ta-îtci tê'lXam
she was found where she was at she sang a conjurer's song. Give up they did those people

kē'nuwa itgōnā'xLam. A'qa wi igō'Xoak!oa. Igē'k·îm
try they went to search for her. Then again they went home. He said

iLā'Xak!Emana GiLā'unaLX: "A'yaq, alxk!uā'ya." A'qa iLE'Xk!oa
their chief the GiLā'unaLX: "Quick, let us go home." Then they went home

GiLā'unaLX. Tā'ntxo tgā'k!iLau Lq!elā'wulX aqLō'kLx
the GiLā'unaLX. Therefore it is forbidden a girl menstruating for the first time she is carried

Suwalalā'xost, qē'wa wu'Xi aq!ēlā'wulXt aqā'gitga kōpa'.
Saddle mountain, because that girl menstruating for the first time she was taken by a spirit there.

IkEnuwakcō'ma qatcā'gitga.
The Thunderbird he took her.

The Man who was Transformed into a Snake (told 1894)

The people moved. Now a man and his wife were left behind. He was a canoe builder. He used to build canoes all the year round. Then his wife gathered fern roots. Now his wife went to dig roots, but they were all bad. They stayed there a long time. Then she went digging again. Now she found many good fern roots. She took them and went home. She reached home. In the evening her husband came home. Then she said to him: "I found good fern roots." She roasted them and gave them to her husband to eat. Her husband said: "These fern roots are good. Gather many; we will take them along when we move. We will move after I have finished my canoe. Gather roots every day." He rose early and went to work on his canoe. His wife rose and went to gather roots. She gathered fern roots—some small ones and some large ones. She

---

Nukuaʟā'yux ta-îtci tê'lXam. Kōpa' aqcgᴇlō'kʟqax ayā'kikal
They moved those people. There they two were left his wife

ya'Xi ēXā't igoaʟē'lX akᴇ'nim iā'xotckǀēna. Ka'nauwē ʟkā'etax
that one person canoes he knew how to build them. All days

nigō'qtcqa-itx. A'qa akǀē'cana agopǀiā'ʟxa-îtx wu'Xi ayā'kikal.
he made canoes. Then fern roots she gathered them that his wife.

Ēwā' kē'nuwa ʟᴇ'kʟᴇk agiō'xoaxîX. Ā'ema itcā'mᴇla wu'Xi
There try dig she always did. Only their badness those

akǀē'cana. Iō'ʟqtîX qacxēlā'îtx kōpa'. A'qa wi nō'îx, aqa wi
fern roots. Long they two stayed there. Then again she went, then again

ʟᴇ'kʟᴇk agiō'xoaxîX. A'qa agucgā'mx atǀō'kti wu'Xi akǀē'cana.
dig she always did. Then she found them good those fern roots.

ʟgā'pᴇla agupǀiā'ʟxax, a'qa naxkǀoa'x. Naxkǀoā'mam tᴇ'ctaqʟ.
Many she gathered them, then she went home. She came home their two selves' house.

Tsō'yustîX nîXkǀoā'mam ya'Xi itcā'kikal. IgiolXā'mx a'qa:
At dark he came home that her husband. She said to him then:

"Inō'cgam akǀē'cana, atǀō'kti akǀē'cana." A'qa aguckǀu'ʟx wu'Xi
"I found them fern roots, good fern roots." Then she roasted them those

akǀē'cana. Aga-îlqoē'mx itcā'kikal. Nigē'mx itcā'kikal: "Ō,
fern roots. She gave him to eat her husband. He said her husband: "Oh,

atǀō'kti gi akǀē'cana. ʟgā'pᴇla amopiā'ʟxa ā'ʟqē. Atxgō'kᵘla
good these fern roots. Many gather them later on. We shall carry them

ma'nîx atxkʟā'yuwa. Ma'nîx anʟigō'ʟqa ya'Xi itcî'Xanim,
when we shall move. When I finish it that my canoe,

a'qa atxkʟā'yuwa. Ka'nauwē ʟkā'etax amopǀiā'ʟxa gi akǀē'cana."
then we will move. All days gather them these fern roots."

Kawī'X igixᴇ'latck. Igigō'qckam, ikᴇ'nim itciō'xoam. Igaxᴇ'latck
Early he arose. He went to work, the canoe he made it. She arose

ayā'kikal. Igō'ya, igagᴇ'loya akǀē'cana. Igupǀē'yaʟx akǀē'cana.
his wife. She went, she went to gather fern roots. She gathered them fern roots.

gathered two bundles, then she went home. Then she made a roasting frame and dried the fern roots. In the evening her husband came home. Then she roasted the roots and gave them to him to eat. Her husband said: "Oh, those fern roots are good. Gather many of them. We shall give them to the people when we move." Then she gathered fern roots every day, and one side of the house was full of them. They were tied in bundles, and the roasting frames were full of them. Then she gathered large fern roots. She dug large ones out of the ground. In the evening her husband came home. She told him: "Ah, I gathered large fern roots." He said to her: "Go again to-morrow. Soon I shall have finished that canoe. Maybe that I shall have finished that canoe at which I am working in four days' time." The man rose early and went to work on the canoe. The woman went afterward to gather fern roots. Now the house was full

---

Iā'newatîX ksE'mmax wu'Xi ak¦ē'cana. A'qa qawa itcā'qaēLax.
First small those fern roots. Then part large.

Mā'kctîX k¦au nakē'x igup¦ē'yaLX wu'Xi aqagē'lak. A'qa
Twice tied they were what she had gathered that woman. Then

igā'Xk¦oa. A'qa sts¦ē'lqaL igE'cux. Kōpa' igaxcā'mit wu'Xi
she went home. Then a roasting frame she made it. There she dried them those

agā'k¦ēcana. Tsō'yustîX igîXk¦oā'mam itcā'kikala. A'qa wi
her fern roots. At dark he came home her husband. Then again

igō'ck¦uL wu'Xi ak¦ē'cana. Igayî'lqo-îm itcā'kikala. Itcō'lXam
she roasted them those fern roots. She gave him to eat her husband. He said to her

itcā'kikala: "Ō, at¦ō'kti ak¦ē'cana. Lgā'pEla amōp¦iā'Lxa
her husband: "Oh, good fern roots. Many gather them

gi ak¦ē'cana. Ā'Lqē atxgawiqoē'mniLa tê'lXam, ma'nîx
these fern roots. Later on we two will give them to eat the people, when

atxkLā'yuwama." A'qa ka'nauwē Lkā'etax igōp¦ē'yaLx wu'Xi
we arrive after moving." Then all days she gathered them those

ak¦ē'cana. PāL igō'xoax ēwa tE'nat tE'ctaqL. K¦au, k¦au, k¦au,
fern roots. Full became there one side their house. Tied, tied, tied,

k¦au nakē'X wu'Xi ak¦ē'cana. PāL ctā'Xi sts¦ē'lqaLpa. Ā4, a'qa
tied were those fern roots. Full that roasting frame on. Ah, then

itcā'qa-iLax igō'cgam wu'Xi ak¦ē'cana. Iā'qa-iLîX aqa LE'kLEk
large she found them those fern roots. Large then dig

igī'yux ya'Xi ēlX. IgaXk¦oā'mam. Xā'pîX igîXk¦oā'mam
she did it that ground. She came home. In the evening he came home

itcā'kikala. Igaxa-ilgu'Lîtck itcā'kikala: "Â, a'qa itcā'qa-iLax
her husband. She told him her husband: "Ah, now large

gi ak¦ē'cana nE'wula." "Ō'la wi amō'ya," itcō'lXam. "A'qa
these fern roots I worked at them." "To-morrow again go," he said to her. "Then

nō'L¦katîX a'qa anLigō'Lqa ya'Xi ikE'nim. Lxuan lakt Lkā'etax
a little while only then I shall finish it that canoe. Perhaps four days

a'qa anLigō'Lqa ya'Xi iqiniōxō'l ikE'nim." Kawī'X igixE'latck
then I shall finish it that what I am working at the canoe." Early he arose

ya'Xi ē'kala, igigō'qckam. Kē'qEmtqîX igō'ya aqagē'lak
that man, he went to work. Afterward she went the woman

ak¦ē'cana igagE'loē, a'qa pā4L ta'Xi tE'ctaqL wu'Xi ak¦ē'cana.
fern roots she went to gather them, then full that their two selves' house those fern roots.

of them. She came home in the evening, and her husband came home when it was dark. She said to her husband: "Oh, the fern roots are large." He said to her: "Go tomorrow and gather many." The man went early; the woman went afterward. She gathered fern roots. Now she found a large root. She took that one. It was *that* large [putting thumbs and forefingers of the two hands together], and, behold, it had branches under ground. She worked at it. Then she cut it and thought: "I will show this to my husband. I will take it home. Maybe I am working at something supernatural. It is too large for a fern root." Then she went home. She carried this large fern root. She was going to show it to her husband. Now she came home and dried her fern roots. She placed that large one at the side of the house. In the evening her husband came home and said to her: "We will move the day after to-morrow. My canoe is nearly finished." She said: "I am frightened; I found an old fern root. I brought it to show it to you. Maybe it is something supernatural and

---

IgaXk!oā'mam tsō'yustîX. IgîXk!oā'mam itcā'kikal Xā'pîX.
She came home at dark. He came home her husband in the evening.

Igiō'lXam itcā'kikala: "Ō, a'qa itcā'qa-iʟax gi ak!ē'cana."
She said to him her husband: "Oh, now large these fern roots."

Itcō'lXam: "Ō'la wi amō'ya. ʟgā'pᴇla amup!iā'ʟxa." Kawī'X
He said to her: "To-morrow again go. Many gather them." Early

iō'ya itcā'kikal. Kē'qᴇmtcîX alā'xtax igō'ya aqagē'lak.
he went her husband. Afterwards last she went the woman.

Igup!ē'yaʟx wu'Xi ak!ē'cana. Ō, itcā'qa-iʟax wu'Xi ak!ē'cana.
She gathered them those fern roots. Oh, large those fern roots.

A'qa ikcō'cgam cta'Xi ctēXt. Ä'wi ctā'qa-iʟ. Qōct, ā'Xka
Then she found it that one. That large. Behold, that

ctā'ʟpukc cta'Xi gictā'qa-iʟ ck!ē'cana wu'Xi gō'ᴇla wu'Xi
its branching roots that large fern root that she worked at them those

ak!ē'cana. A'qa ʟq!up igᴇ'côx cta'Xi gictā'qa-iʟ ck!ē'cana.
fern roots. Then cut she did it that large fern root.

IgaxʟŌ'Xoa-it: "Itcî'kikal ancîxēnemā'ya. Ancō'kᵘla, ʟXuan
She thought: "My husband I shall show it to him. I shall carry it, perhaps

iqcxē'ʟau ta'yax nē'wula txāl itcā'qa-iʟax gi ak!ē'cana." A'qa
a monster that I worked at too large these fern roots." Then

igā'Xk!oa. Igᴇ'cukᴛ cta'Xi gictā'qa-iʟ ck!ē'cana. Akcîxnēmā'ya
she went home. She carried it that large fern root. She was going to show it to

itcā'kikal. IgaXk!oā'mam. IgaXcā'mit agā'k!ēcana. ʟxē'leuX
her husband. She came home. She dried them her fern roots. At side of house

ikcxē'ma cta'Xi gictā'qa-iʟ ck!ē'cana. Xā'pîX igiXk!oā'mam
she threw it that large fern root. In the evening he came home

itcā'kikal. Itcō'lXam: "Iawē'k a'qa atxkʟā'yuwa. A'qa
her husband. He said to her: "The day after to-morrow then we shall move. Then

q!oā'p anʟigō'ʟqa ya'Xi ikᴇ'nim." "Iqanoq!oē'xaēmaʟx,"
nearly I finished it that canoe." "I am scared,"

igiō'lXam. "Incō'cgam ck!ē'cana, ctā'q!eyuqt ck!ē'cana cta'Xi
she said to him. "I found it a fern root, its old age a fern root that

camxatnēmā'mam. ʟXuan tānki iqcxē'ʟau nîcqē' ck!ē'cana.
I brought it to show it to you. Perhaps something monstrous, not at all a fern root.

not at all a fern root. I never saw any of that size." Then her husband said to her: "You went to gather roots and are afraid of a fern root. How can that food be anything supernatural? Quick! roast it. I will eat it." Then she showed him that fern root and roasted it for her husband. When it was done, it was swollen. Then her husband ate it. He said to her: "Come, I will give you to eat. That fern root is good." But she replied: "No, eat it alone, I am afraid." He laughed at his wife and said: "You are afraid of food. You eat those small fern roots. When you eat those small fern roots, you are not at all afraid of them." Then night came. They lay down to sleep. They slept feet to feet. When it was nearly daylight the woman awoke. Then the house was warm. The woman felt hot. Now there was a noise of something hissing in the house. She tried to push her husband with her feet, but she did not find him at her feet. Then she lighted the fire. It began to burn. Behold, the house was full of snakes, and part of them were knotted together and rolled about. Part

---

Nîct qantsî'x qancqElkE'lx ck¡ē'cana kopE't ictā'qa-iL." Itcō'lXam
Never I saw it a fern root as large." He said to her

ayā'kikal: "Iā'mkîX qamxulk¡ē'wulalEmx, k¡wac mxā'cxôx
his wife: "Else you gather roots, afraid you are

ck¡ē'cana. Qantcî'x Lqa pō iqcxē'Lau ya'Xi iLxE'lem. A'yaq
a fern root. When maybe if a monster that food. Quick

cî'ck¡uL, acînxElEmō'xuma." A'qa ikcixE'nēma cta'Xi ck¡ē'cana.
roast it, I will eat it." Then she showed it to him that fern root.

A'qa ikcōck¡uL ikcē'lôx itcā'kikal cta'Xi ck¡ē'sana. Ictō'kst, a'qa
Then she roasted it, she did it for him her husband that fern root. It was done, then

ictutā'wulX cta'Xi ck¡ē'cana. A'qa icixE'lEmux ya'Xi itcā'kikal.
it swelled that fern root. Then he ate it that her husband.

Itcō'lXam ayā'kikal: "Tcu'xoa yamElqoē'ma. Ō, ct¡ō'kti gi
He said to her his wife: "Well I will give you to eat. Oh, good this

ck¡ē'cana." Igiō'lXam: "Ma'ēma cEmxE'lEmuX. K¡wac
fern root." She said to him: "You only eat. Afraid

nxā'cxôx." Itcuqoā'nîmtck wu'Xi ayā'kikal, itcō'lXam: "K¡wac
I am of it." He laughed at her that his wife, he said to her: "Afraid

mxE'xôx iLxE'lEm, k¡a wu'Xi ksE'max ak¡ē'cana amxelā'x.
you are of it food, and those small fern roots you eat.

Nîcqē' k¡wac mxā'xôx." Ā'2qa igō'ponEm. IckLqā'yuXuit.
Not at all afraid you are of them." Then it grew dark. They two lay down.

Cq¡EnEmō'qtcqix·it. Q¡oā'p ē'k^{u}tElîL, a'qa igaXE'qo-îtq wu'Xi
They lay feet to feet. Near morning star, then she awoke that

aqagē'lak. A'qa L¡o4 ta'Xi tE'ctaqL, ō'tcqa-it wu'Xi aqagē'lak.
woman. Then warm that their two selves' house, she felt warm that woman.

Tc¡Ec4 tā'nki ixElā't ta'Xi tE'ctaqLpa. Kē'nuwa igigE'Ltq
Hissing something moved that their two selves' house in. Try she kicked him

itcā'kikal. K¡ā nîct igiō'cgam LE'gapcpa. Wax igō'xoa actā'tōL.
her husband. Nothing not she found him her feet at. Light she did it their two selves' fire.

Wax igā'xôx wu'Xi ā'tōL. Ō4, Lqōct, tc¡iā'ukc pāL ta'Xi
Light she did it that fire. Oh, behold, snakes full that

tE'ctaqL. Kā k¡au noxoā'xa-îtx qatqxu'ta-îtx; qā'wa a'qa nîct
their two selves' house. When tied they were they rolled; part then not

were not knotted together. Then she lighted a torch and saw a large snake which had just reached the door. Its face was the size of the moon. When it became daylight the large snake went out and all the small ones followed. Then the woman followed the large snake. It went into the woods to the place where she had dug fern roots. Then the large snake went into the ground and all the small snakes went in also. The woman went down to the water, and she cried going. Her husband had become a snake.

Therefore the Klatsop do not gather large fern roots. They gather only small ones. When a large one is found, they do not take it.

Then the woman went to her relatives. She told them: "My husband became a snake. He ate a large fern root. If you do not believe me, go with me. I will show you the place where he went into the ground." The people said: "Let us go and see." On the following day the people went, following the woman. She showed them where

---

k¡au'k¡au. Wax igᴇ'ʟux ʟq¡axō'cgan. A'qa icī'qēpa iō'yamt
tied. Light she did it a torch. Then the door at it arrived

ya'Xi giā'qa-iʟ itc¡ī'yau. ʟXuan ʟa ʟkʟmenā'kc ciā'xôst
that large snake. Perhaps like the moon its face

ictā'qa-iʟax. Nī'ktcō'ktxīX, a'qa iupā'x ya'Xi giā'qa-iʟ itc¡ī'yau.
large. Day came, then it went out that large snake.

A'qa kē'qamtqīX qatgiwā'x ta'Xi ksᴇ'max tc¡iā'ukc. A'qa
Then afterward they followed those small snakes. Then

agiwā'x ya'Xi igiā'qa-iʟ itc¡ī'yau wu'Xi aqagē'lak. Kōpā'
she followed it that large snake that woman. There

qayō'īx ʟXᴇ'leu ya'Xi gō'lapa ak¡ē'cana. Kōpā' qayō'īx ya'Xi
it went inland that where she worked at fern roots. There it went that

giā'qa-iʟ itc¡ī'yau. Nilō'pqaxīX ēlX, qatilō'pqaxīX ka'nauwē
large snake. It entered the ground, they entered all

ta'Xi ksᴇ'max tc¡iā'ukc. A'qa nō'ʟxax wu'Xi aqagē'lak. Ō'qulqt
those small snakes. Then she went down to the water that woman. She cried

nō'ʟxax. Itc¡ī'yau nīxō'xoax itcā'kikal.
she went down to the water. A snake he became her husband.

Tā'ntxo nīct gīctā'qa-iʟ ck¡ē'cana aqcup¡iā'ʟxax Tiā'k¡ēlakē.
Therefore not a large fern root is gathered Klatsop.

Ā'cma ksᴇ'max ak¡ē'cana aqōp¡iā'ʟxax. Manī'x gīctā'qa-iʟ
Only small fern roots are gathered. When a large one

aqcucgā'mx, a'qa nāct aqcup¡iā'ʟxax ck¡ē'cana.
it is found, then not it is gathered a fern root.

A'qa nō'īx wu'Xi aqagē'lak tgā'cuXtīkcpa. Naxkᵘʟē'tcgoax:
Then she went that woman her relatives to. She told them:

"Itc¡ī'yau igē'xôx itcī'kikal. Ck¡ē'cana icixᴇ'ʟᴇmux, ictā'qa-iʟ
"A snake he became my husband. A fern root he ate it, a large

ck¡ē'cana. Ma'nīx amcgᴇngē'q¡anēma, a'qa alxō'ya. Ayamcxᴇnemā'ya
fern root. When you disbelieve me, then we will go. I shall show you

qā'xpa ya'Xi ēlX igē'lōpqīX." "Alxgiō'ketama," igugoā'k·īm
where that ground he entered it." "We will go and see," they said

tē'lXam. Igē'tcuktīX. A'qa itgī'ya ta-ītci tē'lXam kā wu'Xi
the people. Day came. Then they went those people and that her husband had crawled into the ground. They looked at the ground. There was a hole there. Then the people went home and burned the house.

---

aqagē'lak.	A'qa	igiuxoā'nema	qā'xpa	ya'Xi	itcā'kikal	ya'Xi	ēlX
woman.	Then	she showed them	where	that	her husband	that	ground

igē'lopqîX.	iqē'qElkElîX	ya'Xi	ēlX	Lxoa'p	igē'xôx.	Ā'qa
he entered it.	it was seen	that	ground	hole	it was.	Then

igō'Xoak;oa	ta-îtci	tê'lXam.	IgōXuē'giLx	tE'ctaqL.
they went home	those	people.	They burned it	their two selves' house.

How the Klatsop were Killed by Lightning (told 1894)

A long time ago the Klatsop were burned. Many women went picking huckleberries, and camped for several days. Then one slave girl laughed when she heard a clap of thunder far away. That slave girl laughed at it. The Thunderbird thundered twice. Then that slave girl imitated the thunder. A stroke of lightning came and burned the whole camp. All were dead; only one youth remained alive. He had gone digging when his companions were burned. All were burned and died. Only that one youth remained alive.

After some time the Klatsop were burned again. They went digging parsnip roots. Early in the morning they rose. First they ate. Then the Thunderbird thundered. Two girls had gone already to dig roots near the creek. Then the women laughed at the thunder. They laughed "hahahā'!" Again the Thunderbird thundered and the women

---

ʟā'k¡ēlak	ā'nqa	nō'XumaʟXa.	Ikanacpᴇ'q	tgē'wula	itā'qola-îm
The Klatsop	long ago	they were burned.	Huckleberries	they gathered	they camped

ʟgā'pᴇlatîkc	ta-îtci	tᴇ'nᴇmckc.	A'qa	hē'hē	nᴇxō'xoax	aeXā't
many	those	women.	Then	laugh	she did	one

alā'etîX.	Kᴇlā'îX	ikᴇnuwakcō'max	igē'xôx.	A'qa	agiuqoā'nim
slave woman.	Far	Thunderbird	was.	Then	she laughed at him

wu'Xi	alā'etîX.	Mâ'kctîX	nixᴇltcō'x	ikᴇnuwakcō'max.
that	slave woman.	Then	he spoke	the Thunderbird.

Agikxō'lalᴇmxîX	wu'Xi	alā'etîX.	Ē'gîlkc	nîxō'xoax,	· a'qa
She imitated him	that	slave woman.	Lightning	it was,	then

nōXumaʟXā'X	ta-îtci	gitā'qulayîm.	Kanauwē'	nuXuaʟā'itx.
they were burned	those	who camped.	All	they were dead.

ĒXā'tka	iq¡u'lîpX	iā'XanatiX.	YaXī'	kᴇlā'îX	iq¡aʟxoē'ma	tcī'wula
One only	a youth	his life.	There	far	roots (sp. ?)	he gathered them

qa	nōXumaʟXā'x	giʟā'cgēwal.	Kanauwē'	nōXuaʟᴇ'lx,	kanauwē'
where	they were burned	his companions.	All	they were burned,	all

nōXuaʟā'îtx.	Iā'ema	ya'Xi	ēXā't	iq¡u'lîpX	iā'XanatîX.
they were dead.	Only	that	one	youth	his life.

A'qa	mank	k¡oalagē'	wī't'ax,	a'qa	wī't'ax	nō'XumaʟXa.
Then	a little	some time ago	again,	then	again	they were burnt.

Icanā'taXuē	tgē'wula.	Kawɪ'X	nuXualā'yutckoax,	a'qa
Parsnip(?) roots	they gathered them.	Early	they arose,	then

nuXuik¡e'tcînktamîtx.	A'qa	ikᴇnuwakcō'max	nixᴇltcō'x.	Ā'nqa
they took their breakfast.	Then	the Thunderbird	spoke.	Long ago

qactō'îx	cta'Xi	cmôkct	shā't¡au.	Q¡oā'p	ē'qaʟpa	ckʟōlā'lpʟ;
they went	those	two	two maidens.	Near	the creek at	they two dug with digging sticks;

icanā'taXuē	cgē'wula.	A'qa	nuXoak¡ayā'wulalᴇmx	ta-îtci
parsnip(?) roots	they two gathered them.	Then	they laughed at it	those

tᴇ'nᴇmckc.	Hahahā'	nuxoā'xax.	Wī't'ax	nixᴇltcō'x
women.	Hahahā'	they did.	Again	he spoke

laughed again "hahahā'!" They laughed heartily. Then one of the two girls who had gone digging said: "It is forbidden. My mother told me that it is forbidden to laugh at the Thunderbird. He will burn the people." Indeed, a stroke of lightning came and almost burned those girls. The Thunderbird thundered so that the ground shook. Then she said to her relative: "Let us go into the water." They stayed in the water, their heads only emerging. The Thunderbird thundered, and the women became silent. They stayed in the water until the Thunderbird became quiet. They went to the fire and there lay their relatives, all dead. They said: "Behold! our relatives are dead." They went home to their town and told the people: "Our companions have been burned; they are all dead. They laughed at the Thunderbird." Thus they said, telling the people. An old person said: "Oh, it is forbidden to laugh at the Thunderbird. Long ago people who had gone to pick huckleberries, and who were camping

---

ikEnuwakcō'ma. Wi k¡oaLqē' nugoagē'mx ta-îtci tE'nEmcke.
the Thunderbird. Again thus they said those women.

Hahahā' nuxoā'xax. Qayuxoalā'-itx. Nagē'mx wu'Xi aeXā't
Hahahā' they did. They laughed heartily. She said that one

abā't¡au cta'Xi ckLōlā'lpL: "Tgā'k¡iLau. AgE'qō agEnulXā'mx.
maiden those two they two dug with digging sticks: "It is forbidden. My mother she told me.

Tgā'k¡iLau. Aqiuk¡oā'nîmx ikEnuwakcō'maX, nuXumaLXā'x
It is forbidden. He is laughed at the Thunderbird, they are burned

tê'lXam." A'qa ā'qanuwē ē'gîlket nîxō'xoax. Ā'koapō
the people." Then indeed lightning was. Almost

qacXEmLXā'x cta'Xi chā't¡au. NîxEltcō'x ya'Xi ikEnuwakcō'max.
they two were burned those two two maidens. He spoke that Thunderbird.

Nau'i nixElā'lalEmx ya'Xi ēlX. AgōlXā'mx wu'Xi agā'cuX:
At once it shook that ground. She said that her relative:

"Aya'q, Ltcu'qoapa atxō'ya." A'qa cxēlā'itX Ltcu'qoapa. Ta'ēma
"Quick, water in we two will go." Then they two stayed water in. Only

ctā'q¡aqctaquks Lā'xLax ōguakē'x Ltcu'qoapa. NîxEltcō'x ya'Xi
their two selves' heads visible were the water in. He spoke that

ikEnuwakcō'max. Qān nōxoā'xax ta-îtci tE'nEmckc. Lā'2lē a'qa
Thunderbird. Silent they were those women. Long then

cxēlā'itx Ltcu'qoapa. Qān nîxō'xoax ya'Xi ikEnuwakcō'max.
they two stayed the water in. Silent he was that Thunderbird.

Qactō'îx cta'Xi cqagē'lak aLā'tōLpa. Ka'nauwē ō'xoaxt ta'Xi
They two went those two two women their fire to. All they lay there those

tetā'cuXtîke, oXoā'La-it. Qacgē'mx: "Ō2, iguXoā'La-it L¡gi
their relatives, they were dead. They two said: "Oh, they are dead behold¡

txā'cuXtîke." QacXk¡oā'x iLā'lXampa. QacXkᵘLē'tegoax:
our two selves' relatives." They two went home their town to. They two told:

"Igō'XumaLXa gintcā'cgēwal. Ka'nauwē iguXoā'La-it.
"They are burned our companions. All they are dead.

Itgiuqoā'nîmtck ikEnuwakcō'max," qacgē'mx, qackᵘLē'lalEmx.
They laughed at him the Thunderbird," they two said, they two told.

QaLgē'mx LēXā't Lq¡eyō'qt: "Ō, tgā'k¡iLau, aqiuqoā'nîmx
He said one old man: "Oh, it is forbidden, he is laughed at

ikEnuwakcō'max. Ā'nqa wi nō'XumaLXa tê'lXam itā'qola-îm
the Thunderbird. Long ago also they were burned people who camped

out, were burned." Then the girl's mother said to her: "I always told you that people were burned long ago." And the girls spoke: "If we had not gone into the water we should not be alive now." Then they went to see the dead ones. They were carried away in two large canoes. All the corpses were put into the canoes and were carried into the town.

Not long ago a band of elks were burned in Klatsop. A woman went to dig roots. She went a long distance to the prairie. Then she saw something red. She went to look at it, and approached. She thought: "Perhaps these elks are asleep." She thought: "I will tell the hunters to shoot them." Then again she hesitated. She thought: "I will not tell them." She crept toward them secretly. She was quite near, but the elks did not rise. They did not rise at all. She threw her digging stick. There was one elk quite near the woman, but it did not move. She threw her digging stick again against its

---

ikanacpᴇ'q tgē'wula." Igō'lXam wā'qaq wu'Xi ahā't¡au:
huckleberries they gathered them." She said to her her mother that maiden:

"Qayaxamᴇlk^{u}ʟē'lalᴇmx gwā'nîsum. Nō'XumaʟXa tê'lXam ā'nqa."
"I told you always. They were burned people long ago."

Icî'k·îm cta'Xi chā't¡au: "Qē nēketx ʟtcu'qoapa intxē'la-it, tā'ntxo
They two said those two two maidens: "If not water in we had been, therefore

intā'Xanatē." A'qa iqtōgoā'lᴇmam ta-îtci tmēmᴇlō'ctîke, iqō'k^{u}ʟa
our life." Then they were fetched those bodies, they were carried

môket gitcā'qa-iʟax akᴇ'nim. Iqtā'kXatq ka'nauwē ta-itci
two large canoes. They were put into the canoes all those

tmēmᴇlō'ctîke. Iqᴇ'tuk^{u}ʟ iʟā'lXampa.
bodies. They were carried their town to.

Näct ā'nqa a'qa wi kōpa' Tiā'k¡ēlakîX nē'XᴇmaʟXa imō'lᴇkumaX.
Not long ago then again there Klatsop they were burned elks.

ĒXt iā'Xtamala imō'lᴇkumax. Qaʟō'îx ʟqagē'lak. Iq¡aʟxoē'ma
One herd elks. She went a woman. Roots (sp.?)

qaʟigᴇlō'îx. Qaʟō'îx ē'wa kᴇlā'îX ta'Xi tᴇmqā'emapa. A'qa tā'nki
she went to gather. She went there far that prairie to. Then something

ē'xôxt ʟpᴇ'lᴇmax. Qaʟō'îx qaʟgiō'qstamx. A'qa q¡oā'p
there was red. She went she went to see. Then near

qaʟgiō'xoamx. QaʟXʟoXoā'itx ʟqagē'lak: "ʟXuan ikqē'witᴇm gi
she arrived. She thought the woman: "Perhaps they sleep these

imō'lᴇkumax." QaʟXʟoXoā'-itx: "Anxk^{u}ʟē'tcguama, tiā'maq
elks." She thought: "I will tell them, shoot

atktēlō'xoa tgā'xēqʟax." A'qa wi môket qaʟktō'xoax ʟā'xataguax.
they will do them the hunters." Then again two became her mind.

QaʟXʟoXoā'-îtx: "Qā txō nîct anxk^{u}ʟē'tcguama." Qaʟxik¡ᴇnukʟuwā'x
She thought: "How perhaps not I tell." She crept near secretly

q¡oā'pîX; näct nixᴇlā'tckoax ya'Xi imō'lᴇkumax. Nî'cqē
near; not they rose those elks. Not at all

nixᴇlā'yutckoax. Qaʟgigᴇltcē'mx ya'Xi ē'ʟaʟqē. Näct nîxᴇlā'lalᴇmx
they rose. She threw at them that digging stick. Not it moved

belly, but it did not move. Then the woman thought: "Perhaps the elks are dead." She arrived and struck the head of the elk. It did not move. She looked to see where it was hit, but it was not hit anywhere. She looked at all those elks. They were all dead. They were burned. Then the woman went home to tell the people. She came to the town and said to her husband: "I am afraid. I found a whole band of dead elks. They are lying dead on that prairie. Their hair is burned." Then her husband ran to another house and said: "My wife found dead elks. Their hair is burned." Then one person said: "Oh, last night the Thunderbird thundered. You all heard it; the ground shook. Maybe it burned those elks. The Thunderbird has done it." Then the people went. They skinned the elks, and cut only the fat ones; they did not cut the lean ones. The people dried

---

ya'Xi ēXt q;oā'pîX Lā'Xkapa La'Xi Lqagē'lak. Wī't'ax qatgigElgā'x
that one near her at that woman. Again she took it

ya'Xi ē'LaLqē. Wī't'ax qaLgigEltcē'mx iā'wanpa. Nā2ct
that digging stick. Again she threw at it its belly at. Not

nixElā'lalEmx. QaLXLoXoā'itx La'Xi Lqagē'lak: "LXuan ixE'La-it
it moved. She thought that woman: "Perhaps they are dead

gi imō'lEkumax." ALigō'qoamx La'Xi Lqagē'lak qaLgiuqoē'lXEmx
these elks." She reached them that woman she struck it

iā'q;aqctaqpa ya'Xi imō'lak. Nāct nixElā'lalEmx. QaLgiuk;umā'nanEmx
its head on that elk. Not it moved. She looked at them

qā'xpa iā'maq. K;ā nīct iā'maq. Ka'nauwē qaLgiuk;umā'nanEmx
where shot. Nothing not shot. All she looked at them

ya'Xi imō'lEkumax. Ka'nauwē iXE'La-it, ka'nauwē ia'qsō ixLE'llt.
those elks. All they were dead, all their hair it was burned.

QaLXk;uā'x La'Xi Lqagē'lak, qaLxk^uLē'tcgamx. Qa-iLō'yam
She went home that woman, she went to tell. She arrived

iLā'lXampa. AgiōlXā'mx itcā'kikal wu'Xi aqagē'lak:
her town at. She told him her husband that woman:

"QEnuq;uē'xaēmaLx. Iniō'cgam imō'lEkumax iXE'La-it. Ē2Xt
"I am scared. I found them elks they are dead. One

iā'Xtamala kanauwē' iXE'La-it ta'Xi tEmqā'emapa. IxLE'llt
herd all they are dead that prairie on. It is burned

tē'yaqcō." Nixē'ngux itcā'kikal tēXt tqu'Lipa: "Igiō'cgam
their hair." He ran her husband one house to: "She found them

imō'lEkumax agE'kikal; iXE'La-it. Ka'nauwē ia'qsō ixLE'llt."
elks my wife; they are dead. All their hair it is burned."

QaLgē'mx Lēxā't LgoaLē'lX: "Xā'pîX igē'xEltcō ikEnuwakcō'max.
He said one person: "In the evening he spoke the Thunderbird.

Megîltcī'mElētEmtck ka'nauwē mE'caika. Igîxlā'lalEmtck gi ēlX,
You heard it all you. It shook this ground,

LXuan Igē'XEmLXa ya'Xi imō'lEkumax. IkEnuwakcō'max ā'kua
perhaps they are burned those elks. The Thunderbird thus

itcī'yux." A'qa itgī'ya ta-îtci tē'lXam. Iqē'yuxc ya'Xi imō'lEkumax.
he did them." Then they went those people. They were skinned those elks.

Iā'ema ya'Xi igayā'pXEleu iqī'yuxc. IuL;E'lyuxt nāct iqī'yuxc.
Only those those having fat they were skinned. The lean ones not they were skinned.

Kōpā' a'qa itgîXcā'mit ta-îtci tē'lXam. Ttsîlqā'Lke iqE'tôx kōpa'.
There then they dried it those people. Drying frames they were made there.

them and made drying frames. Then the elks were dried. When all the meat was dried, the people went home.

Therefore the Klatsop are afraid of the Thunderbird.

Kōpa'	iqîXcā'mît	ya'Xi	imō'lᴇkumax.	Kanauwē'	igîXᴇ'caq,	tcXua
Then	they were dried	those	elks.	All	they were dry,	then

igō'Xoak!oa	ta-îtci	tê'lXam.
they went home	those	people.

Tā'ntxō	k!wac	ʟā'k!ēlak	ikᴇnuwakcō'max.
Therefore	afraid	the Klatsop	the Thunderbird.

WAR AGAINST THE KLATSOP (TOLD 1894)

The T!uwā'nxa-îkc [a tribe speaking a Shahaptian dialect] came down to fight the Klatsop. There were many people. They came down to Niā'k!ewanqîX. [That is the middle town of the Klatsop.] They were seen at Skippanon. Then a youth said: "Oh, people are coming. They are going to make war against us. Go and tell at Niā'k!ewanqîX." Thus spoke one person. They went to tell the people: "You are staying here quietly. People are coming to make war against us." And all the people ran away inland to ʟiā'menaʟuctē [a large town on a lake]. That town had five blocks. It was a town of the Klatsop. The Klatsop were there. They did not sleep until it became daylight again. They held their arrows in readiness. The T!uwā'nxa-îkc went down to the beach at Niā'k!ewanqîX. They came to the town in the evening. Early in the morning they made an attack upon the town, but there were no people. They found

---

A'qa itgā'tēt T!uwā'nxa-îkc. Igugoatk!ē'saqoamam Tiā'k!ēlakîX.
Now they came the Klikitat. They came to make war upon them the Klatsop.

ʟgā'pᴇlatîkc ta-îtci tê'lXam. A'qa iʟgᴇ'ʟxam Niā'k!ēwanqîXpa
Many those people. Then they came down to the water Niā'k!ēwanqîX at

iā'xalcuX ya'Xi ēlX. Iqō'quikᴇl Sqēpanā'wunX: "Ā, tê'lXam
its name that country. They were seen Skippanon: "Ah, people

tgatē't," iʟᴇ'k·îm ʟēXā't ʟq!u'lîpX. "Sāq° qᴇlxᴇ'txam." "A'yaq
are coming," he said one youth. "War they come to make upon us." "Quick

mck^{u}ʟē'tcgam Niā'k!ēwanqîX," iʟᴇ'k·îm ʟēXā't ʟgoaʟē'lX.
tell them Niā'k!ēwanqîX," he said one person.

Icxauik^{u}ʟē'tckoam ta-îtci tê'lXam Niā'k!ēwanqîXpa: "P!ā'la
They went to tell them those people Niā'k!ēwanqîX at: "Quietly

amcxēlā'etîX, tgatē't tê'lXam. Sāq° qᴇ'lXôxt." Itguā'Xit
you stay, they are coming people. War is made upon us." They ran away

ka'nauwē ta-îtci tê'lXam. Itgī'ya ʟxᴇ'lcuX ʟiā'menaʟuctēpa.
all those people. They went inland ʟiā'menaʟuctē to.

Kopā' qui'nᴇma iXᴇ'mo-itt ya'Xi ē'lXam ʟiā'mᴇnaʟuctēpa, ʟā'k!ēlak
There five blocks that town ʟiā'mᴇnaʟuctē at the Klatsop

iʟā'lXam. Kōpā' igō'xoax ta-îtci tê'lXam ʟā'k!ēlak. Näct
their town. There were those people the Klatsop. Not

nuguaqē'witXîtx ac wāx niktcō'ktxîX. Itgōguigā't tgā'qamatcX
they slept and the next day day came. They held them their arrows

guā'nᴇsum ta-îtci tê'lXam. Itgē'ʟxa T!uwā'nxa-îkc Niā'k!ēwanqîX.
always those people. They went down to the water the Klikitat Niā'k!ēwanqîX.

Itxē'k!ᴇnukʟuwā ya'Xi ē'lXam. Tsō'yustîX. Kawī'X igē'xoxîx,
They crept up secretly to that town. It was dark. Early it became,

sāq° itgī'yux ya'Xi ē'lXam. K!ā'ya tê'lXam, tā'ema tqʟā'2max.
war they made upon it that town. None the people, only houses.

only the houses. They entered and said: "Where may those people have gone to?" Now there was something round and as long as a finger lying near the fire. Then one Clackama spoke (part of them were Clackama): "These are the excrements of these people. They defecate near the fireplace." It is said that the Klatsop defecate near the fireplace. One of the men took it up and said: "You lie. Those are not excrements; it is something else." [It was the refuse of a root which they chew and spit out.] The people went down to the sea and one of them went to the water. He saw an abalone in the water and took it. He put it under his blanket next to his stomach. Then it bit him with both its claws and made a large hole in his stomach. He fell down and died. The people said: "Let us go inland. Perhaps there are monsters in the water." Behold, a crab had bitten that person and he thought it was an abalone.

The people went inland to search for the town. They crossed that creek and went inland. Then they came out of the woods and arrived

---

Itgᴇ'pqa ta-îtci tê'lXam. Igugoā'kim ta-îtci tê'lXam: "Qā'mta
They entered those people. They said those people: "Whither

aʟgētgī'ya tkci tê'lXam?" Kopa' q¡oā'p itā'tōʟpa tā'nki ixō'Xtax
they went those people?" There near their fire something was there

lō'ᴇlōmax k¡a iā'ʟktax. ʟēXā't iʟᴇ'k·îm Giʟā'q¡ēmas, aqa'watîkc
round things and long. One he said a Clackama, part of them

Gitā'q¡ēmas ta-îtci tê'lXam: "Itā'qēxalē tkci tê'lXam. Q¡oā'p gi
Clackama those people: "Their excrements these people. Near this

ē'tōʟ ka'nauwē qatkʟotsā'tsax." K¡oaʟqē' aqtōlXā'mx: "ʟā'k¡ēlak
fireplace all they defecate." Thus they said: "The Klatsop

kōpā' itā'tōʟpa itā'qēxalē." Qaʟgigᴇlgā'x ʟa'Xi ʟēXā't. Qaʟgē'mx:
there their fireplace at their excrements." He took it that one. He said:

"Ēmē'ʟ¡mēnXut. Nîcqē igē'xalē taya'x; ixᴇlō'ita." Qatgᴇ'ʟxax
"You lie. Not at all excrements that; it is different." They went to the water

mā'ʟnîX ta-îtci tê'lXam; qaʟō'îx ʟtcu'qoapa ʟaXi ʟēXā't.
seaward those people; he went the water to that one.

Qaʟgiqᴇlgᴇ'lx iktē'lowa-îtk ʟtcu'qoapa. Qaʟgigᴇlgā'x ya'Xi
He saw it an abalone the water in. He took it that

iktē'lowa-îtk. NîʟXmō'tkax iʟā'wanpa. Qatcʟō'qcx kanā'mtᴇmax
abalone. He put it under his blanket his belly at. It bit him both

tē'yaxō iʟā'wanpa. Nau'i ʟxoa'pʟxoap nîxō'xoax iʟā'wanpa. Kōpā'
its hands his belly at. At once holes became his belly in. There

qaʟxē'maxitx qaʟō'mᴇqtx. Nōguagē'mx tê'lXam: "A'yaq,
he fell down he died. They said the people: "Quick,

alxō'ptcga, ʟXuan tqcxēʟā'uke ʟtcu'qoapa ōguakē'x." Qō'ct
let us go inland, perhaps monsters the water in are." Behold

ʟqaʟxē'la ʟa'Xi qaʟkʟō'qcx ʟa'Xi ʟgoaʟē'lX. Iʟxʟō'Xoa-ît
a crab that it bit him that person. He thought

iktē'lowa-itk.
an abalone.

Qatgᴇ'ptckax ta-îtci tê'lXam qatgionā'xʟam ē'lXam.
They went inland those people they went to search for it the town.

Qatigᴇlguā'kuax ya'Xi ē'qaʟ. Qaʟgᴇ'ptcgax ʟxē'leu, a'qa wī't'ax
They went through the water that creek. They went inland inland, then again

aqtgᴇ'ʟxax. A'qa itigᴇlō'ʟxamx ikakꜝō'ʟîtîx·. Iā'qa-iʟ ikak¡ō'ʟîtîX.
they went down to the water. Then they reached it a lake. Large the lake.

at the lake. They saw a large lake and a town on the other side. They said: "Behold, there is the town of the Klatsop. When it gets dark, one man shall swim across. He shall go and take a canoe." That lake is large. Its name is ʟiā'menaʟuctē. The girls were bathing in front of the town. Their heads were covered with dentalia. They wore hair ornaments and ear ornaments. Then one of these people said: "I wish it would grow dark quickly that we may attack these people." When it grew dark, one of them said: "I will go and fetch a canoe." That person wore a head ornament made of feathers. The faces of all the T¡uwā'nxa-îkc were painted black and red. When it began to be dark, they went down to the water and this man said to his companions: "You stay here. I will go and take a canoe." He walked into the water of the lake. It was shallow. At some places it was deep. Sometimes it reached to his armpits, sometimes to his knees, and sometimes it went over his head.

Qatgiqᴇ'lkᴇlx ya'Xi ē'lXam ē'wa k¡anatē'tōʟ. Nōguagē'mx: "Qōct!
They saw it that town there on the other side. They said: "Behold!

gipā'tîX iʟā'lXam ʟā'k¡ēlak. Ma'nîx alupō'nᴇma, a'qa ʟēXā't
here their town the Klatsop. When it grows dark, then one

aʟuk¡uē'x·a. Ikᴇ'nim aʟgiugoā'lᴇmam." Iā'qa-iʟ ya'Xi ikak¡ō'ʟitîX,
he shall swim across. A canoe he shall go to fetch it." Large that lake,

ʟiā'mēnaʟuctē iā'xaleuX. A'qa ōxuaqwā'yōtuʟ ta-îtci thā't¡aunana
ʟiā'mēnaʟuctē its name. Then they bathed those maidens

ya'Xi ē'lXam ayā'maʟnapa. Pāʟ tgā'ktemax ta-îtci thā't¡aunāna
that town toward the water from it at. Full their ornaments those maidens

tgā'q¡aqstaxukcpa. Tqoxuā'lXtax tā'wîxt, ick¡ᴇ'la iā'wîXt ta-îtci
their heads on. Hair ornaments were on them, ear ornaments were on them, those

that¡aunā'na. Igugoā'kim ta-îtci tê'lXam: "Qō'i aya'q igō'ponᴇm,
maidens. They said those people. "Oh, if quick it grows dark,

sāq° ilxgᴇ'tux ta-îtci tê'lXam." Igō'ponᴇm, iʟᴇ'k·îm ʟēXā't:
war we will make upon them those people." It grew dark, he said one:

"Nai'ka aniogoā'lᴇmam ikᴇ'nim. ʟā'k¡ēcgᴇla ʟa'Xi ʟgoaʟē'lX.
"I I will fetch it a canoe. A head ornament of feathers that person.

ʟᴇguē'matckuîX stā'xōst, anā' ʟᴇlX, anā' ʟpᴇl ka'nauwē stā'xōstpa
Painted their faces, sometimes black, sometimes red all their faces on

ʟt¡uwā'nxa. Gā4p igō'ponᴇm. A'qa iʟō'ʟxa ʟa'Xi ʟt¡uwā'nxa.
the Klikitat. Late in the afternoon it grew dark Then he went to the water that Klikitat.

Iʟktō'lXam giʟā'cgewal: "Tē'ka amcxō'xoa; aniugoā'lᴇmam
He said to them his companions: "Here you stay; I go to fetch it

ikᴇ'nim. Iʟigᴇ'lkoago-îX ya'Xi ikak¡ō'ʟîtX. A'qa cpāq ya'Xi
a canoe. He went into the water that lake. Then shallow that

ikak¡ō'ʟitîX, anā' ʟ¡lap nîxō'xoaxîx, anā' ʟā'xᴇmalapqîX, qoā't
lake, sometimes under water he became, sometimes his armpits, thus (far)

ʟ¡lap qaʟō'îX, anā' ʟā'q¡ôxʟᴇmax saxala', pāt ʟ¡lap qaʟō'îx.
under water he went, sometimes his knees up, really under water he went.

He said to his companions: "Behold, the lake is shallow." Sometimes he found warm water and sometimes cold water. When he came to the middle of the lake, it changed all of a sudden. Noise was heard under water. It began to boil; waves arose on the lake, and that person went down. He came up again crying "Eh," and clapping his mouth. He came up five times. Then his cries ceased. He ceased to clap his mouth. Then he was heard under water in that lake. Noise was heard from below. Then the warriors said: "Let us go home. This land is monstrous; it helps the people. Two of our companions are dead." Now that person remained in the lake. When it gets foggy, he is heard in the lake. Not very long ago he was seen swimming. People were digging up a beaver dam, and there he was seen coming out of it. He is heard when it becomes windy.

QaLktōlXā'mx ta-îtci gitā'cgewal: "Me'ctē! iXî'caqtîX, Lqōct."
He said to them those his companions: "Come! dry, behold."

Anā' L¦ōł La'Xi Ltcu'qoa qaLkLucgā'mx, anā' tsEs Ltcu'qoa
Sometimes warm that water he found it, sometimes cold water

qaLkLucgā'mx. Qēq¦ayaqpa ya'Xi ikak¦ō'LîtX qaLō'yamx. A'qa
he found it. The middle in that lake he arrived. Then

ixElō'ita nîxō'xoax ya'Xi ikak¦ō'LîtX. Ā'yaXulam na-ixElō'xoax
different it became that lake. Its noise came to be on it

gē'gualîX. A'qa ē'LaLEmLEm nîxatElō'xoax La'Xi Ltcu'qoa. A'qa
below. Then its foam it was on it that water. Then

ayā'kolal na-ixElō'xax ya'Xi ikak¦ō'LitîX. L¦lap qaLō'îX La'Xi
its waves they were on it that lake. Under water he went that

LgoaLē'lX. Lāx qaLxō'xoamx La'Xi LgoaLē'lX. Ē'nxeaXul
person. Visible he became that person. Crying "Eh"

qaLgiō'xoax La'Xi LgoaLē'lX. Ē'wa qaLgio'xoax iLā'kucXat.
he did that person. Thus he did his mouth.

NiLxElqē'lXEmX iLā'kucXat. Qoā'nEmîX Lāx qaLxō'xoax,
He always clapped it his mouth. Five times visible he became,

kopā'tîX ē'nxeaXul qaLgiō'xoax, kopā'tîX niLxElqē'lXemX
as often crying "Eh" he did, as often he always clapped it

iLā'kucXat. A'qa gē'gualîX aqitcî'mElitEmx, ya'Xi ikak¦ō'LîtX
his mouth. Then below he was heard, that lake

ā'yaxolam na-ixElō'xoax gē'gualîX. Nōguagē'mx ta-îtci gitā'k¦ēsaq:
its noise it was on it below. They said those warriors:

"Alxk¦oā'ya; qōct iqcxē'Lau gi ēlX. Qatcuguigē'cgama-itx tê'lXam.
"We will go home; behold monstrous this land. It always helps them the people.

A'qa mâ'kctîkc gîlxā'cgēwal iguXuā'la-it." A'qa gwā'nEsum iLE'xôx
Then two our companions are dead." Then always he was

La'Xi LgoaLē'lX ya'Xi ikak¦ō'LîtXpa. Manîx na-ikxaLā'qxoaXîX
that person that lake in. When it gets foggy

aqLîltcî'mElitEmx kōpa' ya'Xi ikak¦ō'LitXpa. Năcqē' ā'nqa pEt
he is heard there that lake in. Not at all long ago really

aqLqElkE'lx LukuēXala. Tqo-inē'nē tE'kxaqLpa LE'kLEk
he was seen swimming. Beavers their house at dig

aqiō'xoaXîX, kōpā' aqLqElkE'lx qaLopā'x. Manē'x ikā'qamtq
it was done, there he was seen he went out. When wind

He always cries "Eh." Now the T¡uwā'nxa-îkc were afraid. They never came again to fight. They all went home. They came home. Then the Clackama said: "We reached Skippanon." Then one person said: "Did you jump much?" He replied: "We came to the place where the sun goes down into the water." Thus spoke the Clackama. They have no sense; they are foolish.

---

nîxō'xoax aqʟîltcî'mᴇlitᴇmx. Ē'nxeaXul qaʟgioxō'lalᴇmx. Kopā't
it becomes | he is heard. | Crying "Eh" | he always does. | Enough

qacuXuigᴇnā'x T¡uwā'nxa-îkc. Nîct qantsî'x nuguak¡ēsaqoamx.
they became afraid | the Klikitat. | Never | they went to attack them.

NuXuak¡uā'x ka'nauwē ta-îtci tê'lXam T¡uwā'nxa-îkc. NuXuak¡uā'-
They went home | all | those | people | the Klikitat. | They came

mamx. Nuguakē'mx Giʟā'q¡emas: "Intcō'yam Sqēpanā'wunX."
home. | They said | the Clackama: | "We arrived at | Skippanon."

A'qa iʟᴇ'k·îm ʟēXā't ʟgoaʟē'lX: "K¡a tcō'xoa
Then | he said | one | person: | "And | well

imcksopᴇnā'wunᴇnXʟtck?" Iʟᴇ'k·îm: "Kōpa' aqaʟā'x ʟ¡lap nxō'la
did you jump much (at the enemies)?" | He said: | "There | the sun | under water | goes

intcō'yam. ʟtcu'qoapa ʟ¡lap nō'îx aqaʟā'x intcō'yam," Giʟā'q¡emas
we arrived. | The water in | under water | goes | the sun | we arrived," | the Clackama

iʟᴇ'k·îm. Nîcqē' ʟā'Xatakoax Giʟā'q¡emas. ʟ¡alā'wēyîkc.
he said. | Not at all | their reason | the Clackama. | They are foolish.

How the Kathlamet Hunt Sea-lions (told 1894)

In February the sea-lions drive the smelts, and the bay gets full of them. Then the hunters say: "Quick, get your hunting canoes ready." Then the hunting canoes are made ready. Their outer sides are burned. The paddles are put in order. When it is calm, they go up the river at half ebb tide. Sometimes twenty canoes go, sometimes ten, and sometimes fifteen. As soon as they see many sea-lions the hunter says: "Let us stay here." The people remain there and after a short time it is low water. Then he asks his companions: "Whose canoe is the fastest?" One person says: "Mine is fastest." "And whose next?" "Mine," says another man. "Then go with your canoes to both ends of our line." They go first, and they all go down toward the sea. Now they find sea-lions toward the sea. The hunter says: "Let us drive them. Many sea-lions are

---

Tcaʟxᴇ'na-îX qaʟgiuwā'x iʟxᴇ'na ʟgipē'Xʟukc, ac pāʟ
In February | they drive them | the smelts | the sea-lions, | and | full

nîxō'xoax ē'maʟ. Qaʟgē'mx kʟā'xēqʟax: "A'yaq, t!aya't!aya
becomes | the bay. | He said | the hunter: | "Quick, | good

amcî'kax amcā'xēcitîX." A'qa t!aya't!aya aqō'xôx aqicē'tîX.
make them | your hunting canoes." | Then | good | they were made | the hunting canoes.

Aqakamʟᴇʟā'lᴇmx aqicē'tîX. T!ayā't!aya aqʟō'xoax ʟcî'kē.
They were burned (outside) | the hunting canoes. | Good | they were made | the paddles.

Ma'nîx ʟlō nîxō'xoaxîX qatgᴇ'suwîlXᴇmx. Kā'tcᴇk pᴇt
When | calm | it got | they went up the river. | Middle | real

qatxᴇltā'kuax, môkctʟā'ʟ aqicitī'yuXᴇmax. Ē'XtᴇmaXîX
ebb tide, | twenty | hunting canoes. | Sometimes

itcā'ʟēlXam, ē'XtᴇmaXîX itcā'ʟēlXam agō'n qui'nᴇm. Qaʟgē'mx
ten, | sometimes | ten | others | five. | He said

kʟā'xēqʟax: "Tē'ka tcXua alxō'xoa," ma'nîx aqʟqᴇlkᴇ'lx ʟā'pᴇla
the hunter: | "Here | then | we will be," | when | they were seen | many

ʟa'Xi ʟgipē'Xʟukc. Kōpa' nîxoā'xax ta-îtci tê'lXam. Mank q!ōl
those | sea-lions. | There | were | those | people. | A little | low water

nîxō'xoaxîX, qatctuqu'mtcXōqoax giʟā'cgewal: "ʟān iā'q!oalasᴇna
it became, | he asked them | his companions: | "Who | the quickest

iʟā'xēcitîX?" Qaʟgē'mx: "Nai'ka," ʟēXā't ʟgoaʟē'lX. "K!a ʟān
his hunting canoe?" | He said: | "Mine," | one | person. | "And | who

wī't'ax?" "Ā, nai'ka," ʟgōn ʟēXā't qaʟgē'mx. "Mᴇ'taika
also?" | "Ah, | mine," | another | one | he said. | "You two

kᴇ'mkitē amtgō'xoa amtā'xēcitîX." Ā'newa alaxō'xoa. A'qa
at both ends | you two be | your two selves' hunting canoes." | First | they will go. | Then

qatgᴇ'ʟxax ē'maʟpa. Qakʟucgā'mx ʟgipē'Xʟukc mā'ʟnē. Nigē'mx
they went down toward the sea | the bay to. | They found them | sea-lions | seaward. | He said

ya'Xi ktiā'xēqʟax: "ʟaʟā'x alxkʟXuwā'ya." ʟā'pᴇla ʟaʟā'x
that | their hunter: | "There | we will drive them." | Many | there

there." Then they surround them. These two canoes go first, and after them the others. The sea-lions dive. When they come up again, the people make a noise by beating their canoes and crying: Ah, ha, he, he, he, he! The sea-lions dive again. When they emerge again, the hunters make noise by beating their canoes. Sometimes they do so often, sometimes only for a short while. Then the people say: "The water is being stirred up by them farther down the river." Then they drive these sea-lions. They try to drive them toward a sandy island. The hunter says: "Let us drive them to this island." Sometimes the people are deceived and the sea-lions stay in the water. The water is not being stirred up down the river. Then the people wait on the water and drift in their canoes until they emerge. When the water is being stirred up down the river they follow them again. Then they make noise by beating their canoes near the sand island. Now the

---

ʟgipē'Xʟukc aqʟxʟā'koax. Ā'newa aqō'xoax wu'Xi môkct
sea-lions they surrounded them. First they were made those two

aqicē'tîX. A'qa kē'xᴇmtqîX wu'Xi qa'wa. ʟ!la'pʟ!lap qaʟxō'xoax
hunting canoes. Then behind those part. Under water they became

ʟa'Xi ʟgipē'Xʟukc. Kōpā' wi ʟā'xʟax qaʟxō'xoax. Qu'lqul
those sea-lions. There again visible they became. (Noise of beating canoes)

aqiʟgᴇlō'xoaXîX. Aqʟōlxā'mx: "Ā4, ha, he, he, he, he."
it was made. They said: "Ah, ha, he, he, he, he."

Wī't'ax ʟ!lap qaʟxō'xoax. Wī kōpa' qaʟktā'yōtcgᴇmx.
Again under water they became. Again there they emerged.

Wī't'ax qu'lqul aʟgiʟgᴇlō'xoaXîX. Ē'Xtᴇmaxîx ē'xauwitîX
Again (noise of beating canoes) they did. Sometimes often

qu'lqul aqiʟgᴇlō'xoaXîX. Ē'XtᴇmaXîX nō'ʟ!katîX qu'lqul
(noise of beating canoes) it was made. Sometimes a little only (noise of beating canoes)

aqiʟgᴇlō'xoaXîX. Nugoagē'mx ta-îtci tê'lXam: "A'qa ō'it
it was made. They said those people: "There go

aʟā'kolal qā'eqamîX." A'qa aqʟuwā'x ʟa'Xi ʟgipē'Xʟukc. Qiā'x
their waves down the river." Then they were driven those sea-lions. If

tgᴇ'tc!îqʟk tqamilā'lᴇq ʟXoē'max, tcXua kōpa' aqʟXuwā'q.
across their way a sand island, then there they were driven.

Nigē'mx ya'Xi ktiā'xēqʟax: "Tau yaXī'pa tqamilā'lᴇqpa, kōpa'
He said that their hunter: "That that at sand on, there

alxkʟXuwā'ya." Kē'nuwa lā'xlax qaʟktō'xoax ta-îtci tê'lXam
we will drive them." Try deceive they did them those people

qaʟxelā'-ltx ʟtcu'qoapa. Năct nō'îx aʟā'golal qā'eqamîX qac kōpā'
they stayed water on. Not they went their waves down the river and there

qatkXinē'tckoax ta-îtci tê'lXam. Qaʟktā'yutckᴇmx kōpa' wu'Xi
they stayed on the water those people. They emerged there those

akᴇ'nim nuXu'nîtck^{u}t. Ma'nîx aʟā'golal nō'îx qā'eqamîX, a'qa
canoes they drifted. When their waves they went down the river, then

wī't'ax aqʟuwā'x. Qu'lqul aqiʟgᴇlō'xoaXîX. Q!oā'p ta'Xi
again they were driven. (Noise of beating canoes) it was made. Near that

sea-lions come to that beach. They go ashore and jump up the land. Then the people follow them and shoot them. When one is hurt and stays ashore, all the sea-lions gather around him and there they are all killed. They are shot. Sometimes twenty are killed, sometimes ten. The meat is all distributed and all the people eat. When there are many people in a town, four are given to them. When there are few people in a town, two are given to them. All through the month of February they hunt sea-lions in this manner.

Some hunters spear the sea-lions when it is dark. Although their canoe is small, they spear large sea-lions. A skillful youth is placed in the stern of the canoe. As soon as the sea-lion is speared, it swims quickly down the river. Then the companion of the harpooner is told: "Shout." The steersman shouts, and is almost crying for fear. He becomes afraid. Xu'lElElElElElE goes the harpoon line [which is about

---

tqamilā'lEqpa,	a'qa	qaLō'ptcgax,	qaLsōpEnā'yux	LXE'leuX.
sand at,	then	they went inland,	they jumped	inland.

AqaqLuwā'X	LXE'leuX,	Lā'maq	aqLElō'xoax.	Ma'nîx	ēXt	iā'tcqEm
They were driven	inland,	shoot	they were done.	When	one	his sickness

nîxElō'xoax	qayuLā'-itx	q!oā'p	LXE'leuX	qaLXtā'koax	kanauwā'
came to be on it,	they stayed	near	inland	they surround it	all

La'Xi	Lgipē'XLukc	qaLigEmElā'itx	ya'Xi	iLā'cuX.	A'qa	kōpa'
those	sea-lions	they stand around it	that	their relative.	Then	there

ka'nauwē	aqLōtē'nax.	Lā'maq	aqLElō'xoax.	Ē'XtEmaXîX	môkctLāL
all	they were killed.	Shoot	they were done.	Sometimes	twenty

aqLōtē'nax,	ē'XtEmaXîX	iLā'LēlXam	aqLōtē'nax.	Kanauwē'
they were killed,	sometimes	ten	they were killed.	All

aqLōmā'kuax,	ka'nauwē	tê'lXam	qaLōXuimō'Xumx.	Ma'nîX
they were distributed,	all	the people	they ate.	When

Lgā'pElatîkc	ēXt	itā'lXam,	lākt	aqLawiqoē'muX;	ma'nîX
many	one	their town,	four	they were given to them to eat;	when

anō'L!katîkc	ēXt	itā'lXam,	mâkct	aqLawiqoē'muX.	Kanauwē'
few only	one	their town,	two	they were given to them to eat.	All

tcaLXE'na-îX	pEt	aqa ā'koa	aXkLō'xoax	La'Xi	Lgipē'XLukc.
February	really	thus	they did	those	sea-lions.

Aqā'watîkc	tgā'xēqLax	a'qa	Xā'pîX	qatkLlō'qcgalalEmx	La'Xi
Several	hunters	then	in the evening	they speared them	those

Lgipē'XLukc.	Iō'k!oa-its	iqisē'tîX,	tatc!a	aqilgē'qcqax	giā'qa-iL
sea-lions.	Small	a hunting canoe,	but	it was speared	a large

igē'pîXL.	Qiā'x	kLctā'xēlalak,	tcXua	LE'qēamē	aqLō'xoax
sea-lion.	If	skillful,	then	the steersman	he was made

Lq!u'lîpX.	Ma'nîx	aqilgē'q^{u}ckax	ya'Xi	igē'pîXL,	nau'i	qā'eqamîX
a youth.	When	it was speared	that	sea-lion,	at once	down the river

nîktā'x	qayuXtk!ē'q.	Kē'nuwa	qaLkLōlXā'mx	gictā'cgewal:
it ran	it swam.	Try	he said to him	his companion:

"Amgē'loma!"	Kē'nuwa	qaLgēlō'max	LE'qēamē,	as
"Shout!"	Try	he shouted	the steersman,	and

qatsîlq!E'lqtkuatcgoax.	K!wac	qaLxō'xoax.	Xu'lElElElElElE
he was almost crying for fear.	Afraid	he was.	Xu'lElElElElElE

two hundred fathoms long]. Many people are fishing sturgeon at this time. The fishermen hear it and see that a sea-lion has been speared. They go to see. When they reach them, two canoes are tied to that sea-lion. Then it goes slowly. When three canoes are made fast to it, then it gets tired. It is speared again and is killed. After a while it is hauled ashore. When a person who has tabus is steersman, then the harpoon line snaps and is lost.

Then the sea-lion is cut. When it comes from Nehelim, green stones are found in its stomach. When it comes from Quinaielt, gray or whetstones are found in its stomach. Then the game is all distributed. Thus did the Kathlamet in olden times.

---

qaLō'îx Lā'Xi LE'pa-ît. Lgā'pElatîkc tê'lXam nuXuamō'ktia-itx
goes that line. Many people they fished sturgeon with the hook

qatcîltcimā'kuax. Nōguagē'mx gatā'mukt¡ēna: "Igē'pîXL ya'Xi
they heard him. They said the fishermen: "A sea-lion that

iqē'lqîqcku." A'qa aqcgō'qoamx. Ma'nîx aqctā'qoamx, a'qa mākct
is speared." Then they went to see. When they reached them, then two

k¡au aqa-igō'xoax wu'Xi akE'nim ya'Xi igē'pîXL. A'qa mank
tied they were done those canoes that sea-lion. Then a little

LAwa' qayō'îx. Manē'x Lōn k¡au aqa-igō'xoax akE'nim, a'qa
slowly it went. When three tied they were done canoes, then

tEll nixō'xoax. A'qa wī't'ax aqilgē'quckax qa-ikXawā'qaquax;
tired it became. Then again it was speared it was killed after being harpooned;

qēwā'qoax. A'qa aqiō'kuix LXE'leu. Manē'x Lā'k¡iLau LE'qēamē
it was killed. Then it was carried inland. When one having tabus the steersman

Lq¡u'lîpX, a'qa Lq¡up qatcLō'xoax La'Xi Llē'pax, aqa nîcxâ'îx.
a youth, then cut it was that hunting line, then it was lost.

Manē'x aqeyō'xex igē'pîXL, ma'nîx ē'wa Naqē'lēm qayō'yamx
When it is cut a sea-lion, when there Nehelim it arrived from

ya'Xi igē'pîXL, a'qa ptsāx LqE'nakc qaLēlā'eta-îtx ē'yamōguipa.
that sea-lion, then green stones are in it its stomach in.

Manē'x ē'wa Kwinaiū'L nigē'pîXL a'qa cpēq iqE'nakc niLā'eta-îtx,
When there Quinaielt a sea-lion from there then gray stones are in it,

anā' ē'qac niLā'eta-îtx. QaLgiumā'koax kLā'xēqLax iLā'k¡ētēnax.
sometimes whetstones are in it. He distributes it the hunter his game.

Ka'nauwē nîxLX·ō'mx qaLgiumā'koax. K¡oaLqē' ā'nqa nuxoā'xa-îtx
All it is finished he distributes it. Thus formerly they did

tê'lXam GaLā'mat, Wā'qa-iqam, QLā'cgEnEmaxîX, GiLā'xaniak,
the people Kathlamet, Wā'qa-iqam, QLā'cgEnEmaxîX, Qā'niak,

k¡oaLqē' itā'k¡ēwula Lgipē'XLukc.
thus they hunted them sea-lions.

Cultee's Ancestor Conjures the Sea-lion (told 1894)

My grandfather sang a conjurer's song. He had one hundred conjurer's songs. His town was ʟaxanakcō'ngut. The people assembled in his house when he sang. The people danced for four nights and then the singer spoke: "That old man will come to listen and to see the dance." The people thought: "Where may that old man come from. Perhaps he will come from Nehelim to see the dance. Perhaps he will come from Klatsop to see the dance." It grew dark and then the people danced again. At midnight they became tired. They slept. One old woman slept when it began to be dark. When it was nearly daylight she awoke. Then something was happening. She heard a noise as if a door were being opened. Something was standing in the doorway. The old woman thought: "Maybe we are going to be attacked. I will wake the people."

ĒXā't nē'qatcXᴇm nai'ka tgᴇ'q!ēyuqtîkc. Tqēqʟax
One he sang conjurer's songs I my ancestors. One hundred

qatciuxoā'watcguîX. ʟaxanakcō'ngut iʟā'lXam. NoXuā'koax
he sang conjurer's songs. ʟaxanakcō'ngut his town. They assembled

ta-îtci tê'lXam ta'Xi tᴇ'ʟaqʟpa ya'Xi iqē'qtcxam. Lākt ʟpō'lᴇmax
those people that his house at that the one who sang conjurer's songs. Four nights

noXuiwī'yutckuax ta-îtci tê'lXam. A'qa nigē'mx ya'Xi
they danced those people. Then he said that

iqē'qtcxam: "A'qa ʟxatō'guala ʟa'Xi ʟq!ēyō'qt, aʟxētᴇlō'tcxama."
the one who sang conjurer's songs: "Now he will come to hear that old man, he will see the dances."

IgoXuiʟō'xoa-it tê'lXam: "Qā'mta ʟqa ʟtē'mama ʟaX ʟq!eyō'qt?
They thought the people: "Whence maybe he will arrive that old man?

ʟXuan ē'wa Naqē'lēm aʟtē'mama aʟxitᴇlō'tcxama, ʟXuan ē'wa
Perhaps thus Nehelim he will arrive he will see the dance, perhaps there

Tiā'k!ēlakîX aʟtē'mama aʟxitᴇlō'tcxama." Igō'pōnᴇm. A'qa
Klatsop he will arrive he will see the dance." It grew dark. Then

wī't'ax iguXuiwī'yutck ta-îtci tê'lXam. Qē'q!ayaq wā'pōlpa, a'qa
again they danced those people. Middle night at, then

tᴇll igō'xoax ta-îtci tê'lXam. Iguqoaqē'witx·it. ʟēXā't ʟq!eyō'qt
tired they were those people. They slept. One old

ʟqagē'lak as nō'ʟ!îX igō'ponᴇm a'qa iʟoqō'pti. Q!oā'p ē'ktᴇliʟ
woman and a little it was dark then she slept. Nearly morning star

qiʟXᴇ'qo-îtq ʟa'Xi ʟq!eyō'qt ʟqagē'lak. A'qa tānki igē'xax.
she awoke that old woman. Then something there was.

Iʟgiltcᴇ'maq q!a'ē, q!a'ē, q!a'ē, tā'nki igē'xax icî'qēpa. Iʟxʟō'Xoa-it
She heard it (noise of an opening crack), something was the door at. She thought

ʟa'Xi ʟq!ēyō'qt: "ʟXuan sāq° iqantcî'txam. Nî'Xua
that old woman: "Perhaps war they come to make on us. Well

She waked them. The people remained quiet. They rose and made themselves ready. They took their arrows. One of them was told: "Light the fire." That person lighted the fire, and something became visible in the doorway. Its face was as large as the moon. The people said: "Oh, a monster has come to our house;" but the singer said: "Is it a monster? It is that old man who comes to see the dance. He has come to give you food." Behold, a sea-lion came to see the dance. He was shot, and was dead. Far up from the sea was their town. Nevertheless that sea-lion went up. Then the people who had gone to attend the singing ate it. Thus was my grandfather's supernatural helper at Laxanakcō'ngut.

---

antutqō'yutcxEma tê'lXam." A'qa iLtuqō'yutc, ac qEnE'mkatîX
I awake them the people." Then she awoke them, and they remained quiet

ta-îtci tê'lXam. IguXoā'qo-îtq ta-îtci tê'lXam. Iguxoalā'yutck.
those people. They arose those people. They made themselves ready.

Itgō'guiga tgā'qamatcX. IqLō'lXam La'Xi LēXā't: "WaX ā'xa
They took them their arrows. He was told that one: "Light do it

wu'Xi ā'tōL." WaX iLE'kôx La'Xi LgoaLē'lX. A'qa tā'nki
that fire." Light he did it that person. Then something

Lāx igē'xôx icî'qepa. LXuan ā'wima îctā'qa-iLax siā'xôst La
visible became the door at. Perhaps thus large its face like

LktemEnā'kstē. Igugoā'k·îm ta-îtci tê'lXam: "IqcxēLau ya'Xi
the moon. They said those people: "A monster that

alîlxgē'tpqa." Igē'k·îm ya'Xi iqē'qtcxam: "IqcxēLau tci? Lā'Xka
he will come in." He said that the one who sang conjurer's songs: "A monster [int. part.]? He

La'Xi Lq¡eyō'qt iLxētElō'tcxam iLgEmcîtqoē'mam." Qōct igē'pîXL
that the old man he came to see the dance he came to give you food." Behold a sea-lion

yaXī'yaX igixElō'tcxam. Tiā'maq iqtē'lôx, kōpa' iō'maqt.
that he came to see the dance. Shoot then he was done, there he died.

KElā'îX cā'xalîX ya'Xi ē'lXam, tatc¡a iuquē'wulXt ya'Xi
Far up that town, but he went up that

igē'pîXL. Aqa itgixE'lEmuX ta-îtci tê'lXam, ta-îtci igē'taxelōtcxē.
sea-lion. Then they ate those people, those who had come to see the dance.

Oxuē'lutcx ya'Xi ē'tcxampa. K¡oaLqē' Lā'yuLEmaX ā'nqa
They saw the dance that song at. Thus their supernatural helper long ago

Laxanakcō'ngut nai'ka tgE'q¡ēyuqtîkc.
Laxanakcō'ngut[1] I my ancestors.

---

[1] A Nehelim village.

Cultee's Grandfather Visits the Ghosts (told 1891)

My grandfather wanted to take a woman from Oak point for his wife. They tried to give him another girl, but he did not like her. He used to make canoes. As soon as he had finished a canoe, he bought a slave with it. He had many slaves. Then an epidemic came. He had a pretty slave girl. She looked just like a chieftainess. Now he heard that the girl whom he wanted to have for his wife had died. The epidemic took the people away. Two days they were sick, then they died. Sometimes they died after three days' sickness. Now his people also were attacked by the epidemic. Several died each day, sometimes three died, sometimes four. Now my grandfather felt sick. After three days he died.

Then he went to the country of the ghosts. He reached that trail. He saw two people carrying a stick. When he came near, he saw that

---

AēXā't q|āxs qayaxā'kXatx, Qā'niak itcā'lXam wu'Xi
One wanting to marry he wanted her, Oak point her town that

ahā't|au. Kē'nuwa aqʟᴇlō'tx ʟhā't|au itcī'k|ak|ō, nēct tq|ēx
maiden. Try she is given to him a maiden my grandfather, not like

qatcʟō'xoax. Guā'nᴇsum akᴇ'nim qatcuxō'lalᴇma-îtx. Acqᴇmō'ʟ
he did her. Always canoes he always made them. Kathlamet canoes

qatcuxō'lalᴇma-îtx. ĒXt qatcʟigō'ʟkax icqamō'ʟ, ʟēXā't ʟlā'etîX
he always made them. One he finished it a Kathlamet canoe, one slave

aqixamᴇlā'lᴇmx. Iā'xotck|ēna, ka ʟgā'pᴇlatîkc tiā'qeXᴇltgeukc.
he was bought. He worked, and many his slaves.

A'qa iō'îx ē'mᴇq|t. AeXā't ayā'la-etîX at|ō'kti, ʟ|a ʟkak|ᴇmā'nate
Then it went the epidemic. One his slave girl pretty, just as a chief

itcā'lkuilē. Naēxᴇltcîmā'koax wu'Xi q|āxs qiaxā'kôx, nō'mᴇqt.
she resembled. He learned that wanting to marry who was wanted, she was dead.

Akᴇmā'ʟa-it iktō'ktcan ta-îtci tê'lXam. Mâ'ketîX qaʟuqō'îX
Cholera (?) took them those people. Twice they slept

iʟā'tcqᴇm niʟxᴇlō'xoax, qaʟō'mᴇqtx. Ē'XtᴇmaxîX ʟō'nîX
their sickness was on them, they died. Once three times

qaʟōqō'îX qaʟō'mᴇqtx. Ā'qa ʟā'itîkc iʟā'tcqam niʟxᴇlō'xoax,
they slept they died. Then those their sickness was on them,

aqā'watîkc nuXoaʟā'itx ēXt ē'koa; anā' aʟō'nîkc, anā' ala'ktîkc.
several died one day; sometimes three, sometimes four.

A'qa iā'tcqᴇm nixᴇlō'xoax. ʟō'nîX qayuqō'îX iā'tcqᴇm
Then his sickness was on him. Three times he slept his sickness

nixᴇlō'xoax qayō'mᴇqtx.
was on him he died.

A'qa iō'îx ē'wa tᴇmēmᴇlō'ctîkc. Qatcugoatā'qoamx tê'lXam
Then he went there the ghosts. He arrived at them people

wu'Xi ā'eXatkpa. Itgiuqoā'nat ē'mqō. Tê'lXam qatctūgolā'qʟqax,
those the road at. They carried it a log. People he saw them from a distance,

they were posts of a house. These people looked just like posts. Then he came to a person who dragged his intestines on the ground. When he came near, he saw that it was a mat made of rushes. The road was full of tracks of people. Now he came down to a large creek. He looked across and saw a large town. He heard people making canoes. Then a person came up to him. He recognized one of his mother's relatives who had been dead long ago. He said: "Did you come at last? They are waiting for you. The news of your arrival has come already. They will buy for you the girl whom you like. She and her mother have come across." Then that person left him. The grass at that place was three fingers wide and was more than man's height. It was moved by the wind and sounded like bells. He heard it ringing all the time. The grass told the people on the other side what was going to happen. Now he saw that woman and he thought: "I do not like her. She looks just like her mother. Her face

---

qayugoatā'qoamx, aqa tElapā'tkc. K¡oaLqā' tEnqiā'wac tā'lXam

he reached them, then house posts. Just so side posts of the house people

qatcōquikE'lx; qatcugoatā'qoamx, a'qa tE'mqō. QatcLktā'qoamx

he saw them; he reached them, then sticks. He met him

LgoaLē'lX iLktuLā'tat Lā'q¡amcukc. Q¡oā'p qatcLō'xoamx, a'qa

a person he hauled them his intestines. Near he reached him, then

icō'lEk. K¡oaLqā' iq¡ā'pEnX, k¡oaLqā' ilk¡uā'tē. Tc¡Emm

a mat. Thus a small rush mat (with ornamented margin), thus a single rush mat. Variegated

tgā'Xatk tê'lXam wu'Xi ā'eXatk. Qayō'Lxamx ē'qxaL; iā'qa-iL

their tracks people that road. He came down to the water a creek; a large

ē'qxaL. Nigē'kctx ēwa k¡anatē'tōL, a'qa ē'lXam, iā'2qa-iL ya'Xi

creek. He looked thus the other side, then a town, large that

ē'lXam. Qoā'o, qoā'o, qoā'o, akE'nim itguxō'lal. QaLigō'qoamx

town. (Noise of making canoes) canoes they worked. He reached him

LgoaLē'lX. Itciugu'laqLk wā'yaq Lgā'cux ā'nqa qaLE'tEmEqt.

a person. He recognized him his mother her relative long ago he was dead.

ILgiō'lXam: "IqamuLā'wina, amtē'mama? Ā'nqa tEmē'xakElaxElt

He said to him: "You were awaited, did you come? Already your news

itgatē'mam amtē'ia. Ma'nîx amtē'mama a'qa aqumElā'lEma wu'Xi

arrived you would come. When you arrive then she will be bought that

tq¡ēx qEmō'xt. K¡a etax·ī'yax ctēt, ictē'kastîX k¡a agā'kxo."

like whom you do. And these came, they went across and her mother."

A'qa wi iLEqE'loqLq La'Xi LgoaLē'lX. Ä'wēmax iLā'xalXtax La'Xi

Then again he left him that person. Thus its width that

Lgē'wan. GipE'tEmax iLā'Lqtax. ILxElā'lalEmtck La'Xi Lgē'wan.

reed. Thus its height. It was waving that reed.

Ya'Xka L¡agi tā'ntēn aqiyō'xoaxîX. ItcLEtcî'mElitEmtck La'Xi

That just as bells it did. He heard it much that

Lgē'wan. ILxgu'Lîtck La'Xi Lgē'wan ē'wa k¡anatē'tuL. Itcā'qElkEl

reed. It told that reed there at the other side. He saw her

wu'Xi aqagē'lak. A'qa ē'yamxtcpa: "NEct tq¡ēx ntcō'xoa. K¡oaLqā'

that woman. Then his heart in: "Not like I do her. Just as

wu'Xi wā'qaq. Istā'tsqEm sgā'xôst guā'nEsum." K¡oaLqā' ya'Xi

that her mother. Its sickness her face always." Just so that is sore all the time." He saw her in that manner. Then another person came to him. He recognized his uncle. They all came up the river. His uncle spoke: "Let us go to catch seals." His uncle took a line. They gave him something that looked just like soap. "Eat that," he said. He ate it, but he did not like it. Then he turned his head toward the land and spit out what was given to him. His uncle, who was looking toward the water, said: "What does he want to eat? He refuses what I give him." Then he thought: "I just came here and they scold me already. I will return." Then the sun shone on his right side. He did not walk. He just turned round and then he fell in a swoon. Now he recovered. He heard people crying. Early in the morning when he had died the people had gone to fetch his aunt from Klatsop. In the evening she arrived and brought two sea-otters which she intended to tie to his body. They had cut their hair and his slaves had been divided. One of his uncles had taken that pretty

---

itcā'qᴇlkᴇl. A'qa wi ʟgōn ʟgoaʟē'lX iʟigā'tqoam. Itciugu'laqʟq
he saw her. Then again another person reached him. He recognized him

gi iā'mōtX. Guā'nᴇsum ē'wa caxalata' qaʟō'yamx. Itciō'lXam ya'Xi
this his uncle. Always there up the river they came. He said to him that

iā'mōtX: "Aqē'sgoax atxagᴇlō'ya." ʟᴇ'pa-īt itcʟgᴇlgā't ya'Xi
his uncle: "Seal we will go to hunt." A rope he took it that

iā'mōtX. Iqē'lōt ya'Xi tā'nki ʟ!agi icō'p iā'lkuile. "Imxᴇ'lᴇmux
his uncle. It was given to him that something just like soap alike. "Eat

iā'Xauē." Itcī'yuqc igixᴇ'lᴇmux. Nēct anī'yaqtckc. Igixᴇ'ʟxēgua
this here." He bit it he ate. Not he liked the taste. He turned

ē'wa ʟxᴇ'leu. Itciō'mqo-it ya'Xi tā'nki iqē'lᴇqo-îm. Ē'wa
there inland. He spit it out that something it was given to him to eat. There

mā'ʟnîX ixᴇ'ʟxîk ya'Xi iā'mōtX, itciō'lXam ya'Xi iā'mōtX:
toward the water turned that his uncle, he said to him that his uncle:

"Tāntxa alēxᴇlᴇmō'xuma tcqi igē'tē. Itciq!ᴇ'leyipX ya'Xi
"What will he eat just he came. He refuses that

inē'lqo-îm." Igîxʟō'Xoa-it: "Ē'yaʟqtîX ʟq intē'mam aqa
I gave it to him to eat." He thought: "Long maybe I arrived then

iqᴇnō'mēla. AnXtā'k!oa," igîxʟō'Xoa-it. Nau'i gataeyā't
I am scolded. I will return," he thought. At once here then

igaēgᴇnxā'xit wu'Xi aqaʟā'x qēnk!ēama'. Nā2ct itcXō'tkakoa,
he struck him that sun on his right side. Not he walked,

nigē'mx, ac igixā'ʟxēgua, a'qa k!ᴇm igō'xax tiā'Xatakuax. ʟ!pāq
he said, and he turned, then nothing became his reason. Recover

igē'xôx. Igoxoē'nim tê'lXam itcauitcᴇ'maq. Kawī'2X ya'Xi
he did. They cried people he heard them. Early that

iō'maqt; iqugoā'lᴇmam ayā'ʟak Tiā'k!elakîXpa. Xā'pîX iqō'kʟam,
he died; she was sent for his aunt Klatsop at. In the evening she was brought,

igiō'kʟam môkct iqalagē'tᴇmax, agixᴇniā'goa. ʟqoā'pʟq!up iqᴇ'tôx
she brought them two sea otters, she was going to tie them to him. Cut were done

tiā'q!akctaqukc. Pā'qpaq iqᴇ'tôx ta'Xi tiā'qēxᴇltgeukc. A'qa
their heads. Divided they were those his slaves. Then

eXā't iā'mōtX itcā'gᴇlga wuXī' qat!ō'kti alā'etîX. A'qa igaXᴇ'ʟXak
one his uncle he took her that pretty slave girl. Then she became angry

slave girl. Now his aunt was angry. She wished to have that slave girl. She went home and took the sea-otters along. In the morning his breath had given out. It became night and became day again. The sun was low when he recovered. The people were crying all the time and said: "To-morrow we will bury him." Then that one woman was quiet and looked at him. It looked just as if the mat were moving. She looked at him again and said: "It is an evil omen for me; I see the mat moving." They lifted it. They felt his heart. He was warm and his heart was beating. His feet and his hands were cold. Then they called the conjurers. They warmed his hands at the fire and blew water on his face. He recovered. They gave him water. They poured some into his mouth. It ran down as far as his throat, but ran out of his mouth again. His throat and his chest were dry. Finally he swallowed the water. He drank much and recovered.

---

wu'Xi ayā'ʟak. Tq!ēx igō'xoa wu'Xi alā'ctîX. Igā'Xk!oa.
that his aunt. Like she did her that slave girl. She went home.

Igē'yukʟ ya'Xi iqalagē'tᴇmax. Kawu'X ya'Xi igaxᴇ'ʟXōm
She carried them those sea otters. Early that it was at an end

ayā'ʟutk; igō'ponᴇm; igē'tcuktîX. Gē'gualîX wu'Xi aqaʟā'x, a'qa
his breath; it grew dark; day came. Low that sun, then

itcîlXā'takoa. Igoxoē'nîmtck ta-îtci tê'lXam. Aqiō'lXam: "Ō'la
he recovered. They cried those people. He was told: "To-morrow

a'qa aqiō'tga." Qān iʟᴇ'xôx ʟa'Xi ʟēXā't ʟqagē'lak. A'qa
then he will be buried." Silent became that one woman. Then

iʟgiō'qumîtck. Yā'xka ʟ!agi ixᴇlā'la ya'Xi icō'lᴇk. Mā'kctîX
she looked at him. Then just as though moved that mat. Twice

iʟgē'qᴇlkᴇl ʟa'Xi ʟqagē'lak. A'qa iʟᴇ'kîm: "Iqenōq!oē'xaemaʟx
she saw it that woman. Then she said: "It is an evil omen for me

yā'Xka ʟ!agi ixᴇlā'la ya'Xi icō'lᴇk." Iqiō'latck ya'Xi icō'lᴇk.
that just as though moved that mat." It was lifted that mat.

Ē'wa iqē'yôx ē'yamxtc, a'qa iō'tcqa-ît ya'Xi ē'yamxtc. A'qa
Thus it was done his heart, then warm that his heart. Then

ā'qanuwē ixᴇlā'la ya'Xi ē'yamxtc. Tsēs tē'yakci; tsēs tiā'qo-it.
indeed it moved that his heart. Cold his hands; cold his feet.

Iqtugoā'lᴇmam tgā'qewamax tēXt tqu'ʟē. A'qa ʟ!āʟ!a iqī'yux
They were fetched shamans one house. Then warm it was made

ē'yamxtc. ʟ!āʟ!a iqā'elux ā'tōʟ. Pō'pō iqʟē'lux ʟtcu'qoa sī'axôst.
his heart. Warm it was made by the fire. Blow it was on him water his face.

ʟ!pāq igē'xôx. Kē'nuwa iqʟē'lōtx ʟtcu'qoa. Kē'nuwa wāx
Recover he did. Try it was given to him water. Try pour out

aqʟēlō'xoax iā'kcXa. Gipā' qaʟō'yamx, a'qa wi qaʟXtā'koax.
it was done on him his mouth. Here it arrived, then again it ran back.

Q!ᴇ'cq!ᴇc igā'x ā'yamōkuē k!a ayā'qatcX, ac tcXoa aqitcʟō'wîlq!
Dry became his throat and his chest, and then he swallowed it

ʟa'Xi ʟtcu'qoa. ʟā'2Xoē itcʟō'qumct, a'qa t!ayā' igē'xôx.
that water. Much he drank it, then well he became.

Many people died. Sometimes five died in one day, sometimes four, sometimes three. The epidemic killed them.

Then the seers learned what he had seen when he went to the country of the ghosts and saw everything there. Formerly the seers did not know it, but when he had been dead they learned about it.

Oxoeʟā'it ta-îtci tê'lXam; aqoā'nᴇmîkc nuxoaʟā'itx ēXt wē'koa; ē'Xtᴇmaxî̂X ala'ktîkc, ē'Xtᴇmaxî̂X aʟō'nîkc. Akᴇmā'ʟa-ît iktōtē'nax.
They died those people; five died one day; sometimes four, sometimes three. The cholera (?) killed them.

Kō'pa a'qa ā'qanuwē aqugōmaʟō'Xoa-it gitā'kikᴇlal ya'Xi iqatctᴇ'tqamîtck, ya'Xi tǀō'tsnîX nē'tē ē'wa tᴇmaʟā't, qatctᴇ'tqamîtck ka'nauwē tā'nᴇmax. Ā'nqa näcᵗ aqugōmaʟōxoā'-itx gitā'kikᴇlal, qā'nᴇq ya'Xi nē'tᴇmqt, tcXua ā'qanuwē aqugōmaʟō'xa-ît gitā'kikᴇlal.
There then indeed they knew it the seers that what he had seen, that first he came there the country of the ghosts, he saw them all things. Long ago not they knew it the seers, when that he died, then indeed they knew it the seers.

ABSTRACTS OF MYTHS

1. AQ¦ASXĒ'NASXĒNA—A woman who has a baby boy leaves her husband and builds a small house outside the village. In the evening, when the people dance, she desires to join them, but hesitates to leave her child. Finally she goes, and the child is carried away by Aq¦asXē'nasXēna, who takes him to the house in which she lives with the Crane. The boy grows up, and is informed by the Crane that Aq¦asXē'nasXēna is not his mother. The Crane tells him how to kill her. The boy does as instructed. He asks Aq¦asXē'nasXēna to carry him up the mountain. When they reach a region grown with white pine, he cuts her neck. Her soul comes out, and he breaks it. Then he climbs a white pine and shoots his arrows toward the sky, making a chain. He ties his bow to the lower end and climbs up. He meets the Darkness, who carries darkness in her bag. He meets different kinds of insects, who are descending to the earth. He meets a man in whose body two arrows are sticking. Soon he meets the Evening Star, who asks if he has seen his game, and explains that he is hunting men. He reaches a parting of trails, and, going on to the left, finds the trail strewn with human bones. He reaches a house, takes a basket down, in which he finds a woman. In the evening her five brothers come home, throwing their game—dead people—down in front of the door. Finally the father, the Evening Star, returns. They offer him human eyes to eat. The daughter is the Moon. He leaves them and returns, reaches the parting of the roads, and turns to the right. He finds the trail strewn with mountain-goat bones. The same thing happens as in the house of the Evening Star. The woman in this house is the Sun, the daughter of the Morning Star. The Moon's brothers make war upon them and are defeated. One day the man looks down and sees his village. He becomes homesick, and is let down to the earth with his wife. He finds his little brother blind, and being maltreated by Blue-jay. He restores his eyesight and punishes Blue-jay. His wife has twin children who are united in the middle. Blue-jay cuts them apart, and they die; then the woman returns to the sky. The twins are the sundogs.

2. NIKCIAMTCĀ'C—Blue-jay advises a girl to marry the Panther. She goes to the house of the animals, and by mistake marries the Beaver. She notices that the fish that he catches are really willow branches. She leaves the Beaver, who sends all the animals to bring

her back. Finally he sends the Panther, who marries the woman. Then the Beaver cries, and produces a deluge. The animals save themselves in their canoes. Finally they dive to bring up some mud. Blue-jay, Mink, Otter, and Muskrat try; the last succeeds. Then the waters begin to disappear, the canoes are left on the dry land, and the animals jump out of them. They all knock off their tails at the gunwale. Those that do not return to get them have short tails.

3. MYTH OF THE SUN—A chief has many pairs of moccasins and leggings made, and walks eastward to visit the Sun. After ten months, he reaches the Sun. He sees war implements hanging on one side of his house, dresses and shell beads on the other side. The sun is hanging near the entrance. He sees a girl, who tells him that all these things are her grandmother's property. The sun is carried by this old woman, who leaves the house every morning and returns late in the evening. He marries the girl, and asks the old woman to give him her blanket. Finally she gives it to him, and it fits his body like a shirt. She gives him a stone ax and sends him home. As soon as he sees people, he loses his senses and is compelled to kill them. After he has killed all his friends, the old woman visits him. She takes away the garment and the ax and leaves him.

4. MYTH OF THE SWAN—The Swan marries a chief's daughter, and during a famine gives her pounded salmon bones to eat, while he himself eats dried salmon. Then she goes home. She goes to bed and lies for five days on one side, then she turns over and lies for five days on the other side. All her hair comes off. Then she conjures the smelt which the people catch. Then she makes the river freeze so that the Swans cannot obtain any food. The Swans go to visit her. She orders the people to roast smelt over a fire of pitchwood; then she lets the Swans come in and they dislike the smoky taste of the fish. She curses them, saying: "You shall fly away when the smelts arrive."

5. THE COPPER IS SPEARED—A bright piece of copper is seen at sea. All the people try to spear it, but are unsuccessful. Finally two girls, who disguise themselves as youths, hit it. They instruct their father to invite the people, and produce the copper. They cut it to pieces and give it to the people. It has many different colors, and they put it onto their garments. These people are the birds, and this accounts for their different colors. The Blue-jay was given the best part of the copper. He showed it to the Clam, who took it away from him, and since that time has the mother-of-pearl color, while to Blue-jay was given what little remained of the copper.

6. MYTH OF THE COYOTE—Coyote and the Snake go up the river. He is instructed by his excrements in the taboos referring to the catching of salmon on the upper part of the river.

7. Myth of the Salmon—There is a famine. The Skunk-cabbage and other plants see the Salmon coming up the river. They say: "If it had not been for us, the people would have starved before you came." The Salmon gives them presents for having saved the people. The Crow, who is in a canoe with Blue-jay and the Flounder, is met by the Salmon. She says: "We are going up to the Cascades with the flood tide and shall return with the ebb tide." This makes the Salmon angry. He stops them, twists the head of the Flounder, and pulls the Crow and Blue-jay into their present shape, and determines that it shall take five days to go up to the Cascades.

8. Myth of the Elk—The eldest of five brothers meets an old man in his house, and is asked to hunt for him. The old man goes out, transforms himself into an elk, and kills the young man. The next three brothers fare no better. The youngest one transforms stone arrowpoints into a dog. His grandmother assumes the shape of a crow. He is told in a dream what has happened to his elder brothers, and is instructed to scratch the fat from an elk skin that he will see in the house. When he does so, the old man cries for pain. He leaves the house with his dog and makes five lakes, placing one quiver filled with arrows near each. Then he re-enters the house. When the Elk comes, he begins to shoot, and, when he cannot kill it, he jumps into the first lake, which the monster empties. He jumps into the next lake. Finally the monster swallows the youth with the water of the last lake. The Crow advises him to cut the Elk's heart, which he does, thus killing him. The skin is cut up and transformed into prairies.

9. Myth of the Southwest Winds—In the beginning there were five Southwest Winds, who lived in the sky. Blue-jay advises the animals to make war upon them. They sing until the sky tilts so that it approaches the earth, and they go up. Blue-jay advises the Skate to go home, because he is so wide. He has a shooting contest with Blue-jay, in which he escapes by turning sidewise, showing his narrow side, while Blue-jay is wounded. The Beaver steals fire from the house of the Winds, allowing himself to be caught, and then running away with the fire. The Skunk is sent as a scout. Next Robin is sent, who enters one house and remains sitting near the fire, which causes his breast to turn red. The bowstrings and the apron-strings of the Winds are cut by the Rats and Mice. Then the Birds attack the Winds, who are chiefs of the village. Only the youngest one escapes. The people return to the earth, but Blue-jay cuts the rope holding the sky to the earth before they are all down. The animals remaining above form the constellations.

10. Rabbit and Deer—The Deer is the Rabbit's mother. While she gathers roots and berries, he gathers branches, which he ties into a bundle and hides near the house. The next day he puts the branches into his canoe so that they look like people, and goes down

the river to a town. He makes the people believe that a war party is coming. They run away, and he steals all their salmon. When his mother returns, she begs him to desist. After five days he goes again to make war upon the people. This is repeated four times. The fifth time an old man does not run away, but hides and sees that it is nobody but the Rabbit. The people catch him and skin him. His body is thrown into the water. His mother finds him. She takes him into her canoe and resuscitates him. He says that he has no blanket and feels cold. He goes back to the village of his enemies and asks for his blanket. They are afraid because he has come back to life, and offer him all sorts of skins, which he refuses. Finally the people give him half of his own skin, the other half having been used for some purpose. He stretches it and puts it on. For that reason the Rabbit's skin is very thin.

11. Coyote and Badger—Coyote and Badger were catching birds all the time. One day they agree to invite various animals in order to kill them. Coyote steps near the water and invites the Sturgeon. When he enters the house, Badger lies down and pretends to be sick. Coyote asks his visitor to help him to carry Badger out of the house. When they do so, the Badger breaks wind, and the stench kills the Sturgeon. In this manner they kill the Seal, the Porpoise, and the Sea-lion. Then the people become suspicious, and nobody ventures near their house. They begin to shoot birds again. Badger is successful, while Coyote is unsuccessful. Badger kills them by means of his wind. Coyote asks for the loan of his anus, and finally induces Badger to give it to him; but he does not know how to use it, and is unsuccessful. Then Badger grows angry and throws Coyote's anus into the river. Coyote pursues it, and sees the children at the various villages trying to hit it with sticks and spears. Finally, when he succeeds in obtaining it, it is all torn. He curses Badger, saying that the stench of his wind shall be feared, but that he shall not be able to kill anything with weapons.

12. Panther and Lynx—The Panther goes out hunting every day, while the Lynx is watching the fire. He plays, and when on his return he finds the fire extinguished, he swims across the river and steals a firebrand from the fires of the Grizzly Bears, which were watched by an old woman. When she feels that one of the firebrands has disappeared, she accuses her vulva of having eaten it. When the Panther returns, he notices by the smell that a new fire has been started in his house. The next morning the Grizzly Bear, who had learned that his fire was stolen, swims across the river to fight with the Panther. The Lynx is covered with a dish. The Grizzly Bear attacks the Panther, and when the latter is almost killed the Lynx jumps out from under the kettle and breaks the Bear's leg with an ax. Thus all the five bears are killed, and then the Panther burns their house. He curses the Lynx for having caused so much trouble, and leaves him.

13. Seal and Crab—The Seal and the Crab are sisters. The Seal catches salmon and asks her sister to carry them up to her house. They break her fingers off. The Seal puts them on again. Then the Crab teases her sister, saying that she will eat the whole salmon. After they have eaten, the Seal closes the door and all the chinks of her house, and forbids her sister to go outside. She, however, disobeys and goes down the river, where she is seen by the people. The Seal goes to catch her and they hide. The people go and find them. They make the Seal vomit the salmon and take it home, where they eat it.

14. Myth of the Mink—Mink is maltreated by the people with whom he has gambled. He is hungry, and Panther, his brother, sends him to a lake, instructing him to stretch out his hands. When he does so, a dish filled with food stands near him. He thinks it is not enough, but is unable to empty the dish, for as soon as he has eaten its contents it becomes full again. His brother tells him to take the dish back to the lake. Then Mink and Panther begin to travel. They meet a person who is sitting on a log overhanging a river. Mink tries to push him into the water, but the man takes hold of him, kills him, and throws him away. His brother resuscitates him. They come to a person who threatens to kill them with his long nails. Mink tries to push him into the water, but is killed. His arm is torn out. Then his brother takes a squirrel's arm, puts it onto him, and resuscitates him. Next they go to a lake on which a two-headed swan is swimming. Mink tries to catch it, but is devoured by a monster that lives in the lake. The brother dries up the lake by throwing red-hot stones into it, cuts up the bodies of the monsters that he finds on the dry bottom, finds his brother, and resuscitates him. In the evening they camp, and Mink is hungry. He is instructed to strike the spruce trees in order to make a deer come out. He mistakes various animals for deer, and is instructed by his brother. Finally the deer comes, and is shot by his brother. He demands the antlers, which look greasy when brought near the fire. When they are going to sleep, he asks the name of the place, but his brother tells him that if the name is mentioned it will begin to rain. Mink learns the name and at once shouts it at the top of his voice. It begins to rain. Mink's brother gathers a large pile of sticks, on top of which he sits down. Mink is too lazy to do so, and is carried away by the floods. He is drowned, after which he is resuscitated by his brother. They reach the house where the brother's wife is living. Mink teases her father, who tries to kill him. They go out intending to fell a tree, and the old man tries to make a tree fall on him. They load the wood into their canoe, and the old man places Mink with the stone hammer in a basket on top of the wood. He makes the basket fall into the water, hoping to drown Mink, who, however, escapes. They try who is able to stay awake longest, and Mink

deceives the old man by placing rotten wood on his eyes. Then the old man asks him to fetch his playmates, the wolves. Mink does so, and they bite and scratch the old man, who begs Mink to take them back. In the same way he brings bears, raccoons, and the grizzly bears. In all these contests he shows himself stronger than the old man.

15. Robin and Salmon-berry—Robin and Salmon-berry are sisters. The latter is very successful in picking berries, while the former is not. Salmon-berry suspects that her sister intends to kill her, and she warns her five children, telling them what to do. She has five boys, while Robin has five girls. Robin kills her sister and tells the children that she has lost her. The next day the Salmon-berry's children propose to the other children to play. They make a hole, cover it, and make a fire over it, pretending that they are being steamed. Soon they say that they are hot, and Robin's children open the hole and let them out. Then they heat the Robin's children in the hole and kill them. They place them in various positions on the house, so that their mother shall not suspect any evil when seeing them from a distance. When she comes home, she finds the children in these various positions, and discovers that they are dead. Salmon-berry's children escape through a hole that they make in the ground. They place their dog at the entrance. When Robin asks the dog where the children have gone, it points in various directions, thus detaining her. Finally she finds their tracks. When they see her coming, they place two kettles on the trail, in one of which they place a rope made of elk skins; in the other they place the antlers; then they command the kettles to boil. When the Robin reaches them, she finds the kettles very hot, waits, and eats the skins and the antlers, which give her serious pain. The children reach a creek, where the Crane is standing, who stretches out his leg and allows them to walk across. When Robin reaches the creek, the Crane stretches out his leg for her, but turns it over and makes her fall into the water. He curses her, and transforms her into a bird. Her body drifts ashore, and the Crow picks at it. Then she recovers and smears the blood that is flowing from her wound over her belly. She visits all the trees, and asks them if they like her looks. She tells those that like her that they will be useful to man, while she tells the others that they will be of no use to man.

16. Panther and Owl—The Owl was the Panther's slave. Blue-jay induces a chief's daughter to visit the Panther. She crosses five prairies and sees the Owl dancing and catching mice. As soon as he is looked at, a stick hits his nose. He searches and finds the woman, whom he marries. The house is full of fat. On the one side is nice-looking fat, on the side where the Owl is living is bad-looking fat. The Owl takes some of the good-looking fat, telling the woman that

it belongs to him. In the evening the Panther comes home and orders the Owl, his slave, to carry in the elk, which the latter does reluctantly. After three days the woman, who is hidden behind a matting, makes a hole and sees the Panther. She discovers that she has made a mistake. The Panther wonders why the Owl obeys him reluctantly, and one day returns at noon. The Panther asks him why he is whispering every evening, and the Owl replies that he is dreaming. One night the Panther hears him talking to the woman, and becomes very suspicious. The woman is tired of her husband. She pulls out two hairs, which she ties round a piece of elk's marrow. The Panther, when eating the marrow, finds the hairs, and thus learns that a woman is hidden in the house. On the following day he returns before the Owl, searches all over the house, and finds the woman. The Owl is very angry and prepares to fight with the Panther. They put on their armor, and in fighting fly upward. They tear each other. Their flesh is falling down. The woman keeps all the red flesh, and burns all the green flesh. She burns all the green bones, and keeps all the white bones. The intestines look just alike, and she cannot distinguish them. She burns part of them. Then she throws the meat and bones that she has preserved into the water, and the Panther arises, but by mistake she has burned his intestines. He sends her to all the animals to ask for half of their intestines. They do not fit, and are returned, until finally those of the Lynx fit. After a while the woman has two children, an Owl and a Panther, who grow up as friends.

17. THE RACCOON—Raccoon and his grandmother are hungry. She offers him all kinds of food, but the Raccoon refuses everything except acorns. She tells him to get some from their cache. She has five caches of acorns. Raccoon eats all the contents of the caches. The Crow observes him and tells what he is doing. His grandmother takes a stick to strike him, but he hides among the wood in the fireplace. She finds him, and strikes his face with a firebrand. He climbs a hawthorn tree. His grandmother follows him, searching for him. She asks him to throw down some fruit to her. He tells her to lie on her back and open her mouth. Then he puts thorns into the haws and throws them into her mouth. She cries for water. Wings grow on her, and she is transformed into a bird. Raccoon travels on and reaches the house of the Grizzly Bear. He tells the Bear that somebody painted him and made him look pretty. The Grizzly Bear requests that the same be done to him. Then Raccoon boils some pitch and pours it over his face. Raccoon runs away, pursued by the Bear. He meets Coyote and asks him to let him pass, and promises to gather food for him. Coyote directs him to his house, and orders him to heat ten stones and to cover himself with a kettle. When Bear comes, Coyote spits and makes his saliva look like the Raccoon, thus making the Bear believe that he has eaten the Raccoon.

He invites the Bear to his house, and bets that he cannot swallow hot stones. Coyote puts a reed into his mouth so that it passes right through his body. He swallows five red-hot stones, which fall right through the reed. The Bear tries the same, and dies. Coyote and Raccoon eat the Bear. After this, Raccoon gathers fruits for Coyote, as he has promised. Later on he wishes every morning to find certain food under his pillow, and his wish comes true, because he himself places the food there every evening. Coyote tries the same, but is unsuccessful. Coyote becomes envious and resolves to kill Raccoon. He warns him not to go to a certain place, saying that there are dangerous warriors there who look just like him. Raccoon disobeys. Coyote, disguised as one of the supposed warriors, wounds Raccoon so that the fat comes out of the wound. When Raccoon comes home, Coyote, under the pretense of curing him, pulls out the fat and kills him. Then he is starving because he is not able to procure any food himself.

ABSTRACTS OF TALES

1. Tiā'pexoacxoac—A girl has a bitch. While she is away, it is killed and the fat is given her to eat. She is deserted by the tribe. Then she gives birth to five male dogs and one female. When she is away, the dogs assume the shape of children. Finally she discovers their transformation and burns their dogskin blankets. The boys become great hunters. Tiā'pexoacxoac hears about her daughter. He is a great chief who eats his wives. He kills all his male children. The brothers kill a sea monster, and give the blood to him to drink. He cannot drink it all, and for that reason makes peace with the brothers. He marries the girl, who gives birth to a boy. She escapes with the baby. The boy grows up in the woods and becomes stronger than his father, whom he resembles in every respect. One day he goes to his father's house, and is mistaken for Tiā'pexoacxoac himself. The latter sends slaves to search for him. The son kills all the people. Then Tiā'pexoacxoac requests him to come back. The boy agrees, and when he returns, his sons shoot their grandfather.

2. Ēmōgoā'lekc—A chief's son falls in love with a slave girl. His father scolds him, and he resolves to leave his people. He jumps into a lake and is transformed into a water monster. He invites his friend to come and see him, but enjoins him not to tell the other people what has become of him. The people track the friend and discover the chief's son. They try to catch him, and when they do not succeed, they try to shoot him with arrows, but they are not able to hurt him.

3. The brothers—A number of brothers maltreat their youngest brother. They give him refuse of their own meals to eat. He goes and catches birds and lies down, singing shaman's songs. His brothers find him in this state and try to reconcile him, but he pays no attention to them and is transformed into a spirit of the sea, the protector of whale hunters.

4. The war of the ghosts—Two men are met by a canoe, the occupants of which invite them to join in a war expedition. One of them refuses, the other one goes, and in combat is wounded, though he does not feel any pain. The people carry him home and he discovers that they are ghosts. The next morning he dies.

5. The TkulXiyogoā'ikc—A chief, Pō'XpoX, kills all his male children. One of his wives saves her male child, who is placed in charge of her mother. He attains supernatural powers by finding dentalia in a pond. The old woman borrows sinew to string them. Then she invites all the people and distributes the dentalia among

them. The boy becomes a warrior by seeing the thunderbird. He invites the people to a great feast, and outdoes his father so much that the latter loses his rank.

6. Pē'lpel—Pē'Lpel is a chief on North river, who robs the people farther south. A young man trains to become a warrior. When Pē'Lpel attacks him, the young man kills him.

7. The Nīsa'l—A man has a wooden figure representing a supernatural being, which he makes dance. Two young men hide near the door, and strike the figure with a club when it is passing. Then snow begins to fall and it gets very cold. Two eagles are seen drifting down the river on an ice floe. The two young men try to catch them and are drowned. Thus is the spirit revenged.

8. The Spirit of Hunger—There is a famine. Two friends are starving. Both have the Famine for their guardian spirit. One of them sees her coming and entering all the houses. Then the people die. The other one is not able to see her, except from a distance. The first goes to meet the Famine and has a struggle with her. He takes away her mat, in which she carries bones and shells. He shows them to the people, and from that time on there is plenty of game.

9. Winter all the year round—A boy plays with his excrements, although it is forbidden to do so. As soon as he has done so, a cold winter sets in. The people propose to expose the boy on the ice, but his parents protect him. A bird is killed which carries a strawberry in its beak, from which the people conclude that it is cold only in their country. Then the parents give the boy up. He is exposed on the ice, where he dies. Then it rains, the snow melts, and it becomes summer.

10. The girl who was carried away by the Thunderbird—The Indians used to hunt elk on Saddle mountain near Astoria. They frightened them and drove them down a certain trail which ended in a precipice. Girls are forbidden to pass over the prairie at the foot of this precipice. A girl disobeys this law and is carried away by the Thunderbird. The people search for her and see many birds flying around the rocks. The girl has become a supernatural being.

11. The man who was transformed into a snake—The wife of a canoe builder finds a very large root. He eats it and is transformed into a large snake. The roots are transformed into small snakes, which follow him when he leaves the house. Hence people do not now eat large roots.

O

Reprint Publishing

For People Who Go For Originals.

This book is a facsimile reprint of the original edition. The term refers to the facsimile with an original in size and design exactly matching simulation as photographic or scanned reproduction.

Facsimile editions offer us the chance to join in the library of historical, cultural and scientific history of mankind, and to rediscover.

The books of the facsimile edition may have marks, notations and other marginalia and pages with errors contained in the original volume. These traces of the past refers to the historical journey that has covered the book.

ISBN 978-3-95940-196-8

Facsimile reprint of the original edition
Copyright © 2016 Reprint Publishing
All rights reserved.

www.reprintpublishing.com

www.ingramcontent.com/pod-product-compliance
Lightning Source LLC
Chambersburg PA
CBHW081346280326
41927CB00042B/3123

* 9 7 8 3 9 5 9 4 0 1 9 6 8 *